משנה

ArtScroll Judaica Classics®

THE THREE

Published by
Mesorah Publications, ltd

FESTIVALS

Ideas and Insights of the SFAS EMES on Pesach, Shavuos, and Succos

Anthologized and Adapted by

Rabbi Yosef Stern

FIRST EDITION
First Impression . . . March 1993
Second Impression . . . July 1994
Third Impression . . . May 1997

Published and Distributed by
MESORAH PUBLICATIONS, Ltd.
4401 Second Avenue
Brooklyn, New York 11232

Distributed in Europe by
J. LEHMANN HEBREW BOOKSELLERS
20 Cambridge Terrace
Gateshead, Tyne and Wear
England NE8 1RP

Distributed in Israel by
SIFRIATI / A. GITLER—BOOKS
10 Hashomer Street
Bnei Brak 51361

Distributed in Australia & New Zealand by
GOLDS BOOK & GIFT CO.
36 William Street
Balaclava 3183, Vic., Australia

Distributed in South Africa by
KOLLEL BOOKSHOP
22 Muller Street
Yeoville 2198, Johannesburg, South Africa

ARTSCROLL JUDAICA CLASSICS®
THE THREE FESTIVALS

ISBN:
0-89906-429-9 (hard cover)
0-89906-430-2 (paperback)

Typography by CompuScribe at ArtScroll Studios, Ltd.
4401 Second Avenue / Brooklyn, N.Y. 11232 / (718) 921-9000

Printed in the United States of America by Noble Book Press Corp.
Bound by Sefercraft Inc., Quality Bookbinders, Brooklyn, N.Y.

תשורת שי לזכות, זכרון לנפש

רפאל יצחק בן אפרים ליפר ז״ל

Raphael I. Laifer

נפטר כ״ז טבת תש״נ

מאת

אשתו מרת מלכה תחי׳

בנו אפרים וריעתו חיה פעשא שיחיו

ונכדיו אריה ורעיתו חנה אסתר שיחיו

ובתם תמר עטרה שתחי׳

אברהם חיים ורעיתו יעל דפנה שיחיו

צבי דוד ורעיתו טובה שיחיו

נקדש לזכר נשמות

אנשים נאמנים לה׳ ולתורתו

שנדדו לארה״ב וזכו להרבות האור ולדחות החשך

ר׳ אברהם דוב ב״ר שמואל נטע ע״ה

א׳ דשבועות תשכ״א

ורעיתו ליבא בת ר׳ זאב ע״ה

ו׳ שבט תשכ״ט

החבר אפרים בן הר״ר רפאל ע״ה

א׳ דר״ח תמוז תש״כ

תנצב״ה

מכתב ברכה מאת כקש״ת אדמו״ר מגור שליט״א

ב״ה ה׳ שמות תשנ״ב לפ״ק

לכב׳ ידידי היקר והנכבד הרה״ג חו״ב נותן טעם לשבח הרב דוד אלעוווסקי שליט״א

שלום רב!

בנידון הספר המבאר את השפ״א לסוכות אשר חיבר הרב יוסף שטערן שליט״א – הנה כידוע לך אינני נותן הסכמות באופן עקרוני. ובפרט כאשר השפה האנגלית אינה שגורה בפי לא שייך בכלל שאני אעבור ע״ז ואסכים עליו. אבל כפי ששמעתי מכם שאנשים חשובים שבחו את הספר הנני מצרף גם ברכתי להרב המחבר שליט״א שיצליח.

והנני בזה ידידך הדושו״ט

פנחס מנחם אלטר

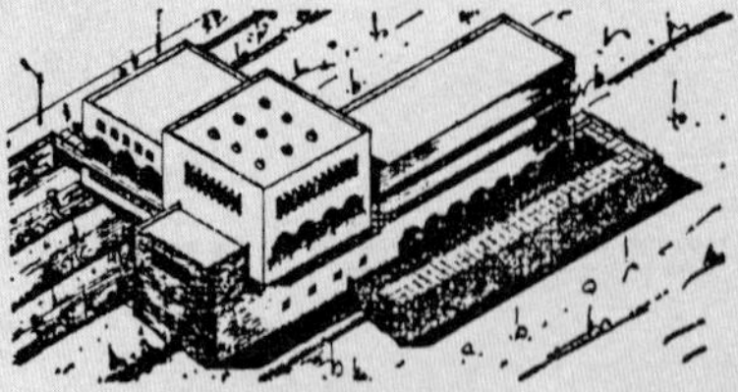

ישיבת "תורה-אור" בעיה"ק ירושלים
בנשיאות מרן הרב הגאון רבי **חיים פנחס שיינברג** שליט"א
"TORAH-ORE" SEMINARY
THE AMERICAN SEMINARY IN ISRAEL
Kiryat Mattersdorf — קרית מטרסדורף
Tel. 373049 טל. ★ P.O.B. 6979 ת.ד.
Tel. Students 371400, 372200 טל. תלמידים
JERUSALEM, 91150 ISRAEL

מכתב ברכה

עש"ק לפרשת "ושמרתם את חקתי ואת משפטי אשר יעשה אותם האדם וחי בהם"
בא לפני הה"ג מבחר רבנן ת"ח ר' יוסף שכטר שליט"א רב דביהכ"נ
אגודת אחים בפלטבוש, וספרי עמלו בידו.
כבר נודע בשערי ישראל מעלות ספרי השפת אמת זצ"ל על התורה
ומועדים אשר לרוב עמקותם היו כספר החתום לפני קהל ועדה. ואפילו
לפני ת"ח אשר שגו בעמקי דברי השפ"א המובאים בשאר ספרים.
ומפני חומר הענין והקוצר דברי השפ"א לא הצליחו לראות את עמקות
המכוון הדברים.
ע"כ אפריון נמטיה להמחבר הנ"ל אשר אסף כעמיר גורנו וליקט
מדברי השפ"א על השלש רגלים דבר דבור על אופניו, ד"ת אשר
יש בהם תועלת הרבה לשומעים המקשיבים לזה וגם לרבות ת"ח
ורבנים המטיפים לעדתם ועוד תרגם אותו לשפה אנגלית המדוברת.
ולחבר שאות גם ומפתח וציין ציונים למאמרי חז"ל המובאים בתוך
הספר.
על כן אמינא לפעלא טבא יישר ויה"ר שיתקבל חיבורו היקר
בתוך תפוצות ישראל וזכות השפת אמת זצ"ל יגן עלינו
שנזכה להגדיל תורה ולהאדירה.

הכו"ח לכבוד התורה ותומכיה
המצפה לישועת ה' הקרובה
חיים פינחס שיינבערג

American Office : 818 Central Ave. ★ Far Rockaway N.Y. 11691 ★ Tel. (718) 471-5132

Publisher's Preface

To publish this work is a high honor. *Sfas Emes* is a name that has evoked respect and awe for a hundred years, as a commentary on the Talmud and as a collection of penetrating insights on the Torah and Festivals. One of the last generation's great *roshei yeshiva* said:

> "There is hardly a Torah commentary that I have not studied, but always I come back to the *Sfas Emes*. Every year I go through it again and I never fail to see new ideas that I never noticed before."

Rabbi Yosef Stern is one of the countless *talmidei chachamim* whose fascination with *Sfas Emes* has enriched his own life and, through him, the lives of many who attend his classes and lectures. Now, he goes a giant step further. He has taken the major ideas of *Sfas Emes* on Pesach, Shavuos, and Succos and presented them in clear, cogent, stimulating essays, topic by topic. At the very least, this book will vastly enrich all who read it. At best, it will introduce many of its readers to the original, so that they too will mine its vast storehouse of ideas and comments.

This book is not a translation, for the *Sfas Emes* cannot be translated. It pulls together strands of thought on individual topics from the over thirty years of comment collected in the *Sfas Emes*, and weaves the ideas into a clear and coherent tapestry. To those familiar with the original, it will be a reminder, a refresher, and a treasury of insights they may have overlooked. To those unfamiliar with the *Sfas Emes*, the book will be an electrifying adventure in Torah thought.

We express our appreciation to Rabbi Stern for undertaking this challenging work.

We likewise are grateful to all those whose talents have been harnessed in producing a work so significant. They may all be proud to have made an important contribution to the Torah growth of countless people.

Rabbis Meir Zlotowitz/Nosson Scherman

Rosh Chodesh Nissan, 5753
March, 1993

Author's Preface

◆§ The Purpose of This Volume

Though I attempted more than one hundred times, I never even began to understand the teachings of your father (the Sfas Emes).

Hashem spoke to Israel through the Sfas Emes. Anyone who maintains that he had any comprehension of the Sfas Emes was mistaken, save for a few exceptional individuals.

I prayed to Hashem numerous times that He should grant me the wisdom to comprehend the Sfas Emes' teachings.

Generally, a person understands his teacher after forty years. I have studied his words for more than fifty years and I have not yet begun to comprehend my master.

Every year that I came to visit the Sfas Emes, I realized that during the previous visit I had understood nothing.

[If I have learned anything from the Sfas Emes] it is to know that we do not know.

(From the letter of R' Yaakov Yitzchak of Zolzobock to R' Avraham Mordechai Alter, the *Sfas Emes'* son, quoted in *Rosh Gulas Ariel,* p. 482)

While these excerpts from the letter of a venerable scholar present one perspective regarding the depth and greatness of the teachings of the *Sfas Emes,* it would also be valuable to consider the comments of others:

"While my father's writings are so profound that no one can comprehend them, there is also something in them for every kind of person. Any Jew can derive from the writings of the *Sfas Emes* something of personal relevance to himself." (R' Avraham Mordechai Alter, son of the *Sfas Emes*)

When a noted kabbalist and scholar in Jerusalem attempted to write a commentary based on the mystical aspects of the teachings of the *Sfas Emes,* his son and successor, R' Avraham Mordechai Alter (known as the *Imrei Emes*) discouraged him, on the ground that his father had intended that everyone derive something of value from his work. (ibid.)

The motivation underlying the present work, an anthology of the teachings of the *Sfas Emes* on the Festivals, dedicated in loving memory of Mr. Rafael Laifer, ע"ה, can best be expressed with yet another statement of the *Imrei Emes*: "Every Jew can find himself in the teachings of the *Sfas Emes.*" If the reader finds ideas that are personally relevant to him in this volume, words of comfort and inspiration, then we will feel we have accomplished a great deal.

On what basis does this writer, hardly an expert in the voluminous and profound works of the *Sfas Emes,* venture to attempt the daunting project of making accessible more than thirty-five years of his thoughts to the English-speaking public? The answer to this question lies in the teachings of the *Sfas Emes* himself, indeed in his very last public statement.

On the final Shabbos of his life, the *Sfas Emes* proclaimed, "No one should boast that Hashem has chosen him [for a sacred mission] because of his spiritual greatness. On the contrary, [Hashem chose] even a hornet [to eradicate the Canaanite nations] or a frog [of the Ten Plagues] as a suitable agent to perform Divine missions." (ibid. p. 158)

In this, his final pronouncement, the *Sfas Emes* left a profound legacy: *Anyone* who has drawn meaning from his teachings, who has found something of himself in the *Sfas Emes,* can share morsels and nuggets of this vast treasure with others.

In attempting this pioneering work, an anthology of the *Sfas Emes'* writings on the Pilgrimage Festivals, this writer hopes to share with a broader audience some of the inspiration and personal growth he has been drawing from the *Sfas Emes* for over a decade. This work is being attempted in order to repay a debt and to express heartfelt appreciation for all that the *Sfas Emes* has meant to us.

☙ How to Use This Volume

By stating from the outset what this book is *not,* we can hope to give the reader a clearer appreciation of what *it is.*

- ☐ This work is not a translation of the *Sfas Emes.* Such a project, even if it were judged to be an appropriate undertaking, is well beyond the capabilities of this writer.
- ☐ This work makes no attempt to follow the sequence presented in the writings of the *Sfas Emes.* Instead we have selected, rearranged, and often "expanded" insights that were first said at Chassidic gatherings (*tischen*) over a period of thirty-five years, from 5631 to 5665 (1871-1905), in an attempt to render them more easily accessible to the contemporary reader.
- ☐ This work makes no attempt to present an exhaustive treatment of the *Sfas Emes'* insights on any particular topic, much less on the Pilgrimage Festivals as a whole. Apart from considerations of space, the sheer volume and profundity of the *Sfas Emes's* writings preclude the possibility of reproducing everything he wrote about the Festivals. Wherever

possible, we have provided references to the original sources in the writings of the *Sfas Emes* on the Torah and Festivals so that those readers with a command of Hebrew can appreciate his insights in their original format. Even for such readers, however, we feel that this work will be a valuable digest and commentary on concepts that are often difficult to grasp fully in their original, very terse, style.

☐ Perhaps most importantly, while we have done everything possible to present the thoughts of the *Sfas Emes* in easily accessible form, we make no claim that this volume will make for light reading. As with most works on the basic principles of Torah, it is best read in small portions, and requires time to absorb and assimilate. Over the course of time, however, it is hoped that such an approach will yield substantial cumulative effects. It is the author's fervent wish and prayer that the reader will pick up this book again and again, each time finding a new idea to be treasured and savored by a Jew thirsting to drink from the rich spiritual springs of the Festival cycle.

The writings of the *Sfas Emes* contain far more than an amalgam of Torah thoughts. Instead, we feel that the serious reader will be able to glean from them a comprehensive and profound summary of the Torah's approach to *every aspect* of life. While we have attempted to present a sampling of his key thoughts in the Biographical Introduction, a complete picture of his overall *weltanschauung* will require time and patience to develop. Lest the reader be daunted by this task, we can promise that the time spent will be both rewarding and enjoyable. This book contains countless tasty morsels of the *Sfas Emes'* world view; if the reader is able to savor only a few of them, his and our efforts will not have been in vain.

☐ Finally, many of the *Sfas Emes'* writings, by virtue of their profundity and obscurity, are subject to varying interpretations. While many people have assisted in the preparation of this volume for publication, the author alone assumes responsibility for its interpretations of this Torah classic, which are his own and most likely mirror his perceptions. May Hashem protect us from errors.

Acknowledgments

No book, let alone one as challenging as this one, could be completed by any one individual alone. I am indebted to many, many others for their assistance and support.

To the sponsor:

To Dr. Franklin Laifer, and his *Eishes Chayil,* for their generous support enabling the publication of this volume. This project was undertaken in loving memory of his cherished father, Mr. Raphel I. Laifer ז״ל, who not only was a pillar of *chesed* and integrity but also served as a link to the generation of the *Sfas Emes*. He derived great enjoyment from sharing his memories of that special world and its great men.

To my family:

To my dear parents Mr. and Mrs. Stern, who have made their lives into an embodiment of *ahavas Hashem* and *ahavas Torah*. Not only did they nurture me in the way of Torah, but their constant encouragement and support has helped keep this project alive from its very beginnings. May Hashem grant them long and healthy years.

To my dear parents-in-law, Rabbi and Rebbetzin Scheinberg. My father-in-law, with the constant encouragement of his *eishes chayil,* has raised an entire generation of *talmidim* in his more than four decades in *chinuch.* May Hashem grant him continued success in his latest endeavor, Yeshivas Migdal Torah, of Nevei Yaakov.

To my dear brother Rabbi Elchanan Stern, whose constant interest in this project has never flagged and whose *divrei Torah* have always been particularly valuable to me.

To my brothers-in-law for their support and warmth, especially to Rabbi Meyer Scheinberg, whose efforts on behalf of this project are particularly appreciated.

Of course אַחֲרוֹן אַחֲרוֹן חָבִיב, to my *eishes chayil,* who has given me constant encouragement to complete the project in the face of the numerous challenges and distractions of daily life. Her efforts to maintain a comparatively tranquil working atmosphere, despite the enormous responsibilities of raising a family, can never be forgotten. May Hashem grant us the merit to witness together בָּנִים וּבְנֵי בָנִים עוֹסְקִים בַּתּוֹרָה וּבְמִצְווֹת

To all those who have contributed to this volume:

To Rabbi Osher Mandel, who helped edit an earlier draft of the section on Shavuos.

To my dear friend, Rabbi Eliezer Gevirtz, who made major contributions to the sections on Shavuos and Succos. An educator, writer and thinker *par excellance,* Rabbi Gevirtz took time from his busy schedule to edit much of this volume. יְמַלֵּא ה׳ כָּל מִשְׁאֲלוֹת לִבּוֹ לְטוֹבָה.

To Rabbi Yehoshua Fulda, whose sharp editorial eye and talent for precision and detail left an indelible imprint on the book.

And especially to my editor, R' Pinchos Osher Rohr. In spite of having known him only a few months and having met him in person only once, I feel an extraordinary closeness to him. Through his tactful and subtle yet cogent critique of this volume, not a page lacks the imprint of his eloquent writing style. I look forward, with Hashem's help, to complete more works in close collaboration with this immensely gifted *talmid chacham.* He has asked that his efforts in this project be dedicated to the memory of his mother, Zlata bas Kalman (Lois Simon Rohr), ע"ה, who passed away Erev Rosh Chodesh Teves of this year. May Hashem grant that her soul be bound in the bond of eternal life.

To the staff of Mesorah Publications:

To Rabbi Nosson Scherman, a Torah educator, writer and lecturer of great note who has championed this project through many vicissitudes. Were it not for his constant involvement and accessibility, in spite of his frenetic schedule, this book would never have seen the light of day.

To the entire staff of Mesorah Publications, including but not limited to Rabbis Meir Zlotowitz, Sheah Brander and Avi Gold, for the help they have given the project. Rabbi Moshe Lieber read the manuscript, made many helpful suggestions and coordinated the final production of the book. Also to the typesetting department — Mrs. Estie Dicker, Mrs. Esther Feierstein, Mrs. Chavie Friedman, Yehuda Gordon, Mindy Kohn, Chaya Gitti Zaidman, and especially Nichie Fendrich, who coordinated the production of the book with skill, poise and infinite patience. Mrs. Bassie Gutman's painstaking care and aesthetic taste in typesetting make this book as pleasing to the eye as it is to the mind. I thank Mrs. Ethel Gottlieb who proofread the entire book, checked sources, edited and shepherded the entire project. Mrs. Judi Dick read and commented. *Yasher Koach* to Avrohom Kay who designed the beautiful cover, and R' Eli Kroen whose graphic skills enhance the beauty of this volume. Shmuel Blitz of the the Artscroll Jerusalem office deserves special thanks for invaluable and cheerful logistical support. Apart from the competent typing staff of Mesorah Publications, Mrs. Elky Goldgrab and Mrs. Mirel Weisel typed earlier drafts of certain sections. They all have my thanks.

To Rabbi Dovid Olewski, Menahel of Mesivta Beis Yisrael, who commented on parts of the section on Succos and served as an invaluable liaison with the Gerer chassidic community. Also to Rabbi Yitzchak Meir Schorr, who graciously read much of the section on Shavuos.

To the members of Congregation Agudas Achim of Midwood, and its president Mr. Arthur Pearlman, who were often the first audience for the present form of the Torah thoughts contained in this work. Also to my "fellow travelers," Reb Mechel Stern and Reb Moshe Yaroslawitz, who served patiently as a "sounding board" for many of these Torah thoughts. May Hashem grant them all peace, prosperity and pleasure in all their endeavors.

To K'hal Adath Yeshurun of Washington Heights, where my formative years were happily spent. My first awareness of the concept of *sfas emes* (words of integrity) was formed long before the idea of the present work entered my mind, by the Siddur of that name that was used in that *Kehillah,* long known for its devotion to the highest standards of *chessed* and *emes.* My special thanks go to its *Rabbonim,* Rav Shimon Schwab and Rav

Zechariah Gelley, and to my *Roshei Yeshiva,* Rav Naftoli Friedler, Rav Yaakov Perlow, the Novominsker Rebbe, as well as to my mentors, Rav Krieger, Rav Glucksman and Dayan Posen. Also to Rabbi Mordechai Stern of Congregation Kehillas Yaakov of Washington Heights, who introduced me to the beauty of the *Sfas Emes*, and many other friends too numerous to mention, in that extraordinary community.

Above all, I must express my total gratitude to Hashem. No human effort, certainly not a pioneering work of this nature, could possibly reach fruition were it not for Hashem's unceasing help in every minute detail of the project.

Since this volume is nearing completion before Pesach, I would like to close with an appropriate thought from the *Haggadah.*

In the blessing recited after the first segment of the *Haggadah* we thank Hashem "that this *night reache*d *us*" — וְהִגִּיעָנוּ הַלַּיְלָה הַזֶּה. This unusual phrase stands in stark contrast to the traditional *berachah* of וְהִגִּיעָנוּ לַזְּמַן הַזֶּה, in which we thank Hashem for *letting us reach* the Festival.

The distinction between the two renditions may be explained quite simply. On all other occasions, we can attain, with Hashem's help, a measure of the Festival's sanctity — we can reach the Festival. Not so, the night of the Seder. This occasion is so far removed from the mind-set of ordinary mortals that Hashem Himself has to bring the occasion down to our level. The night reaches us — we cannot reach it.

As we are זוֹכֶה to present a few rays of the *Sfas Emes'* luminescence, we pray for סַיַּיתָּא דִשְׁמַיָּא that He bring these rarefied teachings to כְּלַל יִשְׂרָאֵל.

Yosef Stern
Shushan Purim, 5753

Table of Contents

Succos

Biography: The Sfas Emes His Life and Thought

◆§ Background and Childhood

As a *bochur,* R' Yehudah Aryeh Leib Alter of Ger, better known as the *Sfas Emes,* would often stay up all night studying Torah. After one such session, he returned to his room for some much-needed rest when it was already day. A short while later, his grandfather, the revered *Chiddushei HaRim,* happened to notice his grandson apparently sleeping the day away. Quickly he roused the slumbering scholar and gently admonished him for wasting precious time that could be better used for Hashem's service. Throughout the benign dressing-down Yehuda Aryeh Leib remained firmly quiet, and when his grandfather finished, gave his solemn word to do better in the future.

News of this encounter reached one of Yehuda Aryeh Leib's comrades, who could not understand his friend's silence. "Why didn't you say anything when the Rebbe spoke to you?" he asked him. "Couldn't you have told him the truth, that you'd learned through the night and had earned a short rest?"

"What? And miss such an opportunity?" was the response.

"What do you mean?"

"Every word a wise man speaks is precious. The Torah tells us that when Moshe scolded the tribes of Reuben and Gad for asking to settle on the east bank of the Jordan River, thinking that they wanted to get out of the battle to conquer *Eretz Yisrael,* they listened patiently. Only after he finished did they explain that they had no intention of abandoning the other tribes, and that their soldiers would lead the fight to take the Land.

"Why didn't they speak up to defend themselves at the beginning of Moshe's lecture? Because they were eager to hear every word that their leader Moshe had to say, even if it was misdirected chastisement.

"So when my holy grandfather told me how to improve myself, I considered it a great opportunity, not an insult. Not every day am I privileged to receive personal advice from such a sage, and I didn't want to miss it by interrupting with excuses."

This keen perceptiveness displayed by the *Sfas Emes* already in his youth continued to develop much more as he matured. His veneration of the Torah tradition and the living vessels who preserved it, as well as his unrelenting quest for new insights into Hashem's teachings, characterized his life and work until his last days.

Rabbi Yehuda Aryeh Leib Alter was the scion of a noble Rabbinic and Chassidic family. His family tree included such Torah luminaries as Rabbi Meir of Rothenberg, Rabbi Yoel Sirkes (known as the *Bach*), and Rabbi Yonasan Eibuschutz. His grandfather, Rabbi Yitzchak Meir Alter of Ger, was known as the *Chiddushei HaRim*, after the title of the illustrious series of novellae he published. Rabbi Yitzchak Meir was a devoted disciple of such chassidic leaders as the Maggid of Kozinitz, Rabbi Simcha Bunim of P'shischah, and Rabbi Menachem Mendel of Kotzk. It was he who founded the chassidic dynasty of Ger.

While Rabbi Yitzchak Meir appeared in public to be an esteemed leader with a large and devoted following, his personal life was clouded with tragedy. He and his rebbetzin had thirteen children, all of whom died very young. The last child, Rabbi Avrohom Mordechai, was a sickly person and by the age of thirty his condition had deteriorated to such an extent that the doctors expected the worst. When the end seemed inevitably at hand, his father came to his sickbed and urged him to cling to life. "The Torah commands us," he said, *'Choose life!'* (*Devarim* 30:19) If you have the will to live, then I am confident that Hashem will reward you with additional years, and with a child to carry on your legacy."

These words boosted Rabbi Avrohom Mordechai's spirits and his condition began to improve. Although his constitution remained weak, he lived on and within a year his prayers were answered. On the 29th of Nissan 5607 (1847), he and his wife were blessed with a son whom they named Yehuda, as an expression of thanks to Hashem for His compassion (cf. *Bereishis* 29:35). On this joyous occasion the *Chiddushei HaRim* wrote of his newborn grandson, "May the spirit of the Lord be upon him: the spirit of wisdom and understanding, of courage and purpose. And may all his endeavors in life be successful."

Because of Rabbi Avrohom Mordechai's continuing weakness, it was agreed that the *Chiddushei HaRim* would himself supervise the child's upbringing. Thus a strong bond grew between the Rebbe and his grandson, especially after Rabbi Avrohom Mordechai's tragic death when the child was only eight. Under the Rebbe's guidance, the boy received a thorough Torah education, with both the personal instruction and the forceful example of one of the greatest scholars and leaders of the time. The Rebbe took pains that his only grandson should grow up with a pure and honest character.

This was accomplished through a careful upbringing that included a sagacious mixture of love and discipline. For example, once it happened that the boy was served barley for lunch. As children are wont to do, he shook his head and refused to eat until food more to his taste could be found. Recognizing that such arrogance could not be left unchecked, the Rebbe saw to it that the boy's lunches consisted of nothing but barley for the next *four weeks*. Eventually, Yehuda Aryeh Leib came to understand the point, never to be ungrateful to Hashem for the gifts He gives us.

At the age of eight, the boy went with his grandfather on a lengthy journey to visit the Kotzker Rebbe, who recognized in the youngster a wondrous prodigy. When asked why he had subjected the youngster to such long and arduous travel, the Gerer Rebbe replied, "I wanted him to see and learn from a real Jew." From this visit, Yehuda Aryeh Leib developed a life-long respect for the Kotzker Rebbe.

As Yehuda Aryeh Leib approached the age of *bar mitzvah*, his enormous potential as a scholar became increasingly obvious. His grandfather, who by now had assumed the role of Rebbe of the chassidic court in the town of Ger near Warsaw, derived deep satisfaction from the boy's progress. When Yehuda was married at the age of fifteen in 5622 (1862) to the daughter of Rabbi Yudel Kaminer, a highly respected *talmid chacham*, the Gerer Rebbe told Rabbi Kaminer, "It is customary for someone who gives a gift to inform the recipient of its value. I can tell you with great pride that my grandson Leibele is a very valuable prize indeed!"

Before his passing, the *Chiddushei HaRim* made it clear that he wanted his gifted grandson, still barely out of his teens, to assume the mantle of leading his *chassidim* after he would no longer be able to do so. The young man, in his great modesty, expressed reservations about his fitness to assume this great responsibility at such a young age. In reply, the *Chiddushei HaRim* told him the following parable:

Once a mountain climber set himself the goal of climbing to a very high and difficult-to-reach peak. After long exertion, he finally arrived and was dismayed to find a group of small children playing there. "How on earth did you ever get here?" he asked them. "I struggled so long and hard to ascend to this peak, surely you are too young to achieve such a feat."

"Ah!" said one of the children. "You had to stuggle because you started from the foot of the mountain. For us it was no problem. You see, we were born here."

With this parable, the *Chiddushei HaRim* intended to convey to his grandson that, in spite of his tender years, he had been born to greatness. Once he assumed the role of Rebbe, he would see that he was naturally suited for it.

Four years after his grandson's wedding, Rabbi Yitzchak Meir passed away. His last words were, "Leibele *Kaddish,*" which his chassidim understood to mean that Yehuda Aryeh Leib should recite *Kaddish* for him, and take over as his successor. However, the retiring grandson felt that he was too young and inexperienced for such a weighty position and, despite the pleas of the chassidim, he begged off.

Instead, he left Ger and found a mentor in Rabbi Chanoch HaKohen, the Rebbe of Alexander. For four years he studied at his master's feet, preparing for the challenges he knew lay ahead. When Rabbi Chanoch died in 5630 (1870), Yehuda Aryeh Leib could no longer turn down the renewed requests from his grandfather's chassidim and reluctantly agreed to serve as their Rebbe.

Once having accepted the position, however, he devoted himself wholeheartedly to his duties. The Gerer chassidim quickly came to appreciate not only his sagacity but also the pure motives that governed all of his actions. He abolished the custom, prevalent in many chassidic circles, of accepting monetary gifts (*pidyonos*) from his chassidim, and relied instead for his livelihood on the meager proceeds of a tobacco shop run by his wife. Though he was not involved in the day-to-day operation of the business, he maintained careful supervision to ensure that it was run with scrupulous honesty. When he noticed that a wholesaler, who numbered among his chassidim, was selling his wares to the shop at a lower than normal price, he quickly put an end to the practice out of fear that the seller might, perhaps unconsciously, be inviting favoritism from the Rebbe.

Rabbi Yehuda Aryeh Leib and his family (including ten children — four of whom died in infancy) lived frugally, giving all of their income to charity apart from what they needed for the most basic necessities. He frowned on costly and extravagant celebrations and constantly reminded his chassidim that conspicuous consumption has no part in the lifestyle of Jews who wish to sanctify themselves. He and his family were sustained in their asceticism by their devotion to Torah study and community service. As much as he could, he tried to inculcate these values in his followers as well.

A chassid from a distant town once came to him complaining that he grew lonely because there were no other chassidim living near him.

Said the *Sfas Emes*, "If you have a *Gemara* with you, then you can never be lonely."

When people called on him to seek his advice (he usually received visitors between nine thirty and eleven o'clock in the morning), they invariably found him sitting before a volume of the *Shulchan Aruch* (Code of Law), which he studied every free moment. "How can one give advice without a *Shulchan Aruch* at hand?" he explained. The *Sfas Emes*'s extraordinary proficiency in all aspects of Torah was acquired in large part by his insistence on not wasting a minute.

Somehow, the *Sfas Emes* found time to commit his own profound thoughts to writing, in commentaries on such holy books as *Tehillim, Koheles, Mishlei, Esther, Pirkei Avos,* and the *Gemara.* Posthumously his writings were given the name *Sfas Emes* by his children based on the verse (*Mishlei* 12:19): שְׂפַת־אֱמֶת תִּכּוֹן לָעַד וְעַד אַרְגִּיעָה לְשׁוֹן שָׁקֶר, *The lips of truth will be established forever, but a lying tongue exists for only a moment.* This was the closing line in the last section he wrote in his commentary on the Torah and festivals (*Parashas VaYechi,* 5665), before he was stricken with his final illness. This title provided the Gerer Rebbe with the name by which he is commonly known.

The following story helps us understand why the *Sfas Emes'* writings are characterized by such a cryptic and abbreviated style. Once he suggested to a certain *talmid chacham* that he write down his *chiddushei Torah* (original Torah thoughts). The latter replied that he would like to but he simply did not have the time.

Said the *Sfas Emes*, "If you write tersely, as I do, it won't take so much of your time."

The *Sfas Emes* rarely agreed to leave his home, but on one occasion he had to travel to another city by train. When he arrived at his destination, he found a large crowd waiting to greet him. Reluctantly he accepted this honor but when one person in the crowd addressed him with the title "Rebbe," the *Sfas Emes* could not restrain himself.

"I'm not your rebbe!" he exclaimed. "I've never taught you anything."

The *Sfas Emes'* grandson, R' Yisrael Alter[1] later remarked, this was the only time he knew of that his grandfather was in error. "He was the Rebbe of the whole Jewish people."

Despite near-total absorption with his studies, writings, and Rabbinic duties, the *Sfas Emes* also found time to take a deeply concerned interest in world events, especially those that affected the Jewish people. The suffering of Russian Jewry in the pogroms of the 1880's caused him deep anguish, as did the conscription of Jews to fight in the Russo-Japanese War of 1905. To those forced to fight in the Russian army he offered compassionate encouragement and heartfelt advice, urging them not to be tempted away from the tenets of Judaism in their time of trial.

These cares took a toll on his health, however, and shortly after Russia's disastrous defeat by Japan he took ill. He passed away on the 5th of Shevat, 5665 (1905), at the age of fifty-eight. In retrospect, we can speculate that Hashem wished to spare this luminary and *tzaddik* the anguish of witnessing the suffering that the First World War was to have on European Jewry.

His years on earth were relatively short, but as his son, Rabbi Avrohom Mordechai, noted after the funeral, "He lived a full lifetime of complete days." In that lifetime, he helped build the town of Ger into the Jerusalem of Polish *chassidus*. Through his leadership, writings, and personal example, he gave powerful expression to the ideals of devotion to Torah and commitment to the Jewish people.

---

1. Author of the *sefer Beis Yisrael* and Gerrer Rebbe until 5738 (1978).

⁂ Themes in His Thought

The voluminous essays of the *Sfas Emes* weave together hundreds of different strands of thought. The following is intended not so much as a comprehensive review of his philosophy, but rather a sampling of his unique insights, especially as they pertain to the ideas expressed in this volume. The sequence presented here attempts to follow the progression of the spiritual development of a Jew, from the early recognition of his inner potential to the realization of the complete capabilities of the Jewish people.

⁂ פְּנִימִיוּת – Personality and Inner Strength

Hashem chose the Jewish people because of the inner spark of spirituality that resides in every Jewish soul. Every Jew has an obligation to fan that spark and nourish it through *mitzvos* and good deeds.

This inner spark, which originates from Abraham, is present in all Jews, even those who stray far from Judaism. Hashem protects it from dying out; this is the meaning of the name *Magen Avraham* the Shield of Abraham. (*Lech Lecha* 5635)

The Torah says that when a *Kohen* removed the smoldering embers of burnt-offerings from the Altar, וְאֵשׁ הַמִּזְבֵּחַ תּוּקַד בּוֹ, *the flame of the Altar burned in* **him** (*Vayikra* 6:2). One would have expected the Torah to say that the flame burned *on the Altar*. However, the Torah here alludes to the spark that smoldered in the heart of the *Kohen*, especially at the time he was performing Hashem's commandments. (Cited in *Maayonos HaNetzach, Parashas Tzav*)

⁂ Growth

Hashem told Abraham to leave his homeland and proceed to the land Hashem would show him (*Bereishis* 12:1). Really this message was not just for Abraham, Hashem calls continuously to every Jew in every generation, "Leave behind your errant ways and return to Me." Alas, we allow ourselves to be distracted by the temptations of the world and do not listen to this inner voice, even though we know it is there. Abraham (and the *tzaddikim* of all times) were sensitive enough to hear Hashem's message clearly and hearken to it. Every Jew has the potential to nurture the same sensitivity in himself, if he would only make the effort.

(*Lech Lecha* 5632)

The third of the Ten Commandments states, *You shall not take the Name of HASHEM, your God, in vain.* Hashem's name is embedded in the soul of every Jew and it is our duty to arouse it rather than squander our potential for spiritual greatness. (*Shavuos* 5636)

The Torah records that when the Jews left Egypt, they traveled from Ramses to Succos. This passage can be understood allegorically to refer to the spiritual "journey" from the degradation and abject slavery they suffered building the city of Ramses to the lofty spiritual level they achieved under the protection of the Clouds of Glory in the Wilderness, which we recreate every year during the festival of Succos.

(*Succos* 5641)

According to Beis Hillel, we kindle an additional candle every night of Chanukah. This serves to remind us that we must seek to elevate ourselves ever higher in a life-long quest to fulfill our potential.

(*Chanukah* 5654)

◆§ Teshuvah (Repentance)

The concept of *teshuvah* (literally "return") refers not only to the expiation of sins but also to the process of returning to the roots of one's soul. Even someone who has not sinned can be a *Baal Teshuvah* by striving to return to his spiritual roots. (*Nitzavim* 5650)

A complete *tzaddik*, someone who has never sinned, has such a strong fear of Hashem engraved in his heart that he can function in the material world without sinning. The *Baal Teshuvah*, on the other hand, having once sinned, must "stand" before Hashem constantly aware every moment Who is watching him, in a way that is not necessary for the complete *tzaddik*. This explains the saying of the Sages (*Berachos* 34b) "In a place where *Baalei Teshuvah* stand, even complete *tzaddikim* cannot stand." In order to maintain this constant perception of Hashem, a *Baal Teshuvah* must have special help from Heaven, help that the complete *tzaddik* does not require.

(*Nitzavim* 5633)

There is at least one portion in the Torah that relates directly to the needs of each generation. For our generation, the final portion of the Torah dealing with the exile and future redemption, calling for Jews to correct their actions and elevate their souls in order to hasten the redemption is especially appropriate. (*Vayelech* 5644)

The *Zohar* notes that a *Baal Teshuvah* can accomplish in one minute what often takes someone else years to master. The greatness of a *Baal Teshuvah* comes from the fact that he redirects the passion he previously used for sinning and now applies it to doing *mitzvos.*

(*Succos* 5636, *Vayakhel* 5635)

◈§ Generation to Generation

The Patriarchs underwent trials that were not necessary for their own spiritual growth but were solely for the sake of setting an example for future generations. For example, Abraham agreed without hesitation to sacrifice his own son in order to impress upon his descendants the need to make personal sacrifices at Hashem's bidding. Hashem, Who sees into the depths of all hearts, could have known that Abraham would give Him unquestioning obedience without subjecting him to such a trial. Likewise, the Jews of Egypt bore a great deal of suffering to minimize the agony of future generations.

(*Vayeira* 5659, Pesach 5640)

Even today we can aspire to the level of previous generations. Ephraim and Menashe were Jacob's grandchildren, yet they merited equal status as tribes alongside their uncles, as Jacob said (*Bereishis* 48:5), "Ephraim and Menashe will be like Reuven and Shimon to me." We and our children are no less capable than they were of rising to the greatness of our predecessors. (*Vayechi* 5632)

Our generation is called the *eikev* (heel) of history, in the sense that in our time the world has descended to an unprecedented low level of moral standards (may Heaven protect us). At the same time, this term offers hope, for just as the heel supports the rest of the body, so can today's generation provide the foundation for future greatness. Thus our time is called *Ikvasa D'Mishicha,* "the *heel* of *Moshiach,*" since our service, difficult and discouraging as it may be, is the support that will bring *Moshiach,* may he come soon. (*Succos* 5636)

In this vein, the verse וְהֵשִׁיב לֵב־אָבוֹת עַל־בָּנִים, *And the hearts of the fathers will be returned to the sons* (*Malachi* 3:24) can be understood as a promise that Hashem will return Jewish children to the spiritual level of their fathers. (*Pesach* 5658)

The Special Role of Jewish Women

The Torah recounts that Jacob received the blessings of his father Isaac indirectly, since Isaac believed he was really blessing Esau. Why could these blessings not have been granted in a more direct manner? The way it actually occurred was preferable because it allowed Jacob's mother Rebecca to play a pivotal role in the drama by redirecting her husband's blessings to the proper recipient. The kindness of her nature helped to mitigate the strict justice that characterized Isaac.

(*Toldos* 5641)

According to some opinions (cf. *Shabbos* 55a), the merits of the Patriarchs have been totally depleted. Those of the Matriarchs, however, still continue. Thus, the Jewish nation will eventually be liberated on the merit of the good deeds of the heroines of Jewish history.

(*Pesach* 5642)

The Power of Love

Israel has a unique and powerful love for its Creator. Even though Hashem says, through the prophet Yirmiyahu (3:8), "I have divorced Israel," we can never accept the concept of being abandoned by Hashem and, however many times He sends us away, we return to stand and wait for Him to have mercy on us. Just as the Torah does not allow a man to divorce his wife if she is mentally unbalanced and will not understand that she is no longer married, so also we can never accept being finally separated from Hashem and always come back to Him.

(*Shoftim* 5647)

Unity Through Torah

Rabbi Akiva's insightful comment, וְאָהַבְתָּ לְרֵעֲךָ כָּמוֹךָ זֶה כְּלָל גָּדוֹל בַּתּוֹרָה, "*You shall love your friend as yourself* is a central rule of the Torah," (*Yerushalmi Nedarim* 9:4) can also be translated in a different manner. The word כְּלָל, (*k'lal*) may refer to *K'lal Yisrael*, the Jewish nation. Thus, Rabbi Akiva's observation may also mean, "The commandment to love your friend as yourself makes Israel into a nation great in Torah." Conversely, common adherence to Torah promotes unity among Jews.

(*Shavuos* 5662)

The fact that the Torah prefaces the laws of the Sabbatical Year with a mention of the Giving of the Torah at Sinai (cf. *Vayikra* 25:1-2) teaches an important lesson. Both served as equalizers of the nation. The observance of *shmittah* demonstrated the economic equality of the people by reminding them that all property belongs to Hashem rather than humans. By the same token, Sinai raised all Jews to the same spiritual plateau, united and equal in their resolve to accept the Torah. Thus, both Sinai and *shmittah* removed all causes for rivalry, and in this way fostered the elusive goal of Jewish unity. (*Behar* 5641)

◆§ Relations Between Jews and Gentiles

One of the key tasks of the Jewish nation is to have an impact on all of humanity through our observance of Torah, to set an example that will inspire the gentiles to *want* to seek Hashem. This is why the Megillah of Ruth is read on Shavuos, to show that even non-Jews like Ruth have within them sparks of sanctity that can be kindled through contact with Jewish ideals. (*Shavuos* 5649)

Ideally, a special relationship could exist between Jews and Arabs because Ishmael, the ancestor of the Arabs, served as a bridge between Israel and the rest of the world, helping to spread knowledge of Hashem among the masses of people. To explain the special role of Ishmael, let us note that the world was created in four categories, *silent* inert matter, *growing* vegetation, *living* animal life, and *speaking* man. Israel, through its study and practice of Torah, constitutes a fifth category, above the processes of nature to which the other four are subject. Between each of the categories are intermediates, which have characteristics in common with the creatures above and below it. For example mushrooms grow but nonetheless resemble inert stones; and monkeys approximate human use of arms and legs but cannot talk.

Ishmael, a son of Abraham but born before he was circumcised, constitutes an intermediary between Israel and the rest of humanity. Thus he is called פֶּרֶא אָדָם, *a wild man* (*Bereishis* 16:12). Though he has the ability to be "wild" like the other nations, if he utilizes his capacity to do good, he becomes a "man," in the sense that only Israel is called man. (*Vayeira* 5650)

◆§ A Spirit of Undying Optimism

Even the seemingly negative events depicted in the Torah contain positive elements and many of the apparently hardened sinners the Torah describes had saving graces. For example, although the leader Elimelech set a bad example by abandoning his followers and fleeing to Moab during a famine, his move eventually brought his Moabite daughter-in-law Ruth to join the Jewish people and bring King David into being. (*Shavuos* 5652)

We should view ourselves not as the generation of the Destruction, but rather the generation of the Rebuilding. Every *mitzvah* we perform is a brick in the reconstruction of the *Beis HaMikdash*. When the Sages said (*Yerushalmi Yoma* 4b) that any generation in whose time the *Beis HaMikdash* is not rebuilt is considered to have contributed to its destruction, they were referring to those generations that do not add their merits to the rebuilding. We hint at this gradual accumulation of merits in the blessing in *Shemoneh Esrei* that says "Who *builds* Jerusalem" rather than "Who *will* build Jerusalem." (*Devarim* 5634)

◆§ Eretz Yisrael

Egypt is compared to an *orlah* (foreskin), in that both are inherently evil and can never be corrected, only excised. Canaan is compared to *pri'ah* (the foreskin that is lifted to reveal the good underneath). That is why the *mitzvah* of *pri'ah* was given only in *Eretz Yisroel.*

(*Acharei* 5651)

While on occasion Eretz Yisrael's temporary inhabitants (e.g. Cannanites) were evil, this is only a surface phenomenon. The land itself only radiates goodness. (*Pesach* 5637)

◆§ Moshiach

The wait for the *Moshiach* can be compared to the search for the *afikomen* during the Pesach Seder. The *afikomen* is the highlight of the meal, but it comes only after extensive preliminaries and searching. However, the long wait only makes the *afikomen* taste that much more delicious when we finally come to it. (*Pesach* 5637)

Though the latest exile has been painfully protracted, perhaps even this may have a silver lining. Hopefully, to compensate us for the difficulty of our wait, Hashem will minimize the calamitous disruptions that have been predicted to accompany *Moshiach's* arrival, and they will prove to be far less painful than we have been led to expect.

(*Pesach* 5642)

The foregoing selections from the writings of the *Sfas Emes* will hopefully serve to whet the reader's appetite for the more extensive presentation of his insights contained in this volume.

While it would be very worthwhile to comprehensively anthologize all of his voluminous writings, (and we hope this will be accomplished with Hashem's help), the focus of this volume will be on examining the Pilgrimage Festivals in the light of his teachings. Few areas of his writing are richer in symbolism and imagery, and also contain more Torah insights, than his comments on the Festivals. In the next section we offer an overview of the significance of the Festivals, both in the time of the *Beis HaMikdash* and in the contemporary era. Following that is a detailed examination of a wide variety of topics relating to the Pilgrimage Festivals, Pesach, Shavuos and Succos.

Monument at gravesite of Sfas Emes

THE THREE FESTIVALS

Introduction to the Shalosh Regalim

שָׁלוֹשׁ פְּעָמִים בַּשָּׁנָה יֵרָאֶה כָל־זְכוּרְךָ אֶת־פְּנֵי ה׳ אֱלֹהֶיךָ בַּמָּקוֹם אֲשֶׁר יִבְחָר בְּחַג הַמַּצּוֹת וּבְחַג הַשָּׁבֻעוֹת וּבְחַג הַסֻּכּוֹת

Three times a year all your males are to appear before HASHEM, *your God, in the place He shall choose, on the Festival of Matzos, on the Festival of Shavuos, and on the Festival of Succos* (*Devarim* 16:16).

This terse account of the requirement to make a pilgrimage to Jerusalem three times a year, together with a few similar descriptions elsewhere (cf. *Shemos* 23:17), is virtually everything that is said in the Torah about what was one of the greatest events in Jewish life at the time of the *Beis HaMikdash.*

How did the pilgrimages affect the people, both during and after their visits to Jerusalem? Did each stay leave a lasting impact, and if so, what? How can Jews of today relate to the concept of presenting oneself before Hashem in Jerusalem, since we are unable to fulfill this commandment as the Torah gave it?

"To Appear Before Hashem" — The Impact of the Pilgrimage

The Torah phrases the obligation to visit Jerusalem three times a year in the following terms: שָׁלוֹשׁ פְּעָמִים בַּשָּׁנָה יֵרָאֶה כָל־זְכוּרְךָ אֶת־פְּנֵי ה׳ אֱלֹהֶיךָ, *Three times a year all your males are to appear before* HASHEM, *your God.* The emphasis seems to be on the *appearance* of a Jew in the *Beis HaMikdash* more than on any other aspect of the pilgrimage. No creature of flesh-and-blood, certainly no one of our generation, which has been deprived of the radiance of the *Beis HaMikdash* for nearly two thousand years, can grasp the full implications of presenting oneself before Hashem on a Festival. Let us attempt, however, to understand the Torah's insistence that we "appear before Hashem" as it relates to the Divine inner spark latent in every Jew.

Hashem's promise to Abraham, אָנֹכִי מָגֵן לָךְ, *I will shield you* (*Bereishis* 15:1), was a promise to protect not only Abraham's person, but also his "inner spark" that we spoke of above. While that spark may lie hidden throughout the year as a Jew goes about his day-to-day activities, on the Pilgrimage Festivals his inner potential for spiritual greatness, his "spark of Abraham," emerges in its true glory. Thus the word זְכוּרְךָ, usually translated *your males*, literally means *your manhood*, the essential inner spark in every Jew. It is that spark that appears before Hashem on the Festivals.

A number of customs that are still observed in some fashion, even now that the *Beis HaMikdash* is in ruins, attest to the impact the Festival had on the Jews of those times. For example, in the time of the *Beis HaMikdash* every Jew was required to immerse in a *mikveh* before the Festival. This custom, which is still widely observed today, was derived by the Sages (*Rosh Hashanah* 16b) from the following verse: וּבְנִבְלָתָם לֹא תִגָּעוּ, *you shall not touch their carcass [of non-kosher animals]* (*Vayikra* 11:8). Figuratively, the Sages may be suggesting that particularly on the Festivals, a Jew must make himself immune ("you shall not touch") from the materialism (the "carcass") that intrudes on his life during the year so that his potential for spirituality can come to the fore. Similarly, the custom of wearing more lavish clothing on the Festivals than on Shabbos points to a significant change that comes over a Jew's body when his inner spark emerges.

Individuals grow at different rates and each Jew is affected by the Festival experience in a unique manner. Moreover, the effects of the Festivals are cumulative so that each Festival adds to the residual impact from the previous ones. Thus the level of sanctity attained on Pesach becomes the starting point from which Shavuos begins. We see an allusion to this phenomenon in the well-known Mishnah (*Peah* 1:1), אֵלּוּ דְבָרִים שֶׁאֵין לָהֶם שִׁעוּר ... הָרֵאָיוֹן, *These precepts have no prescribed measure ... the appearance [which a Jew is required to make on the Pilgrimage Festivals]*. However often one appears in Jerusalem on the Festivals, each time one enters into Hashem's Presence it makes an additional impression on the inner soul.

The *mitzvah* of presenting oneself before Hashem on the Festivals must have been an awesome, overwhelming experience. Consider the dread and fear an ordinary Jew would feel as each Festival approached: "Here I am, an average Jew. How can I show myself in Hashem's Presence with all the sins I've done?" [Even if no one else knows about them, and even if Hashem forgives me, as He always does, I still won't be able to hide from myself.] It required enormous courage — almost to the point of martyrdom — to travel to Jerusalem. Thus in one place the Torah mentions the Festivals (*Vayikra* 23:2) next to a section dealing with martyrdom, implying that appearing in the *Beis HaMikdash* was an act of personal sacrifice.

Such great sacrifice deserved to be rewarded — and indeed it was. In addition to the material blessings that came with the Festival, the pilgrim was granted potent spiritual powers that made his appearance in the *Beis HaMikdash* an exhilarating, growth-oriented experience. We live in a world of passion and physical wants that often conflict with the wishes of the Torah. The pilgrim was promised that the lofty heights he attained on the Festival would not be compromised after he went back to his normal life.

This thought is alluded to in one of the few blessings the Torah gives in connection with the Festivals: לֹא־יַחְמֹד אִישׁ אֶת־אַרְצְךָ בַּעֲלֹתְךָ לֵרָאוֹת אֶת־פְּנֵי ה׳ אֱלֹהֶיךָ שָׁלֹשׁ פְּעָמִים בַּשָּׁנָה, *No man will covet your land when you go up to appear in the Presence of* HASHEM, *your God, three times a year* (*Shemos* 34:24). This verse is usually interpreted as a promise that no one, not even the neighboring nations, would have designs on Jewish property over the Festivals. It can also be understood figuratively, as a promise that no temptations will be allowed to deflect our desire to maintain the spiritual growth we achieved during the Festival.[1] The Festivals, far from being transitory in their impact, permanently changed the life-patterns of a Jew.

The Mishnah (*Avos* 5:7) notes another dimension to the blessings of the Festivals: עוֹמְדִים צְפוּפִים וּמִשְׁתַּחֲוִים רְוָחִים, *[the Pilgrims] stood crowded together, yet prostrated themselves in ample space.* Normally this Mishnah is understood to refer to the extreme crowding experienced in the *Beis HaMikdash.* Yet, when it was necessary to prostrate themselves, they had ample room. Homiletically, however, it also alludes to the relationship between the Festival itself and its

---

1. The word אַרְצְךָ *your land* is understood here to be interchangable with the similar-sounding word רְצוֹנְךָ, *your desire.*

aftereffects. In Jerusalem the Jew stood rooted to his place not because of crowding, but because of his awe at the change that Hashem's Presence wrought on his personality. During the following months he could "spread out" the spiritual advances of the Festival into tangible blessings in the material world.

Similarly, the Psalmist captures the Festival's ongoing effects in the following verse (118:27): אִסְרוּ חַג בַּעֲבֹתִים עַד קַרְנוֹת הַמִּזְבֵּחַ, *Bind the Festival offering with cords until the corners of the Altar.* This is an appeal to every Jew: "Nothing can match the Jewish soul's potential for sanctity; nowhere on earth has the extraordinary ambiance of the *Beis HaMikdash*; and certainly no time of the year approaches the unique opportunity of the Festivals. You, Israel, are blessed with an innate yearning for sanctity that can bind these elements together — the Festival, that most sacred of days, with the Altar, that most sublime of places. (*Pesach* 5636, 5639, 5641, 5646, 5653, 5662)

☙ The Festivals Today

Thus far we have discussed the impact of the Festivals on the Jew in the time of the *Beis HaMikdash*. What does the Festival mean for the contemporary Jew who lives nearly two millennia after the destruction of the *Beis HaMikdash*?

In answer, let us look at another Mishnah in *Avos* (3:15), הַמְבַזֶּה אֶת הַמּוֹעֲדוֹת . . . אֵין לוֹ חֵלֶק לָעוֹלָם הַבָּא, *One who disgraces the Festivals . . . has no portion in the World to Come.* Logically, we may assume that the converse is also true — just as those who disparage the Festivals are so severely punished, those who yearn for the Festivals, even though they may not be able to observe them in the ideal fashion, will be amply rewarded.

The relationship between observance of the Festivals in the time of the *Beis HaMikdash* and in the present time may be expressed as follows. Our forefathers experienced the outer manifestations of the Festivals — the *Beis HaMikdash* with its services and the festivities in Jerusalem. At times, unfortunately, they failed to render proper appreciation and respect for the experiences they enjoyed, as we see often in the admonishments of the prophets. We, on the other hand, want passionately to see the *Beis HaMikdash* rebuilt so that we can personally feel the spiritual effects of the Divine Service. Perhaps, with our painfully frustrated yearnings, we are better off than those who did not value the *Beis HaMikdash* and the Holy City they had the privilege of enjoying first hand. Thus our prayers for the restoration of the *Beis HaMikdash* act as a substitute for the offerings brought by our forefathers.

In this light, the Sages' institution of a second day to the Pilgrimage Festivals in the Diaspora reveals Israel's powerful yearning to retain as much of their effects as possible, even today. While in the time of the *Beis HaMikdash* one day was sufficient to absorb the lessons of the Festival, now two days are needed.

Moreover, the sensitive contemporary Jew who constantly prays for the rebuilding of the *Beis HaMikdash* can still experience, even now, a ray of the light that emanated from the *Beis HaMikdash* on the Festivals. By learning about the Festivals and discussing their impact on us today, we can make up at least in part for the absence of the *Beis HaMikdash*. As the Talmud notes (*Megillah* 32a), Moshe established the custom to study about the Festivals, insuring that some of the impact of these days could be experienced at all times, even today.

The verse we cited to introduce this essay, *Three times a year all your males are to appear before HASHEM, your God,* (*Devarim* 16:16), can also be read, *All your males shall* **see** *Hashem's Presence*. During the Festivals, a Jew could actually perceive Hashem's Presence in the *Beis HaMikdash*. Today's Jew, although he can no longer perceive that Presence, is still "seen" by Hashem on every Festival.

(*Pesach* 5632, 5636, 5646, 5662)

⸙ Shabbos and the Festivals

Israel observes two kinds of special days, the weekly Shabbos and the Festivals. While the two may appear similar in some ways, fundamentally they are quite different.

Shabbos enhances the Jewish soul with an extra dimension of holiness through the additon of an "additional soul" (*neshamah yeseirah*). On the Festivals, an even more momentous phenomenon occurs. The *body* of the Jew is not only consecrated, it is actually transformed and revitalized. Thus certain additional kinds of "work" are permitted on the Festivals — those connected with preparing food. On *Yom Tov* the Jewish body is no longer merely the "casing" for the soul. It, too, becomes so hallowed that by preparing food on the Festival one is simply enabling the body to discharge its sacred functions.

Other significant differences exist between the comparatively subdued Shabbos and the far more joyful Festivals. Whereas Shabbos is inherently sacred, the Festivals must be consecrated by Israel's action in proclaiming the New Moon. Inasmuch as every Shabbos God grants us the privilege of celebrating His creation of the world (cf. *Beitzah* 16b), on the Festivals we commemorate events that happened to us. While Shabbos commemorates an event that occurred in total privacy, the Festivals are an observance of events that took place in full public view. (5660, 5664)

Unlike the Festivals, which could be fully appreciated only in Jerusalem and therefore required several grueling treks each year, on Shabbos the Jew basks in the sanctity of the day in the comfort of his home. This is implied in the verse, שַׁבָּת הִוא לַה׳ בְּכֹל מוֹשְׁבֹתֵיכֶם, *It is a Shabbos for HASHEM in all of your dwelling places* (*Vayikra* 23:3). Observing Shabbos properly does not require going to Jerusalem, because Hashem enters every Jewish home in the world on Shabbos. (5647)

Finally the effect of Shabbos is transient whereas the Festivals leave a permanent impact. The pilgrim was forever changed by his visit to Jerusalem. This may explain why we do not savor fragrant spices in the *havdalah* service at the end of a Festival, even when a festival coincides with *Motzaei* Shabbos. *Tosafos* suggests (*Pesachim* 102b) that the function of spices in *havdalah* is to compensate for the loss of the "additional soul" that departs at the conclusion of Shabbos. The "additional soul" granted on a Festival, however, never departs at its conclusion. (*Emor* 5647)

◆§ Names Denoting the Festivals

In the Torah and Rabbinic literature, numerous names are used to denote the Pilgrimage Festivals. They are called מוֹעֵד (cf. *Vayikra* 23:2), a term connected with the concept of bearing witness (עֵדוּת). The mass pilgrimage of Jews to Jerusalem, as well as the profound impact on the souls and bodies of Jews on the Festivals, all "bear witness" to the unique relationship between the Creator and Israel. Thus the Torah uses the expression מוֹעֲדֵי ה׳, "Hashem's festivals." In the liturgy, however, the holidays are described with reference to their role *vis a vis* Israel — "the time of *our* freedom," "the time of the giving of *our* Torah," "the time of *our* gladness." This change in perspective testifies to Israel's unique relationship with the Creator. Only a "couple" with so close an association could "exchange" holidays. (*Pesach* 5662)

The word מוֹעֵד contains the same root letters as דַעַת, *da'as* (knowledge). The Festivals provide a great opportunity for Jews to acquire knowledge of the Creator. (*Pesach* 5634)

The Festivals are also called חַגִּים, a cognate of the word חוּג, *circle*, suggesting that the Festivals are pivotal times of the year, focal points of the "circle" of Jewish life. (*Pesach* 5662)

The Torah additionally refers to the Festivals by the word רְגָלִים (cf. *Shemos* 23:14). While this word literally means "feet," indicating that the Jews made their journey to Jerusalem by foot, it also has the connotation of "habit" from the word רְגִילוּת. The Festivals were the most propitious times of the year to shake off one's lethargy, and make the needed changes in one's accustomed lifestyle. (*Pesach* 5632)

Similarly, the Festivals are called פְּעָמִים (cf. *Shemos* 23:17). This word means not only "time," but also "bell" (פַּעֲמוֹן), because they rouse us from our lethargy and awaken in us the higher spiritual aspirations that lie dormant most of the year. (*Pesach* 5656)

Another name in the Torah for the Festivals is (*Vayikra* 23:2), מִקְרָאֵי קֹדֶשׁ, *holy convocations* (from the word מִקְרָא, *reading*). On these days one can "read" the aura of holiness, that is, one can perceive the holiness in whatever place one finds oneself. (*Pesach* 5631)

Finally, Rabbinic literature's established custom refer to these Festivals as *yamim tovim*, "good days." This term may be a reference to the light Hashem created at the beginning of time, the light of which the Torah says, וַיַּרְא אֱלֹהִים אֶת־הָאוֹר כִּי־טוֹב, *and* H*ASHEM* *saw that the light was good* (*Bereishis* 1:4). Although Hashem hid this light from humans to keep it in reserve for the World to Come, since it was too holy and potent for this earth, during the Festivals, a glimpse of its sanctity penetrate through to the earth. This "good light" can be perceived and enjoyed in some small measure. (*Pesach* 5631)

Pesach

The Pesach Seder

לֵיל סֵדֶר / A Night of Order[1]

We begin this essay "A Night of Order" with a brief discussion of two traditional names associated with this night, לֵיל שִׁמּוּרִים, *night of watching*, and סֵדֶר, *order*.

Chiddushei HaRim suggests that calling the ritual of this night "Seder" conveys a message of great significance. Miracles are not simply haphazard events — rather there is a methodical symmetry to the way Hashem arranges the wonders He does. Expanding on this thought, we may say that a function of the Seder is to instill a sense of "order" to the events of the Exodus, as we shall explain.

The Exodus occurred with such rapidity — even the Paschal Lamb was eaten in haste — that the Jews had no time to absorb its significance. Therefore we are given an opportunity each year to relive the events we could not appreciate as they were happening by discussing them, performing *mitzvos* that commemorate them, and praising Hashem for them. The Seder is far more than a replay of the same rituals year after year; on the contrary, each successful Seder adds meaning to the original events and brings us closer to the Final Redemption.

Thus the prophet Yeshayahu proclaims (52:12): כִּי לֹא בְחִפָּזוֹן תֵּצֵאוּ, *You will not leave in haste*. Unlike the Exodus from Egypt, when *Moshiach* arrives, our departure from exile will not be in such haste. Perhaps this refers not only to physical haste, but also to the conceptual haste, spoken of above, that left our ancestors no time to contemplate and absorb the meaning of their liberation. The final redemption cannot take place until we fully understand the meaning of the Exodus. By finding a new meaning in the story of the Exodus each year, and giving *seder* — order — to our understanding of that first night of our freedom

1. Introductory Note: This essay on "A Night of Order" is intended only as a general overview of a few comprehensive issues related to the Seder.

as a nation, we bring closer *Moshiach's* arrival and the final redemption.

The Torah itself teaches us the importance of understanding the Exodus: *I am* HASHEM, *your God, Who brought you out from the the land of Egypt to be a God to you* (*Bamidbar* 15:41). Only through the Seder, the annual reorganization and re-evaluation of our national freedom, can we further the objective of the Exodus, to make Hashem into our God and bring the final redemption. We find this point in the Haggadah: כָּל יְמֵי חַיֶּיךָ לְהָבִיא לִימוֹת הַמָּשִׁיחַ — *[You should relate the story of the Exodus] all the days of your life to bring the time of Moshiach.*

In light of the above, the questions posed by the Four Sons also play a central role in the Seder by elucidating the lessons of the Exodus.

Expanding on this theme, we may suggest that the Seder brings a new "order" to the universe, as we shall explain. Hashem's plan at the time of the Exodus was to fashion a perfect world in which mankind, led by the Jews, would accept His sovereignty. This dream, which should have been realized in the period following the Exodus, was thwarted by the attack of Amalek, which dampened Israel's ardor to serve Hashem. Thus Israel's hatred for Amalek stemmed not so much from the physical threat they posed as from the spiritual damage they caused by delaying, by several millenia, the dream of unifying humanity under Hashem's banner.

Every year at the Seder, we seek to undo the lingering damage Amalek caused, by retracing our steps out of Egypt and bringing closer the original dream of an ideal world openly ruled by Hashem. In other words, we rearrange our universe, giving it a new *order* closer to specification. The damage Amalek did cannot be undone all at once. However the cumulative effect of yearly incremental achievements will over time bear rich fruits, as the Mishnah says, (*Berachos* 1:5) לְהָבִיא לִימוֹת הַמָּשִׁיחַ, *to bring the days of Moshiach.* (5642, 5635)

◆§ לֵיל שִׁמּוּרִים / A Night of Watching

This phrase could also be translated *a night of protection* (based on a common meaning of the word שׁוֹמֵר, "to guard"). Let us consider the implications of this interpretation. The protection generated by the Seder night is actually sufficient to last for an entire year, as the Torah says, (*Shemos* 12:42) שִׁמֻּרִים לְכָל־בְּנֵי יִשְׂרָאֵל לְדֹרֹתָם, *a protection for all the Children of Israel for their generations.*

The *afikoman,* which we keep intact until the end of the Seder instead of eating it earlier with the required portions of *matzah,* is symbolic of the protection generated this night that continues beyond this one night. Our ability to persevere in the face of the challenges we encounter throughout the year is undoubtedly in the merit of this protection. (5652)

We may further suggest that *matzah* itself accords Divine protection for the rest of the year, as the Torah says (*Shemos* 13:10) וְשָׁמַרְתָּ אֶת־הַחֻקָּה הַזֹּאת לְמוֹעֲדָהּ מִיָּמִים יָמִימָה, which can be paraphrased, "You will be protected by observing this statute [i.e. *matzah*] in its designated time from day to day."

The simple meaning of this phrase, however, is that this night has a built-in protection against the normal perils of the nighttime hours. Even this protection extends to all the nights of the year, as indicated by the plural form שִׁמּוּרִים, *protections*, one for each night. (5653)

A second meaning of this phrase, "a night of watching," alludes to the anticipation every Jew feels approaching the night of the Seder. Not only Israel, but Hashem as well, awaits this evening anxiously, as indicated by the plural form לֵיל שִׁמּוּרִים, *a night of waitings.* Waiting for the Seder is not merely a prelude to the event but actually adds to its meaning — the more one anticipates this greatest of nights, the greater the spiritual uplift he will be privileged to derive from it.

It is significant that the verse describing the night of waiting contains two different words for "night": לֵיל and לַיְלָה. The addition of the letter *heh* (ה) in לַיְלָה connotes a more potent kind of night. Before the Exodus, miracles on such a scale of magnitude were unknown. The night of Passover was a לֵיל, a future dream waiting to be realized. After the Exodus and the precedent Hashem set for rearranging the natural order of His universe for Israel's benefit, the dream wistfully voiced by לֵיל became the potent reality indicated by the additional *heh* of לַיְלָה. The Jew can dream of *Moshiach* on Seder night with confidence; since the vision of liberation (לֵיל) was realized once, it has achieved the status of לַיְלָה, and will certainly become reality again. (5651)

◆§ Haggadah Recitation: Why No Blessing?

The question arises why we do not recite a blessing on observing the Torah's commandment of retelling the story of the Exodus. One possible answer is that blessings are recited only on those commandments that we would not have known to do on our own. Therefore the blessing recited before most *mitzvos* emphasizes that *Hashem* commanded us to perform the commandment, to show that we would not have performed it on our own. Retelling the story of the Exodus, however, is something we would surely do simply on the basis of gratitude, without being formally commanded. As the Sage Rav observed (*Pesachim* 116a) "A servant whose master releases him from bondage and gives him gold and silver [as the Jews received at the time of the Exodus and the Splitting of the Sea] should praise his master." So too, we would praise and thank Hashem for our freedom on our own, even if He had not commanded us to do so. (5640)

Similarly, we may ask why we do not recite, the traditional blessing commemorating miracles, שֶׁעָשָׂה נִסִּים לַאֲבוֹתֵינוּ, *Who has wrought miracles for our forefathers,* as we do on Chanukah and Purim? The text of this blessing, however, implies that we are thanking Hashem for performing miracles on behalf of our forefathers and suggests that those miracles were undeserved gifts. By contrast, the Exodus was important not only to our ancestors but to the universe itself, whose continued existence was in jeopardy until then. As we discuss at length in the section on Shavuos, without a nation devoted to serving the Creator, the universe would have no reason for continued existence. Thus it would be inappropriate to make a blessing that implies that our ancestors were the main beneficiaries of the miracles when in reality the entire universe depended on them.

We see that the continued survival of the universe was dependent on the Exodus from the stipulation Hashem made with the Sea at the time He created it: "Split your waters for the Jews or you will cease to exist."[1]

Alternatively, the Sages (*Pesachim* 118a) say that the phrase כִּי לְעוֹלָם חַסְדּוֹ, *For His kindness endures forever* is repeated twenty-six times in *Psalm* 136 parallel to the twenty-six generations from the Creation until the Giving of the Torah that were kept alive exclusively through Hashem's kindness. This Psalm lists all the miracles done in connection with the Exodus, indicating that these miracles were necessary for the continued survival of the world.

This understanding of the importance of the Exodus in the survival of the universe gives us a better appreciation of the Jews' idealism at the

1. For a fuller discussion of this idea, see our commentary on the the verse (*Shemos* 14:27), וַיָּשָׁב הַיָּם ... לְאֵיתָנוֹ, *The Sea returned to its power,* in the essay on the "Preparations for the Song" (*Yalkut Shemos* 237).

time. The last section of the Song recounts the fearful reaction of various nations — the Philistines, the Caananites, Edom and Moab. The Jews wanted primarily, for these peoples to accept Hashem's sovereignty so that His open eternal reign could start immediately. Their intention to intimidate these nations was only secondary. How did the Jews come to have such lofty ideals? They realized that, since the universe's existence was renewed as a result of the Splitting of the Sea, this was an opportune moment to revitalize all of Hashem's creations — mankind as well as heaven and earth. (5637)

❧ אַרְבַּע כּוֹסוֹת / The Four Cups of Wine

The Seder commences with *Kiddush*, which is recited over the first of the Four Cups of wine. Let us consider the significance of these cups, which recur throughout the evening and are central to the symbolism of the Seder.

The most common explanation of the Four Cups is that of the Palestinian Talmud, in which each of the cups corresponds to one of the four expressions of redemption used by Hashem in His promise to Moshe at the beginning of *Parashas Vaeira* (*Shemos* 6:6-7): וְהוֹצֵאתִי אֶתְכֶם מִתַּחַת סִבְלֹת מִצְרַיִם וְהִצַּלְתִּי אֶתְכֶם מֵעֲבֹדָתָם וְגָאַלְתִּי אֶתְכֶם בִּזְרוֹעַ נְטוּיָה . . . וְלָקַחְתִּי אֶתְכֶם לִי לְעָם — *I will take you out from the burdens of Egypt and I will save you from their slavery and I will redeem you with an outstretched arm .. and I will take you to Me as a nation.*

At the time this promise was made, the Jews were totally unable to absorb such lofty ideals, as the Torah reports (v. 9), *They did not listen to Moshe because of shortness of spirit and harsh labor.* Yet Moshe's appeal was not in vain. Even though that generation could not accept the concept of redemption, we as their proxies drink the Four Cups every year to demonstrate our appreciation to Hashem for fulfilling His promise; given with these four expressions. As a free nation — free to serve Hashem — we celebrate our ability to appreciate that which our forefathers were too burdened to accept at the time. (5644)

Why is wine the best medium for expressing redemption? Wine enjoys a peculiar trait — the ability to bring ordinarily hidden matters into the open, as the Sages said (*Sanhedrin* 38a), נִכְנַס יַיִן יָצָא סוֹד, *when wine goes in, secrets come out.*

It is not enough merely to understand the concept of redemption on an intellectual and theoretical level — we must feel our freedom as an emotion arising from the depths of our souls. Wine has the power to bring out these "secret" feelings, to make us feel every year that *we* ourselves are being liberated on this night.

In the *Beis HaMikdash,* the *Korban Pesach* (Paschal Lamb) had even more power to elicit appreciation of the miraculous nature of our freedom. As we discuss elsewhere the word "Pesach" can be understood as a combination of the two words פֶּה and סָח — the mouth that talks. The offering and eating of the *Korban Pesach* aroused the people's capacity to verbalize their joy at being free to serve Hashem.

Seemingly, the requirement to drink the Four Cups was instituted only after the destruction of the *Beis HaMikdash*. Just as the *Korban Pesach* had inspired Jews to sing of the joy they felt in the story of the Exodus, the Four Cups of wine, to a lesser extent, aroused the same feelings.

In this light we can give a figurative interpretation to the Mishnah (*Pesachim* 10:1) that states *Even the poorest man of Israel ... [the administrators of the charities] must provide him with no less than four cups of wine*: Even our spiritually destitute generations (the "poor man" of Israel) must still strive for the same Divine revelation once obtained from the *Korban Pesach*. How do we do this? By drinking the Four Cups. Spiritually impoverished as we may be, the Four Cups elicit the same emotions once elicited by the Paschal Lamb. (5653)

But what is the significance of the number *four*? — *four* cups corresponding to *four* expressions of redemption.

The *Zohar* states that "the power of speech" (symbolizing the ability to speak Hashem's praises, as we discuss at length in the essay on the Ten Commandments in the section on Shavuos, see page 250) was also "in exile" in Egypt. There are five principal organs of speech: the lips, teeth, tongue, palate, and throat. Of these the matzah symbolizes the teeth, since it must be finely chewed before it can be digested, and the other four are represented by the Four Cups.

The Four Cups, then, and the four expressions of redemption, both connote the ability of the liberated Jew to praise Hashem that was a primary accomplishment of the Exodus. Thus King David sings (*Tehillim* 81:11), אָנֹכִי ה׳ אֱלֹהֶיךָ הַמַּעַלְךָ מֵאֶרֶץ מִצְרָיִם הַרְחֶב פִּיךָ וַאֲמַלְאֵהוּ, *I am* HASHEM*, your God, who raised you from the land of Egypt, open wide your mouth and I will fill it*. Hashem brought us out of Egypt to free us to open our mouths so that He could fill them with His praises. (5633)

These groupings of four may also correspond to the four senses by which Hashem "perceived" the Jews' suffering in Egypt, as the Torah says (*Shemos* 2:24-25): וַיִּשְׁמַע אֱלֹהִים אֶת־נַאֲקָתָם וַיִּזְכֹּר אֱלֹהִים אֶת־בְּרִיתוֹ אֶת־אַבְרָהָם אֶת־יִצְחָק וְאֶת־יַעֲקֹב: וַיַּרְא אֱלֹהִים אֶת־בְּנֵי יִשְׂרָאֵל וַיֵּדַע אֱלֹהִים: — *God **heard** their groaning, and God **remembered** His covenant with Abraham, with Isaac, and with Jacob. God **saw** the Children of Israel and God **knew.*** While the senses of sight and hearing are easily understood, the other senses require further examination.

The Torah refers to that part of the *minchah* offering that was burned (for Hashem to *smell*) as an אַזְכָּרָה, *a remembrance*, (*Vayikra* 2:2), indicating a connection between Hashem's sense of smell and His memory. Also, we find that the reasoning power is often referred to in Rabbinic literature as טַעַם, *taste*, suggesting a connection between that sense and Hashem's "knowledge."

By drinking the Four Cups, we demonstrate our appreciation of Hashem's concern for the plight of the Jews in Egypt. This is expressed by the four "senses" the Torah uses in describing Hashem's perception of the Jews' suffering in Egypt.

To carry this further, the sense of *touch* is symbolized at the Seder by the requirement to recline on the left side as we drink the Four Cups and perform other *mitzvos* symbolic of our freedom. This in turn corresponds to the *tefillin* worn on the left hand. Our reclining reminds us of the protectiveness Hashem displayed for the Jews as they left Egypt. We find an allusion to *touching* in connection with the left side, as an expression of protectiveness in *Shir HaShirim* (2:6): שְׂמֹאלוֹ תַּחַת לְרֹאשִׁי וִימִינוֹ תְּחַבְּקֵנִי, *His left hand is under my head and His right hand embraces me.* We lean on Hashem's protective left hand, as His right hand envelops us affectionately.

We can also draw a parallel between the Four Cups and the four *parashios* of *tefillin.* The first cup, over which we say Kiddush, corresponds to the *parashah* קַדֶּשׁ־לִי כָל־בְּכוֹר, *Sanctify to Me every firstborn* (*Shemos* 13:1-10). The second cup, which we pour as we begin to recite the *Haggadah* and leave in front of us throughout the recitation, until after the climax of the redemptive process וְהִכְנִיסָנוּ לְאֶרֶץ יִשְׂרָאֵל corresponds to the *parashah* וְהָיָה כִּי־יְבִאֲךָ, *And it shall be when* Hashem *will bring you* (ibid. v. 11-16), which speaks of our coming to *Eretz Yisrael.* Even though the second *parashah* gives greater emphasis to our freedom, the first *parashah* alludes to the fact that the whole purpose of the Egyptian exile was to prepare us for eventual sanctification. For this reason it appears first in the Torah.

The third cup, which we drink upon reciting *Birchas HaMazon* (Grace After Meals), corresponds to the *parashah* of *Shema.* Just as we thank Hashem for the physical sustenance He gives us, the *Shema* proclaims our appreciation for the spiritual sustenance that flows from Him.

Finally, the fourth cup, after which we pronounce the blessing *For the land and for the fruit of the vine,* corresponds to the second *parashah* of *Shema,* (*Devarim* 11:13) וְהָיָה אִם שָׁמֹעַ, which speaks of the conditions necessary for survival and prosperity in *Eretz Yisrael.*

(5655)

Alternatively, the four cups symbolize the four kinds of lasting effects the Exodus had, as seen by their placement in the Seder. The first cup, *Kiddush*, suggests that Hashem's Name was sanctified through the Exodus. The second, poured prior to the four questions and over which we recite the *Haggadah*, celebrates the Exodus itself. The third cup, consumed with Grace After Meals, represents the material well-being we received from the wealth of the Egyptians. Finally the fourth cup, over which we beseech Hashem to pour out His wrath on the wicked, alludes to the destruction of Egypt's wicked during the Exodus.

(5646)

Finally, we may say that the Four Cups symbolize the four exiles to which the Jewish people have been subjected, Egypt, Persia, Greece and Rome, and the punishment that will be visited upon them. It is thus very fitting that over the fourth cup, corresponding to the present exile, the longest and bitterest of all, we beseech Hashem, שְׁפֹךְ חֲמָתְךָ אֶל הַגּוֹיִם אֲשֶׁר לֹא יְדָעוּךָ, *Pour Your wrath upon the nations that do not recognize You.* May He soon have mercy on His people and punish those who have pushed us, physically and spiritually, and propelled us so far away from the Kingdom of Heaven. (5636)

קָרְבַּן פֶּסַח / The Pesach Offering

פֶּסַח שֶׁהָיוּ אֲבוֹתֵינוּ אוֹכְלִים בִּזְמַן שֶׁבֵּית הַמִּקְדָּשׁ הָיָה קַיָּם עַל שׁוּם מָה? עַל שׁוּם שֶׁפָּסַח הַקָּדוֹשׁ בָּרוּךְ הוּא עַל בָּתֵּי אֲבוֹתֵינוּ בְּמִצְרַיִם.

The Pesach offering eaten by our forefathers during the period when the Temple stood — for what reason was it eaten? Because the Holy One, Blessed is He, passed over the houses of our fathers in Egypt.

What is the significance of the Pesach offering? As the Haggadah states, by partaking of the offering our forefathers commemorated how God had passed over the Jewish homes in Egypt. The question remains, however, why would the festival and the offering derive their name from this event?

The Haggadah may well be alluding to some of the less obvious — and equally critical — ramifications of God's passing over the Egyptian homes. As Solomon suggests, (*Shir HaShirim* 2:8) קוֹל דּוֹדִי . . . מְדַלֵּג עַל־הֶהָרִים, *the voice of my lover . . . making [me] skip on the mountains* [i.e. God helping Israel to surmount all obstacles]. When God "skipped" over the Jewish homes in Egypt on the night of our liberation, He enabled the Jewish people to do likewise and "skip" over every obstacle that had impeded their spiritual growth. By revealing a new dimension of His interaction with our world He allowed man to emulate that "skipping." Rather than using the expected form דוֹלֵג, *He skips*, Solomon says מְדַלֵּג, *He made [me] skip*. The overriding message of the name Pesach is "skipping" — making a quantum leap and growing spiritually. At the Sea, beleaguered by Pharaoh's armies, the Jewish people seized the "profession" of their forefathers (תָּפְסוּ אוּמָנוּת אֲבוֹתָם) and prayed. In a larger sense every Passover, we leap to attain the standards and the high moral levels achieved by our forefathers. This may be the intent of that well-known verse וְהֵשִׁיב לֵב־אָבוֹת עַל־בָּנִים, *God will return the hearts of fathers to the children*, (*Malachi* 3:24), which we understand to mean that God will grant children the hearts of their fathers. He will grant them the wherewithal to leap beyond their own limitations to follow the ways of their fathers. (5643)

Not only do the Jewish people "leap" every Passover, but so does God "leap," as it were, over His own customary procedures, ignoring His mode of guiding history because of His love for Israel, as will be detailed. Passover is a time of Divine Judgment (דין), as symbolized by the blood of the Pesach offering. The roasting of the lamb over fire represents the wrath God reserves for evildoers. On that first Passover God "leaped" over His customary practice and transmuted the very symbols of strict judgment, blood and fire, into factors that spared the Jewish people. While blood is ordinarily a symbol of harsh judgment culminating in death, Israel would *live* by its blood. Indeed, night is usually a time of Divine justice, but on the night of Pesach, it was transformed into a period of mercy.

The verse כַּחֲצֹת הַלַּיְלָה אֲנִי יוֹצֵא בְּתוֹךְ מִצְרָיִם, *At about midnight I shall go out in the midst of Egypt*, (*Shemos* 11:4) may be reinterpreted in this light. The night, which is ordinarily a time of strict justice, was tempered by kindness on this night. God Himself personifies justice blended with mercy, for He described both as a אֵשׁ אוֹכְלָה, *consuming fire*, (*Devarim* 4:24), and the source of our life [וְאַתֶּם הַדְּבֵקִים בַּה׳ אֱלֹהֵיכֶם חַיִּים כֻּלְּכֶם], (ibid 4:4).

Upon further reflection, one need not view the above process as a transformation of justice into Divine kindness. Rather it should be seen as the removal of a harsh outer layer in order to reach inner goodness. In other words, that which may appear as harsh justice on the surface (חִיצוֹנִיוּת) is, in reality, Divine kindness. Those who are prescient to appreciate how events that often appear to be detrimental to us are really blessings in disguise. Why is this outer surface, this "facade" of harsh justice, even necessary? Because Divine kindness — like anything else that is valuable — must be protected by an exterior covering. This covering is "justice." While other nations may not be able to penetrate beyond the surface and are thus subject to strict justice — Israel is able to peel away such outer trappings.

In this context, we can also appreciate why the Torah places great emphasis on the entrance of the Jewish doorway [וּפָסַח ה׳ עַל־הַפֶּתַח, *And Hashem will pass over the entrance* (*Shemos* 12:23)]. The doorpost symbolizes the home's *outer* surface. It is only the outer surface, harsh justice, that could prove dangerous to Israel — and therefore God "leaps" over that surface and spares Israel. Once that barrier has been surmounted, the inner treasure-trove of Divine kindness is attained. It is noteworthy how often the outer perimeter of a Jewish entity is inhibited or actually removed. The foreskin (עָרְלָה), representing the human being's surface appearance, is circumcised. The *mezuzah* guards the doorpost of the Jewish home, and the night of protection (לֵיל שִׁימּוּרִים) protects the Jewish people at the year's beginning [see our commentary on סוּכּוֹת page 343 for the relationship between עוֹלָם, (place) שָׁנָה, (time of year), and נֶפֶשׁ (most enlightened souls)]. In this instance, the *mezuzah* symbolizes protection for the place (עוֹלָם); the *milah*, the soul (נֶפֶשׁ); and the Passover night, the time (שָׁנָה). If we consider God's admonition to Cain, לַפֶּתַח חַטָּאת רוֹבֵץ, *sin* [i.e. the Evil Inclination — יֵצֶר הָרָע] *lies [waiting] by the opening* (*Bereishis* 4:7), we can appreciate even more the need for the opening of every entity to be guarded. The opening is the point of vulnerability from a spiritual standpoint. Even the opening to Eden itself is guarded by the cherubs and the blade of the rotating sword! (5654)

The term Pesach (as has been discussed in the section on the Four Cups and elsewhere) may also be an acronym spelling out פֶּה סָח, *the mouth that talks*. While in Egypt, the Jewish people were unable to articulate God's praises, but after they were redeemed, they could assume their role of praising God and propagating His word.

David sings: (*Tehillim* 81:11) אָנֹכִי ה׳ אֱלֹהֶיךָ הַמַּעַלְךָ מֵאֶרֶץ מִצְרָיִם הַרְחֶב פִּיךָ וַאֲמַלְאֵהוּ — *I am* HASHEM *your God who raised you from the land of Egypt — open wide your mouth and I will fill it*. As this indicates, the Exodus enabled Israel to sing God's praises freely.

On Passover night we open our mouth — we voice our first words as Jews, by reciting and expounding upon the Haggadah. God, in turn, promises to fill our mouths with words of Torah (וַאֲמַלְאֵהוּ) on Shavuos. As the Talmud (*Succah* 42a) states, once a child begins to talk his father should teach him Torah. Paralleling this dictum, as soon as we were able to sing His praises, on Pesach, God responded by teaching us the Torah on Shavuos. This process is repeated yearly.

This progression from the halting first words of Passover to the Torah-imbued speech of Shavuos may explain the significance of the reading and fulfillment of a Torah passage relating to these two festivals. On Passover, we quote extensively from the portion that a Jew was to read while offering the first fruit: אֲרַמִּי אֹבֵד אָבִי. On Shavuos, we celebrate the actual bringing of those fruits. In this context, on Passover as we "re-learn" the art of speech we choose the selection from the *Bikkurim* ceremony describing our first days as God's people. On Shavuos, by actually bringing the First Fruits we commemorate Israel's maturity, the fulfillment of its Divine mission. It is even possible that both modes of speech — the initial halting speech of Passover and the Torah imbued speech of Shavuos — are alluded to in the introduction to the First Fruits ceremony — וְעָנִיתָ וְאָמַרְתָּ, *you should answer* (*Devarim* 26:5), [i.e. respond feebly] *and you should say* [your Torah thoughts on Shavuos]. (5639)

◆§ מַצָּה / Matzah

מַצָּה זוּ שֶׁאָנוּ אוֹכְלִים עַל שׁוּם מָה? עַל שׁוּם שֶׁלֹּא הִסְפִּיק בְּצֵקָם שֶׁל אֲבוֹתֵינוּ לְהַחֲמִיץ עַד שֶׁנִּגְלָה עֲלֵיהֶם מֶלֶךְ מַלְכֵי הַמְּלָכִים הַקָּדוֹשׁ בָּרוּךְ הוּא וּגְאָלָם. . .

This matzah that we are eating — for what reason [is it eaten]? Because the dough of our fathers did not have time to become leavened, before the King of Kings, the Holy One Blessed is He, revealed Himself to them and redeemed them. . .

We eat *matzah* to commemorate that our forefather's dough did not rise. Let us consider why this event is so significant that we commemorate it annually with a week-long prohibition of *chametz?* What great tragedy was averted when God revealed Himself so hastily that our forefathers' dough was not yet leavened?

Apparently, time was of the utmost essence that first Passover night. Had Israel tarried even for moments, they would have become assimilated into Egyptian society to the point of no return. As the Midrash states, Israel would have sunk into the fiftieth gate of defilement — the lowest abyss of impurity, from which they could never have emerged. God's revelation came just in time to avert a national catastrophe — the end of the Jewish people forever. (5639)

To elaborate further on the potential tragedy of Israel sinking into the fiftieth level of impurity, consider the ideal counterweight to the Jewish people's backsliding, — Moshe. According to the Talmud, (*Rosh Hashanah* 21b) Moshe had ascended to the forty-ninth gate of knowledge of God (מ״ט שַׁעֲרֵי בִּינָה). Only the fiftieth gate, complete comprehension of God's ways, eluded him. Had the Jewish people been permitted to descend into the lowest level of defilement, no leader, not even Moshe, despite his enormous erudition, could have brought about Israel's redemption. [A leader must be able to extricate his people from their defilement and he can accomplish this only through personal achievement. Each gate of Moshe's knowledge of God corresponded to an equivalent level of the nation's defilement.]

In this light, we can understand Moshe's reluctance to accept the mantle of Jewish leadership. He feared that the Jewish people would sink to the fiftieth gate of defilement, thus hampering his ability even at the exalted forty-ninth level of Divine understanding to aid in their liberation.

The Messiah, however, will reach levels of Divine comprehension attained by no mortal not even Moshe, including the fiftieth gate of Divine understanding. As Yeshaya describes Israel's future leader: (52:13) יָרוּם וְנִשָּׂא וְגָבַהּ מְאֹד, *He will be high and very exalted,* the term "very" indicating a level of achievement even higher than Moshe's.

In fact, when Moshe asked God to designate someone else as the Redeemer — *send through whomever You will send* (*Shemos* 4:13, cf. Midrash on שְׁלַח־נָא בְּיַד תִּשְׁלָח) — he meant that a better Redeemer would be the ultimate Messiah, for Moshe knew that he **could** effect Israel's liberation, regardless of their spiritual level.

This comparison between Moshe and the Messiah may explain why the Exodus from Egypt had to occur in haste, whereas the final redemption (see *Yeshayah* 52:12) [spearheaded by the Messiah, who will have ascended to the highest level of understanding,] need not occur hastily. (5659).

Yet a question remains. Why is the concern about Israel's near assimilation portrayed in terms of dough rising? Couldn't another metaphor or a direct statement that God released them before they could assimilate — be equally valid? The response to this question helps explain the prohibition of *chametz*: Had the dough risen, the Evil Inclination (יֵצֶר הָרָע), symbolized by the yeast that causes dough to rise, would have been permanently embedded in the Jewish personality. By not permitting the dough to rise, God gave Israel the opportunity to extricate itself from the *Yetzer Hara's* clutches.

But why is the *Yetzer Hara* likened to yeast and leavened dough (שְׂאוֹר שֶׁבָּעִיסָּה). Possibly, as Rav Schneur Zalman of Liadi suggested, because fluffy, leavened bread symbolizes haughtiness (גַּאֲוָה), the precursor of many sins. Unleavened bread, matzah, on the other hand, epitomizes humility and simplicity. God's revelation was not only a hurried action preventing Israel from letting the matzah rise, but far more profoundly, it meant symbolically how could the Jews manifest haughtiness (symbolized by leavening) in the presence of God?

Even the spelling of the words matzah (מַצָּה) and *chametz* (חָמֵץ) bespeak their nature. In essence, these two contrasting bread-forms are spelled identically except that מַצָּה contains a ה (*hei*) and *chametz* a ח (*ches*). Examine the shape of a ה. Its short left foot represents an inner segment (נְקוּדָה פְּנִימִיּוּת), symbolizing the inner spark implanted by God in every Jew. However, in the case of the ח (as in *chametz*), that inner spark is elongated and become attached to the rest of the letter. This suggests that the individual has subsumed the Divine spark in his quest for self-aggrandizement. Why else would one take the Divine imprint, the soul that is distinct from the body and truly unique, and relegate it as a secondary adjunct to one's own materialistic drives? (5631)

God insisted that the Pesach offering be eaten in haste. Likewise, He "hurried" the Jewish people through the bread baking process not permitting it to rise. We follow this practice every year at the Seder. The Talmudic requirement that we hurry the eating of matzah at the Seder חוֹטְפִין מַצָּה בְּלֵילֵי פְּסָחִים (*Pesachim* 109a), usually interpreted "to hurry the Seder," and by doing so ensure that the children will remain awake throughout the Seder — symbolizes our own determination to speedily take advantage of God's Revelation on this night. It bespeaks our determination not to fall into the abyss of assimilation, not to forget the Divine spark in our midst. (5639)

In light of our discussion (in the segment on the Pesach offering), emphasizing the distinction between the surface manifestation of harsh justice (מִדַּת הַדִּין) and the inner reality of Divine kindness (מִדַּת הַחֶסֶד) we can derive additional meaning from God's determination not to let the matzah leaven. Matzah, simple flour and water that it is, symbolizes an inner core of Divine kindness. On the other hand, leavened bread consists of that same inner base of ingredients comprising matzah — but with the addition of an extraneous outer layer, reminding us of justice. At the time when Divine justice is transmuted into Divine kindness, we dare not even possess, let alone eat or benefit from any trace of *chometz* — the outer layer of strict justice. In this context, one can understand better why prohibitions do not extend to the *chametz* of a Gentile. Since Passover is indeed a time of judgment for mankind, as it was when the Egyptian firstborns were slain, *chametz* is a particularly appropriate symbol at this time of year for the world at large. *Chametz* is inappropriate only for Jews, for whom justice was transmuted into mercy. (5654)

One final comment on this passage: In the Haggadah we read of God's Revelation. When did this occur? While one may think that the Haggadah is referring to the Seder night, in reality the verse cited by the Haggadah, וַיֹּאפוּ אֶת הַבָּצֵק, *They baked the dough* (*Shemos* 12:39), occurred on the following day. Apparently, the Haggadah is referring to the Divine cloud by which God revealed Himself to the Jewish people in Rameses. This, too, was called redemption because of the spiritual liberation that

Israel felt as their souls were released from the utter despondency of slavery to the sublime pleasure of becoming God's servants. (4640)

◆§ לֶחֶם עוֹנִי / Bread of Poverty

הָא לַחְמָא עַנְיָא דִי אֲכָלוּ אַבְהָתָנָא בְּאַרְעָא דְמִצְרָיִם

This is the bread of poverty that our forefathers ate in the land of Egypt.

An important aspect in understanding the concept of מַצָּה fully is to explore the reasons for it being called לֶחֶם עֹנִי — "the bread of poverty" (*Devarim* 16:3)

In contrast to the "poverty" that characterizes the *matzah* of Egypt, the Torah speaks of *Eretz Yisrael* in the following terms (*Devarim* 8:9): אֶרֶץ אֲשֶׁר לֹא בְמִסְכֵּנֻת תֹּאכַל־בָּהּ לֶחֶם, *a land in which you shall not eat bread in poverty.* Underlying this contrast is a profound spiritual distinction: When our forefathers left Egypt, taking *matzah* with them, they took no active part in bringing about their liberation. In this sense their liberation was one of poverty, not sustained by their own merits. Furthermore, they barely understood the miraculous events connected with it. The spiritual darkness that enveloped Egypt all but obscured the light of Torah; Egyptian bread was the bread of *intellectual* poverty.

By eating *matzah* we evoke the merit of our forefathers, who followed Hashem into the wilderness, in spite of the fact that His plan was totally beyond their comprehension at that time. As the prophet Yirmiyahu sang (2:2), זָכַרְתִּי לָךְ חֶסֶד נְעוּרַיִךְ . . . לֶכְתֵּךְ אַחֲרַי בַּמִּדְבָּר בְּאֶרֶץ לֹא זְרוּעָה — *I remember for you* [Israel] *the kindness of your youth . . . your walking after me into the wilderness, in a land that was unsown.*

When they entered *Eretz Yisrael,* however, our forefathers were charged with a new mission — to serve Hashem in an atmosphere of Torah knowledge and intellectual sophistication, as well as material prosperity. (This is the deeper meaning of the phrase we say in Grace After Meals, אֶרֶץ . . . טוֹבָה וּרְחָבָה, *a good and broad land* — a land conducive to intellectual breadth and scope.) This shift in mission is alluded to by the Mishnah (*Avos* 4:11): כָּל הַמְקַיֵּם אֶת הַתּוֹרָה מֵעֹנִי סוֹפוֹ לְקַיְּמָהּ מֵעֹשֶׁר, *Anyone who observes the Torah despite poverty will eventually observe it in wealth.* In reward for following Hashem out of

Egypt and accepting the Torah in spite of their lack of comprehension of its depth (intellectual poverty); the Jewish people were given the privilege and responsibility of studying and observing it amidst the intellectual wealth of *Eretz Yisrael*.

If so, why do we begin the Seder by emphasizing that *matzah* is "the bread of poverty"? The reason emerges from the same Mishnah in *Avos*: כָּל הַמְבַטֵּל אֶת הַתּוֹרָה מֵעֹשֶׁר סוֹפוֹ לְבַטְּלָהּ מֵעֹנִי, *Anyone who neglects the Torah amidst wealth will eventually neglect it in poverty*. Because the Jews did not fulfill their mission in spite of the rich intellectual atmosphere of *Eretz Yisrael* and the *Beis HaMikdash*, they were exiled and returned to their earlier "impoverished" intellectual status. Thus the *matzah* we eat symbolizes our (at least partial) return to the intellectual darkness that enveloped our forefathers in Egypt, and our trust and faith that Hashem will again have mercy on us and redeem us as He did then.[1]

(5663)

Alternatively, by calling *matzah* "the bread of poverty" the Torah may be hinting to a powerful lesson about the Jew's relationship to material matters. In the words of the Mishnah (*Avos* 1:17), לֹא מָצָאתִי לְגוּף טוֹב אֶלָּא שְׁתִיקָה, *I have found nothing better for [the body] oneself than silence*. To paraphrase this, where material matters are concerned, there is nothing better than "silence" — a humble and simple approach. The more we avoid the honors and creature comforts that accrue with wealth, the more we will subordinate our bodies to our souls. Indeed, body and soul collaborate best in their common mission to serve Hashem when each reaches its potential, the body through humility and self-negation, and the soul through joy.

Thus just a week after leaving Egypt the Jews were able to sing the Song at the Sea, with all its splendid insights ordinarily beyond the reach of most Jews, because of the *matzah* they ate, with its message of physical humility and spiritual exaltation. (5660)

This humility and self-negation implicit in *matzah* was particularly important for the generation of the Exodus. They had been charged with the difficult task of making themselves into servants of Hashem, a task which would have been impossible — how can a newly-liberated nation

---

1. *Editor's note*: Lest the objection be raised that the present Torah atmosphere which flourishes in yeshivos throughout the world, through the kindness of Heaven, could hardly be called "intellectual darkness," we can only say that we, in our generation, have no conception of the brilliant light that shone from the *Beis HaMikdash* and lit up the whole world with knowledge of Hashem.

voluntarily subject itself to yet another master — were it not for their experience with servitude in Egypt. Having sampled Pharaoh's brand of subjugation, of which the *matzah* they ate was a constant reminder, the Jews were now prepared to accept Hashem's sovereignty. Thus it was *matzah*, the bread of slavery, that enabled Israel to subjugate themselves to Hashem.

Matzah is a pointed reminder not to become haughty. Not infrequently, newly-liberated nations let power go to their heads. But *matzah*, with its taste of humility and servitude, reminds us of our humble origins as slaves. Indeed, we may say that all the suffering and anguish we have endured in our history has had the same purpose: to humble us so that when Hashem shows us the great miracles that will accompany His salvation (in the near future, we hope) we will react with joy and enthusiasm rather than arrogance. (5633)

There is another historical dimension to the concept of "bread of poverty." Adam, in the aftermath of his sin, was given a curse: בְּעִצָּבוֹן תֹּאכֲלֶנָּה כֹּל יְמֵי חַיֶּיךָ . . . בְּזֵעַת אַפֶּיךָ תֹּאכַל לֶחֶם — *You will eat in sadness all the days of your life . . . By the sweat of your brow you shall eat bread* (*Bereishis* 3:17,19).

Israel, through two hundred ten years of toil and frustration, was not only preparing for a glorious future but was also rectifying Adam's sin of eating the Forbidden Fruit (as we discuss in the essay on the Offering of the Omer; pg. 70). Consequently, Hashem's curse to Adam, that man eat bread under stress and that the earth itself would resist him, was lifted when Israel completed its period of slavery. According to this approach, the suffering of Egypt (symbolized by *matzah*) transmuted all "bread," (i.e. the entire material world) from a cursed commodity into a source of blessing. (5651)

The Talmud, however, interprets the term לֶחֶם עוֹנִי, *bread of poverty*, as being related to the similar word עוֹנֶה, *to answer*: לֶחֶם שֶׁעוֹנִין עָלָיו דְּבָרִים, *Bread on which one answers words* (*Pesachim* 115b). This statement is usually understood to mean that the Haggadah should be recited in the presence of *matzah*. In the following discussion, however, we will consider other possible interpretations of this Rabbinic saying. In particular, we will discuss whether pronouncing words (עוֹנִין עָלָיו דְּבָרִים) is a *means* towards the end of partaking of *matzah* or, on the contrary, eating *matzah* is a means to achieve the ability to pronounce sacred words.

In the first approach, reciting the Haggadah is seen as a way to enhance the spiritual benefit we derive from eating *matzah*. The *Zohar* calls *matzah* מִיכְלָא דְאַסְווּתָא, the food of healing, suggesting that eating *matzah* provides spiritual healing. Nevertheless, not everyone who eats *matzah* merits to experience so dramatic a change; the spiritual healing that *matzah* brings must be *earned.* Those who ate the first *matzah* earned it through the suffering they experienced in Egypt. The Jew of today needs the merit of retelling the story of the Exodus to derive the spiritual benefit of eating *matzah*. (5655)

Conversely, eating *matzah* is also a way to enhance the words of Torah we say over it. As we discussed in the essay on the Four Cups, (pg. 48) the Jews lacked the ability to describe Hashem's wonders articulately until they partook of the *Korban Pesach* (Paschal Lamb) on the night of the Exodus, (alluded to in the word *Pesach,* which can be broken down into the component words פֶּה and סָח, *the mouth that talks*).

Eating *matzah* and reciting the Haggadah is spiritually therapeutic for the contemporary Jew as well. By eating matzah the Jew helps to rectify any improper acts associated with eating (e.g. eating non-kosher food or eating without making proper blessings). Reciting the Haggadah in the presence of *matzah* gives a Jew the ability to articulate Hashem's praises.

Why does the Talmud use the plural form דְּבָרִים, *words*? This may indicate an additional blessing that comes from *matzah,* the *words* of Torah, an enhancement of our ability to study Torah and to pray to Hashem. This propensity of matzah to enhance both prayer and Torah study may be discerned from a discrepancy between the written and spoken form of the term "bread of poverty." It is written deficient, without a *vav* — עֹנִי — but read as if it had one. This is strikingly similar to Isaac's description of Jacob's voice — הַקֹּל קוֹל יַעֲקֹב, *the voice is Jacob's voice,* (*Bereishis* 27:22) — the first time without a *vav* and the second time with. The *Zohar* says that קֹל without a *vav* refers to prayer, while קוֹל alludes to learning Torah. In this instance also, we may infer that by eating *matzah* we can merit to the benefits of both עֹנִי without a *vav,* the enhanced ability to pray, as well as עוֹנִי with a *vav,* help in Torah study. (5652)

◆§ מָרוֹר / Maror

מָרוֹר זֶה שֶׁאָנוּ אוֹכְלִים עַל שׁוּם מָה? עַל שׁוּם שֶׁמֵּרְרוּ הַמִּצְרִים אֶת חַיֵּי אֲבוֹתֵינוּ בְּמִצְרַיִם

Why do we eat this bitter herb? Because the Egyptians embittered the lives of our fathers in Egypt.

It is often presumed that eating the *maror* is a sad and discordant note in our night of national jubilation. Upon further contemplation, however, we begin to realize that every activity performed at the Seder even the eating of *maror* reflects our sense of gratitude to God for His miracles. If partaking of the Pesach offering and matzah are joyous acts, so, too, is the eating of *maror*. By eating the *maror* we are expressing gratitude for all of the bitterness associated with the Egyptian exile.

Consider some of the benefits accruing from our forefather's suffering. The Egyptians' hatred prevented the Jewish people from totally assimilating. As David states, (*Tehillim* 105:25) הָפַךְ לִבָּם לִשְׂנֹא עַמּוֹ, *He turned their* [the Egyptians] *hearts to hate His nation* [Israel]. Furthermore, during those bitter days in Egypt we learned to cry (see our discussion on the Prelude to the Splitting of the Sea pg. 132). The anguish and torment of the Jewish people engendered the Redemption, as it says (*Shemos* 2:23), וַיֵּאָנְחוּ בְנֵי יִשְׂרָאֵל מִן הָעֲבֹדָה וַיִּזְעָקוּ וַתַּעַל שַׁוְעָתָם אֶל הָאֱלֹהִים *And the Children of Israel groaned from the toil and they cried out, and their pleas went up to God.*

During this bitter period the Jewish people underwent a purification process, removing impurities [the wicked] and attracting sparks of sanctity. Prior to this purification, we were a family. Having gone through the crucible of Egypt we emerged purer than ever, and became a nation. As the Torah says, (*Devarim* 4:20) וַיּוֹצִא אֶתְכֶם מִכּוּר הַבַּרְזֶל מִמִּצְרָיִם לִהְיוֹת לוֹ לְעַם נַחֲלָה *God took you from Egypt, out of the iron crucible to become His nation of heritage.*

We thank God for the bitterness in Egypt and even for the bitterness of the contemporary exile. By eating *maror* and remembering the benefits of Egyptian slavery, we are able not only to cope with, but to actually *sweeten*, the misery and bitterness of our exile. Partaking of the *maror* is a powerful demonstration of the Jew's belief that all our bitterness is a mere prelude to eventual liberation. (5644, 5632, 5636)

By eating matzah and *maror* together, we are also demonstrating the consistency of God's ways. One might contemplate (ח״ו) that the Exodus was a break with the previous pattern of slavery, that they contradicted one another. To refute this mistaken contention, we combine matzah and *maror*, indicating that bitterness enabled liberation. True, the suffering epitomizes death (*maror's* numerical equivalent, 446, is identical with that of מָוֶת, *death*). But the virtual demise of the Jewish personality decreed in Egypt had the effect of creating a new and better less assimilated and more loyal Jew, a nation prepared for the

Exodus. By eating *maror,* we express our profound belief that our contemporary bitterness, deadly though it may be, is the prelude to revival and redemption. As we say in our daily prayers: מֶלֶךְ מֵמִית וּמְחַיֶּה וּמַצְמִיחַ יְשׁוּעָה, *O [G-d is a] King who causes death [so that He can then] restore life and make salvation sprout.* (5653)

Our discussion thus far has focused on the individual *mitzvos* of the *Seder.* However, in order to obtain a fuller appreciation of the Seder and its practices, we should consider the relationships between these *mitzvos,* as well.

✎§ כּוֹרֵךְ / Matzah and Maror

One of the most significant relationships is that of the matzah and *maror,* a relationship already stipulated by the Torah: עַל מַצּוֹת וּמְרֹרִים יֹאכְלֻהוּ, *one should eat it* [i.e. the Pesach offering] *with matzah and bitter herbs* (*Bamidbar* 9:11).

The significance of eating matzah and *maror* together may be deduced from God's promise to Jacob as the Patriarch prepared to enter Egypt: (*Bereishis* 46:4) אָנֹכִי אֵרֵד עִמְּךָ מִצְרַיְמָה וְאָנֹכִי אַעַלְךָ, *I will go down with you to Egypt and I will also bring you up.*

By eating matzah with *maror,* we underscore that God is present not only during periods of freedom (symbolized by the matzah) but even during the most bitter periods of exile, (*maror*) as well. God protected Jacob's descendants even as they were enslaved in Egypt. While His rule may not have been as *apparent* during Israel's period of torment, God was present in Egypt. In fact, the term אֵרֵד, used to connote going down, also is used to express "reigning" (such as in וְיֵרְדְּ מִיָּם עַד יָם) *dominate from sea to sea* (*Tehillim* 72:8). Hashem reigns even in the bitterest periods of Jewish history. This is expressed by the combined matzah and *maror* sandwich (כּוֹרֵךְ). This thought is echoed in *Tehillim,* (91:15) עִמּוֹ אָנֹכִי בְצָרָה, *I am with him in his times of suffering.* Likewise, Solomon sings, צְרוֹר הַמֹּר דּוֹדִי לִי בֵּין שָׁדַי יָלִין, *My lover is a bundle of myrrh. He lies between my bosom,* (*Shir HaShirim* 1:13) which is homiletically interpreted, אע״פ שֶׁמֵּיצַר וּמֵימַר לִי בֵּין שָׁדַי יָלִין, (*Yalkut Shimoni Shir HaShirim* 984) *even though He lets me suffer and causes me bitterness, He still rests between my bosom.*

The love between Israel and Hashem has not abated, even during difficult periods. While other rulers appear to have total control over the Jewish people, this is so only because God authorized them to do so for a limited period. As David notes, מַלְכוּתְךָ מַלְכוּת כָּל עֹלָמִים, *your kingdom [is the source] of all world kingdoms* (*Tehillim* 144:13).

It is noteworthy that מְרוֹרִים, *bitter herbs*, has the identical numerical equivalent (גְּמַטְרִיָא) as that of מַלְכוּת (kingdom), to emphasize that God's sovereignty is in full force even under the most bitter circumstances. The plural form מְרוֹרִים, *bitter herbs*, suggests that not only during the Egyptian exile but throughout each of the other bitter periods of exile, the message of matzah, of freedom and Divine control, remains paramount. (5663)

The relationship between matzah and *maror* may also be expressed in the following manner. It was the *maror*, the bitterness of Egypt, that enabled the Jewish people to retain their true character in Egypt. Such unyielding loyalty to authentic tradition is represented by the matzah, simple flour and water that has not been transformed nor processed. By eating matzah and *maror* together (as Hillel did with כּוֹרֵךְ), we are suggesting that it was the *maror's* bitterness that enabled us to attain matzah-like characteristics. If the Jewish people didn't adopt Egyptian names or the Egyptian language, it is because the *maror*-like ambiance of Egypt didn't permit it. In fact, each aspect of Abraham's vision at the Covenant (בְּרִית בֵּין הַבְּתָרִים) eventually emerged as a blessing. As compensation for their period of sojourning and second-class citizenship, the Jewish people were granted the most desirable habitat, the Land of Israel. The enforced servitude to Pharaoh was attenuated by their becoming God's servants, and the oppression of Egypt was a vital prerequisite for receiving the Torah at Sinai. The Talmud states (*Megillah* 6b) that Torah insights and true understanding can only be achieved through exertion (יָגַעְתִּי וּמָצָאתִי תַּאֲמִן). The toil and torment of Egypt substituted for the intensive efforts usually required to attain mastery of Torah. As David states, (*Tehillim* 119:71) טוֹב לִי כִּי עֻנֵּיתִי לְמַעַן אֶלְמַד חֻקֶּיךָ, *It is good for me that I was oppressed, so that I may learn Your statutes*. Perhaps, homiletically, the term לֶחֶם עוֹנִי, *bread of poverty* (see our notes on this topic) may refer to the Torah [often compared to bread לְכוּ לַחֲמוּ בְלַחְמִי; (*Mishlei* 9:4)], which was attained through affliction. (5658)

It is also possible that the "sandwich" of matzah and *maror* expresses the feeling of the contemporary Jew reflecting upon the first exile and the first redemption. By partaking of this combination, we affirm that we survived all the tribulations of millennia of exile because God sustained us throughout the bitterness of the Egyptian exile, symbolized by *maror*. If we will merit liberation, it will be because the liberation from Egypt set the stage for all future liberations. (5647)

קָרְבַּן פֶּסַח, מַצָּה, וּמָרוֹר / Pesach Offering, Matzah, and Maror

The contemporary Jew, bereft of the Temple, partakes only of matzah and *maror*. While the Temple stood, however, our forefathers ate all three, the Pesach offering, matzah, and *maror*. What could this "triple sandwich" signify? Perhaps each of these items represents one aspect of the Exodus: Matzah signifies how the Jewish people did not substantially change while in Egypt; *maror* represents the downfall of the wicked Egyptians who caused us so much bitterness, and the offering (derived from *pasach*, to leap; see the Pesach offering pg. 51) symbolizes God's "liberation," for God not only extricated Israel, but departed Himself from Egypt's vile society. Which aspect of the Exodus is cause for greatest celebration? The Torah itself suggests the answer עַל מַצּוֹת וּמְרֹרִים יֹאכְלֻהוּ, *eat [the Pesach offering "over" the] matzos and bitter herbs* (*Bamidbar* 9:11), implying that our joy over God's departure from Egypt (symbolized by the Pesach offering) should be even greater than that of our liberation. (5661)

מַצָּה וְיַיִן / Matzah and Wine

These two aspects of the Seder may also be related. As stated the Exodus and its process of separating good from evil had the effect of atoning for Adam's first sin of eating from the Tree, which blurred the distinction between good and evil and caused them to merge in mans psyche (עֵץ הַדַּעַת טוֹב וָרָע).

Both matzah and wine represent the process of carefully watching, so that good (desirable and halachically permitted food) and evil (prohibited substances) do not become mixed. Matzah must be carefully guarded so that it does not rise. Wine is zealously watched so that it does not become prohibited through contact with an idolater. By partaking of both matzah and wine, we help atone for Adam's sin of confusing good and evil. In fact, the Talmud states (*Berachos* 40a) various opinions as to the nature of the Forbidden Fruit eaten by Adam, among these opinions are grapes (producing wine) and wheat (the source of bread). By partaking of matzah and wine at the Seder, we assist in rectifying Man's first sin. (5663)

Finally, one may deduce a relationship between three components of the Seder: *maror*, the Pesach offering, and telling about the Exodus (סִפּוּר יְצִיאַת מִצְרַיִם). An analogy can be drawn between these three commandments and three major sins, the performance of each of these *mitzvos* helping to rectify a particular sin.

The slaughter of the Pesach offering involves blatant defiance of Egyptian paganism, under whose tenets the lamb had been revered. The eating of *Maror*, whose numerical equivalent is identical to death (מָוֶת) [thus reminding us of the bitterness associated with murder], helps atone for murder (שְׁפִיכַת דָּמִים). Discussion of the Exodus, a *mitzvah* performed verbally, counteracts the sin of evil speech, which is committed by mouth. (5662)

The Omer Sacrifice

◆§ Introduction

וַיְדַבֵּר ה׳ אֶל מֹשֶׁה לֵּאמֹר דַּבֵּר אֶל־בְּנֵי יִשְׂרָאֵל וְאָמַרְתָּ אֲלֵהֶם כִּי־תָבֹאוּ אֶל־הָאָרֶץ אֲשֶׁר אֲנִי נֹתֵן לָכֶם וּקְצַרְתֶּם אֶת־קְצִירָהּ וַהֲבֵאתֶם אֶת־עֹמֶר רֵאשִׁית קְצִירְכֶם אֶל הַכֹּהֵן וְהֵנִיף אֶת־הָעֹמֶר לִפְנֵי ה׳ לִרְצֹנְכֶם מִמָּחֳרַת הַשַּׁבָּת יְנִיפֶנּוּ הַכֹּהֵן

HASHEM spoke to Moses saying: Speak to the Children of Israel and say to them: When you arrive in the Land that I give you and you reap its harvest; you are to bring an Omer from your first harvest to the Kohen. He is to wave the Omer before HASHEM to gain acceptance for you; on the morrow of the rest-day the Kohen is to wave it (*Vayikra* 23:9-11).

The above verses state the Torah's requirement to bring an offering from the first fruits of the harvest each year on the second day of Pesach. Before discussing the details of this offering, let us look at several comments by the Sages about this *mitzvah,* which highlight its importance.

הֵבִיאוּ לְפָנַי עוֹמֶר בַּפֶּסַח כְּדֵי שֶׁתִּתְבָּרֵךְ לָכֶם תְּבוּאָה שֶׁבַּשָּׂדוֹת

[Hashem said] Bring before Me the Omer on Pesach so that the grain in the fields should be blessed for you (*Rosh Hashanah* 16a).

,,וְאַתָּה אֶת בְּרִיתִי תִשְׁמֹר" זוּ מִצְוַת הָעוֹמֶר שֶׁלֹּא זָכָה אַבְרָהָם אָבִינוּ לִירוּשַׁת הָאָרֶץ אֶלָּא בִּזְכוּת הָעוֹמֶר

And you shall observe My covenant (Bereishis 17:9*); this refers to the commandment of the Omer. Abraham inherited the land of Israel only in the merit of the Omer.*

הִיא שֶׁעָמְדָה לָהֶם בִימֵי הָמָן

This [the merit of Omer] is what stood for [i.e. saved] them [the Jewish people] in Haman's time (cf. *Midrash Rabbah Vayikra* 28:6*).*

As the passage from the Torah says, (ibid., v. 10) on the second day of Pesach an *omer* of barley (a dry measure equivalent to a tenth of an *ephah* or the volume of approximately 43.2 average eggs) was harvested and then brought to the *Kohen* as an offering. The selections from the Talmud and Midrash suggest that the Jewish people attached great importance to this offering since not only the coming year's harvest depended on it, but also the fate of *Eretz Yisrael* and the ongoing struggle with Amalek.

In the following essay we discuss the significance of "the morrow of the rest day," the apparently redundant phrase "to gain acceptance for you," the relationship between the Omer and *Eretz Yisrael,* the connection between the Omer and prosperity, and the impact of Israel's ongoing battle against Amalek. Finally, we will consider the timing of the Omer offering.

מִמָּחֳרַת הַשַּׁבָּת / The Morrow of the Rest Day

According to tradition, the Omer was offered on the second day of Pesach, which the Torah calls מִמָּחֳרַת הַשַּׁבָּת, *the morrow of the rest day (Sabbath).*

What is the relationship between the weekly Sabbath and Pesach? Even superficially we can see certain resemblances between the two occasions. For one thing, the Torah prescribes both of them with the same two words, זָכוֹר, *remember*, and שָׁמוֹר, *guard*.[1]

To understand the significance of these words, let us relate them to the inner spark of every Jew (*pintele yid*) that, while it may lie hidden during the week, comes alive every Shabbos. "Remember the Sabbath day to keep it holy" (*Shemos* 20:8), can be rephrased, "Remember the Sabbath — remember who you are every Shabbos and allow that part of your personality that is the essence of *you*, that is always remembered and can never be forgotten any more than your name can be forgotten, let that element of you emerge at least on Shabbos, if not during the rest of the week. On the other hand, protect (שָׁמוֹר) your soul — don't let it dissipate in an environment inappropriate for Shabbos."[2]

On Pesach also, the *pintele yid*, the spark of Godliness in every Jew, finds new expression. *Matzah*, called the "bread of poverty," with its purity and simplicity, is a moving symbol of the undefiled soul that emerges afresh each year on Pesach. By "watching" *matzah* to protect it from rising (שְׁמִירָה), וּשְׁמַרְתֶּם אֶת־הַמַּצּוֹת, *You shall watch the matzohs* (*Shemos* 12:17), we symbolically protect our souls from corruption. By remembering the Exodus (זָכוֹר), we remind ourselves that our souls, which have been transplanted into this world, are given new life every Pesach. The verse (*Shemos* 12:14) וְהָיָה הַיּוֹם הַזֶּה לָכֶם לְזִכָּרוֹן, *this day should be a remembrance for you*, alludes to the fact that Pesach is a particularly auspicious time to remember our purpose in life — to do Hashem's bidding. (5657)

Additionally, Pesach and Shabbos both give us the opportunity to testify that it was Hashem, the living God, Who created the universe. By refraining from work on Shabbos, we affirm that Hashem created the world in six days and rested on the seventh. Until the Exodus, however, we were unable to articulate our belief that Hashem rules the world. As we have said in several places in this section, the name "Pesach" is a composite of the two words פֶּה and סָח, "the mouth that talks." Only after the Exodus were we free to praise Hashem openly as the Creator of the universe. Were it not for Pesach, then, Shabbos would be only an

---

1. וְהָיָה הַיּוֹם הַזֶּה לָכֶם לְזִכָּרוֹן *this day shall be a remembrance for you* (*Shemos* 12:14), לְמַעַן תִּזְכֹּר אֶת־יוֹם צֵאתְךָ מֵאֶרֶץ מִצְרַיִם כֹּל יְמֵי חַיֶּיךָ, *that you may remember the day of your departure from the land of Egypt all the days of your life* (*Devarim* 16:3), and also וְזָכַרְתָּ כִּי עֶבֶד הָיִיתָ בְּמִצְרָיִם וְשָׁמַרְתָּ . . . אֶת־הַחֻקִּים הָאֵלֶּה, *Remember that you were a slave in Egypt and guard these statutes.* (*Devarim* 16:12)

2. For a fuller discussion of the connection between זָכוֹר and שָׁמוֹר, see our essay on the Ten Commandments in the section on Shavuos (pg. 250).

abstraction. Pesach is rightfully called a "rest-day" — only because of it does the sacred message of Shabbos have any meaning in the world.

(5657)

The relationship between Shabbos and Pesach may be explained homiletically as follows. The Mishnah (*Avos* 5:8) teaches that destructive spirits, symbolic of all evil, were created in the twilight of the first Shabbos. The Talmud (cf. *Chagigah* 16a) notes that, these beings were not properly formed and remained as souls without bodies. The *Zohar* (*Parashas Terumah* 155b), comments that the onset of Shabbos brings with it a certain cessation of the power of evil.

Similarly, at the time of the Exodus the Jews had served only two hundred and ten of the four hundred years of exile that Hashem foretold to Abraham. This was sufficient because Hashem overruled the forces of evil to suspend Israel's sentence. Hashem's love for Israel — especially when it is based on our merits — has the power to shorten any decree. Thus both Pesach and Shabbos represent the abrupt cessation of evil. May Hashem soon grant that the remaining forces of evil in the world, which cause all of our suffering in the current bitter exile, soon be abruptly terminated.

The Talmud relates that if the final redemption comes as a result of Israel's merit, it will occur before its designated time. Pesach, Shabbos, and the day of Israel's final redemption (described by the Mishnah (*Tamid* 7:4) as "the day which is entirely Shabbos") are all times when evil, and all that accompanies it comes to an abrupt termination.

(*Shabbos Hagadol* 5656)

◆§ Waving the Omer

Let us now turn our attention to the larger significance of the Omer Service. Why should waving a few select kernels of barley have such a great impact that Israel considers its viability and prosperity to be dependent on the proper performance of this service?

◆§ Separating Good From Evil

In answer, let us consider the signficance of the Omer in the context of man's first sin and the lasting effect it left on the world. After partaking of the Forbidden Fruit, Adam was admonished, וְקוֹץ וְדַרְדַּר תַּצְמִיחַ לָךְ, *Thorns and thistles shall sprout for you* (*Bereishis* 3:18).

When Adam ate from the Tree of the Knowledge of Good and Evil, the distinction between good and evil became blurred — figuratively, the chaff intermingled with the grain.[1]

There were other implications of this blurring of good and evil as well, such as the dispersal among the non-Jewish world of "sparks of sanctity," for example sacred souls such as Ruth and Yisro. Similarly, alien influences have found their way into the Jewish world and must be purged. Much of this process occurred during the Egyptian exile, which was described as an "iron furnace" that smelted out spiritual impurities.

By *separating* a small quantity from the first harvest (רֵאשִׁית קְצִירְכֶם) and offering it to Hashem, we symbolically undo (at least partially) the confusion between good and evil caused by Adam's sin. Thus the elaborate sifting process that produced the barley brought as the Omer offering symbolizes the sifting of good from evil that reverses the effects of Adam's sin.[2]

There could be no better time than Pesach to offer the Omer, which has the effect of undoing mankind's basic sins. The Exodus was the end of our dual enslavement — both to the struggle to eke out a living from the earth by the sweat of our brow, and to the Egyptian oppressor. Once we were finally liberated from Adam's curse, we could begin to take steps to reverse his sin by bringing the Omer offering.

Pesach, and the other festivals, give us an opportunity to correct another aspect of this curse, בְּעִצָּבוֹן תֹּאכְלֶנָּה כֹּל יְמֵי חַיֶּיךָ, *with anxiety shall you eat all the days of your life* (*Bereishis* 3:17). The festivals are also a source of blessing for the Jewish farmer. As the Talmud reminds us (*Rosh Hashanah* 16a), on Pesach grain is blessed, on Shavuos fruit trees, and on Succos we are blessed for an abundant supply of rainfall. Thus the festivals, with their blessings for prosperity, transform the grief that since Adam's curse has come to be associated with survival, into joy. The joy of the festivals comes not only from the joyous

1. Before he ate the forbidden fruit, Adam was able to distinguish clearly between good and evil. Even though it was possible to disobey Hashem, as he did, at least he was aware that he was doing wrong. After the sin, however, the distinction between good and evil blurred and it became possible for people to justify their misdeeds with the claim that they were doing good.

2. *Avos* (5:18) voices a similar theme: A Torah scholar is, at times, blessed with the ability to act as a sieve. A sieve is so constructed that it allows the coarse grain to pass through and retains only the fine flour. So, too, is a good Torah student who retains the essence of his Torah studies and disregards the irrelevant.

historical events they commemorate but also from this reversal of Adam's decree of sadness. (5662)

The above discussion helps us appreciate the connection between the Exodus, with its message of purging evil from good, and the offering of the Omer. But how do later generations, long removed from the Exodus, set the stage for the Omer simply by recounting the story of the Exodus every year? Reciting the *Haggadah*, with its dominant theme of the emergence of good from evil — the Patriarchs from early idol worship and the evil Laban, and the Jews from Pharaoh's Egypt — is an excellent preparation for the sifting of good from evil represented by the Omer offering. The *Haggadah* also sets the tone for rectifying Adam's sin.

One of the names given in the Torah for *matzah*, "the bread of affliction" alludes to this role of the Exodus in rectifying Adam's sin. As we discuss in the essay on the Seder (pg. 59), the affliction of Egypt transformed that bread, and by extension the struggle for material survival, from a curse into a source of blessings. The Talmudic play on words לֶחֶם עוֹנִי שֶׁעוֹנִין עָלָיו דְּבָרִים, "the bread on which we answer words," suggests that reciting the *Haggadah* fulfills the function that Egyptian slavery once performed, separating good from evil. Thus the Torah uses the phrase כֹּל יְמֵי חַיֶּיךָ, *all the days of your life*, to describe both Adam's curse and the *mitzvah* of remembering the Exodus every day. The very name most commonly used for festivals (whose origin is in the Talmud), *yom tov*, literally "a good day," also suggests this process of separating good from evil that occurs on the festivals.[1] (5651)

The process of harvesting barley and preparing it to be eaten is also symbolic of the Omer's role in separating good from evil. Winnowing chaff from grain represents the differentiation of evil from good. Thus it is fitting that the Torah sets the annual commemoration of the Exodus at the time that the barley harvest ripens. Pesach represents not only the redemption of mankind, but also the liberation and consecration of the entire material world that ocurs when the inedible portions are separated from life-sustaining food. Not only Israel but the entire natural world is redeemed every Pesach. By removing the coarse components and leaving only that which is edible, we liberate the grain and illustrate that

---

1. While our remarks here focus on the impact of the Omer ceremony in separating good from evil, similar effects were also achieved by the Two Loaves on Shavuos and the Water Libation Ceremony on Succos.

the material world can serve a higher purpose: sustaining man for Divine service. (5636)

◆§ Maintaining Purity

The necessity of separating good from evil is particularly important at harvest time for yet another reason. As long as it is attached to the ground, vegetation retains the natural purity with which it was created and is not subject to the laws of ritual defilement. Only when it is detached from the ground, exposed to outside forces, can it become impure. In this light the harvest is a time of danger, when the grain Hashem created pure is exposed to the contaminations of the world. It is just at this moment when we consecrate the newly-cut grain to Hashem, that we express our wish that He help us preserve as much of the original purity of the natural world as is possible, even though we have to face the temptations of a corrupt world. (5655)

◆§ Good Beginnings Ensure a Good Verdict

This process of separating good and evil that occurs at the beginning of the harvest underlines the need to dedicate our first efforts in any endeavor to Hashem. By consecrating the harvest from its very beginning, we ensure that no bad will be mixed in with the good at any time in the future.

This is true not only in a material sense, in terms of protecting the year's grain from blight; it can also be applied to our spiritual endeavors. By dedicating our first efforts of the year to Hashem, we protect *ourselves* from the temptations of the *yetzer hara* in the months ahead. Thus the Zohar (*Parashas Tetzaveh* 183b) says that if Israel properly performs the offering of the Omer on Pesach and the waving of the Two Loaves on Shavuos, it need have no fear of negative judgments on Rosh Hashanah. After all, all sin replicates Adam's sin in mingling good and evil. By being strict about both the letter and the *spirit* of the Omer, by not commingling good and evil, we can obviate the need for punishment on the Day of Judgment.

King Solomon alludes to this power of the Omer to forestall harsh judgments in the following verse (*Koheles* 9:7): אֱכֹל בְּשִׂמְחָה לַחְמֶךָ וּשְׁתֵה בְלֶב־טוֹב יֵינֶךָ כִּי כְבָר רָצָה הָאֱלֹהִים אֶת מַעֲשֶׂיךָ, *Go, eat your bread with joy and drink your wine with a good heart for Hashem has already accepted your deeds. "Eat your bread with joy"* — if you have offered the Omer properly then your grain harvest is assured to be a good one. *"Drink your wine with a good heart"* — your vineyards and fruit orchards will produce good crops in the merit of the Two Loaves. Hashem has already accepted your good deeds in performing these two ceremonies and you may be assured of a good judgment on Rosh Hashanah. (5660)

Similarly, we learn from the verse in *Parashas Emor* that follows the description of the ceremonies of the Omer and the Two Loaves that a good ending is also critical to the success of an endeavor: וּבְקֻצְרְכֶם אֶת־קְצִיר אַרְצְכֶם לֹא תְכַלֶּה פְּאַת שָׂדְךָ בְּקֻצְרֶךָ וְלֶקֶט קְצִירְךָ לֹא תְלַקֵּט לֶעָנִי וְלַגֵּר תַּעֲזֹב אֹתָם אֲנִי ה׳ אֱלֹהֵיכֶם, *And when you harvest the harvest of your land do not completely harvest the corner of your field and the standing grain do not scatter leave them for the stranger and the poor person I am* H*ASHEM*, *your God* (*Vayikra* 23:22).

Not only the beginning of the harvest is offered to Hashem, through the Omer and the Two Loaves; the end corner is also sanctified. This symbolizes that although those souls that are far removed from sanctity (so to speak on the outer edge), such as our generations, they can come close to Hashem, even without a *Beis HaMikdash*.[1] (5646)

⁂ קָרְבַּן עוֹמֶר / The Omer Sacrifice

This theme of consecrating the beginning of the harvest and especially the relationship between the Omer and the Two Loaves can be appreciated by noting the Midrash that describes both the Torah and the Jewish people as a beginning. בִּשְׁבִיל יִשְׂרָאֵל שֶׁנִּקְרְאוּ רֵאשִׁית שֶׁנֶּאֱמַר רֵאשִׁית תְּבוּאָתוֹ וּבִשְׁבִיל הַתּוֹרָה שֶׁנִּקְרָא רֵאשִׁית שֶׁנֶּאֱמַר רֵאשִׁית דַּרְכּוֹ *[The world was created] in the merit of Israel which is called the beginning as it says "the beginning of His grain"* (*Yirmeyahu* 2:3) *and in the merit of Torah which is called the beginning as it says "the beginning of His way"* (*Mishlei 8:22*) (*Yalkut Bereishis*).

The Omer and the Two Loaves correspond to Israel's beginning and to the beginning of Torah, as we shall explain. Originally the universe consisted of תֹהוּ וָבֹהוּ, "desolation and chaos," (*Bereishis* 1:2) with Hashem's spirit hovering over the waters. It was in the merit of Israel,

1. See the essay on *Hoshana Rabbah* for a lengthy discussion of the linkage between distant generations.

who would later separate good from evil by consecrating the first grain in the Omer ceremony that the earth emerged from its initial confused status. Thus the earth's beginning is linked directly with Israel.

Similarly, the heavens were created for the sake of the Torah, symbolized by the Two Loaves offered on Shavuos, the day the Torah was given. While the full depth of Torah is infinitely beyond human comprehension, a spark of Torah was revealed to Israel on Shavuos, described as "a beginning of Hashem's way" (*Mishlei* 8:22).

(5647)

◆§ Why Israel's Prosperity Depends on the Omer

In the introduction to this essay, we cited a Midrash saying that Abraham inherited the land of Israel in the merit of the Omer. The Midrash derives this from Hashem's statement to Abraham just before his circumcision (*Bereishis* 17:9), וְאַתָּה אֶת־בְּרִיתִי תִשְׁמֹר *And you shall observe my convenant.* In the following section, we discuss the connection between the Omer and possession of *Eretz Yisrael.* We shall also consider Abraham's unique role, as well as the Torah's description of the Omer as a covenant.

◆§ Only "Men" Can Inherit the Land

We can approach the connection between the Omer and *Eretz Yisrael* in the light of David Hamelech's description of those who are to inherit the Land (*Tehillim* 115:16): הַשָּׁמַיִם שָׁמַיִם לַה׳ וְהָאָרֶץ נָתַן לִבְנֵי אָדָם, *The heavens are Hashem's but the earth He has given to mankind.* The following verse then explains why this description applies only to Israel: לֹא הַמֵּתִים יְהַלְלוּ יָהּ וְלֹא כָּל יֹרְדֵי דוּמָה וַאֲנַחְנוּ נְבָרֵךְ יָהּ מֵעַתָּה וְעַד עוֹלָם, *Neither the dead can praise God, nor any who descend into silence; but we will bless God from this time and forever.*

The wicked are considered to be dead even during their lifetime. Only Israel, who praises Hashem, may inherit *Eretz Yisrael.* The Land is only given to Israel who bless God forever.

Without question, Abraham proclaimed Hashem's praises as much as anyone else who has ever lived, as we see from Yehoshua's description (14:15), אָדָם הַגָּדוֹל בָּעֲנָקִים, *the greatest man among giants.* And if a nation was ever capable of singing Hashem's praises, it was the Jewish people after the Exodus. Once liberated, the nation was finally free to speak Hashem's praises. The Omer is an expression of our consecrating our productivity to the praise of God. We recognize that He gave us the earth and all its produce.

Now we can understand the intent of the Midrash. Only Abraham, and his descendants the Jewish people, deserve to inherit *Eretz Yisrael* — in the merit of bringing the Omer each year immediately after celebrating their freedom to praise Hashem.[1]

But how does this relate to Hashem's covenant with Abraham? We may say that the ability to praise Hashem is not something that man *happens* to possess. Rather, like everything else we have, it is a gift bestowed upon us by Hashem in the form of a covenant. Even though Abraham had declared Hashem's existence to an unknowing mankind before his circumcision, when he was still called Abram, he was able to spread his message far more effectively after the covenant of circumcision. In addition to the covenant of circumcision, he was given another covenant granting him the ability to speak Hashem's praises. Similarly, the Jewish people became aware of their full potential to praise Hashem only after they were circumcised on the night of the Exodus. (5658)

◆§ Tempering Strict Justice

The Midrash linking the Omer with Abraham and *Eretz Yisrael* also hints at the Jewish people's ability to *sustain* themselves from the soil of the Land. Generally, livelihood comes to people on the basis of strict judgment, as we say in the blessing recited upon seeing a Jewish cemetery, "Who nourished and sustained you with justice." This is especially true in *Eretz Yisrael*, which the Torah says is watched by Hashem from the beginning of the year until the end of the year.

The nation of Israel, descended from Abraham who personified kindness, possesses the ability to mitigate and sweeten the harsh effects of strict justice. Abraham won this ability by his unceasing devotion to kindness in the world, as evidenced by his efforts to evoke Hashem's kindness on behalf of the wicked people of Sodom. It is entirely fitting

1. This interpretation of the verse *the earth He has given to mankind* is supported by the Talmud's statement (*Berachos* 35a) that we have the right to derive pleasure from the world only after reciting a blessing. Only Israel, who recognizes that Hashem is the true Owner of the Land and blesses Him, deserves to dwell on sacred soil.

that he was entrusted with a son like Isaac, who symbolized strict justice.[1]

As Abraham's descendants, we also have the ability to mitigate the harsh justice through which sustenance is normally meted out. The Torah teaches us how to transform justice into mercy: וַהֲבֵאתֶם אֶת עֹמֶר רֵאשִׁית קְצִירְכֶם אֶל הַכֹּהֵן וְהֵנִיף אֶת הָעֹמֶר לִפְנֵי ה׳ לִרְצֹנְכֶם *And you shall bring the Omer, the first of your harvest, to the Kohen, and he should wave the Omer in the presence of* H*ASHEM* (*Vayikra* 23:10,11). These two actions — bringing the first barley kernels to the *Kohen* (an agent of Hashem's kindness by inheritance from his ancestor Aaron, who was renowned for his love of peace) and waving the barley in the *Beis HaMikdash* to show our belief that all of our sustenance comes from Him — transform justice into a showering of Hashem's kindness.

This then is the message of the Midrash: The Jewish people sustained themselves in the land in the merit of Abraham and the Omer ceremony, both of which had the power to sweeten Divine justice. Only a liberal outpouring of Hashem's kindness makes it possible for us to survive on the sacred soil of *Eretz Yisrael.*

Why is Pesach the most appropriate time for this? As we discussed in the section on the Paschal Lamb, the name Pesach itself implies that Hashem "passes over" the ambiance of strict justice that prevails at this time of the year and commutes it to kindness. Indeed, were it not for this "commutation," the Jews would have met the same fate as their Egyptian neighbors. From this we see that Pesach is a propitious time to convert justice into kindness. (5657)

◆§ Why Hashem Tells Israel to Bring the Omer

הָבִיאוּ לְפָנַי עוֹמֶר בַּפֶּסַח כְּדֵי שֶׁתִּתְבָּרֵךְ לָכֶם תְּבוּאָה שֶׁבַּשָּׂדוֹת
Bring the Omer in My presence on Pesach so that the grain in the fields will be blessed for you (*Rosh Hashanah* 16a).

In this section we explore the relationship between Hashem's request that Israel bring the Omer and Israel's prosperity. We will also discuss the connection between dew, for which we pray on Pesach, and rainfall, for which we pray on Succos.

1. Abraham educated Isaac to channel his natural inclination to favor strict justice over kindness in such a way that it would become a vehicle for Divine service.

◆§ Pesach's Dew — A Deserved Blessing Succos Rainfall — Hashem's Kindness

To better understand the significance of Hashem's commandment to offer the Omer, let us examine the word לָכֶם, *for you,* that appears in that commandment. Hashem asks us to offer the Omer so that the grain will be blessed *for us.* Apparently He wants us to be *worthy* to receive our sustenance, rather than to have to receive it as an unearned gift, as the non-Jewish world does. The seemingly redundant word לָכֶם, *for you,* implies that *our* grain is blessed differently from that of any other people.

What are the implications of sustenance received on the strength of merit? For one thing, our livelihood comes even at times when Divine justice, rather than kindness, prevails. As we said above, the blessings of Pesach must be earned; while it is possible to mitigate Divine justice and transform it into kindness, there must still exist some measure of *merit* for this process to work.

Thus, Hashem pleads with Israel, "Offer the Omer to demonstrate your faith that all worldly blessings, even your harvest, originate from Me. In the merit of that faith, I will bless you." In contrast, the blessings of the non-Jewish world come at Succos, when Hashem's kindness prevails.[1]

The very symbol of Pesach's blessing, dew, stands in contrast to the rainfall of Succos. Dew never ceases throughout the year; it is given even during the Pesach season, when Divine blessings must be deserved. Thus dew is symbolic of the Jews (cf. *Hosea* 14:6, אֶהְיֶה כַטַּל לְיִשְׂרָאֵל, *I will be as the dew to Israel*) since its blessings continue to flow even during times when strict justice prevails.

In contrast, rain, representing the outpouring of Hashem's kindness, falls in *Eretz Yisrael* only during the season beginning with Succos, a period marked by Divine kindness.[2]

King David differentiates between the deserved dew of Pesach and

1. As we discuss extensively in the section on Succos, the nations have a large portion in that festival, as evidenced by the seventy bulls offered, corresponding to the seventy cultures of the world.

2. In the essay on *Shemini Atzeres* we point out that the Jewish people do not pray for rain until that festival, a time of justice, in order to distinguish themselves from the other nations by showing that they want even their rainfall to come on the basis of merit.

the unrequited rainfall of Succos in the verse (*Tehillim* 68:10) גֶּשֶׁם נְדָבוֹת תָּנִיף אֱלֹהִים, *A generous rainfall did you lavish, O God.* The Midrash (*Yalkut Tehillim* 795) comments on this, "If it [the land] requires rain, an act of [Divine] generosity is needed; if it needs dew, Hashem will bestow it." Clearly Hashem decrees rain on Succos even to the non-deserving, if necessary, while Pesach's dew comes in the merit of an Israel deserving of Hashem's blessings.

Not just Pesach but also the entire Omer period is characterized by strict justice, because blessings are granted then only to the worthy. The Torah describes this period as שֶׁבַע שַׁבָּתוֹת תְּמִימוֹת, *seven complete weeks,* on which the Midrash (*Vayikra Rabbah* 28) comments, "When are they 'complete'? When Israel does Hashem's will." Anything less than complete devotion to Hashem's will is especially perilous at this time. On the other hand, if we succeed in elevating ourselves to the exacting standard of this period, we will be spared a harsh verdict on Rosh Hashanah. We can do this by totally devoting ourselves to the Torah, the source of all completeness, as the Psalmist says (19:8) תּוֹרַת ה׳ תְּמִימָה, *the Torah of HASHEM is perfect.* We cannot help but do this if we only recognize that all of our material as well as spiritual blessings flow from the Torah.

What else can we do to *merit* Divine blessings at this time? The Torah itself gives an answer — lift up the Omer. By raising the first produce of the new agricultural year to Hashem, we demonstrate our belief that all material abundance is really His gift. In one sense, the Omer ceremony can be viewed as a "reversal" of Creation. The Sages frequently said that Hashem created the universe יֵשׁ מֵאַיִן, "something from nothing." By waving the Omer, we, so to speak, return the יֵשׁ, a material "something," back to אַיִן, "nothing," the totally spiritual state from which it originated, thereby affirming that everything we are and everything we have was created by Hashem. It is interesting to note that the *gematria* (numerical value) of the word עֹמֶר *omer* (310) is equivalent to that of יֵשׁ, "something."

In conclusion, waving the Omer in order to "earn" blessings ensures our prosperity not only during this period but throughout the year. The Torah describes this time as "seven complete weeks" — weeks whose merit sustains us for a complete year. (5654)

Miraculous Sustenance

A Midrash that compares our livelihood to liberation sheds light on another aspect of the Omer ritual (*Bereishis Rabbah* 97): מַה פַּרְנָסָה בְּכָל יוֹם אַף גְאוּלָּה בְּכָל יוֹם וּמַה גְאוּלָּה פְּלָאִים אַף פַּרְנָסָה פְּלָאִים, *Just as our livelihood is given every day, so also we are liberated every day. And just as liberation occurs miraculously, so also does our livelihood.* Our waving of the Omer affirms that our daily bread is a miraculous gift from Hashem.

Once we comprehend this miraculous nature of our livelihood, then the second phase of the comparison in the Midrash comes into play: Every day we are *redeemed* from the false belief that the natural world functions independently of Hashem. What more valued liberation can there be than to be extricated from the clutches of such falsehood? Hashem asks us to bring the Omer on Pesach, "the time of our freedom," to remind us that our livelihood, symbolized by the Omer, is as miraculous as our freedom and equally important. On Pesach we are liberated from the belief that our sustenance is solely the product of our natural efforts. The very name of the festival, "the time of our freedom," suggests that even *time* — the linchpin of the material world — is liberated on Pesach.

In this light, we may propose yet another interpretation of the phrase מִמָּחֳרַת הַשַּׁבָּת, *the morrow of the rest-day,* which the Torah designates as the time of the Omer offering. The *Zohar* (*Parashas Yisro* 88a) notes that each week's sustenance comes from the blessing of the preceeding Shabbos, even though work is forbidden on Shabbos itself. So also, the miraculous days of Pesach, days of redemption, also provide sustenance for the entire year that follows — "the day(s) after the rest-day," the festival of Pesach. (5647)

The Omer and Haman

The third Midrash cited at the beginning of this essay teaches that Israel was spared from Haman's machinations in the merit of the Omer. What is the connection between the Omer and Haman?

As a preface to our answer, let us note the timing of Amalek's attack on Israel. Amalek was aware that the Exodus was a preliminary to the giving of the Torah, as Hashem had told Moshe (*Shemos* 3:12), "When you take the people out of Egypt you will serve God on this mountain" and was therefore determined to do whatever he could to foil this plan. Though he could not prevent the Torah from being given, he could at least dampen Israel's enthusiasm, as the Torah says (*Devarim* 25:18), אֲשֶׁר קָרְךָ בַּדֶּרֶךְ, "that he chilled you [your enthusiasm for Torah] on the way [to Sinai]."

Each year we are again redeemed on Pesach and each year Amalek's contemporary agent, the *yetzer hara*, again attempts a frontal attack on the Jews as they proceed to Sinai. Unlike our forefathers who waited to defend themselves until Amalek had attacked, we have to take the initiative. The Omer, which is described (*Yeshaya* 30:32) as מִלְחֲמוֹת תְּנוּפָה, *the battle of waving*, is a particularly potent defense against Amalek. By offering a symbol of our material abundance to Hashem, we show our enthusiastic commitment to Torah, thereby protecting ourselves against Amalek's attack.

The Sages said (*cf. Sanhedrin* 72b), "When someone comes to kill you, get up and kill him first." This is surely true of spiritual attacks. In this light, the Omer may be seen as a pre-emptive strike against Amelek. Haman issued his decrees against the Jews in the month of *Nissan* (though the lot he cast postponed the intended annihilation until the following *Adar)* in order to suppress their enthusiasm for Torah when it was at its peak in the Pesach season. Once again, the merit of the Omer (which, since there was no *Beis HaMikdash* at the time, meant studying the laws of the Omer offering) protected the Jews and prevented Haman's schemes from reaching fruition. To the contrary, Haman's downfall led to a renewed commitment to Torah at the time of the Purim miracle. (5643)

We may suggest an even deeper connection between the Omer and Haman's downfall. As we said earlier in this essay, the Omer offering helped to rectify Adam's sin of obfuscating good and evil. The deadly enemy Haman drew all of his power from the confusion of good and evil, as the Sages said (*Chulin* 139b): הָמָן מִן הַתּוֹרָה מִנַּיִן דִּכְתִיב הֲמִן הָעֵץ, *Where in the Torah is there a reference to Haman? From the verse, 'Have you eaten from (הֲמִן) the tree* of the knowledge of good and evil?' Only in an atmosphere where good and evil are blurred, can the wicked like Haman fester. And only the Omer ceremony, with its power to separate good from evil and to clarify the spiritual roots of the physical world, could foil Haman's diabolical plans. Haman's existence is predicated upon Israel repeating mankind's first sin, blurring good and evil. (5653)

It is interesting to note the striking similarities in the Torah's descriptions of the Omer ceremony and the battle of Amalek. Both of these mention a "lifting up" of the hands: יְנִיפֶנּוּ הַכֹּהֵן, *the Kohen is to wave it*; and likewise Moshe had to lift up his hands to vanquish Amalek וְהָיָה כַּאֲשֶׁר יָרִים מֹשֶׁה יָדוֹ וְגָבַר יִשְׂרָאֵל, *and it was when Moshe lifted his hands, Israel prevailed* (*Shemos* 17:11) The similarity in wording cannot be coincidental. By attributing everything to Hashem, both material abundance and military might, we can triumph over our deadliest enemy Amalek.[1] (5641)

◆§ According to Your Will

Finally, we will consider the significance of a seemingly unnecessary word in the Torah's description of the Omer ceremony: וְהֵנִיף אֶת־הָעֹמֶר לִפְנֵי ה׳ לִרְצֹנְכֶם, *[the Kohen] shall wave the Omer before Hashem's Presence* ***according to your will*** (*Vayikra* 23:11). What does the word לִרְצֹנְכֶם, *according to your will*, add to our understanding of this verse?

This term may be included to clarify the meaning of the phrase that follows it, מִמָּחֳרַת הַשַּׁבָּת, *the morrow of the rest-day*. The Saducees, a heretic sect who accepted the written Torah but rejected the Oral Law passed down from Sinai, contended that this expression was to be interpreted literally, that the Omer had to be offered on Sunday, "the day after the Sabbath."

To refute this erroneous view, the Sages highlighted this otherwise unexplained word, לִרְצֹנְכֶם, *according to your will*. Clearly on Pesach, when the Jews followed Hashem blindly and unquestioningly into the Wilderness, there was unequalled good will between Hashem and His People, especially on the morrow of that first Pesach. Thus the term לִרְצֹנְכֶם, *according to your will*, shows clearly that the phrase מִמָּחֳרַת הַשַּׁבָּת, *the morrow of the rest-day*, must refer to the day after Pesach, when Israel's "will" to serve Hashem was at its greatest.

The term לִרְצֹנְכֶם may refer also to the Jews of every generation in which the Omer was offered. This day is depicted by our Rabbis as יוֹם

1. The hand-raising in both cases indicates an attribution of what man produces be it his food or military victory to its ultimate Source.

הֶנֵף, *a day of elevation* (cf. Mishnah *Rosh Hashanah* 4:3), suggesting that this day, the second day of Pesach, itself can be elevated by the actions of the Jews. If our efforts to sanctify this day are sufficiently sincere, then the day *itself* is exalted to make a greater impression on us. Thus the term לִרְצֹנְכֶם, *according to your will,* also tells us that the spiritual uplift we receive on this day is dependent on *our will* to make it into a higher day. (5642, 5644)

Shir HaShirim

◆§ Shir HaShirim and Pesach

Although *Shir HaShirim* contains no explicit reference to the festival of Pesach, it is read at this time by Jews all over the world. Why is this? What connection is there between the message of Pesach and *Shir HaShirim*?

The Jewish people's capacity for clear, articulate praise of Hashem originated with the miracles of the Exodus. Brutally suppressed under Egyptian tyranny, they had no outlet for their pent-up emotions. Only at the Exodus were they able to fulfill the mission Hashem gave them to speak His praises. Indeed, the word Pesach is a combination of the words פֶּה and סָח, *the mouth that talks,* an allusion to the newly found ability to marvel at Hashem's creations granted at the Exodus.

There is no better time to read *Shir HaShirim* than "the time of our freedom." The term freedom here implies not only physical freedom, but also release from the *yetzer hara*. When one is set free from the temptation to sin, not only can he realize his own personal potential, he also has the ability to catalyze the whole physical world to sing Hashem's praises, to realize *its* potential. The Psalmist alludes to this link between the Exodus and man's ability to influence nature: בְּצֵאת יִשְׂרָאֵל מִמִּצְרָיִם ... הָיְתָה יְהוּדָה לְקָדְשׁוֹ יִשְׂרָאֵל מַמְשְׁלוֹתָיו (114:1-2). *When Israel went out of Egypt ... Judah became His sanctuary, Israel His dominions.* When the Jewish people left Egypt, they not only attained sanctity for themselves (יְהוּדָה לְקָדְשׁוֹ) but they also gained the ability to influence the entire universe to accept Hashem's sovereignty (מַמְשְׁלוֹתָיו). (5635)

Finally, and most profoundly, it is only at the "time of our freedom," from both physical and spiritual danger, that the true meaning of *Shir HaShirim* can be appreciated. While *Shir HaShirim* sings the beauty of the physical world, this is only a superficial metaphor. King Solomon's true intent is to show that the universe, with all of its complexities, is no more than a parable to express the love every Jew is expected to have for Hashem. Thus the prevalent image of a man's love for his spouse is really just an allegory, in terms understandable to human ears, for how we are to properly love Hashem.

The rest of the year, the surface penetrating to meaning of *Shir HaShirim* is so attractive that it distracts us from the book's true intent. Only on Pesach, liberated from the temptations of materialism, can we penetrate beneath the surface to *Shir HaShirim's* true profundity; only on Pesach can we focus on the inner meaning rather than the metaphor that enclothes it. King Solomon, the wisest of all men, understood the spiritual roots of every physical phenomenon; he saw how everything on earth is rooted in Heaven, how ultimately the entire universe was created by Hashem. On Pesach, the ordinary reader also can grasp some part of what the wise King Solomon constantly saw with such clarity. (5631)

◆§ Introduction

שִׁיר הַשִּׁירִים אֲשֶׁר לִשְׁלֹמֹה

The Song of Songs of Solomon (1:1)[1]

The opening words of this beautiful paean, which give it its name, *Shir HaShirim*, Song of the Songs, may be understood in their most literal sense: *A song of King Solomon's songs*, a song to be sung by the songs King Solomon wrote. No mere mortal could properly sing Hashem's praises, only the letters of the Torah, whose roots originate in the highest places in Heaven.

Evidently, *Shir HaShirim* was composed in two phases. Acting under Divine inspiration, King Solomon wrote the letters of the song. Then

1. Unless otherwise indicated, all verse references in this essay are to *Shir HaShirim*.

those sacred letters themselves were fanned to life by the very intensity of his devotion and burst out singing Hashem's praises to the heights of Heaven.

Another instance of inert words coming to life to sing Hashem's praises occurs at the end of *Pesukei D'Zimrah,* the section of the Morning Prayer Services composed of selections from *Psalms* and other verses praising Hashem. Near the end of the concluding blessing, we say that Hashem is הַבּוֹחֵר בְּשִׁירֵי זִמְרָה, the One Who chooses "chanting songs," songs that the song itself sings. This implies that if only we were to enunciate the songs with proper intensity and devotion, they themselves would burst forth with life and sing their own words in Hashem's presence.

King Solomon expresses a similar thought elsewhere: לֵב חָכָם יַשְׂכִּיל פִּיהוּ, *the wise man's heart [i.e. his intense devotion] allows his mouth [i.e. his speech] to succeed* (*Mishlei* 16:23). Someone who truly desires to cling to the Torah is given the ability to discourse meaningfully about concepts that would ordinarily be too profound for him to understand, let alone express. How is this possible? When one sincerely yearns to praise Hashem's greatness, Hashem helps him articulate the appropriate words. The deep thoughts he expresses may have been even beyond his original ability to grasp. The letters seem to take on a life of their own and to form thoughts never dreamed of by their speaker. All that is required is an intense desire to do Hashem's will, and to sing His praises.

So also, the letters and words King Solomon spoke were arranged by Hashem to voice the sublime thoughts of *Shir HaShirim,* the song composed by itself, that sings itself. (5634)

Another possible meaning of the name *Shir HaShirim* is "the song that is comprised of all other songs." According to tradition, all natural creations sing Hashem's praises. Though we are not always aware of it, the natural world, by its infinite beauty and perfect harmony, attests continually to the grandeur and beauty of Hashem's creation — in effect singing His praises. For this reason many Jews recite every day *Perek Shirah,* an anthology of the songs "sung" by flora and fauna as recorded in *Tanach.* The entire world — animals, plants, fish, and fowl — sings Hashem's praises.

Man also sings Hashem's praises, by his striving for moral perfection. Man's role, however, is not confined to his own song; his mission goes far beyond the challenge of perfecting himself. By mastering his own evil impulses and channeling his actions towards Divine service, man inspires the rest of nature to greater perfection. While it is true that nature "sings" Hashem's praise through its perfection and harmony, nonetheless its ability to realize its full potential is inextricably bound to man's pursuit of greatness. If man achieves to the utmost of his ability, if his "song" is loud and true, all of nature will follow suit.

Shir HaShirim is the song composed by the earthly maestro, the supreme natural conductor-man. It is composed of all the songs sung by Hashem's creations; within its folds are contained all the beauty and perfection of the universe. This is the meaning of Rabbi Akiva's statement (*Shir HaShirim Rabbah* 111) that *Shir HaShirim* is the holiest of all holy songs (*kodesh kadoshim*). All other songs tell of nature's praise for the Creator — *Shir HaShirim*, by contrast, is an ode to man's ability to arouse nature to sing its own dormant song which lies waiting to emerge. (5634, 5635)

The Midrash (*Yalkut Shimoni* 980) comments: שִׁיר הַשִּׁירִים לְמִי שֶׁעֲשָׂנוּ שָׁרִים בָּעוֹלָם, *Shir HaShirim is dedicated to Hashem, Who made us singers in the world*. This Midrash, and in particular the term *sharim* (singers), are subject to various interpretations. One approach suggests that *Shir HaShirim* is a tribute to Hashem, Who gave the Jewish people the unique mission, and with it the requisite ability, to sing His praises. As the prophet says "This nation I have created, to tell My praises" (*Yeshaya* 43:21). According to this interpretation, the word שָׁרִים is properly written with a *shin*.

Shir HaShirim may also be seen as a praise of Hashem for teaching us *how* to sing His praises. This concept applies also to *Pesukei D'Zimrah*, which consists primarily of King David's praises of Hashem for His manifold wonders. By reciting *Pesukei D'Zimrah*, we praise Hashem not only for His numerous accomplishments, but also for giving us the ability to say *Shema* and *Shemoneh Esrei*. Similarly, *Shir HaShirim* praises Hashem for giving the Jewish people the opportunity to praise Him. (5635, 5641)

Alternatively, this Midrash may also refer to the Jew's ability to control his destiny by curbing his evil impulses. In this interpretation, the word שָׁרִים should be read with a *sin*, שָׂרִים, *princes*, masters of our fate. We are able to inspire the universe to "sing," to realize its potential to praise Hashem, only because we, in turn, are able to master our actions and direct them to realizing *our* potential, to act as princes in every sense. By making ourselves into *princes*, we arouse the whole universe to sing. (5635)

יִשָּׁקֵנִי מִנְּשִׁיקוֹת פִּיהוּ כִּי־טוֹבִים דֹּדֶיךָ מִיָּיִן
He will kiss me from the kisses of His mouth, for your friendship is more precious than wine (1:2).

The expression *kiss me from the kisses of His mouth* may be an allusion to the *neshamah* (soul), the Divine Presence in every Jew. The Jewish people plead with their Loved One (i.e. Hashem) to let spiritual values, namely the soul prevail. The symbolic connection between man's soul and Hashem's "mouth" can be traced back to the first soul, which Hashem implanted in Adam. וַיִּפַּח בְּאַפָּיו נִשְׁמַת חַיִּים וַיְהִי הָאָדָם לְנֶפֶשׁ חַיָּה. *He [HASHEM] blew into his nostrils the soul of life; and man became a living being* (*Bereishis* 2:7). According to *Onkelos*, man acquired the ability of speech only when Hashem "breathed" from His "mouth" into Adam's nostrils.

This plea for enhanced spirituality, for Hashem to allow the soul to shine forth with its light, belongs here at the beginning of *Shir HaShirim*. As we have said, above, man began to speak only *after* Hashem "breathed" a soul into his nostrils. This sublime song is feasible only if spiritual concerns push the material world into the background.

The Midrash (*Yalkut Shimoni* 981) suggests that Hashem's "kisses" are a metaphor for Hashem's response to the Jewish people's acceptance of the Torah at Sinai. The Midrash presents a dialogue that occurred between the angels and the people when the Torah was given:

א״ר יוחָנָן מַלְאָךְ אֶחָד יוֹצֵא לִפְנֵי כָּל דִּבּוּר וְדִבּוּר וּמְחַזֵּר עַל כָּל אֶחָד מִיִּשְׂרָאֵל וְאוֹמֵר לוֹ מְקַבֵּל אַתָּה עָלֶיךָ אֶת הַדָּבָר הַזֶּה. כַּךְ וְכַךְ מִצְוֹת שֶׁיֵּשׁ בּוֹ . . . כַּךְ וְכַךְ שְׂכַר יֵשׁ בּוֹ וְאוֹמֵר לוֹ הֵן וְחוֹזֵר וְאוֹמֵר מְקַבֵּל אַתָּה עָלֶיךָ אֱלֹהוּתוֹ שֶׁל הקב״ה וְאוֹמֵר לוֹ הֵן הֵן. מִיַּד הוּא נוֹשְׁקוֹ עַל פִּיו

Rabbi Yochanan said that an angel went forth [as each of the Ten Commandments was pronounced] asking each Jew, 'Are you willing to accept this statement, with so many mitzvos . . . and so much reward connected to it?' Each Jew responds affirmatively, then he [the angel] asks will you accept God's sovereignty. [Again] Each Jew responds affirmatively. The Angel immediately kisses each Jew.

This Midrash sees in our verse a yearning for the halcyon days at Sinai, especially for the moment when the angels showed Hashem's appreciation for their acceptance of the Torah by "kissing" each individual Jew (see *Rashi ad loc*).

A question arises, however. The angels urge the people to accept the Torah because of the great reward offered to its adherents. There is a well-established principle of Judaism (cf. *Avos* 2:1) that the reward for observing *mitzvos* is not revealed in this world. If so, how could the angels offer such rewards for accepting the commandments when no one can know what the reward is for observing them?

It may be that the rule against revealing the reward for *mitzvos* came into effect only after the people had sinned with the Golden Calf. In the diminished state of sanctity that ensued, it became difficult for the Jewish people to understand the boundless reward associated with *mitzvos*.

Before that sin, however, and especially at the time the Torah was given, our forefathers were on such a high spiritual level that they *were* able to grasp the rewards of *mitzvos*.[1] Moreover, this verse can be interpreted as talking about the hidden, esoteric parts of Torah, and especially the *reasons*, the inner rationale for *mitzvos*. The Jewish people yearn for the day when Hashem will reveal the inner secrets of Torah, as He did once at Sinai.

The Midrash sheds further light on this question. Our generation must content itself with Torah's simple meaning; it would therefore be wholly inappropriate for us to seek to understand the reasons for the *mitzvos* or the reward due to those who observe them. The generation that received the Torah, however, was different — they *could* comprehend both the reason for *mitzvos* and their reward. (5635)

It is noteworthy that our verse uses an unusual word פִּיהוּ, *his mouths*, rather than the more common form פִּיו, *his mouth: May Hashem kiss me from His mouths*. What is the significance of this plural form? In a similar vein, the prophet Yirmiyahu speaks of Hashem's "mouths" (*Eichah* 1:18): צַדִּיק הוּא ה׳ כִּי פִיהוּ מָרִיתִי, *Hashem is righteous! For I have disobeyed His utterance (His mouths)*. The Midrash (*Eichah Rabbasi* 1:61) suggests that the plural word "mouths" in this verse refers to King Yoshiyahu's confession that he betrayed not only Hashem's words but also those of His prophets. In our verse as well, the Jewish people yearn not only for Hashem's "kisses," but also for those of his greatest prophet,

1. *Editors Note:* Being on the spiritual level of Adam before the sin they could appreciate reward in this world much like Adam whose arena for spiritual toil was Gan Eden, the place of his reward.

Moshe. While the Written Law was transmitted to the Jewish people through a "Divine kiss," and the Ten Commandments, were heard directly from Hashem, the Oral Law was given through the intermediary of Moshe as he had been taught by Hashem. Thus, the "kisses" of His mouth is a metaphor for the Divine kiss (i.e. the Written Law) that the Jews so yearned for, as well as for Moshe's unforgettable teaching of the Oral Law. (5651)

מָשְׁכֵנִי אַחֲרֶיךָ נָּרוּצָה הֱבִיאַנִי הַמֶּלֶךְ חֲדָרָיו

Attract me, I will follow you. The king has brought me to His chambers (1:4)

This verse, and in particular the word נָרוּצָה (literally *we shall run*), can be interpreted in two ways.

Firstly, *attract [literally, pull] me and I shall run after you.* The Jewish people plead with Hashem, "Pull us out of Egypt — we are suffering so much from physical deprivation and spiritual assimilation that we cannot even take the first step. We cannot leave Egypt or commit ourselves to Torah and *mitzvos* without Your help. "Pull me" from Egypt's misery, give me the impetus and then "we will run after You" with renewed vigor."

Their plea was answered and they were "pulled" out of Egypt with a "strong hand" without being spiritually or physically prepared for liberation. We were pulled from Egypt prematurely, after only two hundred ten years of servitude rather than the four hundred years foretold to Abraham. We were pulled away forcibly from any lingering attraction we may have felt to the pagan ways of Egypt.[1] Above all, we were *pulled* to leave Egypt on the basis of pure *emunah* (faith), without any understanding of what it meant to be Hashem's servants. Simple unleavened *matzah*, the bread of poverty, is called by the *Zohar* נַהֲמָא דְהֵימְנוּתָא, *the bread of faith,* reflecting our simple unflinching loyalty to Hashem.[2]

Thus, at the beginning we had to be pulled, with halting and slow first steps, but soon afterwards נָרוּצָה, *we ran.* Within a few short days, we were vaulted from the mud and bricks of Egyptian slavery to the inspired recitation of the Song of the Sea.

---

1. Indeed, the same term מִשְׁכוּ, *pull yourselves,* is used to command their sudden withdrawal from pagan worship just days before the Exodus (*Shemos* 12:21).

2. The theme of leaving Egypt solely on the basis of faith is also discussed in the essay on the *Succah,* which the *Zohar* calls צִילָא דְהֵימְנוּתָא, *the shade of faith.*

Really, the Jewish people had always been destined for great things. Their hearts were always prepared for redemption by the tradition they received from their fathers and kept alive the whole time they were in Egypt. Once the barriers were removed, the people proceeded with giant strides all the way to the King's inner sanctum at the Splitting of the Sea.

The Jewish people were made for Divine service, to be troops in Hashem's army. Once liberated from Egypt, they naturally assumed the positions in Hashem's forces that had been prepared for them from birth. Thus, in describing the Exodus the Torah says (*Shemos* 12:51): הוֹצִיא ה׳ אֶת בְּנֵי יִשְׂרָאֵל מֵאֶרֶץ מִצְרַיִם עַל צִבְאֹתָם, *Hashem took the Children of Israel from the land of Egypt in* ***their*** *legions*. Hashem enlisted the Jews in *their legions* rather than *His legions*. They were merely assuming the roles in Hashem's army that had been prepared for them since birth. (5639)

Another interpretation is, מָשְׁכֵנִי, *pull me* out of Egyptian slavery (if need be forcibly), and then נָרוּצָה, we shall *want* (from the word רָצוֹן, *will*). The initial impetus to freedom emanated from Hashem but once they were liberated our forefathers exhibited enormous willpower to follow Him and to remove the negative effects of years in Egypt.

The Torah uses the expression עַל צִבְאֹתָם, which can be translated "above their legions," to indicate the great advances the people made. As *ba'alei teshuvah*, returnees to the faith of their fathers, the Jews of the Exodus were able to attain a higher level than they would have otherwise, a spiritual level beyond their capacities. No Jew is ever really lost or cut off — while he may drift temporarily, intrinsically he always clings to Hashem.

The Jewish people yearned to follow in the footsteps of the Patriarchs but their aspirations were thwarted while they were in slavery. As soon as they were redeemed, however, they were able to reach the lofty heights that had been denied to them in captivity. The forefathers were not merely theoretical role models, people one *desires* to follow: now in the merit of the Patriarchs, the Jewish people could become instantly great, they could be transformed from slaves to servant of the living Hashem within days. (5639)

שְׁחוֹרָה אֲנִי וְנָאוָה בְּנוֹת יְרוּשָׁלָיִם כְּאָהֳלֵי קֵדָר כִּירִיעוֹת שְׁלֹמֹה
I am black with sin, but I am beautiful nonetheless, daughter of Jerusalem. Even if I appear to be as dirty as

the tents of Kedar, I will be as immaculate as the draperies of Shlomo (1:5).

אַל תִּרְאֻנִי שֶׁאֲנִי שְׁחַרְחֹרֶת שֶׁשְּׁזָפַתְנִי הַשָּׁמֶשׁ בְּנֵי אִמִּי נִחֲרוּ־בִי שָׂמֻנִי נֹטֵרָה אֶת הַכְּרָמִים כַּרְמִי שֶׁלִּי לֹא נָטָרְתִּי

Do not view me with contempt despite my blackness, for it is but the sun which has glared upon me. The children of my mother were incensed with me and make me a keeper of the vineyards of idols, but the vineyard of my own true God I did not keep (1:6).

These verses are a plea to penetrate beyond surface appearances and to grasp the true inner nature of the world. Though he may appear black on the surface, every Jew possesses an inner spark of beauty. Even in the most wretched exile, depicted by the blackness of Kedar's tents, that inner spark still flickers: Jews remain loyal to Hashem under the most difficult circumstances. As the Psalmist says (44:21): אִם שָׁכַחְנוּ שֵׁם אֱלֹהֵינוּ וַנִּפְרֹשׂ כַּפֵּינוּ לְאֵל זָר, *We never forgot our God's Name or ever raised our palms to an alien deity.*

While this inner spark is always present, it is especially prominent on Shabbos.

As the Midrash says (*Yalkut Shimoni* 983), שְׁחוֹרָה בִּימֵי מַעֲשֶׂה וְנָאוָה בְּשַׁבָּת שְׁחוֹרָה אֲנִי בְּמַעֲשַׂי וְנָאוָה בְּמַעֲשֵׂה אֲבוֹתַי, *All week long I may be besmirched, but on Shabbos I am beautiful. Even if I am besmirched by my own deeds, I am still beautiful because of the deeds of my fathers the Patriarchs.* These two statements express the same thought: On Shabbos, I am beautiful because of the merit of the Patriarchs. While a Jew may draw close to Hashem at any time, on Shabbos the merit of the Patriarchs brings him even closer. Then the spark of the Patriarchs rises to the surface and illuminates the Jewish soul.

The simile with the draperies of Solomon (v.5) is particularly apt. The transition from the "blackness" of the weekday to the beauty of Shabbos is like cleaning the besmirched outer surface of immaculately clean curtains. So too on Shabbos, the outer veneer of the Jew, black with sin, is washed clean and his pure interior becomes sparklingly visible.

While the Jew's inner spark, derived primarily from the Patriarchs, is evident on Shabbos, it is far more prominent on the festivals. In the time of the *Beis HaMikdash* a radical transformation occurred, as the people shed their outer "material" appearance to reveal their inner goodness. As we say in the the *Mussaf* prayer of Yom Tov (cf. *Devarim* 16:16): שָׁלוֹשׁ פְּעָמִים בַּשָּׁנָה יֵרָאֶה כָל־זְכוּרְךָ. *Three times a year all your males are to appear [in the Beis HaMikdash.]* While this verse is usually understood to refer to the requirement that all males appear in Jerusalem, it can be translated more literally to say that a person's "manhood," his inner personality comes to the forefront on Yom Tov.

Similarly, every Jew was obligated to immerse himself in a *mikveh* prior to Yom Tov. As the Sages said (*Rosh Hashanah* 16b), חַיָּיב אָדָם לְטַהֵר עַצְמוֹ בָּרֶגֶל, *a person is required to purify himself for the festival.* Symbolically, this means that we must remove all barriers to the sanctity of Yom Tov so that the festival's inner spirit can penetrate the personality. Of course, the process of shedding the exterior self and revealing what lies within does not occur instantaneously. As the Mishnah tells us (*Peah* 1:1): הָרַאֲיוֹן אֵין לוֹ שִׁיעוּר, presenting oneself before Hashem on Yom Tov is among the *mitzvos* that have "no prescribed measure" — revealing one's true self is a limitless task, a lifetime pursuit.

(5641)

Later in *Shir HaShirim* (3:11) King Solomon hints again at this need to shed the outer barriers to sanctity in order to allow the inner spark to prevail: צְאֶינָה וּרְאֶינָה בְּנוֹת צִיּוֹן בַּמֶּלֶךְ שְׁלֹמֹה, *Go out, daughters of Zion, and you will perceive King Solomon.*[1] In order to perceive Hashem's sanctity on Yom Tov, it is necessary first to "go out", to remove all external layers that prevent sanctity from penetrating into the soul, and then you will "perceive" Hashem's Presence.

If Judaism puts such great emphasis on the inner core of a person, the dynamic spark we call the soul, why did Hashem even bother to create an outer garb for us and to make it so important in our lives? Why did He not create man with only a soul, and none of the external trappings? The answer is that externalities also have a purpose in Hashem's plan. By observing the *mitzvos* that pertain to the material world, a Jew elevates it and infuses it with a sacred quality. Thus the role of the Jew is to show the rest of the world that they too, beset with material concerns as they are, can lead sacred lives.

In order to do so, however, it is critically important to keep our priorities clear in our minds. It would be a grievous error to ignore the soul and devote all of one's attention and effort to the demands of material life, pressing as they sometimes are. Unfortunately, the

---

1. Throughout *Shir HaShirim* "King Solomon" always alludes to Hashem.

tribulations of life in exile have often caused Jews to confuse these priorities. Setting an example for the Gentile world must be secondary to our primary task of nurturing our souls through Torah and *mitzvos*. As *Shir HaShirim* proclaims (1:6), שָׂמֻנִי נֹטֵרָה אֶת־הַכְּרָמִים כַּרְמִי שֶׁלִּי לֹא נָטָרְתִּי, *They have made me a keeper of vineyards, but my own vineyard I did not keep.* I have tended everyone else's vineyard and dealt extensively with material concerns — the outer trappings of the secular worlds, but I have forsaken my own vineyard — the Torah, and the inner strength it gives me.[1] (5643)

לְסֻסָתִי בְּרִכְבֵי פַרְעֹה דִּמִּיתִיךְ רַעְיָתִי
To my horse amongst Pharaoh's chariots I have compared you, my beloved (1:9).

The key to this very puzzling verse lies in the word דִּמִּיתִיךְ. While literally it means *I have compared you*, it may also be related to the word דֹּם, *silence*. This verse actually describes the Jews' reaction to the Splitting of the Sea, as we shall explain.

Throughout the period of Egyptian servitude our forefathers wondered why they were enslaved. They were so embittered and wretched in spirit that they could not take seriously Moshe's reassurances that the redemption was imminent, as the Torah says (*Shemos* 6:9), *They did not listen to Moshe because of their frustrations and hard labor.*

From Hashem's perspective, however, the tribulations of Egypt were not punishments but rather agents in the process of purification. As a result of the suffering they underwent in Egypt, when the Exodus finally came the Jews were able to ascend to even higher levels than would otherwise have been possible.

At the time, however the people could not grasp the purpose of their suffering. Hashem knew that, in the words of the prophet Yechezkel (16:6), וָאֶרְאֵךְ מִתְבּוֹסֶסֶת בְּדָמָיִךְ וָאֹמַר לָךְ בְּדָמַיִךְ חֲיִי, *I saw you wallowing in blood [i.e. suffering], and I said to you 'In your blood is My life.'* It was precisely this suffering that purged their impurities, serving as a source of life, so that they would eventually live (בְּדָמַיִךְ חֲיִי) as liberated subjects of Hashem.

It was only at the Splitting of the Sea, when the Exodus came to a

1. The problem of keeping a balance between reaching out to the nations and our development as Torah individuals is also discussed in the essay on *Na'aseh Ve'Nishma* in the section on Shavuos.

glorious climax with the final destruction of Pharaoh's hordes, that the doubters among the Jewish people were forever silenced. Finally they could understand the purpose in all the suffering they had undergone — to give them merit so that they would deserve the miracles they had just witnessed. In the "eyes" of Hashem, Who sees the ultimate truth in everything, their misery in Egypt was a jewel that made possible a brighter day in the near future.

Now we can better interpret our verse לְסֻסָתִי בְּרִכְבֵי פַרְעֹה דִּמִּיתִיךְ רַעְיָתִי: When the Jewish people beheld Pharaoh's horses and chariots drowning in the Red Sea, they saw the real meaning of all their suffering, and all their complaints, were silenced. At that moment they would have willingly undergone such suffering over again in order to attain spiritual heights like those reached at the Red Sea.[1] (5643)

We can also interpret the word דִּמִּיתִי in a way more in keeping with its usual meaning, *I compared You*. In this sense, our verse compares our slavery at Pharaoh's hands with our eventual emergence as servants of Hashem. The Jewish people tells Hashem, "My relationship with You is like the relationship I had with Pharaoh."

Similarly when the Jews first went into slavery, the Torah recounts (*Shemos* 1:12) וְכַאֲשֶׁר יְעַנּוּ אֹתוֹ כֵּן יִרְבֶּה וְכֵן יִפְרֹץ, *as they afflicted it [the people], so it grew and so it expanded.* This verse teaches that the growth of the Jewish people in freedom parallels their sufferings. What is the similarity?

Let us consider some of the comparisons between Pharaoh's servitude and our homage to Hashem. The misery of the Egyptian slavery was total; no slave had ever been able to escape from it to the extent that the Torah describes Egypt as a כּוּר הַבַּרְזֶל, *an iron forge* (*Devarim* 4:20). So too, our commitment to Hashem is total, a link forged so strongly that it could never be severed — even if, Heaven forbid, we wanted to do so. Thus the prophet Yechezkel writes (20:33): אִם־לֹא בְּיָד חֲזָקָה . . . אֶמְלוֹךְ עֲלֵיכֶם, *I will rule over you with a strong hand*, even by coercion if necessary.

Our relationship with Hashem is immutable, much as our relationship with the arch opponent Pharaoh seemed to be.

Both reflect total commitment: one of human bondage, the other of an eternal relationship with the living God. Even though other nations

1. *Editor's Note:* This theme, an important one in the writings of the *Sfas Emes*, is developed further in the essay devoted to the Song of the Sea (pg. 171).

have attempted to follow in Pharaoh's footsteps and enslave the Jewish people, and have at times had some success, their success will never be more than limited and superficial. At our core, we have remained steadfast in our service of Hashem ever since the Exodus, even in the worst of times.

The comparison between enslavement to Pharaoh and our commitment to Hashem can be developed further. We were enslaved in the most miserable culture the world has ever known, both physically and spiritually. In contrast, after our liberation. Hashem settled us in the finest of lands, *Eretz Yisrael*. While Egypt was called the "House of Bondage," *Eretz Yisrael* and the *Beis HaMikdash* are truly royal homes.

There is still another comparison that can be made between the Egyptian enslavement and our servitude to Hashem: both occurred on a gradual, sequential basis. Pharaoh did not enslave us all at once, rather the people were first asked to volunteer for work. As the Torah says (*Shemos* 1:13): וַיַּעֲבִדוּ מִצְרַיִם אֶת־בְּנֵי יִשְׂרָאֵל בְּפָרֶךְ, *Egypt enslaved the Jewish people softly* [at first]. (This translation is based on the interpretation of the word פָּרֶךְ as a combination of the two words פֶּה and רַךְ, *with a soft mouth.*)

Just as this initial "softness" escalated into brutal, back-breaking slavery, so also our relationship with Hashem "grew" and developed over time. Our initial acceptance of Torah was a classic example of volunteerism.

At first we accepted the Torah because we wanted to, as we see from the well-known proclamation, נַעֲשֶׂה וְנִשְׁמָע, *we will do and we will listen* (*Shemos* 24:7). After this initial willingness, however, Hashem "suspended Mount Sinai like a vat" over our heads, virtually compelling us to accept the Torah. This coercion was necessary to drive home the point that we have no alternative other than to observe the Torah, even though at times Hashem's Presence may not be as palpable as it was at Sinai. (For a fuller discussion of this compulsion, see the essay entitled *Na'aseh VeNishma* in the section on Shavuos.) (5652, 5662)

תּוֹרֵי זָהָב נַעֲשֶׂה־לָּךְ עִם נְקֻדּוֹת הַכָּסֶף
Let us make for you circlets of gold with spangles of silver (1:11).

The Midrash (*Yalkut Shimoni* 983) interprets this verse as an allusion to the treasures the Jews took upon their departure from Egypt and at the Sea of Reeds. Comparing these two windfalls, the Sages said, גְּדוֹלָה

בִּיזַּת הַיָּם מִבִּיזַּת מִצְרַיִם, *The spoils of the sea were greater than the spoils of Egypt.* The "spoils of the sea" are the treasures carried by the Egyptian soldiers that were washed ashore after they drowned and collected by the Jews. While the Torah does not mention them specifically, *Rashi* cites them in his commentary on *Shemos* 15:22). The "spoils of Egypt," however, are specifically mentioned in the Torah (*Shemos* 12:35): וּבְנֵי־יִשְׂרָאֵל עָשׂוּ כִּדְבַר מֹשֶׁה וַיִּשְׁאֲלוּ מִמִּצְרַיִם כְּלֵי־כֶסֶף וּכְלֵי זָהָב וּשְׂמָלֹת, *The Children of Israel carried out the word of Moshe; they borrowed from the Egyptians silver vessels, golden vessels, and garments.* Even so, all this largess was inferior to the booty obtained at the Sea. Our verse alludes to the relative worth of these treasures by calling the spoils of Egypt *spangles of silver* while those of the Sea are called *circlets of gold.*

Why is this distinction emphasized? In what sense was the booty of the Sea more significant than that of Egypt?

Generally something we earn has more value to us than something we receive as a present. The spoils of the Sea, as well as the great miracles associated with the Splitting of the Sea, were amply deserved by the Jewish people. Just before that miracle, they had been judged and found worthy of being saved (cf. *Rashi Shemos* 14:19). Thus the Torah calls the the splitting of the Sea a *salvation,* since the people merited it (*Shemos* 14:30): וַיּוֹשַׁע ה׳ בַּיּוֹם הַהוּא, *HASHEM **saved** on that day.*

By contrast, the Exodus was accomplished by Hashem's outstretched hand, as the Torah says: (*Devarim* 4:34), בְּיָד חֲזָקָה וּבִזְרוֹעַ נְטוּיָה, *with a strong hand and an outstretched arm*. The people were extricated from their misery *in spite of* their unworthiness and unreadiness for freedom.

Thus the spoils earned by the Jews in reward for their willingness to plunge into the sea are described as "gold"in comparison to the "silver" they were given in Egypt as an undeserved gift from Hashem.

A question arises, however. Why did Hashem shower the Jewish people with gifts at the time of the Exodus? Why was simply being freed from the terror of Egypt not sufficient by itself? The Talmud answers that Hashem wanted to fulfill His promise to Abraham (*Bereishis* 15:14), וְאַחֲרֵי־כֵן יֵצְאוּ בִּרְכֻשׁ גָּדוֹל, *after this [four hundred years of suffering] they will leave with great wealth.* Hashem did not want the *tzaddik* Abraham to be able to argue that the Egyptian enslavement He foretold in Egypt was fulfilled, but the promise of great wealth was not. In order to forestall such a claim, Hashem showered the wealth of Egypt on his descendants (*Berachos* 9a).

It is entirely appropriate that it was concern for Abraham's sensitivity that caused them to benefit from Hashem's boundless kindness. Abraham himself was an exemplar of kindness to the extent that the Sages called him the "Pillar of Kindness." Abraham unfailingly acted beyond the kindness that was required of him and extended himself both to those who deserved his kindness and to those who did not. In return, Hashem extended his kindness to his descendants and allowed them to leave Egypt and even to exploit the bounty of that land.

Yet only a week later, after the people proved themselves by following Hashem into the Wilderness and plunging into the Sea, they had accumulated enough merit of their own to *deserve* the miracles of the Splitting of the Sea and treasures which were not mere unearned gifts. Earned gifts are of far greater value than unearned.

There is another significant difference between the spoils taken in Egypt and those obtained a week later at the Sea. The former were taken reluctantly, as we see from the fact that Hashem *pleads* with the Jewish people to ask the Egyptians for gold, silver, and garments (cf. *Shemos* 11:2). On the other hand, only a week later, Moshe had to order the Jewish people to cease their plundering.

Why were they so reluctant at first and so eager later? Apparently there were drawbacks associated with the spoils of Egypt such as the risk of spiritual "contamination" associated with wealth that emerged from the moral depravity of Egypt. During the period between the Exodus and the splitting of the Sea, however, significant changes occurred. The residual bonds between the newly liberated nation and their former masters were washed away by the raging waters of the Sea and the ecstasy of the song they sang. Now it was safe to partake of Egypt's wealth without fear of ill effects.

Later in *Shir HaShirim* there is an allusion to this purification, the washing away of lingering ties with Egyptian culture by the waters of the Sea: שִׁנַּיִךְ כְּעֵדֶר הַקְּצוּבוֹת שֶׁעָלוּ מִן־הָרַחְצָה, *Your teeth are like sheep that are counted as they come up from a washing* (4:2). The plural form of the word קְצוּבוֹת, *counted*, is a reference to the two opportunities the Jews were given to consume (teeth-like) the booty of their foes. While in Egypt the treasures were still contaminated by the immorality of Egyptian culture, at the Sea any links with the past had been washed away leaving them as sheep emerging from a washing, cleaner than ever before.

This, then, is the meaning of the Sages' observation, that "The spoils of the sea were greater than the spoils of Egypt'': The possessions the Jews acquired at the Sea were greater in that they had been cleansed of Egyptian influence and became truly Jewish, as opposed to the *Egyptian* bounty they had been made to take at the Exodus. (5653)

Finally, we may consider the bounty of Egypt and the Sea not just as material possessions, but also as allusions to spiritual treasures extracted on each occasion. *Ohr HaChaim* (*Shemos* 19:6) comments that the purpose of the dispersion of Jews to so many lands is so that sparks of sanctity (נִיצוֹצֵי קְדוּשָׁה) scattered throughout the world may be gathered and restored to Torah.[1] The Jewish people endured two hundred ten years of Egyptian exile in order to liberate sparks of sanctity (i.e. non-Jewish souls) and bring them closer to Torah. While the suffering of Egypt — two hundred ten years of misery — recovered some of those dispersed sparks, many more can be gathered through Torah. The *Ohr HaChaim* describes Torah as a magnet to attract sparks of sanctity dispersed throughout the universe. The Torah the Jews created at the Sea (i.e. the song they sang to praise Hashem) attracted more souls to Judaism and retrieved more sparks of sanctity than all the suffering of Egypt.

Thus the Sages' comment that ''the spoils of the sea were greater than the spoils of Egypt'' applies also to the souls they attracted, the sparks of sanctity gathered. Much more was accomplished by the events of the Sea and the joy of Torah generated there than by two hundred ten years of pain and distress endured in Egypt.

The Psalmist alludes to the relationship between suffering and joy in the following phrase (68:7), מוֹצִיא אֲסִירִים בַּכּוֹשָׁרוֹת, *[God] releases those bound in fetters*, a reference to the liberation of the Jews from Egypt. The Midrash (*Yalkut Shimoni* 795) interprets the word בַּכּוֹשָׁרוֹת as a composite of the words בְּכִי, *tears*, and וְשִׁירוֹת, *and song*. As used here, the concept of song refers to words of Torah created through the medium of song. These do more to capture stray sparks of sanctity and returning stray souls than the tears of suffering.

The Torah also hints at the impact of the Splitting of the Sea on the universe (*Shemos* 14:17): וְאִכָּבְדָה בְּפַרְעֹה, *I will be honored through Pharaoh*. The demise of Pharaoh's hordes at the Red Sea contributed

1. This is a deep Kabbalistic idea which is prevalent in Chassidic thought. Oversimplified, it sees the function of a Jewish presence in Gentile surroundings as God's method to harness any positive elements of those surroundings toward His service. The Jewish people serve as a ''magnet'' to draw those elements into the Godly orbit.

greatly to the awareness of the Creator and served as a harbinger of the day when all men will recognize His greatness. (5659)

עַד־שֶׁהַמֶּלֶךְ בִּמְסִבּוֹ נִרְדִּי נָתַן רֵיחוֹ
While the King was yet at his table my nard gave forth its scent (1:12).

This verse is generally understood as a criticism of the Jewish people for the sin of the Golden Calf, which occurred so soon after the Divine Revelation at Mount Sinai. However, we may also see it in a more positive vein, as a praise of the Jews for contributing a segment of the Torah on their own initiative — the song they sang upon witnessing the splitting of the Sea of Reeds and the destruction of Pharoah's army.

In this interpretation, the verse should be understood as follows: While the King was yet in Heaven, (before the Torah was revealed to man) the fragrance of Torah (the resonant, sweet soul of the Song) was already diffused by the Jewish people (i.e. they sang the Song).

The Torah was not given in a formal sense until Shavuos, seven weeks after the Exodus from Egypt. Before this, however, a very important section of the Torah, the Song, emanated from the hearts and minds of the Jewish people themselves. Our verse suggests that while the Torah was still in Heaven (at the "King's table"), the Jews were able to bring to earth a bit of its fragrance ("the nard gave forth its smell") in the form of the Song. A small but important sample of Torah was already revealed to man.

While it is true that before it was given the Torah was situated in Heaven and not on earth, at the moment of the splitting of the Sea, the Jewish people felt as if they were in Heaven. When they exclaimed זֶה אֵלִי, *This is my God,* they sensed that the Creator was right there. Whereas when the Torah was given at Sinai, Hashem "descended" to a level even with the earth, at the Sea the people "ascended" to Heaven and were thus able to compose a portion of the Torah on their own initiative, even before the Torah came down to earth.

This capacity to innovate a segment of Torah before Sinai attests to the extraordinary relationship between the Torah and the Jewish people. Jews do not merely study Torah — they are attached to it with an inexorable bond.[1] This is what enabled them to bring to earth portions of the Torah that were still in Heaven. The relationship between the

1. "Torah is a commentary on the Jewish soul" (*R' Tzadok HaKohen, Tzidkas HaTzadik*).

Song and the events of Sinai is indicated by the future tense of the opening verb of the Song (*Shemos* 15:1): אָז יָשִׁיר־מֹשֶׁה וּבְנֵי יִשְׂרָאֵל, *Then Moshe and the Children of Israel* **will sing** *this song*, suggesting that the Song was a foretaste of the Torah that would later be given at Sinai.

According to the Midrash (*Shemos Rabbah* 23:4), the verse (*Mishlei* 31:26), פִּיהָ פָּתְחָה בְחָכְמָה *She [the Jewish people] opened her mouth in wisdom,* alludes to the Song. In light of the above explanation we can say that the *first words* of Torah (wisdom) spoken by the Jewish people prior to Sinai were the Song.

אֲנִי חֲבַצֶּלֶת הַשָּׁרוֹן שׁוֹשַׁנַּת הָעֲמָקִים

I am a rose of Sharon, a rose of the valley (2:1).

The Midrash (*Yalkut Shimoni* 985) interprets this verse as a reference to the plight of the Jewish people during the Egyptian exile and all future exiles. חֲבִיבָה אֲנִי שֶׁהָיִיתִי חֲבוּיָה בְּמִצְרַיִם. . .דָּבָר אַחֵר שֶׁהָיִיתִי חֲבוּיָה בְּצִילָן שֶׁל מַלְכֻיוֹת, *I am precious because I was hidden by* H*ASHEM's protecting shade during the Egyptian exile. Also, I was hidden in the shade of other kingdoms.*

This Midrash describes the role of the Jewish people among the nations and, by extension, the reason of their dispersion throughout the world. The nation of Israel, scattered among many cultures is to be a role model for a confused and often corrupt human race. In order to accomplish our mission in exile, we were given an additional name appropriate for this task, יְשֻׁרוּן , *Yeshurun* (cf. *Devarim* 32:15) from the word יָשָׁר (*straight, honest*): That which *straightens* and *makes honest* everything that is corrupt, and is destined to help mankind rectify its errors.

By sending the Jewish people out among the nations, Hashem seeks to help mankind find a new, straight path in a world that is otherwise perverse and devious. Thus, Israel in exile is called *Yeshurun,* or in this verse *Sharon.* I am the protected one whose function in exile is to perfect mankind and to straighten (שָׁרוֹן) the corrupt ways of the world. Elsewhere in *Shir HaShirim* the Jewish people is given another name appropriate to its role in exile, שׁוּלַמִּית, *Shulamith* the peacemaker nation whose function is to make peace between Hashem and mankind, by bringing all men closer to their Creator. This mission applies at all times and under every circumstance in which we find ourselves.

In spite of our zeal to perfect humanity, however we never lose our identity, and never completely assimilate among our temporary hosts.

Later in *Shir HaShirim*, King Solomon hints that Jewry refused to assimilate in each of the four kingdoms to which it was subjugated by repeating the word שׁוּבִי (*return*) four times: (7:1) שׁוּבִי שׁוּבִי הַשּׁוּלַמִּית שׁוּבִי שׁוּבִי וְנֶחֱזֶה בָּךְ, *Return, return, you peacemaker; return, return and we will see you.* This fourfold expression hints at Israel's survival in each of the four exiles it has been subjected to. In each of the three that have ended (we are still in the fourth exile, that of Rome, may it soon end), not only did we emerge intact, we also succeeded in bettering the world. (5643)

כְּשׁוֹשַׁנָּה בֵּין הַחוֹחִים כֵּן רַעְיָתִי בֵּין הַבָּנוֹת
As a rose among the thorns, so is my beloved among the maidens (2:2).

This verse refers to the Egyptian exile, the first occasion that Israel not only emerged intact, but also influenced its surroundings, by releasing sparks of sanctity subsumed in Egypt. We were a rose amongst thorns, a beacon of morality in an immoral world who truly fulfilled the role of *Yeshurun* (straightening out the crooked) during those difficult years of servitude. Having completed their mission of rectifying Egyptian society by correcting what could be salvaged and destroying the rest, we could sing the Song of the Sea. Such an accomplishment deserves reward, some Divine indication of approval and appreciation. The reward was nothing other than the Torah we were given at Sinai, as indicated in the following verse: כְּתַפּוּחַ בַּעֲצֵי הַיַּעַר כֵּן דּוֹדִי בֵּין הַבָּנִים *As an apple tree amongst the trees of the forest, so too is my beloved [HASHEM] among the sons [idols]* (2:3).

The apple tree is known for its shade; its mention here alludes to Hashem's Presence at Sinai, hovering over us to reward us for our spiritual accomplishments.

Another approach to these verses sees them metaphorically as a dialogue between Hashem and the Jewish people. Israel yearns for the halcyon days in the Wilderness when we were shrouded by Heavenly clouds that protected us like a rose is protected in the valley. Hashem responds, "As a rose among the thorns, so is my beloved among the maidens." Much as we wish for His protecting shelter, we are more important in Hashem's eyes when we remain strong in our faith in Him even though we are pierced on all sides by the "thorns" of exile. (See *Sfas Emes* 5647)

Yet another approach sees these verses as a dialogue with Hashem about Shabbos and the Festivals. On the Festivals Hashem appreciates Israel's worth. On Shabbos, we appreciate His greatness.

כְּשׁוֹשַׁנָּה בֵּין הַחוֹחִים, *Like a rose among the thorns,* suggests that much as a rose is hidden among the thorns, so too, only Hashem appreciates Israel's true worth. Among the nations the Jewish people is reticent to bare its soul. Only on the Festivals, when we appear before our Creator in the *Beis HaMikdash* is our true worth appreciated.

Israel responds: "Only you can appreciate my worth (on the Fesitvals) and only I can appreciate your greatness on Shabbos, because כְּתַפּוּחַ בַּעֲצֵי הַיַּעַר כֵּן דּוֹדִי בֵּין הַבָּנִים בְּצִלּוֹ חִמַּדְתִּי וְיָשַׁבְתִּי וּפִרְיוֹ מָתוֹק לְחִכִּי, *As the apple tree among the trees of the forest, so is my beloved among the sons. I coveted His shade and His fruit was sweet to my palate* (2:3).

In reality, the apple tree has no pronounced shade. As the Midrash (*Yalkut Shimoni* 986) says, the apple tree's shade is faint and cannot always be noticed. Mankind fled from this shade in refusing to accept the Torah at Sinai but Israel persisted and accepted the truth.

The apple tree's subtle shade may also be a metaphor for Shabbos, which is a source of protection, as we say in the Shabbos and Festival prayers, הַפּוֹרֵשׂ סֻכַּת שָׁלוֹם עָלֵינוּ וְעַל כָּל עַמּוֹ יִשְׂרָאֵל, *Hashem spreads a shelter of peace on us and on all of His people Israel.* On these occasions every Jew is graced with a *neshamah yeseirah,* an additional dimension of spirituality.[1] On Shabbos, the universe is managed directly by Hashem, rather than by the angels He empowers during the week. These crucial distinctions between Shabbos and the week are barely noticeable to someone limited by the material world. Much like the subtle shade of the apple tree, they are apparent only to Israel; so too Shabbos can be experienced only by Israel. A careful examination of the end of this verse reveals further allusions to Shabbos:

> בְּצִלּוֹ חִמַּדְתִּי וְיָשַׁבְתִּי וּפִרְיוֹ מָתוֹק לְחִכִּי
> *I coveted His shade and I sat [there], and his fruit was sweet to my palate* (2:3).

I "sat in His shade," I remained in my place as one is required to do on Shabbos (cf. *Shemos* 16:29). His "fruit," the rarified spiritual atmosphere of Shabbos, was sweet to my palate.

On the Festivals the rose emerges from among the thorns — Hashem can appreciate our worth while on Shabbos we appreciate His greatness.

1. The presence of a *neshamah yeseirah* on Yom Tov is discussed in *Tosafos Pesachim* 102b.

Shabbos is an apple tree with its subtle shade, a taste of the World to Come that can be appreciated only by Israel. The Festivals, on which Hashem shows His appreciation of Israel highlight their beauty, a rose amongst the thorns of the universe. (5647)

סַמְּכוּנִי בָּאֲשִׁישׁוֹת רַפְּדוּנִי בַּתַּפּוּחִים כִּי־חוֹלַת אַהֲבָה אָנִי

HASHEM supported me with His fires, he adorned me with his apples, for I am sick with love (2:5).

A Jew's love for his Creator is intrinsic in his heart. The Patriarchs, Abraham, Isaac, and Jacob, loved Hashem with all their heart, even though they had not yet received the Torah. In inspired moments, even later generations sometimes burst forth with spontaneous expressions of love for Hashem. The Song of the Sea is an example of the inner love that every Jew feels for Hashem. This inner enthusiasm came to the surface in the merit of the trust the Jewish people displayed in Hashem by plunging into the Red Sea.

The ability of the Jew to show love for Hashem even before they received the Torah is indicated by the Midrash מַחֲשַׁבְתָּן שֶׁל יִשְׂרָאֵל קָדְמָה לַתּוֹרָה, *The thoughts of Israel [i.e. their love of Hashem] preceded Torah.*

Not every generation is able to reach such exalted levels, however. More often, the Jew requires some form of Divine assistance to realize his potential for loving Hashem. This may be the intent of the words in our verse, *He supported me with fires* — my own *internal* flame, my own love of Hashem, was found wanting, thus *I was sick with love.* Hashem however, kindled a Heavenly fire which joined together with my own innate potential and aroused my love for Him.

The Jew in exile, unable by himself to realize his potential for Divine love, is assisted by Hashem and His Torah to fulfill one of the most fundamental precepts of the Torah, וְאָהַבְתָּ אֵת ה׳ אֱלֹהֶיךָ, *You shall love HASHEM, your God (Devarim* 6:5). (5660)

קוֹל דּוֹדִי הִנֵּה־זֶה בָּא מְדַלֵּג עַל־הֶהָרִים מְקַפֵּץ עַל־הַגְּבָעוֹת

The voice of my beloved has come leaping over mountains, skipping over hills (2:8).

The Midrash understands this verse to refer to Hashem's hastening of the redemption from Egypt. Even though Hashem had told Abraham that his descendants would be enslaved in a strange land for four hundred years, after only two hundred ten years He surmounted all obstacles (leaping over mountains") to give us an early release from our servitude.

How was such a maneuver justified? If a sentence of four hundred years was predetermined, how could it have been reduced to two hundred ten years? The Midrash (*Yalkut Shimoni* 986) suggests that the mountains and hills of this verse refer to Patriarchs and Matriarchs of the Jewish people. Hashem "leaped" (i.e. reduced the four hundred years to two hundred ten) in the merit of the Patriarchs and "skipped" in the merit of the Matriarchs. The concept of giving later generations the merit of their predecessors is mentioned in *Shemoneh Esrei*: וְזוֹכֵר חַסְדֵי אָבוֹת, *[Hashem] recalls the kindness of the fathers,* וּמֵבִיא גוֹאֵל לִבְנֵי בְנֵיהֶם, *and brings a Redeemer to their children's children.*

This concept must be properly understood, however. Why should Hashem have redeemed unworthy children from Egypt prematurely in the merit of earlier righteous generations?

The answer may lie in the Patriarch's willingness to do more than Hashem required of them, specifically to observe the Torah even before it was given at Sinai. Because of this it was reasonable for Hashem also to override strict principles of justice and to liberate them one hundred ninety years early in order to repay their Patriarchs and Matriarchs for doing more than they were obliged. If so, why does our verse use expressions like "leaping" and "skipping," that imply that difficult hurdles had to be surmounted, when early liberation was really in keeping with normal Divine procedures? Had not Hashem considered the Patriarch's willingness to do more than required when He ordained four hundred years of servitude?

The answer is that the figure of four hundred years was actually justified, even considering the Patriarchs' virtues. However, once Divine mercy came into play the reckoning was altered. Thus both calculations are correct: Four hundred years was just a figure based on a strict appraisal of the Patriachs' merits, but two hundred ten years was an appropriate reduced sentence that took into account Hashem's mercies.

The connection between the Patriarchs and their descendants may be even more profound, as a careful examination of our verse will indicate. Normally the word "to leap" would be in the simple construction (דוֹלֵג). The use of the causative (מְדַלֵּג) suggests that Hashem made others leap. Similarly the word מְקַפֵּץ implies that Hashem made the Jewish people "skip." At the time of the Exodus, Hashem made it possible for the

Jewish people to "vault" spiritually to levels higher than those they had previously attained.

Thus these two words, מְדַלֵּג and מְקַפֵּץ indicate a particular relationship between Hashem's actions and ours. Hashem "vaulted" over the obstacles of history to condense four hundred years into two hundred ten; we in turn "skipped" over the barriers of our hearts, overcoming the limitations of a slave mentality to become servants of the living God. At the time of the Exodus we "grew" all at once. In one short day, we journeyed from Ramses, site of the most abject slavery (where the Jewish people built storehouses for Pharaoh) to Succos, where Hashem's Divine clouds first protected the Jewish people (as is discussed at greater length in the essays on *Succah*).

The use of the form מְדַלֵּג, *to cause to jump,* indicates that this quantum leap — from Pharaoh's slaves to Hashem's servants — would have been impossible without Divine assistance and without role models to follow. If there ever were individuals who "leaped" — who rose to exalted levels through self-sacrifice, they were the Patriarchs and Matriarchs. This may be the true meaning of the Midrash cited above. Hashem hastened the redemption not only in the *merit* of the Patriarchs and Matriarchs, but also because they served as role models to show us how to rise quickly to exalted levels upon our redemption. By reading *Shir HaShirim* on Pesach, we voice our firm conviction that every year at that time, we too will follow the example of the Patriarchs and "leap" to ever higher spiritual levels.

Can there be a better and more timely form of redemption than spiritual growth? As the prophet Malachi foretold (3:24), וְהֵשִׁיב לֵב אָבוֹת עַל בָּנִים, *And he [Elijah] will return the heart of the fathers to the children* — he will cause future generations to aspire to the great spiritual heights of their forefathers. Hashem hastened the redemption once; we have every reason to believe that He will do so again, as the prophet Michah says (7:15), כִּימֵי צֵאתְךָ מֵאֶרֶץ מִצְרָיִם אַרְאֶנּוּ נִפְלָאוֹת, *I will show you [i.e. perform on your behalf] wonders as I did during the days when you left Egypt.*

This verse refers to both the past redemption from Egypt and the future redemption when *Moshiach* comes. The opening segment of our verse in *Shir HaShirim* pertains to the redemption from Egypt — He "leaped" over the mountains to release us from Egyptian slavery. However, the closing phrase "skipped over the hills" tells us that the final redemption will also be hastened. In fact, *Moshiach's* redemption may be even more accelerated than the one from Egypt. The term "skipping" (מְקַפֵּץ) is taken by Rabbi Schneur Zalman (*Likutei Torah Shir HaShirim*) to refer to rapid movement with *both* feet, whereas "leaping" implies motion with only one foot. Hashem helped us "leap" from Egypt but will allow us to "skip," at a much faster pace, during the final redemption.

In what sense will the final redemption be at an even more rapid pace than the first one? Certainly the Midrash is not referring to the length of time served in exile. While the Egyptian exile was shortened (from four hundred to two hundred ten years), no one can determine precisely when the final redemption will occur. Indeed, many *tzaddikim* and scholars have attempted to predict when *Moshiach* will arrive without success. The present exile has lasted far beyond expectations; certainly in a quantitative sense the final redemption has not been accelerated.

The concept of hastening the future redemption may relate instead to lessening the intensity of the suffering that precedes the exile's end. The Egyptian slavery may have been shortened, but the suffering, especially in its final phase, grew more intense to compensate for the reduced sentence. The reverse may well hold true for the final redemption. In exchange for the apparent lengthening of the exile, the intense suffering associated with the period immediately prior to *Moshiach's* arrival, suffering so intense that many great Rabbis have declared that they do not want to be present during that period, will be mitigated.

In what merit will the final redemption be hastened? Whereas the redemption of Egypt was accelerated in the merit of the Patriarchs, this merit may no longer be available for contemporary generations. The Talmud (*Shabbos* 55a) states that the merit of the Patriarchs has been exhausted by previous generations in times of distress. However, the final redemption will still occur in the merit of the Matriarchs, the mothers of the Jewish people. Hashem will skip over the "hills," the obstacles to Moshiach's arrival, in the merit of the gentle compassionate women who built and nurtured the Jewish people, for their merit is eternal. We know and trust that the Matriarchs of the Jewish people will pray from their place of repose in Heaven for a hastening of the final redemption. (5642, 5655, 5658)

הִנֵּה־זֶה עוֹמֵד אַחַר כָּתְלֵנוּ מַשְׁגִּיחַ מִן־הַחַלֹּנוֹת מֵצִיץ מִן־הַחֲרַכִּים
He was standing behind our wall, observing through the windows, peering through the lattices (2:9).

This verse suggests that even when the Jewish people is dispersed in exile, Hashem does not forsake them. He observes them from behind the wall, through the windows, or through the lattices. People standing on both sides of a window can see each other, but a crack in the wall allows only one-way vision — the person peering through it cannot be seen by someone on the outside.

In life, too, sometimes Hashem looks at us without being "seen," (at times when His presence is veiled) while at other times a reciprocal perception occurs: He looks at us through His "windows" while we can "visualize" His presence as well and are aware that He sees us. These two kinds of perception can be found in many aspects of Jewish life. For example, Hashem's relationship with *tzaddikim* is comparable to that of people on either side of a window who can see each other. The less pious are seen by Hashem, but are not privileged to perceive His Presence so clearly.

This metaphor can be understood in terms of the human body also: Hashem sees inside every crevice of our bodies, and we in turn can perceive Him through seven apertures — two eyes, two ears, two nostrils, and a mouth. These sensory organs allow as to perceive the material world, which testifies to the existence of its Creator.

The metaphor of our verse applies also to the Jewish calendar year. During the week He looks at us through "cracks" that do not allow us to see Him in return. On Shabbos and Festivals, however, there is mutual perception, as through a "window." This was especially true on the pilgrimages to the *Beis HaMikdash,* but even now we have some awareness of the enhanced sanctity of these occasions.

The Talmud (*Chagigah* 2a) notes that the verse requiring that all males be seen on Festivals, יֵרָאֶה כָּל זְכוּרְךָ, can also be read יִרְאֶה, *all your males* ***will*** *see,* that is, will perceive Hashem's Presence. On Festivals, we are increasingly aware of Hashem's Presence through our new-found windows. Thus the seven orifices mentioned above can be seen as coinciding with the seven Festivals days of the year (two days of Pesach, two days of Succos, one day each of Shavuos, Rosh Hashanah and Yom Kippur). Finally, this metaphor also relates to specific locations. While Hashem sees everything that happens everywhere in the universe[1] only in certain specific locations (e.g. the *Beis HaMikdash,* Jerusalem, *Eretz Yisrael*) can we sense His presence as He observes us. (5643,5647)

1. This seemingly simple statement, if we contemplate it for even a few seconds, should leave us dizzy with awe of Hashem's greatness.

יוֹנָתִי בְּחַגְוֵי הַסֶּלַע בְּסֵתֶר הַמַּדְרֵגָה הַרְאִינִי אֶת מַרְאַיִךְ הַשְׁמִיעִנִי אֶת־קוֹלֵךְ כִּי קוֹלֵךְ עָרֵב וּמַרְאֵיךְ נָאוֶה

My dove, trapped in the clefts of the rock, the concealment of the terrace. Show Me your countenance, let Me hear your voice, for your voice is sweet and your countenance beautiful (2:14)

The Midrash (*Yalkut Shimoni* 986) suggests that this verse refers to that moment at the Sea of Reeds when the Jewish people, their backs pinned to the sea by the Egyptian army, prayed and beseeched Hashem to save their lives. A short while later, after witnessing the annihilation of Pharaoh's hordes, they sang the Song. The prayer at the Sea and the Song were not separate events. According to the Midrash, Hashem precipitated the crisis at the Sea to bring out Israel's potential for prayer, its hidden capacity to beseech Him.

"My dove in the cleft of the rock" refers to the Jewish people (often compared to the benign dove) whose potential for heartfelt prayer was latent, hidden in the cleft of the rock. Hashem begs us "Let me hear your voice," let your prayer and song prevail. Even today, the Song is recited by Jews around the world every day before the *Shema* and *Shemoneh Esrei* to arouse our powers of prayer. In fact, the Rabbinical requirement that a prayer for redemption be recited before *Shemoneh Esrei* (cf. *Berachos* 4b), may allude to the Song whose recitation helps ensure that the following prayers, including *Shemoneh Esrei*, will be said with full devotion.

Prayer has always been our inner strength, our secret weapon. As Isaac said "The voice is Jacob's voice" (*Bereishis* 27:22) — Jacob's descendants pride themselves on the power of their prayers — whereas Esau (the non-Jewish world and Esau's descendants in particular) is known for physical prowess and military might.

Much of the suffering that Hashem allows to happen to Jews is intended not as punishment but rather to bring out the inner voice of Torah, the voice that first spoke at the Sea of Reeds. A meaningful relationship with Hashem is possible only when the Jew's latent power of prayer is actualized, both on a community and individual level. As King Solomon says, (*Koheles* 6:7) כָּל עֲמַל הָאָדָם לְפִיהוּ, *A person's effects are directed to his mouth*

The singing of the Song, when the Jewish people displayed their latent potential for prayer, ensured that all future prayers of the Jewish community, as well as individual Jews, will be said with true devotion. (5643, 5647)

זאת קוֹמָתֵךְ דָּמְתָה לְתָמָר וְשָׁדַיִךְ לְאַשְׁכֹּלוֹת אָמַרְתִּי אֶעֱלֶה בְתָמָר אֹחֲזָה בְּסַנְסִנָּיו וְיִהְיוּ־נָא שָׁדַיִךְ כְּאֶשְׁכְּלוֹת הַגֶּפֶן

Such is your stature, likened to a palm tree, and your bosom is like clusters of grapes I said I will climb tree, I will hold onto its branches; your bosom is like clusters of grapes on the vine. (7:8-9)

Why is the comparison of Israel's "bosom" repeated in these verses? We may say that this emphasizes Israel's humility even in times of glory. Though we ascend to the peak of the lofty palm tree, and are still laden with the sweet juice of Torah and good deeds, we still perceive ourselves as low hanging clusters of grapes and remain with our humility.[1] (5640)

The Seventh Day

שֵׁשֶׁת יָמִים תֹּאכַל מַצּוֹת וּבַיּוֹם הַשְּׁבִיעִי עֲצֶרֶת לַה׳ אֱלֹהֶיךָ לֹא תַעֲשֶׂה מְלָאכָה

For six days you are to eat matzos and the seventh day shall be an assembly to H*ASHEM*, *your God, you may not perform labor* (*Devarim* 16:8).

This verse raises several questions: Why does it limit the *mitzvah* of eating matzah to only six days? Furthermore, in *Parashas Bo,* the Torah says, מַצּוֹת יֵאָכֵל אֵת שִׁבְעַת הַיָּמִים, *Matzos should be eaten throughout the seven days* (*Shemos* 13:7); why in one place does the Torah specify six days and in another seven? What is the role of the seventh day of Passover — why was the ultimate victory against the

1. This image is often used in Torah to represent Torah scholars, from whom flow the nurturing sustenance of Torah teachings.

Egyptian armies at the Sea of Reeds and the Song at the Sea deferred until that day?

We will suggest several simple keys to resolve all of these questions. For one thing, the word *matzah* may be understood to mean *strife*.[1] Furthermore, the Exodus may be seen not merely as a physical liberation from slavery but also as a process of spiritual freedom from the *yetzer hara* (evil inclination), a theme we develop more extensively elsewhere in this book. In light of these assumptions, the phrase *six days shall you eat matzos* may be construed as follows: "Six days shall you *fight* the *yetzer hara* and on the seventh day, there shall be an assembly, at which the elusive goal of Jewish unity shall be attained as the Torah says, עֲצֶרֶת לַה' אֱלֹהֶיךָ, *an assembly for HASHEM, your God.*

The process of fighting the *yetzer hara,* which constitutes the task of the first six days, cannot be undertaken on a unified basis. Each individual has his own deficiencies and weaknesses to combat. Only on the seventh day, after a week of *struggling* against the *yetzer hara,* can a united Jewish people celebrate the Festival of Gathering. There was no greater demonstration of Jewish unity than the Song of the Sea, which was composed and sung by every Jew in perfect unison. Such an accomplishment would have been impossible prior to the seventh day of Pesach, an occasion of profound unity. We find an allusion to this in the words of the Psalmist (34:15) סוּר מֵרָע וַעֲשֵׂה־טוֹב, *turn from evil* by fighting the *yetzer hara* in the first six days, *and do good* on the seventh day, a time of intense unity. (5664, 5638)

Alternatively, we may see in this verse a reference to the primary message of *matzah* — humility. By its simple, stark, and unleavened shape *matzah* pleads to the Jewish people — be more humble! Humility is among the primary values of Judaism.

But how is humility to be attained? *For six days you are to eat matzos* — we are to strive for humility by emulating the message of the simple flat contours of *matzah* — utter negation of the physical world.

Matzah reminds us of our frailties, our mortality. But another route to humility exists: By contemplating Hashem's majesty, we come to realize our own shortcomings. Indeed, Moshe, the most unassuming of men, enjoyed the most intimate relationship with Hashem any mortal has ever known and the more he perceived of Hashem's splendor, the more humble he grew.

---

1. Cf. (*Devarim* 25:11) כִּי־יִנָּצוּ אֲנָשִׁים יַחְדָּו, *when men shall fight together.*

This is the message of the seventh day of Pesach, when the Jewish people saw the glory of Hashem at the Sea and sang their Song — that humility can be attained not only through self-denial but also by appreciation of Hashem's grandeur. It is thus appropriate that it was Moshe, whose whole life reflected the humility he attained through his intimate knowledge of Hashem, who led Israel in singing the Song. As the Torah says (*Shemos* 14:31-15:1) וַיַּאֲמִינוּ בַּה׳ וּבְמֹשֶׁה עַבְדּוֹ: אָז יָשִׁיר־מֹשֶׁה וּבְנֵי יִשְׂרָאֵל אֶת־הַשִּׁירָה הַזֹּאת לַה׳, *They had faith in* HASHEM *and in Moshe, His servant. Then Moshe and the Children of Israel sang this song to* HASHEM.

We can find the theme of the seventh day of Pesach embodied in the *matzah* itself. While ordinary *matzah*, with its flat shape consisting merely of flour and water, suggests self-negation, "enriched *matzah*" (מַצָּה עֲשִׁירָה), that is made with liquids other than water, also called egg *matzah*,[1] represents humility attained through a "richer" and more sophisticated understanding of Hashem. According to this approach, our verse is to be interpreted as follows: "*Six days shall you absorb the lesson of matzah*, but on the seventh day observe an *atzeres*." (The term *atzeres* as discussed at length in the section on Shavuos, alludes to Hashem's sovereignty.) Our initial interpretation brings us to an awareness of Hashem's glory via struggle with the *yetzer hara* and trodding the path of the humble. With this construction on the seventh day, you achieve the same objectives of humility — but this time through an appreciation of Hashem's splendor.

The relationship between the first six days and the seventh is analagous to that of the six weekdays and Shabbos. All week long, we strive for humility through self-negation; on Shabbos, a day of intense spirituality, we achieve it through intimacy with Hashem. (5662)

The above approaches assumed that *matzah* symbolizes humility and self-negation. The uniqueness of the seventh day of Pesach can also be understood in light of another aspect of *matzah*, freedom. Freedom implies not only liberation from slavery but also accepting Hashem's sovereignty over us, as indicated in the opening words of *Hallel*, הַלְלוּ עַבְדֵי ה׳, *Praise [Hashem] servants of* HASHEM (*Tehillim* 113:1). This has been interpreted only servants of Hashem may praise Him, וְלֹא עַבְדֵי פַרְעֹה, *but not servants of Pharaoh* (*Megillah* 14a). Both sides of this coin

1. Egg matzos may be eaten on Pesach except for the obligatory *matzah* portion eaten at the Seder. However, an ancient Ashkenazic custom cited in *Shulchan Aruch Orach Chaim* 462 prohibits its consumption.

are equally critical in Judaism: Release from the bondage of Pharaoh and becoming a servant of Hashem. The *matzah* we eat the first six days of Pesach commemorates liberation from Egypt, while the seventh day of Pesach, and especially the Song of the Sea, symbolize acceptance of Hashem's sovereignty. Thus the verse *For six days you are to eat matzos and the seventh day shall be an assembly to HASHEM, your God* may be interpreted as follows: Six days celebrate your freedom from Pharaoh by eating *matzah* and on the seventh day celebrate your new status as servants of Hashem. (*Sfas Emes* 5651)

In a similar vein, we may understand this verse as a reference to the healing process by which Hashem "cured" Israel from the wounds inflicted on them in Egypt. Hashem is twice described in connection with the Exodus as the Ultimate Healer of Israel. The prophet Yeshayahu describes the Jewish people's liberation from Egypt in the following terms (19:22): וְנָגַף ה׳ אֶת־מִצְרַיִם נָגֹף וְרָפוֹא וְשָׁבוּ עַד־ה׳ וְנֶעְתַּר לָהֶם וּרְפָאָם, *HASHEM plagued Egypt and [while plaguing Egypt] He will heal, and they will return to HASHEM and He will answer them and heal them.*

The *matzah* eaten during the final six days of Pesach is also described by the Zohar as the bread of healing (נַהֲמָא דְאַסְוּוּתָא). It was only through the destruction of Egypt that Israel was healed. Even today, spiritual growth, the "healing" of the soul, is possible only through protracted struggle with the *yetzer hara.* In the aftermath of the Splitting of the Sea and the Song, however, we entered into an entirely new phase of Divine healing. Henceforth, healing could occur even without recourse to the destruction of the foe. Soon after the Song Hashem says, כָּל־הַמַּחֲלָה אֲשֶׁר־שַׂמְתִּי בְמִצְרַיִם לֹא־אָשִׂים עָלֶיךָ כִּי אֲנִי ה׳ רֹפְאֶךָ, *I will not bring upon you any of the diseases that I brought upon Egypt, for I am HASHEM, your Healer* (*Shemos* 15:26). The seminal events of the seventh day of Pesach mark the beginning of a new phase in our relationship with Hashem: In return for being His servants, He will heal us and nurture our spiritual growth.

Thus far we have compared the relationship between the seventh day of Pesach and the first six days to the relationship between Shabbos and the six days of the week. A careful examination of the Midrash (*Shemos Rabbah* 19:8) reveals an even more striking similarity, however. The seventh day of Pesach is actually the climax of six working days and is called a Sabbath. Just as each week enjoys its Sabbath, so too the special week of Pesach enjoys its own Sabbath which serves as the climax of the Pesach week.[1] Let us consider the first Shabbos observed by the Jewish people, described in the *parashah* of the manna: שְׁבוּ אִישׁ תַּחְתָּיו אַל־יֵצֵא אִישׁ מִמְּקֹמוֹ בַּיּוֹם הַשְּׁבִיעִי, *everyone is to remain in his location, no one is to go out of his place on the seventh day [i.e. do not abandon your tents in search of the manna]* (*Shemos* 16:29).

The Jews rested on that first Shabbos. Likewise, after six days of being pursued by Pharaoh's forces and the *yetzer hara,* lacking the leisure and peace of mind to fully appreciate G-d's miracles they can finally come to rest on the seventh day. Now they were secure in the knowledge that their mortal foes were no longer a threat. (5643, 5645)

Further contemplation reveals an even more profound relationship between the seventh day of Pesach and Shabbos. The faith of a Jew rests on two pillars representing two historical events: the Creation and the Exodus from Egypt. While Hashem created the universe in total isolation, the Exodus was a public event that revealed Hashem's undeniable presence to all mankind. The first *six* days of Pesach we celebrate and affirm our belief in Divine creation. By celebrating the *seventh* day, however, the Jew identifies Shabbos as the completion (*shleimus*) of Creation. While a Jew is granted an "extra soul" every Shabbos, on the "Shabbos" of Pesach, the seventh day, the Jewish people was granted the spiritual energy to sing the Song. Just as Hashem derived pleasure from the creation He completed just prior to the first Shabbos, so too He drew satisfaction from the fact that the enormous threat posed by the Egyptian armies was obliterated by His miracle at the Sea. (5640)

---

1. This comparison of the seventh day of Pesach with Shabbos could explain why in two instances the Torah prohibits *all* work on that day, while on the other Festivals only laborious work is spoken of. In fact, the seventh day of Pesach is identical with the other festivals (except for Yom Kippur) with regard to the prohibition of work. Nonetheless, the different terms used to describe the prohibitions of the seventh day of Pesach imply an affinity between that day and the weekly Sabbath.

The Exodus and the Splitting of the Sea

Any interpretation of the Pesach story must deal with the following questions: Why did the miracles associated with the Exodus occur in two phases: the departure from Egypt and the splitting of the Sea of Reeds? Why did Hashem choose not to wipe out the Egyptians in one quick stroke? To answer these questions, we must say that both of these events were vital components in His plan for Israel's liberation, as the following discussion will show.

◆§ Exodus: Physical Liberation Splitting of the Sea: Spiritual Freedom

Clearly, the Exodus marked the physical liberation of the Jewish people. To commemorate this we eat *matzah*, the embodiment of simplicity, as the Mishnah says (*Avos* 1:17), לֹא מָצָאתִי לְגוּף טוֹב אֶלָּא שְׁתִיקָה, *I found nothing better for oneself than silence. Matzah* reminds us that the body should be humble and subjugate itself to the influence of the soul.

This was merely the first phase, however. The Song of the Sea, sung in unison by all Jews, was possible because of a unique transformation of the Jewish soul. The soul, representing the potential of the Jew to reach ever greater spiritual heights, reached its apex at the Sea. The Psalmist alludes to this relationship between body and soul (118:5): מִן־הַמֵּצַר קָרָאתִי יָּהּ עָנָנִי בַמֶּרְחָב יָהּ, *From the straits did I call upon God; God answered me with expansiveness.* The body should be confined to narrow *straits*, while Hashem gives the soul unlimited *expansiveness*.

(5660)

The deference of the body to the soul is also symbolized by the *tefillin* of the arm and head. While the arm *tefillin*, representing physical actions, is placed on the weaker hand and is usually covered, the head *tefillin* is openly displayed.

Similarly, Jacob's two names reflect the relationship between body and soul. On one hand, he was called *Yaakov*, from the word *eikev* (heel), suggesting the inferior position of the material world. His other name, *Yisrael*, emphasizes the superior position of the Jewish "head," the intellectual and moral powers of the soul. The letters of this name can be rearranged to form the words לִי רֹאשׁ (literally *the head is mine*) — for the Jew, matters of the mind are most significant.

In this light, the verse cited earlier takes on new meaning. שֵׁשֶׁת יָמִים תֹּאכַל מַצּוֹת וּבַיּוֹם הַשְּׁבִיעִי עֲצֶרֶת לַה׳ אֱלֹהֶיךָ לֹא תַעֲשֶׂה מְלָאכָה, *For six days you are to eat matzos and the seventh day shall be an assembly to* HASHEM, your God, you may not perform labor* (*Devarim* 16:8). For the six days that we celebrate our physical liberation, we eat and heed the message of *matzah*. The seventh day, however, is an *atzeres*, a time of spiritual intimacy, of gathering and rapprochement between the Jewish soul and its Creator. (5660)

☙ Exodus: Becoming Hashem's Servants Splitting of the Sea: Becoming Hashem's Children

Alternatively, we may suggest that the Exodus and the Splitting of the Sea represent dual aspects of the relationship between the Jew and the Creator. The Exodus brought not so much unbridled freedom as a challenge to make ourselves into Hashem's servants. At that time, the Jewish people were called (*Shemos* 12:41) צִבְאוֹת ה׳, *HASHEM's hosts*. The same term is used to describe all of the creations of the universe who serve Hashem with unquestioning loyalty: וַיְכֻלּוּ הַשָּׁמַיִם וְהָאָרֶץ וְכָל־צְבָאָם, *The heaven and the earth were finished and all their hosts* (*Bereishis* 2:1). When Israel was released from Egypt, it took upon itself to serve Hashem with the same loyalty as the natural world.

On the seventh day of Pesach, however, as the sea split and the Jewish people sang the Song, something even greater happened. The Jewish people rose to the level of being Hashem's children. Thus, the passage in the *Maariv* prayer describing the Splitting of the Sea contains several references to Israel's status as Hashem's children: מַעֲבִיר בָּנָיו בֵּין גִּזְרֵי יַם סוּף, *He brought His children through the split parts of the Sea of Reeds*; וְרָאוּ בָנָיו גְּבוּרָתוֹ שִׁבְּחוּ וְהוֹדוּ לִשְׁמוֹ, *When His children perceived His power, they lauded and gave grateful praise to His Name*; and, מַלְכוּתְךָ רָאוּ בָנֶיךָ, *Your children beheld Your Majesty.*

(5658)

Exodus: Release From the Foe Within Splitting of the Sea: Vanquishing the Enemy Without

The Midrash (*Shemos Rabbah* 22:4) offers further insights into the relationship between the two phases of the liberation from Egypt:

> שָׁנוּ רַבּוֹתֵינוּ הַקּוֹרֵא אֶת שְׁמַע צָרִיךְ לְהַזְכִּיר יְצִיאַת מִצְרַיִם קְרִיעַת יַם סוּף וּמַכַּת בְּכוֹרוֹת בֶּאֱמֶת וְיַצִּיב וְאִם לֹא הִזְכִּיר אוֹתָם מַחֲזִירִין אוֹתוֹ וּמַה בֵּין יְצִיאַת מִצְרַיִם לִקְרִיעַת יַם סוּף שֶׁיְּצִיאַת מִצְרַיִם קָשֶׁה שֶׁנֶּאֱמַר „אוֹ הֲנִסָּה אֱלֹהִים לָבוֹא לָקַחַת לוֹ גוֹי מִקֶּרֶב גּוֹי." תֵּדַע לְךָ שֶׁזּוּ קָשֶׁה מִזּוּ שֶׁבִּיצִיאַת מִצְרַיִם כְּתִיב אָנֹכִי ה' אֱלֹהֶיךָ אֲבָל בִּקְרִיעַת יַם סוּף אֵינוֹ מַזְכִּיר אֶת הַשֵּׁם.
>
> *Our Rabbis learned: One who reads the Shema is required to mention the Exodus, the Splitting of the Sea and the Plague of the Firstborn in the section Emes VeYatziv. If one neglected to mention any one of them, he must repeat the prayer.*
>
> *How is the Exodus different from the Splitting of the Sea? The Exodus was more difficult, as the Torah says (Devarim 4:34): "Has God ever before come to take for Himself one nation from the midst of another nation?" The Midrash proves that the Exodus was more difficult, since the Torah says, "I am* Hashem *your God Who took you out of Egypt," while concerning the Splitting of the Sea Hashem's Name is not [so closely] identified.*

In what sense was the Exodus more difficult than the Splitting of the Sea? The Midrash mentions the difficulty of extricating a people that is subsumed within another nation. In Egypt, the Jewish people had nearly lost their identity as a distinct and holy nation. On the other hand, the Splitting of the Sea, while a formidable accomplishment, involved only the elimination of a clearly defined external force, the army of Pharaoh.

In one respect, however, the miracle at the Sea was more significant. The Exodus was a one-time phenomenon never to be repeated. Never again were Jews to be so thoroughly submerged within another nation.

However, the annihilation of the Egyptian army set a precedent often to be repeated, demonstrating to the world that Hashem will save the Jewish people from its pursuers.

Hashem is called *the redeemer and the savior* (פּוֹדֶה וּמַצִּיל), referring to these two events: He *redeemed* us from Egypt's clutches and *saved* us from Pharaoh's forces at the sea. (5655)

◆§ Exodus: Hashem's Gift Splitting of the Sea: Israel's Merit

Another distinction is that while the Splitting of the Sea occurred at least partially in the merit of the Jewish people, the Exodus was entirely a Divine gift granted to an undeserving nation. The Torah alludes to this distinction in numerous places. For one thing, by the time they arrived at the Sea, the Jews already had many *mitzvos* to their credit: offering the *Korban Pesach* (Paschal Lamb), *matzah*, *maror*, and *bris milah*. This had not been so at the time Hashem first decided to take the Jews from Egypt, when He revealed Himself to Moshe at the burning bush, or the beginning of the Ten Plagues. Then Israel had virtually no merits to its credit. Moreover, Israel's courage in plunging into the sea before it had parted revealing their great trust in Hashem, was also a major source of merit.

The Torah describes the Exodus as the work of Hashem's "strong hand," implying that greater force was required to liberate an undeserving people. In contrast, according to *Rashi* (*Shemos* 14:19), just before the Splitting of the Sea the people was judged by Hashem and found worthy to have such a miracle performed for them.

A subtle but significant nuance in the Torah's account conveys this point: וַיּוֹשַׁע ה׳ בַּיּוֹם הַהוּא אֶת־יִשְׂרָאֵל מִיַּד מִצְרָיִם, *HASHEM saved — on that day — Israel from the hand of Egypt* (*Shemos* 14:30). The word *saved* used in this verse connotes the help that is given to those deserving of it, implying that the Jews *deserved* the miracle Hashem did for them. King David pleads הַרְאֵנוּ ה׳ חַסְדֶּךָ וְיֶשְׁעֲךָ תִּתֶּן־לָנוּ, *Show us Your kindness, HASHEM, and grant us Your salvation* (*Tehillim* 85:8). "Show us Your *kindness*" refers to the unwarranted gift Hashem gave at the Exodus, "and grant us Your *salvation*, refers to the Splitting of the Sea, which the Jews deserved.

Before smiting the Egyptian first-born, Hashem commanded the Jews not to leave their homes, so that they would not see the Egyptians dying.

At the Splitting of the Sea, on the other hand, the Torah emphasizes that וַיַּרְא יִשְׂרָאֵל אֶת־מִצְרַיִם מֵת עַל־שְׂפַת הַיָּם, *Israel saw the Egyptians dead on the seashore* (*Shemos* 14:30). Only a deserving nation may actually witness the downfall of its foes, while those who benefit from an unearned miracle are not allowed to see their enemies in defeat.

As King David sings, ה׳ לִי בְּעֹזְרָי וַאֲנִי אֶרְאֶה בְשֹׂנְאָי, *HASHEM is with me through my helpers; therefore I can face my foes* (*Tehillim* 118:7). When Hashem *helps* me on the basis of my own merit (because I have acted in my own behalf), then I deserve to witness the downfall of my enemies. (5655)

Another allusion to Israel's merit is the phrase וּפַרְעֹה הִקְרִיב (*Shemos* 14:10). While it is usually translated, *Pharaoh approached*, literally this means, *Pharaoh brought [something] close*. This can be interpreted to mean that by pursuing the Jews, Pharaoh caused them to repent and *brought them close* to Hashem, giving them additional merit by which they would deserve the miracle of the Splitting of the Sea.

One question remains, however. We have said that between the Exodus and the Splitting of the Sea Israel rose quickly to a lofty spiritual level. If so, why did Hashem, Who can arrange all the events of the world to suit His purposes, not cause Israel to repent while still in Egypt? To restate this question, why was it as important that the Exodus be unmerited as it was that the Jews be worthy of the miracle of the Splitting of the Sea?

We can say that Hashem may have arranged matters as He did to show that He still maintains His unique relationship with the Jews even though they do not repent and act as they should. Thus two of the greatest miracles ever performed, the Exodus and Splitting of the Sea, attest to two basic precepts of Judaism: the power of repentance and the special bond between Hashem and all Jews, even those who have not yet repented. (5636)

☙ Exodus: Love of Hashem
Splitting of the Sea: Fear of Hashem

The Exodus and the Splitting of the Sea were important not only for their intrinsic historical significance, but also because of certain character traits they implanted in the Jewish people, in particular love of Hashem and fear of Hashem. The Jews' conduct at the time of the Exodus provides one of the most impressive demonstrations of their love for Hashem in the course of their history. Only a people filled with love of its Creator would follow Him blindly into the Wilderness, with no provisions for the basic necessities of life such as food and water.

The Song of the Sea, while also motivated by feelings of affection, was inspired primarily by fear of Hashem, as we see from the verse immediately preceding the Song: וַיִּירְאוּ הָעָם אֶת־ה׳ וַיַּאֲמִינוּ בַּה׳ וּבְמֹשֶׁה עַבְדּוֹ, *the people feared* HASHEM, *and they had faith in* HASHEM *and in Moshe, His servant* (*Shemos* 14:31).

◈ Exodus: Gradual Process Splitting of the Sea: One Broad Sweep

There is a fundamental difference between the Exodus and the Splitting of the Sea. The former was a process that lasted a year and a half, from the beginning of the plagues to the smiting of the first-born and the departure from Egypt, while the latter totally ended the Egyptian threat in one broad sweep. The Exodus conclusively demonstrated Hashem's mastery over every component of the natural world, from the waters of the Nile which He turned to blood, to the reptiles and beasts He caused to overrun Egypt and turn it back into a jungle, and even to the heavens, from which He rained down hail on the fields of Egypt. After these events, there could be no doubt of Hashem's unlimited power in the world.

The Torah describes Pharaoh's mobilization of his forces in the following verse (*Shemos* 14:7): וַיִּקַּח שֵׁשׁ־מֵאוֹת רֶכֶב בָּחוּר וְכֹל רֶכֶב מִצְרָיִם וְשָׁלִשִׁם עַל־כֻּלּוֹ, *He took six hundred elite chariots and all the chariots of Egypt, with officers on them all.* The Midrash (*Yalkut Shimoni, Shemos* 230) interprets the end of this verse with a play on words, עַל מְנַת לְכַלֵּם, *for the purpose of destroying them.* We see from this that Pharaoh unwittingly arranged for his own total annihilation by engaging Israel in this final confrontation.

The Talmud states (*Chulin* 127a), כָּל מַה שֶּׁיֵּשׁ בַּיַּבָּשָׁה יֵשׁ בַּיָּם, *Whatever exists on dry land exists on the sea.* In terms of our discussion, we may interpret this to mean that the miracles that occurred gradually over a long period of time on the *land* of Egypt occurred all *at once* at the Sea.

(5647)

◆§ Exodus: Purging Egypt's Visible Forces Splitting of the Sea: Purging Egypt's Underlying Core

Another explanation of why Hashem in His wisdom arranged the destruction of Egypt in two phases has to do with the destruction of Egyptian idolatry. The Sages said (*Avodah Zarah* 45b), "אַבֵּד תְּאַבְּדוּן", הָעוֹקֵר עֲבוֹדָה זָרָה צָרִיךְ לְשָׁרֵשׁ אַחֲרֶיהָ, *"You shall surely destroy"* (*Devarim* 12:2); *from this we learn that one who seeks to uproot idolatry must also destroy its roots.* It is known that the root of all idolatry in the world was in Egypt.

This is why the Splitting of the Sea had to follow the Exodus, in order to destroy the idolatry of Egypt down to its deepest roots. At the time of the Exodus, Hashem destroyed only the exposed forms of idolatry, the idols themselves and their "sanctuaries" and trappings. Only one idol remained, the one called *baal tzafon* (cf. *Shemos* 14:9), which stood at the border as a symbol of Egyptian invincibility. This idol survived the destruction at the time of the Exodus because the root of Egyptian idolatry remained intact beneath the surface.

Indeed, this was the reason for Hashem's concern that the Jews might have a change of heart and return to Egypt if they were to encounter warfare on the way through the land of the Philistines (cf. *Shemos* 13:17). Hashem wanted to totally annihilate even the source of idolatry, and therefore arranged for a final confrontation at the Sea.

There Hashem made sure that the Jews would see the downfall of Egypt's guardian angel, the kingpin of Egyptian paganism. When the people first saw this angel, the Torah says they were "very frightened" and cried out to Hashem. In the end, however, this angel was destroyed along with his people, and there was nothing left to Egypt, not even the root of their idolatry.

While the Jews may have been capable of battling their Egyptian counterparts, only Hashem himself could best Egypt's angel. Thus, the Jews were instructed: ה׳ יִלָּחֵם לָכֶם וְאַתֶּם תַּחֲרִשׁוּן, *Hashem shall do battle for you, and you are to remain silent* (*Shemos* 14:14).

In light of the above discussion we can better appreciate why no mention was made of the Splitting of the Sea in Hashem's covenant with Abraham[1] (cf. *Bereishis* 15:13). Hashem's promise to the Patriarch

1. Hashem foretold to Abraham the entire period of Egyptian exile and the Exodus culminating in the promise that the Jews would leave with considerable possessions. No mention is made of the final stage of the liberation, the Splitting of the Sea.

concerned only those events that pertained to Israel. The Splitting of the Sea involved something even more profound — Hashem's battle against Egypt's spiritual protector. (5645)

◈ Exodus: Miracles Occur
Splitting of the Sea: Israel Absorbs the Miracles

Miracles and other great events can occur quickly and sometimes are over in an instant. Once the *momentary* excitement of a miracle subsides, however, it is often difficult to retain the impression it makes and to preserve the lessons to be learned from it. Great events fade into the distant recesses of history, and usually the ones who participated in those events are left largely unaffected.

In order to strengthen the impact of the miracles the Jews had seen, Hashem arranged for them to occur in a planned sequence. Firstly, the hasty departure from Egypt, which occurred so swiftly that the people did not have time to absorb its significance (since they were required to eat the *Korban Pesach* hastily, poised for an immediate departure). The period after their departure from Egypt was an ideal opportunity for them to absorb the miracles they had just experienced.

During that period, moreover, they acted in a manner that reinforced the lessons of the Exodus. For example, at Hashem's command, they turned around *to face* the advancing Egyptian armies. Later, they plunged into the sea *before* it split. Above all, they did it *deliberately*, on a premeditated basis, whereas on the night of the Exodus they had little control of events. (*Parashas Beshalach* 5631)

◈ Exodus: Oral Law
Splitting of the Sea: Written Law

The ultimate objective of the Jews' departure from Egypt was the Giving of the Torah at Mount Sinai. This understanding helps us appreciate the significance of both the Oral Law and the Written Law. Freedom from Egyptian servitude was only the first phase in the process that culminated in accepting Hashem's sovereignty.

While this may seem apparent with hindsight, immediately after the Splitting of the Sea, our forefathers wanted to return to Egypt to conquer their former masters. Moshe had to convince them that they had a much greater mission to accomplish — receiving the Torah.

In this light, both the Exodus and the Splitting of the Sea can be seen not only as miraculous events, but also as vehicles for transmitting the Torah's teachings. Before Hashem sent Moshe to Pharaoh He told him (*Shemos* 10:2), וּלְמַעַן תְּסַפֵּר בְּאָזְנֵי בִנְךָ וּבֶן־בִּנְךָ, *So that you may relate in the ears of your children and grandchildren.* From this verse we see that the Exodus story must be passed on orally from one generation to the next. However, the Splitting of the Sea was an event of such enormous magnitude that anyone who had not seen it himself could not begin to understand its significance. The Torah repeatedly emphasizes that the Jewish people *saw* Hashem's might in action at the Splitting of the Sea. In similar fashion, the Torah relates that the Jews *saw* the dramatic supernatural phenomena associated with the giving of the Torah (*Shemos* 20:15): וְכָל־הָעָם רֹאִים אֶת־הַקּוֹלֹת וְאֶת־הַלַּפִּידִם וְאֵת קוֹל הַשֹּׁפָר וְאֶת־הָהָר עָשֵׁן וַיַּרְא הָעָם וַיָּנֻעוּ וַיַּעַמְדוּ מֵרָחֹק, *The entire people saw the thunder and the flames, the sound of the shofar, and the smoking mountain; the people saw and trembled and stood from afar.*

These events left far too profound an impression on the Jews to be expressed verbally. It was only because of a special grant of *ruach hakodesh* (Divine Spirit) that the Jews were able to sing the Song, which then became part of the Written Torah. The generation that beheld the Splitting of the Sea certainly remembered the sight and the impression it left on them throughout their lives. And while they tried to pass that memory on to their children as best they could, the contemporary Jew can grasp its significance only through learning about it in the Torah. Thus, events such as the Splitting of the Sea and the Giving of the Torah persevere through the Written Law, while memory of the Exodus is better transmitted by word of mouth.[1]

⁂ Exodus: This World Splitting of the Sea: The World to Come

In a broader sense, the Exodus and Splitting of the Sea symbolize our world and the World to Come. In order to appreciate this insight, let us consider carefully the meaning of the word עוֹלָם, *world.* It has

1. There is an important underlying principle in this. Whenever possible, it is preferable to transmit the Torah's teachings orally, by word of mouth. This point can be inferred from the *Nishmas* prayer we say on Shabbos: אִלּוּ פִינוּ מָלֵא שִׁירָה כַּיָּם . . . אֵין אֲנַחְנוּ מַסְפִּיקִים לְהוֹדוֹת לְךָ, *Were our mouth as full of song as the sea . . . we could still not thank You sufficiently.* From the fact that the Men of the Great Assembly mention oral praises but not written ones in this prayer, we see that oral praises of Hashem are preferable to written ones (*Sfas Emes* 5639).

sometimes been connected to the word הֶעְלֵם, *hidden*, implying that something is hidden in this world. Spiritual values are obscured by the "veil" of materialism. The World to Come, however, is itself "hidden" because the intense spiritual atmosphere that prevails there is far above the grasp even of those who dwell there.

The liberation from Egypt resembled Torah life in this world. Despite the intense spiritual void and crass materialism of Egypt, which could have caused the Jews to forget Hashem totally, He helped them see light amidst the darkness. At the Exodus, Godliness and spirituality emerged out of a setting devoid of such values. Only one week later, at the Sea, the Jews had already risen to the level of the World to Come.

But then other challenges, other mysteries (הַעֲלָמוֹת), surfaced. How could the Jews relate to the intense spirituality that engulfed them at the sea? Here too, with the Splitting of the Sea, an overwhelming demonstration of His power, Hashem's light pierced through the darkness. At the Exodus, the people learned how to cope with this world — at the Sea they came face-to-face with the World to Come. As the Psalmist sings (118:5): מִן הַמֵּצַר קָרָאתִי יָּהּ עָנָנִי בַמֶּרְחָב יָהּ, *From the straits did I call upon God; God answered me with expansiveness.* The beginning of this verse refers to the Exodus when Israel, trapped in a hostile environment, found Hashem. Its ending, however, hints at the World to Come, in whose manifold spiritual possibilities the Jew inevitably finds Hashem. (5637)

Exodus: First Redemption Splitting of the Sea: First Battlefield Triumph

Both the Exodus and Splitting of the Sea set major precedents. Since the Exodus was Israel's first redemption, the people were still unready to cope with the stresses of battle, as we see from Hashem's decision not to lead them through the Philistine land so that they would not turn faint-hearted when they saw belligerent local tribes. Similarly, at the Splitting of the Sea, the people were so terrified at the prospect of battle that Hashem *insisted* that they play no role in the battle, as Moshe said (*Shemos* 14:14), ה׳ יִלָּחֵם לָכֶם וְאַתֶּם תַּחֲרִשׁוּן, *HASHEM shall do battle for you, and you are to remain silent.* It was only after the Splitting of the Sea that the Jewish people were able to join in *battle* against their foes.

What was their fear of fighting the Egyptian army? Why did Hashem have to perform such a miracle, before Jewish armies would enter into battle? Perhaps it was because of the sudden nature of war: Amalek attacked Israel *suddenly*. So too, the Egyptian army appeared *suddenly*, as the Torah says (*Shemos* 14:10), וּפַרְעֹה הִקְרִיב וַיִּשְׂאוּ בְנֵי־יִשְׂרָאֵל אֶת־עֵינֵיהֶם וְהִנֵּה מִצְרַיִם נֹסֵעַ אַחֲרֵיהֶם וַיִּירְאוּ מְאֹד וַיִּצְעֲקוּ בְנֵי־יִשְׂרָאֵל אֶל־ה׳, *Pharaoh approached; the Children of Israel raised their eyes and behold! — Egypt was journeying after them, and they were very frightened; the Children of Israel cried out to HASHEM.* Having begun to taste freedom, the Jews were totally unprepared for Egypt's surprise attack. (5634)

◆§ Exodus: Consciously Following Hashem (דִבּוּר) Splitting of the Sea: Subconscious Following of God (קוֹל)

The *Zohar* (*Parashas Vaeira*) contains an insight that may provide the key to understanding why both miracles, the Exodus and the Splitting of the Sea, were needed. According to the *Zohar*, the purpose of the Exodus was to "liberate" the Jews' capacity for *dibbur*, the spoken word. In light of this approach, we may suggest that the Splitting of the Sea performed a similar but even higher function, to "release" *kol*, the Jewish voice. In the following discussion we will attempt to clarify the meaning of these abstract concepts.

The term *dibbur*, as utilized in the *Zohar*, refers to willful, deliberate action. (While the word *dibbur* literally means "speech," the *Zohar* extends it to mean all forms of deliberate behavior, the highest of which is the ability to speak.)[1] The phrase in the *Shema* (*Devarim* 6:7) וְדִבַּרְתָּ בָּם, while it is usually translated as *you shall speak in them [words of Torah]*, actually implies much more than mere speech, that one's entire conduct should be based on the Torah. At the Exodus, Israel accepted Hashem's sovereignty upon themselves — as His servants, they would guide their every action by His will. In the *Zohar's* terms, the *dibbur* ability of Israel to follow the Divine will consciously began at the Exodus.

At the Splitting of the Sea an even more profound phenomenon occurred — the Jewish People found their *voice*. As the Torah says, *the Children of Israel cried out to HASHEM*. Terrified by the advancing Egyptian armies, afraid of drowning in the sea, the Jews abandoned the

1. *Editors Note*: We may conjecture that the *Zohar's* understanding of this word is related to a variant meaning of the root דבר, *dabeir*, which is sometimes used in the sense of *to lead*, as in the verse (*Tehillim* 47:4), יַדְבֵּר עַמִּים תַּחְתֵּינוּ, *He shall lead nations under us*. The act of leading is simply the imposition of one's "willful, deliberate action" on others.

careful, premeditated behavior they had just learned. Instead, a subconscious cry rang out from the inner recesses of the Jewish heart, the voice of Jacob (קוֹל יַעֲקֹב) that Isaac heard, that inner voice of the *pintele yid.* The same inner voice that leads a Jew to turn to his Creator in moments of anxiety and depression burst forth in united song at the Sea.

There is no other plausible way to explain how millions of men, women, and children could sing an exactly identical song, except that somehow an inner spark was ignited simultaneously in all of them by the sight of the Splitting of the Sea. The emergence of this inner voice marked the second phase of Israel's acceptance of Torah, in which they proclaimed *Na'aseh VeNishma* (as we shall discuss extensively in the section on Shavuos). נַעֲשֶׂה, — "We will do" and conduct our lives *rationally,* according to His will, the ideal of *dibbur.* As a result, our subconscious will become so suffused with Torah values that even without conscious effort נִשְׁמַע, — "We will hear" and feel *kol haTorah,* the voice of Torah in every fiber of our body. Consciously, and even subconsciously, our lives will become one with the Torah.

This same transition from conscious fulfillment of the Divine will (*dibbur*) to subconscious and intuitive "hearing" of the voice of Torah (*kol*) occurs every week. The six work days represent *dibbur,* as the Jew conducts himself in a Torah-true fashion amidst the pressures of daily life. Then on Shabbos, physical activity subsides and the subconscious *kol,* abetted by the נְשָׁמָה יְתֵרָה, the extra dimension of spirituality every Jew enjoys on Shabbos, takes over. After struggling all week to lead a rational Torah life, the Jew can rest on Shabbos, secure in the knowledge that spiritual gains will come with almost no effort on this day.

In the essay entitled "The Seventh Day" we discussed a number of similarities between the seventh day of Pesach and Shabbos. Now we can propose yet another comparison: On both of these days, the seventh day of Pesach when the Song was first sung, as well as the weekly Shabbos, the subconscious and emotional dominate. (5633)

◆§ Exodus: Liberation for the Righteous Splitting of the Sea: Freedom Even for the Wicked

On a simple yet appealing level, the distinction between the Exodus and the Splitting of the Sea may best be appreciated in terms of those who beheld the associated miracles. Only righteous Jews left

Egypt.[1] Four-fifths of the people, those who did not live up to a minimum standard, perished during the Plague of Darkness. However, the miracle of the Splitting of the Sea was witnessed by even the worst elements of the Jewish people, based on nothing more than their very Jewishness. Even those who moments before had proclaimed their desire to return to Egypt, crossed the sea.[1] (5632)

◆§ Exodus: Appreciation of Freedom
Splitting of the Sea: Gratitude for all the Suffering in Egypt

Something very profound occurred at the Splitting of the Sea: Israel learned to appreciate the bad as well as good. While the Jews left Egypt as free men, they still carried with them the emotional baggage of suffering, too much to be eradicated all at once. Thus they bore mixed emotions — gratitude for their deliverance coupled with remorse over what they had endured in Egypt.

It was only when they saw Hashem's might unleashed at the Sea that the Torah could proclaim (*Shemos* 14:31), וַיַּאֲמִינוּ בַּה׳ וּבְמֹשֶׁה עַבְדּוֹ, *they had faith in* HASHEM *and in Moshe, His servant.* Their faith encompassed not only Hashem's ability to redeem them, but ascended to the much higher level that they could say with a full heart, "All the suffering we experienced was worthwhile for the miracles we are now witnessing!" Only after the Splitting of the Sea could the people actually *believe* that all the tribulations of Egypt had been justified in order to bring them to the miracles of the Sea.

The Midrash (*Shemos Rabbah* 20:11) alludes to this concept in relating that Hashem Himself was not comforted (וְלֹא נָחָם אֱלֹהִים) over the suffering the Jews endured in Egypt until the Splitting of the Sea.

(5637)

◆§ Exodus: Hashem Performs Miracles
Splitting of the Sea: Israel Attributes Its Miracles to Hashem

The Talmud (*Berachos* 38a) offers an additional insight: כַּד מַפִּיקְנָא לְכוּ עֲבִידְנָא לְכוּ מִלְתָא כִּי הֵיכִי דְיַדְעִיתוּ דְאֲנָא הוּא דְאַפֵּיקִית יָתְכוֹן מִמִצְרַיִם,

---

1. Even the *eirev rav*, a group of converts who would later cause much grief, were still considered righteous at the time of the Exodus.

2. The Midrash (*Shemos Rabbah* 41:1) suggests that even an idol — the molten image of Micah — traveled with them.

When I will take you out from Egypt, I will do something [the Splitting of the Sea] so that you know that it was I Who took you out. While Hashem performed great miracles in the course of the Exodus, Israel could not appreciate their source until the Splitting of the Sea. Then every Jew could proclaim זֶה אֵלִי, *This is my God!* in full appreciation of the fact that it was Hashem Who had performed those miracles. (5640)

◆§ Exodus: Israel Separated From Oppressor Splitting of the Sea: The Oppressor Ceases

Let us point out one final distinction between the Exodus and the Splitting of the Sea. Even though at the Exodus Israel was finally separated from the enemy Pharaoh, as long as he survived and as long as the confining narrowness of Egypt (indicated by the name *Mitzraim*, derived from the word *meitzar*, narrow strait) remained in place, they would always threaten to reclaim the Jews. Only when Pharaoh and all his forces were destroyed at the Sea could the Jews be totally secure in their freedom. (5631)

Events Preceding the Splitting of the Sea

In the following essay we will review a number of insights regarding the events that preceded the Splitting of the Sea.

> וַיְהִי בְּשַׁלַּח פַּרְעֹה אֶת־הָעָם וְלֹא־נָחָם אֱלֹהִים דֶּרֶךְ אֶרֶץ פְּלִשְׁתִּים
> *And it happened when Pharaoh sent out the people that God did not lead them by way of the land of the Philistines* (*Shemos* 13:17).

The *Zohar* on this verse states that וַיְהִי, *and it was*, always indicates a situation of suffering (cf. *Megillah* 10b). Why would the Torah refer to the Exodus with an expression of suffering?

In a spiritual sense Israel did suffer as a result of the Exodus. In Egypt the Jewish people were a shining beacon of morality, at least in comparison to the promiscuous Egyptians. Once they were on their own, however, their deficiencies became more noticeable. However, this spiritual unease did not last long. In the following week, culminating in the splitting of the sea, not only did they witness unprecedented miracles, they also underwent a major spiritual reawakening.

At the sea, Moshe instructed the people: הִתְיַצְּבוּ וּרְאוּ אֶת יְשׁוּעַת ה׳ אֲשֶׁר־יַעֲשֶׂה לָכֶם הַיּוֹם, *Stand fast and see the salvation of Hashem that He will do for you today* (*Shemos* 14:13). The phrase "He will do for you" implies that Hashem revitalized the Jewish soul in addition to liberating their bodies with the splitting of the sea.

Elsewhere the Torah uses a similar expression to describe the impact on the Jew of observing Hashem's commandments אֲשֶׁר יַעֲשֶׂה אֹתָם הָאָדָם וָחַי בָּהֶם (*Vayikra* 18:5), *which man shall carry out and by which he shall live*. (5642)

וַחֲמֻשִׁים עָלוּ בְנֵי־יִשְׂרָאֵל מֵאֶרֶץ מִצְרָיִם

The Children of Israel were armed as they went up from Egypt (*Shemos* 13:18).

The *Zohar* interprets this verse as a reference to the "fifty gates" of Egyptian impurity that were shed all at once at the time of the Exodus.[1] Indeed, the Exodus is mentioned exactly fifty times in the Torah, suggesting that liberation from Egypt was not only physical but also a spiritual process of fifty ascending stages.

A question arises: If Israel had already attained such a high level of sanctity at the time of the Exodus, why was a further period of growth necessary before the Torah could be given?

Evidently, two phases were required. At the Exodus, Israel was catapulted to the apex of the fifty levels of purity giving them a temporary "taste" of the highest level. Then, at the end of the first day of Pesach, one day after the Exodus, Hashem charged Israel with a far more daunting task — to make the long climb from the abyss of defilement to the highest levels of purity totally on their own. This period, which we now

1. The term "fifty gates of impurity" is used frequently by the Kabbalists to describe the moral depravity of Egypt. At the time of the Exodus, the Jewish people had sunk to the forty-ninth level and would have descended even further had Hashem not liberated them in time.

observe as *Sefirah,* is an opportunity for personal growth, while on the first day of Pesach Hashem pulls Israel from the brink of spiritual devastation. (5637, 5640)

וַיִּקַּח מֹשֶׁה אֶת עַצְמוֹת יוֹסֵף עִמּוֹ כִּי הַשְׁבֵּעַ הִשְׁבִּיעַ אֶת־בְּנֵי יִשְׂרָאֵל לֵאמֹר פָּקֹד יִפְקֹד אֱלֹהִים אֶתְכֶם וְהַעֲלִיתֶם אֶת־עַצְמֹתַי מִזֶּה אִתְּכֶם
Moshe took the bones of Joseph with him, for he had firmly adjured the Children of Israel saying, God will surely remember you, and you shall bring up my bones from here with you (*Shemos* 13:19).

Why does the Torah mention Joseph's remains at this point? Apparently it wishes to convey not merely that Joseph's bones were brought out of Egypt, but also to emphasize that the Exodus occurred in his merit, as we shall explain.

One of the few merits the Jewish people possessed at that time was a sense of morality, as we see from the fact that they never intermarried with Egyptians (see *Rashi* on *Bamidbar* 26:5). The Jews inherited this concern for moral values, and the strength to overcome the temptations of Egypt, from Joseph, who firmly rejected the overtures of Potifar's wife (*Bereishis* 39:8). Moreover, it is well-known that circumcision protects against immorality (cf. *Yehoshua* 5:9). Joseph was a firm advocate of circumcision, as seen from the fact that as long as he lived, he made sure that all of his descendants were circumcised. He was so adamant about preserving this rite that he even insisted that Egyptians who wished to purchase grain from him be circumcised (see *Rashi* on *Bereishis* 41:55).

The connection between circumcision and liberation can also be seen in the passage in the Grace After Meals where the two concepts are juxtaposed: עַל שֶׁהוֹצֵאתָנוּ מֵאֶרֶץ מִצְרַיִם . . . וְעַל בְּרִיתְךָ שֶׁחָתַמְתָּ בִּבְשָׂרֵנוּ, *[We thank You] because You removed us from the land of Egypt . . . and for Your covenant [of circumcision] which You sealed in our flesh.*

Joseph's critical role in the Exodus is alluded to in the reassurance Hashem gave Jacob that his children would eventually leave Egypt: וְאָנֹכִי אַעַלְךָ גַם־עָלֹה וְיוֹסֵף יָשִׁית יָדוֹ עַל־עֵינֶיךָ — *I will surely bring you up [from Egypt] and Joseph will place his hand on your eyes* (*Bereishis* 46:4).

The final phrase, "Joseph will place his hand on your eyes," may be interpreted homiletically as an intimation that by lifting up his hand to reach Jacob's eyes, Joseph would rise to his father's spiritual level and thereby give Jacob's descendants the merit they would need to be redeemed.

In a similar vein, Joseph's role in the Exodus may be inferred from the expression הַשְׁבֵּעַ הִשְׁבִּיעַ, *caused to swear*, which suggests the number seven (שֶׁבַע), an allusion to the seven personal qualities Joseph attained.[1]

The apparently redundant expression פָּקֹד יִפְקֹד, *he surely will remember*, may hint at the two figures who made their children swear to remove their remains from Egypt, Jacob and Joseph. Each possessed qualities that would assist their descendants at the time of the Exodus. Joseph, as we have said, set a high moral standard for the Jewish people in Egypt. Jacob, on the other hand, symbolized the ability of the Jew to speak with the dignity befitting a repository of Torah. This gift of Jewish speech was first recognized by his father Isaac, who exclaimed, הַקֹּל קוֹל יַעֲקֹב *The voice is the voice of Jacob* (*Bereishis* 27:22). The importance of this dignified quality of Jewish speech in the Exodus is reflected in the name of this festival, Pesach, which may be understood as a composite of two words — פֶּה and סָח — meaning "the mouth that talks [properly]."

These traits of moral fortitude and measured speech may have played a role in the two great miracles Hashem performed for the Jewish people: the Exodus and the Splitting of the Sea. The Exodus occurred in the merit of proper speech, as the name פֶּסַח *(Pesach)* indicates. On the other hand, the sea was split in the merit of Joseph's moral purity' as the Midrash (*Yalkut Tehillim* 793) relates: "הַיָּם רָאָה וַיָּנֹס", מַה רָאָה אֲרוֹנוֹ שֶׁל יוֹסֵף, *The sea saw and fled [split]* (*Tehillim* 114:3) *What did the sea see [that caused it to split]? The coffin of Joseph*. Just as Jospeh overcame his natural feelings about Potifar's wife, the Sea overcame its natural impulse not to split for the Jews. (5635, 5641, 5655)

> דַּבֵּר אֶל בְּנֵי יִשְׂרָאֵל וְיָשֻׁבוּ וְיַחֲנוּ לִפְנֵי פִּי הַחִירֹת . . . לִפְנֵי בַּעַל צְפֹן
> *Speak to the Children of Israel and let them turn back and encamp before Pi Hachiroth ... before Baal Zephon* (*Shemos* 14:2).

This order from Hashem is one of the most puzzling aspects of the story of the Exodus. The Jewish people, well on their way out of Egypt, were suddenly told to return towards Egypt, and to encamp in the presence of the last surviving Egyptian deity, Baal Zephon[2]

1. These traits include חֶסֶד, kindness, גְּבוּרָה, moral strength, תִּפְאֶרֶת, glory, נֶצַח, permanence, הוֹד, grandeur, יְסוֹד, foundation [i.e. Hashem bringing the world into formation], and מַלְכוּת, sovereignty.] They are generally used as descriptions of Hashem. However, the *tzaddikim*, who emulate Hashem, can also attain these characteristics in a manner appropriate to them.

2. All other Egyptian gods had been eliminated at the time of the Exodus (see *Shemos* 12:12); as we discuss at length in the essay comparing the Exodus to the Splitting of the Sea.

One answer is that by retracing its steps and marching into and out of Egypt again, a *repeat* of the Exodus, the Jews were given another opportunity to assimilate the miracle of the Exodus. The first time, the night that the Egyptian firstborn were slain, Israel was forced to eat its Paschal lamb in great haste and did not have the opportunity to appreciate the great events of the Exodus. Only by repeating the departure from Egypt could the Jews properly absorb the full impact of the Exodus. In this light, the expression וְיַחֲנוּ (*they should camp*) may refer to the process of solidifying and internalizing the events of the Exodus.[1] (5643)

Why was the newly-liberated nation instructed to make the seemingly suicidal move of marching straight into the hands of the oncoming Egyptian army?

The key to another explanation for the return to Egypt may lie in the word וְיָשֻׁבוּ, *they should return.* Homiletically, this word may refer to spiritual return — *teshuvah*. While the Jews had only a passive role in the miracles of the Exodus, at the Splitting of the Sea they had reached the point of taking important initiatives. (For a fuller discussion of this topic, see the essay comparing the Exodus and the Splitting of the Sea.) By returning to Egypt and then marching out again and into the sea, despite the great risks involved, the Jews took an active role in their liberation. (5631, 5637)

In other words, the people's return and subsequent departure from Egypt considerably dampened whatever desire they may have had ever to return there again. Though liberated from abject servitude, they may still have retained certain fond memories of their former subjugators. However, a people released *twice* will have no desire to return. [Even though, individuals and groups of malcontents may later have desired to go back, the entire nation never did so.]

In this light, the following verse assumes additional meaning: כִּי אֲשֶׁר רְאִיתֶם אֶת־מִצְרַיִם הַיּוֹם לֹא תֹסִפוּ לִרְאֹתָם עוֹד עַד־עוֹלָם, *for as you have seen Egypt today, you will not see them ever again* (*Shemos* 14:13).

In these words, Moshe not only foretells Egypt's impending downfall, but also assures the people that they will never *want* to return to Egypt. (5636)

1. Thus, this was a conceptual encampment, allowing extraordinary events to percolate in the collective memory and understanding.

Israel Reacts to the Egyptian Army's Advance

וַיִּשְׂאוּ בְנֵי־יִשְׂרָאֵל אֶת־עֵינֵיהֶם וְהִנֵּה מִצְרַיִם נֹסֵעַ אַחֲרֵיהֶם וַיִּירְאוּ מְאֹד וַיִּצְעֲקוּ בְנֵי־יִשְׂרָאֵל אֶל ה׳. וַיֹּאמְרוּ אֶל־מֹשֶׁה הֲמִבְּלִי אֵין־קְבָרִים בְּמִצְרַיִם לְקַחְתָּנוּ לָמוּת בַּמִּדְבָּר מַה־זֹּאת עָשִׂיתָ לָּנוּ לְהוֹצִיאָנוּ מִמִּצְרָיִם

The Children of Israel raised their eyes and behold! — Egypt was journeying after them, and they were very frightened; the Children of Israel cried out to H*ASHEM*. *They said to Moshe: "Were there no graves in Egypt, that you took us to die in the wilderness? What have you done to us to take us out of Egypt?"* (*Shemos* 14:10-11).

Why was Israel afraid of the Egyptian armies? Hashem had assured them that Pharaoh and his forces would be vanquished, as the Torah says, *I will be glorified through Pharaoh and his entire army, through his chariots and through his horsemen* (*Shemos* 14:17). Even if we were to say that only Moshe was aware of Hashem's assurance, the question would still remain in light of Hashem's response to Moshe (*Shemos* 14:15), מַה־תִּצְעַק אֵלָי, *Why are* **you** *crying to Me?* suggesting that Moshe cried also, in spite of Hashem's assurance to him.

To answer this question, let us point out that the verse does not say that the *Egyptians* were journeying after the Jews, but rather that *Egypt* was journeying. The Midrash (cf. *Rashi* 14:10), says that whenever the word "Egypt" is used in the singular, it refers to the heavenly angel who ruled Egypt. It was the sight of this angel that caused the Jews such dread. Throughout history, the Jewish people has always had more to fear from spiritual conflicts than from physical battle. A prime example of this is Jacob's fear of confronting Esau, culminating eventually in his struggle with Esau's angel and spiritual mentor. Once he overcame that battle, Esau himself was easy to deal with. (5662)

It is also possible that the Jews were afraid because of their own inadequacies. They realized that Hashem would save them at the Sea only if their merit would be sufficiently great (a theme discussed extensively in the essay comparing the Exodus with the Splitting of the Sea). Thus, their real worry was that they would not merit liberation. (5631)

Perhaps also their fear stemmed from the bewilderment that gripped them based on a certain inconsistency they perceived. Because they felt no lingering intellectual or emotional ties with Egypt, they wondered why the Egyptians seemed to feel differently, to the extent of pursuing them.

Hashem's response to their concern — and indeed His rationale for granting the Egyptians one final attempt to defeat their former slaves — lies in the very phrase that describes the Jews' fear, וְהִנֵּה מִצְרַיִם נֹסֵעַ אַחֲרֵיהֶם, *And behold! — Egypt was journeying after them* (*Shemos* 14:10). The expression "after them" implies that their current troubles did not stem from lack of merit on their part; they did not need more adversity in order to merit liberation. Rather, Pharaoh and his armies were lured to the Sea for the purpose of teaching a lesson to future generations of Jews that would be on a lower spiritual level. Pharaoh's downfall showed that no attempt of pursuing the Jews would ever succeed. The expression "after them" implies that the Jews' anxiety and anguish was necessary preparation for the great victories that would be won by generations *after* them. (5652)

Finally, their fear may have been caused by the the Egyptian army's united attack, as indicated by the singular form "Egypt **was** journeying," which *Rashi* interprets 'with one heart, as one person."

This appearance of unity, however, was soon proved to be nothing more than a mirage as the Psalmist says (92:10), יִתְפָּרְדוּ כָּל פֹּעֲלֵי אָוֶן, *all evildoers will be dispersed.* The Egyptians met their end as a fragmented people, not as a proud and united nation while the Jews crossed the Sea of Reeds and sang the Song in perfect unison. Thus the *Zohar* describes the forces of evil: שָׁארֵי בַּחֲבוּרָא וְסַיְּים בְּפִרוּדָא, *They begin with unity and end in dispersion.* (5647)

וַיִּצְעֲקוּ בְנֵי יִשְׂרָאֵל אֶל־ה׳
The Children of Israel cried out to Hashem (*Shemos* 14:10).

Rashi offers a terse but powerful comment on this verse: תָּפְשׂוּ אוּמְנוּת אֲבוֹתָם, *[the Jews] seized the craft of their fathers [i.e. prayer].* This is one of the first instances in which Israel prayed. From where did they learn about the power of prayer?

The answer is that a Jew does not need formal instruction in prayer. We are all scions of Abraham, Isaac, and Jacob, whose strong faith in Hashem implanted the seed of prayer in their descendants. Even though this ability may have weakened in the sinful atmosphere of Egypt, it remained latent in their souls so that in time if need be the stirrings of the coming redemption could awaken it. Thus once again they "seized the craft of their fathers."

The Midrash (*Yalkut Shir Hashirim* 982) interprets a verse in *Shir HaShirim* (1:5): שְׁחוֹרָה אֲנִי בְּמַעֲשַׂי וְנָאוָה בְּמַעֲשֵׂה אֲבוֹתַי, *Even though I am black with my own actions, I am still beautiful with the deeds of my forefathers.* Even though the Jews had sinned in Egypt, they had not fully lost their fathers' power of prayer. This is hinted at also in the well-known verse (*Malachi* 3:24): וְהֵשִׁיב לֵב־אָבוֹת עַל־בָּנִים, *And He will return the heart of the fathers onto the children.* Children can learn to emulate the hearts of their fathers. Thus the Children of Israel knew instinctively how to embrace the heartfelt prayers of the Patriarchs.

(5658)

The Jews returned to their ancestors' ways and soon afterwards the Egyptians were vanquished as Israel marched through the Sea. This sequence of events is hardly coincidental: The Jews' return to the Patriarchs' legacy of prayer was a forerunner of the great redemption about to occur. We are told that the final redemption will follow the same pattern. First, the children will embrace their father's hearts and pray as their ancestors did; then the prophet Elijah will come to herald the redemption itself.

One final observation on this subject: While it is certainly significant that the Jews adopted their fathers' ways as the redemption unfolded, an even greater revelation occurred in the final stages of the Splitting of the Sea with the proclamation (*Shemos* 15:2)': זֶה אֵלִי וְאַנְוֵהוּ, *This is my God, and I will glorify Him.* They not only recognized Hashem as the God of their fathers, but after they beheld His wonders proclaimed *This is **my** God* as well. Every day in *Shemoneh Esrei* we note both these aspects of our relationship to Hashem in the words, אֱלֹהֵינוּ וֵאלֹהֵי אֲבוֹתֵינוּ, *our God and the God of our forefathers.* (5658)

How then can we explain the sudden turnabout from emulating the prayers of the Patriarchs to the clamoring to return to Egypt? The Midrash (cf. *Yalkut Shemos* 231) uses the image of "adding yeast to dough" to explain this shift: כֵּיוָן שֶׁהִטִילוּ שְׂאוֹר בְּעִיסָה בָּאוּ אֵצֶל מֹשֶׁה וְאָמְרוּ הֲמִבְּלִי אֵין קְבָרִים בְּמִצְרַיִם לְקַחְתָּנוּ לָמוּת בַּמִּדְבָּר, *Once the the yeast was placed in the dough, they came to Moshe and said, 'Were there no graves in Egypt that you took us to die in the wilderness?'*

The expression, "yeast in the dough," seems to refer to their rational awareness of what was happening to them. Emotionally, they were prepared for the Splitting of the Sea after having unquestioningly accomplished remarkable feats of obedience — marching back towards Egypt at Hashem's command and offering prayers even though they were not accustomed to do so. Rationally, however, they could not yet assimilate the implications of their liberation. Without yeast, dough does not rise and quickly assumes the form of matzah. When yeast is added, the process is slowed down and the bread takes much longer to bake. Thus, once they were given the opportunity to contemplate, the Jews rebelled. (5654)

הֲלֹא־זֶה הַדָּבָר אֲשֶׁר דִּבַּרְנוּ אֵלֶיךָ בְמִצְרַיִם לֵאמֹר חֲדַל מִמֶּנּוּ וְנַעַבְדָה אֶת־מִצְרָיִם כִּי טוֹב לָנוּ עֲבֹד אֶת־מִצְרַיִם מִמֻּתֵנוּ בַּמִּדְבָּר
Is this not the statement that we made to you in Egypt, saying: 'Let us be and we will serve Egypt, for it is better for us to serve Egypt than that we should die in the wilderness!' (*Shemos* 14:12).

How could the Jews, just a week after the Exodus, suddenly complain to Moshe that they would rather have stayed in Egypt? The Midrash suggests that it was only the *eirev rav*, a group of converts who joined the Jews at the time of the Exodus, who complained (see *Shemos* 12:38). This suggestion is supported by the complaint offered in the previous verse, מַה זֹּאת עָשִׂיתָ לָּנוּ לְהוֹצִיאָנוּ מִמִּצְרָיִם, *What have* **you** *[Moshe] done to us to take us out of Egypt?* Really it was Hashem rather than Moshe Who took the Jews out of Egypt; however, the decision to permit the *eirev rav* to join their ranks was Moshe's. Thus, only the *eirev rav* could properly attribute *their* Exodus to Moshe (*Rashi, Shemos* 32:7). (5642)

The assertion made earlier that the sea would split only if Israel merited it also explains the Jews' complaint that they would have done better to stay in Egypt. Whereas the Splitting of the Sea was contingent upon Israel's merit, Hashem promised Abraham to redeem his descendants from Egypt without reference to their merit. Aware of their own shortcomings, the Jews preferred to remain in Egypt and enjoy liberation based on Hashem's promise to previous generations, rather than run the risk that they might not have enough merit to earn the miracles at the Sea. (*Sfas Emes* 5631) We may also note that this is the only instance we know of that Moshe ordered the Jews to travel in a particular direction. All their other journeys in the Wilderness were guided by the pillar of cloud. In this case, however, Hashem wanted to give the Jews an opportunity to demonstrate their faith in Moshe by turning back towards Egypt and therefore did not use the pillar of cloud to lead them.

It was this that later caused the complainers ("Were there no graves in Egypt?") to suspect that Moshe had given these orders on his own, without Hashem's assent. Fortunately, the mere fact that they originally trusted him wholeheartedly gave them enough merit to be saved from the Egyptians and to come to have faith in him again as a faithful servant of Hashem. We see this in the Torah just before the Song where it says, וַיַּאֲמִינוּ בַּה׳ וּבְמֹשֶׁה עַבְדּוֹ, *they believed in Hashem and in Moshe His servant.* (*Parashas Beshalach* 5638)

> וַיֹּאמֶר מֹשֶׁה אֶל־הָעָם אַל־תִּירָאוּ הִתְיַצְּבוּ וּרְאוּ אֶת יְשׁוּעַת ה׳ אֲשֶׁר־יַעֲשֶׂה לָכֶם הַיּוֹם כִּי אֲשֶׁר רְאִיתֶם אֶת מִצְרַיִם הַיּוֹם לֹא תֹסִפוּ לִרְאֹתָם עוֹד עַד עוֹלָם ה׳ יִלָּחֵם לָכֶם וְאַתֶּם תַּחֲרִשׁוּן
> *Moshe said to the people: 'Do not fear! Stand fast and see the salvation of HASHEM that He will perform for you today; for as you have seen Egypt today, you will not see them ever again! HASHEM shall do battle for you, and you shall remain silent'* (*Shemos* 14:13).

Moshe responds to the complaints of "the people," (הָעָם), a term that normally refers to the *eirev rav* rather than to the Children of Israel. (5642)

Initially Moshe reassures the people and tells them not to fear. Later, however (v. 31), the Jews are praised for their fear of Hashem: *the people feared HASHEM*. Why is fear discouraged in one place and praised in another?

We must understand that two different kinds of fear are being discussed. Moshe urged the Jews not to let themselves be paralyzed by fear of Hashem's punishment. While some measure of this kind of fear is desirable to prevent sin, Moshe was warning them not to be excessively afraid, as the Torah relates (v. 10) וַיִּירְאוּ מְאֹד, *they were very frightened*, presumably of Hashem's strict justice, according to which they might well have drowned in the Sea.

On the other hand, awe of Hashem's majesty and manifold wonders is highly meritorious; it was this kind of fear that put the people in a joyous frame of mind to sing the Song. The Torah clarifies this relationship in the sequence of events: וַיִּירְאוּ הָעָם אֶת־ה׳ . . . אָז יָשִׁיר־מֹשֶׁה וּבְנֵי יִשְׂרָאֵל אֶת־הַשִּׁירָה הַזֹּאת לַה׳, first *the people feared HASHEM*, followed by *then Moshe and the Children of Israel chose to sing this song for HASHEM* (*Shemos* 14:31-15:1).

The *Ikkarim* (a major medieval philosophical work) delineates this relationship by observing "My fear is derived from my joy and my joy from my fear." (יִרְאָתִי מִתּוֹךְ שִׂמְחָתִי וְשִׂמְחָתִי מִתּוֹךְ יִרְאָתִי), True fear of Hashem's awesomeness can only lead to joy, as the Psalmist notes (34:10): יְרְאוּ אֶת ה׳ קְדֹשָׁיו כִּי אֵין מַחְסוֹר לִירֵאָיו, *Fear HASHEM, you — His holy ones — for there is no deprivation for His reverent ones.*

Nothing, not even the ultimate feeling of joy is lacking for one who reveres Hashem's majesty. (5658)

הִתְיַצְּבוּ וּרְאוּ אֶת־יְשׁוּעַת ה׳ אֲשֶׁר־יַעֲשֶׂה לָכֶם הַיּוֹם

Stand fast and see the salvation of HASHEM that He will perform for you today (*Shemos* 14:13).

The syntax of this verse is interesting. First it tells what Hashem *will* do in the future but then speaks of His intentions in the present, *this day*. This switch from future to present suggests that the Jews witnessed not only their own miracles at the Splitting of the Sea, but also all the miracles that Hashem would perform on their behalf in the future. (According to this interpretation the verse should be understood as if the wording was rearranged as follows: הִתְיַצְּבוּ וּרְאוּ הַיּוֹם אֲשֶׁר יַעֲשֶׂה לָכֶם, "behold today what Hashem will do in the future.

There is a famous Rabbinic observation on the Splitting of the Sea (cf. *Yalkut Shemos* 244): רָאֲתָה שִׁפְחָה עַל הַיָּם מַה שֶּׁלֹּא רָאוּ נְבִיאִים, *A maid-servant by the sea beheld what the prophets could not see.* Prophecy is subject to finite limits, as the Talmud says (*Berachos* 34b): כָּל הַנְּבִיאִים לֹא נִתְנַבְּאוּ אֶלָּא לִימוֹת הַמָּשִׁיחַ אֲבָל לָעוֹלָם הַבָּא עַיִן לֹא רָאֲתָה זוּלָתְךָ אֱלֹהִים יַעֲשֶׂה לִמְחַכֵּה לוֹ, *All the prophets prophesied only until the arrival of Moshiach. About the World to Come [after Moshiach], however, it is said, (Yeshayahu 64:3) 'No eye has beheld, but You, Hashem, Who will make [i.e. grant a portion] to those who await Him.'*

In contrast, the horizons of the simplest maid-servant at the Sea knew no limits and she could see even Hashem's future miracles in the World to Come. The very word יַעֲשֶׂה, *He will do*, suggests that the Jews at the

Sea could see *everything* Hashem will do in the World to Come.[1] Also the opening word of our verse, הִתְיַצְּבוּ, *stand forth,* is interpreted by the Midrash (*Yalkut Shemos* 232) as an allusion to *Ruach HaKodesh,* the sacred spirit of prophecy. (5662)

We can further say that Moshe's command, רְאוּ, *see!* suggests that Hashem granted the people an unparalleled vision of miracles He intended to perform in the remote future. No prophet has ever been privileged to see the World to Come, yet ordinary people at the Sea could do just that. When Hashem commanded Israel to "see," He allowed the whole people to envision what none of the prophets, men and women of sublime spiritual sensitivity, were granted to see.[2]

(5642)

ה׳ יִלָּחֵם לָכֶם וְאַתֶּם תַּחֲרִישׁוּן

HASHEM shall do battle for you, and you are to remain silent (*Shemos* 14:13).

While we can easily appreciate why Moshe told the people to let Hashem take charge in the battle against Egypt, the need for Israel to *remain silent* seems baffling. How could Israel's cries be harmful to Hashem's efforts? We will suggest two approaches to answering this question, based on interpretations we have presented already.

Earlier we said that the verse *The Children of Israel raised their eyes and behold! — Egypt was journeying after them, and they were very frightened,* (*Shemos* 14:10) describes the fear that the sight of Egypt's guardian angel inspired in the Jews. In this light, Moshe's response was entirely appropriate: "Only Hashem can meet Egypt's spiritual mentor in battle. You, as mortals, must remain silent. The slightest involvement on your part, even one word of prayer, would intrude on what must be a purely heavenly battle. Your salvation must come entirely from Hashem." (5645)

According to another approach, Moshe's answer was addressed to the *eirev rav,* that had instigated this revolt at the Sea: "Hashem will fight for you, and you will be compelled to remain silent while the Jews sing

---

1. The same word, יַעֲשֶׂה, *He will make,* is understood by this Midrash to refer to the mysteries of the World to Come as we see from the verse, אֱלֹהִים יַעֲשֶׂה לִמְחַכֵּה לוֹ, *He will [grant a portion] to those who await Him.*

2. For additional commentary on the phrase אֲשֶׁר יַעֲשֶׂה לָכֶם, *which He will perform,* emphasizing in particular the impact of the Splitting of the Sea on the people's souls, see our commentary on the verse וַיְהִי בְּשַׁלַּח פַּרְעֹה אֶת הָעָם, *And it happened when Pharaoh sent the people,* at the beginning of this section.

their Song of praise to Hashem." Thus the Song begins with a very pointed reference, *Then Moshe and the* ***Children of Israel*** *sang this song*. Only the Children of Israel were allowed to sing the Song, not the converts of the *eirev rav* who had caused so many problems. (5642)

A more profound answer to our question, however, is that by overcoming their natural urge to scream, the Jews underwent a transformation as radical and far-reaching as the Sea itself. Every instinct in their minds strained to scream, yet they remained silent. Every fiber in the Jewish body fought against plunging into the turbulent waters — and yet they followed the lead of Nachshon ben Aminadav, *Nasi* of the tribe of Yehudah, and leaped into the Sea.

Only after they submitted themselves totally to Hashem's will by remaining silent did the Sea split. As the Psalmist sings (114:3) הַיָּם רָאָה וַיָּנֹס, *the Sea saw and fled* — when the Sea saw the magnificent courage of Israel's silent acceptance of Hashem's will, then it split. "If these humans," the Sea must have thought, "whom Hashem endowed with free choice — the ability to defy His commands — overcame their natural inclinations to obey Him, then I, a mere inanimate entity, must certainly comply with His will."

In this light, the opening phrase of our verse takes on new meaning: *Stand fast and see the salvation of HASHEM that He will perform for you today*. Moshe was telling the Jews, "Stand erect, don't scream, and you will behold Hashem's salvation. He will save you from what you thought was certain death so that His name be revered by all of humanity."

This message applies to us in all situations, particularly in times of crisis. Whenever things look difficult, our task is simply to understand what Hashem wants of us and accept His will silently and completely. If we do this, if we genuinely trust that He will help us, then we will have the inestimable privilege of seeing His salvation unfold, and seeing His might and power revealed in the world. (5632)

◆§ Hashem's Response

וַיֹּאמֶר ה׳ אֶל־מֹשֶׁה מַה־תִּצְעַק אֵלָי דַּבֵּר־אֶל בְּנֵי־יִשְׂרָאֵל וְיִסָּעוּ

HASHEM said to Moshe, 'Why do you cry out to Me, speak to the Children of Israel and let them journey forth!' (*Shemos* 14:15).

An obvious question presents itself on this verse: Throughout Torah we find that prayer is considered a desirable response to any problem. Why here does Hashem discourage Moshe from praying to Him?

The following Midrash (*Shemos Rabbah* 21) suggests an answer to this question:

> הֲדָא דִכְתִיב וְהָיָה טֶרֶם יִקְרָאוּ וַאֲנִי אֶעֱנֶה כָּל מִי שֶׁהוּא עוֹשֶׂה רְצוֹן הַמָּקוֹם וּמְכַוֵין אֶת לִבּוֹ בִּתְפִילָה שׁוֹמֵעַ לוֹ בָּעוֹלָם הַזֶּה וְכֵן לֶעָתִיד לָבֹא שֶׁנֶּאֱמַר וְהָיָה טֶרֶם יִקְרָאוּ וַאֲנִי אֶעֱנֶה בָּעוֹלָם הַזֶּה שֶׁנֶּאֱמַר וּלְעָתִיד לָבֹא הֵם מְדַבְּרִים וַאֲנִי אֶשְׁמָע
>
> *This is what is written in the verse (Yeshayahu 65:24): "And it will be before they call and I will answer." Anyone who does Hashem's will and directs his heart in prayer, Hashem hears him in this world and in the World to Come, as it says, "And it will be before they call and I will answer," this refers to our world. But about the World to Come, it says, "While they are still speaking, I will listen."*

This Midrash teaches that suffering is only a surface phenomenon. While a Jew may sometimes seem to undergo unrelenting misery for a period of time, in reality his suffering is only a preliminary to great events that are about to follow. Sometimes we do not merit to witness the liberation that follows the suffering in this world and we must wait until the next world to understand the purpose of our anguish and misery.

However, the Jews at the Sea merited an almost immediate explanation for the purpose of *their* suffering. Moshe in effect told them, "You are wondering, why I took you out of Egypt? Within a few short moments, you will realize that your present anguish is only a prelude to the Splitting of the Sea and to the Song you will sing." Since this was already determined, Hashem could tell Moshe that no further prayers were necessary, only to journey forward and they would see that their suffering would be short lived.

This, then, is the intent of the verse cited by the Midrash: *First they will call out* in their anguish, *and I will answer them* at the Sea. *While they are still speaking* words of joy — the Song — *I will listen.* Hashem assures Moshe that Israel's desperate call will shortly be transformed into the sublime Song of the Sea.

This theme of anguished cries being answered with speedy relief is voiced by the Psalmist (118:5): מִן הַמֵּצַר קָרָאתִי יָּהּ עָנָנִי בַמֶּרְחָב יָהּ, *From the straits [of my suffering] did I call upon God, God answered me with expansiveness* of Divine relief, by showing me that all my suffering was only a preliminary to His salvation that would quickly follow.

There is another allusion to these two settings of prayer, cries of anguish and bursts of joy, in one of the first mentions of Jewish prayer in the Torah (*Bereishis* 27:22): הַקֹּל קוֹל יַעֲקֹב, *the voice is Jacob's voice.* The first time it appears, the word קֹל is written without the usual *vav*, suggesting confused and anguished cries of suffering. The second time, however, it is written in its full form, קוֹל, suggesting happy and fully formed songs of gratitude and joy. (5655)

Alternatively, according to the above Midrash, Hashem may have been telling Moshe that further prayer was unnecessary because He already knew Moshe's *thoughts.* In this world, Hashem desires that we serve Him via the three channels of thought, speech and action. The Actions we do in the performance of *mitzvos* and the Words we speak in prayer or the study of Torah are usually required to generate pure Torah Thought, which is the ultimate goal of our service.

In the World to Come, however, we will be able to serve Hashem with our thoughts *alone,* which will then encompass all the power that our speech and actions have now. In this sense, the verse cited by the Midrash, *And it will be before they call and I will answer; while they are still speaking, I will listen,* implies that in the World to Come Hashem will consider Israel's noble thoughts as if they had been materialized in speech and action.

However, not only in the World to Come but even in rare moments in *this* world that give a foretaste of the next world — such as the Splitting of the Sea — Hashem gives the *thoughts* of Jews the same power that is normally granted only to words and actions. Thus Hashem asks Moshe, "Why do you cry out to me? I've already heard your thoughts and answered your prayers." (5633)

A similar interpretation of our Midrash suggests that Hashem is telling Moshe that further prayers are unnecessary because he has already succeeded in awakening the *inner* voice of the Jewish soul, whose cries are far more powerful than the external prayers that can be heard in the material world. Another Midrash (*Bereishis, Midrash Rabbah* 6) states that the cry of this inner voice at the moment the soul leaves the body can be heard from one end of the world to the other.

While mortals cannot hear the sound the soul makes as it leaves its temporary casing, Hashem perceives it with special acuteness. This is the inner voice of the Jew — unable to scream any longer — preparing to meet his Creator.

Thus when Moshe told the Jews *you are to be silent*, he meant that their *inner* voice, silent to the mortal ear, would speak for them more effectively than their loud prayers. (5636)

Finally, another version of Midrash comments (*Shemos Rabbah* 21):

> הָדָא דִכְתִיב צָעֲקוּ וַה׳ שָׁמֵעַ מַהוּ כֵן אֶלָּא ב׳ יְרוּשׁוֹת הִנְחִיל יִצְחָק לְבָנָיו הִנְחִיל לְיַעֲקֹב הַקּוֹל וְכֵן הוּא אוֹמֵר הַקֹּל קוֹל יַעֲקֹב וְהִנְחִיל לְעֵשָׂו הַיָּדַיִם עֵשָׂו הָיָה מִתְגָּאֶה בִּירוּשָּׁתוֹ יַעֲקֹב מִתְגָּאֶה בִּירוּשָּׁתוֹ
>
> *This is what is written (Tehillim 34:18), "[The righteous] cried out and* H*ASHEM hears." What does this mean? Isaac bequeathed two legacies to his children. To Jacob he bequeathed the voice [of prayer] as it says (Bereishis 27:22): "The voice is the voice of Jacob," and to Esau he bequeathed the "hands" [i.e. physical might]. Esau prided himself over his legacy Jacob prided himself over his legacy.*

According to this Midrash, the Jews at the Sea were merely doing what comes naturally to any Jew, crying to Hashem with "the voice of Jacob." If Israel lives up to its legacy it receives another reward: In addition to their traditional "weapon" of prayer, they are also given Esau's legacy — the sword, as Isaac said to Esau (*Bereishis* 27:40), וְעַל־חַרְבְּךָ תִחְיֶה, *by your sword shall you live.*

The Torah says that the Jewish people left Egypt armed (see *Shemos* 13:18). As we have said, armaments are not Israel's typical means of defense, rather prayer is. However, in reward for its observance of the Torah, Israel is also given Esau's portion, physical might as well. Thus the Midrash concludes, "Jacob prides himself over his legacy," knowing that Esau's portion will eventually also be his.

In this light, Hashem's response to Moshe, "Why do you cry out to Me?" may be understood quite simply: "It is no longer necessary to cry. Your prayers have already identified you as Jacob's descendants and you have a right to his legacy, the voice of prayer. You need do no more. (5633, 5635)

וַיֵּט מֹשֶׁה אֶת־יָדוֹ עַל־הַיָּם וַיָּשָׁב הַיָּם לִפְנוֹת בֹּקֶר לְאֵיתָנוֹ

Moshe stretched out his hand over the sea, and toward morning the water went back to its power (*Shemos* 14:27).

The Midrash (cf. *Yalkut Shemos* 236) comments that by rearranging the letters of the word לְאֵיתָנוֹ (literally, *to its power*) we obtain the word לִתְנָאוֹ, *to its original condition,* to the condition that was stipulated with it during the six days of creation.

The Midrash continues, א״ר יוֹנָתָן הִתְנָה הקב״ה תְּנָאִים עִם הַיָּם שֶׁיְּהֵא נִקְרָע לִפְנֵי יִשְׂרָאֵל, *Rabbi Yonasan said: Hashem stipulated with the Sea [at the time of its creation] that it should split before Israel.*

An obvious question arises: Shouldn't there be an allusion to Hashem's stipulation with the Sea at the time the Sea split, rather than when it returned to its former strength? By reversing the order, however, the Midrash is hinting at a profound insight: Not only the Splitting of the Sea, which occurred in miraculous fashion, but even its return to its natural state, was possible only because of Hashem's stipulation at the time He created it.

Contrary to popular misconception, "nature" is not outside Hashem's control, nor is it distinct from that part of Creation normally considered to be "above" nature. The celestial bodies, the earth and sea all follow their regular routines only because nature did Hashem's bidding at the Splitting of the Sea. The natural world, including the Sea, at that time were in a state of quasi-rebellion and their continued existence depended on obeying Hashem's command. Only after the Sea heeded Hashem's will could it, together with the rest of nature, be secure in its existence. Thus the lesson of the Sea is that the stability of the natural world is directly proportional to its submissiveness to Hashem.

When the Psalmist asks (114:5), מַה לְּךָ הַיָּם כִּי תָנוּס, *What ails you, O Sea, that you flee?* he is really giving the Sea (and the rest of nature with it) a subtle reminder that not only at the time that it split but at all other times also it is compelled to do the will of Hashem. As the Psalmist answers his own question (v. 7), מִלִּפְנֵי אָדוֹן חוּלִי אָרֶץ מִלִּפְנֵי אֱלוֹהַּ יַעֲקֹב, *Before the Presence of the Master — Who created the earth — before the presence of the God of Jacob.* The natural world exists on Hashem's sufferance and the Jewish people only remind nature that it is subservient to the wishes of those who fulfill Hashem's commandments.

We may say further that the Sea was given its force at the time of Creation only to strengthen the effect of the miracle that would later be done for the Jews. Had the Sea not abided by the stipulation that was made with it, the whole purpose of its existence would have been shown, retroactively, to be in vain. In that case Hashem would have no need for it to continue in its powerful state. (5635)

וַיָּשֶׂם אֶת הַיָּם לֶחָרָבָה וַיִּבָּקְעוּ הַמָּיִם

[And HASHEM] made the sea dry land, and the waters were divided (*Shemos* 14:21).

What is the significance of making *the sea dry land* and dividing the waters?

The Midrash (*Bereishis Rabbah* 5) sheds a new light on the connection between the Splitting of the Sea and the Jews' Song. The Midrash is commenting on the verse (*Bereishis* 1:9), יִקָּווּ הַמַּיִם *Let the waters gather.*[1]

אָמַר הקב"ה יִקָּווּ לִי הַמַּיִם מַה שֶׁאֲנִי עָתִיד לַעֲשׂוֹת בָּהֶם מָשָׁל לְמֶלֶךְ שֶׁבָּנָה פַּלְטִין וְהוֹשִׁיב בְּתוֹכָהּ אִלְּמִים וְהָיוּ מַשְׁכִּימִים וְשׁוֹאֲלִים בִּשְׁלוֹמוֹ שֶׁל מֶלֶךְ בִּרְמִיזָה וּבְאֶצְבַּע אָמַר הַמֶּלֶךְ אִילוּ הָיוּ פִּקְחִין עאכ"ו אֶתְמַהָא הוֹשִׁיב בָּהּ הַמֶּלֶךְ דִּיוֹרִין פִּקְחִין עָמְדוּ וְהֶחֱזִיקוּ בְּפַלְטִין אָמְרוּ אֵין פַּלְטִין זוֹ שֶׁל מֶלֶךְ שֶׁלָּנוּ הִיא אָמַר הַמֶּלֶךְ תַּחֲזוֹר פַּלְטִין לִכְמוֹ שֶׁהָיְתָה כַּךְ מִתְּחִילַּת בְּרִיָּיתוֹ שֶׁל עוֹלָם לֹא הָיָה קִילוּסוֹ שֶׁל הקב"ה עוֹלֶה אֶלָּא מִן הַמַּיִם . . . אָמַר הקב"ה מַה אִם אֵלוּ שֶׁאֵין לָהֶם לֹא פֶּה הֲרֵי הֵן מְקַלְּסִין אוֹתִי כְּשֶׁנִּבְרָא אָדָם עאכ"ו עָמַד דּוֹר הַמַּבּוּל וּמָרַד בּוֹ. . . אָמַר הקב"ה יִפְנוּ אֵלוּ וְיַעַמְדוּ וְיָבוֹאוּ אוֹתָן הה"ד וַיְהִי הַגֶּשֶׁם עַל הָאָרֶץ אַרְבָּעִים יוֹם וְאַרְבָּעִים לָיְלָה

Hashem said, "There is hope for the waters because one day I will disperse them again."

This is like a king who built a palace to house mute people. Every morning they greeted the king with gestures. The king thought, "If these were normal people, surely they would sing my praises."

So he placed talking people there. Eventually they rebelled, claiming that the palace belonged to them, not the king. After that, the king said, "I will return the palace to its previous mute occupants."

So too, Hashem's praises at first originated from the waters, in a universe dominated by water. Hashem

1. We present the English of this Midrash in very free translation, adapted for the purposes of this discussion.

> reasoned, "If the inanimate world praises Me, then if I transform the water into dry land and populate it with speaking people, they would certainly praise Me." However, man shirks his responsibility and claims the universe belongs to him, not to Hashem. Finally, when the generation of the Flood rebelled, Hashem allowed the water to fill the universe again, since man forfeited his right to live on dry land.

This Midrash shows us the relationship between singing Hashem's praises and the transformation of the sea to dry land. If so, at the time of the Exodus when Israel superbly fulfilled its mission of praising Hashem by singing the Song, Hashem rewarded them by splitting the Sea, so that the waters once again became dry land. (*Parashas Beshalach* 5661)

וְהַמַּיִם לָהֶם חֹמָה מִימִינָם וּמִשְּׂמֹאלָם

And the water was a wall for them on their right and on their left (*Shemos* 14:29).

What purpose did a "wall" of water serve? There is a precedent for such a protective shield in the *Zohar*'s suggestion that Noah's Ark was a shield against the Angel of Death. Similarly, at the Splitting of the Sea, the Angel of Death was kept busy furiously slaying the Egyptians. Israel, however, was shielded behind a wall of water, and thus protected from his destructive powers.[1] (5635)

◆§ Prelude to the Song

וַיּוֹשַׁע ה׳ בַּיּוֹם הַהוּא אֶת־יִשְׂרָאֵל מִיַּד מִצְרָיִם וַיַּרְא יִשְׂרָאֵל אֶת־מִצְרַיִם מֵת עַל־שְׂפַת הַיָּם וַיַּרְא יִשְׂרָאֵל אֶת־הַיָּד הַגְּדֹלָה אֲשֶׁר עָשָׂה ה׳ בְּמִצְרַיִם וַיִּירְאוּ הָעָם אֶת־ה׳ וַיַּאֲמִינוּ בַּה׳ וּבְמֹשֶׁה עַבְדּוֹ . . . אָז יָשִׁיר־מֹשֶׁה וּבְנֵי יִשְׂרָאֵל

Hashem saved — on that day — Israel from the hand of Egypt, and Israel saw the Egyptians dead on the seashore. Israel saw the great hand that Hashem inflicted upon Egypt and the people feared Hashem, and they had faith in Hashem and in Moshe, His servant. Then Moshe and the Children of Israel chose to sing. (*Shemos* 14:30-15:1).

---

1. See also our commentary on the final verse of the Song כִּי בָא סוּס פַּרְעֹה, *When Pharaoh's cavalry came.*

This brief passage sets the stage for the Song of the Sea by highlighting those factors that enabled the Jews to sing the Song. The most important requirement for the Song was *emunah* (faith).Thus, the statement of the Jews' faith, *they had faith in* HASHEM *and in Moshe, His servant*, immediately precedes the beginning of the Song.

It is noteworthy that the Torah does not say וְהֶאֱמִינוּ, which would mean simply that they believed,[1] but rather וַיַּאֲמִינוּ, which is grammatically a causative (*hif'il*) form — they caused others to believe. At the moment of the Splitting of the Sea, Israel brought all of mankind to recognize Hashem's rule in the world. Even more, they brought the concept of faith into the world. As a result of such idealism, the Jews were able to sing the Song. (5662)

Another Midrash elucidates the unique quality of the Jewish people's *emunah* just prior to the Splitting of the Sea:

> אע״פ שֶׁכָּתוּב כְּבָר שֶׁהֶאֱמִינוּ עַד שֶׁהָיוּ בְּמִצְרַיִם שֶׁנֶּאֱמַר וַיַּאֲמֵן הָעָם חָזְרוּ וְלֹא הֶאֱמִינוּ שֶׁנֶּאֱמַר אֲבוֹתֵינוּ בְּמִצְרַיִם לֹא הִשְׂכִּילוּ נִפְלְאוֹתֶיךָ כֵּיוָן שֶׁבָּאוּ עַל הַיָּם וְרָאוּ גְּבוּרֹתָיו שֶׁל הקב״ה הֵיאַךְ עוֹשֶׂה מִשְׁפָּט בָּרְשָׁעִים מִיַּד הֶאֱמִינוּ בַּה׳ וּבִזְכוּת הָאֱמוּנָה שָׁרְתָה עֲלֵיהֶם רוּחַ הַקּוֹדֶשׁ וְאָמְרוּ שִׁירָה.
>
> *Even though the Torah says the Jews believed [in Hashem] while they were still in Egypt, as it says (Shemos 4:31): "The people believed," their faith later weakened, as it says (Tehillim 106:7): "Our fathers in Egypt did not contemplate Your wonders."*
>
> *Once they came to the Sea and beheld* HASHEM*'s mighty deeds, how He metes out justice to the wicked, immediately they believed in* HASHEM. *In the merit of this faith, Ruach HaKodesh [the prophetic spirit] descended on them and they said the Song* (*Shemos Rabbah* 23:2).

As this Midrash notes, the Splitting of the Sea was not the first time the Jews had exhibited faith in Hashem. Already in Egypt, after Moshe performed the various signs Hashem had given him, they trusted in Hashem, but this faith was short-lived. Even the Ten Plagues, miraculous as they were, left little lasting impact on the people, as the verse cited in the Midrash says, *they did not contemplate [i.e. absorb the*

1. *Editor's note*: Literally "they brought themselves to believe," cf. *Bereishis* 15:16 and *Shemos* 4:8.)

meaning of] Your wonders. Ramban (cf. *Ramban, Shemos* 13:16) states that the occasional miracles performed by Hashem signify to the world at large that even the natural order of things (Hebrew, *teva*) is controlled and sustained by Hashem.

This lesson however, was not learned by our fathers in Egypt, possibly because Pharaoh's kingdom remained intact in spite of all of the supernatural occurrences. Only when they witnessed Egypt's final downfall at the Sea were they able to fully absorb the message inherent in what they had been seeing all along — that the entire natural world is conducted through hidden miracles. (5651)

Alternatively, we may interpret this Midrash in a way somewhat less critical of our forefathers in Egypt than what we have suggested until now. Even though the Jews in Egypt believed in Hashem, their belief was on a relatively simple level, commensurate with their lack of knowledge. A Jew who knows little of Torah and thus has little appreciation of Hashem's wonders has no option but to hold on to his simple faith. The versed cited by our Midrash describes this primitive state of *emunah* as not comprehending the basis for Hashem's miracles.

At the Sea, however, they came to a far more sophisticated form of *emunah,* based on a more advanced understanding of Torah they derived from having seen how Hashem openly controls the world. As the Psalmist sings (106:12): וַיַּאֲמִינוּ בִדְבָרָיו יָשִׁירוּ תְּהִלָּתוֹ, *they believed His words, they sang His praise,* as a result of believing Hashem's words, the words of Torah, they could sing His praise, the praise of the Song. The rudimentary form of *emunah* they achieved in Egypt is called a lack of faith only in comparison with the much loftier form they attained at the Sea. Still, the *emunah* they had in Egypt was not entirely without value — the simple faith of uninitiated Jews who believed in Hashem without understanding His ways was a necessary prerequisite for the more exalted *emunah* they achieved at the Sea. (5645)

The concept of dual levels of faith can be derived from *Rashi's* commentary on the Talmud (*Sanhedrin* 90a) which insists that it is not sufficient merely to believe in the resurrection of the dead, but rather one's belief must be based on the fact that the Torah teaches it.

Indeed, it is possible to say that both simple *emunah* and more sophisticated faith based on extensive knowledge of the Torah are requirements for the salvation of the Jewish people. The Song at the Sea was produced by a people at the pinnacle of faith, as *Shir HaShirim* notes (4:8), תָּשׁוּרִי מֵרֹאשׁ אֲמָנָה, *Sing from the peak of faith.* At the same time, Hashem has a special affinity for simple trusting faith, even that displayed by learned, sophisticated Jews. Someone who attains high levels of knowledge and faith must still retain the simple faith of his earlier years, as the Talmud states (*Chullin* 5b): אָדָם וּבְהֵמָה תוֹשִׁיעַ ה׳" אֵלוּ,, בְּנֵי אָדָם שֶׁעֲרוּמִין כְּאָדָם וּמְשִׂימִין עַצְמָן כִּבְהֵמָה, *"You save both man and beast,* HASHEM*" (Tehillim 36:7). This verse refers to those who are sophisticated [in their faith] like humans but who make themselves like animals [in the simplicity of their faith].*

In light of this understanding, the verse immediately preceding the Song, *they had faith in* HASHEM, assumes additional significance. Having attained a higher level of faith, Israel now fully realized that the entire universe is dominated by Hashem's Presence. Ultimately, all mankind will reach this lofty level, as the prophet Zechariah says (14:9), בַּיּוֹם הַהוּא יִהְיֶה ה׳ אֶחָד וּשְׁמוֹ אֶחָד, *On that day,* HASHEM *will be One and His Name will be One* — all men will recognize that Hashem controls everything in the natural world. However, the generation of enlightened believers that stood victorious at the Sea was already able to *believe* that which will become the shared belief of all mankind only sometime in the (we hope not too distant) future. (5644)

We may say further that the *emunah* the Jews attained at the Sea surpassed that which they had in Egypt in another respect. In Egypt, the people placed their faith in Hashem, as the Torah says, וַיַּאֲמֵן הָעָם, *the people believed.* At the Sea, however, by trusting Moshe as well, they reached the achievement of *emunas chachamim,* belief in the teachings of Torah scholars. (This concept is discussed more fully in the essay on the Book of Ruth in the section on Shavuos).

Even though *emunas Hashem* is more important than *emunas chachamim, emunas Hashem* can bring one to have trust in the teachings of Torah scholars, which in turn leads to a much higher level of faith in Hashem, the level of *true* faith. This was the progression followed by the Jews at the Sea: The Torah first says, וַיַּאֲמִינוּ בַּה׳, *they had faith in* HASHEM, then it says וּבְמֹשֶׁה עַבְדּוֹ, *and in Moshe, His servant,* and then they sang the Song, showing that they had reached the level of *true* faith in Hashem. (5639)

Furthermore, the *emunah* the Jews felt in Egypt was on a lower level than that which they achieved at the Sea because the former was conditional on the fulfillment of a particular promise. Thus the Torah says (*Shemos* 4:31), וַיַּאֲמֵן הָעָם וַיִּשְׁמְעוּ כִּי־פָקַד ה׳ אֶת־בְּנֵי יִשְׂרָאֵל וְכִי רָאָה אֶת־עָנְיָם, *The people believed and they heard [what Moshe told them] because Hashem had remembered the Children of Israel, and because He had seen their poverty.* The wording of this verse suggests that their belief in Hashem, as well as their willingness to listen to Moshe, existed only because he offered them realistic hope that their redemption was near.

Later, however, the Torah says (*Shemos* 6:9), וְלֹא שָׁמְעוּ אֶל־מֹשֶׁה מִקֹּצֶר רוּחַ וּמֵעֲבֹדָה קָשָׁה, *they did not listen to Moshe [i.e. did not believe what he told them], because of shortness of spirit and hard work.* Because their workload had been increased, it was harder for them to believe Moshe and to have faith in Hashem's ability to redeem them.

At the Sea, however, their faith attained the level of unconditional submission, independent of any reward they may have expected in the future. (5638)

Thus far we have contrasted the high level of *emunah* the Jews attained at the Sea with the simpler *emunah* they felt in Egypt. Yet this concept of *emunah* seems to clash with the traditional notion of faith as a complete confidence or trust capable of withstanding any challenge or adversity. The experience at the Sea, when the Jews witnessed the unprecedented spectacle of their enemies first being drowned and then spit out on the seashore, could hardly be considered a "challenge"to their faith. How, then, can we say that this experience revealed their faith to be on such a high level?

Evidently, their *emunah* at the Sea included all future generations so that even in the darkest and most despairing days of future exiles their descendants would never fall completely away from belief in Hashem's might. In this regard, all Jews fit the *Rambam's* description of a complete penitent (*baal teshuvah gamur*) as someone of whom וְיָעִיד עָלָיו יוֹדֵעַ תַּעֲלוּמוֹת שֶׁלֹּא יָשׁוּב לָזֶה הַחֵטְא עוֹד, *the One Who knows secrets [i.e. Hashem] will testify that he will never return to this sin* (*Hilchos Teshuvah* 2:2). Just as the true *ba'al teshuvah* will never again succumb to the *yetzer hara's* enticements, so also we will not be deflected from our faith by the most difficult trials Hashem sends us. Even though we may find it impossible to maintain the high level of idealism achieved at the Sea on a constant, unwavering basis, our national faith in Hashem can never be extinguished.[1]

1. For a fuller discussion of the spiritual linkage between generations, see the essay on *aravah* in the section on Succos.

◆§ Fear of Hashem at the Sea

Thus far, we have focused on the *motif* of *emunah* in the Song of the Sea. Now we wish to consider the role of *yiras Hashem,* fear of Hashem, in motivating the Jews to sing Hashem's praises. As the Torah itself emphasizes (*Shemos* 14:31), וַיִּירְאוּ הָעָם אֶת־ה׳, *and the people feared* H*ASHEM.*

At first glance, fear and song seem to contradict each other — how can someone experiencing fear break into joyous song? Upon contemplation, however, we can suggest several ways to understand the relationship between the two. For one thing, the Jews may have sung the Song in gratitude for the ability to maintain their previous level of fear of Hashem even after witnessing such amazing miracles. Other nations would let such a spectacle go to their heads and boast arrogantly of *their* might and prowess.

Israel, however, remained strong in its fear of Hashem and its recognition of Whose servant it was. The Song would have been worthwhile if only as an expression of gratitude for this humility, for the ability to remember to fear Hashem even in glorious triumph.[1]

We may even say that fear of Hashem is a necessary precondition to singing His praises. The song of a less pious nation than Israel would be full of coarse and vainglorious boasting. It is only the song of those who truly fear Him that Hashem deems acceptable. (5642)

וַיַּרְא יִשְׂרָאֵל אֶת־הַיָּד הַגְּדֹלָה אֲשֶׁר עָשָׂה ה׳ בְּמִצְרַיִם

And Israel saw the great hand that H*ASHEM did in Egypt* (*Shemos* 14:31).

One last part of the introduction to the Song requires clarification. The Talmud (*Berachos* 58a) suggests that "Hashem's great hand" in this verse actually refers to the Creation of the world. Only after seeing Hashem's great power revealed at the Sea was Israel wholeheartedly convinced that Hashem created the world and continues to direct every detail of everything that happens in it. (5638)

Most of the commentators are puzzled by the reference to the miracles

---

1. The Jewish ability to retain one's fear of Hashem in spite of great success may be the legacy of our father Jacob, who responded to a vision of angels ascending to Heaven not with gloating but rather with fear, as the Torah says (*Bereishis* 28:17), וַיִּירָא וַיֹּאמַר מַה־נּוֹרָא הַמָּקוֹם הַזֶּה, *He was afraid, and he said, 'How awesome is this place!'*

Hashem did *in* Egypt, inasmuch as this verse was written in the context of the Splitting of the Sea. We may say, however, that "the great hand that Hashem did in Egypt" refers to the course of the Jewish exile in Egypt. At the Sea, the people could finally appreciate retroactively and accept with complete faith that all the misery and suffering Hashem had caused them to undergo in Egypt, from beginning to end, was entirely to the good because it had brought them to that exalted moment at the Sea. On the verse וַיַּרְא יִשְׂרָאֵל אֶת־מִצְרַיִם מֵת עַל־שְׂפַת הַיָּם, *Israel saw Egypt dead on the seashore,* the Midrash (cf. *Yalkut* 240) comments that the word מֵת, *dead,* appears in the singular because each Jew saw the wicked Egyptian who had subjected *him* to hard labor. As a result, they realized and accepted with a full heart that Hashem had meant their trials for their good, in order to bring them to this moment of glory.

(5643)

Az Yashir

אָז יָשִׁיר מֹשֶׁה וּבְנֵי יִשְׂרָאֵל

Then Moshe and the Children of Israel will sing (*Shemos* 15:1).

◆§ Introduction

In the following section, we will discuss the implications of the use of the future tense in this verse, אָז יָשִׁיר, *then Moshe 'will' sing,* rather than the more standard אָז שָׁר, *Moshe 'sang.'* We will explore two approaches proposed by *Rashi* and suggest a number of innovative interpretations of our own.

Let us first take a look at *Rashi*. אָז כְּשֶׁרָאָה הַנֵּס עָלָה בְלִבּוֹ שֶׁיָּשִׁיר הַשִּׁירָה ... זֶהוּ לְיַשֵּׁב פְּשׁוּטוֹ אֲבָל מִדְרָשׁוֹ אָמְרוּ רז״ל מִכַּאן רֶמֶז לִתְחִיַּת הַמֵּתִים מִן הַתּוֹרָה — *Then when he [Moshe] saw the miracle it entered his heart to sing the Song... This is to explain the simple meaning. In the Midrash, however, our Rabbis said: From here [we can deduce] that the [concept of] the Resurrection of the Dead is based on the Torah.*

Two questions arise about *Rashi's* "simple meaning," that the future tense is used to indicate Moshe's future intention to sing the Song. Firstly, why was Moshe's intention of any importance? While normally we say that the desire to perform a good deed is as good as performing the deed itself, that is of significance only if the deed itself is never accomplished. In our case, however, it would seem that the singing of the Song itself would far overshadow Moshe's earlier intention. Furthermore, how does the future tense imply that Moshe had such an intention; this is at best an unusual way of expressing it?

We can say, however, that *Rashi* is teaching a lesson about the enormous significance of the desire to perform a *mitzvah.* Even the loftiest deeds, normally the exclusive province of a handful of righteous Jews, can be within the reach of ordinary individuals if they set their aspirations high enough. On the surface it seems inconceivable that millions of Jews, including everyone from infants to renegades who wanted to return to Egypt, should simultaneously sing the identical song without the slightest deviation. Perhaps even more incomprehensible is the fact that the emotions of so many Jews should be recorded in a fundamental portion of the Torah. Evidently, it was the heartfelt desire to sing the Song, despite their limitations, that proved crucial. As *Rashi* notes, the thought alone — the wish to sing — made it possible for myriads of Jews to contribute the Song, one of the Torah's most moving portions.

Upon careful examination, we can see that the Song itself contains numerous references to Israel's enthusiasm to speak Hashem's praises. The letter *aleph* (א) that prefaces several of the Song's key phrases expresses this longing. Thus, we have אָשִׁירָה, *I wish to sing;* זֶה אֵלִי וְאַנְוֵהוּ, *this is my God and I 'wish' to glorify Him;* and אֱלֹהֵי אָבִי וַאֲרֹמְמֶנְהוּ, *the Hashem of my father and I 'wish' to exalt Him.*

This relationship between great wishes and the deeds they inspire is important to the contemporary Jew also. In effect, *Rashi* is suggesting that every Jew can attain lofty spiritual levels. If he only has sufficient desire, there are no limits to his potential for spiritual growth. (5632)

This *Rashi* also makes a statement about great thoughts that *never* reach fruition. The soul of every Jew has a share in the Song, yet many have never been able to realize their desire to sing it and remain with frustrated preparations. Still, their heartfelt intentions to sing Hashem's praises are as valuable to Him as if they had actually accomplished them. Even those who did actually sing probably articulated only a small part of all their sublime thoughts. By couching the song in the future tense, the Torah emphasizes that Hashem values an unspoken or only partially rendered song as much as a finished product. (5639)

❧ ❧ ❧

We are left with the question of why the *future* tense is used to convey the Jews' intention to sing the Song. In a few words, *Rashi* tells us that the world of Jewish thought is beyond temporal limitations. Normal language allows for only three tenses — past, present and future. In these terms, it would surely be inappropriate to describe a past historical event in the future tense. In the world of Jewish imagination, however, the finite limitations of time do not exist. Events yet to happen may be perceived as if they have already occurred and past events, replete with meaning for all generations, such as the Song, are appropriately expressed in the future tense. (5631)

Let us consider the implications of *Rashi's* statement that the use of the future tense alludes to the singing of the Song by the resurrected dead. By relegating the Song to the distant future, the Midrash on which this *Rashi* is based seems to contradict the Torah's plain meaning that the Song was *already* sung at the Splitting of the Sea.

However, in light of *Rashi's* first approach, emphasizing the Jews' *desire* to sing the Song, this Midrash becomes much more understandable. Only *some* of Israel's sublime thoughts were articulated at the Splitting of the Sea, but most were deferred until the conclusion of world history, to that glorious moment when the Song will be heard again. *Then* (אָז) the Song will be complete, with both the *words* sung at the Sea and all the sublime thoughts that had to be held in abeyance.

An important lesson emerges from this: Sincere efforts at Divine service and moral growth are never in vain. While they may not reach fruition in our lifetime in this world, ultimately they will succeed. (5646)

Careful examination of this *Rashi* reveals further insights. *Rashi* emphasizes that *from here* can be derived the Resurrection of the Dead, suggesting that the singing of the Song by itself is an indication of the Resurrection. In its time, the Song was actually a powerful resurrection of a spiritually dormant generation. The lowliest maid and the recent sinner (who had just pleaded to return to Egypt) suddenly became prophets, magnificently singing Hashem's praises. As the prelude to the Song indicates, when Israel "saw Hashem's *hand*," they were lifted out of their moral torpor and put into direct connection with the Creator. If such a powerful spiritual resurrection occurred that first Pesach (let us remember that the Song was sung on the seventh day of Pesach), perhaps a future Pesach is a likely time for the great physical resurrection that we all await.

It is also possible that a physical, as well as spiritual, resurrection occurred at the Splitting of the Sea. The Song's opening phrase, *Then Moshe and the Children of Israel will sing,* might mean not only the Jews of that generation, but literally Jacob's actual children — his twelve sons. Surely the ones who went down to Egypt, as described in the first verse of *Shemos, These are the names of the Children of Israel who came to Egypt,* richly deserved to witness their descendants' liberation in person.[1] (5642)

Apart from these two approaches of *Rashi,* we may suggest additional insights to be gleaned from the use of the future tense. The word יָשִׁיר, *he will sing,* may be understood grammatically as a causative form, indicating that the Jews *created* the song! No mortal — and certainly no nation made up of millions of individuals — could compose such a sublime song, and then merit to have that song become an integral component of the Torah. Although, the letters comprising the Song were composed by Hashem Himself, they remained in Heaven (as did the entire Torah before the Revelation at Sinai) until the Jews, under Divine inspiration, desired to sing the Song. Then these letters found a *physical* expression in the form of the Song. Thus, Israel seized the initiative by taking the building blocks of the Song — spiritual entities still in Heaven — and converted them into the physical entity of the Song. (5635)

The future tense also implies that various entities — as we shall describe — were anxiously awaiting the moment when Israel *would* sing the Song. Consider some of the "players" who watched anxiously for the moment when the Song would be sung. All of Hashem's creations (including heaven and earth), each in its own fashion, clamored for the day when they would be able to praise Hashem. Only man — and especially Israel — could make that wish possible. The Jews, by singing the Song, fulfilled the universe's fondest wish.

1. *Rashi* (*Taanis* 5b) suggests a somewhat similar concept — Yaakov himself, and not the שְׁבָטִים witnessed קְרִיעַת יַם סוּף.

Indeed, Israel itself, through the long Egyptian oppression, waited for the day when it would be able to speak Hashem's praises openly. At the Sea, the Jews expressed their gratitude not only for the liberation but for everything that had occurred to them, for the difficult days as well as the triumphant one. They realized that their suffering in Egypt was a necessary preliminary to their liberation and therefore they praised Hashem even for Pharaoh's evil designs, as they sang (*Shemos* 15:9), *the foe said, 'I will pursue and overtake them and divide the spoils.'*

(5637, 5647)

Finally, the future tense attests to Israel's primary mission of singing Hashem's praises, as the prophet says (*Yeshayahu* 43:21), עַם־זוּ יָצַרְתִּי לִי תְּהִלָּתִי יְסַפֵּרוּ, *This nation I have created for Me, they will tell My praise.* The Song was the Jews' initiation to their Divine vocation, a precedent-setting experience. As slaves in Egypt their lips were sealed. Henceforth, as the future tense indicates, they *will* achieve their mission of singing Hashem's praises.

אָז־יָשִׁיר מֹשֶׁה וּבְנֵי יִשְׂרָאֵל אֶת־הַשִּׁירָה הַזֹּאת
Then Moshe and the Children of Israel sang [lit. *will sing*] *this song* (*Shemos* 15:1).

The Midrash analyzes every aspect of this opening verse of the Song, starting with the word אָז.

☙ Trust

אֵין אָז אֶלָּא לָשׁוֹן בִּטָּחוֹן שֶׁנֶּאֱמַר „אָז תֵּלֵךְ לָבֶטַח דַּרְכֶּךָ״
The word אָז can only mean trust [in Hashem], as it says: *Then* [if you heed the Torah's teaching] *you will go on your way with trust* (*Mishlei* 3:23).

The Song marked not merely a moment of rare bliss but also the forging of a trusting relationship between Hashem and the Jews. Many battles lay ahead of the people; deadly snakes and scorpions roamed the parched wilderness. Beyond the desert awaited armies determined to thwart their hopes of occupying the Promised Land. As the Midrash informs us, however, the very first word of the Song, אָז, indicates Israel's determination to fight all of Hashem's foes until the day all men accept Hashem's sovereignty. True, the obstacles were many and great, but the people trusted that Hashem would help them prevail over their foes as He had helped them against Pharaoh.

Thus, the Jews' new-found trust in Hashem was shown by their total willingness to enter into battle if necessary. This was in marked contrast to their previous fear of even witnessing the internal battles of the Philistines, as was revealed at the beginning of *Parashas Beshalach* (*Shemos* 13:17), *lest the people have regret upon seeing war.* (5660)

⌁§ Hashem's Throne is Established

אָז יָשִׁיר מֹשֶׁה – הָדָא דִכְתִיב נָכוֹן כִּסְאֲךָ מֵאָז א״ר בֶּרֶכְיָ׳ בְּשֵׁם ר׳ אַבָּהוּ אַע״פ שֶׁמֵעוֹלָם אַתָּה לֹא נִתְיַשֵּׁב כִּסְאֲךָ וְלֹא נוֹדַעְתָּ בְעוֹלָמְךָ עַד שֶׁאָמְרוּ בָנֶיךָ שִׁירָה . . . מָשָׁל לְמֶלֶךְ שֶׁעָשָׂה מִלְחָמָה וְנָצַח וְעָשׂוּ אוֹתוֹ אַגוּסְטוּס אָמְרוּ לוֹ עַד שֶׁלֹּא עָשִׂיתָ הַמִּלְחָמָה הָיִיתָ מֶלֶךְ עַכְשָׁיו אַגוּסְטוּס. מַה יֵּשׁ כָּבוֹד בֵּין הַמֶּלֶךְ וְאַגוּסְטוּס. אֶלָּא שֶׁהַמֶּלֶךְ עוֹמֵד עַל הַלּוּחַ וְאַגוּסְטוּס יוֹשֵׁב. כַּךְ אָמְרוּ יִשְׂרָאֵל. בֶּאֱמֶת עַד שֶׁלֹּא בָרָאתָ עוֹלָמְךָ הָיִיתָ אַתָּה וּמִשֶּׁבָּרָאתָ אוֹתוֹ אַתָּה הוּא אֶלָּא כִּבְיָכוֹל עוֹמֵד שֶׁנֶּאֱמַר עָמַד וַיְמוֹדֵד אָרֶץ אֲבָל מִשֶּׁעָמַדְתָּ בַּיָּם וְאָמַרְנוּ שִׁירָה לְפָנֶיךָ בְּאָז נִתְיַשְּׁבָה מַלְכוּתְךָ וְכִסְאֲךָ נָכוֹן הֱוֵי נָכוֹן כִּסְאֲךָ מֵאָז בְּאָז יָשִׁיר

This is what is written: "Your Throne is henceforth established" (Tehillim 93:2). Rabbi Berechya said in the name of Rabbi Abahu: Even though You are eternal, Your throne was not established, nor were You known in Your world until Your children [the Jewish people] said the Song . . . This is compared to a king who emerged victorious from battle and as a result was coronated emperor. They said to him: Before you fought the battle you were a king; now you are an emperor. What is the distinction between a king and an emperor? A king is portrayed as standing "above" his throne, whereas an emperor is portrayed as sitting [on his throne].

So said the Jewish people: In truth, You [Hashem] are always the same, both before You created the world and since the world was created. But [before the Song] it is as if You were standing, as it says (Habakuk 3:6), "He stood and measured the earth." But once you stood at the Sea [to vanquish the Egyptians] and we sang before You the Song with the word אָז, *Your kingdom became "settled" and Your throne became established, as it says (Tehillim 93:2), "Your throne became established" with the word* אָז, *[when we sang]* אָז יָשִׁיר.

This Midrash perceives the Song as a turning point in the relationship between Hashem and mankind. Prior to the Song, Hashem ruled the universe like a King standing *above* his throne; after the Song He became an Emperor *sitting* on his throne.

What does this mean? Prior to the Exodus, Hashem's presence was known only in Heaven, "above" Hashem's throne. Israel's purpose is to make Hashem's sovereignty known to the world below as well as to the angels in Heaven. As long as they were enslaved in Egypt, however, they could not accomplish this purpose. Only as free men, free to sing Hashem's praises and proclaim His sovereignty, could they "enthrone" Hashem and "seat" Him on His throne in the presence of all mankind. This is what Israel accomplished by beginning the Song with the word אָז.

The Song's impact on mankind is also seen in the use of the word וַיַּאֲמִינוּ, *they caused others to believe*, rather than the simpler form וְהֶאֱמִינוּ, *they believed*. That the Song "enthroned" Hashem is also apparent in its concluding verse: ה׳ יִמְלֹךְ לְעֹלָם וָעֶד, *Hashem will reign forever and ever*. Just as Abraham determined to "coronate" Hashem before mankind, so too the Jewish people at the Sea pledged to proclaim His power to the world. (5662)

However, "coronating" Hashem implies that not only does He rule the heavens but also He controls every minute detail of the daily life of mortals. Before the Song, Hashem was perceived by mankind as "standing," distant and remote from daily concerns. Only at the Splitting of the Sea, when Pharaoh's hordes were drowned and the Jews triumphed against all odds, did humanity realize that all human affairs great and small are under Hashem's command, that He sits on earth as well as stands in Heaven. As the Psalmist sings (113:4-6): רָם עַל כָּל גּוֹיִם ה׳ עַל הַשָּׁמַיִם כְּבוֹדוֹ. מִי כַּה׳ אֱלֹהֵינוּ הַמַּגְבִּיהִי לָשָׁבֶת הַמַּשְׁפִּילִי לִרְאוֹת ... — *Hashem is exalted above all nations, above the heaven is His glory. Who is like Hashem our God, who sits so high, who looks so low ...*

(5631, 5655)

A question remains, however: Why did the proclamation of Hashem's sovereignty have to wait until the Sea? While Israel may not have been able to propagate its ideals while they were in Egypt, why could they not have affirmed Hashem's sovereignty through the miracles of the Exodus? Why did Hashem's "coronation" have to wait another week, until the Splitting of the Sea?

The answer is simple and also helpful in clarifying the nature of

Hashem's sovereignty: No ruler can exist without followers. Hashem was not perceived in His role as Emperor until the Splitting of the Sea because only as a free nation could the Jews accept Hashem as their King. While Egypt still existed, this was not possible.

In this light, the verse on which the above Midrash is based assumes new meaning: ה׳ מָלָךְ גֵּאוּת לָבֵשׁ לָבֵשׁ ה׳ עֹז — *Hashem reigned, He clothed Himself with majesty, girded Himself with strength* (*Tehillim* 93:1). Only when Hashem was coronated by the Jewish people did he gird Himself in majesty. In a world of non-believers, it was unnecessary and inappropriate for Him to assume the mantle of a King. Only when the Jews proclaimed their loyalty at the Sea did He enclothe Himself in regal "vestments," the majesty that was as extrinsic to His essence as clothing is extraneous to the body of a person.

With this new understanding of Hashem's Sovereignty, let us now look at a powerful, if somewhat cryptic, Midrash: כְּבוֹד אֱלֹהִים הַסְתֵּר דָּבָר כְּבוֹד מְלָכִים חֲקוֹר דָּבָר כְּבוֹד אֱלֹהִים הַסְתֵּר דָּבָר עַד „וַיְכֻלּוּ״ כְּבוֹד מְלָכִים חֲקוֹר דָּבָר מִ„וַיְכֻלּוּ״ וְאֵילָךְ — *God's glory is to hide the matter. The glory of monarchs is to investigate the matter. The phrase "Hashem's glory to hide the matter" refers to the story of Creation until "And the heaven and earth were completed" (Bereishis 2:1). "The glory of monarchs is to investigate the matter" refers to the events from "And the heaven and earth] were completed" and beyond.*

This abstruse Midrash actually reveals a fundamental principle of Torah scholarship: No mortal, however great his learning, can investigate Hashem Himself ("The glory of Hashem is to hide the matter"). On the other hand, Hashem's relationship with man, expressed in the phrase "the glory of kings," which is apparent only when man accepts His sovereignty, may be thoroughly investigated. It was only when Adam was created and accepted Hashem's sovereignty that Hashem, so to speak, "entered" a more comprehensible phase in His relationship with man. The first full day of this new phase was Shabbos, when Heaven and earth were complete and man was prepared to pay Hashem full tribute. Thus, Shabbos became a refuge from the concerns of the material world, a time when we can relate again to our Maker, and Hashem's sovereignty "reasserts" itself.

This point is emphasized in the liturgy of Shabbos: יִשְׂמְחוּ בְמַלְכוּתְךָ שׁוֹמְרֵי שַׁבָּת, *Those who observe the Sabbath shall rejoice in Your kingdom*. Let us reinterpret this short phrase in the context of our discussion: On Shabbos, we can rejoice in our understanding of

Hashem's ways, His sovereignty over mortals, a perception normally unattainable during the week when His presence is hidden. For this reason Shabbos is called a "testimony", because then we can clarify Hashem's relationship to us. This is also a reason we read the Torah every Shabbos, to exploit at this special time the most effective means at our disposal to understand Hashem's sovereignty over us, the Holy Torah.

In this light we can better understand why few if any of Hashem's praises were sung (and, indeed, why no songs were chanted) before the Splitting of the Sea. Until then, it would have been presumptuous for mortals to even attempt to sing Hashem's praises, or to reveal His hidden glory. Only after we accepted Hashem's sovereignty at the Sea could we sing the Song and declare His intimate relationship with us.

(5654)

An additional meaning can be gleaned from the Midrash's interpretation of נִתְיַשְּׁבָה כִּסְאֲךָ, that Hashem's throne was established with the term אָז at the beginning of the Song.

Until now, we have emphasized the enhanced awareness of Hashem's presence mankind underwent when the Jews chanted the Song. Now we will expand on this theme by proposing that not only humanity but also the entire universe was "enhanced" by the miracles associated with the Exodus, culminating in the Song. The Mishnah in *Avos* (5:1) implies a strong relationship between the actions of *tzaddikim* and the universe's achievement of its potential:

With ten utterances the world was created [e.g. Hashem created light by saying "Let there be light"]. Indeed, could it not have been created with one utterance? This was to exact punishment from the wicked, who destroy the world that was created with ten utterances, and to bestow goodly reward upon the righteous, who sustain the world that was created by ten utterances.

This Mishnah shows clearly that the purpose of the universe can be accomplished only through the obliteration of the wicked and the vindication of the righteous; this is precisely what occurred for the first time at the Splitting of the Sea. Only then did Hashem's sanctity become apparent on earth, only then did it become clear that the normal conduct of nature is no more than a manifestation of Hashem's stewardship which can be easily overridden at His behest. When the righteous Jews sang their Song as the wicked fell, the purpose of the universe could finally be fulfilled.

The Midrashic expressions *sitting* and *standing* can also be interpreted in this light. As long as Hashem "stood" above the universe, the earth seemed to be subject to immutable laws of nature. Then as the wicked met their end and the righteous prevailed at the Splitting of the Sea, it was shown that the earth was also within Hashem's "supernatural" realm—His throne was established and He, so to speak, "sat" on it.

This concept clarifies an otherwise abstruse passage in the Shabbos prayers: לְאֵל אֲשֶׁר שָׁבַת מִכָּל הַמַּעֲשִׂים בַּיּוֹם הַשְּׁבִיעִי הִתְעַלָּה וְיָשַׁב עַל כִּסֵּא כְבוֹדוֹ, *To God Who rested from all works, Who on the seventh day was elevated and sat on the Throne of His Glory*. On Shabbos Hashem's Presence, which had been "hovering" in Heaven, was finally revealed on earth, as the universe became suffused with sanctity and Hashem sat on His throne.

With this in mind, the relationship between Shabbos and the Exodus becomes considerably clearer. The version of the Ten Commandments in *Parashas VaEschanan* expresses a clear linkage between Shabbos and the Exodus (*Devarim* 5:15): *And you shall remember that you were a slave in the land of Egypt . . . therefore HASHEM, your God, commanded you to do* [i.e. observe] *the Sabbath day*. On the first Shabbos Hashem's Presence could be perceived on earth, but only to to those sophisticated enough to appreciate sanctity. Until the Jewish people was released from Egypt Shabbos lacked a partner. Then, as on the first Shabbos, Hashem's Presence was felt on earth: Hashem *sat* on His throne.

A renowned verse in *Tehillim* also alludes to this theme (22:4): וְאַתָּה קָדוֹשׁ יוֹשֵׁב תְּהִלּוֹת יִשְׂרָאֵל, *You are the Holy One, enthroned upon the praises of Israel.* While Hashem is always sacred, ordinarily He "stands" above the earth. Only when Israel sings Hashem's praises on earth, as in the Song, does He "sit" and make His Presence acutely felt.

Another approach to understanding the distinction between sitting and standing is as follows. The Midrash cited the verse *He stood and measured the earth.* When Hashem is "standing," His power appears to be limited because He leaves the natural order to function normally and does not override it on behalf of His people. When He "sits," however, His presence is perceived so acutely that all previous limitations fall by the wayside. Sitting on earth Hashem will do anything, even perform supernatural feats, for His people Israel. (5647)

An additional interpretation of the phrase *Your throne became established* emerges from the Torah's account of the world's infancy (*Bereishis* 1:2): וְרוּחַ אֱלֹהִים מְרַחֶפֶת עַל פְּנֵי הַמָּיִם, *And the Spirit of God hovered on the face of the waters.* Hashem's original plan was to create a world in which His Presence would be perceived clearly. After Adam sinned, however, He changed His plan and made the majesty of His Presence more distant from His creations. Then, at the moment that Israel sang the Song, the universe returned to the glory of Creation and Hashem's throne was established and returned to its original position of prominence. (5654)

Another interpretation of the phrase *Your throne became established* is suggested by another Midrash (see *Rashi* on *Shemos* 17:16) אֵין כִּסְאוֹ שָׁלֵם עַד שֶׁיִּמְּחֶה זֶרַע שֶׁל עֲמָלֵק, *[HASHEM's] throne will not be complete until the seed of Amalek is obliterated.* As long as Amalek, the arch-enemy of Hashem and Israel, continues to pose a threat, Hashem's throne will not be complete, that is, He does not desire that His Name be revealed. Only at the Splitting of the Sea, when it appeared momentarily that even Amalek had succumbed to Hashem's might could Hashem's throne be completely established and His Majesty fully grace the earth.[1] (5635, 5639)

The phrase נִתְיַשְּׁבָה כִּסְאֲךָ, *Your throne was established,* may be understood also by reference to a Talmudic use of the word יָשׁוּב, meaning to answer questions or to resolve doubts. The Patriarch Abraham first posed the question מִי הוּא בַּעַל הַבִּירָה, *Who is the owner of [i.e. who controls] the palace [this universe]?* While the obvious answer is that Hashem is the owner of the palace, for centuries it was possible for mortals to entertain doubts. Only at the Splitting of the Sea was the question definitively answered: Hashem was indeed the Master of the palace, beyond any shadow of doubt. (5638)

The phrase נִתְיַשְּׁבָה מַלְכוּתְךָ, *Your sovereignty was established,* may also be understood in terms of the concepts of *sitting* and *standing,* as discussed earlier. Prior to the Splitting of the Sea, Hashem was compelled to "stand," to rule the universe from an "erect position" to ensure that mortals would not rebel. Now, however, Hashem's kingdom has been established by His victories in war and He may "sit," that is He no longer has to guard the universe from the threat of rebellion. Even those who appear to deny Hashem's existence most strongly accept His rulership in times of distress (as the saying going, "there are no atheists in foxholes").

---

1. See our comments on the verse, *Then the chieftans of Edom were confounded* (*Shemos* 15:15) at the end of this essay on the Song of the Sea.

The Word אָז — Moshe's Repentence

אָמַר מֹשֶׁה לִפְנֵי הקב״ה יוֹדֵעַ אֲנִי שֶׁחָטָאתִי לְפָנֶיךָ בְּאָז שֶׁנֶּאֱמַר ,,מֵאָז בָּאתִי אֶל פַּרְעֹה״ וַהֲרֵי טָבַעְתָּ אוֹתוֹ בַּיָּם לְכַךְ אֲנִי מְשַׁבֵּחַךָ בְּאָז . . . דֶּרֶךְ הַצַּדִּיקִים בְּמַה שֶּׁהֵם סוֹרְחִים הֵם מְתַקְּנִים כַּךְ מֹשֶׁה לֹא קָנְטֵר אֶלָּא בְּאָז וּבַמָּה שֶּׁסָּרַח תִּיקֵּן מַעֲשָׂיו

Moshe said before Hashem, "I know that I sinned with the word אָז, as it says (*Shemos* 5:23), 'And from when (מֵאָז) *I spoke to Pharaoh' You caused this people to suffer even more. Now that You have sunk Pharaoh in the sea, I will praise You with the word* אָז, *as it says* אָז יָשִׁיר מֹשֶׁה, *'Then Moshe sang . . .' Such is the nature of the righteous, through the very thing with which they sin, they rectify their sin. So too, Moshe provoked Hashem with the word* אָז, *and with that with which he sinned, he rectified his sin.*

This Midrash, far from being a mere play on words, expresses a profound point. When Moshe complained that his demand that Pharaoh release the Jews only aggravated the situation, he certainly did not doubt Hashem's ability to liberate the people. Rather he was asking Hashem to liberate the Jews Himself, rather than through a human agent, who would be subject to the constraints of time and nature. Moshe's question (*Shemos* 3:11), מִי אָנֹכִי כִּי אֵלֵךְ אֶל-פַּרְעֹה, "Who am I that I should go to Pharaoh?" was really intended to remind Hashem of His promise to Jacob (*Bereishis* 46:4), וְאָנֹכִי אַעַלְךָ, "*I* will bring you up."

Hashem, however, wanted to show that even events within the domain of time and nature could have an effect on the worlds above nature, and therefore insisted on making Moshe His agent to liberate the Jews. By beginning the Song with the word אָז, *then,* Moshe rectified his earlier error and admitted that even events which were *then,* at a specific point in time, such as the Splitting of the Sea, could ascend to sing Hashem's praise in worlds far above nature and time.

Only after Moshe's efforts to initiate the process of liberation were constantly frustrated by Pharaoh, did Hashem conclude the process at the Sea. (5632)

The Midrash also notes the unprecedented nature of the Song:

הַדָא דִכְתִיב „פִּיהָ פָּתְחָה בְחָכְמָה וְתוֹרַת־חֶסֶד עַל־לְשׁוֹנָהּ״. מִיּוֹם שֶׁבָּרָא הקב״ה אֶת הָעוֹלָם וְעַד שֶׁעָמְדוּ יִשְׂרָאֵל עַל הַיָּם לֹא מָצִינוּ אָדָם שֶׁאָמַר שִׁירָה לְהקב״ה אֶלָּא יִשְׂרָאֵל . . . הֵצִיל אַבְרָהָם מִכִּבְשַׁן הָאֵשׁ וּמִן הַמְּלָכִים וְלֹא אָמַר שִׁירָה וְכֵן יִצְחָק מִן הַמַּאֲכֶלֶת וְלֹא אָמַר שִׁירָה וְכֵן יַעֲקֹב מִן הַמַּלְאָךְ וּמִן עֵשָׂו וּמִן אַנְשֵׁי שְׁכֶם וְלֹא אָמַר שִׁירָה. כֵּיוָן שֶׁבָּאוּ יִשְׂרָאֵל לַיָּם וְנִקְרַע לָהֶם מִיַּד אָמְרוּ שִׁירָה לִפְנֵי הקב״ה שֶׁנֶּאֱמַר „אָז יָשִׁיר מֹשֶׁה״

This is what is written (Mishlei 31:26), "She opens her mouth with wisdom, and the Torah of kindness is on her tongue." From the day that Hashem created the world until Israel stood at the Sea, we do not find that anyone said a song to Hashem except the Jewish people . . . He saved Abraham from the furnace and from the [four] kings and he did not say a song. Likewise, Isaac was saved from the knife and he did not say a song. Jacob, too, was saved from [Esau's] angel, and from Esau, and from the people of Shechem [who had abducted Dinah] and he did not say a song. When Israel came to the Sea and it split for them, they immediately sang a song before Hashem.

An obvious question arises: The Song at the Sea was certainly not the first time that anyone sang a song of praise to Hashem. Adam, for example, praised Hashem when he was created. Likewise, the Jews chanted parts of *Hallel* on the night of the Exodus.

Upon closer examination, however, the true intent of the Midrash becomes apparent. It does not say that no one ever sang a song, but rather "we do not *find* anyone that sang a song" — individuals may have sung songs praising Hashem but they were not incorporated into the Torah. The Song at the Sea is the first one that was written into the Torah. In this light, the end of the Song's introduction, וַיֹּאמְרוּ לֵאמֹר, *they said in order to say,* (*and they said the following*) takes on new meaning. This song was said at the time in order to be repeated by future generations of Jews; every day when a Jew repeats the Song, he finds new meaning and inspiration in it. This is what the Midrash meant by citing *the Torah of kindness is on her tongue*—the Jews responded to Hashem's kindness by making their song part of the Torah.

Furthermore, this Song marked the first time that an entire nation sang Hashem's praises. Previous songs had been sung by individuals —

Adam, Abraham, Isaac, or the numerous *individual* Jews who sang in their homes on the night of the Exodus — but until the Splitting of the Sea never had an entire community sung together. (5644)

But what is the significance of the Midrash's opening phrase, "she opens her mouth in wisdom"? Rabbi Simcha Bunim of Pshischa (a prominent Chassidic thinker of the early Nineteenth Century) said that while most great works can be appreciated only in their entirety, the greatness of this Song can be discerned even from its very first words. The very word אָז is laden with great significance.

Perhaps the Midrash means to suggest that it was "wise and noble thoughts" that enabled the Jewish people to "open their mouths" to sing the Song. Only because Hashem rewarded the Jews for their fervent desire to praise Him by "opening" their mouth could hundreds of thousands of individuals sing this great song simultaneously. (5640)

Finally, by citing this verse the Midrash may also be alluding to the willing nature of the song. Unlike the anguished cry the Jews sounded when they saw the Egyptian army pursuing them, the Song emerged in spontaneous joy: "She [Israel] *opened* her mouth in song; the Torah of kindness on her tongue." Israel's Song was an act of kindness on her part, done of her own volition.

It was the Patriarch Isaac who first noted the power of Jewish prayer in the phrase *Bereishis 27:22* הַקֹּל קוֹל יַעֲקֹב, *the voice is the voice of Jacob*. The double expression הַקֹּל קוֹל suggests the dual nature of prayer: Sometimes a Jew's prayer emerges from the depths of his suffering, while at other times he is infused with the "Torah of kindness," and simply bursts forth in joyous song to thank Hashem for His many kindnesses. (5653)

מֹשֶׁה וּבְנֵי יִשְׂרָאֵל

Moshe and the Children of Israel (15:1)

The Song marks an important phase in the status of the Jewish people as Hashem's Chosen People. Prior to the Splitting of the Sea, singing Hashem's praises had no special connection to Israel or to *Eretz Yisrael*. Anyone could sing in any location. From the time of the Song however, the Jewish people assumed a special mission of praising Hashem that overshadowed the efforts of the other nations. Similarly, once they took possession of *Eretz Yisrael*, that became the optimal location for expressing Hashem's praise.[1] Thus Hashem selected the ideal people, the best location, and the most suitable time for His praises to be sung.[2] (5659)

אֶת־הַשִּׁירָה הַזֹּאת

'This' song (15:1).

The word הַזֹּאת, *this*, implying that the song had been composed previously, adds force to the assertion we made earlier that the Song (in some rarified spiritual fashion) was already present in Heaven. Israel succeeded in transplanting the Song to earth by virtue of its fervent desire to sing what had been a Divine song. (5644)

וַיֹּאמְרוּ לֵאמֹר

And they said saying (15:1).

The Midrash interprets this apparent redundancy as a reference to future generations. The Song of the Sea was only the first of many songs Israel would sing in fulfillment of its historic mission described by the prophet Yeshayahu, as we have seen above. Indeed, the Song itself attains additional meaning with each generation of Jews. The word לֵאמֹר, then implies that Moshe and his generation incorporated the Song and its message as a permanent part of Israel's heritage.

We said above that many of Israel's more esoteric thoughts could not be articulated at the Splitting of the Sea and had to be deferred until the Resurrection. In this light the Sages' expression לֵאמֹר לַדּוֹרוֹת takes on new meaning. Each generation adds to the Song incrementally, until it reaches a climactic completion at the culmination of history — the final Resurrection.

With this in mind, we can better understand the significance of the universal custom of reciting the Song daily. Each day it takes on a new meaning, greater than its meaning of the day before, as we come one day closer to the fulfillment of its — and our — mission. Moreover, the thoughts and emotions of Jews who recite the Song are necessary to its development, a process that began at the Sea and will culminate with the Resurrection. Thus it is fitting that the word *shir* is used in Mishnaic

---

1. Thus the singing of *Hallel* was instituted to commemorate the miracle of Chanukah, which occurred in *Eretz Yisrael*, but not for Purim, which occurred *chutz la'aretz*.

2. See the overall Introduction to the Festivals for further discussion of this theme, based on the principles of עוֹלָם (ideal geographical locations) שָׁנָה (most conducive time of year) and נֶפֶשׁ (select individuals or nation to fulfill the Divine mission).

Hebrew to mean "chain."[1] וְכָל בַּעֲלֵי הַשֵּׁיר יוֹצְאִים בְּשֵׁיר, *And all that wear a neck chain may go out with a neck chain.* The Song is a chain, first started by the generation of the Exodus with additional links contributed by devout Jews in every generation. (5640, 5645)

אָשִׁירָה לַה׳ כִּי גָאֹה גָּאָה

I shall sing to HASHEM for He is exalted above the arrogant. (15:1)

Rashi offers several explanations for the repetition of the word גָּאָה. We shall discuss the concept of Hashem's "highness" in the light of *Rashi*'s insights, as well as several original interpretations. כָּל הַשִּׁירָה תִּמְצָא כְּפוּלָה, עָזִּי וְזִמְרָת יָהּ וַיְהִי לִי לִישׁוּעָה, ה׳ אִישׁ מִלְחָמָה ה׳ שְׁמוֹ וְכֵן כּוּלָם — *In the entire song you will find double expressions, such as 'my strength and my song is HASHEM and He was my salvation,' 'HASHEM is a man of war, HASHEM is His name,' and similarly with all the others.*

Rashi is not merely noting a stylistic tendency of the Song, but rather is telling us about a double triumph that occurred at the Sea. As we noted in the essay on the Prelude to the Song (on the words וְהִנֵּה מִצְרַיִם נֹסֵעַ אַחֲרֵיהֶם, *and behold, Egypt was journeying after them*, 14:10), Hashem's primary battle was waged against Egypt's angel. The defeat of the Egyptian forces was secondary to this. The use of doubled phrases throughout the Song alludes to these two aspects of the battle.

Also, the word שִׁירָה, *song*, suggests the word יָשָׁר, *to straighten*, implying that the Song balances between a person's conduct on earth and the demands of his soul bestowed upon him from Heaven. Hopefully by reciting the Song every day, we help to elevate and sanctify our bodies' physical needs to subordinate them to our souls' craving for spirituality. (5659)

Rashi continues: דָּבָר אַחֵר עַל כָּל הַשִּׁירוֹת וְכָל מַה שֶּׁאֲקַלֵּס בּוֹ עוֹד יֵשׁ בּוֹ תּוֹסֶפֶת — *Above all the praises and everything with which I praise Him, there is still more to Him,* more than I can possibly grasp, much less articulate into praises. For this reason the Jews were afraid even to attempt to sing Hashem's praises, since it was impossible to sing them all. Their fear was resolved when, as the *Rashi* we cited above says, "it came in their hearts to sing." From this we learn that, however great is our fear of Hashem, we should always let the joy of our love for Him overcome our fear and arouse us to sing His praises. However high He

---

1. See the Mishnah (*Shabbos* 5:1).

is above His creation, He is still close to His people and desires our praises.

Why is it so important that Israel praise Hashem on a continual basis? Hashem certainly does not need man's praises. We can say, however, that the Jewish people praises Hashem not for His sake, but rather to give the world, and in particular the wicked who claim that Hashem pays no attention to His creations, a vivid demonstration of His interest in world Jewry. Thus, Israel's continuous praise attests to Hashem's permanent bond with the Jewish people. Really this verse should be interpreted: "I sing to Hashem to demonstrate how close He is to me, in spite of His elevated status." (5642)

Rashi also refers us to the translation of *Onkelos*: אֲרֵי מִתְגָּאֵי עַל גֵּוְתָנַיָּא וְגֵאוּתָא דִּילֵהּ הִיא — *Because He is high over the haughty and highness is His*. The intent of this is that all haughtiness — even the arrogance of the wicked and certainly the power and prestige of the righteous — stem from Hashem. While a *tzaddik* always attributes his high position to his Maker, the wicked who pursue power are also instruments of the Divine Will. Hashem elevates evildoers to positions of great prestige so that, when they fall from their lofty heights His Name will be sanctified. (5632)

This *Onkelos* — *Hashem is high over the haughty* — also alludes to Hashem's battle with Egypt's angel. Unlike mortal rulers who try to weaken their foes before engaging them in battle, Hashem elevated the Egyptians — even allowing their angel to intercede on their behalf — to make their eventual downfall even more precipitous and a greater glorification of His Name. Not only the Egyptian armies on earth but also their mentor in Heaven met their end at Hashem's hands.

In this light, we can understand the verse, סוּס וְרֹכְבוֹ רָמָה בַיָּם, *the horse and its rider were thrust into the Sea*, as a reference to the power that propelled the Egyptian army, their angel that rode in Heaven. (5645)

In a similar vein, the double expression גָאֹה גָּאָה may refer to the unique nature of Hashem's high position. The haughtiness of humans has meaning only insofar as it demonstrates Hashem's grandeur, whereas Hashem's loftiness exists entirely for its own sake. Thus Hashem elevates the wicked to high positions only to make their eventual downfall a more striking demonstration of His power. When the righteous receive honors, they are so overwhelmed by Hashem's loftiness that they acknowledge His greatness even more. In contrast

Hashem's honor and glory exist in and of themselves, and are not dependent on any other end or purpose.

The expression גָאֹה גָּאָה also conveys the uniqueness of Hashem's grandeur which is totally beyond comparison to human haughtiness. Had the word גָּאָה appeared only once, it would have implied merely that Hashem's high position is quantitatively superior to the power and prestige of mortals. The double expression, however, indicates that there is no basis for comparison with anything else. Hashem's greatness is radically different from any attributes that pertain to mortals. (5631)

Alternatively, the double expression suggests that Hashem's greatness is, so to speak, enhanced by Israel's high position, or rather by the fact that the higher He raises them, the more they humble themselves to Him. This loftiness, arising from the greatness of those who lower themselves before Him, is the truest kind because it comes from the willing submission of loyal subjects, rather than the humiliation of a vanquished opponent. (5634)

Finally, the double expression teaches that Hashem granted the Jewish people power and prestige in order to give the rest of mankind some grasp of His exalted position. It is difficult for mortals even to imagine Hashem's glory. By raising one nation up, Hashem gave everyone else a glimpse of His grandeur. In this approach, the phrase *I will sing to HASHEM for He is surely exalted*, can be paraphrased: "I sing to Hashem for giving me the opportunity to exhibit His greatness through my own high position." The similarity between the words שִׁירָה, *song*, and יָשָׁר, *straighten*, that we mentioned earlier here suggests that humanity's moral conduct was "straightened out" by Israel's liberation. (5635)

עָזִּי וְזִמְרָת יָהּ וַיְהִי־לִי לִישׁוּעָה

My strength and my praise is God and He was for me a salvation (15:2).

The term *my strength* in this verse alludes to the Torah, as we find in the verse (*Tehillim* 29:11), ה׳ עֹז לְעַמּוֹ יִתֵּן, *HASHEM will give strength to His nation*. Likewise the term *my song* alludes to prayer. Thus this verse is an acknowledgment by Israel that its salvation depends on its embracing the Torah and offering continual prayers. (5643)

זֶה אֵלִי

This is my God (15:2).

As we have said, these words mark a radical transformation just completed by the Jewish people. Moments before, many of them were crying to return to Egypt. Now, they became not only totally loyal to Hashem, but also sensed an intense intimacy with Him, greater than that achieved by any of the prophets. Indeed, the greatest aspect of the Splitting of the Sea was the "tearing" of the Jewish heart, an act even more impressive than the parting of the sea itself.

This insight gives us a new understanding of the future tense of the word יָשִׁיר, *will sing*. As Israel's true personality emerged, it realized that not only did it want to sing to Hashem then, it always *will* want to sing His praises. (5632, 5633)

Equally significant, by proclaiming, *This is my God*, the Jews finally attributed the miracles they experienced in Egypt to Hashem. Possibly it was the medium of song that brought them to this realization. Mere talk about liberation somehow did not arouse sufficient awareness of Hashem's role in the events they had seen and it took a song to forge an emotional connection with their Maker.

There is a parallel between Israel's reaching to Hashem through the song and the role played by King David's Psalms in drawing the people closer to Hashem. While the Patriarchs laid the foundations of the Jewish nation and it was in their merit that the Exodus occurred, nonetheless, it was through the songs of King David that the Jewish people was able internalize the teachings of the Patriarchs and to *retain* them permanently.

This, then, was the fulfillment of the promise Hashem had made after Moshe's first confrontation with Pharaoh (*Shemos* 6:7), *I will take you to Me for a people and I will be for you a God, and you shall know that I am HASHEM, your God, who takes you out from beneath the burdens of Egypt*. Now, as the Jews watched the Egyptians drowning, they could truly proclaim, *This is my God and I will glorify Him!*

The following Midrash (*Midrash Rabbah* 23:15) gives a better insight into the scope of Israel's vision at the Sea:

אָמַר רַבִּי בְּרֶכְיָ׳ בֹּא וּרְאֵה כַּמָּה גְדוֹלִים יוֹרְדֵי הַיָּם מֹשֶׁה כַּמָּה נִתְחַבֵּט וְנִתְחַנֵּן לִפְנֵי הַמָּקוֹם עַד שֶׁרָאָה אֶת הַדְּמוּת שֶׁנֶּאֱמַר הַרְאֵנִי נָא אֶת כְּבוֹדֶךָ. . .

וְעוֹלֵי הַיָּם כָּל אֶחָד וְאֶחָד מַרְאֶה בְאֶצְבָּעוֹ וְאוֹמֵר זֶה אֵלִי וְאַנְוֵהוּ.

Rabbi Berechya said, "Come and see how great were those who entered [plunged] into the Sea. Moshe had to prostrate himself and beseech God in order to perceive God's likeness, as it says (Shemos 33:18) 'Show me your Countenance' "

Everyone who entered [plunged] into the Sea could point with his finger and say "This is my God and I will glorify Him."

If the Midrash equates Moshe's plea to perceive Hashem's countenance to the Jews' vision at the Sea, we can appreciate the clarity with which our forefathers perceived Hashem. (5631)

וְאַנְוֵהוּ

I will glorify Him.

The Talmud interprets (*Shabbos* 133b) this expression as follows: אֶתְנָאֶה לְפָנָיו בְּמִצְוֹת, *I will adorn myself in His presence with mitzvos.*

A question arises: If the Talmud interprets this verse to mean that Israel will observe *mitzvos*, why does it not say explicitly, "I will observe *mitzvos*"? The indirect phrase, *I will adorn myself with mitzvos*, however, implies a more esoteric and powerful concept — that the Jewish body makes itself into a repository for the soul through the observance of *mitzvos*.

We see this also in the correspondence between the two hundred forty-eight positive commandments and the two hundred forty-eight limbs of the body. Thus, the phrase *I will adorn myself with mitzvos* implies that we sanctify our bodies by observing the *mitzvos*. In the *Mussaf* prayer of Festivals we make a request using the same word נָוֶה, which can mean either *dwelling* or *beauty*: וְהָשֵׁב יִשְׂרָאֵל לִנְוֵיהֶם, *return Israel to their dwellings*. In the context of our discussion, we can understand this not only as a request to return to our actual physical dwellings, but also to our spiritual dwellings, the fibers of the soul, which we have beautified and sanctified through the performance of *mitzvos*.

The Midrash interprets the word וְאַנְוֵהוּ as a plea to witness the building of the *Beis HaMikdash*. We can reconcile this explanation with that of the Talmud as follows: Before the sin of the Golden Calf the body of every Jew was a miniature *Beis HaMikdash*, which one could make into a dwelling for Hashem's Presence by adorning oneself with *mitzvos*. The brush with idolatry, however ruptured this direct connection and made it necessary to build the *Mishkan* (Tabernacle) as a physical setting for Hashem's Presence, to ensure Israel's survival." (5643, 5646)

A simpler interpretation of the word וְאַנְוֵהוּ sees it as a request: Moshe and the Jewish people beseech Hashem for the opportunity to make Him beautiful. Yet how can mortals hope to adorn the Almighty? The answer is both simple and stark: In the normal course of things, it is impossible for human's to "adorn" Hashem; and even difficult to conceive what that might mean. Presumptuous as this wish was, however, because they wanted so sincerely to adorn Hashem, He granted their request, as He proclaims through the prophet *Yeshayahu* (49:3), יִשְׂרָאֵל אֲשֶׁר בְּךָ אֶתְפָּאָר, *Israel, I pride Myself in you.*

No wish of the Jewish people, no matter how improbable, is beyond Hashem's ability to fulfill. We need only to desire to serve Him with all our hearts. (5647)

יְמִינְךָ ה׳ נֶאְדָּרִי בַּכֹּחַ יְמִינְךָ ה׳ תִּרְעַץ אוֹיֵב

Your right hand, HASHEM, is adorned with strength; Your right hand, HASHEM, smashes the enemy (15:6).

Rashi comments on this verse: שְׁנֵי פְּעָמִים כְּשֶׁיִּשְׂרָאֵל עוֹשִׂין רְצוֹנוֹ שֶׁל מָקוֹם הַשְּׂמֹאל נַעֲשֵׂית יָמִין — *[The word for 'Your right hand' is written] twice to teach that when Israel fulfills Hashem's will, even His left hand becomes a right hand.*

The terms right and left hand are obviously not to be understood literally in speaking of Hashem. Instead *Rashi* is referring to angels of the "right" who proclaim Israel's merits, and those of the "left" who indict the Jews for their faults (cf. *I Melachim* 22:19, *Rashi* s.v. מימינו). When Israel does Hashem's will, even its accusers speak its praises.

In fact, the only purpose of prosecuting angels is to humble the wicked. When people emulate the "left" by dredging up each others' faults, then even "right" angels, who are normally advocates turn to the left and accuse them.

While it may sometimes appear that the "left" is prevailing, whatever suffering it causes is merely a prelude to the great liberation that lies ahead. As the prophet Yirmiyahu wrote describing the long period of exile, הֵשִׁיב אָחוֹר יְמִינוֹ, *He turned back His right hand* (*Eichah* 2:3). After we are liberated, however we will realize that all the anguish of the exile was necessary to bring our eventual redemption and the arrival of *Moshiach*.[1] (5652)

אֱלֹהֵי אָבִי וַאֲרֹמְמֶנְהוּ

The God of my father and I will exalt Him (15:2).

Immediately after Israel proclaims its desire to adorn Hashem, it tempers this statement by voicing a determination to elevate Him as well. "Adorning" Hashem, developing an intimate relationship with Him, does not in any sense "lower" Him to the level of mankind. On the contrary, the closer Hashem draws us to Him, the more we can perceive His sanctity and the more exalted He becomes in our eyes. Hashem's Presence is felt everywhere at all times, and even so He is exalted above all His creations. (5647)

The Torah does not say וַאֲרֹמְמֵהוּ, *I will raise Him*, because it would be impudent for a mortal to suggest that he has the power to "raise" Hashem. Instead, it says וַאֲרֹמְמֶנְהוּ, which may be understood as a combination of the two words וַאֲרוֹמֵם מִמֶּנוּ, *I will be raised through association with Him*. Out of His love for the Jews, Hashem allows them to perceive His sanctity even in the material world. A Jew grows in a spiritual sense by drawing closer to Hashem, and in turn comes to appreciate Him on an even higher level. In this sense, the word וַאֲרֹמְמֶנְהוּ implies also that we will appreciate Him on a loftier level. (5653)

וּבְרֹב גְּאוֹנְךָ תַּהֲרֹס קָמֶיךָ

In Your abundant grandeur You shatter Your opponents (15:7).

Rashi comments on this verse, מִי הֵם הַקָּמִים כְּנֶגְדּוֹ אֵלּוּ הַקָּמִים עַל יִשְׂרָאֵל — *Who are those who arise against You? The ones who arise against Israel*. Even though it would be arrogant of any other nation to claim that its enemies are Hashem's enemies, it was entirely appropriate for Israel to say so at the Splitting of the Sea, when their sole desire was to serve Him. Physical torture and mental oppression mattered nothing to them unless such suffering interfered with Divine service. Such a selfless people — lacking any identity of its own — could genuinely claim that its enemies were also Hashem's foes.

Additionally, in this verse Israel proclaims the utter *impossibility* of

1. In this context, see also our commentary on the verse *Israel saw the great hand that* H*ASHEM inflicted upon Egypt* in the essay on the Prelude to the Splitting of the Sea.

any tyrant ever rebelling against Hashem. The Jews reasoned that the only rationale for the existence of Hashem's enemies must be for Israel's ultimate benefit. Therefore, when those who profess to be Hashem's enemies threaten us there is no reason to succumb, or even to weaken in our resolve against them. Instead, we need only strengthen our commitment to do Hashem's will in order to win an even greater reward for ourselves. Thus it is correct to conclude that Hashem's self-styled opponents exist only for the purpose of testing Israel's resolve, and ultimately of increasing Israel's reward. (5644)

אָמַר אוֹיֵב אֶרְדֹּף אַשִּׂיג אֲחַלֵּק שָׁלָל

The enemy declared: 'I will pursue, I will overtake, I will divide plunder' (15:9).

Endowed with the *Ruach HaKodesh* that inspired the Song, the Jews could read their enemies' minds. The question arises, however, why mention the enemy's strategies and intentions in the Song, which is primarily a praise of Hashem. We can say that there was an interplay between Egypt's grandiose plans and Israel's salvation. While Pharaoh boasted to his army how he would vanquish the Jews, Hashem deflated his bravado not merely by defeating him but by totally routing all of his forces. Pharaoh's boasting only built up Israel's name in the world, as his promises to his troops were all turned against them. In the end the Jews *pursued* the Egyptians, *overtook* them, and *divided their plunder.* (5639)

Thus, the Jews mentioned Pharaoh's diabolical design in order to thank Hashem not only for their victory, but even for Pharaoh's enmity. Now they could see that, bitter as it was, the Egyptian exile was a build-up to the great miracles that would be done for them later.[1] This is another implication of the word אָז, *then*: After experiencing the exile and the Splitting of the Sea, Israel was prepared to praise Hashem for *everything* they had experienced, even the suffering. (5642)

There is another question on this verse: Why is it placed in the middle of the Song? Chronologically the Song should start with a statement of Pharaoh's intentions, and afterwards give Hashem due praise for thwarting those intentions.

If the purpose of the Song were merely to thank Hashem for

1. This topic is discussed further in the commentary on the verse *Israel saw the great hand . . . and they believed in HASHEM* in the essay on the Introduction to the Song.

liberation it would have been appropriate to mention Pharaoh's designs at the beginning. The main theme of the Song, however, is the close connection that developed between Hashem and His people at the Sea. As the Sages said (*Bereishis Rabbah* 55:11) : אַהֲבָה מְקַלְקֶלֶת אֶת הַשּׁוּרָה, *Love corrupts [supersedes] the accustomed order.* After experiencing the heady feeling engendered by that closeness, the natural, chronological order did not matter to the Jews. Determined to share its newfound relationship with all mankind, they hoped that the Song would bring the rest of the world to share their ideals and convictions, and their love for Hashem.

It was therefore appropriate to start the Song *I shall sing to HASHEM for He is exalted above the arrogant*, placing Hashem's creatures before their own salvation. As the Midrash says, love supersedes the natural order and someone in love praises his loved one's virtues before thinking of his own needs. Thus Israel began the Song with praise of its beloved God, and only then mentioned its salvation. (5635)

מִי כָמֹכָה בָּאֵלִם ה׳ מִי כָּמֹכָה נֶאְדָּר בַּקֹּדֶשׁ נוֹרָא תְהִלֹּת עֹשֵׂה פֶלֶא
Who is like You among the heavenly powers, HASHEM! Who is like You, mighty in holiness, too awesome for praise, doing wonders (15:11).

The Talmud (*Gittin* 56b) reinterprets the beginning of this verse by adding one letter: מִי כָּמֹכָה בָּאִלְּמִים, *who is like You among the mute.* What is the significance of this change? In what way may Hashem be considered mute?

We can say, however, that this slight change makes a significant statement about Hashem's stewardship of the universe. Even though Hashem's rulership of the world is sometimes evident in the miracles He performs, as the verse ends, *doing wonders,* such deviations from the natural order of the world are rare and exceptional. Exceptional as they are, Hashem's miracles are testimony that all physical phenomena, those we call "natural" as well as the supernatural, are His doing. Just as Hashem can radically change the fundamental order of the universe, He can accomplish His purposes while conducting it on a "normal" basis as well.

It is in this sense that the Talmud calls Hashem mute: Although most of the time He conceals His actions in the mantle of "nature" and may not appear to answer our prayers immediately, He is always active behind the scenes. And the proof of this is that He sometimes "does wonders." At all times, however, we must continually ask, "Who is like You?" (5647)

The Midrash (*Mechilta Beshalach* 8) notes that the Song does not say that Hashem did wonders but rather that He *does* wonders. In this statement, the Jews at the Sea (and we who repeat their words every day) fulfill the mission Hashem gave us, as expressed by the prophet *Yeshayahu* (43:21), עַם־זוּ יָצַרְתִּי לִי תְּהִלָּתִי יְסַפֵּרוּ , *I created this nation for they will tell My praise.*

All life consists of miracles, though we do not always recognize their existence; as long as they were enslaved, the Jews could not appreciate Hashem's *daily* miracles. A major effect of the Exodus was to give the Jewish people the sensitivity to recognize Hashem's ongoing and unceasing miracles.

In this light Hashem's promise through the prophet Michah (7:15), כִּימֵי צֵאתְךָ מֵאֶרֶץ מִצְרָיִם אַרְאֶנּוּ נִפְלָאוֹת, *As in the days you left Egypt, I will show you wonders*, takes on new meaning. Although the world is always suffused with wondrous deeds, it is only at extraordinary moments of Jewish history that we are given the ability to see and appreciate these hidden miracles, as the Psalmist pleads (119:18), גַּל עֵינַי וְאַבִּיטָה נִפְלָאוֹת, *Unveil my eyes that I may perceive wonders.*

Let us now reconsider each fragment of our verse: *Who is like You among the heavenly powers, HASHEM!* This refers to the physical bodies of living creatures, which are created by Hashem and continually draw life force from Him. *Who is like You, mighty in holiness.* Hashem also created a sacred component in every mortal, a soul which is "mighty in holiness," separated from the body by its holiness. עֹשֵׂה פֶלֶא, *doing wonders*, *Rema*, (*Orach Chaim* 6:1) in his commentary on the blessing *Asher Yatzar*, observes that one of Hashem's greatest wonders is the maintenance of body and soul together in one entity.

(5631, 5647, 5658)

אָז נִבְהֲלוּ אַלּוּפֵי אֱדוֹם

Then the chieftains of Edom [Esau] were confounded (15:15).

How could the Jews at that time know how Esau reacted to the Splitting of the Sea? In *Parashas Haazinu* (*Devarim* 32:8, and *Rashi* there) Moshe says that Hashem established the boundaries of the seventy nations of the world to correspond to Jacob's seventy offspring who went down to Egypt. We see from this that the nations were created to oppose Israel's service of Hashem. When their power to do so was weakened, the sensitive Jewish soul, whose only purpose is to serve Hashem, instinctively felt relieved.

Actually, as we discuss above, the Jews had hoped that the Song would inspire the whole world to submit to Hashem's greatness; and were it not for the wickedness of Esau's descendant Amalek, their hope might have been realized. Alas, Amalek's confusion was only temporary, and very soon afterwards he regrouped and attacked Israel with full force, in spite of the clear lesson learned by the world when Hashem destroyed the Egyptian army in the Sea. It is no wonder that the Torah says of Amalek that "he did not fear God" (*Devarim* 25:18). (5638)

תִּפֹּל עֲלֵיהֶם אֵימָתָה וָפַחַד

Let fear and dread befall them (15:16).

What is the meaning of this seemingly redundant expression, *fear and dread*? We can understand it, however, in light of our earlier assertion that Hashem's primary battle was against Egypt's angel, and only secondarily against Egypt itself. Thus *Rashi* comments, "Fear on those who are far" the angels in Heaven who are close to Hashem, "and dread on those who are close," the Egyptians on earth who feel instinctively when their angel was afraid. (5659)

תְּבִאֵמוֹ וְתִטָּעֵמוֹ בְּהַר נַחֲלָתְךָ . . . מִקְּדָשׁ ה׳ כּוֹנְנוּ יָדֶיךָ

You shall bring them and implant on the mount of Your heritage ... the Sanctuary, my Lord, that Your hands established (15:17).

Moshe beseeches Hashem to bring the Jews to the Promised Land — the mountain of Your inheritance — and then refers to the *Beis HaMikdash*. While it is not immediately apparent what connection these future events have to the Splitting of the Sea, we will see that they are closely related. The Jews' later ability to occupy *Eretz Yisrael* and to build the *Beis HaMikdash* had its origins in the Splitting of the Sea and the Song, as the prophet Yeshayahu hints (51:16), וָאָשִׂים דְּבָרַי בְּפִיךָ וּבְצֵל יָדִי כִּסִּיתִיךָ לִנְטֹעַ שָׁמַיִם וְלִיסֹד אָרֶץ, *And I placed My words in your mouth* [when Israel sang the Song], *and I covered you with the shadow of My hand* [the heavenly cloud hovering over the Jews] *to plant heaven* [to receive the Torah given from heaven] *and to establish the earth* [entering the Land and building the *Beis HaMikdash*].

This description implies that at the same time that Hashem inspired the Jews to sing the Song, He also gave them permission to enter the Land and erect the *Beis HaMikdash*. Thus at the end of the Song, Moshe asks Hashem to allow the people to fulfill the remainder of their potential just as they had realized the first part of it. (5645)

ה׳ יִמְלֹךְ לְעֹלָם וָעֶד . . . כִּי בָא סוּס פַּרְעֹה
HASHEM shall reign for all eternity ... when Pharaoh's cavalry came [into the Sea] (15:18,19).

In one sense, the phrase *when Pharaoh's cavalry came* can be seen as a summation of the entire Song, which was sung upon seeing the Egyptians drowning in the Sea. In another sense, however, its position immediately following the declaration of Hashem's eternal sovereignty indicates that Pharaoh's downfall was a prerequisite for mankind's acceptance of Hashem's Kingship. By proclaiming *Hashem shall reign!* the Jews were following in the footsteps of Abraham, who resolved to announce Hashem's majesty to the whole world.

The Midrash (*Yalkut* 253) notes that had the Jews said ה׳ מֶלֶךְ, *Hashem reigns* in the present tense rather than the future, no nation would have been able to conquer them. Why, then, did they not do so?

In answer, we can say that the Jews at the Sea had a dream that all mankind would join them in acknowledging Hashem's sovereignty, as the prophet Zechariah foretells (14:9), וְהָיָה ה׳ לְמֶלֶךְ עַל כָּל הָאָרֶץ בַּיּוֹם הַהוּא יִהְיֶה ה׳ אֶחָד וּשְׁמוֹ אֶחָד, *Then HASHEM will be King over all the world, on that day HASHEM will be One and His Name will be One.* They knew that proclaiming Hashem's sovereignty in the present tense, while it would have made them invulnerable to the nations, would also have denied the world the opportunity to accept Hashem's Kingship of their own free will. Therefore they willingly accepted a secondary status in the world in order to leave a possibility open for the nations to be exposed to the Torah and come embrace Hashem on their own.

(5640, 5645)

This was the Jews' rationale for deferring Hashem's kingdom into the future. On the other hand, had Israel proclaimed ה׳ מֶלֶךְ, *Hashem reigns now*, this by itself would have completed the perfection of their souls, which in turn would have influenced the entire Gentile world to embrace Hashem. Thus, they would have refrained from attacking Israel, as the Sages said, not so much out of fear of Israel as because they would have totally accepted Hashem's sovereignty on themselves.

(5654)

וַיַּסַּע מֹשֶׁה אֶת־יִשְׂרָאֵל מִיַּם סוּף

Moshe caused the Children of Israel to journey from the Sea of Reeds.[1]

We will conclude this essay on the Song with some insights on those who sang Hashem's praises and those who chose not to sing.

The Talmud (*Kesubos* 7b) notes that even the fetuses in their mothers' wombs sang the Song: מִנַּיִן שֶׁאֲפִילוּ עֻבָּרִים שֶׁבִּמְעֵי אִמּוֹ אָמְרוּ שִׁירָה עַל הַיָּם שֶׁנֶּאֱמַר בְּמַקְהֵלוֹת בָּרְכוּ אֱלֹהִים ה׳ מִמְּקוֹר יִשְׂרָאֵל — *From where does one know that even the fetuses in their mother's womb said the Song at the Sea as it says, (Tehillim 68:27) "In congregations bless God," HASHEM [should be blessed] from Israel's womb.*

Perhaps the reference to "fetuses" actually means future generations. While the Song was said by Moshe's generation, in reality every generation — all Jews — to be born in the future — had a stake in the Song. In the same manner that a fetus lies dormant in its mother's womb waiting to emerge, so too the sentiments of future generations are all included in the Song. Each day we repeat the Song, new sentiments, and a new level of purity, is revealed, as we say שִׁירָה חֲדָשָׁה שִׁבְּחוּ גְאוּלִים, *the ones who were redeemed praised [Hashem in] a new song.*

The verse cited by the Talmud points out a key factor that makes the Song relevant to all generations, the factor of unity. Only when a united congregation blesses Hashem, the "fetuses" — unborn generations — also bless Hashem. Unity among Jews and unity among generations of Jews is a crucial prerequisite to the Song. (5645)

On the other hand, one of Israel's greatest monarchs, Chizkiyah, did not sing *shirah* (cf. *Sanhedrin* 94a). At the moment of his triumph over Sancheriv's army, his curious reticence to sing God's praises can be rationalized as a result of the deficiencies of his generation. Unlike Moshe's contemporaries who rose to an exalted level at the Sea, Chizkiyah's generation did not merit that their leader sing *shirah*.

Alternatively, Chizkiyah felt so close to Hashem at all times — even while conducting his daily activities — that he was not overly impressed by a miracle. For him, it was obvious that the natural course of events was nothing but a series of miracles. (5631)

---

1. For a fuller description of why Moshe had to coerce Israel to leave the Sea, and the significance of the booty gathered by Israel at the Sea, see our commentary on the verse תּוֹרֵי זָהָב נַעֲשֶׂה לָּךְ עִם נְקֻדּוֹת הַכָּסֶף, *Let us make for you circlets of gold with spangles of silver*, in the essay on *Shir HaShirim* (1:11).

Shavuos

Shavuos' Many Names

◆§ Introduction

In this essay we will consider the relationship between Shavuos and the other Festivals, and suggest that Shavuos occupies a pivotal place between Pesach and Succos, not only chronologically but philosophically as well. We will demonstrate that Shavuos is the most beloved of the Festivals, and discuss the special link that exists between Shavuos and Simchas Torah.

No other festival has as many names as Shavuos. Apart from the name Shavuos itself, it is called זְמַן מַתַּן תּוֹרָתֵינוּ, *the time of the giving of our Torah*, עֲצֶרֶת, *convocation*, זְמַן חֵרוּתֵנוּ, *the time of our freedom*,[1] עֶצֶם הַיּוֹם הַזֶּה, this very day (*Vayikra* 23:21), and יוֹם הַבִּכּוּרִים, *the day of the first fruits* (this name is discussed at length in a separate essay), and יוֹם הַקָּהָל, *the day of congregational unity*. In the following discussion we will offer various explanations for these names.

◆§ Relationship to Other Festivals

The Festival cycle is one of the most popular topics of discussion within the Jewish world. Even those not generally knowledgeable about other matters of halachah talk readily about the laws of the Festivals. The verse we read in the daytime *kiddush* on the Festivals contains a hint to the widespread interest they arouse: וַיְדַבֵּר מֹשֶׁה אֶת־מֹעֲדֵי ה׳ אֶל־בְּנֵי יִשְׂרָאֵל, *And Moshe declared HASHEM's appointed festivals to the Children of Israel* (*Vayikra* 23:44). Apart from its

1. The relevance to Shavuos of this name, which is more commonly associated with Pesach, will be explained below.

obvious meaning, this verse suggests that Moshe imparted to the Jewish people the ability to discourse on the Festivals.[1]

Similarly, the Rabbinical instruction (*Megillah* 32a) שֶׁיְּהוּ שׁוֹאֲלִין וְדוֹרְשִׁין בְּעִנְיָנוֹ שֶׁל יוֹם, *[the people] should inquire about and expound upon the matters of the day,* implies not only that one *must* talk about the Festivals (as this saying is usually taken to mean), but also that anyone, however much knowledge he may possess, *will* readily discuss them. (5634)

Although all the festivals have great importance in Jewish life, Shavuos occupies a special place in the Festival cycle. For one thing, it comes between the two other Pilgrimage Festivals, Pesach and Succos. In Jewish tradition, the middle is an especially coveted position. In this sense, Shavuos is compared to the בְּרִיחַ הַתִּיכוֹן, *the middle beam* (*Shemos* 26:28) that miraculously held up the walls of the *Mishkan*, much as Shavuos bolsters the period between Pesach and Succos.

This analogy between Shavuos and the beam that supported the *Mishkan* can be taken further. The boards that made up each wall of the *Mishkan* were held up by five beams. Four of them were positioned on the side of the boards, two near the top and two near the bottom, and were held in place by rings. The middle beam ran inside the boards, hidden from sight but effectively supporting all the others. So too, the two days of Pesach (the first and last) and the two days of Succos and Shemini Atzeres, at either end of the Festival cycle, are supported by the middle day of Shavuos. (5652)

Various references in *Tanach* also attest to the unique status of Shavuos. For example, King Solomon said (*Mishlei* 3:15), יְקָרָה הִיא מִפְּנִינִים, *She is more precious than pearls.* The Midrash interprets this to mean that the Torah is more precious than a first-born son or than the *Kohen Gadol.* Both interpretations are suggested by the word פְּנִינִים meaning most precious or first. Metaphorically, we can understand this Midrash to mean that the festival on which the Torah was given is more beloved than the first (literally *innermost*) treasure given the Jews — the festival of Pesach.

Elsewhere, King Solomon said (*Shir HaShirim* 1:4), הֱבִיאַנִי הַמֶּלֶךְ חֲדָרָיו נָגִילָה וְנִשְׂמְחָה בָּךְ, *The King has brought me into His chambers; we will be happy and rejoice in you.* Our Sages interpret this verse as follows:

---

1. In this approach, the word וַיְדַבֵּר is interpreted to mean *lead* or *bring,* as we find in *Tehillim* (47:4), יַדְבֵּר עַמִּים תַּחְתֵּינוּ, *He will lead nations under us.* Here also, Moshe *brought* the light of the festivals to Israel.

Though Hashem brought me into His abode (the *succah*), we rejoice more in בָּךְ (*gematria* twenty-two), the twenty-two letters of the *alef-beis* that are the building blocks of Torah. This also suggests the uniqueness of Shavuos in contrast to Succos or Pesach. (5647)

We find a reference to Shavuos in another verse יוֹם־אֶחָד הוּא יִוָּדַע לַה׳, *one day will be known to HASHEM* (*Zechariah* 14:7). Though Hashem created many days, He keeps one of them for Himself, namely Shavuos.

Another approach pairs the three Pilgrimage Festivals with the three levels of human expression: word, thought and deed. Pesach represents Hashem's great *actions* such as the the splitting of the Sea, as the Torah says (*Shemos* 14:31), הַיָּד הַגְּדֹלָה אֲשֶׁר עָשָׂה ה׳ בְּמִצְרַיִם, *the great hand that HASHEM inflicted upon Egypt*. Shavuos corresponds to the *words* Hashem spoke in giving the Torah on Mount Sinai. Finally Succos, called זְמַן שִׂמְחָתֵנוּ, *the time of our gladness*, symbolizes the *thoughts* we have following the High Holy Days, when not only actions and speech but even the *thought* of every Jew is sanctified. Perhaps for this reason Succos is called *the time of our gladness*, since the Jew attains some of the spiritual level that will be enjoyed when *Moshiach* arrives, when we will be able to truly sanctify our minds as well as our words and deeds.[1]

The Mishnah in *Avos* (3:18) also hints at the importance of Shavuos. The Mishnah first expresses the love Hashem has for all humanity because the first man was created in His image, followed by His special affection for the Jewish people, whom He calls His children. Finally, the Mishnah speaks of the *extraordinary* attachment He showed for His people by giving them the "cherished utensil" with which the world was created, the Torah. Homiletically, each of these levels may be said to correspond to one of the *sholosh regalim*: The respect due to all humans is a basic theme of Succos, which celebrates Hashem's assistance in surmounting the natural obstacles of the elements. The seventy bulls offered during this festival correspond to the seventy basic cultures of humankind. The second stratum alludes to Pesach, when Hashem led the newly-formed nation, still defenseless children, out of the bondage of Egypt. Shavuos, however, represents the full blossoming of the Jews as Hashem's people. It was at this time that God revealed the full depth of His devotion to His people by lavishing upon them His paramount gift, the Torah. (5640)

---

1. The essay entitled "The Time of Our Gladness" in the section on Succos discusses this theme at greater length.

◆§ Shavuos and Shemini Atzeres — A Special Connection

While there are clear links between Shavuos and the other Pilgrimage Festivals as we have seen, there is a special relationship between Shavuos and Shemini Atzeres which in *Eretz Yisrael* is celebrated together with Simchas Torah and in the Diaspora is observed as a two-day festival, Simchas Torah being the second day. Both occasions celebrate the glory of Torah, and both are called by the name *Atzeres*. King Solomon calls the Torah Hashem's ultimate delight in which He revels two days a year (*Mishlei* 8:30): וָאֶהְיֶה שַׁעֲשׁוּעִים יוֹם יוֹם, *And I was His delight day by day*. The two days mentioned refer to Shavuos and Shemini Atzeres, the festivals focused directly on Torah.

◆§ Shavuos' Many Names: Shavuos

The primary name of this festival, Shavuos, signifies not only that it is the Festival of Weeks, crowning the seven-week counting of the *Omer* that began on Pesach, but also that it is the Day of the Great Oath, (since the word *shavuah* also means "oath"). On this day Hashem swore eternal devotion to us, and we in turn pledged everlasting loyalty to Him.

While the Torah does not mention these oaths explicitly, it does contain hints to them. The Talmud (*Shavuos* 36a) suggests that repeating "yes" or "no" twice indicates an intent to swear. Hashem's declaration, אָנֹכִי ה׳ אֱלֹהֶיךָ, *I am* H*ASHEM*, *your God*, is repeated in the Torah twice, once in *Parashas Yisro* (*Shemos* 20:2) and once in *Parashas Va'eschanan* (*Devarim* 5:6), thereby certifying His sworn commitment to the Jewish people. Correspondingly, at Mount Sinai, the Jews twice declared their intention to keep Hashem's word: כֹּל אֲשֶׁר־דִּבֶּר ה׳ נַעֲשֶׂה, *Everything that* H*ASHEM has spoken we shall do* (*Shemos* 19:8), and also כָּל־הַדְּבָרִים אֲשֶׁר־דִּבֶּר ה׳ נַעֲשֶׂה, *All the words that* H*ASHEM has spoken we will do* (*ibid*. 24:3).

The name "Shavuos" implies not only that we pledge our allegiance to Hashem, but also that we testify to His Omnipotence. The name is understood in the sense of שְׁבוּעַת הָעֵדוּת, the oath of a witness. By listening attentively at Sinai, we became witnesses to His existence and His awesome power. (5655)

When the prophet Shmuel said (*I* 12:22), כִּי לֹא־יִטֹּשׁ ה׳ אֶת עַמּוֹ . . .כִּי הוֹאִיל ה׳, *for* *HASHEM* *will not abandon His people for* *HASHEM* *agreed,* he was referring to the oath (see *Rashi* on *Shemos* 2:21) that Hashem swore at Sinai. The expression מוּשְׁבָּע וְעוֹמֵד מֵהַר סִינַי, *already sworn from Mount Sinai* (*Shavuos* 21b) also alludes to the oath taken at Sinai that bound the Jews irrevocably to the Torah. (5663)

The timing of Israel's oath is also signficant. Generally the prerogative of swearing is reserved for the unusually devout, as indicated in the verse (*Devarim* 10:20) אֶת־ה׳ אֱלֹהֶיךָ תִּירָא אֹתוֹ תַעֲבֹד וּבוֹ תִדְבָּק וּבִשְׁמוֹ תִּשָּׁבֵעַ, *You shall fear* *HASHEM*, *your God, you shall serve Him, and you shall cling to Him, and in His Name shall you swear.* Only those who fear Hashem, and serve Him and cling to Him may swear in His Name.

And indeed the Jews progressed through this order: They *feared* Him in Egypt as a result of the plagues but could not *serve* Him until after they had left Egypt. During the forty-nine day period between leaving Egypt and receiving the Torah they *clung* to Him. Finally on Shavuos, at Mount Sinai, they *swore* their loyalty to Him. (5664)

Why was Israel able to swear only on Shavuos, not before? The Talmud states (*Niddah* 30b), כִּי לְךָ תִּכְרַע כָּל בֶּרֶךְ – זֶה יוֹם הַמִּיתָה, תִּשָּׁבַע כָּל לָשׁוֹן – זֶה יוֹם הַלֵּידָה, *"[All the world's inhabitants will recognize and know that] to You every knee should bend" — this refers to the day of death, "every tongue should swear" — this refers to the day of birth.* Only at these two intensely spiritual moments, when the soul is about to enter the world and when it has just departed from the body, can one perceive Hashem so closely that he can swear by His Name. So too, on that first Shavuos when the souls of the Jews expired (as discussed in the essay on the Aftermath of the Giving of the Torah), they could perceive Hashem clearly enough to swear by His Name.

Based on the concept of swearing, one can clarify the relationship between Pesach and Shavuos. On Pesach, the Jews became Hashem's servants and pledged that their *physical* instincts would also serve Him. On Shavuos the soul, with its intellectual abilities, also swore submission. This is analogous to the submission symbolized by the two kinds of *tefillin*: the *shel yad* (arm-*tefillin*) represents submission of the body to Hashem's service and the *shel rosh* (head-*tefillin*) represents submission of the soul and intellectual capacities. (5642)

◆§ Your Oaths

It is noteworthy that this festival is also referred to as שְׁבֻעֹתֵיכֶם, *your oaths.* When the soul swears, the Jew is able to arouse the roots of *his* soul and to realize *his* full potential. Thus this is the Festival of *Our* Oaths (*Bamidbar* 28:26). (5647)

◆§ The Time of the Giving of the Torah

The time of the giving of the Torah — זְמַן מַתַּן תּוֹרָתֵנוּ — this phrase can be understood to refer not only to the historical event that occurred at Mount Sinai, but also to the *re-giving* of the Torah we still experience every year. Likewise, preparation for receiving the Torah repeated itself every year. We see this also in the opening verse of the day's Torah reading: בַּיּוֹם הַזֶּה בָּאוּ מִדְבַּר סִינָי, *on* **this** *day they arrived at the Wilderness of Sinai.* (*Shemos* 19:1) Every year on *this* day we renew our acceptance of the Torah. (5643)

Ideally a Jew should be prepared to receive the Torah anew every day of the year. All we need is to strip away the veneer of materialism to allow the spiritual core to shine through. In the period before Shavuos, the Jews were told to wash their clothing (*Shemos* 19:10). Clothing is an exterior garb and thus washing is an act that symbolized purification of the connection with the material world, a procedure we need to engage in every year. (5641)

◆§ Rosh Hashanah of the Fruit of the Trees

Shavuos is also called the "Rosh Hashanah of the Fruit of the Trees" (*Megillah* 31b). We may understand this not only in the literal sense that many trees blossom at this time of year, but also symbolically. The first Mishnah in tractate *Peah,* which we read every morning after reciting the Blessings on the Torah, reminds us that the principal reward for our earthly endeavors comes in *Olom HaBa* and in this world we enjoy only the fruits of our efforts. On Shavuos, when we work to strengthen our commitment to Torah, we are reminded that we will realize no more than a glimpse of Torah's rewards during our lifetime.

The image of fruit trees may also allude to the concept of creativity. Hashem created the earth so that man, armed with Torah, could perfect it, and participate in the creative process. This idea is expressed in the verse (*Bereishis* 2:3), אֲשֶׁר־בָּרָא אֱלֹהִים לַעֲשׂוֹת, *which God created to* **make.** Hashem created the world for man to apply his creative ability to make things, to make the world into a better place. Not until the Torah was given, however, could this creativity truly flourish. Thus the first two millenia are called in the Talmud (*Avodah Zarah* 9a) ב׳ אֲלָפִים תֹּהוּ, two thousand spiritually uncreative years. (5642)

Contrary to popular belief, we are not required to limit our attention to spiritual pursuits on Shavuos. Rather, we are urged to consecrate the world we live in by applying Torah insights to all situations we encounter. Torah permeates this world just as much as it pervades the World to Come. Thus, Shavuos links the material and spiritual worlds, when the dividends we earn in this world give us a glimmer of the more important rewards that await us in *Olom HaBa*. In this sense, it is a day when the present and the hereafter are joined together in harmony. (5645)

This helps explain why the Torah was given to mortals on earth rather than to angels in heaven. The angels, who lack the urge to do wrong, have no need for the Ten Commandments. Rather, it is the human being who, because of his frailties and inclinations, needs the structure of the Torah to guide him.

It is because Shavuos celebrates the achievements of the frail human striving to sanctify his life that it merits a unique form of festivity. It is the only festival on which the authorities all agree that we are obligated to satiate our bodies with food and drink, as well as to fill our souls with Torah (cf. *Pesachim* 68b). Even those who hold that the requirement to rejoice on *yom tov* can be fulfilled by study and meditation agree that on Shavuos one is required to indulge in fine foods, as a reminder that Torah is as relevant to this world and its material pleasures as it is to the World to Come. Torah is the key to understanding the holy function of the "mundane." This is symbolized by the waving of the Two Loaves, bread grown on earth, towards Heaven. Through Torah the material universe can be elevated to the spiritual Heavens. (5642)

◆§ Atzeres

In Rabbinic literature, Shavuos is most frequently called *Atzeres*. This ambiguous word may refer to the acceptance of Hashem's sovereignty by the Jewish people that first began on Shavuos. In *Shmuel I* (9:17) we find this word used to mean *rule*: זֶה יַעְצֹר בְּעַמִּי, *This one will rule over My people*. Thus the name *Atzeres* may refer to our acknowledgment of Hashem as our Supreme Monarch on Shavuos. (5657)

More commonly though, the word *Atzeres* is understood to mean ingathering. As we have said, Shavuos is the most beloved of the Festivals. In a sense, then, all of the others gather and cluster around Shavuos, the day of the giving of the Torah, the high point of human history. Furthermore, it is a day of ingathering for Jews, a day to join together in reaffirming their ties to Hashem that were so dramatically forged at Sinai. This link between Hashem and the Jewish people began on Shavuos, another reason the holiday is called *Atzeres*. (5663)

The name *Atzeres* also suggests the word אוֹצָר, *storehouse* or *treasure chest*. In this sense we can say that Shavuos is the day that Hashem's spiritual treasures were removed from His storehouse and bestowed on the Jewish people, after being rejected by the other nations. This is the fulfillment of the promise made to Abraham after the *akeidah* (*Bereishis* 22:17), וְיִרַשׁ זַרְעֲךָ אֵת שַׁעַר אֹיְבָיו, *and your offspring shall inherit the gate of its enemy*. (5660)

It should be emphasized, however, that our acceptance of the Torah was never intended to disenfranchise the rest of the world from access to this spiritual heritage. On the contrary, throughout the *omer* period leading up to Shavuos, we plead that all of humanity be granted the wisdom to forsake the materialistic domination of their existence and embrace Hashem's spirituality. Indeed, as explained earlier, this day is called *Atzeres* because it represents the hope that all humans will be "gathered in" under the embrace of Torah ideals. It is appropriate that the spiritual journeys of both Ruth and Yisro to Judaism occurred during the *omer* period, which is a very favorable time for the ingathering of "sparks of holiness." (See the essay on Ruth for further discussion of this theme.) (5660)

According to this approach, the name *Atzeres* may have the meaning of *negation*. On Shavuos, the entire material world became nullified, when the awesome Presence of Hashem revealed the seven heavens and showed that nothing else existed apart from Him, as the Torah says (*Devarim* 4:35), אֵין עוֹד מִלְּבַדּוֹ, *there is none aside from Him*. This may explain why both Shavuos and Shemini Atzeres are called *Atzeres*. On Shavuos, the Jewish people negated itself to Hashem, as shown by the fact that the Sages, representing the people, called the day *Atzeres*. On Shemini Atzeres, a reverse form of "negation" occurs. Hashem tells

Israel, עֲצֶרֶת תִּהְיֶה לָכֶם, *it shall be an Atzeres for* **you,** only Israel matters to Me the rest of the world is peripheral to Israel. (5645)

◆§ The Time of Our Freedom

Most surprisingly, Shavuos could be called זְמַן חֵרוּתֵנוּ, *the time of our freedom,* a name usually associated with Pesach. Nevertheless, Shavuos can also be thought of as a time of liberation; whereas the Jews obtained physical freedom on Pesach, they did not achieve true spiritual freedom until Sinai, when the Exodus from Egypt reached its true fruition. As the Mishnah says (*Avos* 6:2), אֵין לְךָ בֶּן חוֹרִין אֶלָּא מִי שֶׁעוֹסֵק בְּתַלְמוּד תּוֹרָה, *you can have no freer man than one who engages in the study of the Torah.* Only by integrating the moral lessons of the Torah into one's personality can he truly free himself from the constraints of the material world.

Alternatively, this Mishnah may be suggesting that only through Torah can the eternal struggle between body and soul be settled. The soul implanted by God into the human body has an insatiable thirst for spirituality. The body on the other hand, craves material belongings. It is only through Torah's insights and its lifestyle that body and soul can coexist. As David sings נַפְשִׁי יְשׁוֹבֵב יַנְחֵנִי בְמַעְגְּלֵי צֶדֶק, *He restores my soul, He leads me on paths of justice* (*Tehillim* 23:3) This verse refers not only to the rejuvenation of the soul from its many troubles but to God's placement of the soul within the human body. The Mishnah in *Avos* comparing one who doesn't study Torah to a beautiful woman who lacks grace alludes to the soul replete with potential that cannot be fulfilled unless its bearer studies Torah. (5651)

The relationship between the freedom of Pesach and that of Shavuos was made explicit when Moshe sought guarantees for the viability of the Jews' departure from Egypt in his first conversation with Hashem at the burning bush (*Shemos* 3:11): מִי אָנֹכִי כִּי אֵלֵךְ אֶל־פַּרְעֹה וְכִי אוֹצִיא אֶת־בְּנֵי יִשְׂרָאֵל מִמִּצְרָיִם, *Who am I that I should go to Pharaoh, and that I should take out the Children of Israel from Egypt?*[1] In response, Hashem proclaims (v. 12), וַיֹּאמֶר כִּי־אֶהְיֶה עִמָּךְ וְזֶה־לְּךָ הָאוֹת כִּי אָנֹכִי שְׁלַחְתִּיךָ בְּהוֹצִיאֲךָ אֶת־הָעָם מִמִּצְרַיִם תַּעַבְדוּן אֶת־הָאֱלֹהִים עַל הָהָר הַזֶּה, *And He said, 'This will be a sign that I have sent you, when you bring the people out of Egypt,*

1. *Rashi* comments on Moshe's second question, "Even if I am worthy to go to Pharaoh, what merit do the Jews have that You should perform a miracle for them and have me take them out of Egypt?"

you will serve God on this mountain.' Hashem's giving the Torah at Mount Sinai was the ultimate guarantee that the Jew's freedom would endure. (5660)

◆§ This Very Day

Finally, Shavuos is referred to as עֶצֶם הַיּוֹם הַזֶּה, *this very day.* This expression is usually used in connection with such epochal events as the Flood and Moshe's death, as well as with such ceremonial observances as Yom Kippur and *bris milah.* The common factor in all these occasions is the atonement of sins to achieve purity.

As we progress through the counting of the *omer,* we try to cleanse our souls and our actions of any impurities that stand in the way of achieving total blending with Hashem's holiness. In short, we attempt to re-establish the purity of Sinai. By striving to prepare ourselves to attain this level of purity that is the ultimate purpose of Shavuos, we fulfill the ideal of עֶצֶם הַיּוֹם הַזֶּה, *that very day,* when we can again face our Father as pure and holy children. (5668)

Shavuos Yom HaBikurim

◆§ Introduction

The Torah calls Shavuos *Yom HaBikurim,* the Day of the First Fruits (*Bamidbar* 28:26). *Rashi* understands this as referring either to the offering of leavened bread brought for the first time on Shavuos, or to the first of the ripening crop of one of the seven species brought to Jerusalem on Shavuos.

It is possible, however, to give a different explanation for this name: The word *bikurim* as used here is derived from the word *bechor,* firstborn, implying that Shavuos is a time of rebirth and renewal, when the world's spiritual resources were rejuvenated at Mount Sinai.

We can elaborate on this idea by making a distinction between the superficial aspects of the universe and its internal dynamic which is driven by spiritual forces rather than by material ones. In this world, every Jew is assumed to be intrinsically good. On Shavuos, the day commemorating the giving of the Torah, the Jew undergoes a spiritual renewal, and can take a vital part in seeking out this radiant "interior"-based world.

⸎ The Universe's First Day

The name *Yom HaBikurim* (literally "ripening") suggests that the world reached maturity on the day the Torah was given. Generally, the term *bikurim* is understood to refer to the first ripening fruits of the seven species by which *Eretz Yisrael* is praised in the Torah which were brought to Jerusalem every Shavuos. However, the name also evokes a broader image of a newly-productive world, yielding a ripening "crop" of spiritually-attuned individuals.

In what way is this renewal associated with Shavuos? For one thing, we can look upon Shavuos as marking, in a sense, the first day of the universe. Normally we say that the Creation occurred when Hashem divided the heaven and earth, as recounted in the beginning of the Book of *Bereishis*. Really, however, that refers only to the physical beginning of the world. Spiritual creation, encompassing the concepts of the Torah, predates material creation. Both Torah and the Jewish nation are called *rayshis*, first, suggesting that they were conceived by Hashem before He created a physical world. It is fitting, then, that Shavuos is called the *first* day — the day *before* Creation — for this was the day when Torah and the Jewish people became inexorably linked together.

It is noteworthy that only in regard to the sixth day of Creation do we find the expression טוֹב מְאֹד, *very good*, instead of the word טוֹב, *good*, used to describe the creations of the other days. As *Rashi* comments, the term יוֹם הַשִּׁשִּׁי, *the sixth day* (*Bereishis* 1:31), is a hidden reference to *the* sixth day, the sixth of *Sivan*, on which the Jews eventually received the Torah. It is only the association with Israel's acceptance of the Torah that gives so fundamental an event in world history as the creation of man the right to be called "very good." (5642, 5647)

◆§ The Universe Renewed

The word *bikurim* also suggests *ripening* or *maturing*. In this sense Shavuos can be seen as the culmination of the Creation, the point at which the world reaches its full maturity.

Shavuos marked the emergence of a new dimension of the Creation. For nearly 2500 years before the Giving of the Torah, the world existed only on a superficial, physical plane, with rare exceptions such as the Patriarchs, who were almost not part of this world. The flowering of the world's inner, spiritual, potential — epitomized by the revelation of Hashem's Presence — did not occur until the Giving of the Torah.[1] If the world was created in the merit of Torah, as we are told that Hashem consulted with the Torah before the Creation, then its continued viability must also depend on Torah. The sixth of Sivan, then, commemorates the first day of the universe's true mission, when the world's inner spirituality came to the fore. As *Chazal* teach us the continued existence of the world was contingent on Israel's accepting the Torah on the sixth of Sivan (*Shabbos* 88a). Not only the Torah itself, but also each of the two hundred forty eight positive commandments and the three hundred sixty five negative commandments play an important role in this new inner-motivated world. Every *mitzvah* is a suggestion from Heaven how to perfect the world and maintain it according to the Divine intent.

As discussed elsewhere, *Onkelos* very aptly renders the verse (*Shemos* 19:20) *HASHEM descended upon Mount Sinai* as *Hashem* **revealed** *Himself at Mount Sinai.* This "revelation" indicates that, prior to the Giving of the Torah, the world's true "self" was hidden from humankind. Similarly, the well-known verse פָּנִים בְּפָנִים דִּבֶּר ד׳ עִמָּכֶם, *Hashem spoke to you face to face* (*Devarim* 5:4) alludes to the inner spiritual dynamism of the universe[2] that was first revealed when the people came face-to-face with Hashem at Mount Sinai.

(5631, 5637)

An analogy can be drawn between the revelation of the inner order of

---

1. In order to properly appreciate the significance of the inner, spiritual dimension of the world, consider that the world can continue to exist only because of the spiritual force that Hashem's Presence, and the Torah, infuse into it constantly. While superficially the world seems to have a self-sustaining momentum, really it is lifeless without the inner spark Hashem conveys it through the Torah.

2. The word פָּנִים, *face*, is suggestive of the related word פְּנִימִיּוּת, *inner spiritual element*.

the universe on Shavuos and Moshe's first exposure to the outside world, which also occurred on the seventh of Sivan. Tradition holds that Moshe was born on the seventh of Adar. Thus the three months that his mother hid him (see *Shemos* 2:2) ended on the seventh of Sivan, on which day he was found, i.e., his light was "revealed," on the banks of the river. (5642)

This revelation of the world's inner nature can be understood as a process of return to the true roots of the universe. However, this search for the world's self was not limited to the Jewish people alone. The Torah was transmitted in seventy languages, because all the seventy nations of the world stood to benefit from the renewal signaled at Mount Sinai. Similarly, our Sages said that the entire universe was laden with spices when each of the Ten Commandments was uttered. This is a reference to the sweet spiritual aroma that accompanied the Giving of the Torah, which wafted down to benefit the Gentiles as well.

Each individual experiences this spiritual rebirth every day, as we say in our prayers וּבְטוּבוֹ מְחַדֵּשׁ בְּכָל יוֹם תָּמִיד מַעֲשֵׂה בְרֵאשִׁית, *In His goodness He renews daily, perpetually, the work of creation.*[1] On Shavuos, however, the world's inner meaning was publicly revealed to all, as humanity realized that the universe is preserved only through Torah. It is thus no coincidence that the *Minchah Chadashah*, the first flour offering from the newly harvested grain, is offered on the anniversary of the reflowering of the universe. (5631, 5633)

Fittingly, the process of reclaiming the world's inner self occurred in a manner that mirrored the original Creation, in both cases through the issuing of ten Divine statements. The Creation was effected by means of "Ten Utterances" (cf. *Avos* 5:1), beginning with the words וַיֹּאמֶר אֱלֹהִים, *And God said*. In parallel fashion, the Ten Commandments set into motion the revelation of the inner dynamic of the world at Mount Sinai. The Ten Utterances are the outer garment of Creation. The Ten Commandments reveal their inner meaning. (5631)

The *Zohar*, however, distinguishes between the Ten Utterances of Creation, which were spoken in an uninhabited universe, and the Ten Commandments, which were given in the presence of all humanity, which was forced to realize that its existence was dependent upon Torah. (5631)

---

1. The "goodness" mentioned in this passage refers to Torah, as the Sages said (*Avos* 6:3), אֵין טוֹב אֶלָּא תוֹרָה, *only the Torah is truly good.*

How did this renewal occur? How did the inner spiritual nature of the world emerge?

A prerequisite for this process to occur was the stripping of the veneer of materialism that so often corrodes and obscures a clear vision of the world. The sweeping drama of Mount Sinai stripped away this superficial layer, revealing the sparkling inner content of the world as it was meant to be. As the Midrash cited earlier suggests, the resounding thunder and brilliant lightning at Mount Sinai served to "break the ear." It cut through the superficial impressions of the world gained through our normally limited capacities of sight and hearing.

(5631)

◈§ Dimensions of a Renewed Universe

Sinai marked a seminal change in the order of the world. Henceforth, the universe would be conducted on the basis of inner meanings rather than outward appearances. Likewise, people would be judged not merely on the basis of their visible actions, but also on the basis of their hidden good motives and intentions.

We should take note of certain ramifications of this new order. Firstly, it brought to the fore the essential unity of all Jews. Though we may differ in geographic location or social status from Sinai, we have the same basic spiritual components. When Hashem proclaimed *I am HASHEM, your God,* at Mount Sinai, the same perception of Godliness permeated *every* Jewish heart. At that moment, every Jew became vitally aware of the latent sanctity in his soul.

This is the meaning of King David's rhapsody (*Tehillim* 29:4), קוֹל־ה׳ בַּכֹּחַ, *The voice of HASHEM is in power!* The verse uses the term כֹּחַ, *power*, rather than כֹּחוֹ, *His* power. The Sages (*Shemos Rabbah* 5:9) interpreted this to mean that each person should think the Divine Presence dwells within his psyche. Indeed, as we say in the essay on the Ten Commandments, the third commandment — *You shall not take the name of Hashem in vain* — is an eloquent plea to each of us not to douse the spark of Godliness inherent in every Jewish soul.

(5633, 5637)

Another consequence of the revelation of the inner dynamic of the world was the positing of the idea that people are intrinsically good. Though their actions may often seem to belie this assumption, this is only because negative influences often corrupt people's basically benign intuitions.

Our Sages noted the essential goodness of humans in connection with the acceptance of the Torah through the following play on words (*Menachos* 53a):יָבֹא טוֹב וְיְקַבֵּל טוֹב מִטּוֹב לַטּוֹבִים, *Let a good man [Moshe] come and receive a good thing [the Torah] from [Hashem, the source of] Goodness for good people [the Jews].* Moshe, the epitome of human goodness, received the Torah, the guidebook defining what is good, from Hashem, the Source of all good and bestowed it upon the Jewish people, the best of the nations of the world.

True, not all Jews behave in a morally correct manner at all times. However, in the annual commemoration of the giving of the Torah, our intrinsic goodness emerges. On Shavuos our inner goodness is so pronounced that the *yetzer hara* (evil inclination) is vanquished. The superficial needs and temptations that sometimes misdirect us are overcome, and both body and soul are purified, much as the garments of the Jews were cleansed at Mount Sinai (cf. *Shemos* 19:10).

(5640, 5650)

On this day, the light of Creation which Hashem had hidden only for the use of *tzaddikim* was now brought out for the benefit of all humanity, to vanquish the *yetzer hara*.[1] (5640)

Although individuals may at times be able to arouse this inner goodness on their own, the process is greatly aided through involvement with the community. This was indicated as early in history as the Creation, when the individual creations of each day were described simply as "good," but the supreme accolade of "very good" was reserved for the final day, when all the creations finally acted in unison. For the same reason, Shavuos is called יוֹם הַקָּהָל, *the day of communal unity*. Only through unified effort can the intrinsic goodness of the Jewish community truly surface.[2] (5646)

⌘ Torah: An Antidote to Amalek

On this day, suffused with emerging goodness, the Jews are best equipped to vanquish their arch enemy Amalek, the symbol of evil incarnate. Some of the expressions used to describe Shavuos and, in

---

1. *Editor's note:* As the Baal Shem Tov taught "the original light of Creation was hidden in the Torah."

2. See the section on *Achdus* (p. 197).

particular the term *bikurim*, are strikingly similar to those depicting Amalek. This suggests that Torah acts as an effective antidote to the terror Amalek strikes in our hearts.

For example, the Torah is called *reishis* (foremost among all knowledge); and the day of the Giving of the Torah is called *Yom HaBikurim* — the day of the first fruits. Likewise, Amalek is called (*Bamidbar* 24:20) רֵאשִׁית גּוֹיִם, the first of Israel's antagonists. To give another parallel, a prerequisite for the defeat of Amalek is a sense of inner tranquility among Jews, and this sense of personal calm and confidence in the future was one of the hallmarks of the Giving of the Torah.[1]

◈ Communal Renewal

The Sages relate that at the conclusion of the annual *bikurim* ceremony, closely affiliated with the giving of the Torah, a heavenly voice would ring out as follows: "You offered *bikurim* today; you will bring it next year as well." This renewed lease on life is derived from the phrase, הַיּוֹם הַזֶּה ה׳ אֱלֹהֶיךָ מְצַוְּךָ לַעֲשׂוֹת, *This day HASHEM your God commands you to do* (*Devarim* 26:16), an expression similar to that used in the first two paragraphs of the *Shema*. As is well known, the first *parashah* speaks to the individual, whereas the second is addressed to the community. In our case, too, the verse implies both communal and individual renewal.

Let us now consider the implications of this renewal for the individual. Our Sages say (*Yevamos* 22a) that a convert attains a new status upon conversion, and is considered a newly-born person. It stands to reason that if a convert gains a new persona through his personal commitment to Judaism, a Jew also must renew his lease on life by reclaiming his stake in Torah, especially when he does so together with the entire Jewish people. Moshe alludes to this individualized revival in *Parashas Va'eschanan*, in the question (*Devarim* 4:33) הֲשָׁמַע עָם קוֹל אֱלֹהִים מְדַבֵּר מִתּוֹךְ־הָאֵשׁ כַּאֲשֶׁר־שָׁמַעְתָּ אַתָּה וַיֶּחִי, *Has any people heard the voice of God speaking from within the fire as you heard and still lived?* In this context, the word וַיֶּחִי signifies not merely survival, but also a renewed lease on life, retaining a firm grip on the true life of the World to Come, as Israel did on the occasion of the Giving of the Torah. (5650, 5651, 5659)

1. It is interesting to note tha the *mitzvah* to remember the actions of Amalek recorded at the end of *Parashas KiSeitzei* is immediately followed by the *mitzvah* of bringing *bikurim* at the beginning of *Parashas KiSavo*.

The Sages relate that the Jews' souls expired (*Shabbos* 89a) when they heard the first two Commandments. This statement seems perplexing indeed unless we see it in connection with the above discussion. The Jews' previous lifestyle, based on materialistic values, was negated, giving way to a new life, guided by the much superior Torah-based morality. In that sense, their old, tarnished souls did indeed expire, to give way to new, elevated ones. (5631, 5647)

The renewal of Shavuos can be appreciated better in light of the observation of the *Arizal* that the Exodus from Egypt was not only a physical liberation but also, and primarily, a spiritual emancipation from Egypt's forty-nine "Gates of Impurity." This is why our freedom is not complete each year after Pesach until we undergo the purification of the forty-nine-day period of *sefirah*. Each day we struggle to enter another gate of purity and to withdraw further from the impurity of Egypt. Only when we enter the fiftieth and final gate of holiness, when all the conflicts are behind us, does Hashem *renew* afresh His gift to the Jewish people — the Torah, together with all the tools and faculties we need to study and observe it. (5639)

◆§ The Torah Internalized

With the giving of the Torah, the Jews found a new lifestyle yet, what was the nature of their new-found commitment? What did this spiritual resurgence imply?

While the Jewish people had already observed certain *mitzvos*, up to this point Torah and good deeds were only external phenomena. The commandments were orders to be obeyed and studied but had not yet become part of the Jewish psyche. At Mount Sinai, Jewry was inspired to internalize Torah. As we affirm in the blessing recited following Torah readings, Torah is an integral part of every Jew — חַיֵּי עוֹלָם נָטַע בְּתוֹכֵנוּ, *eternal life planted in our midst*. Through Torah, the Divine Intelligence, Hashem's characteristics, such as mercy and honesty, became incorporated within every Jewish soul. (5650)

◆§ Shavuos — A New Concept of Time

This theme of renewal through Torah is voiced by King Solomon's famous observation (*Koheles* 1:9) אֵין כָּל־חָדָשׁ תַּחַת הַשָּׁמֶשׁ *There is nothing new under the sun*. The Talmud notes that this verse speaks only of developments *under* the sun. However, opportunities for renewed growth definitely exist *above* the sun; i.e., in the spiritual realm.

Koheles likewise makes a distinction between two different aspects of time (3:1): לַכֹּל זְמָן וְעֵת, *To everything there is a time and a season.* According to the Midrash, the word זְמָן, *time*, refers collectively to major moments in the history of the world, such as when Noah entered the ark or when Abraham circumcised himself. However, the term עֵת, *season*, is reserved for one overriding event — the Giving of the Torah. The distinction between these two terms lies in the fact that *time* refers to time in a natural sense: ordinary days consisting of hours, minutes, and seconds. Prior to the giving of the Torah, the world knew only of *time* governed by natural laws. However, in accepting the Torah, the Jewish people was exposed to an entirely new concept of time, typified by the word עֵת — supernatural time, extending beyond the limitations of space and matter. Thus, *time* is that which is experienced by man, while *season* expresses the concept of infinite time, subject only to Hashem's control.

It was at Mount Sinai that the Jews first encountered this phenomenon of spiritual time; here they first learned that the apparent barriers of time and space could be overcome through the study and application of Torah ideals. The prophet Yeshayahu alludes to this ability of the truly dedicated Torah student to overcome "natural" time in the following proclamation (33:6): וְהָיָה אֱמוּנַת עִתֶּיךָ חֹסֶן יְשׁוּעֹת חָכְמַת וָדָעַת, *And He shall be the stability of your times, a store of salvation, wisdom and knowledge.* Those who are are immersed in "wisdom and knowledge" live by supernatural time, with Hashem as the stability of their sense of time, rather than by time that is subject to finite limits.

(5652)

☙ The Torah Scholar Renewed

Finally, we can view Shavuos as a *Yom HaBikurim* for those committed to Torah study, so to speak, their spiritual *Rosh Hashanah.* On this day is determined the spiritual growth each individual will experience during the coming year.[1] (5643, 5651)

The Sages, in a beautiful analogy (*Taanis* 7a), compare Torah to a tree. On Shavuos, the place of every Jew in relation to this Tree of Life

1. This theme is explored at greater length in the essay on *Tikun Leil Shavuos*.

is decided, whether his portion in Torah be drawn from the tree's trunk and roots, or from its periphery — the branches and leaves.

This may explain the prayer of thanks traditionally offered at the completion of a tractate: שֶׁלֹּא שָׂם חֶלְקֵנוּ מִיּוֹשְׁבֵי קְרָנוֹת, *You have not placed me among those who sit on street corners* (cf. *Berachos* 28b). Normally understood as an expression of gratitude that Hashem has not given us a station in life together with idlers, this may also be a fervent plea that we draw spiritual sustenance from the main trunk of the Tree of Life, and not from the corners (קְרָנוֹת). We wish to be close to the mainstream of Torah, not on the periphery. (5634)

As stated earlier, Shavuos represents a return to our inner core, to the world's true underlying nature. As individuals scrape away the outer layers of their lives and penetrate to their own inner selves, they can begin to realize their true portion in Hashem's Torah — their real place in Hashem's worldly design. In effect, then, Torah serves as a mirror. Scrape away the outer layer of materialism, shiny but thin as it is, and we can truly perceive the awesomely great souls contained in each of us. That is where the potential for spiritual growth lies waiting to flourish. (5639)

Achdus

◆§ Introduction

One of the names of Shavuos is *Yom HaKahal*, the Day of Congregational Unity. This name implies that the wondrous events of Mount Sinai would not have occurred had there not been a sense of unified purpose on the part of the entire Jewish people. In this essay, we will trace the sources of Jewish unity (*achdus*), suggesting that our common Torah heritage and belief in Hashem are prerequisites for *achdus*. However, while the study of Torah promotes *achdus*, in turn *achdus* inspires a Torah-based lifestyle. In our conclusion, we will explore the existence of a collective Jewish soul, a single *neshamah* common to all Jews.

◆§ Day of Unity

Achdus, unity, is an indispensable attribute for the survival of Jewish people. Without it, the nation would crumble into easily dispersed fragments. When *achdus* exists, however, we stand ready to outlive all other peoples. And, in fact, *achdus* played a vital role in bringing about the glorious historical event of the Giving of the Torah.

In the account of this event found in *Sefer Devarim*, great emphasis is given to the status of the Jews as a *kahal*, a congregational entity. For example, in *Parashas Ve'eschanan* (5:19) we find, אֶת־הַדְּבָרִים הָאֵלֶּה דִּבֶּר ה׳ אֶל־כָּל־קְהַלְכֶם, *HASHEM spoke these words to all your assembly.* Similarly, Moshe describes יוֹם אֲשֶׁר עָמַדְתָּ לִפְנֵי ה׳ אֱלֹהֶיךָ בְּחֹרֵב בֶּאֱמֹר ה׳ אֵלַי הַקְהֶל־לִי אֶת־הָעָם, *The day you stood before HASHEM your God at Sinai, when HASHEM said to me, "Assemble the people for Me"* (*Devarim* 4:10). Later, in *Parashas Shoftim*, the day the Torah was given is called יוֹם הַקָּהָל, *the day of congregational unity* (*Devarim* 18:16). In *Parashas Yisro* the Torah described the Jew's encampment at Mount Sinai in the following terms, וַיִּחַן־שָׁם יִשְׂרָאֵל נֶגֶד הָהָר, *And Israel encamped there, opposite the mountain* (*Shemos* 19:2). *Rashi* comments that the use of the singular verb וַיִּחַן, *and* **he** *encamped*, teaches that they were "as one man, with one heart." The intrinsic character of Israel is that all individuals are but parts of an organic whole.

The spirit of *achdus* prevalent at Sinai was a prerequisite not only for the original transmission of the Torah, but also for the success of all future assemblies. As the Mishnah teaches (*Avos* 4:14) any conclave that has as its aim the furtherance of Torah causes, rather than personal aggrandizement, will ultimately meet with success. Anytime the Jewish people unite around a common positive purpose, they draw from the power of the original assembly at Sinai. (5649)

According to the Midrash, whenever Hashem uses the word לִי, *for Me*, as in the verse cited above הַקְהֶל־לִי אֶת־הָעָם, *assemble for Me the people*, it implies permanence. If we enter an undertaking purely for Hashem's sake, He promises us that it will endure for all the generations.

We can find the same theme in the oft-quoted verse (which we discuss at length in the essay on *Simchas Torah*), תּוֹרָה צִוָּה־לָנוּ מֹשֶׁה מוֹרָשָׁה קְהִלַּת יַעֲקֹב, *Moshe commanded to us the Torah, a heritage of the assembly of Jacob* (*Devarim* 33:4). Only when Jacob's descendants come together as a united *assembly* can the Torah be their heritage. The gift of Torah was not given to individual Jews. One's share in Torah is commensurate with his connection to all his fellow Jews. (5647)

The name *Atzeres*, often applied to Shavuos, has the connotation of "ingathering" (from its similarity to the word אוֹצָר, *storehouse*).[1] Thus this name also suggests the theme of unity and its bearing on the Giving of the Torah, the day when all factions within the Jewish people unite in supreme *achdus*. This name also suggests the concept of Hashem's Kingship, implying that the only enduring basis of Jewish unity is acceptance of Hashem's sovereignty. This is the true rallying point of our People. (5652, 5657)

Every year on Shavuos, the *achdus* we first experienced at Mount Sinai is reenacted and achieved once again. Somehow, this festival enables the Jewish people to unite. This occurs not only on Shavuos, but also every day when we recite the *Shema*, since the word שְׁמַע also has the meaning of *gather*, as in the verse וַיְשַׁמַּע שָׁאוּל אֶת הָעָם, *and Shaul gathered the people* (*I Shmuel* 15:4). Thus the *Shema* means not only *Hear, O Israel*, but also *Gather Israel* together to proclaim that Hashem is our God, the One and Only! However, on Shavuos we achieve a heightened sense of this *achdus*. (5655)

◆§ Sources of Unity

What is the source of this *achdus*, that seems to be so crucial a factor in all of Jewish life throughout our history?

On the most superficial level, we can say that the Jewish people possesses an innate sense of oneness, a common bond that comes of a shared lineage, as we say in the *Shabbos Minchah* Prayer, וּמִי כְּעַמְּךָ יִשְׂרָאֵל גּוֹי אֶחָד בָּאָרֶץ, *And who is like Israel, one nation on earth.*

◆§ Torah Promotes Unity

Probing a bit further, we find that *klal Yisroel*'s unity is based on a unique heritage common to all Jews — that of Torah. Just as *achdus* is a prerequisite for Torah so through Torah we can achieve *achdus*. Despite occasional internal differences within the Jewish world, allegiance to Torah unites our people in an overriding bond. This ability to forge unity through Torah may be seen in the first verse taught to

1. א and ע are ocassionally interchangeable in *Lashon HaKodesh*.

small children, תּוֹרָה צִוָּה־לָנוּ מֹשֶׁה מוֹרָשָׁה קְהִלַּת יַעֲקֹב, *Moshe commanded to us the Torah, a heritage of the Assembly of Jacob* (*Devarim* 33:4). Only through Torah can disparate elements of Israel be welded into an *Assembly of Jacob*, a unified whole. Indeed, *the assembly of Jacob* may even refer to the Torah itself as the force that unifies the Jewish people.

Torah leads to *achdus* in the sense that since every Jew has a unique portion in Torah. We can hope to realize our potential in Torah only by pooling our portions cooperatively. Torah is the "glue" that holds us all together. (5653, 5662)

Likewise, Rabbi Akiva's renowned saying, וְאָהַבְתָּ לְרֵעֲךָ כָּמוֹךָ זֶה כְּלָל גָּדוֹל בַּתּוֹרָה — *"Love your neighbor as yourself"* (*Vayikra* 19:18), is one of the Torah's quintessential precepts, and may actually be a reference to the relationship between Torah and *achdus*. The Torah tells us to love our fellows not because of their personal qualities, but because זֶה כְּלָל גָּדוֹל בַּתּוֹרָה, (*Yerushalmi Nedarim* 26a), because we are an entity (כְּלָל) great in Torah.[1] The unifying power of our common Torah heritage also explains why the First Commandment, *I am Hashem, your God*, was phrased in the singular rather than the plural (אֱלֹהֵיכֶם). (5662)

Faith Brings Achdus

Thus far, we have traced Jewish unity to our common Torah heritage. Really, however, the source of our unity goes even deeper — to our common belief in the One above, Whose very being is a form of unity far beyond our comprehension.[2] While no material or spiritual entity can begin to approach Hashem's Oneness, by striving to achieve internal unity the Jewish people can become a vehicle to teach the world about *achdus*.

The Exodus from Egypt was the catalyst that originally made Jewish unity possible. As we said in the essay on *succah*, the word *Mitzrayim* connotes not only the land of Egypt, but also a status of confinement (derived from the component word *tzar*, narrow). In a larger sense, then, *yetzias Mitzrayim* (the Exodus from Egypt) symbolizes liberation from

1. We become a great united entity through Torah. The word יִשְׂרָאֵל is the acronym for "יֵשׁ שִׁשִּׁים רִבּוֹא אוֹתִיּוֹת לַתּוֹרָה, there are 600,000 letters in the Torah." Torah is what gives our nation its form.

2. *Editor's Note:* The *Pasach Eliyahu* prayer captures this concept succinctly in the following fragment: אַנְתְּ הוּא חַד וְלָא בְחוּשְׁבָּן ... לֵית מַחֲשָׁבָה תְּפִיסָא בָךְ כְּלָל, *You Who are a Unity, but not in the sense of disparate parts ... no intelligence can have any perception of You.*

all the narrow partisan concerns that serve as obstacles to our working together. With the First Commandment, אָנֹכִי ה׳ אֱלֹהֶיךָ אֲשֶׁר הוֹצֵאתִיךָ מֵאֶרֶץ מִצְרַיִם מִבֵּית עֲבָדִים — *I am HASHEM, your God, Who delivered you from the land of Egypt, from the house of slavery* (*Shemos* 20:2), Hashem eradicated all the confining factors that obstructed the *achdus* of the Jewish people. This removal of barriers that came with the Exodus in a sense made the Jewish people more closely resemble Hashem, Who has no beginning, no end, no measure or number, boundary or limit. (5653)

◈ Torah Promotes Achdus

As we have said, Jewish unity is derived from, among other sources, our allegiance to Torah. The reverse is also true — while Torah promotes *achdus, achdus* just as surely leads to Torah. The light of Torah that shines in any generation is directly proportional to the *achdus* that emits that light. Conversely, when there is dissension, Heaven forbid, Torah learning also suffers.

Not only does *achdus* promote development in Torah, it also brings us to establish a closer relationship with Hashem than that of any other people. This is based on our recognition of His transcendental Unity. Thus the *Shabbos Minchah* Prayer links our unity with Hashem's — אַתָּה אֶחָד וְשִׁמְךָ אֶחָד וּמִי כְּעַמְּךָ יִשְׂרָאֵל גּוֹי אֶחָד בָּאָרֶץ, *You are One, and Your Name is One, and who is like Your people Israel, one nation on earth.* Just as Hashem is One and His Name (i.e. the Torah) is One.[1] This prayer suggests that it is because of Israel's unity that we can fully accept Hashem to the exclusion of any other power — the true meaning of ה׳ אֶחָד, *HASHEM, the One and Only.*

It is noteworthy that the Name אֱלֹהִים is used to describe the relationship between the Gentiles and the Creator. The plural form suggests that different peoples perceive Him at different levels, while only Israel can appreciate His Oneness. This is why only Israel can proclaim שְׁמַע יִשְׂרָאֵל ה׳ אֱלֹהֵינוּ ה׳ אֶחָד, *Hear, O Israel, HASHEM is our God, HASHEM is the One and Only God.*

This is also the intent of the Psalmist in the verse אֱלֹהִים אֱלֹהֶיךָ אָנֹכִי, — *"Although I am God to all mankind, nonetheless I am your God"*

---

1. Cf. *Ramban's* introduction to his commentary on the Torah which says that the whole Torah consists of Names of Hashem.

(*Tehillim* 50:7). Only Israel, when it achieves internal unity, can appreciate Hashem as the one and only God. (5655)

◆§ Jewry's Common Soul

Underlying all these approaches to the concept of *achdus* is the belief that the Jewish people share one common *neshamah* (soul). Thus the Torah describes Jacob and his descendants on their arrival in Egypt in the following terms: כָּל־הַנֶּפֶשׁ לְבֵית־יַעֲקֹב הַבָּאָה מִצְרַיְמָה שִׁבְעִים, *the whole soul of the house of Jacob coming to Egypt was seventy* (*Bereishis* 46:27). From the use of the singular form of the word נֶפֶשׁ, *soul*, we deduce they they were really one common soul divided among seventy bodies. Similarly, the Jewish people as a whole share a common soul which is nourished by Torah, as the Psalmist says (19:8),תּוֹרַת ה׳ תְּמִימָה מְשִׁיבַת נָפֶשׁ— *The Torah of HASHEM is perfect, it restores the soul*. (5662)

Finally, the dream of *achdus* may help explain the Talmud's well-known but perplexing story of the would-be proselyte who asked to be taught the entire Torah while standing on one foot (*Shabbos* 31a). Why was he so insistent on learning in such an awkward and unsteady position?

We can say that the image of standing on one foot represents a degree of consistent unity that is impossible for ordinary individuals to maintain, except by effacing themselves to the unity of Hashem and the Jewish people. Thus Hillel answered the would-be proselyte that if he wanted to achieve that level of consistency in Torah learning, he would have to unite himself completely with the Jewish people. The only way to do that, said Hillel, is to be totally sensitive to the feelings of others — "Whatever is distasteful to you, do not do to your friend." (5663)

Tikkun Leil Shavuos

◆§ All-Night Learning on Shavuos: Origin and Significance

Throughout the world Jews observe the centuries-old custom of conducting an all-night vigil dedicated to Torah learning on the first night of Shavuos. One explanation for this tradition given by the *Mishnah Berurah* (494:1) is that it compensates for a tragic error committed by the Jewish nation as they were about to receive the Torah at Sinai: On the very morning Hashem came to give the Torah, they overslept! Hashem had to arouse them and remind them that it was time to receive the Ten Commandments.

To atone for this blunder, Jews have accepted upon themselves the custom of remaining awake all night. The *Zohar* suggests that staying up on Shavuos night is an especially auspicious act, for one who learns Torah diligently on this occasion is virtually assured of longevity. *Arizal*, cited by the *Mishnah Berurah*, promises that someone who does not sleep at all and learns Torah will live through the year without harm.

In the following essay, we will suggest a number of other explanations for this custom, portraying *Tikkun Leil Shavuos* as a prelude to the purity and holiness of Shavuos. We will also explore how it is a means of demonstrating our thirst for Torah study, which will hasten the arrival of the *Moshiach*.

◆§ Shavuos Night: Culmination of Purity

The custom of conducting an all-night Torah vigil on the first night of Shavuos is cited by the *Zohar* in its commentary on *Parshas Emor* (97b). The *Zohar* describes a process of spiritual purification (*taharah*) that grows in intensity during the seven weeks of *sefirah* until it reaches a climax on the night of Shavuos. This purification is compared to that of a woman who has become impure through a discharge of which the Torah says (*Vaykira* 15:28), וְסָפְרָה־לָּהּ שִׁבְעַת יָמִים וְאַחַר תִּטְהָר, *she shall count for herself seven days and become clean.* Similarly, the purpose of counting seven weeks of *sefirah* is to prepare for the purification of Shavuos.

During these days and weeks, our personal efforts to cleanse ourself of spiritual impurities are critical, as the Torah says (*Vayikra* 23:15), וּסְפַרְתֶּם לָכֶם, *you shall count* **for yourselves.** However, if we make sincere efforts during *sefirah,* we can be assured that Hashem will shower us with an outpouring of *taharah* on the night of Shavuos, as the Sages said (*Shabbos* 104a) הַבָּא לְטַהֵר מְסַיְּעִים אוֹתוֹ, *someone who comes to purify himself will receive [Divine] help.*

The *Zohar* also reminds us that the *taharah* that descends on those who immerse themselves in Torah study on this night is a fragile thing. Unless we take active steps to preserve it throughout the year we cannot be assured that it will remain with us. As the Psalmist says (51:12), לֵב טָהוֹר בְּרָא־לִי אֱלֹהִים וְרוּחַ נָכוֹן חַדֵּשׁ בְּקִרְבִּי, *Create for me a pure heart, O God, and a steadfast spirit renew within me.* There are two steps here. Through our efforts during the seven weeks of *sefirah* we merit the creation of a "pure heart" for ourselves. However, it takes the all-night vigilance of Shavuos to give it permanence and turn it into a "steadfast spirit" that will endure throughout the year. (5662)

◆§ Purity Leads to Torah

What is unique about the aura of spiritual purity that pervades Jews, particularly on the first night of Shavuos?

The *Zohar* speaks of the purification that occurs during the forty-nine-days of *sefirah.* As noted there, there are forty-nine levels of purity that coexist alongside forty-nine levels of defilement. The challenge facing Jews during the *Sefirah* period is to progress from sinfulness to purity at each stage, every night discarding one level of defilement to attain a new level of *taharah.*

This purity is only a beginning, however, a means to an end. In the Shabbos and festival prayers we ask טַהֵר לִבֵּנוּ לְעָבְדְּךָ בֶּאֱמֶת, *purify our heart to serve You with truth.* The true goal of the purification of Shavuos night is to be able to serve Hashem through the truth of Torah.

It is significant that the letters of the word for truth, אֱמֶת, are the first, last, and middle letters of the *alef beis*, indicating that Torah is all encompassing, a part of every aspect of life, every component of the universe. (5663)

Consequently, by the time Shavuos comes the Jew has risen above a blurred world of intermingled sin and virtue and reached a summit of unmitigated purity immune from the onslaught of the forces of evil. Many commentators note that the *yetzer hara* is disabled on the night of Shavuos.

To an extent, the experience of *Tikkun Leil Shavuos* leaves a permanent effect on the Jewish psyche. It is clear that no object, however hallowed, can remain suspended in air with no basis of support. On Shavuos, aided by the purity unique to that day, collective world Jewry is made into a supportive base for Torah, a vessel to receive the Torah. In effect, then, *Tikkun Leil Shavuos* forges a spiritual union between the Jewish people and Torah, making us a foundation for the sturdy establishment of Torah in this world. (5639)

Learning through the night also has the beneficial effect of preserving the integrity of the Torah. While the Torah itself is incorruptible, it is subject to distortion by those whose motives are less than pure. Perturbed by the possibility of deliberate misconstruction of the Torah King David beseeched (*Tehillim* 120:2), ה׳ הַצִּילָה נַפְשִׁי מִשְּׂפַת־שֶׁקֶר מִלָּשׁוֹן רְמִיָּה — *HASHEM, rescue my soul from lying lips, from a deceitful tongue*. Likewise, Aaron was eulogized by the prophet Malachi for his determination to preserve the Torah's integrity (2:6), תּוֹרַת אֱמֶת הָיְתָה בְּפִיהוּ וְעַוְלָה לֹא־נִמְצָא בִשְׂפָתָיו, *the Torah of truth was in his mouth and sin was not found on his lips.*

In fact, the Torah study of Shavuos night can be viewed as a means of better appreciating truth. The paramount importance attached to truth as a Jewish value is indicated by the Aramaic term for this concept קוּשְׁטָא (*kushta*), which is related to a Hebrew word for beauty, קְשׁוֹט (*keshot*). There is no more authentic beauty than the pure truth — in a world saturated with false and ugly values, the true values of Torah stand out in their radiant beauty. (5634)

While the purity that pervades Shavuos is a Divine phenomenon requiring no human intervention, efforts of Jews to purify themselves can certainly enhance the process. In particular, *taharah* is associated with the in-depth study of Torah that is often marked by novel Torah thoughts (*chiddushei Torah*). The prophet Yechezkel (36:25) metaphorically compares *taharah* to the sprinkling of water, וְזָרַקְתִּי עֲלֵיכֶם מַיִם טְהוֹרִים וּטְהַרְתֶּם, *I shall sprinkle pure water upon you and purify you.* The image of water usually alludes to Torah learning, as the Sages said (*Taanis* 7a), נִמְשְׁלוּ דִבְרֵי תוֹרָה לְמַיִם.

Thus, a particularly effective way to merit the purity attainable on this night is to exert oneself to produce creative Torah thought, which is an expression of the particular makeup of his soul's potential. While deriving new concepts in Torah can be arduous, Hashem helps those who dedicate themselves to this task. When He gave us the Torah, He also gave us the ability to use it creatively for personal growth. (5644)

Other dimensions of the learning of Shavuos night are also of great significance. *Tikkun Leil Shavuos* may be considered a rehearsal of an old established tradition, as well as a new means of dialogue between Hashem and Israel. Given that the Torah is accepted anew every Shavuos, *Tikkun Leil Shavuos* gives us an opportunity to review the progress we have made over the past year in preparation for renewed efforts during the coming year. In the days before He first gave the Torah Hashem told the Jews (*Shemos* 19:5), וְעַתָּה אִם־שָׁמוֹעַ תִּשְׁמְעוּ בְּקֹלִי, *and now, if you will hearken well* [literally, *listen and listen*] *to My voice.* The double expression שָׁמוֹעַ תִּשְׁמְעוּ may be an allusion to the two-pronged approach to learning inherent in *Tikkun Leil Shavuos*: review of what one has learned and preview of what one is about to learn.[1] (5640)

◆§ Torah: Communication with Hashem

Tikkun Leil Shavuos is also a tool to prepare us for a new and higher mode of Divine communication. The *Zohar* (*Parashas Va'eira* 25) notes that Divine pronouncements introduced with the Hebrew root *dibbur* did not have full force until *Mattan Torah.* Before then, says the *Zohar*, *dibbur* was in exile. (This may explain why the Jews in Egypt did not accept Moshe's predictions of their imminent redemption, since he prefaced them with the word וַיְדַבֵּר, a term they were not yet ready to comprehend.) Shavuos, then, commemorates the first occasion on which the term *dibbur* was used: The Ten Commandments commence with the words וַיְדַבֵּר אֱלֹהִים, *And God spoke* (with the term *dibbur*). They are called עֲשֶׂרֶת הַדִּבְּרוֹת from the same root.

1. See *Rashi* ad loc.

According to a tradition mentioned in the Talmud (*Succah* 42a), as soon as a child begins to speak he is first taught the verse (*Devarim* 33:4), תּוֹרָה צִוָּה־לָנוּ מֹשֶׁה מוֹרָשָׁה קְהִלַּת יַעֲקֹב, *Moshe commanded us the Torah, the heritage of the congregation of Jacob.* It is not coincidental that a Jew's first *dibbur* should affirm his belief in Hashem and His holy Torah. Likewise, to commemorate the night before the Jews' initiation into *dibbur* via the Ten Commandments, we too speak the *divrei Torah,* of *Tikkun Leil Shavuos.* Learning through the night of Shavuos, like teaching a toddler to repeat תּוֹרָה צִוָּה־לָנוּ מֹשֶׁה, is the beginning of our attempt at serious communication with Hashem.

King David alludes to the relationship between our efforts at discussing *divrei Torah* on Shavuos night and reciting the Ten Commandments the next morning in the following description of the Jewish people (*Tehillim* 103:20): עֹשֵׂי דְבָרוֹ לִשְׁמֹעַ בְּקוֹל דְּבָרוֹ — *who make His speech for the purpose of hearing His speech.* We can understand this reference in light of the preceding discussion. By confining our speech to words of Torah on Shavuos night, we merit to commune with Hashem's Presence the following morning through the Ten Commandments. (5645)

Based on *Ibn Ezra's* interpretation of the concise but very significant expression, אֶת־ה׳ הֶאֱמַרְתָּ הַיּוֹם, *You made HASHEM speak* (*Devarim* 26:17) a connection can be made between our Torah study on Shavuos night and Hashem's response in the Ten Commandments.

Similarly, the Psalmist (68:35) exhorts us to תְּנוּ עֹז לֵאלֹהִים, *Render might to God,* an allusion to our efforts to come closer to Hashem through learning Torah. Our Torah learning so to speak invests Hashem with a power to bring us closer to Him. This reciprocal pattern of human initiative followed by Divine response was set when Moshe ascended Mount Sinai without assurance that Hashem intended to speak to him there (*Shemos* 19:3): וּמֹשֶׁה עָלָה אֶל־הָאֱלֹהִים, *Moshe ascended to God.* He was then rewarded with a direct summons from Hashem, וַיִּקְרָא אֵלָיו ה׳ מִן־הָהָר, *and HASHEM called to him from the mountain.* (5655)

The form of *dibbur* that originated at Sinai can be separated into two components: one characterized by the rough sounds of speech that emerge from the *mouth,* and the articulate speech that emanates from the *tongue.* The first is more of a surface phenomenon, while the second originates from a deeper, not readily evident source.

The composer of the *Nishmas* prayer recited on Shabbos and festivals distinguishes between these two aspects of speech in the following passage, כִּי כָל פֶּה לְךָ יוֹדֶה וְכָל לָשׁוֹן לְךָ תִשָּׁבַע, *Every mouth shall offer thanks to You; every tongue shall vow allegiance to You.* The kind of speech symbolized by the mouth was attained at the time of the Exodus from Egypt, when every mouth offered thanks to Hashem. (Indeed, the word *Pesach* can be broken down into the two words פֶּה סָח, *the mouth that talks,* alluding to the consecration of the power of speech.) However, the consummation of the process of *dibbur,* the ability to articulate deep thoughts symbolized by the tongue, occurred on Shavuos. The period of *sefirah,* marking the progress from the Exodus to the giving of the Torah, is thus a transition from the rudimentary speech skills of Pesach to the profound experience of Shavuos.

On Shavuos, every tongue vowed allegiance to Hashem. Taking an oath (*shavuah*) implies not only acceptance of the primacy of the spiritual realm and acknowledgment of Hashem's rulership, as occurred at *Pesach,* but also complete rejection of materialistic values, the level attained at Sinai. This supreme employment of speech is the goal we aspire to in *Tikkun Leil Shavuos.* (5664)

◆§ Shavuos: A Renewal of Torah

The full night of learning is an intensely personal experience, a time of spiritual renewal. One of the names of Shavuos, *Chag HaBikurim,* the Festival of the First-Fruits, refers not only to the offering of the first fruits or the two leavened loaves offered on Shavuos, but also to the spiritual rejuvenation of Shavuos. On that uplifting day, exhausted individuals are given a new lease on life. The student who earlier had access to only the surface of Torah wisdom now finds, as a result of his exertion in Torah on this night, a new vitality to penetrate beyond superficial explanations.

King Solomon describes this process of rejuvenation in the following terms (*Mishlei* 5:15): שְׁתֵה־מַיִם מִבּוֹרֶךָ וְנוֹזְלִים מִתּוֹךְ בְּאֵרֶךָ, *Drink water from your reservoir, and fresh flowing water from your well.* By drinking the immutable waters of the written Torah on the night of Shavuos, we will merit to drink constantly fresh flowing waters from the springs of the oral Torah throughout the year.[1] This night,

1. The written Torah is compared to a reservoir which has finite boundaries. The Oral Torah is constantly unfolding in a flow of new ideas similar to a spring which constantly gushes forth with fresh water.

which commemorates the giving of the Torah, is the time to begin this process.

Not only students of Torah, but the Torah itself is renewed on this night. While the Written Torah is fixed and definite, the Oral Law with its constantly growing and developing explanations and insights knows no limits. Torah is called the *Eitz Hachayim*, the Tree of Life, because it bears new fruits of intellect and reason every year, and consequently offers humanity an ever-fresh bounty of new perceptions and applications. Shavuos is indeed a "New Year" for the produce of the intellect. Just as our material fortunes are decreed on Rosh Hashanah on the basis of our actions of the past year, and in particular of our service of that day, so also is our intellectual growth for the coming year. The Torah thoughts we will be granted to innovate are determined on Shavuos, the "New Year" of Torah. It is therefore critical that we have the merit of a night of intensive Torah study to prepare us for this momentous day. (5661)

The Mishnah (*Avos* 2:17) notes the need for extensive preparation before renewing our ties to Torah, הַתְקֵן עַצְמְךָ לִלְמוֹד תּוֹרָה שֶׁאֵינָהּ יְרֻשָּׁה לָךְ, *prepare yourself to study Torah, for it is not yours by inheritance.* While the finite Written Torah is מוֹרָשָׁה קְהִלַּת יַעֲקֹב, *the heritage of the congregation of Jacob,* and is certain to be transmitted from one generation to the next *regardless* of our efforts, the novellae and constantly changing applications of Torah principles that give life to learning the Oral Torah depend largely on our own initiative. It is thus of utmost importance to invest untiring effort, however weary we are, into this night full of learning that sets the stage for the coming successful year of Torah achievement. (5661)

Tikkun Leil Shavuos also expresses vividly our incessant thirst for Torah. In most matters, the scarcer a commodity is, the greater is our demand for it; conversely, the more plentiful something is the less pleasure we have from it. Thus, food tastes best on an empty stomach and loses its appeal as we grow full.

One would think, then, that the night before the giving of the Torah, we would want to starve ourselves to increase our appetite for the next morning's "feast." This would be comparable to our not eating *matzah* a few weeks before Pesach to insure our desire for it on Seder night. However, the nature of Torah is exactly the reverse of physical pleasures. The more Torah we learn, the more we want to learn and the greater is our capacity and need for learning.

This is amply displayed on Shavuos night. This is similar to human growth. As one ingests food his stomach and appetite expand and hence his *need* for food increases. Although we learned Torah all year long, on this night we seek to attain an even higher level of Torah knowledge, to the extent that we are willing to forfeit our keenly-desired sleep. What is more, doing so only *increases* our thirst for the Torah we will receive the next morning.

On his deathbed, the Patriarch Jacob blesses his offspring to be like fish, וְיִדְגּוּ לָרֹב בְּקֶרֶב הָאָרֶץ, *may they proliferate abundantly like fish within the land* (*Bereishis* 48:16). Although they live in water fish never drown. Similarly, although the Jewish nation is constantly immersed in Torah, we are never satiated or overwhelmed by it. (5660)

Finally, *Tikkun Leil Shavuos* underscores our yearning for *Moshiach.* Though we are assured that he will come to redeem us eventually regardless of our merits, we can accelerate his coming through our intensive study of Torah. *Proverbs* suggests that, through our immersion in Torah, our fondest wishes — including the arrival of the *Moshiach* — will be realized.

The famous statement (*Pesachim* 6b), אֵין מוּקְדָם וּמְאוּחָר בַּתּוֹרָה, *there is no earlier or later in Torah,* is usually understood to mean that the written Torah we have before us is not always in chronological sequence. We may suggest the additional interpretation, however, that through the medium of *Torah* Jews have the ability to alter the decrees of what is to be earlier or later in the course of history, and to hasten the arrival of *Moshiach.*

We can also advance his arrival through heartfelt prayer. If it is true throughout the year that one should learn before *davening* in order to give his prayers the merit of Torah, how much more so is it true on this day which is so crucial to our learning of the entire coming year! In particular, we should concentrate both our learning and our prayers on bringing the redemption quickly. By following a full night of learning with enthusiastic early-morning prayers,[1] we can hope that the combined effort will expedite *Moshiach's* speedy arrival and the final and complete redemption. (5658)

---

1. *Editors Note:* While the prevailing custom is to *daven "ke-vasikin,"* (so as to begin the silent *amidah* at sunrise) on Shavuos, those who would be too fatigued to concentrate properly on their prayers after a full night of learning would be better advised to sleep for a while. They will then have strength to *daven* later with proper enthusiasm. Each individual must decide what is best for himself.

Megillas Ruth

◆§ Introduction

The custom of reading The Book of Ruth — the moving story of a Moabite woman's odyssey to Judaism — on Shavuos is first mentioned in *Mesechtas Sofrim*, a source dating back to the era of the Gaonim. Judaism's authoritative code of law, the *Shulchan Aruch*, briefly mentions this custom in *Orach Chaim* 490:9.

Numerous reasons have been offered for this practice. *Mishnah Berurah* (ad loc.) suggests that *Ruth* reminds the would-be Torah scholar that achieving greatness in Torah learning is not a simple matter. Torah can be acquired only through constant struggle to overcome challenges. *Yalkut Shimoni* (*Ruth* 590) says that in order to reach the pinnacle of spiritual elevation, one must be prepared to face the obstacles of poverty, deprivation, and humiliation, as Ruth herself did.

In the following essay, we will offer various approaches to explain why *Ruth* was selected as the appropriate *Megillah* to be read on the festival of Shavuos. One suggestion is that this book demonstrates the power of Torah scholars such as Boaz to set halachic standards through their actions. In addition, *Ruth* illustrates the interconnection between Torah study and practical actions such as giving charity, and shows how non-Jews can join the ranks of the Jewish people and make significant contributions to its legacy. Since Ruth was the founder of Davidic dynasty and the root of the Moshiach, reading her story also exemplifies our indomitable belief that the arrival of *Moshiach* will usher in a glorious era to rival the splendor of the giving of the Torah at Mount Sinai. Throughout the essay, we will stress that *Ruth* is not merely a book to be read on Shavuos, but serves as an essential supplement to the Torah.

◆§ Megillas Ruth and Shavuos

Why do we read *Ruth* on Shavuos? Although numerous explanations have been given, all share a common theme. *Ruth* is not merely an appropriate reading for Shavuos, but at the same time a supplementary text that leads to a fuller appreciation of the Torah that was transmitted on Shavuos.

◆§ Deeds of the Righteous

Firstly, *Ruth* dramatizes the theme expressed in the Mishnah (*Avos* 1:17), לֹא הַמִּדְרָשׁ הוּא הָעִקָּר אֶלָּא הַמַּעֲשֶׂה, *Not study but practice is the main thing*. In particular, we must learn from the deeds of *tzaddikim* (righteous individuals), often performed of their own initiative without *halachic* precedent, as well as their reactions to situations not explicitly mentioned in the Torah. The true role models of Torah do not just practice Judaism, they personify it. Their every action is guided by Torah principles, and is worthy of study as much as actual Torah commandments. In fact, the practices of *tzaddikim* are deemed to be a living supplement to the Torah.

Through Torah study, the Jew's soul is so perfected that he is able to conduct all his deeds in accordance with the Torah. Torah is compared to an inner light (cf. *Tehillim* 97:11), אוֹר זָרֻעַ לַצַּדִּיק, *light is sown for the righteous*, the light of Torah is sown in the soul of the *tzaddik*. That light should be nurtured until it brings forth fruit. King Solomon alludes to this in *Mishlei* (4:22): כִּי־חַיִּים הֵם לְמֹצְאֵיהֶם, *For [the teachings of the Torah] are life to those who find them* — those who harness their soul to the study of Torah will merit that all of their actions be in accord with Torah. (5640)

The conduct of Boaz, as depicted in *Ruth*, is a classic example of the personification of Torah through the actions of *tzaddikim*. The very name "Boaz" can be seen as an amalgam of the Hebrew words בּוֹ and עַז, *meaning strength is within him*.[1] He was a man of innate strength and

1. Torah is called עוז (strength) as the Midrash *Tanchuma* explains the words of the Psalmist (29:11) "Hashem will give give strength to His nation" as referring to the giving of the Torah.

courage, someone well equipped to focus the searchlight of Torah on situations not previously clarified.[1] (5647)

Boaz agreed to marry Ruth despite his relative's unfounded contention that marriage with a Moabite woman was forbidden by Jewish law. He was content to rely on the Biblical interpretation and collective wisdom of the Sages of his generation, who ruled that the prohibition against marrying Moabites applied only to males from that nation (*Yevamos* 77). By marrying Ruth, and thus publicly demonstrating his confidence in the Sages, Boaz affirmed *emunas chachamim,* faith in the rulings of contemporary Torah scholars. However, his announced intention to marry Ruth, even before an official decision permitting unions with Moabite women was rendered, indicated that the behavior of *tzaddikim* is inherently correct. Boaz intuitively anticipated the ruling of the Sanhedrin because his own identification with Torah law was complete. This is one reason we read *Ruth* on Shavuos, to demonstrate the power of the authorities of a generation to both interpret and, in some instances, *anticipate* rulings involving *halachah* through their personal conduct.

This is the essence of the Oral Law, the ability of the leaders of each generation to implement ever-new aspects of Torah *orally,* in accordance with the established principles of Torah interpretation. The expression we say in the *Maariv* prayer every night, אֱמֶת וֶאֱמוּנָה, *truth and faith,* alludes to the role of contemporary authorities in the development of the Oral Law. While the Written Law is unquestionably the pure *truth,* as a nation we can arrive at that truth only through *emunas chachamim,* faith in the Torah that the authorities of our generation effect constantly. This particular faith is very difficult to maintain; because it is so vital to our connection with Hashem's Torah, the *yetzer hara* goes to extraordinary lengths to weaken and destroy it. It is therefore important for every Jew who wishes to built his life on Torah to strengthen himself in this particular point, and to consult with teachers and scholars to resolve any doubts the *yetzer hara* may attempt to implant into his mind. (5633)

King David alludes to this ability of Torah sages to set *halachic* precedents through their actions (*Tehillim* 84:6): אַשְׁרֵי אָדָם עוֹז לוֹ בָךְ מְסִילוֹת בִּלְבָבָם, *Praiseworthy is the man whose strength is in You, those*

1. Alternatively, the name Boaz may allude to his strength in resisting the temptation he may have felt when Ruth first came to him at night.

whose hearts focus on the paths leading upwards. (Perhaps this verse, which contains the word עוֹז, specifically alludes to Boaz.) Such a person is a true *ben Torah* (son of Torah) because his *every* action is guided by the Torah. (5651)

Even the misled actions of the righteous can be informative. Ruth's father-in-law Elimelech, who acted improperly in fleeing to Moav at a time of starvation in the Land of Israel, unwittingly initiated a scenario which resulted in the birth of King David, and which will reach its ultimate climax with the arrival of David's descendant, *Moshiach*.

This power of *tzaddikim* to interpret *halachah* may be based on the verse that introduces the Ten Commandments (*Shemos* 20:1): וַיְדַבֵּר אֱלֹהִים אֵת כָּל־הַדְּבָרִים הָאֵלֶּה לֵאמֹר, *And God spoke all of these statements saying*. The apparent redundancy of this verse — since it says וַיְדַבֵּר, *and He spoke*, the word לֵאמֹר, *saying*, is unnecessary — suggests that interpretation of the Torah would be based on the *spoken* rulings and precedents of the authorities of each generation. The expression לֵאמֹר, *to say* indicates that Hashem spoke His statements to be interpreted (לֵאמֹר) by the Torah scholars of every generation.

Similarly, the blessing recited after reading the Torah, וְחַיֵּי עוֹלָם נָטַע בְּתוֹכֵנוּ, *Who implanted eternal life within us*, (suggesting that the Torah is constantly alive within each generation) refers to the power of contemporary Torah leadership to establish *halachah* based on the accepted principles of Jewish law. This blessing also hints at the innate ability of the Jewish people to follow Hashem's will intuitively. This is the concept of *daas Torah*. By itself the study of Torah out of pure motives, will cause one's actions to reflect Hashem's wishes.

(5645, 5652)

The centerpiece of the Sinai experience we celebrate on Shavuos — Israel's acceptance of the Torah with the words נַעֲשֶׂה וְנִשְׁמָע, *we will do and we will listen* — also alludes to this theme. The word נַעֲשֶׂה suggests the actions of the leaders of each generation that render *halachic* decisions that all Jews must listen to and obey — נִשְׁמָע.

By extension, not only the deeds of *tzaddikim* but also the actions of any Jew can be made to harmonize with the Torah. For this reason we read *Ruth* on Shavuos, to emphasize the significance of each individuals' actions and to highlight the Jewish people's partnership in Torah with Hashem. This partnership is implied in Moshe's statements to the Jews (*Devarim* 26:17-18), וַה׳ הֶאֱמִירְךָ הַיּוֹם לִהְיוֹת לוֹ לְעָם, *And* HASHEM *said of you today to become His people*, making it possible for the actions of Jews to be stated in Torah, and אֶת־ה׳ הֶאֱמַרְתָּ הַיּוֹם לִהְיוֹת לְךָ לֵאלֹהִים, *you said of HASHEM today to be your God*, making it possible for abstruse concepts of Godliness to be realized through words of Torah. (5644)

Our reading of *Ruth* on Shavuos underscores two values closely related to the concept of Torah study: *tefillah* (prayer) and *tzedakah* (charity). The Book of Ruth ends with the birth of King David, Ruth's great-grandson, who described himself as the personification of prayer (*Tehillim* 109:4): וַאֲנִי תְפִלָּה, *I am [my] prayer*. King David's last words to his son Solomon also reflect the close relationship between Torah and prayer — דַּע אֶת־אֱלֹהֵי אָבִיךָ וְעָבְדֵהוּ, *Know the God of your father and serve Him* (*I Divrei HaYamimim* 28:9).[1]

The converse is also true, however — Torah study is required in order to offer the highest form of prayer. This concept is hinted at in King David's words to Solomon cited above, *Know the God of your father and serve Him*. Before one can properly *serve* Hashem (through prayer), one must first come to *know* Him through Torah study. Another reference to this concept can be found in Hashem's first conversation with Moshe at the burning bush. There Hashem said (*Shemos* 3:12), בְּהוֹצִיאֲךָ אֶת־הָעָם מִמִּצְרַיִם תַּעַבְדוּן אֶת־הָאֱלֹהִים עַל הָהָר הַזֶּה, *When you bring the people out of Egypt, you will serve God on this mountain*. By accepting the Divine service of learning Torah at Mount Sinai, they will come to the level of being able to perform another form of service, that of prayer. Thus this verse makes a clear connection between Torah and prayer. (5647)

In another place the Psalmist also calls our attention to the linkage between Torah and prayer (145:18): קָרוֹב ה׳ לְכָל קֹרְאָיו לְכֹל אֲשֶׁר יִקְרָאֻהוּ בֶאֱמֶת, *HASHEM is close to all who call upon Him — to all who call upon Him in truth*. Those whose call to Hashem is based on the *true* principles of Torah will be answered readily. (5643, 5647)

Our reading of *Ruth* also reminds us of the intimate relationship between Torah and *tzedakah* (charity). The Midrash (*Yalkut Shimoni* 601) suggests that the principal reason for reading *Ruth* is to show us the example of magnanimous individuals like Boaz. In fact, the son of Boaz and Ruth was named Oved, suggesting the word *avodah* (service).

1. Similarly Moshe's parting blessing to Yehudah (*Devarim* 33:7) שְׁמַע ה׳ קוֹל יְהוּדָה, *HASHEM, hear the voice of Yehudah*, may also be a prophetic allusion to the prayers of Yehudah's descendant David. In order to achieve any mastery of Torah or to come to meaningful knowledge of Hashem, service, in the form of prayer, is required.

Conversely, Elimelech was severely punished precisely because, as a community leader, a descendant of Yehudah and forerunner of the Royal House of King David, he should not have abandoned his people at a time when the need for charitable deeds was greatest. (5643)

Indeed, we must remember that the Royal House of David owed its very existence to many instances of Divine kindness. Not only David's survival in his struggle with Goliath and his selection to be king over his brothers point to this, but looking back into his lineage we can find many other examples. Peretz, David's patrilineal ancestor nine generations previously, was born only because of Hashem's benevolence in saving Tamar from burning. Similarly, only Hashem's kindness in saving Lot from the destruction of Sodom made the existence of his descendant Ruth possible. One whose existence is so dependent on Hashem's kindness (as we all are, though we do not always remember it) must make especially sure to be kind to others.

Thus we read *Ruth*, with its underlying theme of kindness, to remind ourselves that Torah and *chesed* should not be seen as two separate entities, but rather as interdependent elements of one broad concept. King Solomon praised the "woman of valor" for having "the Torah of kindness on her lips" (*Mishlei* 31:26). The Sages (*Succah* 49a) interprets this passage as a reference to the study of Torah *lishmah* — for its own sake, without expectation of reward. Seemingly, they mean to suggest that learning Torah *lishmah* makes the study more palatable. Although Torah can indeed be very demanding, those who approach it without ulterior motives find in it a palpable sweetness and beauty, and indeed, the custom of eating tasty dairy foods on Shavuos may be related to the idea of "sweetening" the sometimes harsh taste of Torah by approaching it *lishmah*.

Ruth has many examples of great personalities performing acts of *chessed* for purely altruistic reasons: *chessed lishmah*. Consider the kindness performed on Ruth's behalf by Boaz. When Ruth arrived in *Eretz Yisrael* as a destitute and famished emigre from Moab, she was treated very solicitously by Boaz. She came to his field to partake of the leavings reserved for the poor, and was urged by him to keep all grain not harvested by his own workers. Boaz invited her to join his workers in a meal and he gave her parched grain to eat. The Sages (*Yalkut Shimoni* 604) observed that had Boaz known that this episode would be recorded for posterity, he would have offered her fattened calves rather than parched grain.

Why, then, did Boaz give her grain rather than calves? In his defense, we can point out that he was totally uninterested in the prestige that might have come from public notice of his generosity. Rather, Boaz offered Ruth a meal of parched grain that was sufficient for her needs, rather than a more elaborate but unnecessary repast. This concern for the needs of the individual, rather than pursuit of honor or fame, is one of the hallmarks of a true *tzaddik*. How sadly lacking is this quality in contemporary society. (5650)

Another way to interpret this Midrash is to say that Boaz would have been more lavish if he had realized that his action would become an integral part of Torah, as we said above, the actions of a *tzaddik* are Torah. Alternatively, we can say that had Boaz been more generous, the purity of his intention to do kindness would have brought *Moshiach* immediately. (5644, 5656)

Ruth also illustrates the dual nature of our relationship with Hashem. On the one hand, Hashem is like a father and we are His children, as the Torah says (*Devarim* 14:1) בָּנִים אַתֶּם לַה׳ אֱלֹהֵיכֶם, *You are children to HASHEM, Your God.* On the other hand, *Ruth* ends with the birth of King David, who was known as the "servant of Hashem." In a larger sense, then, as Jews we must relate to our Heavenly Father and Master in the double role of children and servants, as we say in the prayers of Rosh Hashanah אִם כְּבָנִים אִם כַּעֲבָדִים, *whether we are children or servants.*

This transition from the status of servant to that of child is particularly appropriate to Shavuos. At Pesach, we first entered into the role of Hashem's servants, as signified by the lowly barley offering brought at the start of the counting of the Omer. Only at Shavuos is the more "refined" wheat offering of the Two Loaves brought, befitting the elevated status as children earned by accepting the Torah. The prophet Yeshayahu alludes to this change in status (*Yeshayahu* 49:3): עַבְדִּי־אָתָּה יִשְׂרָאֵל אֲשֶׁר־בְּךָ אֶתְפָּאָר, *You are My servant, Israel, in you I will glory.* Starting out as servants, we rise to become Hashem's children, in whom He will glory. Not only David, but also his descendant *Moshiach* is called Hashem's servant, as the prophet says soon afterwards (*Yeshayahu* 52:13), עַבְדִּי יָרוּם וְנִשָּׂא וְגָבַהּ מְאֹד, *Behold, My servant will be raised up and lifted and very elevated.* (5646)

Ruth also emphasizes the global role of the Jewish nation. As Hashem's "Chosen People," our mission is to proclaim His rulership to the whole world. This mission does not preclude us from accepting into our ranks enlightened individuals from other backgrounds or creeds. Just as Ruth made an important contribution to Judaism, so can anyone from any origin. Indeed, Hashem actively waits for strangers to emerge from the clutches of the non-Jewish world, as the Psalmist writes (146:9), ה׳ שֹׁמֵר אֶת גֵּרִים, *HASHEM watches for strangers.* The word שֹׁמֵר also means expectantly await as in וְאָבִיו שָׁמַר אֶת הַדָּבָר, *and his father awaited the happening* (*Bereishis* 37:11). After all, at Mount Sinai, all Jews were *geirim*: novices to Judaism.[1]

There are sacred seeds dispersed throughout the world, holy souls destined to gravitate to Judaism. While this ingathering can be a long and difficult process, it is inherent in the phenomenon of exile, in which Jews are scattered throughout the world in order to attract enlightened Gentiles to their ranks.[2] (5647)

This dream that all humanity might embrace Torah voluntarily is voiced by the prophet Yirmiyahu (16:19): ה׳ עֻזִּי וּמָעֻזִּי וּמְנוּסִי בְּיוֹם צָרָה אֵלֶיךָ גּוֹיִם יָבֹאוּ מֵאַפְסֵי־אָרֶץ וְיֹאמְרוּ אַךְ־שֶׁקֶר נָחֲלוּ אֲבוֹתֵינוּ הֶבֶל וְאֵין־בָּם מוֹעִיל, *Hashem is my strength and my stronghold, and my refuge in the day of affliction; nations will come to You from the ends of the earth and they will say, "Only falsehood did our forefathers inherit, emptiness that has no gain."* If we remain loyal to Hashem, then the nations will flock to us.

⚜ Moshiach's Arrival: Culmination of Sinai

Reading *Ruth* on Shavuos also reminds us of the final Revelation Day, a day as glorious as that on which the Torah was given, when *Moshiach ben Dovid* will appear. The word אָנֹכִי, *I*, was spoken once at Mount Sinai, at the start of the Ten Commandments, and will again be spoken to herald the arrival of *Moshiach*: אָנֹכִי אָנֹכִי הוּא מְנַחֶמְכֶם, *I, I am He Who comforts you* (*Yeshayahu* 51:12). If Shavuos marked the onset of Jewish history, then *Moshiach's* arrival will be its splendid climax, when all of humankind will flock to Hashem.

In our first encounter with Hashem as a nation, the people were afraid to ascend to Mount Sinai. When *Moshiach* comes we will all be aroused to repent and return to Hashem, and the whole nation will climb

1. The term *ger* may be related to the word נִגְרָר, *to be dragged*, suggesting that until a *ger* joins the ranks of Judaism he is "pulled back," held forcibly among the Gentiles.

2. In this light we can explain why no *geirim* will be accepted in *Moshiach's* time (*Yevamos* 24b). All those souls that were destined to join the Jewish People will have already done so.

to the top of Mount Sinai, as Hashem told Moshe (*Shemos* 19:13), בִּמְשֹׁךְ הַיֹּבֵל הֵמָּה יַעֲלוּ בָהָר, *with an extended blast of the shofar they will go up on the mountain.*

How fitting it is that on the first day of Shavuos, which is called *Yom HaBikurim*, we read about the final day of *Moshiach*. As King Solomon wrote (*Koheles* 7:8), טוֹב אַחֲרִית דָּבָר מֵרֵאשִׁיתוֹ, *The end of a matter is better than its beginning.* Thus on the festival that commemorates the beginning of Israel's status as the people of Torah, we read about the day that will be the culmination of that status, may it come soon.

(5649)

Not only does reading *Ruth* turn our gaze toward *Moshiach*, it lays out for us various scenarios for his arrival, as we see in the following words spoken to Ruth by Boaz (3:13): אִם־יִגְאָלֵךְ טוֹב יִגְאָל וְאִם־לֹא יַחְפֹּץ לְגָאֳלֵךְ וּגְאַלְתִּיךְ אָנֹכִי חַי־ה׳ שִׁכְבִי עַד־הַבֹּקֶר, *If he will redeem you, then good, let him redeem. And if he does not desire to redeem you, then I myself will redeem you. [I swear] as* HASHEM *lives, lie until the morning.* Apart from the obvious meaning of this verse in the story, we may offer a homiletic interpretation: "May HASHEM redeem you, Israel, quickly in the merit of your Torah, which is called 'good.' But if not, then wait patiently until the 'morning' [symbolic of liberation], when *Moshiach* will surely arrive at his appointed time." (5658)

Finally, the reading of *Ruth* on Shavuos reminds us of *Techiyas HaMeisim* (resurrection of the dead). Boaz's redemption of the property of his relative Elimelech and his sons Machlon and Kilyon, and the *yibum* ceremony[1] he performed with Ruth, with its impact on the souls of Elimelech and his sons Machlon and Kilyon, evoke our faith in *Techiyas HaMeisim*. Thus when Boaz proposes to marry Ruth, he speaks in terms of restoring the name of her late husband (*Ruth* 4:5).

Similarly the concept of a redeemer appears in *Ruth*. Upon the birth of Oved, the son of Boaz and Ruth, Naomi is told that she now has a redeemer to restore the soul of her late husband Elimelech (*Ruth* 4:14). Although the union of Boaz and Ruth was not technically the *yibum* referred to in the Torah, since Ruth was the widow of a relative but not his brother, the concepts of redemption and restoration of the deceased soul are unquestionably relevant here.

It is clear from all the above that, as we say in the *Shemoneh Esrei*

---

1. When a man dies childless, the Torah (*Devarim* 25:5) requires his widow to marry her deceased husband's brother. This procedure, called *yibum*, is understood by the Kabbalists (cf. *Ramban Bereishis* 38) to have the power to resurrect the soul of the deceased brother.

Prayer בְּאוֹר פָּנֶיךָ נָתַתָּ לָנוּ ה׳ אֱלֹהֵינוּ תּוֹרַת חַיִּים, *with the light of Your countenance You gave us,* HASHEM, *our God, the Torah of life.* Torah indeed serves as the Life Source of all existence.

We may still ask, nonetheless, why the message of resurrection is relevant to Shavuos. For it is only through the merit of Torah that resurrection will occur. Boaz, the epitome of Torah, merited to have the opportunity to perform the *yibum* ceremony, bestowing *chessed* on the souls of his relatives Elimelech and Machlon. In this sense, the term commonly used for kindness done to the deceased, *chessed shel emes,* the kindness of truth, alludes to the forms of kindness we are allowed to do in the merit of Torah, which is called *emes.*

The Sages taught (*Chullin* 142a) that every letter of Torah has the power to bring about the resurrection of the dead, if we only knew how to interpret it properly. Thus Boaz, who was an exemplar of Torah, was able to perform a ritual causing such a resurrection.

The institution of *yibum,* in turn, is not possible without the Torah that was given on Shavuos. As we discuss at length elsewhere, the Jewish people's souls expired and then revived at the time the Torah was given. This demonstrates that the Torah has the power to resurrect. For this reason also, Torah was given to mortals rather than to angels, because only mortals have need for Torah's restorative powers. (5656)

Two Loaves

❧ Introduction

In the time of the *Beis HaMikdash,* a major part of the rituals of Shavuos was the offering of the Two Loaves. This procedure is first mentioned in the Torah in *Parashas Emor* (*Vayikra* 23:17): מִמּוֹשְׁבֹתֵיכֶם תָּבִיאוּ לֶחֶם תְּנוּפָה שְׁתַּיִם שְׁנֵי עֶשְׂרֹנִים סֹלֶת תִּהְיֶינָה חָמֵץ תֵּאָפֶינָה בִּכּוּרִים לַה׳, *From your dwelling-places you shall bring two loaves of waving, two esronim of fine flour shall they be, leavened shall they be baked, a first-fruit offering to* HASHEM.

In the following essay we will discuss the symbolism of these two loaves, and in particular the question of why there were *two* of them. We will examine many of the dual relationships that exist in Jewish life, including the link between individual efforts to provide for one's livelihood and Hashem's help in that area, and the bond between Hashem and the Jewish people. Also the connection between learning Torah and the character traits that aid in that learning, and two preeminent personalities of Jewish history, Moshe and *Moshiach*, will be discussed.

The Torah requires that the Two Loaves be waved in all four directions as well as above and below. We will explore the significance of this waving ceremony, and reasons for the requirement that these loaves be made *chometz* (leavened). As in many of the essays in this book, many other issues of Jewish thought will prove to be of relevance to our primary theme.

◆§ Two Loaves: Heavenly and Earthly Sustenance

A central feature of Shavuos in the *Beis HaMikdash* was the ceremony in which the Two Loaves, (which had to be *chometz*), were waved in all four directions, as well as up and down. The Torah calls the entire ritual (*Vayikra* 23:16) מִנְחָה חֲדָשָׁה, *a new flour offering.*

Several questions arise: Why did there have to be *two* loaves and why did they have to be *chometz*? What does the *waving* of the bread symbolize? Why does the Torah emphasize the *newness* of the offering?

Why two loaves? Bread is very commonly used as a symbol for sustenance and livelihood. These two loaves of bread, then, can be taken as symbolic of two means of providing one's livelihood. The first may be called *heavenly bread* (cf. *Shemos* 16:4, לֶחֶם מִן־הַשָּׁמָיִם), the manna that sustained an entire generation in the Wilderness for forty years. Such a lifestyle, while acceptable temporarily, is not the ideal means of livelihood. As the *Zohar* observes (*Parashas Behar*), מַאן דְּאָכִיל דְּלָאו דִּילֵיהּ בָּהִית, *someone who eats that which is not his feels ashamed.*

The Jewish ideal of livelihood, was the agricultural lifestyle that became established in *Eretz Yisrael*. There, in spite of many difficulties faced by struggling farmers, their efforts to live off the land, forged a close relationship between Hashem and each individual.[1]

1. Not only the Jew but even the Land itself "clings to Hashem," since the farmer realizes that his efforts are fruitless without Hashem's blessing. This is especially true in the *shmitah* year, when the Land itself, and not just its occupants, rests, as the Torah says (*Vayikra* 25:2), וְשָׁבְתָה הָאָרֶץ שַׁבָּת לַה׳, *the Land shall rest, a Sabbath for HASHEM.*

This lifestyle, which relies on Divine blessing for our efforts and reminds us that we are rewarded in consequence of good actions, may be called that of *earthly bread* (לֶחֶם מִן הָאָרֶץ).

Thus the Two Loaves symbolize the relationship between these two forms of livelihood, *heavenly bread* and *earthly bread.* Waving the Two Loaves towards Heaven reminds us that both of them, including the *earthly bread* that seems to depend only on our physical efforts, require the blessings of Heaven in order to succeed and, indeed, that the two are really both from Heaven. (5631, 5634)

It may appear paradoxical that the material world is given a blessing on Shavuos, a day we normally associate with the highest level of spirituality. However, we can understand this by way of an analogy to Shabbos. Shabbos is considered the source of all blessings, and in particular the material blessings of the week that surrounds it, even though no material work may be done on that day, and no manna was given on it.

Hashem does not shower His blessings on the Jewish people unless they also take initiative on their own behalf. Even though He sustains the Gentile world purely out of His generosity, He wants Jews to earn their sustenance with good deeds. By offering the Two Loaves, symbolizing material blessings, on the day that the Torah was given, we acknowledge the linkage between Torah and material livelihood, as the Sages said (*Avos* 3:21), אִם אֵין קֶמַח אֵין תּוֹרָה אִם אֵין תּוֹרָה אֵין קֶמַח, *If there is no flour there is no Torah; if there is no Torah, there is no flour.* This is particularly true because, until the Torah was given, Hashem lavished His blessings on the Jews regardless of their merit, as the Sages said (*Pesachim* 118a) כ"ו דורות שֶׁזָּן בְּחַסְדוֹ, *He nourished twenty-six [from the Creation until the Torah was given] generations in His kindness.* Only after Sinai was a linkage established between Torah and the struggle for livelihood. (This theme is discussed at greater length in the essay called *Eretz Yarah VeShakatah — The Earth Feared and then Grew Calm.*)
(5651)

The following verse in the *parashah* of the *Tamid*-offering provides additional basis for the assertion that Sinai was a turning point, after which Jews had to merit their sustenance: עֹלַת תָּמִיד הָעֲשֻׂיָה בְּהַר סִינַי לְרֵיחַ נִיחוֹחַ אִשֶּׁה לַה׳, *It is the continual elevation-offering that was done at Mount Sinai, for a satisfying aroma, a fire-offering to* HASHEM (*Bamidbar* 28:6). From the fact that Hashem earlier (v. 2) calls this offering לַחְמִי, *My food,* we may infer that some form of "satisfying aroma," that is, some action taken to win favor in Hashem's eyes, would thenceforth be required in order to merit to receive לַחְמִי, Hashem's food. This transformation occurred with the giving of the Torah at Sinai.

Similarly, the fact that the Ten Commandments are introduced by Hashem's Name *Elokim*, typically indicating His quality of judgment, also suggests from then on Hashem applied strict justice in deciding whether the Jewish people was spiritually worthy of its material livelihood. (5651)

Finally on this theme, we may interpret the opening verse of the *parashah* of the *Tamid* offering (*Bamidbar* 28:2) to draw the same message — אֶת קָרְבָּנִי לַחְמִי לְאִשַּׁי רֵיחַ נִיחֹחִי תִּשְׁמְרוּ לְהַקְרִיב לִי בְּמוֹעֲדוֹ, *My offering, My food for My fires, My satisfying aroma, you are to be scrupulous to offer Me in its appointed time.* Homiletically we may paraphrase this as follows: "You should ensure that My bread, the sustenance I give, shall came through My satisfying aroma, the satisfaction I have when Israel's actions are pleasing." (5651)

☙ Two Loaves: Challenge of Divine Service

Bread also denotes challenge and struggle, as indicated by the similarity between the words לֶחֶם, *bread*, and מִלְחָמָה, *war*. The Two Loaves, may be said to symbolize the two primary challenges that together make up our mission in the world: First, the struggle against the *yetzer hara* (evil inclination), the vanquishing of the negative and also the challenge of seeing that the World to Come underlies everything that we do in this world, the infusing of life with positive meaning. These two challenges also correspond to the twin declaration of the Jewish people at Sinai, *Na'aseh v'Nishma* (we will do and we will listen). We must fight the *yetzer hara* with our *doing* (*na'aseh*), and through *listening* to the teachings of Torah (*nishma*) we will bring an awareness of the World to Come into our material world. (5635)

☙ Two Loaves: Hashem and Israel Come Closer

Additionally, the Two Loaves symbolize Hashem's drawing close to His people. Sharing bread together is always a good catalyst to bring people together, as the Sages said (*Sanhedrin* 103b), גְּדוֹלָה לְגִימָה שֶׁמְּקָרֶבֶת אֶת הָרְחוֹקִים, *great is the power of giving food to guests, for it brings together those who are far apart.*

On Shavuos a dual process occurs — Hashem embraces His children, who in turn draw closer to Him. Thus Hashem calls Shavuos *Yom HaBikurim*, the Day of the First Fruits, to emphasize our gifts to Him, and we call the festival *The Season of the Giving of Our Torah*, pointing out His gift to us.[1] (5636)

☙ Two Loaves: Torah and Prayer

The Two Loaves also allude to two pillars of our service of Hashem, Torah and *tefillah* (prayer). Not only did we receive the Torah on Shavuos, but with it we also received the gift of *tefillah*, the power to pray to Hashem. This relationship is illustrated in two nearly parallel verses (*Devarim* 4:7-8): כִּי מִי־גוֹי גָּדוֹל אֲשֶׁר־לוֹ אֱלֹהִים קְרֹבִים אֵלָיו כַּה׳ אֱלֹהֵינוּ בְּכָל־קָרְאֵנוּ אֵלָיו: וּמִי גּוֹי גָּדוֹל אֲשֶׁר־לוֹ חֻקִּים וּמִשְׁפָּטִים צַדִּיקִים כְּכֹל הַתּוֹרָה הַזֹּאת אֲשֶׁר אָנֹכִי נֹתֵן לִפְנֵיכֶם הַיּוֹם — *For what nation is so great that it has a God close to it like* Hashem*, our God, whenever we call to Him? And what nation is so great that it has righteous statutes and laws like this entire Torah that I am giving before you today?* In the first verse, Moshe tells Israel to exult in the fact that Hashem always listens to their prayers. In the second, he boasts of the righteousness of the laws of the Torah. From this we see that Torah and *tefillah* are mutually dependent.

The Talmud also calls attention to the interconnection between Torah and *tefillah* in the following dictum (*Berachos* 31a): אֵין עוֹמְדִין לְהִתְפַּלֵּל ... אֶלָּא מִתּוֹךְ הֲלָכָה פְּסוּקָה, *One should stand up to daven ... only after learning halachah.* Similarly, King Solomon warned that someone who spurns learning Torah will not merit to have his prayers accepted: מֵסִיר אָזְנוֹ מִשְּׁמֹעַ תּוֹרָה גַּם־תְּפִלָּתוֹ תּוֹעֵבָה, *One who avoids listening to Torah, even his tefillah will be an abomination* (*Mishlei* 28:9). (5650)

☙ Two Loaves: Renewal in Torah

The requirement that the Two Leaves be made from new produce suggests growth and renewal, a widespread theme in Jewish thought. Our efforts in Torah (symbolized by bread which, as we saw above, hints at the *war for Torah*, from the similarity of the words לֶחֶם and מִלְחָמָה) are merely the starting-point for the renewal in Torah we

1. *Editor's Note:* This dual process is paralleled by Moshe ascending the mountain and Hashem descending to Mount Sinai.

experience. Our halting and feeble attempts to originate new Torah thoughts here on earth serve only to arouse an outpouring of Heavenly wisdom, the real source of all growth in Torah.

Thus King Solomon sings (*Mishlei* 31:23), נוֹדָע בַּשְּׁעָרִים בַּעְלָהּ, *her husband is renowned at the gates.* The serious student of Torah who applies himself diligently to learning and growth through Torah, will win renown in the gateways of Heaven, where his efforts will be rewarded with Divine help to succeed in his learning. The more we push ourselves to learn Torah, the more Divine assistance we will be given, as the *Zohar* says (*Parashas Vayeira*), נוֹדָע בַּשְּׁעָרִים בַּעְלָהּ כְּפוּם מַה דִּמְשַׁעֵר בְּלִבָּא, *Her husband [the Torah student] will win renown [and become versed in Torah] according to the estimation he gives it in his heart,* that is, he will be helped to succeed in accord with the place of importance it occupies in his heart.

Similarly, the Psalmist alludes to this Divine grant of wisdom in the exclamation (24:7), שְׂאוּ שְׁעָרִים רָאשֵׁיכֶם וְהִנָּשְׂאוּ פִּתְחֵי עוֹלָם וְיָבוֹא מֶלֶךְ הַכָּבוֹד, *Raise up your heads, O gates, and be uplifted, you everlasting entrances and the King of Glory will come.* This verse urges us to elevate the "gates" of our hearts, to prepare ourselves for Torah. When we do this, the "everlasting entrances" of our people — Moshe and Aaron who made openings into the World to Come with their Torah and service — are uplifted and made into conduits to bring Hashem's Presence into our midst. Then "the King of Glory" will come to us. In other words, our efforts in Torah and prayer give the leaders of the generation the power to bring Hashem's Presence into our midst.

This relationship between Torah study in our world and Divine assistance may underlie the following dictum of the Sages (*Sanhedrin* 99b), כָּל הָעוֹסֵק בְּתוֹרָה לִשְׁמָהּ מֵשִׂים שָׁלוֹם בְּפַמַּלְיָא שֶׁל מַעֲלָה וּבְפַמַּלְיָא שֶׁל מַטָּה, *Whoever occupies himself with Torah study for its own sake brings peace between those who initiate Torah study on earth and the One who promotes and inspires learning from His place in Heaven.*

(5652)

◆§ Two Loaves: The Torah Personality

The Two Loaves may symbolize two aspects of the Giving of the Torah at Sinai: Not only were the laws of the Torah given there, but also the qualities of personality needed to accept and incorporate them were also given.

King Solomon emphasizes the impact of Torah on the Jewish personality by pleading (*Mishlei* 9:5) לְכוּ לַחֲמוּ בְלַחְמִי, *Come and eat My bread.* While this verse has no literal translation in English, the phrase לַחֲמוּ בְלַחֲמִי has the connotation that by partaking of Hashem's "bread" (i.e. Torah), by our diligent efforts to acquire Torah, we become imbued with the "personality" of the Torah. (5650)

When Hashem spoke the words אָנֹכִי ה׳ אֱלֹהֶיךָ, *I am HASHEM, your God,* in the singular, it implied that He was the God of each individual Jew and not just of the group as a whole. Thus, each Jew *felt* his connection to Torah and to his portion in Heaven and was helped to subdue his *yetzer hara.* The Two Loaves remind us that on Shavuos not only did we receive the Torah, but also were given personal qualities necessary to use Torah as a tool for growth by making it part of ourselves,[1] As we perfect ourselves, the entire universe attains a new, higher, level of perfection. The name *Yom HaBikurim,* the "day of the first fruits" alludes to this renewal of the universe on a higher level. (5637)

In a similar vein, the Two Loaves may represent not only the Torah given to Israel but also the power of Torah scholars to interpret the Torah and to originate new Torah thoughts. This theme is discussed more extensively in the essay on Ruth. (5647)

◆§ Two Loaves: Humility on All Occasions

The dual nature of the Two Loaves also reminds us of the need for humility in all walks of life, since the nature of a *minchah*-offering implies subservience to someone else.[2] The Two Loaves show that not only the *am ha'aretz* (ignorant person) but even the greatest Torah scholar must humble himself before Hashem.

This "double humility" is also symbolized by the flour offerings at the beginning and the end of the count of the *Omer.* The *Korban HaOmer* on the second day of Pesach consisted of barley, a coarse animal food representing the humility of the unlearned Jew. The Two Loaves of Shavuos, however, at the end of the *Omer* period, were made of fine wheat flour, a noble human food, suggesting that even the

1. *Editor's Note:* The Sages clearly had this in mind in their dictum (*Avos* 6:1), וּמְגַדַּלְתּוֹ וּמְרוֹמַמְתּוֹ עַל כָּל הַמַּעֲשִׂים, *[The Torah] makes him great and exalts him above all things.*

2. Thus we find that Jacob sent his brother Esau a *minchah* to show his submission to him.

learned Jew who receives the Torah on Shavuos must subjugate himself to Hashem by offering a *minchah.* Humility is a necessary precondition to meriting Torah. Torah, like water runs from above to below.

The counting of the *Omer* marks the transition from the ignorance and spiritual immaturity of the Jews when they left Egypt (as the *Haggadah* says, וְאַתְּ עֵרֹם וְעֶרְיָה, *you were naked and exposed,* bare of *mitzvos* and spiritual achievements) to the spiritual perfection they attained just fifty days later on Shavuos. This dual humility — the imperative for all Jews, learned as well as ignorant, to remain humble — is the ultimate mission of the Jewish people.

King David referred to the humility required of the sophisticated Jew in the phrase (*Tehillim* 36:7), אָדָם וּבְהֵמָה תוֹשִׁיעַ ה׳, *You save both man and beast,* HASHEM. The Sages (*Chullin* 5b) taught that this passage refers to knowledgeable and sophisticated people who nonetheless hold themselves to be no better than ignorant animals. (5637)

◆§ Two Loaves: Written and Oral Law

The Two Loaves may also be seen as symbolic of the two aspects of Torah, the Written Law and the Oral Law. The verse in *Mishlei* (9:5) discussed earlier, לְכוּ לַחֲמוּ בְלַחְמִי, "*Come and eat My bread [i.e. partake of the Torah],*" clearly defines Torah as "Heavenly nourishment." By waving the Two Loaves together we indicate that neither the Written Law nor the Oral Law can stand alone, but rather they must be considered an inseparable whole. (5638)

Waving the Two Loaves upward indicates that *our* study of Torah elevates both the Written and the Oral Law to greater heights. While this may seem an egoistic attitude, in truth the Torah accomplishes its purpose in the design of creation only when it is learned and practiced by Israel.[1] (5638)

In a similar vein, lifting the Two Loaves, which were produced here on earth, towards Heaven symbolizes the fact that even the new Torah thoughts that seem to originate here on earth actually emanate from the understanding of Torah given by Heaven. (5639)

Alternatively, we may see the Two Loaves as representing the two kinds of *tefillin,* those of the head and the hand. As a result of our

---

1. This understanding of the significance of our Torah study simultaneously inspires and demands responsibility.

efforts here below, especially our efforts to learn the Oral Law (symbolized by the hand-*tefillin*), Hashem will shower us with His blessings from above, in particular with understanding of the Written Law (symbolized by the head-*tefillin*). (5642)

☙ Two Loaves: Two Worlds

The Two Loaves also symbolize the two worlds with which the Jew is concerned, our world and the World to Come. The waving of the Two Loaves on Shavuos signifies that life in both these worlds depends on Torah, as the Mishnah says (*Avos* 6:7), גְּדוֹלָה תּוֹרָה שֶׁהִיא נוֹתֶנֶת חַיִּים לְעוֹשֶׂיהָ בָּעוֹלָם הַזֶּה וּבָעוֹלָם הַבָּא, *Great is Torah, for it confers life on its practitioners, both in this world and in the World to Come.* (5662)

☙ Two Loaves: Downfall of Amalek

The waving of the Two Loaves may also allude to a necessary prerequisite for the arrival of *Moshiach* — the downfall of Amalek. In the first battle with Amalek, whenever Moshe lifted his hands Israel was able to subdue Amalek (cf. *Shemos* 17:11). Similarly, by lifting our hands to wave the Two Loaves, we voice our hope that we will soon be able to vanquish Amalek and everything he represents.

Indeed, the *bikurim*, the first fruits offered on Shavuos, are called (*Devarim* 12:6), תְּרוּמַת יֶדְכֶם, *the offering [lit. the raising up] of your hands.* This is reminiscent of the Torah's description of Moshe's raising his hands in the battle against Amalek (*Shemos* 17:11) — וְהָיָה כַּאֲשֶׁר יָרִים מֹשֶׁה יָדוֹ, *and it was, when Moshe raised his hand.* The *Zohar* (*Parashas VaEschanan*) says that Moshe's battle was only the beginning of the vanquishing of Amalek a prerequisite for Hashem's revelation in the world — while *Moshiach's* arrival will be the culmination, as the Torah says (*Devarim* 3:24), אַתָּה הַחִלּוֹתָ לְהַרְאוֹת אֶת־עַבְדְּךָ אֶת־גָּדְלְךָ וְאֶת־יָדְךָ הַחֲזָקָה, *You have begun to show Your servant Your greatness and Your strong hand.* Just as Moshe's victory over Amalek made possible the giving of the Torah, so the final destruction of Amalek and the eradication of his name from under the Heavens will make possible Hashem's revelation to all the world, may we be privileged to see it soon. (5641)

⌘ Two Loaves: The Challenge of a Better World

In a more novel approach, the waving of the Two Loaves in all directions may represent the Jewish ideal of a better world for all people, Gentiles as well as Jews. The mission of the Jewish people is not only to bring themselves closer to Hashem but also to bring all of humanity into contact with Torah, the Tree of Life.[1] (cf. 5641)

⌘ Two Loaves: A New Offering

The Two Loaves are called מִנְחָה חֲדָשָׁה, *a new offering*. The Talmud (*Menachos* 68b) considers the *halachic* implications of this requirement for "newness." הָעוֹמֶר מַתִּיר בַּמְדִינָה וּשְׁתֵּי הַלֶּחֶם בַּמִּקְדָּשׁ — Whereas individuals in the rest of *Eretz Yisrael* were allowed to partake of the new crop of grain as soon as the *Korban Omer*, the offering of the *Omer*, was brought on the second day of Pesach, flour offerings in the *Beis HaMikdash* could not be brought from new grain until after the Two Loaves were brought on Shavuos. It is entirely fitting that the new cycle of offerings should begin on Shavuos, since all of the offerings are said to be based on the offerings brought at Sinai, as we see in the verse cited above (*Bamidbar* 28:6) עֹלַת תָּמִיד הָעֲשֻׂיָה בְּהַר סִינַי, *the continual elevation-offering that was done at Mount Sinai.*

Similarly, all of our prayers, which are in effect surrogate sacrifices, are closely related to Torah. We see an allusion to this in the words of the Psalmist (145:18), קָרוֹב ה׳ לְכָל־קֹרְאָיו לְכֹל אֲשֶׁר יִקְרָאֻהוּ בֶאֱמֶת, *HASHEM is close to all who call upon Him [who pray to Him] — to all who call upon Him in truth.* The word קָרוֹב, *close*, is closely related to the word קָרְבָּנוֹת, *offerings*, and the word אֱמֶת, *truth*, is often identified in Rabbinic literature with Torah. Thus it is fitting that Shavuos, the day on which the Torah is renewed, also marks the renewal of the offerings, both of which are in turn closely related to *tefillah*. (5643)

⌘ The Two Loaves and the Omer Offering

Let us consider a more profound dimension of the distinction between the *Omer* offering brought on the second day of Pesach and the Two Loaves brought on Shavuos. Pesach marks the liberation of the

---

1. See editor's note 2 on the subsection Torah's Impact on the Nations.

neshamah, the Jewish soul, from the material demands of its corporal encasing. We see an allusion to this in the Rabbinic dictum cited above (*Menachos* 68b), הָעוֹמֶר מַתִּיר בַּמְּדִינָה, which we can interpret homiletically that the materialism (represented by the rest of the land outside of the *Beis HaMikdash*) that too often shackles us is negated on Pesach.[1] On Shavuos, however, an even more significant process occurs, וּשְׁתֵּי הַלֶּחֶם בַּמִּקְדָּשׁ, *and the Two Loaves [permit new offerings] in the Beis HaMikdash].* The goodness inherent in every Jew suddenly blooms in the inner recesses of the Jewish heart (in the *Mikdash,* the sanctuary of the heart).

The Sages said (cf. *Shir HaShirim Rabbah* 5:3), פִּתְחוּ לִי פֶּתַח כְּחוּדוֹ שֶׁל מַחַט וַאֲנִי אֶפְתַּח לָכֶם פֶּתַח כְּפִתְחוֹ שֶׁל אוּלָם, *Open [in your hearts] an opening for Me like the eye of a needle and I will open up to you [to repent and return to Hashem] an opening like the doorway to a grand ballroom.* On Pesach, by overcoming our materialistic limitations, we open ourselves like the eye of a needle. On Shavuos, however, we achieve a spiritual breakthrough that unleashes our inner potential.

The prophet Yechezkel alludes to these progressively wider openings in his description of the opening of the gates of the future *Beis HaMikdash* on Shabbos and Rosh Chodesh (46:1), כֹּה אָמַר ה׳ אֱלֹהִים שַׁעַר הֶחָצֵר הַפְּנִימִית הַפֹּנֶה קָדִים יִהְיֶה סָגוּר שֵׁשֶׁת יְמֵי הַמַּעֲשֶׂה וּבְיוֹם הַשַּׁבָּת יִפָּתֵחַ וּבְיוֹם הַחֹדֶשׁ יִפָּתֵחַ, *So spoke God, HASHEM: 'The Gate of the Inner Courtyard that faces east shall be closed the six days of work and on the Sabbath day it shall be opened and on the day of the [new] month it shall be opened.'* Homiletically we may see in this a reference to the first opening achieved on Pesach (here referred to as "the day of the new month" because the month of Nissan in which it falls was called הַחֹדֶשׁ הַזֶּה לָכֶם רֹאשׁ חֳדָשִׁים, *this month shall be for you the beginning of the months,* see *Shemos* 12:2), and to the subsequent breakthrough achieved on Shavuos, here called "the Sabbath day" because the Torah was given on Shabbos. (5653)

Finally, let us consider why the Torah insists that the Two Loaves be made leavened (*chometz*). *Chometz* is traditonally associated with the

1. The word מַתִּיר means to unshackle.

yetzer hara, the inclination to sin. On Shavuos, however, even the *yetzer hara* is subjugated, directed to a higher purpose, and deprived of its capacity to do evil. Thus we celebrate the subjugation of the *yetzer hara* by taking *chometz* and raising it up to Heaven, symbolic of the fact that the *yezter hara* has been redirected to higher purposes.

This suppression of the *yetzer hara* was a long and difficult process, attained in a succession of forty-nine successive purifications of the counting of the *Omer.* Only on Shavuos, when we attain the fiftieth level of purity, can we be sure that no vestiges of the *yetzer hara* remain.

The requirement that the Two Loaves be offered from *chometz* may also allude to the challenge and struggle faced by all humans in their quest for growth. *Matzah* symbolizes the simple unchanging and unyielding lifestyle of angels. However, as the Sages tell (*Shabbos* 88b), the claim of the angels to retain the Torah was rejected because man, with his constantly fomenting turbulence, had greater need for the growth potential of Torah. *Chometz* represents the constant changing and growth nature of man, that carries with it the potential to transcend all obstacles and ascend continually higher and higher through Torah.

(5639, 5646, 5658, 5659)

Na'aseh Ve'Nishma

✧ Na'aseh Ve'Nishma: Practice Before Wisdom

At Mount Sinai, the Jews' gave a ringing declaration of their loyalty to Hashem (*Shemos* 24:7): כֹּל אֲשֶׁר־דִּבֶּר ה׳ נַעֲשֶׂה וְנִשְׁמָע, *All that HASHEM has spoken we will perform and we will hear!* This teaches us that *doing mitzvos* takes primacy over the study of them. The Jewish people clearly give a higher priority to observing Hashem's law, than to researching it.

Similarly, the Mishnah teaches (*Avos* 1:17), וְלֹא הַמִּדְרָשׁ הוּא הָעִקָּר אֶלָּא הַמַּעֲשֶׂה, *not study, but practice is the prime objective*, in other words observing *mitzvos* is more important than studying about them. Another Mishnah in *Avos* (3:12) observes, כֹּל שֶׁמַּעֲשָׂיו מְרֻבִּין מֵחָכְמָתוֹ חָכְמָתוֹ מִתְקַיֶּמֶת וְכֹל שֶׁחָכְמָתוֹ מְרֻבָּה מִמַּעֲשָׂיו אֵין חָכְמָתוֹ מִתְקַיֶּמֶת, *Anyone whose good deeds exceed his wisdom, his wisdom will endure; but anyone whose wisdom exceeds his good deeds, his wisdom will not endure.*

The principle of *Na'aseh Ve'Nishma* — subordinating study to practice — helps explain the request the Jewish people made to Moses after hearing the first two of the Ten Commandments directly from Hashem. They beseeched Moshe to accept the remaining Commandments from Hashem and transmit them to the people. Their reluctance to receive the Torah directly from Hashem may not have been due to concern that they would misunderstand Hashem's will. Rather, they might have been apprehensive that by receiving Hashem's laws directly, they would put themselves in the position of understanding them *all too well* so that their wisdom would outdistance their psychological capacity to observe the new laws.

Let us examine this in greater detail. Had the Jews heard all Ten Commandments directly from Hashem, they would have benefited immensely in terms of the scope and depth of their intellect. Their wisdom would undoubtedly have far surpassed that of any generation before or since. However, the added sagacity, derived from direct access to Hashem could have had fatal consequences, as the people themselves said (*Devarim* 5:22), אִם־יֹסְפִים אֲנַחְנוּ לִשְׁמֹעַ אֶת־קוֹל ה׳ אֱלֹהֵינוּ עוֹד וָמָתְנוּ, *If we continue to hear the voice of* HASHEM, *our God, we will die!*

Why was this so? Their fear was based on the likelihood that, with a direct channel to Hashem, their knowledge would have far surpassed their *mitzvah* observance and their knowledge would have been not only short-lived but also fraught with danger. As King Solomon said (*Koheles* 1:18), וְיוֹסִיף דַּעַת יוֹסִיף מַכְאוֹב, *he who increases knowledge increases [the danger of causing himself] pain [if he does not fulfill his potential].* Had they heard the Commandments directly from Hashem, and then not been stringent in their performance there was a risk of their perishing. Their level of understanding would demand an unattainable level of performance.

Thus, the generation of the desert acted prudently in asking to hear the remaining Commandments from Moshe, rather than from Hashem, so that their *Nishma* would not exceed their ability for *Na'aseh*.[1]

We may also understand the first sin, eating from the Tree of Knowledge, in this same context. Once he had partaken of the forbidden fruit, Adam's knowledge of Hashem now exceeded his capacity to heed Hashem's directives. This first sin gave Adam a theoretical wisdom, without a corresponding willingness to apply it in practice, that not only caused him to be driven from Gan Eden but also brought death into the world. Likewise, listening to the details of Hashem's Torah (*nishma*) without a commitment to observe it (*na'aseh*) would have been fatal to Adam's descendants, the Jewish people.

King David, in his bequest to his son Solomon, defined the relationship between knowledge and practice by means of the following words: וְאַתָּה שְׁלֹמֹה־בְנִי דַּע אֶת אֱלֹהֵי אָבִיךָ וְעָבְדֵהוּ, *And you, my son Solomon, know the God of your father, and serve [i.e., worship] Him* (*I Divrei HaYamim* 28:9). David urged his son to study the profoundly awesome ways of Hashem not as an end in itself but as a means to an end, namely to *serve Him*. (5651)

This emphasis on the practical observance of Torah has other implications for the Jewish people. According to the Talmud (*Shabbos* 88a), *Na'aseh Ve'Nishma* was a motto preserved as a secret by the angels:

> אָמַר רַבִּי אֶלְעָזָר בְּשָׁעָה שֶׁהִקְדִּימוּ יִשְׂרָאֵל 'נַעֲשֶׂה לְנִשְׁמַע' יָצְתָה בַּת קוֹל וְאָמְרָה לָהֶן מִי גִילָּה לְבָנַי רָז זֶה שֶׁמַּלְאֲכֵי הַשָּׁרֵת מִשְׁתַּמְּשִׁין בּוֹ דִּכְתִיב „בָּרְכוּ ה' מַלְאָכָיו גִּבּוֹרֵי כֹחַ עֹשֵׂי דְבָרוֹ לִשְׁמֹעַ בְּקוֹל דְּבָרוֹ" בְּרֵישָׁא עֹשֵׂי וַהֲדַר לִשְׁמֹעַ:
>
> *Rabbi Elazar said: When the Jewish people said "We will do" before saying "We will hear," a Heavenly voice proclaimed, "Who revealed to My children this secret that the ministering angels use, as it is written (Tehillim 103:20) "Hashem's angels bless Him; those that carry out His word, and those that listen to His word." First it says that they do His bidding, and afterwards it says that they hear it.*

1. *Editor's Note:* This reasoning should certainly not discourage anyone of our generation from learning Torah to the fullest of his abilities. To the contrary, today we need as much help as possible in the struggle against the *yetzer hara*. Indeed, we see that the Jews of that generation did not *cease* to learn, but rather turned to the *gadol hador*, the leader of the generation, to instruct them.

How can we understand the concept that *Na'aseh Ve'Nishma* is a secret means of communication employed by Hashem's heavenly angels? Let us bear in mind, however, that angels do not have the free will that is basic to humans. They are "pre-programmed" to perform Hashem's bidding, for that is the justification for their existence. Consequently, they are not torn by the internal struggle between good and evil that confronts humans.

Thus, by proclaiming, *Na'aseh Ve'Nishma*, Jews usurped the angels' "secret" means of serving Hashem. By announcing their desire to abandon material interests in favor of spiritual goals, the Jews declared themselves ready to follow in the footsteps of the angels, and to accept their assigned mission without the slightest hesitation. They yielded their free will in order to serve Hashem fully.

The ideal of total obedience to Hashem's will was attainable at Sinai, when the Jewish spirit was capable of prevailing over material bonds. Unfortunately, this exalted level of devotion to Hashem declined after Sinai, when they returned to the mundane reality of everyday life where the focus was not on spiritual matters, but on material needs.

Under such conditions, unquestioning fealty to Hashem was all but impossible. In a material world, humans do not normally have the spiritual resources to achieve a true bonding with Hashem. *Na'aseh* alone, is not by itself sufficient, and the spirit of *nishma*, building a relationship with Hashem by delving into His Torah, is required as well.

(cf. 5657)

◆§ Torah's Impact on the Nations

To be sure, we would be happy to remain at the lofty spiritual peak we reached at Sinai. However, this would undermine one of our designated missions, to influence the non-Jewish world to accept the basic tenets of the Torah,[1] a mission which requires active involvement in the world of humans, not that of angels. This is where the *nishma* aspect of life, delving into the study of Hashem's teachings is essential, to help us find spiritual meaning in a life filled with materialistic trappings, in a world clothed in materialism. By carefully studying the lessons of the Torah and applying them to real-life

1. *Editors Note:* This refers to the seven Noachide Laws which apply to all nations.

situations, Jews can set proper examples to be emulated by the rest of humankind.[1]

Yisro, one of the leading luminaries of the pagan world, was willing to join the Jewish people in the Wilderness, and thus give credence to the universal power of Hashem's message. He did so not on the basis of *na'aseh* — instinctive obedience to Hashem — but because of *nishma.* The Torah itself emphasizes that Yisro *heard* of the miracles wrought by Hashem on behalf of Israel (*Shemos* 18:1). He studied the achievements and goals of the Jews, and was sufficiently impressed to cast his lot with his son-in-law's people.

Thus, we can understand these two terms as follows: *Na'aseh* is an ideal intended for the Jewish nation, while *nishma* encompasses the existing reality, and as such is fit for all humanity.

(*Parashas Yisro* 5637)

In light of this, we can understand the word *na'aseh* in its literal sense: to redesign (remake) the world at large in the spirit of the Torah. At Sinai, the Jewish people became the Chosen Nation, implying that they were to be a separate and privileged class, but in fact they were to set an example for the other nations. It is our task to demonstrate that the treasures of the Torah are not limited to a select few but have universal ramifications. The Jewish nation is meant to serve as a conduit of spiritual concepts to the Gentile world. So, when the Jews accepted the Torah, they did so not only on behalf of themselves, but also, in a sense, on behalf of all people.

The proper role of the Jew within a non-Jewish world is very aptly described (in a homiletical sense) by the eighth of the thirteen hermeneutic principles by which the Torah is interpreted: כָּל דָּבָר שֶׁהָיָה בִּכְלָל וְיָצָא מִן הַכְּלָל לְלַמֵּד, לֹא לְלַמֵּד עַל עַצְמוֹ יָצָא אֶלָּא לְלַמֵּד עַל הַכְּלָל כֻּלּוֹ יָצָא, *Anything that was included in a general statement, but was then singled out from the general statement in order to teach something, was not singled out to teach only about itself, but to apply its teaching to the entire generality.*

Although this principle refers primarily to the technical interpretation of the Torah according to traditional guidelines, it also teaches us about the relationship between the Jewish people and the rest of humanity.

1. *Editors Note:* It must be emphasized that our approach to non-Jews is not one of active outreach, but rather of setting a good example and impressing them with our virtuous character and honesty. How much more so must we provide a suitable example to non-observant Jews, whom the Torah *obligates* us to bring close to Hashem's service.

We have been given an extraordinary role to play on the world scene, a role which involves major responsibilities. However, our selection as Hashem's Chosen Nation was never meant to exclude the rest of humankind from Hashem's embrace. On the contrary, our mission is to bring everyone closer to the Creator. By proclaiming *Na'aseh* or, in a similar vein, כֹּל אֲשֶׁר־דִּבֶּר ה׳ נַעֲשֶׂה, *All that Hashem has spoken we will do* (*Shemos* 19:8), the Jews exhibited their willingness to fashion a new world order, in which Jew and non-Jew alike will recognize Hashem. In the words of the prophet Tzephaniah (3:9), כִּי־אָז אֶהְפֹּךְ אֶל־עַמִּים שָׂפָה בְרוּרָה לִקְרֹא כֻלָּם בְּשֵׁם ה׳ לְעָבְדוֹ שְׁכֶם אֶחָד, *For then I will give the peoples a pure language so that all of them may call upon the name of Hashem to serve Him in a unified manner lit., [one shoulder].*

The term *na'aseh* is used in other places in *Tanach* to denote creation of a belief or entity where none was present earlier. When the first man was created, Hashem said, נַעֲשֶׂה אָדָם, *Let us make man!* Likewise, the Torah describes Abraham's efforts to convince his neighbors of the existence of the universal God with the following expression (*Bereishis* 12:5), הַנֶּפֶשׁ אֲשֶׁר־עָשׂוּ בְחָרָן, *the souls which he MADE in Charan.* Because of this, the Midrash describes the Jewish people as the Torah's guarantors (*araivim)* who insure, through the example of their lofty moral standards, that the light of Torah will eventually filter down to all people.

How can we accomplish this? How can we as Jews cause Torah teachings to impact upon all of humanity?

First of all, we should welcome to the fold all Gentiles who sincerely embrace Judaism, for example Ruth the Moabite (discussed further in the essay on the Book of Ruth). The unique relationship we have cultivated with Hashem should not prevent us from accepting the righteous Gentile into their ranks. As the prophet Michah writes (7:20), תִּתֵּן אֱמֶת לְיַעֲקֹב חֶסֶד לְאַבְרָהָם, *Grant truth to Jacob, kindness to Abraham.* While the truth of the Torah applies principally to Jacob and his descendants, the compassion that characterized Abraham should be extended to all those who seek out Hashem. This includes not only those related to him, such as Ruth, a descendant of his brother Lot, but members of all nations, since Abraham was called "the father of many nations." (5664)

◆§ Sanctifying the World Through Torah

These outreach efforts should by no means distract us from our primary function, to absorb and practice Torah. On the contrary, there is a direct relationship between our efforts to welcome sincere Gentiles and our own growth in Torah. The more we are able to influence non-Jews who seek Hashem of their own volition, the greater is the likelihood that Torah will penetrate into every Jewish heart. We can only gain when we spread Torah ideals throughout the world.

This concept can be portrayed through an analogy to the relationship between body and soul. If a Jew seeks to sanctify his body (by limiting his intake of material pleasures), his soul also benefits. Similarly, by benefiting the Gentile world, the Jew gains in spiritual stature. (5664)

Another way of sanctifying this world, and reflecting the light of Torah to all quarters, is simply to dedicate ourselves with renewed purpose to observing the Torah. If we renew our commitment to Torah, eventually all other peoples will follow suit. The concept of *tochachah* (admonishing others) does not mean criticizing someone until he repents. Rather, by working on improving oneself, he can influence others as well. The Sages chastise someone who "has it in his hands to protest the misbehavior of others and does not do so," and who therefore shares the punishment of the sinner because of his non-involvement. This may also apply to someone who should have rebuked *himself* and failed to do so. (5642)

Making contact with an estranged world, then, is one task included in the concept of *naa'seh*. However, there are other challenges in Jewish life, and other possible interpretations of *na'aseh*. Few challenges are more daunting than *aspiring to arrive* at novel insights into the Torah's brilliance. In this sense, *na'aseh* can refer to the formation of new concepts based on Torah. The building blocks of the Torah — the basic matter from which all Torah ideas emanate — are quite simple: they are the twenty-two letters of the *alef beis*. From these elementary tools, one can develop remarkable ideas, based on the spirit of *na'aseh*. These same letters were used by Hashem in fashioning Creation.

Betzalel, the master craftsman who constructed the *Mishkan* (Tabernacle), was more than just an accomplished artist. His skill lay in his ability to fuse the letters of the *alef beis* in a brilliant manner to fashion the Tabernacle, which was primarily a spiritual abode and only secondarily a physical structure.

So, too, Jews can build homes and mansions of their own, not physical entities, but spiritual spheres of novel Torah thoughts, by connecting the building blocks of Torah.

King Solomon praises the Woman of Valor who דָּרְשָׁה צֶמֶר וּפִשְׁתִּים וַתַּעַשׂ בְּחֵפֶץ כַּפֶּיהָ, *seeks out wool and flax to work willingly with her hands* (*Mishlei* 31:13). She spins the wool, creating a great tapestry from simple materials. Similarly, a Torah scholar, of whom this verse speaks metaphorically, creates his own dazzling spiritual fabric from simple materials. The Jewish people have been compared to a silk worm that spins exquisite strands of silk from its mouth. In fact, the popular term *Torah sheb'al peh* (Oral Law) may be understood as a reference to the Torah thoughts that Jewish scholars of all generations will generate with their mouths. (5636)

☙ Torah: A Personal Experience

Probing further, we see that *Na'aseh* confronts the Jew with a striking challenge. To the Jew just beginning to undertake a life of *mitzvos*, Torah observance can be an abstract and distant process. He adheres to the laws because he is told that they are essential and beneficial, even though he may not yet fully understand why that is so. His commitment at this point is based on his teacher's say-so, rather than his own convictions.

With the passage of time, however, he begins to personalize *mitzvah* observance as the beauty and rationale behind the God-given laws grows increasingly evident to him. His relationship with Hashem, previously formal and distant, becomes warm and intense. Whereas earlier he had simply *listened* to the words of Hashem, he now *hears* them. *Na'aseh* has become *nishma*, and *nishma* has taken on an all-inclusive meaning.

When Hashem first gave the Torah at Mount Sinai, every Jew heard His Divine Voice and through this direct connection felt a unique relationship with Him. Likewise, after a period of *mitzvah* observance, a very special bond develops between Hashem and the Jew. One who performs Hashem's precepts becomes aware that Hashem speaks to him personally, bidding him to "keep My holy laws."

This intimacy is referred to in the daily prayer we mentioned above, "Happy is the person who *hears* your *mitzvos*." Although this expression seems to refer to those who *observe* the *mitzvos*, in a more literal sense it really means those who *hear* Hashem's voice as it sounded when He spoke the first commandments at Sinai.

Imagine the majesty and splendor of that encounter in the desert — the unique rapture and unparalleled ecstasy that enveloped the Jews as the Creator of the world Himself spoke with them directly. Amazingly, this same personal encounter with the Almighty can still be experienced today. Every Jew who adheres to the holy laws should hear Hashem's words reverberating constantly in his ears: "Observe My commandments; listen to My voice."

Another verse (*Vayikra* 22:31), may also refer to this phenomenon: וּשְׁמַרְתֶּם מִצְוֹתַי וַעֲשִׂיתֶם אֹתָם אֲנִי ה׳, *And you shall keep my mitzvos and you shall make them, I am HASHEM.* Every time a Jew performs a *mitzvah*, it is as if the *mitzvah* is formulated anew for the individual observing it. The famed Mishnah (*Avos* 4:2), שְׂכַר מִצְוָה מִצְוָה, *the reward for a mitzvah is another mitzvah,* also expresses this concept. The reward for observing a *mitzvah* faithfully is the ability to relate to the *mitzvah* as if one had received it personally from Hashem. Likewise, the Rabbinic teaching that an angel is created from every *mitzvah* (cf. *Avos* 4:13) may refer to the angels created when Hashem *first* commanded the *mitzvos*. Every Jew who devotes himself completely to Torah and *mitzvos* can merit to hear the voices of the angels he has created encouraging him to accomplish even more.

The same point comes across in a verse cited earlier (*Tehillim 103:20*): בָּרְכוּ ה׳ מַלְאָכָיו גִּבֹּרֵי כֹחַ עֹשֵׂי דְבָרוֹ לִשְׁמֹעַ בְּקוֹל דְּבָרוֹ, *Hashem's angels bless Him; those that carry out His word, and those that listen to His word.* By carrying out the word of Hashem, one merits to *hear* His word.

(5652)

◆ Na'aseh Ve'Nishma: Specific Mitzvos

Although the phrase *Na'aseh Ve'Nishma* is generally assumed to refer to the entire package of precepts covering all Jewish experience, it can also pertain to laws applying only in specific times and places. For example, *na'aseh* alludes to Aaron the High Priest, who specialized in performing the offerings of the *Mishkan*, which the Torah describes (*Bamidbar* 28:6) with the expression הָעֲשֻׂיָה בְּהַר סִינַי, *which was made at Mount Sinai.* On the other hand, *nishma* refers to the study of Torah, an undertaking we naturally associated with the lawgiver, Moshe. Thus this interpretation suggests that the words *na'aseh ve'nishma* refer to the two sturdiest pillars of Torah tradition, Moshe and Aaron. (5655)

This expression can be interpreted to refer to other great personalities in Jewish history, and to the *mitzvos* they performed. For example, *na'aseh* represents the service of Hashem through prayer, which is preceded by such physical acts as the donning of *tallis* and *tefillin* and *nishma* represents the Torah that we learn.

Alternatively, *na'aseh* may allude to *tzedakah*, the active allotment of charity. In several cases the Torah terms the giving of charity as an "act". The prophet Yeshayahu (33:17), for example, speaks of peace as emanating from "charitable deeds" meaning the dispensing of *tzedakah*. Similarly, when Boaz assists Ruth, she speaks of him as הָאִישׁ אֲשֶׁר עָשִׂיתִי עִמּוֹ, *the man with whom I worked* (*Ruth* 2:19).[1]

Extending this further, we can view *na'aseh* as referring to *any* of the 613 *mitzvos*. Everything that exists in this world can be raised to a higher level if it is used for the sake of a *mitzvah*. (For example, bread can be sanctified by making it the centerpiece of a Shabbos meal.) *Na'aseh*, then, deals with the elevation of the mundane by incorporating it into the world of *mitzvos*. *Nishma*, on the other hand, refers to the totality of Torah. Although we may try our best to fulfill as many *mitzvos* as we can (*na'aseh*), the individual who can truly maximize his spiritual potential is rare. Nevertheless, in accordance with the requirement of *nishma*, we declare our commitment in principle to accept all of the Torah's commandments. Indeed, the Ten Commandments were also transmitted in this manner: First came a generalized statement (*Shemos* 20:1), וַיְדַבֵּר אֱלֹהִים אֵת כָּל־הַדְּבָרִים הָאֵלֶּה לֵאמֹר, *And God spoke* **all** *these words, saying*, followed by an enumeration of the specific commandments. (5641)

Let us consider yet another interpretation. *Na'aseh* and *nishma* may correspond to the two types of *tefillin* (phylacteries) donned daily by Jewish men: the *tefillin shel yad*, placed on the arm, symbolizing active worship of Hashem; and the *tefillin shel rosh*, placed on the head, signifying intellectual acceptance and comprehension of *mitzvos*. Here again we find a distinction made between action and thought, with both of them combining harmoniously to serve the Almighty. (5641)

---

1. *Editor's Note:* The interplay between *Tzedakah* and Torah (*nishma*) is discussed more extensively in the essay on the Book of Ruth.

◆§ Na'aseh Ve'Nishma: Two Forms of Divine Service

One of the most most profound and widely cited Midrashim associated with the phrase *Na'aseh Ve'Nishma* places these two words in a slightly different context. *Midrash Rabbah* (*Shemos* 27:9) tells of a king who ordered his servant to be especially careful in watching two valuable goblets of the king's while he was away. The servant carried the goblets with him; but before the king's return, a calf running by the palace gate collided with the servant, and one of the goblets was smashed. The frightened servant feared the king's reaction, but when the king appeared, he told the servant not to worry. "One of the goblets is still intact. If you guard it with particular care, the situation can still be salvaged."

In the same sense, says the Midrash, Hashem prepared two cups for the Jews at Mount Sinai: one is represented by *na'aseh*, the other by *nishma*. The Jews shattered the one labeled *na'aseh* by their involvement with the Golden Calf. Hashem then granted them a chance to recoup by making good use of the goblet labeled *nishma*; namely, by drinking deeply of the cup of *mitzvah* performance. As the Midrash expresses it, קִלְקַלְתֶּם נַעֲשֶׂה הִזָּהֲרוּ בְּנִשְׁמַע, *you ruined na'aseh, be careful now with nishma.*

The intent of this Midrash may be better appreciated by remembering that *na'aseh* connotes activity, while *nishma* implies passivity — the Jewish people were *waiting* to hear the Divine Word. At first, Hashem intended for the Jews to take the initiative, and observe the *mitzvos* of their own volition. Then He would reward Israel for its allegiance by granting them the Torah at Mount Sinai. This intention is implicit in Hashem's address to the Jewish people before He gave the Torah in which they were told (*Shemos* 19:5), וְעַתָּה אִם־שָׁמוֹעַ תִּשְׁמְעוּ בְּקֹלִי וּשְׁמַרְתֶּם אֶת־בְּרִיתִי, *And now, if you listen to My voice [i.e. by performing My precepts]], and you will guard My covenants.* Observance of *mitzvos* proceeds] receiving the Torah.

Later, however, when the people clamored to be given a Golden Calf, they showed their diminished capacity to observe *mitzvos* of their own volition. It then became necessary for them to *accept* Hashem's sovereignty (by receiving and studying the Torah) first, and only then could they fully immerse themselves in Torah observance. It is much easier to live the life of a Torah-true Jew (*na'aseh*) after one has first committed oneself to accepting Hashem's Torah (*nishma*).

While Israel at first proclaimed *na'aseh ve'nishma* idealistically, showing an immediate willingness to practice *mitzvos*, Hashem foresaw their proclivity to sin and saw fit to reverse the order. It is significant that two of the most fundamental passages in the Torah, the Ten Commandments and the *Shema*, both begin with references to *nishma*, passive acceptance of Hashem, rather than *na'aseh*. The first of the Commandments focuses not on a specific deed, but on the acknowledgment that Hashem is the One and only Supreme Power (*Shemos* 20:2). This is the epitome of *nishma*, as opposed to *na'aseh*.

Similarly, the opening words of the *Shema* (*Devarim* 6:4), **Hear** *O Israel, HASHEM is our God, HASHEM, the One and Only*, offer a stirring call for Jews to connect with Hashem at first on an emotional and intellectual level. Only then are they exhorted to perform specific *mitzvos*. The *Shema* itself can be seen as a plea from Hashem to heed His voice, the same voice that thundered at Sinai, אָנֹכִי ה׳ אֱלֹהֶיךָ, *I am HASHEM, your God*. That voice has never ceased, as Moshe later remarked (*Devarim* 5:19), קוֹל גָּדוֹל וְלֹא יָסָף, *a great Voice that did not cease*. Even after the Jews moved on, it continues to echo until this very day, speaking to us still in clear and emphatic tones.

The message of this voice remains pertinent: Our performance of *mitzvos* is greatly enhanced by first accepting Hashem's mastery over the world. We do this by reciting (with proper concentration and intention) the appropriate blessing before performing a *mitzvah* (אֲשֶׁר קִדְּשָׁנוּ בְּמִצְוֹתָיו וְצִוָּנוּ . . ., *Who has sanctified us by His commandments and commanded us . . .*), thereby reaffirming our commitment to Hashem and His Torah. (*Parashas Yisro* 5635)

◆§ Amalek: Obstacle to Torah

There is yet another historical context for *na'aseh ve'nishma*, this one set in a futuristic mode. Despite the Jews' overwhelmingly positive response to the pivotal events at Sinai and their willingness to embrace Hashem's laws, one barrier remained to their whole-hearted commitment to Torah life — the nation of Amalek. The skirmish between Israel and Amalek shortly after the Exodus from Egypt left a permanent scar on the people that tempered their enthusiasm for a Torah-oriented existence. This was a major factor in the Jews' astonishing service of the

Golden Calf, which occurred close to the time of the giving of the Torah. In this context, *na'aseh* refers to the destruction of Amalek, and the removal of the final barrier to our unrestricted commitment to Torah.

Indeed, the word "hand" is used in describing the events surrounding Israel's first battle with Amalek. First the Torah tells that Moshe lifted his hand while Joshua battled Amalek (*Shemos* 17:11). Then, five verses later, we read that Hashem's "Hand" is permanently raised against Amalek. This imagery symbolizes the physical act of Amalek's destruction. Although the use of arms is *not* a typically Jewish means of resolving conflicts (cf. *Bereishis* 27:22, *The voice* [of prayer] *is Jacob's and the hands* [of battle] *are Esau's*), in dealing with Esau's descendant Amalek we have to resort to his tactics in addition to our own.

On that glorious day to come when Hashem will determine that the final battle with Amalek is at hand, all barriers to unconditional acceptance of the Torah will be removed. Then *nishma* will apply to all humanity, who will finally acknowledge His mastery over the world. At that moment of exultation, Hashem's name will once again be proclaimed throughout the world, as we pray in *Kaddish*: *May His great Name grow exalted and sanctified!* (5641)

To conclude, it would be appropriate to cite a passage from the Talmud (*Shabbos* 88a) that offers additional insight into the relationship between *na'aseh* and *nishma*:

> מ״ד כְּתַפּוּחַ בַּעֲצֵי הַיַּעַר כֵּן דוֹדִי בֵּין הַבָּנִים לָמָּה נִמְשְׁלוּ יִשְׂרָאֵל לְתַפּוּחַ לוֹמַר לְךָ מַה תַּפּוּחַ זֶה פִּרְיוֹ קוֹדֶם לְעָלָיו אַף יִשְׂרָאֵל הִקְדִימוּ נַעֲשֶׂה לְנִשְׁמַע
>
> "As an apple tree exists among the vegetation of the forest, so is my love [the Jewish people] among the sons" (*Shir HaShirim* 2:3) *in what sense can the Jewish people be compared to an apple tree? Such a tree has the unique characteristic of being able to produce its fruit before its leaves. Similarly, the Jewish people said na'aseh before nishma.*

According to *Tosafos*, the "apple" in this verse actually refers to an *esrog*. A mature *esrog* remains on the tree for several years, even after the leaves of the future crop appear.

What does the Talmud mean by employing the image of "fruits and leaves" for the concept of *na'aseh ve'nishma*? Leaves appear on the tree as a preparation for the emergence of the fruit. Had Israel said *nishma ve'na'aseh* at Mount Sinai instead of the reverse, it would have implied that Torah study (*nishma*) is only a means to achieve the goal of practicing *mitzvos*, in terms of the image, placing leaves before fruit. By placing *na'aseh* before *nishma*, the Jews affirmed their commitment not only to study Torah as a prerequisite to *mitzvah* performance, but also to treat the *mitzvah* of Torah study as an important goal in itself.

(5656)

◆§ Torah Acceptance Under Duress — A Mountain Over Their Heads

וַיִּתְיַצְּבוּ בְּתַחְתִּית הָהָר א״ר אַבְדִּימִי בַּר חָמָא בַּר חָסָא מְלַמֵּד שֶׁכָּפָה הקב״ה עֲלֵיהֶם אֶת הָהָר כְּגִיגִית וְאָמַר לָהֶם אִם אַתֶּם מְקַבְּלִים הַתּוֹרָה מוּטָב וְאִם לָאו שָׁם תְּהֵא קְבוּרַתְכֶם א״ר אַחָא בַּר יַעֲקֹב מִכָּאן מוֹדָעָא רַבָּה לְאוֹרַיְיתָא אָמַר רָבָא אעפ״כ הַדּוֹר קַבְּלוּהָ בִּימֵי אֲחַשְׁוֵרוֹשׁ דִּכְתִיב „קִיְּמוּ וְקִבְּלוּ הַיְּהוּדִים״ קִיְּמוּ מַה שֶׁקִּיבְּלוּ כְּבָר

"And they stood at the underside of the mountain" (*Shemos* 19:17) — *Rabbi Avdimi, the son of Chama the son of Chasa, said, "This verse teaches us that Hashem suspended Mount Sinai over the Jewish people like a vat, and told them, 'If you accept the Torah [you will be spared]; if not, there [beneath the mountain] will be your burial place.' " Rabbi Acha, the son of Yaakov, said, "Based on the above statement, a major complaint can be lodged by the Jewish people [namely, that they were coerced into accepting the Torah]."*

Rava said, "Nevertheless [i.e., despite the element of coercion at the time of the Giving of the Torah], the Jewish people accepted [the Torah] willingly at the time of Achashveirosh, as it says (Esther 9:27) 'The Jews upheld and accepted'; they upheld what they had already accepted" (Shabbos 88a).

This well-known passage in the Talmud conveys the impression that the Jews at Mount Sinai were coerced into accepting Hashem's law as their irreplaceable guide to life. Rabbi Avdimi infers from the unusual word תַּחְתִּית, *at the underside,* rather than the simpler תַּחַת, *under*, that Hashem suspended the mountain above the Jews to confront them with two options: accept the Torah or die.

Rabbi Acha bar Yaakov comments that future generations could justify any lapses in their Torah observance by arguing that their forefathers' acceptance of Hashem's law had been under duress and therefore not totally binding. However, Rava adds that this excuse was valid only until the advent of the Purim miracle. Then, in the euphoria that prevailed after their triumph over Haman, the Jews accepted the Torah wholeheartedly for all time.

The image of a mountain suspended over the heads of the Jews in the desert need not be taken literally. Instead, the coercion may have come from the enthralling atmosphere that prevailed at Mount Sinai. The people were so awed by the grandeur of Hashem's Presence that they virtually relinquished their free will, realizing that not only their lives but also the existence of the whole world depended on their agreeing to become Hashem's Chosen Nation. Although nature may at times appear to function independently, without external control, the Jews now understood that no event is outside Hashem's supervision, and every force of "nature" can be suspended at His will. It is noteworthy that *Onkolos*, whose Aramaic translation of the Torah was Divinely inspired, renders the verse (*Shemos* 19:20), וַיֵּרֶד ה׳ עַל־הַר סִינַי, *And Hashem descended on Mount Sinai* as וְאִתְגְּלֵי ה׳ עַל טוּרָא דְסִינַי, *and Hashem was* **revealed** *on Mount Sinai.* This suggests that the Jews realized at Mount Sinai that Hashem's Presence is revealed in every particle of the universe. It was this realization that compelled the Jews to accept the Torah without any hesitation.

How can we reconcile this interpretation with the comments of Rabbi Acha bar Yaakov? How could the Jews have claimed that they had been coerced into accepting laws that they would later find too difficult to observe?

Perhaps we can say that even though it was the aura of Hashem's power rather than physical coercion that forced the Jews to accept the Torah at Mount Sinai, that aura soon dissipated and the universe returned to its normal state, seemingly propelled by immutable natural laws. While it had been relatively simple to acknowledge Hashem's supremacy and accept His Torah without hesitation under the influence of that aura, it was another matter to maintain that enthusiasm in a world in which His supremacy over nature was no longer so obvious. Jews might in the future claim that lacking that aura they become lax in their commitment.

Sinai and Purim

The Purim experience changed this situation. The events of that time demonstrated to a new generation that Hashem could control every detail of human affairs even acting within the ordinary confines of nature, and not just by acting in supernatural fashion as He had at Mount Sinai. The hidden but easily discernible miracles that produced the Jews' victory over Haman proved that Hashem watched out for His people far afield from Sinai. If He could surreptitiously manipulate the hearts and minds of kings and ministers, as was evident during the Purim story, then it was clear that His might was no longer confined to supernatural events like Sinai. Thus, after the events of Purim the argument that the Torah could not be observed without the stimulus of Sinai-like miracles was no longer valid.

Yet, why was the "coercion" of Sinai necessary at all? After all, the Jewish people had seemed openly *eager* to accept the Torah, to the extent of proclaiming *Na'aseh Ve'Nishma,* "We will do (i.e. observe) and listen to the entire Torah!" What need did Hashem perceive to compel them to accept the Torah?

Hashem foresaw that the Jews' willingness to embrace Torah in time would give way to flirtations with foreign gods and alien ideologies, the first manifestation of which came, after a mere forty days had elapsed, with the incident of the Golden Calf. Consequently, Hashem wanted to make it clear from the beginning that Torah was a serious matter, not to be tossed aside on a moment's whim, and compelled them to accept it as an eternal treasure, to be respected whatever their future preferences might be.[1]

From Sinai until the time of the Purim story, then, the Jews' commitment to Torah was one born of obligation, rather than of free-willed enthusiasm. Once they recognized Hashem's hidden hand working through the normal processes of nature in the defeat of Haman, however, they reapproached the Torah with a renewed avidity and were pardoned at least in part for the sin of the Golden Calf. The mass return to Torah at that time wiped out all residual effects of the original brush with idolatry.[2]

---

1. See *Maharal Ohr Chadash.*

2. The relationship between the Golden Calf and the Purim miracle is explored further in the *Sfas Emes'* comments on Purim.

The relationship between *Na'aseh Ve'Nishma* and Hashem's forcing the Jews to accept the Torah at Sinai can be extended even further. The fact that the Jews were given no choice but to commit themselves to Torah can be viewed as a privilege rather than a punishment. Out of it came a guarantee that they would always possess the Torah, even when they no longer cared to observe it. Can there be any greater privilege than being assured that Hashem's Torah will always remain part of one's heritage? Once the Jews merited this privilege, they *deserved* to have Mount Sinai suspended over their heads, because they had expressed their allegiance to the Torah with the words, *Na'aseh Ve'Nishma*. The generation that voiced such enthusiasm for Hashem's treasure also deserved a forceful reminder of their obligations to preserve it.

This reminder was intended not so much for man's spiritual component as for his materialistic nature. While a Jew's *neshamah* (soul) is permanently wedded to Torah, even in the worst of times, his physical urgings are nevertheless more likely to lead him astray. It was their bodies, and not necessarily their hearts, that strayed after the Golden Calf. As a result, Hashem had to force acceptance of Torah on the Jews, so that even their materialistic impulses would be subservient to Torah principles. It was only at the time of Purim, when the Jewish people acquired a physical salvation, that they realized that the body as well as the soul was bound to the Torah. From then on further compulsion to accept the Torah was unnecessary.

Let us offer one final explanation for the need for coercion at Sinai. While it is clear that the Jews were keenly intent on accepting Hashem's law, the resolute cry of *Na'aseh Ve'Nishma* signified full-fledged acceptance only of the Written Law. Their commitment to the Oral Law (also transmitted to Moses at Sinai and passed down orally through the generations until it was compiled in the Talmud) was more detached. Not until Purim did the triumphant Jews express enthusiasm for the Oral Torah as well, as indicated by the resurgence of Torah study following the miracle of Purim.[1]

It is generally believed that it was on the day of that first Purim celebration that the Jews renewed their acceptance of the Torah. It is possible, however, that this actually occurred on the Shavuos following the downfall of Haman. A careful reading of the Megillah indicates that

1. See *Midrash Tanchuma Noach* 3.

it was only after Shavuos that letters were sent to Jews throughout the kingdom to inform them of their right to defend themselves against Haman's remaining followers. Only when they armed themselves with the force of a renewed commitment to Torah did they feel confident of their ability to vanquish Amalek, their eternal foe. Fittingly, it was on the anniversary of the giving of the Torah that the Jews once again accepted Hashem's Law in its entirety, for all time.

(*Purim* 5636, 5637, 5638, 5643, 5645 and 5647)

☙ Na'aseh Ve'Nishma: Crowns to be Restored

Perhaps the most popular expression associated with Shavuos is *Na'aseh Ve'Nishma*. When Moses read the *Sefer HaBris*, which contained the Torah starting from *Bereishis* until just before the giving of the Torah, the Jews responded נַעֲשֶׂה וְנִשְׁמָע — "We will do and we will listen" (*Shemos* 24:7). Let us take a final look at both the context in which these words were spoken and their content.

The Talmud (*Shabbos* 88a) describes the reward the Jews received for this declaration of loyalty: בְּשָׁעָה שֶׁהִקְדִּימוּ יִשְׂרָאֵל,נַעֲשֶׂה׳ לְ,נִשְׁמַע׳ בָּאוּ שִׁשִּׁים רִיבּוֹא שֶׁל מַלְאֲכֵי הַשָּׁרֵת לְכָל אֶחָד וְאֶחָד מִיִּשְׂרָאֵל קָשְׁרוּ לוֹ שְׁנֵי כְתָרִים אֶחָד כְּנֶגֶד נַעֲשֶׂה וְאֶחָד כְּנֶגֶד נִשְׁמַע, *When Israel said "We will do" before "We will hear," six hundred thousand ministering angels came and tied two crowns on the head of each Jew, one for na'aseh and one for nishma.*

What does this passage mean? We may say that the two crowns each Jew received symbolize the two sources of enlightenment latent in every Jew. Each of us is blessed with an inner spark, the pure unsullied *neshamah* that Hashem placed in us, as we say every day in the Morning Blessings, נְשָׁמָה שֶׁנָּתַתָּ בִּי טְהוֹרָה הִיא, *The soul You placed within me is pure.* The crown of *na'aseh* symbolizes this potential.

However, in addition to the *neshamah*, which represents the individual's innate potential granted by Hashem, there is an ability to grasp beyond the limits of one's abilities, to outdo oneself. The crown of *nishma* alludes to this supercapability. Furthermore, the Sages deliberately described the affixing of these crowns with the word קֶשֶׁר, *knot*, to hint at the tight, intimate, connection between the Jews and these "crowns". (5635)

The above-cited Talmud continues as follows:

וְכֵיוָן שֶׁחָטְאוּ יִשְׂרָאֵל יָרְדוּ מֵאָה וְעֶשְׂרִים רִיבּוֹא מַלְאֲכֵי חַבָּלָה וּפֵירְקוּם שֶׁנֶּאֱמַר,,וַיִּתְנַצְּלוּ בְנֵי יִשְׂרָאֵל אֶת עֶדְיָם מֵהַר חוֹרֵב״ . . . אָמַר ר״ל עָתִיד הקב״ה לְהַחֲזִירָן לָנוּ שֶׁנֶּאֱמַר,,וּפְדוּיֵי ה׳ יְשֻׁבוּן וּבָאוּ צִיּוֹן בְּרִנָּה וְשִׂמְחַת עוֹלָם עַל רֹאשָׁם״ שִׂמְחָה שֶׁמֵּעוֹלָם עַל רֹאשָׁם

When the Jews sinned [with the Golden Calf], one hundred twenty thousand destructive angels came down and removed [the crowns], as it says (Shemos 33:6) *"And the Jews were stripped of their crowns from Mount Horeb" . . . Reish Lakish said, "In the future, the Holy One, Blessed is He, will return them to us, as it says (Yeshayahu* 35:10), *'Those redeemed by* HASHEM *will return and arrive at Zion with glad song and everlasting gladness on their heads.' This refers to the gladness that was previously on their heads."*

We see from this passage that the gladness that was once "on their heads" will again be experienced in the time of *Moshiach.* This may also allude to the ability of the generation that said *Na'aseh Ve'Nishma* to "super achieve" to grasp beyond their abilities. We see this from the traditionally understood meaning of this phrase, "we will do even before we grasp," that is, we will undertake more than our abilities. It is fitting that these *doers* who were willing to perform *mitzvos* without understanding were rewarded with the ability to understand beyond their normal capacity.

As the Talmud says, these crowns were removed when the Jews sinned with the Golden Calf. Every Shabbos, however, the crowns, and the potential they represent, are restored in the form of the *neshamah yeseirah,* the additional soul which is granted to a Jew on Shabbos. Thus Shabbos is an opportunity not only to bring our innate potential to the forefront, but also to strive to achieve beyond our capacities. We have said previously that the *tefillin* worn on the arm and the head represent the ideals of *na'aseh* and *nishma,* respectively. On Shabbos, however, we do not wear *tefillin,* because Shabbos itself gives us the power to achieve these ideals directly. (5639, 5641)

Ten Commandments

⸎ Introduction

The two most fundamental events of Jewish history, the Creation of the World and the Revelation at Sinai, have many features in common. For example, the Torah's account of the two events both begin with general descriptions of what occurred, followed by detailed delineations of the specific events involved. Thus, the story of the Creation starts with a general verse (*Bereishis* 1:1): בְּרֵאשִׁית בָּרָא אֱלֹהִים אֵת הַשָּׁמַיִם וְאֵת הָאָרֶץ *In the beginning of God's creating the heavens and the earth.* Afterwards there is an enumeration of what was formed on each of the six days of Creation. Likewise, the account of the giving of the Torah opens with the statement (*Shemos* 20:1), וַיְדַבֵּר אֱלֹהִים אֵת כָּל־הַדְּבָרִים הָאֵלֶּה, *And G-d spoke all these statements,* referring to the Ten Commandments, which are then listed.

The Mishnah (*Avos* 5:1) explains the elaborate detail of the Creation by noting that the world was created with ten separate utterances, rather than a single command, to justify a greater reward for those righteous people who uphold a world that was created so deliberately, and also to inflict more stringent punishment on the wicked who abuse such a world. In regard to the Giving of the Torah, however, punishment was not a concern. The commandments were given in ten separate statements, rather than as one lengthy declaration, solely to give added credit to righteous Jews who uphold all ten heavenly injunctions.[1] (5645)

The similarity between the Creation of the World and the Giving of the Torah extends further. In each instance, the use of the Divine Name *Elokim*, which connotes Hashem's strict application of justice, precedes

---

1. Alternatively, we can say that various levels of rewards are granted to those who study Torah out of proper motives, while punishment is meted out to those who study Torah to belittle it. In this approach, there is a closer correspondence between the Ten Commandments and the Ten Utterances of Creation.

that of the Name *Hashem*, which indicates His quality of mercy. Thus, for most of the account of the Creation only the Name *Elokim* is used, and only in the second chapter do we find the Name *Hashem* (*Bereishis* 2:4): בְּיוֹם עֲשׂוֹת ה׳ אֱלֹהִים אֶרֶץ וְשָׁמָיִם, *on the day of* HASHEM *Elokim's creating the earth and heavens.* Likewise, the account of the Giving of the Torah begins with the Name *Elokim* in the verse we cited above, וַיְדַבֵּר אֱלֹהִים, *And God spoke ...* Only after this do we find the Name *Hashem* in the first commandment, אָנֹכִי ה׳ אֱלֹהֶיךָ, *I am* HASHEM, *your God ...*

Rashi explains the shift in terminology in the story of Creation by saying that, as originally conceived, the world was to be answerable to the strictest level of judgment. However, Hashem soon realized that the universe could not survive on the basis of such a harsh standard, and therefore tempered His strictness with mercy. Similarly, the Torah was originally intended to exist in an environment of firmly-administered justice, with no leniency for infractions of Hashem's commands. But Hashem felt it necessary to moderate this unbending interpretation of the law with a liberal sprinkling of mercy.

It is noteworthy that another fundamental Divine pronouncement, the *Shema*, also opens with a general statement, followed by specific explanations: שְׁמַע יִשְׂרָאֵל ה׳ אֱלֹהֵינוּ ה׳ אֶחָד, *Hear, O Israel,* HASHEM *is our God,* HASHEM, *the One and Only* (*Devarim* 6:4), an all-inclusive proclamation of Hashem's sovereignty, is followed by וְאָהַבְתָּ אֵת ה׳ אֱלֹהֶיךָ, *You shall love* HASHEM, *your God,* a paragraph that details the observance of many fundamental *mitzvos.*

The opening statement of the Ten Commandments contains a seemingly unnecessary word that is, in fact, very significant. The Torah there states (*Shemos* 20:1), וַיְדַבֵּר אֱלֹהִים אֵת כָּל־הַדְּבָרִים הָאֵלֶּה לֵאמֹר, *And G-d spoke all these statements, saying.* What does the word לֵאמֹר, *saying,* teach us? Originally all of humanity were charged with the mission of singing Hashem's praises. This long-neglected mission was restored to the Jewish people at Mount Sinai. Indeed, all later prophets attained their powers of prophecy from the miraculous transmission of Hashem's Torah at Sinai. Thus, this verse tells us that Hashem spoke *these statements* once, for the purpose of preparing all other forms of prophecy. (5645)

Ideally, all men should have the merit to be able to speak in Hashem's Name. In describing the creation of the first man, the Torah stresses his capacity for speech: וַיְהִי הָאָדָם לְנֶפֶשׁ חַיָּה, *And the man was a living soul*

(*Bereishis* 2:7). *Onkelos* renders these words וַהֲוַת בְּאָדָם לְרוּחַ מְמַלְּלָא, *and the man had powers of speech.* Man was created for the purpose of articulating the praises of Hashem. The same theme was expressed by the prophet Isaiah: עַם־זוּ יָצַרְתִּי לִי תְּהִלָּתִי יְסַפֵּרוּ, *This nation have I created; to Me shall they render My praises* (*Yeshayahu* 43:21).

However, the generation that constructed the Tower of Babel corrupted their powers of speech by using their common language to rebel against Hashem. Consequently, Hashem rescinded the gift of universal communication and limited the ability to articulate His praises to the Jewish nation. The Torah alludes to this transference in the account of the dispersion of peoples at that time (*Bereishis* 11:6), הֵן עַם אֶחָד וְשָׂפָה אַחַת לְכֻלָּם, *Behold, there will be one nation [rather than a unified society of humankind] that will speak in one tongue [in order to express the wonders of the Almighty].* (5645)

❦ ❦ ❦

וַיְדַבֵּר אֱלֹהִים אֵת כָּל־הַדְּבָרִים הָאֵלֶּה לֵאמֹר

Hashem expounded on these words.

Great events had occurred before the Giving of the Torah, and great deeds had been performed. However, the ability to produce great *words* — to inspire and teach through spell-binding speech — was unknown prior to the revelation at Mount Sinai.

Thus, there is a difference between the Ten Utterances of Creation and the Ten Commandments of Mount Sinai. Whereas all of humanity could appreciate the Creation, only the Jewish nation could comprehend the lesson of the Ten Commandments, namely that speech could be used as a vehicle for glorifying Hashem.

The historical mission of the Jews in the world is inextricably linked to words, to their allegiance to the letter of the written law. Such verbal messages as the listing of the *mitzvos* and of Hashem's philosophy are so basic to the Jews' *raison d'etre* that the Torah could conceivably have eliminated all stories of events and given only the details of the *mitzvos*. As the Sages said, the Torah could really have begun with the first *mitzvah*, the first spoken word of Hashem. The stories of Creation and deeds of the Patriarchs were included only to enable Jews to strengthen their faith in times of difficulty, when they lived among the Gentiles, who could relate to Hashem only through His miraculous deeds.

(5650)

While all of the prophets were given this unique power of Divinely-inspired speech, the prophecy of Moshe had a unique role. He not only transmitted the message of Hashem, but actually acted as Hashem's spokesman, to the extent that Hashem's words emanated via Moshe's vocal cords.

According to the Midrash (*Shemos Rabba* 28:3), Hashem asked Moshe to descend from Mount Sinai at the time that the first Commandment, *I am* HASHEM, *your God,* was being proclaimed, to avoid giving the false impression that it was Moshe, rather than Hashem Himself, who was talking. This Midrash can be understood in light of the statement that Hashem spoke through Moshe's voice. If Moshe had remained on the mountain, it would have been difficult for the people to ascertain whether the voice they were hearing was Hashem's voice or that of Moshe, His spokesman. (5659)

❧ ❧ ❧

When the Jews were first apprised of the Ten Commandments, they responded by declaring their eagerness to perform all the positive commandments, and their intention to abide by the prohibitions, as *Rashi* comments on the word לֵאמֹר, *saying,* מְלַמֵּד שֶׁהָיוּ עוֹנִין עַל הֵן הֵן וְעַל לָאו לָאו, *this teaches that they would answer "Yes" to a positive commandment and "No" to a negative commandment.* Their purpose in responding in this fashion was to show that they did not consider the Law to be a mere abstraction, but something to be incorporated into the very fabric of their lives, through positive action and self-control.

Thus, there is a splendid link between the Torah's introduction to the giving of the Commandments, אֵת כָּל־הַדְּבָרִים הָאֵלֶּה, *all these things,* and the first Commandment, אָנֹכִי ה' אֱלֹהֶיךָ, *I am* HASHEM, *your God.* Hashem reminded the Jews that Godliness can illuminate every aspect of life, for אָנֹכִי — Hashem's Presence — is found in *all these things*: all the things that constitute life as we know it. (5652, 5656)

❧ The First Commandment

The use of the singular form of the possessive in the first Commandment, אֱלֹהֶיךָ, *your [singular] God,* rather than אֱלֹהֵיכֶם, is significant. It implies that even during times of rampant assimilation, when only relatively few Jews retain their allegiance to the Commandments, Hashem's sovereignty will still prevail. Another interpretation is that Hashem's Presence is most pronounced when the Jewish nation is one united entity, and not broken up into warring factions.

The singular form, *your [singular] God,* may also allude to the fact that Hashem reveals Himself in different ways, depending on the needs and spiritual status of individual Jews, or on the situation of the Jewish People at any given point in time. As *Rashi* comments on this verse — at Mount Sinai Hashem was revealed as an elder full of mercy, while at the Splitting of the Sea He appeared as a young warrior.[1] If Hashem had said, אָנֹכִי ה׳ אֱלֹהֵיכֶם, *I am HASHEM, your [plural] God,* it would have implied that He is always revealed in the same form, no matter what the circumstances. By using the singular, Hashem meant to imply that however many forms He may take, He is still *your* God, the God Who is relevant to each individual. (5635, 5646, 5653, 5657)

Another implication of the singular form is that all Jews have one single, united soul. Even though some Jews are able to bring the Divine Presence to the forefront, while in others It remains hidden, the source of their souls is all the same. Just as all light in the world emanated from the moment Hashem declared, יְהִי אוֹר, *Let there be light* (*Bereishis* 1:2), and has continued even since, so too the collective Jewish soul originated at the moment Hashem proclaimed, *I am HASHEM, your God*.

(5633, 5637)

There is yet another reason that Hashem phrased this commandment in the singular form. So as to give Moshe a basis to argue, in his defense of the Jews after the sin of the Golden Calf, that *he* alone had been commanded not to worship other gods. (5635)

Hashem describes Himself in the first Commandment as the One Who freed the Jews from Egyptian bondage. This refers to not only the physical liberation of the Exodus but also to the spiritual salvation. In its broadest meaning, the Exodus from Egypt implies freedom from the constraints of the material world. The word *Mitzrayim*, Egypt, contains the word *tzar*, narrow, which can denote a narrow channel or even narrow-mindedness — something that blocks one's ability to progress or achieve his potential. It is in this sense that the *Kiddush* we say on Shabbos and *Yamim Tovim* mentions זֵכֶר לִיצִיאַת מִצְרָיִם, literally *a memorial of the Exodus from Egypt*, but actually a reminder of the *spiritual* freedom the Exodus brought. It would not be necessary to

1. For further development of this theme, see commentaries to the *Song of Glory* recited at the conclusion of Shabbos morning services.

include such a phrase if it referred only to the physical rescue, since a freed slave needs no reminder of his liberation. (5659)

◆§ The Second Commandment

The second Commandment — לֹא־יִהְיֶה לְךָ אֱלֹהִים אֲחֵרִים עַל־פָּנָי, *You shall not recognize the gods of others before My presence,* is not merely an admonition but also a promise. With this, Hashem guaranteed His Chosen People that they would never be totally subjugated by any antagonistic force. His commitment to us will remain firm, under both favorable and adverse conditions, as long as we are faithful to Him. (A similar promise is implied in the first Commandment by the word אָנֹכִי, *I,* an allusion to the verse (*Tehillim* 91:15) עִמּוֹ אָנֹכִי בְצָרָה, *I am with him in distress,* which declares Hashem's empathy towards Jewish suffering). (5661)

◆§ The Third Commandment

The third Commandment, לֹא תִשָּׂא אֶת־שֵׁם־ה׳ אֱלֹהֶיךָ לַשָּׁוְא, *You shall not take the Name of HASHEM, your God, in vain,* is more than the obvious injunction against swearing falsely or using Hashem's Name improperly. It is also a fervent plea for us not to misuse our potential, as symbolized by the Divine Name which is embedded in every Jewish soul. Failing to rise to the spiritual heights within our reach is tantamount to abusing the Divine spirit within us. To ignore our Heavenly spark is to harbor it in vain.

Thus the conclusion of this verse, כִּי לֹא יְנַקֶּה ה׳ אֵת אֲשֶׁר־יִשָּׂא אֶת־שְׁמוֹ לַשָּׁוְא, *for HASHEM will not absolve [literally, cleanse] anyone who takes His Name in vain,* can be seen as a warning that even though Hashem assists those who wish to purify themselves [as the Sages said (*Shabbos* 104a), someone who wishes to purify himself will receive Divine help], this does not apply to those who waste their potential. (5636)

◆§ The Fourth Commandment

The wording of the fourth Commandment, זָכוֹר אֶת־יוֹם הַשַּׁבָּת לְקַדְּשׁוֹ, *remember the Sabbath day to sanctify it,* implies that the Jews had had prior exposure to the concept of Shabbos, and were therefore able to recall it. However the Torah repeats the commandment to observe the Sabbath because of the possibility that it would be forgotten.

Indeed, the Jews had already been taught the basic laws of Shabbos at Marah (see *Rashi* on *Shemos* 15:25). However, something quite different happened at Sinai. Whereas then they had been instructed in the laws of Shabbos, it was only at Sinai that the Jews were fully exposed to the intensity of the Shabbos experience. (5638)

Now let us turn to the last word of this verse, *to sanctify it*. This implies that Jews hallow Shabbos by observing it. What is the relationship between observing Shabbos and making it holy? How can the actions of mere mortals add to the holiness Hashem had already given this day at the time of Creation, as it says (*Bereishis* 2:3), וַיְבָרֶךְ אֱלֹהִים אֶת־יוֹם הַשְּׁבִיעִי וַיְקַדֵּשׁ אֹתוֹ, *And God blessed the seventh day and hallowed it*?

It is possible to say homiletically that the phrase *to sanctify it* here refers not to the Shabbos that comes every week, but rather to that most sacred Shabbos, the one on which the Torah was given to the Jewish nation.[1] Thus the commandment to *Remember the Sabbath day to sanctify it* is a reminder of the glory of the Shabbos on which the Torah was given.[2]

On the other hand, this verse may also be interpreted literally. When a Jew observes the Shabbos, he enhances the sanctity of this most holy day. At the same time, Shabbos nurtures and enhances the holiness inherent in every Jew. Thus, there is an interdependence between the sanctity of Shabbos and that of the Jewish nation — when they observe Shabbos "to make it holy," they in turn cause the aura of holiness inherent in themselves to flourish. (5637, 5638)

The Fourth Commandment undergoes a significant change in wording when it appears in *Parashas Ve'Eschanan* (*Devarim* 5:12-16). Whereas the earlier version reads *Remember the Sabbath day*, the later version says שָׁמוֹר אֶת־יוֹם הַשַּׁבָּת לְקַדְּשׁוֹ, *Observe the Sabbath day to sanctify it*. The Sages taught that these two terms are so intimately

1. This is based on a tradition, cited by the Sages (*Shabbos* 86b), that the Torah was given on Shabbos.

2. Another point: Moshe added a third day of preparation (*sheloshes yimei hagbalah*) to the two days designated by Hashem. Because of this extra day that Moshe sanctified, the Torah was given on Shabbos rather than the day before. Thus the commandment *Remember the Sabbath day to sanctify it* alludes to the Sabbath that Moshe sanctified with the Giving of the Torah.

connected that they were originally spoken simultaneously: זָכוֹר וְשָׁמוֹר בְּדִבּוּר אֶחָד נֶאֶמְרוּ מַה שֶׁאֵין הַפֶּה יָכוֹל לְדַבֵּר וְאוֹזֶן לִשְׁמוֹעַ, *The words "remember" and "observe" were said in one pronouncement, something which a [human] mouth cannot say and a [human] ear cannot hear* (*Shevuos* 20b). What is the connection between the words, and what does each mean?

זָכוֹר, *remember*, refers to an inner feeling of *deveikus*, of clinging to Hashem in the intimate way a devout Jew feels on Shabbos. However, the command שָׁמוֹר, *observe*, ensures that an individual will not be carried away by his ecstatic state to lose himself totally. The word שָׁמוֹר also means *guard*, guard and preserve this inner intimacy and channel it to doing *mitzvos*. (5631)

Further, שָׁמוֹר refers to the preparations that enable a Jew to receive and assimilate the sanctity of Shabbos. Only through such preparations can a Jew merit to perceive the true intimacy of Shabbos. Thus the later version emphasizes the preparations necessary to attain the state of remembrance implied by the earlier version, which was directed at the Jew who has already prepared. (5631)

The word שָׁמוֹר literally means *guard*. Here it refers to the very unique bond established between the Jewish people and Hashem through their *observance* of Shabbos, as the Torah says, (*Shemos* 31:13) אוֹת הִיא בֵּינִי וּבֵינֵיכֶם, *It is a sign* [*of attachment*] *between Me and you*. Not only do the world's Jews observe Shabbos, but they do so in a fashion that guarantees that the Shabbos-related ties between them and Hashem will remain unique. They make sure that the day does not become a banal holiday from work rather than a holy occasion. In this manner, the Jews *safeguard* the special quality of Shabbos. (5660)

Alternatively, the term זָכוֹר refers to the requirement to recall the spirit of Shabbos at every phase of one's life. In the most immediate sense, this means that we should carry the aura of Shabbos into the other days of the week. In this way, we can turn any day of the week into a privileged time period in which we either prepare for the holiness of the upcoming Shabbos, or bask in the lingering holiness of the Shabbos just past. Thus we can bring the spirit of Shabbos into everything we do. Any ordinary undertaking can become uplifting if it is seen as a service performed to sanctify Hashem's world.

(*Parashas Yisro* 5631, 5637)

Therefore, while שָׁמוֹר instructs us to carefully guard the parameters of Shabbos, and keep strictly within the bounds of the law given to Bnei

Yisroel, זָכוֹר encourages us to extend the glory of Shabbos to our entire existence.

As mentioned above, our Sages relate that the Ten Commandments were given on Shabbos. This was no coincidence. Both the Giving of the Torah and Shabbos convey a sense of completion. The Divine act of Creation was not completed until the first Shabbos occurred. In fact, it was the sense of *nachas*, of satisfaction, that Hashem derived from the world's completion that made Shabbos possible; for it was only after He pronounced the world fit that Shabbos came into existence.

Likewise, the Giving of the Torah denotes the spiritual completion of the universe. Without Torah, the people of the world would have wandered along the road of life in abject confusion, forever ignorant of the meaning of human existence.

Furthermore, both Shabbos and the Giving of the Torah mark the return of the Jewish people to their roots. Every Shabbos, physical exertion gives way to spirituality; and from beneath even the plainest exterior of the most menial workman emerges the glowing countenance of the Jewish soul. In this sense, Shabbos is described as מֵעֵין עוֹלָם הַבָּא, *a sampling of the world to come* (*Berachos* 57b), a spiritual occasion so transcendent that it offers a glimpse of the World to Come.

Likewise, the giving of the Torah represents the Jewish people's return to its collective roots — to the Heaven-centered devotion that typified our forefathers. Thus the version of the Ten Commandments in *Parashas VaEschanan* reminds us explicitly of the connection between Shabbos and the Exodus: *You shall remember that you were a slave in the land of Egypt and HASHEM your God took you out from there with a strong hand and an outstretched arm; therefore HASHEM your God has commanded you to make the Sabbath day* [as a remembrance] (*Devarim* 5:15). We may understand this to refer not only to the physical freedom of the Exodus, but also to the spiritual freedom from the pressures of the world which the Jew is granted every Shabbos. (5644)

We may say further that the Torah was given on Shabbos in order to insure that, even at times when the Jews deviate from Torah, they would still study and observe it on Shabbos. (In this context, see also the essay on *Na'aseh Ve'Nishma*, where we say that the two crowns that were taken away from the Jews at the time of the Sin of the Golden Calf are restored every Shabbos). (5637)

Extending the comparison even further, we note that on both Shabbos and *Shavuos* (commemorating the Giving of the Torah), Jews are obligated to partake of festive meals and dress in their best garments. Both days celebrate our life-sustaining link with Hashem, and as such are naturally joyous occasions. Moreover, Shabbos is frequently described in terms of an added dimension of spirituality. This heightened holiness, called the *neshamah yeseirah* (literally, "extra soul"), first became operative on Shavuos. It was through the added impetus of the granting of the Torah that the Jews were able to attain this added aura on Shabbos. (5641, 5661)

According to tradition, each day of the week was paired with a companion (e.g., Sunday and Monday), with the exception of the seventh day, which was left by itself. To appease it, Hashem decreed that Shabbos would indeed have a partner — the Jewish nation. However, this special relationship between Shabbos and the Jews was possible only after the Giving of the Torah. Once they had accepted Hashem's Law at Sinai, the nation imbued with spirituality could fittingly be linked with the most spiritual of days. (5663)

The Fourth Commandment concludes, וַיָּנַח בַּיּוֹם הַשְּׁבִיעִי עַל־כֵּן בֵּרַךְ ה׳ אֶת־יוֹם הַשַּׁבָּת וַיְקַדְּשֵׁהוּ, *He rested on the seventh day, therefore* HASHEM *blessed the Sabbath day and sanctified it*. It would seem that the order of this verse should be reversed — since the day had already been blessed, therefore Hashem chose to rest on it. Evidently the Torah is suggesting that since Hashem rested on this day, therefore the Jewish soul, however tormented it may be, is able to restore itself and return to its roots, to return to Hashem. This is, after all, the true meaning of the concept of blessing.

Elsewhere, the Torah says, וּבַיּוֹם הַשְּׁבִיעִי שָׁבַת וַיִּנָּפַשׁ, *on the seventh day He rested and was refreshed* (*Shemos* 31:17). The word וַיִּנָּפַשׁ, *and He was refreshed*, has the same root as the word נֶפֶשׁ, *soul*. We see in this an allusion that on Shabbos, the Jewish soul is able to return to Hashem. (*Parashas Yisro* 5632)

◆§ After the Torah was Given

וְכָל־הָעָם רֹאִים אֶת־הַקּוֹלֹת וְאֶת־הַלַּפִּידִים וְאֵת קוֹל הַשֹּׁפָר וְאֶת־הָהָר עָשֵׁן וַיַּרְא הָעָם וַיָּנֻעוּ וַיַּעַמְדוּ מֵרָחוֹק

The entire people saw the thunder [voices] and the flames, the sound of the shofar, and the smoking mountain; the people saw and trembled and stood from afar (*Shemos* 20:15).

While the previous essay dealt with the events preceding the Giving of the Torah, in this essay we will consider the events that followed it. The first part of the discussion focuses on the sight the Jewish people saw immediately after Hashem gave the Ten Commandments.

The above verse describes the people's trembling after they *saw* the voices of Mount Sinai. Every word of this verse has meaning. First the Torah stresses that the *entire* people saw the voice, implying that every limb and sinew of each individual saw the light of Torah. It is well-known that each limb of the body corresponds to one of the two hundred forty-eight positive commandments, which are compared to sparks emanating from a source of light, the Torah. Thus, at the time the Torah was given, every limb and sinew of the whole Jewish body not only experienced the aura of the *mitzvos* but was actually infused with the light of Torah.

The phrase אֶת הַקּוֹלֹת, *the voices,* also alludes to the same phenomenon. The word אֶת[1] generally indicates the presence of an added dimension beyond the surface meaning of the words. Here also, we may infer that the phrase אֶת הַקּוֹלֹת, *the voices,* alludes to the penetration of the light of Torah and *mitzvos* into every fiber of the Jewish personality. (5640)

⊰§ Seeing What is Normally Heard

Literally, however, this phrase indicates that the Jews actually *saw* the voices that resounded at Mount Sinai. The Sages described the event with the words (*Mechilta D'R'Shimon bar Yochai*) רוֹאִין אֶת הַנִּשְׁמָע, *they saw what was [normally only] heard.* Why was this miracle necessary? Why would it not have been sufficient had the Jewish people only *heard* Hashem's voice.

Apparently, a dual-sensory experience was needed — both hearing and seeing. Each means of perception has unique advantages lacking in the other. When someone sees an object, he sees it in its exact form without distortion. Sound, on the other hand, can be altered between its source and the party receiving it. Sound is an internal phenomenon that penetrates throughout the body, while sight is only on the surface.

1. This particle has no equivalent in English but is used in Hebrew to introduce a direct object.

When they received the Torah, the Jews had the benefit of both senses: the clear, unaltered perception of sight and the inner penetration of hearing. Perhaps they merited this dual perception by their proclamation of *Na'aseh Ve'Nishma,* we will do and we will listen. In the merit of *doing* before they heard, they were privileged to *see* what is normally only heard. (5635)

It is noteworthy that, in spite of the added element of hearing our verse describes this experience as one of sight. This may be because, when the Torah was given the whole people attained the same level of communication with Hashem that the Patriarchs had enjoyed, as the Hashem says (*Shemos* 6:3), וָאֵרָא אֶל־אַבְרָהָם אֶל־יִצְחָק וְאֶל־יַעֲקֹב, *I appeared to Abraham, to Isaac and to Jacob.* (5636)

An additional purpose of the miracle of dual-perception may have been to underscore the point that the Torah is above all a physical phenomenon, including the senses. In the normal course of nature sounds are perceived by the ears and sight by the eyes; in the realm of Torah, however, this can be reversed. (5631)

The miraculous transcending of the normal sensory processes reveals the intuitive nature of Hashem's relationship with the Jewish people. They *felt* the sanctity of the event they were experiencing with every part of their bodies, not just their eyes or their ears. In this respect they were following the example of Abraham who, according to tradition, felt an intuitive awareness and love of his Creator ["his two kidneys served him as two teachers" (*Bereishis Rabbah* 61:1)] even before he learned Torah. (5641)

The Sages relate that at the moment the Torah was given, the souls of the Jewish people "expired" (a topic we will explore later in this essay). This esoteric concept may be understood in terms of the awareness of the sanctity of the event we described above. The experience may have been so overpowering emotionally that the people simply collapsed and expired.

Specifically this might have occurred when Hashem began to pronounce the Ten Commandments. The words, *I am HASHEM, your God,* which the people not only heard but *felt* with all their senses penetrating into every fiber of their bodies, left an indelible mark on the Jewish psyche. In this sense, perhaps the term שֵׁמוֹת שֶׁאֵינָן נִמְחָקִים, *names which may not be erased* can be understood. It refers not only to those Names by which Hashem is known that may not be erased, but also to this eternal impression His Name left on the people as a whole.

Thus the phrase רֹאִים אֶת הַקּוֹלֹת, *seeing the sounds,* refers to that moment when an inseverable emotional bond was forged with the Creator, a bond that will never allow either side to forsake the other. At that moment, the Jews realized that Hashem was the *source* of their souls, and therefore of their very existence. Much of the time, the material nature of our existence obscures this fact, but those who were privileged to stand at Sinai could actually *see* that their souls were rooted in Hashem.

The Second Commandment then, לֹא יִהְיֶה לְךָ אֱלֹהִים אֲחֵרִים עַל־פָּנָי, *You shall not recognize the gods of others before My Presence,* is not only a prohibition but also a promise that nothing will ever jeopardize this unique relationship between Hashem and His people.

It should also be noted that the permanent imprint of Hashem's Name on the Jewish people remains clear and sharp in all conditions, even in times of exile and distress. The אָנֹכִי (*I*) Who said אָנֹכִי ה׳ אֱלֹהֶיךָ, *I am HASHEM, your God,* is the same One Who said (*Tehillim* 91:15) עִמּוֹ־אָנֹכִי בְצָרָה, *I am with him [the people] in distress,* as well as (*Yeshayahu* 49:15) וְאָנֹכִי לֹא אֶשְׁכָּחֵךְ, *And I will not forget you.*

In the *haftarah* we read on Shavuos, the prophet Yechezkel's account of the flaming "chariot" bearing Hashem's glory, proves the validity of this promise. The fact that Yechezkel had this exalted vision of Hashem in exile in Babylonia shows clearly that our connection with Hashem remains strong and irrevocable, in whatever circumstances we may be.

The drama surrounding the Giving of the Torah was needed more by the rest of humanity than by the Jews. It was they who required incontrovertible proof that Hashem dominated the world. Jews, however, have an innate propensity to see Hashem's Presence in the world and once He announced His will to them they accepted it immediately.

It was fitting that the Jews were chosen to bear witness to Hashem's existence, as the prophet Yeshayahu says (43:10), אַתֶּם עֵדַי נְאֻם־ה׳, *you are My witnesses, says HASHEM.* As a nation, we have an innate conviction of Hashem's existence that makes us worthy to testify to it. A belief that rests on dramatic miracles can be easily eroded by doubts and trials; every miracle has its gainsayers. Intuitive belief in Hashem however, can never be refuted.

This innate conviction, while it exists all the time, is especially compelling on Shabbos. The *neshamah yeseirah* (the "extra soul" given to a Jew on Shabbos) perceives Hashem's Presence more keenly than during the week.

It is noteworthy that the Torah says that the people *see*, in the present tense, rather than *saw*, in the past tense. This suggests that not only those who were present at that time, but also all future generations have this ability to "see" some part of the light of Sinai. Especially the prophets of all generations derive their inspiration from the wellsprings of Torah that first bubbled forth at that spectacular moment.

The use of the present tense, *see*, also alludes to the *neshamah* (soul), a "part" of Hashem that dwells within every Jew. In the same manner that Hashem perceives the past and the future as clearly as the present, so too our souls reside on such a high spiritual level that they can "see" things that are normally only heard.

What, then, do our souls "see" on a day-to-day basis? They see the same thing they saw at Sinai, the words אָנֹכִי ה׳ אֱלֹהֶיךָ, *I am HASHEM, your God,* as clearly as they saw them that first time. We say every day in the *Shema,* אֲשֶׁר אָנֹכִי מְצַוְּךָ הַיּוֹם, *which I command you this day,* every day Hashem commands us to believe in Him as clearly as He did at Sinai. (*Shavuos* 5661, *Parashas Yisro* 5661)

◆§ Seeing and Trembling

The verse we are discussing continues, וַיַּרְא הָעָם וַיָּנֻעוּ, *the people saw and trembled.* Why are we told a second time that the people *saw?*

Perhaps the second use of the word *see* indicates another seeing; they saw future generations that would also be expected to accept and observe the Torah. If so, their trembling may have been out of fear for their descendants, who would have to uphold the Torah without having been infused with the same spirit they received at Sinai. (5640)

Possibly also they saw their own potential to grow in Torah and trembled out of fear that they would not be strong enough to realize their potential. The beginning of our verse also alludes to this recognition of potential: *the entire people saw the voices* (קוֹלֹת means voices and sound i.e. thunder). The people not merely believed but actually saw Hashem's voice saying אָנֹכִי ה׳ אֱלֹהֶיךָ, *I am HASHEM, your God;* at that moment, as we said above, they could see and feel the roots of their souls that is their potential to serve Hashem.

Moshe later described the Giving of the Torah, with the phrase פָּנִים בְּפָנִים דִּבֶּר ה׳ עִמָּכֶם, *face to face Hashem spoke with you* (*Devarim* 5:4).

This image also alludes to the Torah's ability to show each individual his potential. This is based on the idea that [Torah is like] a mirror in which each person sees himself. In the same way a person looks at the Torah, the Torah reflects back on him. The more one is willing to expose his inner self to Torah, and to allow himself to be carried away with desire to understand Torah's depths, the more he will merit to understand his unique portion in Torah, that part of Torah that speaks to the root of his soul.

As is well-known, the Sages frequently compared Torah to water — נִמְשְׁלוּ דִבְרֵי תוֹרָה לְמַיִם, *the words of Torah are compared to water* (*Taanis* 7a). Perhaps they were referring to these mirror-like qualities of Torah, its ability to show someone his true potential. Furthermore, the more one strives to attain one's capacity for Torah, the more the Torah reflects its light on those who study it. (5639)

Why did they tremble? Having sensed their potential as Torah individuals, in spite of their limited powers of reason they were seized with awe and could not help but tremble. As we said above, the Sages taught that they "expired" at that moment. Perhaps the overwhelming vision of their capacity to absorb Torah made their souls, unable to bear the limitations of the material world, fly off to seek the spiritual treasures of the World to Come. As the Sages said (*Avos* 4:29), עַל כָּרְחֲךָ אַתָּה נוֹלָד וְעַל כָּרְחֲךָ אַתָּה חַי, *against your will you were born and against your will you live*; just as the fetus does not want to come into the world and has to be pushed out of the womb, so also the Jews were forced to return to the material world in order to observe the Torah in the context for which it was intended. And just as the soul of each Jew is administered an oath as it enters the world to become a *tzaddik*, (*Niddah* 30b) so also the souls of the Jews swore before they returned to their bodies. This may be the intent of the expression used by the Sages (*Shavuos* 21b), מוּשְׁבָּע וְעוֹמֵד מֵהַר סִינַי, *bound by a standing oath since Mount Sinai.*

Our verse concludes, וַיַּעַמְדוּ מֵרָחוֹק, *they stood from afar*. In its simple meaning, this verse suggests that the people drew back from the mountain, perhaps in fear of the obligation their proximity imposed on them or on future generations. Homiletically, this phrase may also be interpreted in light of a saying of the Sages (*Berachos* 26b), אֵין עֲמִידָה אֶלָּא תְּפִלָּה, *the word "standing" in the Torah always refers to prayer.* Perhaps they "stood" to pray that their future generations (hinted at in the word רָחוֹק, *afar*) would be worthy of the Torah that was given at Mount Sinai.

◌ The Jews Decline A Direct Dialogue

וַיֹּאמְרוּ אֶל־מֹשֶׁה דַּבֵּר־אַתָּה עִמָּנוּ וְנִשְׁמָעָה וְאַל־יְדַבֵּר עִמָּנוּ אֱלֹהִים פֶּן־נָמוּת

They said to Moses, 'You speak to us and we shall hear; let God not speak to us lest we die' (*Shemos* 20:16).

Having seen and heard Hashem's voice giving the first two of the Ten Commandments, the people reacted with fear and asked Moshe to receive the rest of the Torah as their proxy. "Let Hashem speak to you," they pleaded, "if He speaks to us we will die."

In Moshe's recounting of the events of Sinai forty years afterwards the same concern is expressed (*Devarim* 5:22), וְעַתָּה לָמָּה נָמוּת כִּי תֹאכְלֵנוּ הָאֵשׁ הַגְּדֹלָה הַזֹּאת אִם־יֹסְפִים אֲנַחְנוּ לִשְׁמֹעַ אֶת־קוֹל ה׳ אֱלֹהֵינוּ עוֹד וָמָתְנוּ, *Now, why should we die? For this great fire will consume us if we continue to hear further the voice of* HASHEM*, our God, we will die.*

A question presents itself: At the moment they said *Na'aseh Ve'Nishma*, the Jews were obviously willing to give up their lives for Torah, if necessary. Also, as we have discussed in several places, the Sages taught that they did actually "expire" upon receiving the Torah. Why then were they suddenly afraid of dying?

We may suggest several answers to this question. For one thing, even though they were *willing* to die for the sake of the Torah, they recognized that from the Torah's perspective it would be better for them to remain alive, as the Torah says (*Vayikra* 18:5), וָחַי בָּהֶם, *you shall live by them.* This is the meaning of the Sages' statement (*Avos* 4:22), יָפָה שָׁעָה אַחַת בִּתְשׁוּבָה וּמַעֲשִׂים טוֹבִים בָּעוֹלָם הַזֶּה מִכֹּל חַיֵּי הָעוֹלָם הַבָּא, *Better one hour of repentance and good deeds in this world than all of the World to Come.* While they were willing to die for Torah, they felt that they could do more alive. Even if one believes that worldly activities are meaningless in themselves, as they believed when they said *Na'aseh Ve'Nishma*, they still have meaning as opportunities to observe the Torah. They wanted to live in order to continue to hear Torah teachings, as they said to Moshe, "you speak to us and we shall hear."

Possibly however, they came to appreciate the importance of observing the Torah in this world only *after* their souls expired, as described above. Indeed, life in this world is most meaningful for those who are willing to sacrifice themselves totally for Torah. Only *their* "hour of good deeds and repentance" is better than all of the world to come, and of them Hashem said (*Devarim* 5:25), *They have done good in everything which they have spoken.*

Thus their desire to remain alive was really a desire to imbue the world with the teachings of Torah, as the prophet Yirmiyahu suggests (15:19), וְאִם־תּוֹצִיא יָקָר מִזּוֹלֵל, *to bring precious fruits out of a world of lowliness.* (5632, 5636)

Another answer to our question may be found in the words the people themselves spoke. Before asking Moshe to intermediate for them they said (*Devarim* 5:21), הַיּוֹם הַזֶּה רָאִינוּ כִּי־יְדַבֵּר אֱלֹהִים אֶת־הָאָדָם וָחָי, *This day we have seen that God speaks to man and [the man may still] live.* They realized that the privilege of hearing and understanding Torah is granted only to those who are willing to sacrifice their lives for it, as they had been until now. Once, however, they heard Torah directly from Hashem, they began to worry that if such contact with Hashem became too common an occurrence, they would not be able to maintain such a high level of dedication. If that happened, they might not have the merit to hear Torah from Hashem and survive. (5634, 5635)

Additionally we can say that the Jews were not concerned about physical death but rather about spiritual stagnation. Had they received all of the Torah directly from Hashem, they would have had a much greater obligation to remain on the same spiritual level they attained at Sinai. Such an expectation was not one they felt they could live up to. If the Torah was given through (the human) Moshe then even though, as they may well have expected, later generations would grow progressively weaker in their commitment to Torah, their lapses would be better tolerated.

In this light the verse (*Devarim* 33:4), תּוֹרָה צִוָּה־לָנוּ מֹשֶׁה מוֹרָשָׁה קְהִלַּת יַעֲקֹב, *Moshe commanded us the Torah, the heritage of the congregation of Jacob,* takes on new meaning. The Torah can be transmitted from one generation to the next, only because it was originally given through Moshe. Had it come directly from Hashem, its demands would have been so great that neither we nor our children would have the strength to live up to them.

Thus when the Jews said, *Why should we die?* they were referring to the spiritual death that such frustration and lack of confidence causes.[1]

(5636)

---

1. We can see that sinning (and even the potential to sin) is incompatible with high levels of

Still another explanation of the people's fear of hearing Hashem directly involves their great humility. Before the Torah was given, the Jews did not realize how important was the role they were to play in justifying the existence of the world through their acceptance of Torah. However, once Hashem began to speak to them and they *saw* the connection between the roots of their souls and the Torah, they were made aware how vital they were in Hashem's plan for the world. Were they to perish, the world would have no purpose and would cease to exist, as we discuss elsewhere in this work at length. (See *Rashi's* comment on *Bereishis* 1:31). (5638)

Possibly also the people were afraid that their untimely mass death would give the world an unfavorable impression of the Torah. Had the entire Jewish people died immediately upon receiving the Torah, the nations would have thought of Torah as deadly poison, rather than the source of life it actually is. (5633)

Another possibility is that the Jews' concern about dying did not relate to physical death, or even spiritual deterioration, as suggested above. Rather they had a well-founded fear that the heady feeling of perceiving Hashem "face-to-face" would adversely affect their personalities. The Sages warned of this danger in the following Mishnah (*Avos* 3:12): כֹּל שֶׁחָכְמָתוֹ מְרֻבָּה מִמַּעֲשָׂיו אֵין חָכְמָתוֹ מִתְקַיֶּמֶת, *anyone whose wisdom exceeds his good deeds, his wisdom will not endure.* The Jews also were afraid that too much exposure to Hashem's word would bring them to such a high level of wisdom that their characters would suffer. (5651)

A final answer is that had the people received the Torah directly from Hashem, it would have put them entirely on a miraculous level of existence. They were concerned because they knew that open miracles do not leave permanent effects (as we see from the Ten Plagues and the Splitting of the Sea, after which nature returned to its original state).

While it is true that the Jews were willing to die for Torah, the fact that their souls *did* actually expire when the Torah was given was an indication that Moshe, rather than Hashem, should speak to them. Simply the fact that they were afraid, the mere *feeling* of fear, justified their concern. (5633)

---

sanctity from Adam's expulsion from Eden to prevent him from eating from the Tree of Life. So too our forefathers opted not to receive the Torah which is comparable to the Tree of Life, directly from Hashem for fear of potential sin (5636).

קְרַב אַתָּה וּשֲׁמָע אֵת כָּל־אֲשֶׁר יֹאמַר ה׳ אֱלֹהֵינוּ וְאַתְּ תְּדַבֵּר אֵלֵינוּ אֵת כָּל־אֲשֶׁר יְדַבֵּר ה׳ אֱלֹהֵינוּ אֵלֶיךָ וְשָׁמַעְנוּ וְעָשִׂינוּ:

You come close and hear everything that Hashem, *our God, will say and you tell us everything that* Hashem, *our God, tells you and we will listen and we will do it* (*Devarim* 5:24).

The Jews responded to their fear of dying by asking Moshe to go to Hashem and accept the Torah on their behalf. It is difficult at first to understand these words, קְרַב אַתָּה, *you come close*. Seemingly, Moshe remained at the mountain while the Jews withdrew, as we saw earlier וַיַּעַמְדוּ מֵרָחוֹק, *they stood from afar*. In what sense, then, were they telling Moshe to "come closer"?

We can say that they were referring to spiritual closeness rather than physical proximity. Before this, Moshe had acted only on his own behalf, since the Jews also heard the first two commandments directly from Hashem. By appointing him to be their emissary they elevated him to a much higher status. A leader acting on behalf of his people attains a level that no one can reach solely on his own merit.[1]

(5635)

The *Yalkut* (*Yalkut Yisro* 301) suggests that Moshe was reluctant to come close and the angels had to compel him to. The Jews may have felt that as long as they stood and heard Hashem's voice together with Moshe, Hashem would give only a level of Torah that *they* were worthy of and capable of accepting. If Moshe were on his own, Hashem would give him a much higher form of Torah. Thus the reason the people wanted *not* to hear Hashem directly was so that Moshe could come even closer.

1. See *Avos* 2:2

After Matan Torah

◆§ Moshe's Response: Have No Fear

In response to the people's plea that Moshe speak to Hashem on their behalf Moshe answered (*Shemos* 20:17), אַל־תִּירָאוּ כִּי לְבַעֲבוּר נַסּוֹת אֶתְכֶם בָּא הָאֱלֹהִים וּבַעֲבוּר תִּהְיֶה יִרְאָתוֹ עַל־פְּנֵיכֶם לְבִלְתִּי תֶחֱטָאוּ, *Do not fear, for in order to elevate you has God come; and so that fear of Him shall be upon your faces so that you shall not sin.*

This verse seems to contradict itself. Moshe begins by urging the Jews not to be afraid, but then says that Hashem's purpose in revealing Himself to them was precisely in order to inspire fear in them, fear of sinning. Is *yiras Shamayim*, fear of Heaven, a desirable fear, or would it be preferable if they were not afraid at all?

We shall suggest several approaches to resolving this apparent contradiction. First let us understand, though, that *yiras Shamayim* is only a means to achieve a higher goal rather than a goal in itself. This is what Moshe meant when he told them, "Do not fear" — do not make fear an end unto itself; it should be only a surface emotion ("upon your faces"), a first step in bringing you to the higher level of loving Hashem. By loving Hashem, one can reach a higher spiritual level than his own forces would normally allow. Someone motivated primarily by fear of Heaven, however, rises only as high as his personal capabilities permit.

If Israel had been able to reach the level of *loving* Hashem at Sinai, He would have continued to speak to them directly. In this interpretation, Hashem's response to the people's request that He not speak to them directly, הֵיטִיבוּ כָּל־אֲשֶׁר דִּבֵּרוּ, *everything they have said is good* (*Devarim* 5:25), was given only with reluctance, since He would have preferred that they reach the higher level of loving Him, rather than merely fearing Him. (5633)

Another approach to resolving this contradiction relies on the well-known distinction between two kinds of fear: fear of punishment and fear inspired by Hashem's majesty. When Moshe told the people not to be afraid, he meant they should not let themselves be motivated by the fear of punishment, which was unsuitable for them. Thus in recounting the events at Mount Sinai forty years later he said (*Devarim* 5:5), *For you were afraid of the fire and you did not ascend on the mountain.* Had they been deterred not by fear of being burned but rather by fear of the very awesomeness of Hashem's Majesty, he implied, Hashem would have brought them to a much higher level. Such an attitude causes one not just to fear the *punishment* for committing a particular sin, but rather to fear the *sin* itself, a much higher level of Divine service, as we see from Moshe's explanation: *so that fear of Him shall be upon your faces so that you shall not sin.* The fear of Hashem's exaltedness prevents us from sinning.[1]

We see also that Moshe considered fear of punishment inferior, from his use of the passive voice in warning the people against it, not אַל תִּירְאוּ, *do not fear,* but rather אַל תִּירָאוּ, *do not* **be** *afraid.* (5636)

This distinction between fear of punishment and higher forms of fear can be further understood in terms of an individual's level of spirituality. Fear of punishment can be attained by people who are still morally deficient. Fear of Hashem's exaltedness, however, is possible only in those who have achieved spiritual perfection (*shleimus*). This is the level referred to by the verse we say in Grace After Meals, יְראוּ אֶת ה׳ קְדֹשָׁיו כִּי־אֵין מַחְסוֹר לִירֵאָיו, *Fear Hashem, you — His holy ones — for there is no lack for His reverent ones* (*Tehillim* 34:10). True *yiras Shamayim* is achieved only by the highly motivated, completed (אֵין מַחְסוֹר, *not lacking*) person.

Tana D'Bei Eliyahu expressed this theme in a different way: אֵין אוֹמְרִים אַל תִּירָא אֶלָּא לְמִי שֶׁיָּרֵא שָׁמַיִם לַאֲמִיתּוֹ, *do not tell someone not to be afraid unless he truly fears Heaven* (*Rabbah* 25). Only those who have achieve spiritual perfection can attain the highest form of fear, the fear of Hashem's exaltedness.

Indeed, the Torah concludes on this note by describing Moshe's greatest accomplishment as מוֹרָא הַגָּדוֹל, *the extraordinary fear* of Hashem's exaltedness that came over the people at the time the Torah was given. The closer an individual is to Hashem, the more of this kind of fear he can attain. Moshe, who came closer to Hashem's Presence than any individual, was the exemplar of this kind of fear. (5663)

---

1. As with love of Hashem, this higher form of fear is beyond human reach, and is possible only with Divine help, granted to those who totally negate themselves to Hashem's will.

In this context we can understand Moshe's explanation of the display of Hashem's might that accompanied the Giving of the Torah (*Shemos* 20:20). וּבַעֲבוּר תִּהְיֶה יִרְאָתוֹ עַל־פְּנֵיכֶם, *so that fear of Him shall be upon your faces,* as an allusion to the shining countenance of every Jew. This outer "light" corresponds directly to the inner sanctity of the Jew.

(*Parashas Yisro* 5647)

Another resolution of the seeming contradiction in our verse makes a distinction based on the *intent* of the fear. When he told the people *Do not fear,* Moshe was warning them against fear that caused them to distance themselves from Hashem, as it says, *and they stood from afar.* Another kind of fear, that prevents one from sinning, is desirable, and it was this that Moshe praised to them in the phrase, *so that fear of Him shall be upon your faces so that you shall not sin.*

(*Parashas Yisro* 5648)

Our verse continues, לְבַעֲבוּר נַסּוֹת אֶתְכֶם בָּא הָאֱלֹהִים, *in order to elevate you has God come.*: Moshe gave the people an additional reason to have direct dialogue with Hashem — His determination to raise them to a higher level and to lead them in a supernatural manner.

The greater the person, the greater the challenges and trials he must face. At the moment they were given the Torah, Israel was faced with great temptations to reject it as the Gentile world had done. With these words Moshe wanted to reassure the Jews that their fear was not adequate reason to reject the Torah, but merely a superficial challenge they could easily overcome.

Hashem acquiesced to the people's reluctance for direct dialogue: הֵיטִיבוּ כָּל־אֲשֶׁר דִּבֵּרוּ מִי־יִתֵּן וְהָיָה לְבָבָם זֶה לָהֶם לְיִרְאָה אֹתִי וְלִשְׁמֹר אֶת־כָּל־מִצְוֹתַי כָּל־הַיָּמִים, *They have done good in everything they said. If only it were in their heart to fear Me and to keep all of My commandments all of the days.* It is noteworthy that while Moshe urged the people not to be afraid, Hashem Himself praises the people for their fear of Heaven — "If only their inclination to revere Me and to observe My commandments would continue forever."

In particular, Hashem urged the people that *their hearts* should fear Him. The word לְבָבָם is understood to refer to both components of the Jewish heart, the good inclination (*yetzer tov*) and the evil inclination (*yetzer hara,* see *Rashi* on *Devarim* 6:5). This suggests that at Sinai even the *yetzer hara* was prepared to serve a higher purpose and that both the good and evil inclinations can and should be used for service of Hashem. The Jews were prepared to fear Hashem not only in the World to Come, but also in our world, the world in which the two inclinations coexist.

It follows then that the Jews should remain on earth and sanctify it by listening to the Ten Commandments that emanate from Heaven. Moshe, however, having urged the people to continue listening to the Torah directly from Hashem, could not comprehend such a mission for his people. He was a Divine person, totally lacking a *yetzer hara*, and as such could understand only man's potential to soar up to Heaven, but not his mission to serve Hashem on earth. (5647)

◆§ The Fragrance and Dew of Torah

In conclusion we will discuss two poignant Rabbinic teachings concerning the Giving of the Torah (*Shabbos* 88b):

> כָּל דִּבּוּר וְדִבּוּר שֶׁיָּצָא מִפִּי הקב"ה יָצְתָה נִשְׁמָתָן שֶׁל יִשְׂרָאֵל הוֹרִיד טַל שֶׁעָתִיד לְהַחֲיוֹת בּוֹ מֵתִים וְהֶחְיָה מֵתִים
>
> *[Upon hearing] each of the commandments emerge from Hashem's mouth, the souls of Israel expired, [and Hashem] brought down the dew that in the future will resurrect the dead and resurrected these dead ones.*
>
> כָּל דִּבּוּר וְדִבּוּר שֶׁיָּצָא מִפִּי הקב"ה נִתְמַלֵּא כָּל הָעוֹלָם כּוּלוֹ בְּשָׂמִים וְכֵיוָן שֶׁמִּדִּבּוּר רִאשׁוֹן נִתְמַלֵּא דִּבּוּר שֵׁנִי לְהֵיכָן הָלַךְ? הוֹצִיא הקב"ה רוּחַ מֵאוֹצְרוֹתָיו וְהָיָה מַעֲבִיר רִאשׁוֹן רִאשׁוֹן
>
> *As each commandment emerged from Hashem's mouth, the whole world filled with the aroma of fragrant spices. If the world was so filled after the first commandment, where did that aroma go so that it could become filled again after the second commandment? Hashem released a wind from His storehouse whose currents dissipated each wave of fragrance in turn.*

These poetic teachings are as laden with meaning as the fragrance and dew whose image they evoke. Let us consider them רִאשׁוֹן רִאשׁוֹן, first things first. The Midrash dealing with *techiyas ha-meisim* (resurrection of the dead) seems to suggest that there is an intimate connection between that event and the Giving of the Torah. But why did the Jews' souls expire upon hearing the commandments?

To answer this, let us examine the transition the people made at that moment, the transition from righteous Gentiles who were not yet obligated in Torah to Torah-observant Jews. The soul of a Gentile who observes the seven Noachide laws, precious as it may be, is insignificant in comparison to the soul of a Jew who observes all six hundred thirteen commandments. The "transplant" that occurred at Sinai, the grafting of this new, Jewish, soul on to the much smaller soul they had previously, was such a traumatic experience that they lost consciousness, their souls expired. (5649)

More profoundly, their souls expired from simple exposure to Hashem's Presence. While the Jewish *neshamah* is described as a light, as King Solomon said (*Mishlei* 20:27) נֵר ה׳ נִשְׁמַת אָדָם, *HASHEM's light is the soul of a man,* Hashem's Presence is the *source* of all light. In the presence of its own source, any lesser light appears invisible, as if extinguished. In a similar vein the Sages often said שְׁרַגָא בְּטִיהֲרָא מַאי אַהֲנֵי, a candle in daylight is ineffectual. So too, the brilliance of Hashem's Presence outshone the souls of the people and in this sense they "expired."

The Sages expressed a similar point in the following saying (*Pesachim* 8a): לְמַה צַדִּיקִים דוֹמִין בִּפְנֵי שְׁכִינָה? כְּנֵר מִפְּנֵי אֲבוּקָה, *To what can we compare the righteous in the Holy Presence? To a candle in the presence of a torch.*

The "resurrecting dew" the Sages spoke of, then, may allude to the fact that Hashem, so to speak, "adjusted" His light to allow the light of the people, their souls, to continue to shine visibly. The prophet Habakuk alludes to Hashem's "hiding" of His light in the verse (3:4) וְשָׁם חֶבְיוֹן עֻזֹּה, *there is the hiding-place of His strength.* Hashem hides His full power so that man can survive.

Another version of this Midrash (*Shemos Rabba* 29:3) suggests that the Torah itself restored the souls of the Jews: הַתּוֹרָה בִּקְשָׁה עֲלֵיהֶם רַחֲמִים מִלִּפְנֵי הקב״ה. יֵשׁ מֶלֶךְ מַשִּׂיא בִּתּוֹ וְהוֹרֵג אַנְשֵׁי בֵּיתוֹ? מִיַּד הֶחֱזִיר נִשְׁמָתָן, *The Torah asked Hashem for mercy for them, "Is there a king who marries off his daughter and then kills the members of his household?" Immediately Hashem returned their souls to them.*

Thus the Torah is called (*Tehillim* 19:8) מְשִׁיבַת נָפֶשׁ, *the restorer of the soul.* It is only fitting that Jewish souls can survive only by upholding the Torah, which is called תְּמִימָה, *perfect* because all life flows from it. (5633)

When the Midrash calls the Jews "members of Hashem's household," the household it refers to is the World to Come. Hashem's intention is that this world should be only an "entry chamber" to His true dwelling, the World to Come. (5631)

Moreover, the Torah is the only way for Hashem's living force to dwell in a material world. Only through Torah can a Jew cope with the demands and pressures of this world. If so, it is very appropriate that it was the Torah that made it possible for the Jews to continue living in the world. We see an allusion to this in the phrase מְשִׁיבַת נָפֶשׁ, *restorer of the soul (nefesh)*. The *nefesh* is the most mundane part of the soul, the one most involved with material existence, and the fact that this allusion refers to it suggests that the Torah restored Israel's capacity to deal with *this* world especially.

(*Parashas Yisro* 5632)

The image of a fragrance that fills the world before being removed to make way for a new fragrance raises a question: Why was it necessary to dispel each wave? Why couldn't new layers of fragrance be added over the old ones?

We may say that Torah is most effective in a void. If the world were saturated with the spirituality (for which the "fragrance" of the Midrash is an image) of the First Commandment, a second commandment would be unnecessary. The first "aroma" was removed not as a permanent displacement of the lofty spiritual effect of the first commandment, but rather as a temporary measure, what the Sages called a יְרִידָה לְצוֹרֶךְ עֲלִיָּה, (cf. *Makkos* 7b) a step down in preparation for the next ascent, much as one crouches slightly before jumping. In this sense Torah is compared to water, as the prophet Yeshayahu said (55:1), הוֹי כָּל־צָמֵא לְכוּ לַמַּיִם, *All you who are thirsty, go to water!* Water always seeks the lowest places to fill whatever void is there.

We refer to this theme in the *Shemoneh Esrei* prayer by describing Hashem as מֶלֶךְ מֵמִית וּמְחַיֶּה, *the King Who causes death and restores life*. When Hashem takes a life, it is only in order to prepare it for the more permanent life of *techiyas ha-meisim*, the resurrection of the dead.

(5634)

While the fragrance of Sinai eventually dissipated and the spices ascended to their place in Gan Eden, they left a lingering scent in our world — the aroma of Torah. The more spiritual a life one leads in this world, the more of Sinai's residual fragrance he will enjoy upon entering the World to Come. In this sense our world is truly an "entry chamber" to the World to Come, a place to absorb the fragrance of Torah so that we will merit the much more powerful fragrance that awaits us there.

(5636)

Even the non-Jewish world, who rejected the Torah and its spirituality (represented by the spices), is nurtured by the residue of Torah's lingering presence in this world. (5636)

This is like a person who enters a spice shop, even if he touches nothing, he cannot help but enjoy the fragrant aroma that surrounds him and that permeates his clothing even after he leaves the shop. So also the nations of the world still feel, in some weakened form, the residue of Torah that clung to them at the time the Jewish people stood at Mount Sinai. Thus nearly all of them pay lip service to some variant of "monotheism," and give at least token recognition to the existence of ultimate human values that originated with the "Mosaic Code" given at Mount Sinai.

How fortunate are we, the heirs to the still fulsome source of that fragrance, the Torah itself, whose rich pleasures are available to any Jew who opens his soul to its life-sustaining aroma.

Torah Attributes

◆§ Introduction

Despite the many customs and traditions that have come to be associated with Shavuos, the central theme of the festival remains Torah. In the following essay, we will present a general overview of Torah from a variety of perspectives, touching on the praise it is worthy of, its attributes, its impact, and above all its comprehensiveness.

◆§ The Meaning of the Word Torah

The word *Torah* is primarily derived from the root הוֹרָה (*horah*), to show, indicating that Torah's deepest secrets are eventually revealed to those who study it assiduously. It may also be related to the word יוֹרֶה (*yoreh*), rain. Just as rain fertilizes the earth and releases its hidden treasures to promote life-sustaining growth, Torah study also releases man's innate potential and makes him a source of life and growth.

(5635)

The word *Torah* may also be related to the word אוֹרָה (*orah*), light, Torah is a light through which we can perceive Hashem's Presence in every aspect of life. The opening words of the Ten Commandments suggest this meaning: *And God spoke all these things saying, I am HASHEM, your God* — through Torah one can perceive Hashem (*I am HASHEM, your God,*) in every facet of the world (*all of these things*). True fear of Hashem comes only from using the light of Torah to appreciate the sanctity present in all of life and to recognize that all of existence is sustained only by Hashem.

We can also find a connection between the words *Torah* and יִרְאָה (*yirah*), *fear*, suggesting that true fear of Hashem comes from in-depth study of Torah. The Psalmist alludes to this connection in the phrase (111:10) רֵאשִׁית חָכְמָה יִרְאַת ה׳, *The beginning of wisdom is the fear of HASHEM.*

◆§ The Many Levels of Torah

In theory the Torah is not the exclusive domain of the Jewish people. Indeed, we are told (*Yalkut, Zos HaBrachah*) that before Hashem gave the Torah to Israel He offered all the other nations the opportunity to accept it and they all refused. Most likely, had it been given to one of the other nations it would have been in a simpler, lower form than its present one. The Torah is versatile enough to have meaning for all people.

Conversely, the Midrash (*Sifri, Zos HaBrachah*) relates that the angels did not want to relinquish control over the Torah and tried to prevent Moshe from transmitting it to the Jews. We may assume that if they had been successful in retaining the Torah for themselves, it would have been in a higher, more rarefied, form. However, since it was not given neither to the Gentile world or to angels, but rather to the Jewish people, the best possible situation came into being. Not only did the Jews obtain the Torah in the form most appropriate to their needs, they also received all the other possible configurations of the Torah, from the lofty spiritual aspects relevant to the angels to the simpler levels intended for the non-Jewish world.

It is significant that the Torah alludes to the fact that Hashem took the Torah from the angels to give to the Jews with an Aramaic expression (*Devarim* 33:2), וְאָתָה מֵרִבְבֹת קֹדֶשׁ, *and it came from the myriads of holy ones.* Since the angels do not understand Aramaic, this statement is not likely to arouse their jealousy. Even though angels are on a much higher spiritual level than humans, mortals and Jews in particular, have the potential to use Torah to elevate themselves to a higher level than angels. (5636)

❧ Torah: Unity and Perfection

The Torah exists on many different levels and offers meaning to individuals at various stages of spiritual development. Still, it is a unified entity rather than a conglomeration of fragmented phrases and concepts. A sense of unity permeates the Torah, even though it allows for different shades of meaning, relevant to each person's needs and background.

The Psalmist (19:8) describes the Torah as "perfect," suggesting that the entire Torah is implied in each and every letter. Another way of saying this is that Hashem's Presence, which is the essence of Torah, is equally evident from every letter of the Torah. This is also implied in a teaching of the Sages (*Pesachim* 6b), אֵין מוּקְדָם וּמְאוּחָר בַּתּוֹרָה, the events related in the Torah are not necessarily in chronological order. If every letter is a microcosm of the entire Torah, it follows that the entire time span recounted by the Torah is encapsulated in each of the letters, from the creation till Moshe's death. While it may *appear* that some events follow others, in reality the events written later were already implied earlier, thus negating any possible chronological sequence to Torah. (5656)

❧ Torah: Fire and Water

The Torah that we know is merely the outer surface of a much deeper phenomenon. The Sages (*Pesikta Berachah*) hinted at Torah's depth by calling it black fire written on a backdrop of white fire. While much of the Torah may appear mysterious to us, like an opaque ball of black fire, always just below that surface is the true meaning of Torah, with all the clarity of white fire. (5638)

Those who can probe beyond the Torah's surface and begin to penetrate its depth will find great clarity in it. The Torah was given through many elements, in particular cloud and fire. A cloud shrouded Mount Sinai, preventing those who could not properly appreciate and respect it from seeing the transmission taking place. The fire, a destructive agent, camouflaged Torah's true nature as the mainstay of all life. The smoke and fire that obscured Torah conjure up the image of a precious diamond that one surrounds with poison to keep it safe from those not authorized to touch it. (5655, 5659)

The Torah is compared to fire not only because of fire's destructive power but also to suggest the permanence and endurance of the Jewish people. The fire of Hashem's perpetual love for us burns like an eternal flame. As King Solomon rhapsodizes (*Shir HaShirim* 8:7), מַיִם רַבִּים לֹא יוּכְלוּ לְכַבּוֹת אֶת־הָאַהֲבָה, *Many waters cannot quench the love.* All the powers in the world cannot quench the love that burns like a fire between Hashem and ourselves. Indeed, we thrive on adversity, as the Torah says of the relationship between Jacob and Esau (*Bereishis* 25:23), וּלְאֹם מִלְאֹם יֶאֱמָץ, *one nation will struggle with the other.* Esau's attacks on Jacob only give him more strength. Thus the Torah was given soon after the surprise attack of Esau's descendants, Amalek. (5660)

While Torah is compared to fire, it is also compared to water, as the prophet says (*Yeshayahu* 55:1), הוֹי כָּל־צָמֵא לְכוּ לַמַּיִם, *All you thirsty ones, go to water.* Both of these comparisons may refer to Torah's ability to combat the *yetzer hara* (since Shavuos is one of the times when the *yetzer hara* is rendered ineffective), as the Sages said (*Kiddushin* 30b) *I created the yezter hara and I created the Torah as an antidote . . . If the yetzer hara is stone, Torah will dissolve it. If it is iron, Torah will shatter it.*

In what way is the *yetzer hara* comparable to stone and iron? Like stone, it blocks the light of positive commandments from entering the heart. But Torah, like water, dissolves all obstacles in its path and softens the heart of the Jew. Iron, on the other hand, represents that power of the *yetzer hara* to seduce Jews to transgress negative commandments. Like fire, Torah shatters iron, and refines its impurities. As the Sages said, (*Pesachim* 85b) *even an iron barrier cannot separate Israel from its Father in Heaven.* Someone who studies and practices Torah is called Hashem's child, and not even the thickest iron wall can separate him from his Father.

There is another sense in which Torah may be understood with reference to water and fire. Torah teaches us to be humble and lowly of spirit, like water which always seeks out the lowest places. We must understand, though, that this humility applies only to material matters — our bodies and their needs. In this sense the Torah calls Moshe "exceedingly humble, more than any other man on earth." In spiritual matters, however, the reverse is true. Spiritually, we must try to raise ourselves to the highest level possible. The lower we make our bodies, like water which seeks low places, the higher our spirits can soar, like fire. Thus it was only "on earth" that Moshe was humble; when he went to Heaven he was on a higher level than the angels. (5662)

◆§ Prepare Yourself to Learn Torah

One's state of preparedness to learn Torah can have as much influence on our ability to absorb and retain what we learn as the learning process itself. For this reason the Sages attributed the initial success of Amalek's attack to the fact that the Jews' had allowed their commitment to Torah to weaken, as they said עַל שֶׁרָפוּ יְדֵיהֶם מִן הַתּוֹרָה, *because their hands relaxed from Torah* (*Mechilta Parashas Beshalach,* 15). Even though the Torah had not yet been given in a formal sense prior to Sinai, the Jews were nonetheless faulted for not *preparing* themselves adequately to receive the Torah at Mount Sinai.

It is interesting to note that the word *hand* is often used to connote preparation for something, as we see in the Sages' exegesis concerning the attack of Amalek. Another example of this is the Torah's description of the preparations for the installation of Aharon and his sons as *Kohanim,* שִׁבְעַת יָמִים תְּמַלֵּא יָדָם, *for seven days shall their* ***hands*** *be prepared* (*Shemos* 29:35).

Thus it is appropriate that just as the Sages used the word "hand" to imply the Jews' lack of preparedness in Torah, Moshe's hand later played a crucial role in defeating Amalek, as it says (*Shemos* 17:11), וְהָיָה כַּאֲשֶׁר יָרִים מֹשֶׁה יָדוֹ וְגָבַר יִשְׂרָאֵל, *and it was when Moshe lifted his hand, Israel prevailed.* This suggests that Moshe's high level of preparedness to receive the Torah compensated for any deficiency in the rest of the people. The Mishnah also emphasizes the importance of being prepared to learn Torah (*Avos* 2:17), הַתְקֵן עַצְמְךָ לִלְמוֹד תּוֹרָה שֶׁאֵינָהּ יְרוּשָׁה לָךְ, *Prepare yourself to learn Torah, for it is not yours by inheritance.*

(5647)

In order to understand and retain the Torah we learn, we must first make ourselves into suitable vessels to receive it. Thus Torah is described as black fire written on a backdrop of white fire. "White fire" here symbolizes the purity of heart required of us to be capable of accepting Torah. Thus three days before the Torah was given Hashem commanded the Jews to wash their garments (וְכִבְּסוּ שִׂמְלֹתָם), a phrase which *Onkelos* renders as וִיחַוְּרוּן לְבוּשֵׁיהוֹן, *they shall* **whiten** *their garments* (*Shemos* 19:10). (5641)

◆§ Torah: The Source of Life

There is a curious paradox concerning the Torah: On the one hand, it is said to sustain life, as the Torah says וָחַי בָּהֶם, *and one shall live by them [words of Torah].* (*Vayikra* 18:5) On the other hand, a Jew must be prepared to die for the sake of Torah, as the Sages said (*Shabbos* 93a), אֵין הַתּוֹרָה מִתְקַיֶּימֶת אֶלָּא בְּמִי שֶׁמֵּמִית אֶת עַצְמוֹ עָלֶיהָ, *The Torah is preserved only in someone who kills himself over it.*

However both statements are true in a very precise way. The Torah sustains life for those who forego all other amenities for its sake: The verse "and one should live by them" refers to those who live only for Torah and for nothing else. Those who are willing to forego all other pleasures for Torah, to *die* for Torah in a sense, live eternally since they are linked to the source of life, Torah. The Sage Rabbi Akiva, who gave up his life for Torah, is described by the Midrash (*Tanchumah Parashas Ki Savo*) as having a portion in the true eternal life. (5647, 5652)

Indeed, the Torah was given in a situation of martyrdom. As we have discussed earlier, The Jewish people's collective soul expired upon hearing the first words of the Ten Commandments. However, dying for Torah involves not only martyrdom but also, in a more mundane sense, consistent trust in Hashem. The Psalmist wrote of the person who maintains such unwavering trust (1:3), וְהָיָה כְּעֵץ שָׁתוּל עַל־פַּלְגֵי מָיִם, *He shall be like a tree deeply rooted alongside brooks of water.* Every Jew is rooted, in a unique portion of Torah. Someone who genuinely trusts in Hashem is able to cling to those roots, and to reach his full potential. (5647)

◆§ Torah and the Nations

While the Torah is intended primarily for the Jewish people, it has also made a powerful impact on the rest of mankind, and on nature itself. This impact, however, cannot be directly felt in the temporal world. It is only because the Jewish people accepted the Torah that mankind can benefit from it. Thus, world Jewry is a vehicle to bring Torah to the rest of the world.

The Sages explain the Jews' role as a funnel of Torah to humanity in a beautiful Midrash (*Yalkut Shimoni* 286). At the precise moment Hashem said *I am HASHEM, your God,* the entire universe trembled and each and every creation — all the mountains and hills — felt that Hashem was *its* God.

However, when Hashem continued, *Who took you out of the land of Egypt,* they realized that He was speaking only to the Jews. The Exodus from Egypt was a prerequisite for receiving the Torah, not only because it afforded the physical freedom necessary for Torah study, but also because of the spiritual liberation it implied. The natural world, embodying materialistic values, is limited by its belief that the laws of nature are immutable. Only the Jewish people, who experienced the overturning of the natural order of the world when they left Egypt, was able to accept the Torah for itself. Then they could funnel Torah values to the rest of humanity.

The Psalmist alludes to nature's inability to receive the Torah directly in the following passage (114:3-7), *The sea saw and fled ... the mountains skipped like rams.* Nature could not remain erect *before the Lord's Presence .. before the presence of the God of Jacob.* Only the Jews, the people that had experienced the wonders of the Exodus, could accept Torah, as indicated in the Psalm's opening words, *When Israel went out of Egypt.*

Nonetheless the residual scent of Torah was enjoyed by all mankind. As we have discussed in the essay entitled "After the Torah was Given" the Sages relate that aromatic spices saturated the world as each of the Ten Commandments was given (*Shabbos* 88b). These "spices" symbolize, among other things, those fragments of Torah that clung to the other nations of the world. The fact that Hashem gave the Torah in seventy languages shows clearly that He intended for all the nations to have some portion in it, not only the Jews. (5631)

The Jewish role as a funnel of Torah to other nations is analogous to the role of *Eretz Yisrael* in bringing livelihood to the rest of the world. *Eretz Yisrael* is described as *a land which HASHEM, your God, continually scrutinizes* in order to provide for its needs. In its merit, the entire world is blessed in turn with rainfall and sustenance.

(5646, 5653, 5655)

Hashem created all men for His honor, as we say in the blessing שֶׁהַכֹּל בָּרָא לִכְבוֹדוֹ, *Who created everything for His honor*. Still, Israel was especially created for His honor, as we say in the *Uva LeTzion* prayer, *Blessed is He, our God, Who created* **us** *for His glory, separated us from those who stray, and gave us the Torah of truth.* By being different from the rest of mankind and keeping the Torah, we demonstrate that all men were created for His honor. (5643)

The impact of Torah was felt on the whole of nature, yet Torah is greater than nature. The secrets that nature is *not* willing to reveal can be acquired by delving into Torah. This is why the world was created with a letter *beis* (in the word *Bereishis*), which is closed on three sides and open only on one side, to indicate that we are not to reflect too deeply on what is above us or on the inner hidden secrets of the natural world.

The Torah was given, however, beginning with a letter *alef* (אָנֹכִי ה׳ אֱלֹהֶיךָ), which is open on all four sides, because the Torah preceded the world. Thus the Jewish people can come to recognize that Hashem created the world, directly through Torah without having to rely on the evidence of the natural world.

This is why the first commandment does not say *I am HASHEM, your God, Who created the world,* but rather *Who took you out of the land of Egypt (Mitzraim),* to indicate that the Torah knows no boundaries or limits (*metzarim*). (5663)

Apart from any other impact the Giving of the Torah may have had on mankind, it also gave shape to what had been until then an amorphous world. While the physical world had been in existence for over two millennia, until Israel accepted the Torah the world lacked direction and purpose. (5636)

Even more than giving shape and direction to the natural world, Torah is also the foundation of nature's continued existence. We say every morning in *Pesukei D'Zimrah, Blessed is He Who speaks and does.* This phrase refers to the creation of the world through "Ten Utterances" (see *Avos* 5:1). The prayer then continues *Blessed is He Who decrees and sustains* — by decreeing the Torah to His people through the Ten Commandments, Hashem sustains the entire universe. (5633)

Torah has an impact not only on the Jewish nation as a whole, but also on individuals. Only through Torah can an individual grow and come closer to Hashem. While the angels start on a higher plane than mortals since they are removed from material concerns, the Torah gives humans the power to lift themselves above the angels.

Torah not only helps the Jew live in this world, it also prepares him for life in the World to Come. The blessing we recite after a public Torah reading, *Who implanted eternal life within us,* is really a reference to *Olam Haba,* perpetual life which is acquired through Torah study. The Midrash suggests that Gehinnom came into being as a result of the evil deeds of the wicked. In the same spirit we may say that the "eternal life" of the World to Come was created by and for the good deeds of *tzadikkim.* (5636)

Even in this world, however, a Jew can achieve his full potential only through Torah, as we say in the *Uva LeTzion* prayer every day, *May He open our heart through His Torah* — Torah opens the heart of the Jew to *yiras Shamayim* (fear of Heaven). The Talmud (*Shabbos* 31b) compares *yiras Shamayim* to a home in that it is the focal point of Jewish life. The Torah is described as the door through which a Jew may enter this "home," and be able to ascend to the lofty realm of *yiras Shamayim*. (5636, 5639, 5640)

◆ The Torah "Face to Face"

A powerful statement of the Torah's impact on Jewry is contained in the verse (*Devarim* 5:4) פָּנִים בְּפָנִים דִּבֶּר ה׳ עִמָּכֶם, *Face to face* H*ASHEM spoke with you.* This verse has been interpreted in various ways. For example, the Midrash (*Mechilta*) sees in it a reciprocal relationship between Hashem and the Jews. Sometimes a teacher wants to teach but the students do not want to learn, or vice versa. Here, however, Hashem was as eager to teach us Torah as we were to learn from Him.

Similarly, this expression *face to face* suggests that Hashem not only gave us the Torah, but also gave us the strength and the internal resources we needed to receive it. This idea emerges also from the *Haggadah,* "If Hashem had only brought us close to Him at Mount Sinai and not given us the Torah, it would have sufficed." Merely bringing us close to Him and giving us the internal resources we needed to learn Torah, was in itself as important as actually receiving it. (5637)

Additionally, the phrase "face to face" implies that Hashem is engrossed with His people, and thus we are totally absorbed with

Hashem and His Torah. This is based on the similarity of the Hebrew words פָּנִים, *face*, and פָּנָה, *to turn away* — we turn away from all our other concerns to devote ourselves to Torah.

Perhaps most profoundly, the expression "face to face" suggests that Hashem directs all the events of the world, including those that seem to pertain only to Gentiles, in accordance with the physical and spiritual needs, of the Jewish people. Conversely, it may also refer to the fact that we conduct all of our affairs based on our perception of Hashem's wishes.

Can there be a more powerful statement of mutual love, of the unshakable bond that exists between Hashem and His people than these simple words, "face to face Hashem spoke with you"! (5637, 5664)

Finally, this phrase "face to face" indicates that Hashem, in His great kindness, gave us the internal resources to stand "face to face" with Him to receive the Torah. This readiness to accept the Torah is renewed afresh on Shavuos. Thus in his retelling of the event forty years later Moshe said (*Devarim* 5:5), אָנֹכִי עֹמֵד בֵּין־ה׳ וּבֵינֵיכֶם, *I stand between HASHEM and you.* By saying *I stand* rather than *I stood* he prepared us to receive the Ten Commandments anew every year, exactly as if we were hearing them for the first time, and committing ourselves to learn and uphold them with the same loving joy we felt at Sinai. (5635)

◆§ How Do We Honor Torah

In our previous remarks we emphasized Torah's significance and its impact both cosmically and on the individual Jew. Yet, the question remains — how do we repay and acknowledge our massive indebtedness to Torah? Furthermore, how do we honor Torah?

While the details of honoring Torah scholars are specified in the Talmud (cf. *Kiddushin* 30b), the means of honoring the Torah *itself* are not quite as apparent.

Rashi, in *Mishlei* (4:8) commenting on the verse סַלְסְלֶהָ וּתְרוֹמְמֶךָּ, *search for it and it will uplift you*, compares the study of Torah to the process in which paupers plucked undeveloped grapes from the vine (cf. *Vayikra* 19:10).

By drawing this parallel between Torah and undeveloped grapes, *Rashi* reminds us that the Torah in its entirety is well beyond our grasp. We cannot pluck the fully-formed grapes from the vine. On the contrary, we honor Torah and acknowledge our indebtedness by avidly seeking to grasp any morsels; by "munching on its tidbits" like a poor person who seeks any type of sustenance. This is the intent of סַלְסְלֶהָ וּתְרוֹמְמֶךָּ — the Jew who endeavors to grasp *anything* from Torah will be morally and spiritually uplifted by Torah itself.

Lest anyone feel depressed about his inability to grasp Torah's totality they should remember that even the greatest scholar can only enjoy the נוֹבְלוֹת, the "withered gleanings" falling from the great Tree of Life to which Torah is compared. Nor should we feel ashamed of our humble beginnings. At Sinai the Jewish people stood at the foot of the mountain (תַּחְתִּית הָהָר) and yet they ascended to great and lofty levels. If we seek Torah's honor by applying it in all walks of life, it in turn will honor us.

(*Succos* 5664)

Eretz Yarah VeShakatah — The Earth Feared and Then Grew Calm

◆§ Introduction

The Talmud (*Shabbos* 88a) relates that as the Torah was being given, the universe first feared its imminent destruction and then becalmed itself. In this piece, we will discuss this sudden shift in mood. Why was the initial trepidation followed by the subsequent tranquility?

We shall propose that the initial fear and the calm that followed were *not* in conflict with each other but rather the fear was a prerequisite for the ensuing calm. We will discuss why the fear came so suddenly, when seemingly it should have started much earlier. We will also touch on related issues, including the "re-creation" of the universe on Shavuos and the relationship between *yiras Shamayim* (fear of Heaven) and Torah.

☙ Torah and Nature

The Creation and the Giving of the Torah are perhaps the two most significant events of Jewish history which, in a larger perspective, represent two pinnacles of Jewish *emunah* (belief in Hashem). To the thinking Jew, the story of the Creation reminds us that Hashem created the universe in infinite harmony, while the events at Mount Sinai represent an even higher level of Godliness, the ability to perceive Hashem's greatness through Torah.

The Talmud (*Shabbos* 88a) quotes a verse describing the moment the Torah was given (*Tehillim* 76:9), אֶרֶץ יָרְאָה וְשָׁקָטָה, *the earth feared and then grew calm.* The Sages ask why nature exhibited such seemingly inconsistent behavior, אִם יָרְאָה לָמָּה שָׁקְטָה וְאִם שָׁקְטָה לָמָּה יָרְאָה, *If it feared, then why was it calm? If it was calm, why did it fear?*

They answer these questions by recalling that heaven and earth were created on a conditional basis. The natural world was informed at the time of its creation that its continued existence was contingent on the Jewish people eventually accepting the Torah. If they rejected the Torah, however, the universe would return to its previous chaotic state, as described at the beginning of *Bereishis* (1:2) — תֹהוּ וָבֹהוּ, *desolate and void.*

Given this condition inherent in the creation, we can understand why the earth should fear as the time for the giving of the Torah approached. If the Jews were to reject their gift, nature would be thrust back into chaos. When nature realized that the Jewish People agreed to accept the Torah, it could be calm, secure that its future was no longer in danger.

☙ Fear: A Prerequisite for Love

In the traditional interpretation, this discussion of the Sages treats fear and calm as two conflicting emotions, as we see from their question, "If it feared, then why was it calm?" Seemingly they could appreciate the earth's fear and questioned only why, *since* it was afraid, was it able to be calmed.

◆§ Fear that Brings Calm

It is also possible to interpret this discussion in an entirely different fashion. Perhaps the earth's inital fear was an important prerequisite for the Torah to be given successfully. In this understanding, the earth's fear and calm are seen as related rather than conflicting emotions.

It is well known that the celestial world and much of nature opposed giving the Torah to the Jewish people. In order to avert their objections, Hashem made it clear to nature that its continued existence was dependent upon the Jewish people's acceptance of Torah.

We may still ask why the universe should have felt fear of its impending destruction. The Sages taught, after all, that the world would have been better off had it not been created (*Eruvin* 13b). However, Hashem's threat was not to destroy the world totally, but rather to return it to a state of chaos — *desolate void* — a far worse state than never having been created at all. (5634)

Thus the earth's initial fear was in reality an essential part of the process that would lead to its eventual calm, once Israel accepted the Torah and nature could be assured it would not return to chaos.

This discussion contains a powerful lesson for us about the correct attitude toward performing *mitzvos.* Just as the earth's fear was a necessary precondition to its later serenity, so also we should approach every *mitzvah* in fear — fear that our performance of the *mitzvah* will not find favor with Hashem. Only if we start with such an attitude, and then are careful to perform each and every *mitzvah* with a loving desire to come closer to Hashem, will we be able to feel the attachment to Hashem that is the true purpose of *mitzvos.*

The concept that fear is a necessary prerequisite to observing *mitzvos* with love is alluded to in the verse (*Devarim* 4:6) וּשְׁמַרְתֶּם וַעֲשִׂיתֶם, *you shall keep and you shall do.* "Keeping" refers to the fear of doing wrong associated with the negative commandments, and is followed by "doing" the positive commandments to demonstrate one's love of Hashem. Similarly, the commandment to observe the Sabbath is expressed both as שָׁמוֹר, *keep,* referring to the prohibitions of Shabbos, and also as זָכוֹר, *remember,* referring to the positive aspects of Shabbos. "Remembering" Shabbos, clinging to the intimate loving atmosphere every Jew feels on Shabbos, would be difficult if one did not first prepare oneself with the attitude of "keeping" Shabbos, relating to the fear necessary to avoid transgressing any of the laws of Shabbos. (5631)

We can say further that in giving the Torah Hashem sought to perfect not just the Jewish people but all of mankind and indeed the entire natural universe. Therefore nature had to be in a state of awe and fear, so that it would fulfill its purpose by submitting itself to the Torah and to the Jewish people. This was the purpose also of the miracles connected with the Exodus from Egypt — to cause the natural world to accept Torah's sovereignty, as the Torah says (*Shemos* 15:14), שָׁמְעוּ עַמִּים יִרְגָּזוּן *The Peoples heard — they were agitated*. In this approach, then, the awe instilled in nature was intended not so much to thwart its interference with the Giving of the Torah as to set the stage for that majestic moment, which was the culmination of all of creation. (5632, 5634, 5635)

Homiletically it is possible to draw a connection between the words שָׁקָטָה, (*shakatah*), was *calmed*, and קֹשְׁט (*kosht*) *truth* as in (*Mishlei* 22:21) קֹשְׁט אִמְרֵי אֱמֶת, *certainty of the words of truth*. Only the fear of Heaven, followed by serene love of Hashem as we describe above, can bring one to a proper appreciation of the truth of Torah. Also, only those who are constantly afraid of distorting the meaning of Torah will merit to speak and understand its truth with confidence. (5634)

One who does not adopt an initial attitude of fear and caution can easily come to be overwhelmed by his instinctive love of Hashem and thus make serious errors in his zeal to perform *mitzvos*. Thus fear protects someone who serves Hashem out of love from losing his perspective. Indeed, the negative commandments are intended primarily to engender this fear that is a necessary precondition of performing the positive commandments with love.

Thus we may interpret the verse *The earth feared and then grew calm* as a guideline for how to serve Hashem here on earth. To succeed as a Torah Jew, one must first turn away from wrongdoing by adopting an attitude of fear; only then is it possible to do good with the serenity and love that comes from true devotion to Hashem.

◆§ Why the Sudden Fear?

Why did the earth suddenly become afraid just before the Torah was given? If its concern was that the Jews would reject the Torah and thereby return it to chaos, that concern should have been present ever since the Creation. Why did it surface only now, as the time for the giving of the Torah drew near?

Evidently, nature had no cause for concern until that time. As the Talmud (*Pesachim* 118a) explains, נֹתֵן לֶחֶם לְכָל בָּשָׂר כִּי לְעוֹלָם חַסְדּוֹ אֵלּוּ כ״ו דורות שֶׁבָּרָא הקב״ה בְּעוֹלָמוֹ וְלֹא נָתַן לָהֶם תּוֹרָה וְזָן אוֹתָם בְּחַסְדּוֹ, *"He gives nourishment to all flesh, for His kindness endures forever" [lit. for the world] (Tehillim 136:25).* The twenty-six expressions of praise [for Hashem in this Psalm, each concluding with "for His kindness endures forever [for the world]," *correspond to the twenty-six generations that Hashem created in His world before He gave the Torah, that He sustained in His kindness.* Only after the Jews accepted the Torah and began to do *mitzvos* was the world sustained on its own merit (that is, on the merit of Israel's Torah and *mitzvos*) rather than by Hashem's kindness.

In other words, until that time, nature could rest secure that it would continue to exist on the strength of Hashem's kindness. Once, however, its future viability became dependent on the actions of fallible human beings, on Israel's merit in observing the Torah, then it had reason to fear. (5637)

◈ The Earth's Inner Soul Revealed

A deeper approach to understanding this transition from fear to calm is suggested by a concept discussed earlier in the essay entitled *Yom HaBikurim*. While the physical exterior of the universe had existed since the Creation, its inner soul did not come into being until Israel accepted the Torah at Mount Sinai. This event gave the universe a completeness that had been lacking until then, a unification of inner self with outer appearance.

Thus the earth *"feared,"* wondering how it could bear the new inner dynamics it had just been granted. Eventually, however, it grew calm in the realization that precisely this trepidation over whether it was worthy of its newfound sanctity, (in other words its humility,) would allow it to continue in a new order based on Torah. (5638)

◈ Fear and Wisdom

A final approach to understanding this verse lies in the relationship between Torah wisdom and fear of Hashem. King Solomon suggests that unless it is tempered by fear of Hashem, wisdom is dangerous, as he wrote (*Koheles* 1:18), כִּי בְּרֹב חָכְמָה רָב כָּעַס, *For with more wisdom there is more anger.*

The question arises, which is the higher goal — fear of Heaven or Torah wisdom. The Mishnah (*Avos* 3:11) says, כֹּל שֶׁיִּרְאַת חֶטְאוֹ קוֹדֶמֶת לְחָכְמָתוֹ חָכְמָתוֹ מִתְקַיֶּמֶת *Anyone whose fear of sin takes priority over his wisdom, his wisdom will endure*, suggesting that fear is only a means to ensure that wisdom, the most important factor, will endure. On the other hand, the Talmud (*Shabbos* 31a) compares fear of Heaven to a house and Torah wisdom to a gate in front of the house, implying that fear is the end goal.

In reality, however, there is no contradiction between these two sayings. Fear of Heaven is both a prerequisite to wisdom and a goal in itself. Initially fear of sin inspires one to acquire Torah wisdom and thereby evolve to higher spiritual levels. This in turn leads to a more profound fear of Heaven, illustrated by the keys to the inner gates of the Talmud's imagery.

With this in mind, let us return to our verse, *The earth feared and then grew calm*. As the time approached for the Torah to be given, the earth feared that a disproportionate amount of wisdom, without corresponding fear, would only lead to sin. But this very fear experienced by the earth was what was needed to bring it to a higher level of wisdom, a wisdom that would endure because it was preceded by fear, and therefore the earth was calmed. (5652)

Succos

Succah

בַּסֻּכֹּת תֵּשְׁבוּ שִׁבְעַת יָמִים כָּל הָאֶזְרָח בְּיִשְׂרָאֵל יֵשְׁבוּ בַּסֻּכֹּת. לְמַעַן יֵדְעוּ דֹרֹתֵיכֶם כִּי בַסֻּכּוֹת הוֹשַׁבְתִּי אֶת בְּנֵי יִשְׂרָאֵל בְּהוֹצִיאִי אוֹתָם מֵאֶרֶץ מִצְרָיִם אֲנִי ה׳ אֱלֹהֵיכֶם

You shall dwell in succos for seven days, every citizen in Israel shall dwell in the succah so that your generations will know that I caused the children of Israel to dwell in succos when I took them from the land of Egypt; I am HASHEM, *your God* (*Vayikra* 23:42-43).

The Torah here projects a direct link between our forefathers in their Wilderness huts after the Exodus, and the contemporary Jew celebrating the festival in his *succah*. Succos, it appears, is not meant just to evoke ancient events — it is an occasion that should profoundly affect our current lives.

How exactly does the message of the *succah* impact on today's world? To answer this, let us examine the nature of the huts in which our ancestors dwelled.

According to both Rabbi Eliezer (cited in *Succah* 11b) and *Onkelos* (the author of the standard Aramaic translation of the Torah), these huts were, in reality, "Clouds of Honor." These clouds are first mentioned in *Shemos* (13:21): וַה׳ הֹלֵךְ לִפְנֵיהֶם יוֹמָם בְּעַמּוּד עָנָן לַנְחֹתָם הַדֶּרֶךְ, HASHEM *went before them [the Jewish People] by day in a pillar of cloud, to show them the way [through the Wilderness].* Elsewhere (*Bamidbar 10:33-34*) the Torah describes how the Clouds of Honor (also called the "Divine Cloud") went before the people to locate an appropriate resting place in the Wilderness.

According to Rashi on that verse, the Divine Cloud dispersed all obstacles facing the Jews as they trekked through the Wilderness. It flattened peaks, filled in crevices, and exterminated snakes and scorpions.

Shortly before his death, Moshe recalled the wondrous protection afforded the people during their sojourn in the Wilderness by this Divine Cloud: הַהֹלֵךְ לִפְנֵיכֶם בַּדֶּרֶךְ לָתוּר לָכֶם מָקוֹם לַחֲנֹתְכֶם בָּאֵשׁ לַיְלָה לַרְאֹתְכֶם בַּדֶּרֶךְ אֲשֶׁר תֵּלְכוּ־בָהּ וּבֶעָנָן יוֹמָם, *[HASHEM your God] went before you, to search out a place to pitch your tents, in fire by night to show you by what path you should go, and in a cloud by day* (*Devarim* 1:33).

⊰§ Reminder of the Exodus

As we say in the *kiddush* of Succos and in all the prayers of the festival, the purpose of Succos is to remind us of the Exodus from Egypt. How exactly does Succos remind us of the Exodus?

For one thing, the *mitzvah* of dwelling in the *succah* reminds us of the protection from the elements afforded our ancestors by the Divine Cloud that surrounded them in the Wilderness: אֲנִי ה׳ אֱלֹהֵיהֶם אֲשֶׁר הוֹצֵאתִי אֹתָם מֵאֶרֶץ מִצְרַיִם לְשָׁכְנִי בְתוֹכָם, *I am HASHEM, their God, who took them out of the Land of Egypt to dwell in their midst* (*Shemos* 29:46).

We must realize, however, that Hashem's fundamental purpose in taking us out of Egypt was to make us aware of His Presence in our midst. Freedom from slavery by itself would have meant nothing without Hashem's Presence, as symbolized by the appearance of the Divine Cloud just days after the Exodus. By associating Succos with the Exodus, we acknowledge that true liberty can be achieved only by recognizing God's presence in our lives.

Extending this thought, we can argue that not only the Exodus but also the two hundred and ten years of slavery were a prelude to the union of the Divine Cloud (representing Hashem) with the Jewish people.

To this end, King Solomon rhapsodizes, צְרוֹר הַמֹּר דּוֹדִי לִי בֵּין שָׁדַי יָלִין, *My Beloved [i.e. Hashem] is a bundle of myrrh unto me; He dwells between my bossom* (*Shir HaShirim* 1:13). *Yalkut Shimoni* (*Shir HaShirim* 984) interprets this as follows: "Even if it appears that God has caused bitterness among His people (i.e., during the Egyptian slavery), this was only a necessary precursor to His eventually dwelling among them." (5665)

☙ The Succah and Yom Kippur

The Jews of the Wilderness dwelled in *succos* throughout the year. Why, then, do we celebrate the festival of Succos specifically during *Tishrei*, five days after Yom Kippur? Why is the theme of Divine Presence (in relation to the Exodus) especially pertinent to this time of year?

The Days of Awe (Rosh Hashanah and Yom Kippur) are a time not merely of judgment, but also of liberation — from temptation and evil impulses. In fact, the Hebrew word *Mitzraim* (Egypt) means "strait" or "narrow place," a reference to Egypt's spiritual emptiness. Conversely, the Exodus represented not merely physical liberation, but also a release from corrupting forces that prevented the Jews from reaching their full potential.

Thus, during the Days of Awe, every Jew experiences a personal Exodus, as he is cleansed of all defects that hinder his spiritual growth. This follows a re-creation of the slavery experienced in Egypt, engendered by the fasting of Yom Kippur and the awareness of the judgment he faces on Rosh Hashanah. It is only fitting, then, that Succos, which celebrates the appearance of the Divine Cloud/Presence after the Exodus, should come immediately after the Days of Awe, which recall the Egyptian slavery. (5665)

The relationship between Succos and Yom Kippur can be further understood by perceiving the *succah* as a tangible manifestation of the expiation of our sins on Yom Kippur.

On the first Yom Kippur, the Jewish people were granted atonement for worshiping the Golden Calf. This sin was committed on the Seventeenth of Tammuz, but the forgiveness did not come until Yom Kippur, some eighty days later. How did the Jews know that they had, in fact, returned to Hashem's favor? According to the Midrash (cited by *Rashi* on *Shemos* 35:1), Hashem commanded the Jews to build the *Mishkan* (Tabernacle) immediately after Yom Kippur. Once they were told to build this repository for Hashem's Presence, they knew that they were back in Hashem's good graces.

The *succah* is a miniature version of the Tabernacle in that it, too, serves as a dwelling place for the Divine Presence. For this reason the Talmud refers to it as "Hashem's home" (cf. *Succah* 9a: שֶׁחָל שֵׁם שָׁמַיִם עַל הַסֻּכָּה, *the Name of Heaven rests upon the succah*). Thus, by beginning to build our *succos* immediately after Yom Kippur, we give a vivid demonstration that our sins were indeed forgiven on that awesome day.

The relationship between Yom Kippur and Succos can be clarified further by examining precisely how the first Yom Kippur served to restore the Divine Presence. What happened on that day to allow for the forgiveness of the Jews' sins?

We must bear in mind that, among other things, Yom Kippur was the occasion when the Jews received the Torah for the second time. The original transmission, on *Shavuos*, was later marred by the shattering of the *luchos* (tablets) when Moshe descended from Mount Sinai to find the nation sunk in worship of the Golden Calf. Now, eighty days later, Moshe came down again bearing the second *luchos*, giving Yom Kippur the status of a second *Shavuos*. King David had this parallel in mind in the following verse (*Tehillim* 68:19) עָלִיתָ לַמָּרוֹם שָׁבִיתָ שֶּׁבִי לָקַחְתָּ מַתָּנוֹת בָּאָדָם וְאַף סוֹרְרִים לִשְׁכֹּן יָ־הּ אֱלֹהִים, *You [Moshe] ascended to the Heavens, you captured booty [i.e., you obtained the Torah], you received a gift for man [the Torah] so that even the rebellious can dwell with God.*

This verse refers to Hashem's gift of the Torah to the repentant Jewish people on Yom Kippur. After sinning with the Golden Calf, the Jews were in danger of forfeiting their special relationship with the Almighty. Nevertheless, in an act of Divine grace, Hashem offered them the Torah a second time, not on the basis of their merit, but as a Divine gift — an expression of His overwhelming benevolence.

Not only was the Torah given on that Yom Kippur: the One Who gave the Torah, in the form of the Divine Presence as symbolized in the *succah*, also came to dwell among the people. The Midrash (*Shemos Rabbah* 33:1) describes this phenomenon with the following parable:

> מָשָׁל לְמֶלֶךְ שֶׁהָיָה לוֹ בַּת יְחִידָה בָּא אֶחָד מִן הַמְּלָכִים וְנָטְלָהּ בִּיקֵּשׁ לֵילֵךְ לוֹ לְאַרְצוֹ וְלִיטּוֹל לְאִשְׁתּוֹ אָמַר לוֹ בִּתִּי שֶׁנָּתַתִּי לְךָ יְחִידִית הִיא לִפְרוֹשׁ מִמֶּנָּה אֵינִי יָכוֹל לוֹמַר לְךָ אַל תִּטְלָהּ אֵינִי יָכוֹל אֶלָּא בְּכָל מָקוֹם שֶׁאַתֶּם הוֹלְכִים בַּיִת אֶחָד עֲשׂוּ לִי שֶׁאָדוּר בְּתוֹכוֹ שֶׁנֶּאֱמַר וְעָשׂוּ לִי מִקְדָּשׁ
>
> The only daughter of a king was about to marry the scion of another royal family from a different country. Before the wedding, the bride's father pulled his prospective son-in-law aside and said, "I cannot bear to be separated from my beloved daughter. Neither can I ask you not to marry her. Therefore, I beg of you the following favor:

Wherever you settle, build a room in your house for me also, so that I can be with both of you." As it is written: *Make a Sanctuary for me.*

In this Midrash, the King represents Hashem; the daughter is His Torah, and the prince is the Jewish nation. Every Yom Kippur, the Torah is retransmitted to us, just as the second *luchos* were presented to Israel on that tenth day of *Tishrei* over three millennia ago. Unable to bear separation from His Torah, so to speak, Hashem asks us to erect a hut to "house" Him wherever we go. This is why we begin to prepare the *succah*, Hashem's hut, where the Giver of the Torah can reside, immediately after Yom Kippur. In it the Divine Presence can be felt intensely, making the *Yom Tov* a true occasion for rejoicing. (5665)

☙ Succah — Humble Dwelling for Royalty

The *succah's* message is also one of humility, of a people shorn of pride by Yom Kippur, described by the Torah (*Vayikra* 16:29) as a day in which the soul is humbled (תְּעַנּוּ אֶת־נַפְשֹׁתֵיכֶם, *you shall afflict your souls*). The Talmud (*Sotah* 5a) declares that the Divine Presence cannot dwell in the same world as a haughty person, for Hashem epitomizes humility.

After the soul-searching of Yom Kippur, the contrite Jew emulates his Creator. He, too, can no longer bear to live in a world populated by the haughty. Instead, he needs an isolated lodging, a home sealed off from the impurities of humankind. By choosing to dwell in the *succah*, and thus secluding himself from the pervasive arrogance of the world, the Jew emulates not only Hashem, but also Moshe. The most unassuming of men, Moshe received the Torah in Heaven, after forty days on Mt. Sinai in the company of the Almighty. In his humility, Moshe was viscerally uneasy in the world of vanity to which he returned. Following his example, Israel, the humblest of nations (and further chastened after Yom Kippur), needs to be sheltered from the arrogance of this world. It needs the *succah*.

Thus the *succah* is a refuge from a haughty world. Yet, earlier we depicted the *succah* as a royal resting place for the Divine Presence. Which description, then, captures the *succah's* true essence?

Really, there is no contradiction between the two descriptions. The *succah*, which serves as a testimonial to Israel's distinction from the other nations, is indeed a humble dwelling. Yet it is precisely such a dwelling that the Almighty has chosen as a fitting abode for His Presence, and precisely for this reason. As Hashem testifies through the prophet Yeshayahu (57:15), מָרוֹם וְקָדוֹשׁ אֶשְׁכּוֹן וְאֶת־דַּכָּא וּשְׁפַל־רוּחַ *I abide in exaltedness and holiness [in Heaven] — but am with the contrite and lowly of spirit [on earth].* The home of the Jewish nation is also the house of Hashem. (5664)

◆§ Succah and Shabbos: A Taste of the World to Come

The *succah* represents not only a place of honor in this world, but also a taste of what is to be found in the World to Come. In fact, the Talmud (*Bava Basra* 75a) refers to the reward given to the righteous in the hereafter as a *succah.*

During the year, we are too engrossed in material pursuits to be able to focus our attention on the World to Come. However, after the spiritual purification of Yom Kippur just days before, we greet Succos with an elevated sense of what awaits us in life. King David's plea (*Tehillim* 51:12), לֵב טָהוֹר בְּרָא־לִי אֱלֹהִים וְרוּחַ נָכוֹן חַדֵּשׁ בְּקִרְבִּי, *Create for me a pure heart, O God, and renew a proper spirit within me,* is fulfilled. The *succah* represents the dream of the World to Come (*Olam HaBa*) in that it constitutes one place on earth that can provide shelter from the temptations of the material world. In this sense, the *succah* is a microcosm of *Olom HaBa,* a taste of the hereafter, where the Jewish soul can have free rein.

For this reason, the *succah* finds a parallel in the otherworldly spirit of Shabbos. Amidst the drudgeries of the workday week, Shabbos offers a rarefied respite, a special period when the soul can emerge refreshed and suffused with the fragrance of the World to Come. It is significant that the expression פּוֹרֵשׂ סוּכַּת שָׁלוֹם, *[Hashem] spreads His succah* [canopy] *of peace,* is found in reference to Shabbos (in the Friday night service) and to the *succah.* On both occasions, the Jew is sufficiently sheltered from the exigencies of daily life to experience *Olom HaBa.*

Nevertheless, there is a crucial distinction between the "canopy of peace" associated with the *succah* and that connected with Shabbos. Whereas Shabbos protects only the righteous, the canopy of the *succah* welcomes even the penitent Jew. This is alluded to in *Yeshayahu* (57:19): שָׁלוֹם שָׁלוֹם לָרָחוֹק וְלַקָּרוֹב, *Peace, peace for those distant [i.e. the sinner who has now repented] and to those nearby [i.e. the Jew who has remained faithful].* The former is covered by the *succah,* and the latter by Shabbos.

These two categories — the repentant Jew and the constantly righteous one — are not necessarily mutually exclusive. Rather, aspects of both exist in each of us. On the one hand, all of us are guilty of sin, to some extent, as King Solomon says (*Koheles* 7:20), כִּי אָדָם אֵין צַדִּיק בָּאָרֶץ אֲשֶׁר יַעֲשֶׂה־טּוֹב וְלֹא יֶחֱטָא, *For no man is so righteous in the earth that he does only good and does not sin.* Yet, no matter how far one strays, there exists in every Jew a sincere love for the Creator, and a spark of Jewishness that is never extinguished, as the prophet Yeshayahu writes (60:21), וְעַמֵּךְ כֻּלָּם צַדִּיקִים, *Your people are all righteous.* Thus every Jew is, in one respect, totally righteous, in that his *pintele Yid* never ceases to flicker. On the other hand, we all err, and are in dire need of *teshuvah* (repentance). Consequently, both the *succah's* canopy of peace for the returnee to Judaism, and Shabbos' shelter for the righteous are equally necessary. (5664)

⁂ An Isolation Chamber Different But Not Different

Thus far, we have seen how the *succah* serves as a reminder of the Divine Cloud and of the Exodus' ultimate purpose, how it testifies to the forgiveness granted to Jewry on Yom Kippur, and how it grants us a foretaste of the World to Come.

We wish now to consider an additional function of the *succah*: to isolate Israel from the world at large.

Using an unusual expression, the Torah says, כָּל־הָאֶזְרָח בְּיִשְׂרָאֵל יֵשְׁבוּ בַּסֻּכֹּת, *Every citizen in Israel shall dwell in the succah* (*Vayikra* 23:42). This implies that the *succah* is reserved for "citizens of Israel," since it serves as an isolation chamber, shielding Israel from the Gentile environment. However, this should not be construed as implying contempt for non-Jews. We should recall that, as long as the Temple stood, seventy bulls were offered on its Altar each Succos, in recognition of the seventy cultures that comprised the Gentile world (*Succah* 55b).

Israel does not view other nations with disdain. Rather, the greatest service that the Jewish people can provide for humankind is to maintain their unique character. If Israel succeeds in its quest to be distinct, then and only then can it fulfill its mission on behalf of the world. However, being different from the rest of society does not mean being indifferent towards humankind. Thus, while the *succah* (as well as the *Beis HaMikdash*) isolated the Jews from the outside world in one sense, they also gave blessings and delight to all of humankind. The Midrash notes (cf. *Midrash Tanchuma Pinchas* 16) that had the Gentiles realized the benefits that the Temple provided on their behalf, they would have decorated it rather than destroyed it.

The need for the Jewish people to maintain their distance in order to achieve their maximum impact as a nation was demonstrated by Judaism's founding father, Abraham. As a young man, Abraham sought to influence everyone he encountered to worship Hashem rather than idols. These efforts failed, and he won respect for his cause only when he heeded the Divine call to leave his birthplace and separate himself from his idolatrous surroundings (*Bereishis* 12:1). Only then was his impact felt on a universal level. In this respect, as in so many others, Abraham provided an example for his descendants to heed and emulate.

(5664)

◆§ The Home of the Faithful

Where can the faithful grasp Hashem's will? The holy *Zohar*, (*Emor* 103a) describes the *succah* as the shade (i.e. shelter) of faith. Two of the *Zohar's* statements in this connection bear in-depth examination: דְּבָעֵי בַּר נַשׁ לְאַחְזָאָה גַּרְמֵיהּ דְּיָתִיב תַּחַת צִלָּא דְּהֵמְנוּתָא *[while sitting in the succah] everyone should see himself as if he were sitting under the shade of emunah (faith).*

The *Zohar* then chastises those who leave their *succos* (i.e., those who distance themselves from the message of the *succah*): מַאן דְּאַפִּיק גַּרְמֵיהּ מִצִּלָּא דְּהֵמְנוּתָא אִתְחַזֵי לְמֶיהֱוֵי עֶבֶד לְעַבְדֵי עֲבָדִים דִּכְתִיב: ,,וַיִּשְׁבְּ מִמֶּנּוּ שֶׁבִי, *Someone who excludes himself from the shade of emunah is fit to be a slave to a slave of slaves [i.e. consigned to a notably inferior position in life], as the Torah says, [the King of Arad fought the Jewish people] and captured a captive* (*Bamidbar* 21:1).

These statements consist of a positive side — the benefits of sitting in a *succah* — and a negative one — the punishment for abandoning the *succah*. Let us consider each in turn.

Why is the *succah* called the "shade of *emunah*?

As was mentioned earlier, the *succah* evokes memories of the Divine Cloud and of the Jewish people's obedience to Hashem's directives throughout the dangerous trek through the Wilderness. The prophet Yirmiyahu recalled this devotion in the following words (2:2): כֹּה אָמַר ה׳ זָכַרְתִּי לָךְ חֶסֶד נְעוּרַיִךְ אַהֲבַת כְּלוּלֹתָיִךְ לֶכְתֵּךְ אַחֲרַי בַּמִּדְבָּר בְּאֶרֶץ לֹא זְרוּעָה, *Thus spoke HASHEM, I remember the kindness of your youth, the love of your nuptial days, how you followed Me in the Wilderness in a land that was not sown.*

Such allegiance deserved a special reward, granted to that generation and to Jews who follow suit every year by dwelling in the *succah.* This reward is the ability to see and comprehend the supreme ways of the Almighty.

In all times, regardless of our merit, Divine Providence shapes the destiny of the Jewish people. However, we do not always appreciate the stewardship of our Creator and Supreme Guide. We do not ordinarily realize that He is constantly protecting us. The ways of Hashem are, after all, mysterious. However, the generation of the Wilderness, graced with the constant presence of the Divine Cloud, were always aware of Hashem's protection and comprehended His ways. They understood that He was standing guard over them in reward for their loyalty to Him. This intimate relationship with Hashem is noted by Moshe: אֲשֶׁר־עַיִן בְּעַיִן נִרְאָה אַתָּה ה׳ וַעֲנָנְךָ עֹמֵד עֲלֵהֶם, *That You, Hashem, were perceived on an eye-to-eye basis [i.e., Your ways were clearly comprehended by the Jewish nation] and Your Cloud stands over them* (*Bamidbar* 14:14). (5663)

Someone who benefits from a gift is normally ashamed to look his benefactor directly in the eye. Under certain circumstances, however, this may not be the case. In return for the staunch loyalty shown by the Jews during the trying times in the Wilderness, they deserved to comprehend Hashem's ways. Thus, they merited the protection of the Divine Cloud, as is indicated by the following verse (*Shemos* 13:21): וה׳ הֹלֵךְ לִפְנֵיהֶם יוֹמָם בְּעַמּוּד עָנָן, *HASHEM went before them by day with a pillar of cloud.* According to *Rashi* (*Bereishis* 19:24), the word וַה׳, *and HASHEM* always indicates that Hashem acted in consultation with His *Beis Din* (Heavenly Tribunal) that stands in judgment over the Jewish people. Thus we may conclude from the use of this word here that the people received the protection of the Divine Cloud not as an undeserved gift from Hashem, but because they were judged to be worthy of it in return for their loyalty to Hashem. Going even further, this generation was also privileged to see Hashem "eye to eye", in the sense that they were allowed to comprehend the mystery of His ways.

It was at Succos time that that generation began to grasp the significance of the Divine Will. In the Wilderness, the Jewish people were able to "see" (i.e. understand) Hashem's ways, as the Torah states (*Devarim* 1:31), וּבַמִּדְבָּר אֲשֶׁר רָאִיתָ אֲשֶׁר נְשָׂאֲךָ ה' אֱלֹהֶיךָ, *In the Wilderness you saw that Hashem carried you.* This experience was unique to them, but even today a Jew can ascend to this level of revelation every year in his *succah.* After being examined under a searchlight on Yom Kippur and being vindicated, the Jew stands ready at Succos to gain the insight into Hashem's actions that they well deserve. The very word *succah,* which is connected to the concept of seeing (see *Rashi* on *Bereishis* 11:29), conveys this theme itself. The Jew sitting in the *succah* is privileged to *see* and comprehend Hashem's ways.

This may be the intent of the first passage from the *Zohar* quoted above, *One who sits in the succah sees himself in the shade of emunah.* Normally, we grope for meaning in life without beginning to fathom Hashem's Will. We exist by virtue of His mercy, our very lives an undeserved gift. Under such circumstances, it is enough for us to receive Hashem's generosity without understanding His purposes.

On Succos, however, having been *judged* by Hashem (and His *Beis Din*) on Rosh Hashanah and Yom Kippur and found worthy, we can can begin to grasp what we would ordinarily be content to accept on the basis of faith alone.

But what of the *Zohar's* second statement? Why does it offer such hasty condemnation for someone who leaves the *succah*, going so far as to compare him to a slave of slaves?

To answer this, let us consider in depth the meaning of *emunah.* The Jew who is suffused with strong faith can rightfully pride himself regarding his roots, which he knows lie in Heaven. As a result, he also bears fruits (on earth). He is productive in both the material and spiritual spheres. His children walk in his ways, and emulate his good deeds. In contrast, a slave has no roots; his children are not part of his heritage in a legal sense (see *Yevamos* 62a).

When a Jew leaves the *succah* — that is, when he forgets the message of the *succah* — he thereby assumes the identity of a slave. He shows his ignorance of the fact that one can be productive only by realizing that his roots lie in Heaven, and acts as if he has no roots at all. He therefore deserves to be considered as an unproductive slave, and be cut off from his heritage.

Appropriately enough, the *succah's* antecedent, the Divine Cloud of the Wilderness, came to protect the Jews primarily through the merit of Aaron, the *Kohen Gadol* (High Priest) (see *Taanis* 9a). This is why the Cloud disappeared after Aaron's death.

Aaron, and indeed all *Kohanim*, are distinguished by their genealogy and roots — the true message of the *succah* and the fullest implications of *emunah*. For example, Aaron is described as a "trustworthy stake" (*Yeshayahu* 22:23), a loyal stalwart. His children, the *Kohanim* are described in the Talmud (*Kiddushin* 69b) as possessing the best pedigree, the highest possible genealogical status. The *succah* and the Divine Cloud representing *emunah* are aptly traced back to Aaron and his descendants, proud bearers of their links to Hashem and to good deeds on earth.

Based on the above remarks, we can come to a better understanding of the meaning of freedom (חֵרוּת). Those who participate in the *mitzvah* of *succah* and comprehend its message of *emunah* can be said to enjoy true freedom. On the other hand, those who reject the *succah* and its message and instead pursue the base pleasures of the world are not free in any real sense. To the contrary, they are no more than *slaves* to the passions they serve. Happy is our lot, that Hashem has given us a portion among the truly liberated who absorb the pleasures, the freedom, of the *succah*. (5663)

◆§ The Succah as the Home of Jewish Unity

The *succah* conveys an additional message: the need for *achdus* (Jewish unity).

In reality, *achdus* is composed of two distinct elements. There must be unity among the Jewish people themselves, and there must be a oneness — to the greatest extent possible — between the Jews and their Creator. Unfortunately, unity is often a very elusive goal. The reason for this may lie not so much in the incompatibility of people's natures as in their wrongdoings. By committing a sin, a Jew induces a rupture between himself and his fellow Jew, as well as discord between him and God. As the Prophet Yeshayahu remarks (59:2), כִּי אִם עֲוֹנֹתֵיכֶם הָיוּ מַבְדִּלִים בֵּינֵכֶם לְבֵין אֱלֹהֵיכֶם, *But it is only your sins that separate between yourselves and your God [i.e., between God and the Jewish people].*

After the nation has been purified of its sins on Yom Kippur, Succos brings a unique spirit of togetherness, which colors both relations among Jews and between Jews and Hashem. This togetherness is symbolized by the *succah*, an inviting meeting place for Jews of all stations, where they can join together and be at one with Hashem. The Talmud (*Succah* 27b) suggests that, in theory, all Jews could sit in one *succah*. Every Jew, no matter how far he has strayed from his roots during the year, can band together with his fellows in the shelter of the *succah*, reposing in Hashem's embrace. (The *Arba Minim* — Four Species — on the other hand, symbolize unity among different types of Jews, as will be explained at length in a subsequent essay.)

The concept of unity embodied by the *succah* actually stems from the Divine Cloud, which is symbolized by our dwelling in huts, as was explained earlier. The reason that the generation of the Wilderness merited the Divine Cloud was their united stand in accepting Hashem's authority, as He later recalled nostalgically to the prophet Yeremiyahu (2:2), כֹּה אָמַר ה׳ זָכַרְתִּי לָךְ חֶסֶד נְעוּרַיִךְ אַהֲבַת כְּלוּלֹתָיִךְ לֶכְתֵּךְ אַחֲרַי בַּמִּדְבָּר בְּאֶרֶץ לֹא זְרוּעָה, *Thus spoke* H*ASHEM*, *I remember the kindness of your youth, the love of your nuptial days, how you followed Me in the Wilderness in a land that was not sown.*

In this verse, Hashem speaks of their love as being *united*, as indicated by the word כְּלוּלֹתָיִךְ, *nuptial days*, a word whose connotations include the entire Jewish people (כְּלַל יִשְׂרָאֵל).

This, then, is the theme of the Festival: peace among Jews, as well as between Jews and Hashem. The dream voiced by the prophet Yeshayahu (57:19) cited above, שָׁלוֹם שָׁלוֹם לָרָחוֹק וְלַקָּרוֹב, *Peace, peace for those distant and those nearby*, makes use of a double expression of peace: one that applies to human relationships, and one that relates to interactions with the Almighty. Both of these must be conducted on a proper basis for human endeavor to achieve a perfect harmony on this earth.

It is therefore significant that this festival is called (*Shemos* 23:16) חַג הָאָסִף, *the Festival of Gathering*. We can understand this to refer not only to the gathering of the harvest, but also to the gathering together of human souls, all yearning to be reunited with their Father in Heaven.

(5648, 5662)

☙ Reminder of the Temple

The *succah* is also a poignant reminder of another home in which Hashem's presence was keenly felt, the *Beis HaMikdash*. The contemplative Jew sitting in a *succah* is reminded of the magnificence of *Succas Dovid HaNofales*, the fallen center of spiritual splendor. This may be the origin of the widespread custom of decorating the *succah* with pictures of the *Beis HaMikdash*.

Just as Hashem resided in the *Beis HaMikdash*, as the Torah says, *Build for Me a Sanctuary and I will dwell in your midst* (*Shemos* 25:8), so does He dwell in the *succah*. The Talmud (*Succah* 9a) notes, שֶׁחָל שֵׁם שָׁמַיִם עַל הַסֻּכָּה, *Hashem's holy Name is present in the succah*. Because the *succah* serves as testimony to the Divine protection the Jews enjoyed in the Wilderness, it provides a forceful reminder of Hashem's continuing vigilance over us to this very day.

Other associations link the *succah* and the Temple. As discussed earlier, the *succah* has the potential to unite all Jews. Similarly, the holy city of Jerusalem, and especially the *Beis HaMikdash*, contributed greatly to Jewish unity. King David remembered the time when עֹמְדוֹת הָיוּ רַגְלֵינוּ בִּשְׁעָרַיִךְ יְרוּשָׁלָםִ יְרוּשָׁלַםִ הַבְּנוּיָה כְּעִיר שֶׁחֻבְּרָה לָּהּ יַחְדָּו: *Our feet stood in your gates, O Jerusalem. Jerusalem, when it was still being built, was like a city of ingathering* (*Tehillim* 122:2-3). The Talmud (*Yerushalmi Chagigah* 19b) interprets this verse as a reference to the uncanny ability of the Holy City to unify all Jews, in that all of the Jews who came as pilgrims to Jerusalem three times a year (עֲלִיָּה לְרֶגֶל) were treated equally. The Jewish people were a united whole when they congregated in Jerusalem.

This being the case, why do we not mourn the destruction of the *Beis HaMikdash* on Succos, instead of rejoicing? Why is Succos called זְמַן שִׂמְחָתֵנוּ, *the Time of our Rejoicing*?

We do, of course, mourn the destruction every year on *Tishah B'Av*. On Succos, however, we assume a different perspective, and concentrate on the positive. Therefore, we thank Hashem for having given us the spiritual splendor of the *Beis HaMikdash*, and show our appreciation for the time we were granted to enjoy the Divine Presence. This upbeat attitude reflects our quiet confidence that, as soon as we merit it, the *Beis HaMikdash* will be built again.

In celebrating the anticipated restoration of the *Beis HaMikdash* on Succos, we follow the example of King David, who rejoiced when he heard the populace ask when the *Beis HaMikdash* would be constructed (*Tehillim* 122:1). He had been told that he would not live to witness the construction of the *Beis HaMikdash*. Surely, news of the coming construction of the *Beis HaMikdash* must have aroused mixed emotions within him. One would have expected him to be morose over the fact that his own demise was a prerequisite for the building of this holy structure. Nevertheless, he rejoiced. His happiness over the fact that the *Beis HaMikdash* would soon become a reality prevailed over any feelings of personal deprivation. Therefore, on Succos, we too curtail our sorrow over the fact that the *Beis HaMikdash* lies in ruins, and focus on both a sense of gratitude that it once existed, and an eager anticipation of its hopefully imminent return. (5660)

◆§ The Succah as a House of Peace

The dream of unity, of the *Beis HaMikdash*, and also of the ideal of peace, are all symbolized by the *succah*. This is emphasized by the words from the Friday night prayers הַפּוֹרֵשׂ סֻכַּת שָׁלוֹם, *Who spreads His succah [shelter] of peace.*

In order to appreciate the relationship between *shalom* (peace) and the *succah*, let us analyze the virtues of Aaron described in the Mishnah (*Avos* 1:12). As we have said, the Divine Cloud, antecedent of the *succah*, graced the Jewish nation in the merit of Aaron. If we can understand Aaron's mission, and in particular the *Kohen Gadol's* association with *shalom*, we will better understand the relationship between the *succah* and the elusive dream of peace.

The *Mishnah* relates that Aaron undertook his quest for peace in a vigorous manner. He loved peace (אוֹהֵב שָׁלוֹם), but was not content to exhibit his concern for that ideal passively. Rather, he pursued peace actively (רוֹדֵף שָׁלוֹם), taking the initiative to bring quarreling neighbors back together, even if they had no desire to be reconciled. Thus, he won a reputation for seeking out peace even at a distance, among those for whom *shalom* seemed remote. In this manner, he emulated Hashem, Who is also intent on securing peace in all quarters, as we have previously seen in the verse from *Yeshayahu* who proclaims *Peace, peace for those distant and those nearby* (57:19).

The search for peace both near and far is one of the messages of the *succah*. The *Arba Minim*, comprising diverse species of vegetation, are nevertheless taken together on Succos as a unified entity. In the same manner, the Jewish nation, so diverse and varied, must unite as one unified nation, and learn to live together in peace.

However, this human-based initiative is only the start of the search for lasting peace. Jews might clamor for peace only when it is near at hand. At times, the prospects for peace might seem so remote that only

Divine intervention can have any hope of bringing it about. In such circumstances, when human efforts fall short, only Hashem, from His distant vantage point, can stimulate or impose peace. This fact is symbolized by the *succah*, whose canopy provides a peaceful setting from above. Thus, the *Arba Minim* represent man's feeble attempts at procuring peace, while the *succah* represents Hashem's supreme role in fostering peace when humans are unable to attain it.

It would be instructive at this point to examine Aaron's almost Divine ability at peace-making by referring to the Zohar's (*Vayikra* 20a) depiction of the roles of Moshe and Aaron. Moshe is characterized as the שׁוֹשְׁבִינָא דְמַלְכָּא (allegorically the "best man" at Hashem's wedding) whose mission is to bring the Torah to the Jewish people. Aaron's function, on the other hand, is described as שׁוֹשְׁבִינָא דְמַטְרוֹנִיתָא (the "best man" of the "matron," the Jewish people). It was his task to bring the Jews closer to Hashem. This role is captured by the Mishnah, which goes on to describe Aaron as אוֹהֵב אֶת הַבְּרִיּוֹת וּמְקָרְבָן לַתּוֹרָה, *one who loves all beings, and in this way brings them closer to Torah.*

While Aaron's intrinsic nature was to bring Jews closer to Hashem, bridging the gap between the temporal and the Divine, we know that he also eventually attained some of the traits of his brother Moshe as well. (*Rashi* on *Shemos* 4:14 notes that Moshe was originally supposed to have been the *Kohen Gadol* but because of his initial reluctance to take on the mission of liberating the Jews from Egypt, this mantle was given over to Aaron instead. Thus, Aaron's priesthood was derived in large part from Moshe's legacy.) Consequently, Aaron assumed not only his innate role as the people's "best man" — the one to make peace among men — but also the role he assumed from Moshe, which allowed him to serve as Hashem's High Priest, and thus bring Torah closer to man. As the people's emissary to Hashem, Aaron brought peace to the near; as Hashem's representative in the *Mishkan* (Sanctuary) he brought peace for the distant as well.

The Talmud (*Kiddushin* 23b) cites a difference of opinion about the status of *Kohanim*. Are they emissaries of the Jewish people (שְׁלוּחֵי דִידָן) or representatives of Hashem (שְׁלוּחֵי דְרַחֲמָנָא)? In reality, both views are valid, as indicated by the dual role assumed by Aaron, who served both Hashem and his fellow Jews.

The events of Aaron's own life may also help clarify his dual mission. Aaron, of course, was among the Jewish people's most righteous members. At the same time, he was also a consummate penitent, having repented for his role in making the Golden Calf. Such a righteous individual can attain a measure of peace merely by being at peace with himself. Thus, for him, peace may arise from a "nearby" source, namely himself.

On the other hand, the returnee to Judaism requires peace "from afar" — special Divine assistance to help him become one with the Jewish people and their lofty values. Therefore, in both his personality and his life's mission, Aaron embodied the characteristic of peace from near and far.

It is then possible that both manifestations of the Divine Presence discussed above — the yearly *succah* and the majestic Divine Cloud — represent twin aspects of *shalom.* The *succah,* erected by men, brings peace from a nearby source, while the Divine Cloud served as Hashem's gift of peace from afar. (5658, 5660)

◆§ The Succah: A Reminder of Israel's Initiative In the Wilderness

לְמַעַן יֵדְעוּ דֹרֹתֵיכֶם כִּי בַסֻּכּוֹת הוֹשַׁבְתִּי אֶת בְּנֵי יִשְׂרָאֵל בְּהוֹצִיאִי אוֹתָם מֵאֶרֶץ מִצְרָיִם

In order that your generations shall know that I made the Children of Israel dwell in succos when I brought them out of Egypt (*Vayikra* 23:43).

In this verse, Hashem instructs the Jewish people to remember throughout their history that He made them dwell in *succos* upon leaving Egypt. For what purpose must we constantly recall this Wilderness experience?

Perhaps our annual celebration of Succos commemorates not only the Divine protection that generation enjoyed, but also their willingness to set out into the treacherous wilderness at Hashem's bidding. This leap of faith came even before they had a sophisticated understanding of Torah, and their blind obedience was rewarded by Hashem's protection from all harm through the Divine Cloud.

Our annual pilgrimage to the *succah* teaches us that, while Hashem yearns to perform kindness to His people (see *Michah* 7:18, חָפֵץ חֶסֶד הוּא, *He desires kindness*), He delights even more when we ourselves take the initiative to evoke His beneficence.

Numerous commentators raise the obvious question, why is the miracle of the Divine Cloud celebrated annually while other equally awesome miracles (such as the manna and the well of Miriam) are not? We can answer with the verse which we have already cited several times (*Yeremiyahu* 2:2): *Thus spoke* H*ASHEM*, *I remember the kindness of your youth, the love of your nuptial days, how you followed Me in the Wilderness in land that was not sown.*

Let us paraphrase Hashem's words to emphasize their relevance to our question: "More than the other miracles, I remember that of the Divine Cloud, because this miracle was not an unmerited gift I gave you. No! It was a reward for חֶסֶד נְעוּרַיִךְ, *the worthy acts of your youthful years.* The word נעור here may be related to the word עוֹרֵר, *to awaken,* suggesting that the Jews *awakened* Hashem's beneficence. By following Him unquestioningly into the Wilderness — the uncharted path that lay ahead of them until the Torah was given at Sinai — the Jews emphatically deserved the miracle of the Divine Cloud.

The eternal lesson of the Divine Cloud is that, in addition to praying for Hashem to bless us with kindness, we can actively evoke Hashem's wondrous deeds with our own positive initiatives. Following the path blazed by the generation of the Wilderness, who accepted Hashem's word without prodding, we can gain Hashem's favor by seeking out *mitzvos* on our own. (5637, 5658)

◆§ The Succah and the Primacy of Spiritual Values

The *succah* emphasizes the spiritual aspect of the liberation from Egypt. Every time we sit in the *succah*, we are reminded of the Divine Cloud and its lesson regarding the primacy of spiritual values: Hashem's commandments must be followed regardless of any immediate (or long-term) consequences. True, as we mentioned above, it was the Jewish people who took the initiative to follow Hashem — but even that initiative stemmed from Hashem. As King Solomon wrote so eloquently (*Shir HaShirim* 1:4), מָשְׁכֵנִי אַחֲרֶיךָ נָּרוּצָה, *Draw (attract) me, so that we will run after You.* The Jews' desire to follow the Almighty originates with Him.

The *succah* thus reminds us of the innate attraction felt by every Jew towards his Creator, a dream voiced by the prophet Shmuel וְשַׂמְתִּי מָקוֹם לְעַמִּי לְיִשְׂרָאֵל וְשָׁכַן תַּחְתָּיו *I will procure a place for My people, Israel . . . and they will reside below it [i.e. beneath the Divine Presence]* (*II Shmuel* 7:10). The solitary goal of the Jew is to find a resting place beneath the Divine Presence, to be sheltered by Hashem. Both the *succah* and Shabbos symbolize the theme of dwelling under Hashem's protective graces. In one of the Torah's first descriptions of Shabbos (*Shemos* 16:29), the following command is given: שְׁבוּ אִישׁ תַּחְתָּיו, *every man is to remain in his place.* According to its plain meaning, this verse prohibits traveling on Shabbos. Homiletically, however, we may paraphrase it as follows: *Remain every one under Him [HASHEM] — Do not leave His place on the seventh day.* On Shabbos, every Jew attains an intimate relationship with his Creator, an association so close that he is actually living "beneath" Hashem.

On Shabbos, the Jew is sheltered by the Divine Presence. That very apt expression, פּוֹרֵשׂ סֻכַּת שָׁלוֹם, *Hashem spreads His shelter of peace,* is true not only of the *succah,* but also of Shabbos, for both are instances in which mortal man is sheltered by the Almighty, in realms wherein the spiritual prevails over the physical. (5657)

◆§ The Succah: A Bridge to Gan Eden

In the aftermath of Yom Kippur, as Israel's sins stand forgiven, we desire to build a new world, a world far removed from the vanities of daily living. This is a world reminiscent of the serenity that Adam and Eve enjoyed in Gan Eden, and built on the fundamental Jewish value of kindness.

This new, kindness-saturated, world has its own sterling heroes. These include Abraham, who is described by the prophet Yeshayahu (41:2) as the "arouser" (i.e. initiator) of kindness, and Aaron, the implementor of kindness, whose very life personified that virtue. Both the initiator and the implementor assume leading roles during the festival season. Abraham, the initiator, according to tradition was circumcised on Yom Kippur (see *Yalkut Shimoni* 80). This 99-year-old man willingly underwent the painful and dangerous procedure as a display of kindness and love towards his Creator. Aaron, the implementor, is linked with Succos, the festival that immediately follows, because it was in his merit that the Jews of the Wilderness benefited from the Divine Cloud that prefigured our *succos.*

Abraham and Aaron were also unique in their ability to bridge the gap between this world and the World to Come. Abraham, waiting for guests in the blazing heat just days after his circumcision, is depicted as sitting at the opening of the tent. Likewise Aaron, before he was initiated into the Priesthood, watched for seven full days at the opening of the Sanctuary while his brother Moshe performed the dedication ceremonies (see *Vayikra* 8:35). This parallelism is more than coincidental: Both sat in *openings* because they were both *openers*, personalities who bridged the gap between this world and *Olam HaBa*.

Furthermore, the *succah* itself can be considered to make this transition. The Talmud (*Succah* 43b) derives the obligation of eating in the *succah* by both day and night from the example of the Sanctuary, lending the characteristics of the Sanctuary to the *succah*. In fact, the *succah* is described as Hashem's "home" (ibid. 9a), making it a replica of the Sanctuary.

How does one attain the privilege of living in Paradise? What are the characteristics of that first man, Adam, who lived in Paradise, albeit briefly? Adam was formed in a most unusual manner. Though the word וַיִּצֶר, *create*, is normally written with one *yud*, here it contains a double *yud* וַיִּיצֶר (*Bereishis* 2:7), implying that a double creation consisting of a complete soul as well as a complete body (or, as *Midrash Rabbah* 14) suggests, there was a physical creation in this world and a spiritual creation for the World to Come).

Humans, too, can merit the *succah* and its link to Gan Eden only if they attain some measure of the completeness achieved by Adam. Each person must in his own way attain a double creation, consisting of a sacred soul and a sacred body permeated by the soul. There is no better time to achieve perfection of the soul then on Yom Kippur, and no better time to perfect a body permeated by spiritual values then on Succos. (5655)

☙ A Symbol of Man's Potential for Growth

The *succah* reminds us of man's capacity to rise from the lowest depths to the highest peaks in mere moments — if one truly wishes to come closer to Hashem. Let us consider the first time that the term Succos is mentioned after the Exodus, when the Divine Cloud first descended over the Jewish people. The Torah describes this moment as a journey from Ramses to Succos (*Shemos* 12:37). This can be understood not only as a journey from one physical location to another, but also as a rapid yet profound spiritual metamorphosis from abject slavery (Ramses, built by the enslaved Jews) to the supreme protection of the Divine Cloud, which first occurred in Succos.

The Jew who craves a close relationship with his Creator will succeed in achieving a personal migration from the despondency of soullessness to the lofty heights of spiritual contentment — his own journey from Ramses to Succos. He will understand and appreciate the *succah's* message of growth. He will not be alone in his quest for greatness; Hashem Himself will help him overcome his temporal limitations and make the quantum leap from Ramses to Succos, from spiritual poverty to greatness.

The words of Hashem, spoken to Israel just days before the Torah was given (*Shemos* 19:4) וָאֶשָּׂא אֶתְכֶם עַל־כַּנְפֵי נְשָׁרִים *I will lift you on eagle wings*, alludes to the swift passage from slavery to lofty spiritual serenity. This journey of personal growth need not be a lonely trek. Instead, it is an epic undertaking, accomplished through man's efforts bolstered by Hashem's support. Man soars on eagle wings to achieve his potential every Succos.

Let us explore further the relationship between the *succah* and spiritual growth. Is it mere coincidence that the Jewish nation was liberated from slavery at a place called Succos, or does this fact reveal a more profound, innate relationship between the *succah* and freedom from Egypt? Consider the literal meaning of the word *succah*. While it is customarily translated as "hut," it may also be related to the word סוֹכֶה, *to gaze ahead* (i.e. to peer into the future). The *succah* calls upon its occupants to shed their physical limitations, look beyond their shortcomings, and achieve their full potential.

King Solomon voices this same theme — how humans can catapult over self-imposed limitations to achieve growth — in the following proclamation (*Shir HaShirim* 3:11): צְאֶינָה וּרְאֶינָה, *Go out and behold*. We may paraphrase these words as a rousing call to utilize the *succah* to its fullest potential, "Go out from your physical habitat and behold Hashem's grandeur! Put aside your constraints and look ahead to untold possibilities!"

While Hashem can help us achieve this transformation, we can contribute to the process as well by activating our desire for growth. Think of the first words Hashem spoke to the first Jew, Abraham: לֶךְ־לְךָ מֵאַרְצְךָ, *Leave your land* (*Bereishis* 12:1). He meant that Abraham was to leave not only the physical land of his fathers, but also to forsake all the physical comforts enjoyed by his ancestors. The *Zohar* describes a Heavenly voice that beseeches every Jew to "prepare yourself to receive Hashem." While Abraham was the first one to heed this voice, every Jew who successfully migrates from Ramses to Succos, who raises himself from abject slavery of the spirit to the lofty height of the Divine Cloud, also hearkens to that call.

The construction of the *succah* itself proclaims its message. Its makeshift nature, with its cover consisting of discarded vegetation, is clearly intended for temporary use, דִּירַת עֲרַאי. In effect it tells us to leave behind our seemingly "permanent" possessions, the wealth we have accumulated in the physical world, and to migrate to the far simpler, yet unfathomably more precious, world of Torah spirituality.

One problem remains, though. The journey from Ramses to Succos was feasible for the generation of the Exodus, but how can we be expected to do the same? Consider the difference: That first generation experienced miracles on a daily basis; for them the radical transformation from spiritual inexperience to spiritual sophistication was a natural development. This was the generation that, according to the *Zohar* (*Parashas Pinchas*), would have merited a *Beis HaMikdash* that descended directly from Heaven, rather than a man-made Sanctuary, were it not for the sin of the Golden Calf. How can we possibly rise to their level? And if, in spite of the palpable Divinity that encircled them, they nevertheless succumbed to sin, how can we, who are so blinded to Hashem's presence, hope to remain on a high plane without falling?

We can respond in two ways. Firstly, we have the benefit of a precedent: The transformation made by our forefathers proved that it was possible for future generations to accomplish the same. They paved the path for us. Secondly, we should recognize the power of repentance — just as the generation of the Wilderness sinned with the Golden Calf, we also backslide from time to time. At the start of every Succos, however, we are still basking in the purification achieved on Yom Kippur. Therefore, we are free to grow again, and to flee (as Abraham did) from our materialistic tendencies back to our Creator.

Given that the *succah* represents a detachment from material values, we can now understand a seemingly puzzling statement from our Sages. The Talmud (*Avodah Zarah* 2a-3a) relates that in the future Hashem will test humanity's fitness to enjoy the rewards of the World to Come by asking them to fulfill the commandment of dwelling in the *succah*. In the words of the Talmud:

לְעָתִיד לָבֹא מֵבִיא הקב״ה סֵפֶר תּוֹרָה וּמֵנִיחוֹ בְּחֵיקוֹ וְאוֹמֵר לְמִי שֶׁעָסַק בָּהּ יָבוֹא וְיִטּוֹל שְׂכָרוֹ מִיַּד מִתְקַבְּצִים עכו״ם בְּעִרְבּוּבְיָא . . .

אָמַר הקב״ה מִצְוָה קַלָּה יֵשׁ לִי סוּכָּה שְׁמָהּ מִיַּד כָּל אֶחָד וְאֶחָד נוֹטֵל וְהוֹלֵךְ וְעוֹשֶׂה סוּכָּה בְּרֹאשׁ גַּגּוֹ, וְהקב״ה מַקְדִּיר עֲלֵיהֶם חַמָּה בִּתְקוּפַת תַּמּוּז וְכָל אֶחָד וְאֶחָד מְבָעֵט בְּסוּכָּתוֹ וְיוֹצֵא

In the future, Hashem will bring a Torah Scroll and place it in His breast and say that whoever studied it should come to receive his reward. All the Gentile nations will gather in confusion [and demean their portion of the reward in the World to Come. Hashem then tests the Gentiles and says,] "I have one 'easy' [i.e., relatively inexpensive] commandment called succah." The nations all leave Hashem's presence and proceed to build succos on their roofs. Hashem then subjects them to the full fury of the midsummer sun. Immediately, the Gentiles leave the succah, kicking it as they do so.

In light of our earlier remarks, this passage from the Talmud takes on new meaning. Why do the nations hasten to depart from the *succah* as soon as difficulties appear? What is the significance of the sun in the story?

The *succah*, as mentioned above, serves as a reminder to leave the material world behind in favor of a spiritual sphere. It is this transition that the Gentiles reject. In particular, the brilliance of the sun perturbs them. In this context, the sun symbolizes the ultimate Source of spiritual light, and the Creator of all illumination. Exposed to the dazzling presence of the Almighty and made fully aware of the spirituality now expected of them, they find themselves unable to adjust. Instead, they violently reject the *succah*, with all its symbolism, including its message of growth through purity. (5641, 5654)

◆§ The Succah — Home of Peace

In a world torn by strife, the *succah* epitomizes peace. The *succah's* antecedent, the Divine Cloud, was sustained through the merit of Aaron, whose mission was one of peace. The expression "spreading the canopy of peace" is used repeatedly in connection with the *succah*. Let us explore further the relationship between the *succah* (specifically as a symbol for the Divine Cloud) and the dream of peace. In what sense does the *succah* convey the message of peace?

As long as it covered them, the Divine Cloud protected the Jews from all enemies. Even the archenemy Amalek, bent on annihilating the fledgling nation, could attack only those whom the Cloud had ejected from its protection because of their sins (see *Rashi* on *Devarim* 25:18). From then on, the Jews were not once attacked until the Divine Cloud ceased to cover them upon the death of Aaron (see *Rashi* on *Bamidbar* 20:29). Thus we see that the strength Aaron gave the Jews lay not in their ability to prevail in confrontations, but rather in the protection Hashem gave them by means of the Divine Cloud because of their avoidance of sin. We find another allusion to this power in King Solomon's aphorism (*Mishlei* 20:3), כָּבוֹד לָאִישׁ שֶׁבֶת מֵרִיב, *Honor is to the man who refrains from quarrel.*

The message of the *succah*, then, is that while confrontation may at times be necessary, the most effective strategy against Amalek is reliance on Hashem and His Cloud. No foe ever succeeded in piercing the protective armor of the Divine Cloud. Similarly, the *succah* expresses our earnest plea to remain untouched by conflict.

Moshe confronted Amalek; Aaron helped Israel avoid enemies by bringing the sheltering Divine Cloud. King David alluded to these two approaches in his proclamation (*I Divrei HaYamim* 29:11), לְךָ ה׳ הַנֵּצַח וְהַהוֹד, *To You,* Hashem*, belongs the victory and the glory. The victory* is a reference to Moshe's triumph over Amalek, and *the glory* refers to Aaron's ability to shelter Israel from confrontation, which is indeed the greatest glory. (5654)

◆§ The Succah and Its Saintly Guests — Ushpizin

The *Zohar* (*Emor* 103b) interprets the verse (*Vayikra* 23:42), בַּסֻּכֹּת תֵּשְׁבוּ שִׁבְעַת יָמִים, *You shall sit in the succah for seven days,* as a reference to the Jewish people's ability not only to dwell in the *succah,* but also to make it into a habitat for Hashem and His saintly guests known as the *ushpizin.*

> תָּא חֲזִי בְּשַׁעְתָּא דְּבַּר נַשׁ יְתֵיב בִּמְדוּרָא דָא צִלָּא דִמְהֵימְנוּתָא שְׁכִינְתֵּא פָּרְסָא גַּדְפָּהָא עֲלֵיהּ מִלְעֵילָא וְאַבְרָהָם וְחַמְשָׁא צַדִּיקַיָּיא אַחֲרָנִין שַׁוְיין מִדּוּרֵיהוֹן עִמֵּיהּ . . . וְדָוִד מַלְכָּא שַׁוְיָן מְדוּרֵיהוֹן עִמֵּיהּ . . . וּבָעֵי בַּר נַשׁ לְמֶחְדֵי בְּכָל יוֹמָא וְיוֹמָא בְּאַנְפִּין נְהִירִין דְּאוּשְׁפִּיזִין אִלֵּין דְּשַׁרְיָין עִמֵּיהּ
>
> *Come and see, when a person sits in the House of Faith [i.e., the succah], Hashem spreads His wings [i.e., protects*

> *him] from above, and Abraham and the five other righteous ones live with him. King David is also included among them. A person should rejoice every day with these guests in the succah.*

Every time a Jew sits in the *succah,* he merits the presence of Hashem and the *ushpizin.* What is the significance of these guests and what is the quality they add to the *succah*?

A careful examination of the *Zohar's* text here reveals an emphasis on the ability every Jew has to welcome such prestigious guests into his home. By observing the commandment of *succah,* we bring Godliness to earth. When we have these holy guests join us in our *succah,* we are, in effect, causing Hashem Himself to reside with us. This is the fulfillment of the prayer we offered during the High Holy Days, וְיֵדַע כָּל פָּעוּל כִּי אַתָּה פְעַלְתּוֹ וְיָבִין כָּל יָצוּר כִּי אַתָּה יְצַרְתּוֹ, *Let everything that has been made know that You are its Maker, let everything that has been molded understand that You are its Molder.* (5653)

◆§ Separating Good from Evil

On the one hand, the *succah* serves to unite all Jews. However, the *succah,* being a walled entity, also acts as a barrier, setting limits to the dream of Jewish unity. The *succah* is open to all Jews, including the newly observant as well as those who have always been righteous. However, there is no welcome for those wicked people who have forfeited their opportunity to repent during the Ten Days of Repentance. The passage from Tractate *Avodah Zarah* cited above (2a-3a), concerning the Gentiles' rejection of the *succah,* illustrates the same theme. The *succah* can shelter only those who have an innate spark of goodness. Those who reject all repentance are "ejected.".

This theme is exemplified by the fate of Sodom and Gemorrah, as well as the builders of the Tower of Babel. In each instance, Hashem "brought Himself down" (i.e., closely investigated the situation), thus bringing Himself closer to man. Yet, those who did evil did not repent. The destruction of Sodom and Gemorrah, and the dispersal of the people of Babel, resulted not only from their sins, but also from their refusal to take advantage of the opportunity to return to Hashem, Who had made Himself so readily accessible.

In fact the verse cited in previous essays (*Yeshayahu 57:19*) to demonstrate Hashem's closeness to the Jewish people indicates that the incorrigible sinner is not welcome in the *succah*: שָׁלוֹם שָׁלוֹם לָרָחוֹק וְלַקָּרוֹב, *Peace, peace for those distant [the penitent] and those nearby [the righteous]*. Shortly afterward the prophet continues (v. 21), אֵין שָׁלוֹם אָמַר אֱלֹהַי לָרְשָׁעִים, *HASHEM says to the wicked, 'For you, there is no peace.'*

This sense of separation is demonstrated by the Libation of Water Ceremony. Every *Chol HaMoed Succos* in the *Beis HaMikdash*, specially consecrated water was poured down an aperture in the altar. This ceremony, called נִסּוּךְ הַמַּיִם, *Libation of the Water*, symbolized the return of Israel to its pure roots, and the return of the universe to its original form, when Hashem's spirit hovered over the waters (see *Bereishis* 1:2). Water, unlike wine (which was poured as an offering on all other occasions), has not been processed. It remains pure and pristine, symbolizing a return to pure roots. On Succos, Jews return to their roots, as symbolized by the Libation of the Waters. This applies to every Jew except evildoers, for their waters are muddied, and they have repudiated repentance. (5652)

◆§ Succah — The Ideal Place on Earth

Hashem created three spheres for man to partake of and for Israel to consecrate. These are the years, months and weeks that comprise the entity of Time; the sublime harmony of the body, and, especially, its crown jewel, the Soul; and finally, the Universe itself. (See the Introduction for a discussion of these concepts.) Seemingly, all of humankind can partake of each of these entities, but if one penetrates beneath superficial appearances, he can find a special relationship between them and the Jewish people. Whereas all cultures recognize the importance of time, it is only the Jews who acknowledge the supreme time period: Shabbos. While all humans possess a soul, only the Jews use their bodies to adorn the soul through the performance of *mitzvos*. Finally, whereas other nations benefit from the bounties of the universe, only Israel can appreciate sacred locations like the land of Israel, the site of the *Beis HaMikdash*, and the confines of the *succah*.

Shabbos, the soul, and the *succah* share a common element — that Hashem can be found within them. Every Shabbos, Hashem is especially close to His people. The Torah says (*Vayikra* 23:3), שַׁבָּת הִיא לַה׳ בְּכֹל מוֹשְׁבֹתֵיכֶם, *It is Hashem's Sabbath, in all your dwelling places.*

The term *dwelling places* suggests that Hashem reveals Himself in every Jew's home on Shabbos. Similarly, in regard to the *succah*, our Rabbis tell us (*Succah* 9a), שֶׁחָל שֵׁם שָׁמַיִם עַל הַסֻּכָּה *The Name of Heaven rests upon the succah.* Thus, the *succah* enjoys a special distinction, as it takes on an aura of sanctity not found anywhere else on earth. (5650)

◆§ Succah — A Link to Hashem's Throne

In previous sections, the *succah* has been portrayed as a foretaste of the World to Come, or a retrospective glance at the Garden of Eden. The *succah* can also be linked to another supernatural phenomenon, Hashem's Heavenly Throne (כִּסֵּא הַכָּבוֹד). The daily prayers make various references to the Heavenly Throne, such as גָּלוּי וְיָדוּעַ לִפְנֵי כִסֵּא כְבוֹדֶךָ, *It is revealed before Your Heavenly Throne.* The concept of glimpsing the Heavenly Throne usually refers to a uniquely intimate relationship with Hashem. Thus, when sitting in a *succah*, a Jew feels as if he is almost in the immediate presence of the Almighty.

What is the relationship between the *succah* and the Heavenly Throne? The Talmud (*Yoma* 86a) relates that repentance has such a powerful impact on the celestial sphere that it reaches as far as the Heavenly Throne. In the aftermath of Yom Kippur, it can truly be said that all Jews have repented, and that the new repository for their souls, the *succah*, reaches all the way to the Heavenly Throne. This link with the Almighty protects the Jewish people on Succos.

The Talmud (*Succah* 5a) derives the halachic requirement that *succah* must be at least ten handbreadths high from a presumption that the Heavenly Throne never descended lower than that level. If that connection between the *succah* and the Throne can be felt by the contemporary Jew, it was even more keenly felt by our ancestors during the time of the *Beis HaMikdash*. For them, a direct link existed between the *succah* and the Divine Service on Yom Kippur. The *Kohen Gadol* was required to offer incense when entering the *Beis HaMikdash's* innermost sanctuary on Yom Kippur. This offering was called a "cloud" (see *Vayikra* 16:2).

In the merit of this incense cloud offered by the *Kohen Gadol*, the Divine Cloud is bestowed upon man in the form of a *succah* just five days after Yom Kippur. The Talmud commentator *Kapos Temarim* (*Yoma* 86a) suggests another function for the Heavenly Throne which may extend further the linkage between it and the *succah*. The Midrash (*Yalkut Shimoni* 11) relates that Jacob's "image" is engraved on the Heavenly Throne. *Kapos Temarim* suggests that the soul of not only the Patriarchs, but also of every Jew, emanates from the Heavenly Throne. All year long we drift away from our Divine roots. After the purification of Yom Kippur, the slippage ceases and the Jew comes back to Hashem and (while sitting in the *succah*) is again linked to the source of his soul — the Heavenly Throne. (5640, 5644)

◆§ Celebrating the Universe's Creation

Rosh Hashanah and Yom Kippur are not merely Days of Judgment for the universe. They are also the occasions when the world, by being spared a harsh judgment is in effect re-created. In fact, the purpose of the Divine Service of the High Holy Days and Succos is so that mortals can again be called the name that was given to the first man (Adam) on the day he was created (*Bereishis* 5:2): וַיִּקְרָא אֶת־שְׁמָם אָדָם בְּיוֹם הִבָּרְאָם, *He [Hashem] called their name Man on the day that they were created.*

The purpose of the entire High Holy Day service is to make mortals into creatures that can be called *mentschen* — truly ethical people. This can occur only after the repentance required on these days. However, a reward accompanies the title. On the first day of Creation, light was created. According to our Sages (*Yalkut Bereishis* 5), Hashem judged that this primeval light was too sacred for man to behold, especially in later generations, when evil would reign along with the good, and He therefore, hid it from ordinary mortals. On Succos everyone can benefit from this sacred light: The prize reserved for the righteous in the World to Come — the rarefied light of the first days of Creation — may also be felt in the *succah*. (5648)

◆§ "Marriage" of Hashem and Man

The Exodus from Egypt can be considered the "betrothal" of Hashem and the Jewish people, as indicated by the verse (*Vayikra* 22:32-33), וְנִקְדַּשְׁתִּי בְּתוֹךְ בְּנֵי יִשְׂרָאֵל אֲנִי ה׳ מְקַדִּשְׁכֶם. הַמּוֹצִיא אֶתְכֶם מֵאֶרֶץ מִצְרַיִם לִהְיוֹת לָכֶם לֵאלֹהִים אֲנִי ה׳, *I shall be holy in the midst of the Children of Israel; I am HASHEM, Who betrothed you while taking you out from the land of Egypt to be for you a God; I am HASHEM.*

Pursuing this analogy further, the *succah,* which resembles a marriage canopy, may symbolize the marriage ceremony confirming the relationship. After such a betrothal, however, the objection might be raised: Why does Hashem favor one nation over others? To demonstrate His determination to choose the Jews in spite of any such "criticism," Hashem completes the ceremony/selection process by housing us in His "bridal canopy," the *succah.*

The question remains valid, though. Why, indeed, does Hashem give precedence to one nation above all others? Why does He choose a part in preference to the whole? We can reply that Hashem is looking not for the superficial loyalty to be found among many of the nations, but rather for a spark of humility in a world gone astray. That spark is to be found in the nation of Israel. Hashem prefers the distinct quality of Israel, in contradistinction to the rest of the world, as He proclaimed through His prophet (*Yeshayahu* 57:15), מָרוֹם וְקָדוֹשׁ אֶשְׁכּוֹן וְאֶת־דַּכָּא וּשְׁפַל־רוּחַ, *On high and holy I dwell, and with the humble and lowly in spirit.* (5634)

◆§ A Present for the Devout

The loyal Hebrew servant (עֶבֶד עִבְרִי) was given a gift upon the completion of his term of service. Among the items frequently bestowed were grain and wine (cf. *Devarim* 15:14). Throughout the High Holy Days, the devout Jew has involved himself in perfecting his Divine Service, and strived to improve. Before he leaves Hashem's Presence and returns to the mundane activities of the year, he is given the *succah* as a reward for his efforts. Appropriately, the *succah* is made of the same materials — the discards of the grain and wine harvest — that comprised the farewell present given the slave. Moreover, if the High Holy Days remind us of the Exodus, when our forefathers left Egypt with great spoils, then the *succah* reminds us of those treasures, since it is in itself a great treasure. (5639)

◆§ Returning to Hashem

Succos is called a Festival of Gathering (חַג הָאָסִיף). Perhaps the Torah gave it this name to demonstrate the contrast between Israel and the rest of humankind. While other nations leave the fields and gather their harvest to take it back to their homes, Jews leave their homes to seek out

Hashem, by gathering at the *Beis Hamikdash*. Another possible interpretation is that Succos is the day on which Hashem gathers us and brings us to *His* home, the *succah*. (5635)

⇝§ Protection for the "Inner Spark"

Every Jew has within him an inner spark of Godliness that is rekindled every year during the High Holy Days. Such a frail spark needs protection, and the *succah* provides it. It was to this spark that the Psalmist referred in the promise (29:11), ה׳ עֹז לְעַמּוֹ יִתֵּן, *HASHEM will give strength to His people.*

The continuation of this verse, ה׳ יְבָרֵךְ אֶת־עַמּוֹ בַשָּׁלוֹם, *HASHEM will bless His people with peace*, refers to the protection He provides for that spark. In fact, the Hebrew letters for one of Hashem's Names, א־ל־ו־ה, are the same as those in the word for a protective tent, אוֹהֶל. When Hashem calls himself אֱלֹהֵי יִשְׂרָאֵל, *Lord of Israel*, He refers to His giving us the consummate protection. For this reason, the verse in *Parashas Emor* that gives the rationale for the *mitzvah* of *succah* (*Vayikra* 23:43, לְמַעַן יֵדְעוּ דֹרֹתֵיכֶם, *so that your generations should know*) concludes, אֲנִי ה׳ אֱלֹהֵיכֶם, *I am HASHEM, your God*. The primary purpose of the *succah* is to protect a Jew's inner spark by housing it in Hashem's home, the *succah*. (5638)

Succah: Auspicious Beginning for a Good Year

⇝§ Rootlessness

The *succah* conveys a message of rootlessness.

During the present era of our history, the Jew has few if any roots in this world. By leaving our sturdy homes in favor of frail, makeshift *succos*, we demonstrate this lack of permanent roots. Even though after

Succos we will return to more permanent structures and go back to our homes, it is as different people, changed by the lesson of the *succah* and reminded that we have no *material* roots.

We might wonder, what good can be accomplished by a week of rootlessness since we will return to our ordinary routine immediately afterwards. This question, however, betrays a misunderstanding of the power of a short period of time lived under ideal conditions. Consider how our forefathers traversed the wilderness for forty years. Living under the Divine Cloud, partaking of the Manna and freed from material worries, they acquired the spiritual stamina that would be needed by all future generations. Similarly, the week of Succos sets a tone for the entire year. By forsaking our plush homes for a week, we ensure that throughout the rest of the year we will know where our real roots are.

Let us not underestimate the importance of good beginnings. A powerful example of this is Hashem's insistence, at the very moment that the Jews crossed the Jordan River, that they pledge to destroy the seven Canaanite nations and the sites of their idol worship (see *Rashi* on *Bamidbar* 33:51). The total annihilation of the enemy was never accomplished. Nonetheless, the fact that the Jews sincerely intended to do so from the very beginning made possible at least the partial success they had. We see from this the critical importance of having proper intentions from the very outset when pursuing a noble goal.

Another example of the importance of good beginnings came immediately after the Exodus, when Hashem pledged to lead the Jewish people in a supernatural manner. As the Torah says (*Shemos* 13:17), וַיְהִי בְּשַׁלַּח פַּרְעֹה אֶת־הָעָם וְלֹא־נָחָם אֱלֹהִים דֶּרֶךְ אֶרֶץ פְּלִשְׁתִּים, *It happened when Pharaoh sent out the people that God did not lead them by way of the land of the Philistines.* The Midrash (*Yalkut Shemos* 226) interprets a fragment from this verse by reference to a play on words: וְלֹא־נָחָם אֱלֹהִים דֶּרֶךְ אֶרֶץ, Hashem did not take them out according to דֶּרֶךְ אֶרֶץ, in a "natural manner," but rather "supernaturally," through miracles. While there were times that Israel did not deserve such a supernatural existence, the tone set at the beginning ensured that we could live in a miraculous manner throughout the wilderness trek.

Thus Succos, with its forced change of lifestyle, is the best time to remember that our roots are not in the material world. It is easier to forsake the material world with a burst of enthusiasm after the inspiration and purification of Yom Kippur. Then we are all returnees to

Hashem (בַּעֲלֵי תְּשׁוּבָה) and are granted unusual moral strength. We flee from the confines of materialism as one flees from a dangerous fire — with every ounce of his strength.

Beginning the year with such an active symbol of our rootlessness also reminds us how our generation is linked to previous ones. In particular, the *succah* recalls our links to the Patriarchs, who themselves had no material roots, no real connection to this world, as we see from the description, אֶרֶץ מְגוּרֵי אָבִיו, *the land of his father's sojourning,* at the beginning of *Parashas Vayeishev* (*Bereishis* 37:1). In fact, the primary purpose of repentance (תְּשׁוּבָה) is to return to the ways of the Patriarchs, and thereby to attach ourselves to our Heavenly roots.

The words of the Psalmist (39:13), כִּי גֵר אָנֹכִי עִמָּךְ תּוֹשָׁב כְּכָל־אֲבוֹתָי, *For I am a visitor with You, a sojourner like all my fathers,* also stress this point. By abandoning our homes to dwell in the ephemeral *succah* in an attempt to emphasize our lack of roots in this world, we approach the aspirations of the Patriarchs, who have been described as "Hashem's Heavenly Chariots" (see *Rashi* on *Bereishis* 17:22), implying that their existence in this world lacked permanence almost like mobile chariots. Their only goal was the extension of the recognition of Hashem's sovereignty.

Having attained this degree of rootlessness, we can now invite the sacred guests the *Ushpizin* (including the Patriarchs, as well as Moshe and Aaron), for we have risen to their level of sanctity. We, too, have forsaken this world for a more spiritual existence. In this sense, we may conceive of the *Ushpizin* as emissaries from Hashem to help Israel repent and thereby retain its newly realized rootlessness. Perhaps this is the intent of the Psalmist's declaration cited above.

This may also be the message of the prophet Malachi in the following verse (3:24): וְהֵשִׁיב לֵב־אָבוֹת עַל־בָּנִים, *[HASHEM] returns father's hearts to children.* Hashem returns the Patriarchs to this earth to join us in the *succah* to strengthen the hearts of their descendants.

Difficult as it may be to abandon the material comforts of our homes — even in the enthusiasm for repentance that follows Yom Kippur, we may be assured that Hashem will help us to achieve this transformation. Thus, the Psalmist rhapsodizes (113:7,8), מֵאַשְׁפֹּת יָרִים אֶבְיוֹן לְהוֹשִׁיבִי עִם־נְדִיבִים, *He lifts the destitute from the trash heaps to seat them with nobles*. Through repentance the impoverished soul is lifted from the trash heap to sit with the Patriarchs, those nobles of the world. On Succos, with Hashem's help, we become nobles, as the Torah says

(*Vayikra* 23:42), כָּל־הָאֶזְרָח בְּיִשְׂרָאֵל יֵשְׁבוּ בַּסֻּכֹּת, *Every honored citizen in Israel [honored by the presence of the Ushpizin] shall dwell in succos.* (5652)

⌁§ Succah as Spiritual Protection

The *succah* affords protection in many ways. The Divine Cloud, after which the *succah* is modeled, protected the Jews of the Wilderness against many enemies, especially the deadly Amalek (discussed in a previous essay). Even today, the *succah* protects us from the *yetzer hara* (evil inclination), the great spritual foe that constantly tempts us to sin. Vanquished on Yom Kippur and forced to concede Israel's goodness (see *Zohar Emor* 102a), this source of evil now redoubles its efforts to weaken our moral resolve. This is why we seek protection in the *succah,* a sanctuary from the moral and spiritual temptations of this world. The exhortation of the prophet Yeshayahu (26:20), לֵךְ עַמִּי בֹּא בַחֲדָרֶיךָ, *Go my people, come into your chamber,* may be seen as an allusion to Israel's seeking shelter in the *succah*.

Especially after Yom Kippur, the *yetzer hara* does not always pursue its prey in an overt, confrontational manner. It also acts subtly, seeking to harm Israel by praising us and giving us too much publicity. Such was the tactic of the wicked Bilaam, who sought to cast an "evil eye" on us (see *Rashi* on *Bamidbar* 24:2). "Hiding" in the *succah,* we have some measure of immunity from the *yezter hara's* various poses, either as a foe tempting to sin, or as a friend singing our praises. (5646)

Esau symbolizes the force of evil, the *yetzer hara.* After Jacob did battle with his brother, he hid in the *succah,* as it says (*Bereishis* 33:17), וְיַעֲקֹב נָסַע סֻכֹּתָה, *Jacob journeyed to Succos.* We can interpret this verse in a spiritual sense — not only did Jacob go to a geographical location called *Succos,* he fled from the influence of his brother Esau to the spiritual protection afforded by the *succah.* (5646)

⌁§ Why Did the Jews Need Physical Huts If They Had the "Divine Cloud"?

If the Jews of the Wilderness benefited from Divine protection in the form of the Divine Cloud, why did they also need tangible huts? Since they had Hashem's supernatural support, why were they subject even to the symbolic exigencies of the material world?

One possible answer is that the spiritual ecstasy of the Divine Cloud was really attainable only as a result of our own initiative. By leaving secure homes in Egypt to dwell in shabby huts in the Wilderness, the Jews affirmed their resolute willingness to follow Hashem. It was in the merit of the initiative we took to build a physical *succah* that Hashem graced us with the Divine Cloud.

Alternatively, we can say that the Divine Cloud was the ideal and most visible representation of the presence of the Divine — an ideal that could be attained only by the Wilderness generation. By sitting in humble man-made huts which conveyed a feeling of Hashem's presence in a more subtle fashion, that first generation established for us, their descendants, a legacy that would enable us to derive spiritual benefit from the *succah* as well.

The Torah alludes to the *succah's* relevance to our generation in spelling the word דֹרוֹתֵיכֶם, *your generations,* missing a letter *vav* which would normally be written in the first syllable. Homiletically, we may interpret this omission to imply that even "faulty" generations, those "missing" the ability to fully perceive the sanctity of the *succah,* should not give up hope. They too are assured that the festival of Succos will bring them from darkness to light. Those generations that partake of the *succah's* bliss without so strong a feeling of Hashem's presence are even more beloved by Hashem. The *succah* is truly a "house of faith" for them, since they perform this *mitzvah* unable to sense the *succah's* sacred ambiance, yet with full faith in its existence. (5644)

The Talmud (*Taanis* 9a) lists three great miracles that occurred in the Wilderness: the Divine Cloud, Miriam's Well (which gave the Jewish people water) and the Manna. Why is there a festival to celebrate only the Divine Cloud and not the other two miracles?

Perhaps this was done to emphasize the power of repentance. The Divine Cloud came in the merit of Aaron, the great *baal teshuvah.* After collaborating (at least peripherally) in the Sin of the Golden Calf, Aaron decided to repent. A returnee deserves a holiday in his own right,as we see from the opinion recounted in the Talmud (*Avodah Zarah* 4b) that Aaron (and in fact all those who had a part in the episode of the Golden Calf) participated in that sin only to teach Israel the power of repentance. (5651)

Another reason why the other miracles (the well and the manna) are not commemorated with special holidays, is that they were accompanied by grumbling and complaints. There were numerous complaints about lack of water and expressions of dissatisfaction with the manna. However, Israel never complained about the cloud. On the contrary, they willingly followed the cloud regardless of where it lead them; they rested when it rested — whether for a short or long period. This is why it was granted a celebration of its own, as the Talmud says (*Shabbos* 130a), כָּל מִצְוָה שֶׁקִּבְּלוּ עֲלֵיהֶם בְּשִׂמְחָה עֲדַיִין עוֹשִׂים אוֹתוֹ בְּשִׂמְחָה, *Any mitzvah done with simchah will be perpetuated with simchah.* (5647)

☙ A Place to "Preserve" New Sparks of Judaism

The High Holy Days are not only a period of individual judgment, but also a time for review of the future of the Jewish people. There is an annual process that culminates in the renewal of our bonds with Hashem and our selection anew from among the nations to perform His special service. The Torah says in *Parashas Emor* (*Vayikra* 20:26), וָאַבְדִּל אֶתְכֶם מִן־הָעַמִּים לִהְיוֹת לִי, *I will separate you from the peoples to be Mine.* The Midrash comments on the verse, (*Yalkut Shimoni* 626) "I have chosen and I will choose again," implying that Hashem selects the Jewish people again each year as part of the judgment process. As the bond is renewed yearly, and as the Jewish people are liberated from the *yetzer hara* at this time of year, there is a veritable liberation, like the liberation from Egyptian bondage, and נִיצוֹצֵי קְדוּשָׁה (sparks of sanctity), souls of Gentiles seeking out the sanctity of the Jewish nation join our ranks.

At the time of the Exodus from Egypt, numerous Gentile souls (referred to in the Torah as the עֵרֶב רַב, *the mixed multitude*) adhered to the newly liberated Jewish people. The Talmud (*Pesachim* 87b) suggests that the purpose of the millenia-long exile of the Jewish people is to attract proselytes (גֵּרִים) to Judaism. This long and bitter exile will come to an end when all these souls, and the "sparks of sanctity" they contain, will have been extracted.[1]

Just as the Divine Cloud protected that first generation of new souls, so also every year the *succah* shelters those who have joined our ranks. Perhaps we can say that the seventy bulls offered on Succos (see *Rashi* on *Bamidbar* 29:18) in the Temple — corresponding to the seventy basic Gentile nations of the world — may help to preserve these "sparks

1. The concept of extracting "sparks of sanctity" from among the Gentile nations is explored at greater length in the essay on the Book of Ruth in the section on Shavuos.

of sanctity" that have long sought to join the ranks of the Jewish people.

An early indication of this capacity of the *succah* to shelter these new, emerging souls can be found in the Torah's first mention of the word Succos. After Jacob's confrontations with Laban and Esau, the Torah says (*Bereishis* 33:17), וּלְמִקְנֵהוּ עָשָׂה סֻכֹּת, *and for his cattle he made huts.* The word used for cattle, מִקְנֶה can be homiletically interpreted as "acquisitions," suggesting that those souls Jacob persuaded to join his ranks were now sheltered in *succos.* (5653)

The Four Species

◆§ Introduction

וּלְקַחְתֶּם לָכֶם בַּיּוֹם הָרִאשׁוֹן פְּרִי עֵץ הָדָר כַּפֹּת תְּמָרִים וַעֲנַף עֵץ־עָבֹת וְעַרְבֵי־נָחַל וּשְׂמַחְתֶּם לִפְנֵי ה׳ אֱלֹהֵיכֶם שִׁבְעַת יָמִים׃

On the first day you are to take for yourselves the fruit of a citron tree, the branches of date palms, twigs of a plaited tree, and brook willows; and you are to rejoice before HASHEM *your God seven days* (*Vayikra* 23:40).

What purpose do the Four Species serve? Also what does the expression "take for yourself" mean? These words suggest that we derive benefit to ourselves from this taking, what is it that we gain? Further, why do these species engender happiness? The following discussion will elaborate on these questions and offer insights from the Midrash and *Zohar*.

◆§ Bringing out the Inner Joy of Succos

The Midrash (*Yalkut Shimoni Emor* 650) explains this verse by citing the prayer of King David (*Tehillim* 16:11): תּוֹדִיעֵנִי אֹרַח חַיִּים שֹׂבַע שְׂמָחוֹת אֶת פָּנֶיךָ נְעִמוֹת בִּימִינְךָ נֶצַח, *Make known to me the path of life, the fullness of joys in Your Presence, the delights that are in Your right hand for eternity.*

While anyone can rejoice, especially on the festive occasion of Succos, joy can be merely a superficial and short-lived emotion. We can be happy one day and revert to morbidity the next day. The message of the Four Species, and their blessing, (*take for yourselves*) is that each person has the ability to scratch below the surface and appreciate the depth of joy on Succos. The *Yalkut* (652) explains that the Four Species represent different organs of the human body:

> רַבִּי מַנִי פָּתַח כָּל עַצְמוֹתַי תֹּאמַרְנָה ה׳ מִי כָמוֹךָ לֹא אָמַר דָּוִד הַפָּסוּק הַזֶּה אֶלָּא בִּשְׁבִיל לוּלָב הַשֶּׁדְרָה דוֹמֶה לְשֶׁדְרָה שֶׁל אָדָם וְהַהֲדַס דוֹמֶה לְעַיִן וַעֲרָבָה דוֹמָה לְפֶה וְאֶתְרוֹג דוֹמֶה לְלֵב
>
> *Rabbi Mani opened [his discourse]: "All my bones say, 'HASHEM, Who is like You?' King David said this verse refers specifically to the lulav, whose spine resembles a man's backbone; the haddas, which resembles the eye; the aravah, which resembles the mouth; and the esrog, which resembles the heart."*

By fulfilling the commandment of the four Species properly, one causes the joy of Succos to penetrate into every part of the body. The Psalmist's plea to be filled with the joy of Hashem's Presence refers to inner serenity, as we see from the word פָּנֶיךָ, in the Psalm cited above. Literally this word means *Your face*, and in this sense often refers to Hashem's Presence. However the word also has the connotation of בִּפְנִים, (interior), alluding to the *inner* joy of being close to Hashem.

The *mitzvah* of taking the Four Species also ensures that the joy of Succos will continue through the year, in the Psalmist's phrase, *the delights that are in Your right hand for eternity.* (5665)

◈ Consecrating the Entire Body

The Midrash cited above suggests that the Four Species symbolize various parts of the human body. By performing Hashem's will with species representing different organs, we dedicate every part of ourselves to a higher calling. The *Midrash* describes those who take the Four Species as winners of a great battle, obviously referring to a moral victory rather than a physical one. The *yetzer hara* (evil inclination) seeks to make the body resist the soul's quest for spiritual growth. By waving these Four Species towards Heaven, we achieve a true victory and demonstrate that our souls triumph, that Hashem's wishes, not our physical passions, dominate us. (5665)

◆§ Four Types of Torah Personality The Fragrant Haddas

The Talmud (*Menachos* 27a) asserts that each of the species represents a different type of Torah personality. The edible and fragrant *esrog* symbolizes the Jew who is both learned and charitable. The *lulav*, which bears sweet dates but totally lacks fragrance, represents the scholar who is very learned but undistinguished by his good deeds. The fragrant but inedible *haddas* symbolizes the Jew who excels in good deeds but is unlearned. Finally, the unimpressive willow (which is discussed at great length in the essay on *Hoshana Rabbah*) symbolizes the ordinary Jew, lacking both Torah knowledge and good deeds. By binding these species together and holding them at one time, we express the integral unity of all Jews (as will be developed in a later section).

For now let us focus on the meaning of the *haddas* and its fragrance. The Midrash cited above suggests that the *haddas* alludes to the three Patriarchs, Abraham, Isaac, and Jacob. (In order to be halachically acceptable, a *haddas* must be *meshulash*, that is, all its leaves must be grouped in clusters of three.). What is the relationship between the Patriarchs and the powerful fragrance of the *haddas*?

A fragrance is the residue of something rather than the *substance* of the thing itself. It is an indication of something that is about to happen or a reminder of something that has already happened. In this sense, the Patriarchs can be considered a "fragrance" of Torah, in that they observed the Torah before it was given at Sinai. They perceived the Torah intuitively before it became a reality in the world. The Patriarchs set an example of what it means to perceive a "whiff" of Torah without its substance by "previewing" Torah and observing it before it was obligatory to do so. All Jews, even those who through no fault of their own, lack Torah knowledge and therefore cannot partake of the substance of Torah, can benefit from its fragrance. All Jews can profit from a connection with Torah, by associating themselves with the Patriarchs, who were also privy to a whiff of Torah's fragrance.

This relationship between a substance and its fragrance is demonstrated each week at *Havdalah* when we smell spices upon taking leave of the Shabbos. If Shabbos is the substance of Judaism, we ask for at least a whiff, a reminder of the Sabbath day, to linger on with us throughout the week.

In a larger sense, the relationship between our world and the World to Come also resembles that of a fragrance and its substance. Our world is merely a "scent" of the World to Come, which is the true substance of Judaism. Every Jew is assured of a portion in the World to Come (cf. Mishah *Sanhedrin* 10:1). One of the special things about the Jewish people is that they enjoy a whiff of the World to Come even in the here and now. Because a Jew is destined to enjoy great things in the hereafter, he is graced with a "whiff" of the World to Come already in this world.

(5664)

◆§ The Righteous Find a Place for the Wicked

The Talmud (*Chagigah* 15a) offers the following description of the relationship between the *tzaddik* (righteous individual) and the wicked person: Everyone has two portions, one in Paradise and one in *Gehinnom*. If the *tzaddik* merits it (by being vindicated on Rosh Hashanah), he will obtain his own portion in Paradise as well as that of the wicked person. Conversely, if the wicked person is condemned to (spiritual) death on Rosh Hashanah, he will be given not only his portion in *Gehinnom* but also that of the *tzaddik* (i.e., the portion to which the *tzaddik* would have been subjected in atonement for any sins he may have committed).

While a detailed analysis of this subject is beyond the scope of this essay, it seems to emerge that on Judgment Day, *tzaddikim* obtain a "monopoly" on Paradise and the wicked are confined totally to *Gehinnom*. However, because true *tzaddikim* are generous they seek to share their portion in Paradise with the wicked. Thus, when Hashem wanted to eradicate the Jewish people and found a great nation descended from Moshe alone following the sin of the Golden Calf, out of his magnanimity Moshe pleaded with Hashem to save the people, even at his own expense (see *Nedarim* 38a).

So too, after their vindication on Yom Kippur, on Succos the *tzaddikim* of the world graciously relinquish their monopoly on Paradise and restore to the wicked their previous allotment there. As we have said, the Four Species represent different Jewish personality types. Thus we place the *aravah* (symbolizing the wicked who have neither learning nor good deeds) next to the *esrog* (the *tzaddik*, full of fragrance and taste) to show that on Succos *tzaddikim* restore to the wicked their portion in the World to Come.

The Talmud (*Menachos* 27a) calls the Four Species a united bond (אֲגוּדָה אַחַת). Surely there can be no higher expression of unity than the compassion of the *tzaddikim* in returning to the wicked their portion in Paradise that occurs on Succos. Another example of this oneness and kindness is the seventy bulls Israel offers in atonement for the seventy nations of the world. The Four Species, thus, exemplify Israel's compassion and generosity towards individuals, the Jewish community, and to the world as a whole. (5663)

◆§ Return to Torah

In *Mishlei* there is another verse that brings together the two concepts of "taking" and "for yourself" (4:2): כִּי לֶקַח טוֹב נָתַתִּי לָכֶם תּוֹרָתִי אַל תַּעֲזֹבוּ — *For I have given you a good acquisition: Do not forsake My Torah*. The obvious similarity of the words לֶקַח, *acquisition*, and לְקַחְתֶּם, *and you shall take*, suggest that here also, in the case of the Four Species, the concept of "taking for oneself" refers to Torah. The merit we have of taking the Four Species, especially after our participation in *Yom Kippur*, brings about the Jewish people's return to Torah. As we said above, the Midrash interprets the verse (*Tehillim* 16:11), *Make known to me the path of life*, as a reference to the Four Species. Now we can understand this reference more clearly: In the merit of taking the Four species, we ask Hashem to make known to us the ultimate path of life, His holy Torah. Similarly when the prophet Hoshea beseeches Israel to repent (14:3), he speaks first of gaining forgiveness and then of doing good. *Rashi* derives from this verse that a sinner is considered to return to the path of good immediately after his sins are expiated. Every year, Israel's sins are forgiven on *Yom Kippur*; immediately afterward, on Succos, we return to the path of Torah.

The Mishnah (*Rosh Hashanah* 1:2) teaches that the Jewish people is judged concerning the allotment of rainfall that will grace their lands in the following year. This may be understood to refer not only to physical precipitation, but also to Torah, the ultimate source of our spiritual nourishment and growth. Every Jew's portion in Torah, his capacity for growth and self-development, is determined on Succos. (5663)

◆§ Hashem's Image Restored

In the prayer that precedes taking the Four Species, we ask to know how we will so to speak "interface" with Hashem by performing this commandment. While every human being is created in Hashem's image (cf. *Bereishis* 1:27), Israel in particular bears the likeness of the Creator through the visible observance of His Torah. Like any other object of beauty, however, man can forfeit his status as a "likeness" of Hashem through unworthy actions. The sins and errors we commit throughout the year tarnish the luster of this beauty we have been favored with.

On Succos, after the cleansing of Yom Kippur, we return to our original challenge, to act in a way that is worthy of bearers of Hashem's image which is now restored to us. This is achieved by taking the Four Species, symbolic of different parts of the human organism (as discussed earlier), and waving them towards Heaven, symbolizing the fact that everything we have, body and soul, emanates from there. (5662)

◆§ Triumph of the Soul

וּלְקַחְתֶּם לָכֶם בַּיּוֹם הָרִאשׁוֹן פְּרִי עֵץ הָדָר . . . וּשְׂמַחְתֶּם לִפְנֵי ה׳ אֱלֹהֵיכֶם שִׁבְעַת יָמִים

On the first day you are to take for yourselves the fruit of a citron tree . . . and you are to rejoice before H*ASHEM*, *your God, seven days* (*Vayikra* 23:40).

This verse, which commands taking the Four Species, concludes by assuring us that if we observe this *mitzvah* we will merit to rejoice in it.

Why and how does performing this *mitzvah* bring joy? As we saw above, in the prayer recited before taking the Four Species we declare that we are doing the *mitzvah* so that Hashem's Name should be present within us: וְלֵידַע אֵיךְ שִׁמְךָ נִקְרָא עָלַי. This difficult phrase (which we have interpreted as a reference to the return of Hashem's likeness to Israel on Succos) also hints at the dominance of the soul, the manifestation of Godliness in the human being, over the body. This is expressed not only in our waving of the Four Species, representing parts of the body, towards Heaven, but also in our observance of Shabbos.

The Talmud (*Beitzah* 16a) speaks of the *neshamah yeseirah* (literally extra soul) which is also a general reference to the added dimension of spirituality perceived every Shabbos.

This connection may also explain, on a deep level, why the Four Species are not taken when Succos occurs on Shabbos.[1] Shabbos a day of intense spirituality, does not need the extra support of the Four Species.

Herein lies the key to understanding the joy promised by the Torah to those who take the Four Species. There is no greater joy than the revelation of the soul, no greater happiness than the triumph of spirituality over the material world. This joy of resurgent spirituality that comes when we wave the Four Species is the same as the joy of the arrival of the *neshamah yeseirah* every Shabbos. The Midrash (*Yalkut Shimoni* 725) supports this by interpreting the phrase בְּיוֹם שִׂמְחַתְכֶם, *the day of your rejoicing* (*Bamidbar* 10:6) as an allusion to Shabbos. Thus both Shabbos and Succos are days of joy and of enhanced spirituality.

(5660)

The Association Between the Four Species and Succah

◆§ Diversity Amidst Unity

It is generally assumed that the *succah* and the Four Species are distinct *mitzvos* whose performance happens to coincide in the same festival. However, closer examination reveals an underlying relationship between the two. The Four Species are really a catalyst to ensure that the *mitzvah* of *succah* will be performed properly. An important prerequisite for this catalytic relationship to occur is *achdus*, unity among Jews.

1. While the Talmud attributes this to the Sages' concern that someone might carry his Four Species four cubits in a public thoroughfare, an act forbidden by the Torah, we are speaking here of the inner significance of this prohibition.

כָּל־הָאֶזְרָח בְּיִשְׂרָאֵל יֵשְׁבוּ בַּסֻּכֹּת
Every citizen of Israel is to dwell in succos (*Vayikra* 23:42).

The Sages see in this verse the (at least theoretical) possibility that all Jews might dwell in one *succah.*[1] In one sense, we can understand this to mean that only when all Jews can sit together in one *succah*, regardless of their differences, will this *mitzvah* be properly observed.

Unity among Jews is a challenging and elusive goal. If there is ever an auspicious time to unite Jews, it is Succos, when all Jews, having forgiven each other on Yom Kippur, celebrate together in their *succos.* On Succos we take the Four Species, which represent, four distinctive personality types who overcome their individual differences to join together, as we discussed at length in the previous essay. Thus the Four Species symbolize unity among Jews, and teach us that only when Jews learn to subjugate their differences and live with each other can they come close to Hashem.

The *succah* has been described as Hashem's home. Similarly, the Sages (*Succah* 9a) taught that Hashem's Name is manifested in the *succah.* Man can return to his Creator, and take pleasure in sitting in His home, the *succah*, only *after* he has made peace with his peers, symbolized by the Four Species. Unity among men engenders unity between Hashem and His people. Binding the Four Species together demonstrates that Israel's unity as a nation is a vital prerequisite for the *mitzvah* of *succah.*

How can Jewish unity be accomplished? Let us consider the Talmud's response to this question: יֵשׁ שֶׁעוֹשִׂין פֵּירוֹת וְיֵשׁ שֶׁאֵין עוֹשִׂין פֵּירוֹת וְיִהְיוּ נִזְקָקִין הָעוֹשִׂין פֵּירוֹת לְשֶׁאֵין עוֹשִׂין, *Some [of the species] bear fruit and some do not bear fruit: Let those that bear fruit be bound with those that do not bear fruit* (*Menachos* 27a).

Metaphorically, this passage suggests that achieving unity, especially among those with different types of intellects, is a synergistic process. Those who "bear fruit," who are productive, must contribute their talents and resources to help their less endowed brothers. The learned can contribute to unity by "reaching out" to those less fortunate than themselves. Similarly, those who are not as productive, less learned and not as involved in good deeds, must recognize their obligation to follow the leadership of those more gifted and accomplished than themselves.

---

1. This derivation is based on the spelling of the word *succos* without a *vav*, so that the word could be understood as a singular noun, a *succah.*

If the righteous were to contribute time and strength to the less righteous and if the less righteous (or less productive) were to submit themselves to the influence of their righteous brethren, true unity would soon ensue. (5662)

Unity does not require total self-negation or totally homogeneous behavior. On the contrary, the Mishnah places as much value on arguments for the sake of Heaven (i.e. for the sake of Judaism) as on unanimity (*Avos* 5:20). The varying personalities represented by the different species can and should maintain their uniqueness as they unite around a common purpose, much as we bind together the Four Species. Indeed differences among Jews are not only natural but also necessary for the nation of Israel to exist as a total composite.

Let us consider further the underlying rationale for differences among Jews. While Hashem gave the same Torah to every Jew, each individual has his own unique faculties with which to comprehend it. Differing approaches to understanding Torah result in diversity and even disagreement within the ranks of Jewry. In other words, the Torah that is *given* is fixed and invariable, and any differences there may be, lie in the *receiving* of the Torah by individuals. As long as such diversity has as its aim eventual unity, it is acceptable and desirable, since it facilitates the unification of the various approaches to Torah into a coherent whole. It is entirely possible for an individual to retain his unique character and yet be an integral part of the Jewish people. This concept was demonstrated by the twelve tribes of Israel, each had its own unique function yet was very much a part of the larger whole.

The patriarch Jacob, on his deathbed, sensed the importance of diversity coupled with unity. Summoning his children, he told them, הֵאָסְפוּ וְאַגִּידָה לָכֶם אֵת אֲשֶׁר־יִקְרָא אֶתְכֶם בְּאַחֲרִית הַיָּמִים, *Unite and I will tell you what will happen to you at the end of days* (*Bereishis* 49:1). This is a plea for unity, based on each of the children receiving the same tradition from the father. But he continues, הִקָּבְצוּ וְשִׁמְעוּ, *Gather and listen* (v. 2). Now the emphasis is not on what Jacob tells his children, but rather on the fact that they are listening together. This is comparable to the point we made earlier, that while everyone *receives* the same Torah, each individual *understands* it differently.

The word הֵאָסְפוּ, *unite*, suggests fusing into a monolithic whole the individual parts of which are undistinguishable. While הִקָּבְצוּ, *gather*, connotes the merging into a cohesive whole of distinct elements, each of which retains its individual identity.

The relationship between a monolith and a union of distinct parts can be extended to the relationship between the *succah* and the Four Species as well. As we have explained, the Four Species, with their theme of unifying diverse Jews, constitute a necessary prerequisite for performing the *mitzvah* of *succah*, which demands total unity. An important distinction, however, exists between the unity exemplified by the Four Species and that of the *succah*. The Four Species demonstrate unity among diverse elements, corresponding to the "argument for the sake of Heaven" mentioned above. They symbolize Israel's taking diverse ways of understanding Torah (as embodied in the terms הֵאָסְפוּ, *unite*, and הִקָּבְצוּ, *gather*) and uniting them. On the other hand, the *succah*, Hashem's home, allows for no distinctions or gradations. It is the ultimate in unanimity, a כְּנֵסִיָּה שֶׁהִיא לְשֵׁם שָׁמַיִם, "assembly dedicated to the sake of Heaven" (cf. *Avos* 4:14). This relationship between the *succah* and the Four Species can be developed even further. The Four Species symbolize unity among Jews, a peer-to-peer relationship. The *succah*, on the other hand, represents man coming ever closer to Hashem.

The above remarks cast new light on the meaning of the verse וּלְקַחְתֶּם לָכֶם, *You are to take for yourselves*. What is it the Jew takes for himself on Succos? By taking the Four Species, symbolically fusing together different types of Jews, we make every Jew a partner in the entity called the Jewish people. The Talmud interprets the requirement of "taking for yourself" in seemingly contradictory ways. On the one hand, every individual Jew is urged to take the Four Species, לְקִיחָה לְכָל אֶחָד (*Sucah* 41b). At the same time, however, a "perfect" (i.e. complete) taking, לְקִיחָה תַּמָּה (*Menachos* 27a) is required, implying that the entire Jewish people should take these species together.

The resolution of this conflict is clear. By making ourselves into members of the community on Succos through *individual* acts of taking the Four Species, we become merged into one communal entity. There is no dichotomy between the enlightened, dedicated acts of the community-minded individual and those of the community itself.

If taking the Four Species has such great significance, why do we not take them when Succos occurs on Shabbos? The above discussion may help us answer this question. The Four Species are a powerful tool for promoting unity among Jews. In reality, however, a great deal of unity exists even *without* them. The souls of all Jews, their spiritual roots, are by their very nature close together, since they share a common Torah heritage and belief in Hashem. Disputes that arise among Jews are only over *material* matters (e.g. power, money, prestige), which affect the *body*. Even though Jews may differ in appearance and physique, their souls are always united. Shabbos is an intensely spiritual time, when the soul prevails and the Jew is graced with a *neshamah yeseirah*, an added dimension of spirituality. Thus, on this day, unity is attained even without the aid of the Four Species. (5662)

◆§ A Return to Jewish Roots

The Midrash (*Yalkut Shimoni Parashas Emor* 651) draws an analogy between the *lulav*, ("the branch of a date palm") and the *tzaddik*. Similarly, the Psalmist wrote (92:13), צַדִּיק כַּתָּמָר יִפְרָח, *the tzaddik will flourish like a date palm*. Evidently, the Midrash wishes to emphasize that the *lulav* symbolizes the deepest aspiration of the *tzaddik*, a yearning to grow close to Hashem. This is stated more explicitly in a Midrash on this verse (*Yalkut Shimoni Tehillim* 845): מַה תְּמָרָה יֵשׁ לָהֶם תַּאֲוָה כָּךְ הֵם הַצַּדִּיקִים יֵשׁ לָהֶם תַּאֲוָה מַה הִיא תַּאֲוָתָה הקב״ה, *Just like date palms have desire, so also the tzaddikim have desire. What is their desire? The Holy One, Blessed is He.*

While this analogy may be apt concerning the truly righteous, how can an ordinary Jew relate his *lulav* to the desires of the righteous? Dare we consider ourselves *tzaddikim*? Normally it would seem presumptuous to call an ordinary Jew by such a lofty name. After the purification of Yom Kippur, however, the reinvigorated Jew feels the same intense yearning to come close to Hashem that the *tzaddik* feels all the time — an incessant avid desire to return to his spiritual roots, to draw near to his Creator.

Moreover, the repentant Jew (*baal teshuvah*) is, in certain respects, even greater than his peer who never strayed from the path of righteousness. As the above cited Midrash says, מַה תָּמָר אֵין גִּזְעוֹ מַחֲלִיף אֶלָּא לִזְמַן מְרוּבָּה, *a date palm's trunk grows over a long period [i.e., slowly]*. So too, the *tzaddik* grows only through years of striving. On Yom Kippur, the *baal teshuvah* is able to accomplish in a short time, in *moments*, what it took the *tzaddik* years to accomplish.

Hashem loves and showers the repentant Jew with love (cf. *Hoshea* 14:5). How apt then, is the comparison of the *baal teshuvah* to a rose (ibid. 14:6). Unlike the slow-growing palm tree, the rose reaches maturity swiftly. So too, the *baal teshuvah*, (which each of us is on *Yom*

Kippur) with Hashem's help, can shift his spiritual direction with incredible speed.

Even the manner in which we wave the *lulav* proclaims the special role of *teshuvah*. Why do we wave the *lulav* in an upward direction — it would seem to be adequate simply to hold it together with the other species in one hand?

Waving symbolizes acceleration, the ability of the newly-devout Jew to "connect" with Hashem on Succos, even though he has drifted far from his Heavenly roots, and has just recently returned.

The Midrash (ibid.) says that the *tzaddik* whom the verse compares to a date palm is Aaron the *Kohen Gadol*, with particular reference to aspects of his spiritual development. For example, he "flourished" like a date palm when Hashem caused his staff to produce almond blossoms as a sign that Hashem had chosen him to be High Priest rather than the usurper Korach (cf. *Bamidbar* 17:16-24).

The next verse, שְׁתוּלִים בְּבֵית ה׳ בְּחַצְרוֹת אֱלֹהֵינוּ יַפְרִיחוּ, *Planted in the House of* HASHEM, *in the courtyards of our God they will flourish*, alludes to the Seven Days of Dedication of the *Mishkan* (Tabernacle), when Aaron did not once emerge from the Sanctuary for seven days (cf. *Vayikra* 8:35).

The signficance of this Midrash lies not only in its explanation of the analogy of the righteous and a date palm, but also in its lesson that even a *short* time devoted to spirituality can leave a lasting effect. The seven days Aaron spent in Hashem's home at the start of his career gave him a life-long dedication to Hashem. We too, spend seven complete days in Hashem's home, the *succah*. We raise the *lulav* towards Heaven to show our fervent desire to find our roots.

Why do we not take the *lulav* when Succos occurs on Shabbos? In light of the above discussion the answer is apparent. A major purpose of the *lulav* is to direct the Jew to his roots. Since this is also the function of Shabbos, the weekly day of rest, that helps the Jew find himself and his Creator, there is no need for the *lulav* on Shabbos. Indeed, the verse we have been considering, *The tzaddik will flourish like a date palm*, is found in *Psalm* 92, *A Song for the Sabbath Day*. Succos and Shabbos are both times for growth, for finding our roots and striving to accomplish what the *tzaddik* has already attained.

(5658)

◆§ Four Species: Finding One's Self — Discovering One's Soul

Every Jew has a special mission in life and is given unique abilities to enable him to fulfill this mission. He is endowed with a *neshamah* (soul) to assist him in reaching his spiritual goals. We have a great potential for greatness, and yet we often do not come even close to realizing our potential. This failure is caused by sin, which taints our souls and erodes their capacity for spiritual growth. Every time a Jew sins, some component of his soul is weakened.

On Yom Kippur each year, the Jew returns to Hashem. Then on Succos, Hashem returns to the Jew his soul that was cast off by sin. Hashem's plea, expressed through the prophet Malachi (3:7), שׁוּבוּ אֵלַי וְאָשׁוּבָה אֲלֵיכֶם אָמַר ה׳ צְבָאוֹת, *Return to Me and I will return to you, says the God of Hosts*, refers specifically to this period of the year. On Yom Kippur, Israel fulfills the first part of this call by returning to Hashem. On Succos, in the merit of our joy in observing the *mitzvos* of *succah* and the Four Species, Hashem in turn returns to us. On Succos, the sensitive Jew feels that his soul, his unique capacity for spiritual growth, has once again become his own.

In the prayer we recite before taking the Four Species, we ask to know how we will, so to speak, "interface" with Hashem by performing that *mitzvah*. This is a reference to our renewed awareness of our souls, our unique spiritual capacities. When the Torah says, וּלְקַחְתֶּם לָכֶם, *You are to take for yourselves*, it reminds us how great is our capacity for good, and arouses our ability to find ourselves — to rediscover our souls on Succos. (5657)

◆§ Lulav: Cherishing the Truly Important

The *lulav* teaches the Jew to recognize and appreciate what is truly significant and to avoid being misled by superficial appearances even of blessings. Instead we are urged to seek out the hidden potential in everything to be used for the service of Hashem. The following essay discusses how the *lulav* offers this message.

The *lulav* is made up of two words לוֹ לֵב, *to him [i.e. to Israel] is the heart*. We take the *lulav* to demonstrate our ability to get to the heart of a matter, to understand its true signficance. The *Zohar* (*Parashas*

Pinchas) actually compares Israel to a human heart because of this ability to filter out everything but the truly significant. Material achievement, power, fame, wealth, outer appearances, none of these matter.

Our greatest wish is to understand and satisfy the Divine Will and in this respect we resemble a human heart. Only blood, the purest and most refined product of the digestive system, enters the human heart. Nothing coarse, certainly no intact food, is ever admitted. So too, Israel, as the heart of the universe, accepts only the finest and purest of Hashem's bounty. Material blessings mean nothing, only the spiritual matters to us.[1]

The Torah pleads with us: Take the *lulav* and at the same time take its message! The *lulav* is לוֹ לֵב: Look for the heart of things, the essential core. Seek out the heart of Hashem's blessings, the ability they give you to utilize to the utmost your potential to serve Him.

When Hashem invited King Solomon to ask for whatever he wanted, he spurned wealth and longevity and instead asked for wisdom and a good heart. As a result, Hashem gave him not only a good heart, but also wealth and long years (cf. *I Melachim* 3:5-15). This is precisely the message of the *lulav* — appreciate what is truly significant. The Midrash explains this passage with a very fitting analogy: Solomon seeks to "marry" the king's daughter, and by doing so he acquires the key to all blessings. (This analogy, comparing spiritual matters and wisdom to the king's daughter, is discussed at greater length in the essay on *Succah*.)

The Psalmist expresses the same message in the following verse (27:4): אַחַת שָׁאַלְתִּי מֵאֵת ה׳ אוֹתָהּ אֲבַקֵּשׁ שִׁבְתִּי בְּבֵית ה׳ כָּל יְמֵי חַיַּי לַחֲזוֹת בְּנֹעַם ה׳ וּלְבַקֵּר בְּהֵיכָלוֹ, *One thing I asked of* HASHEM, *that shall I seek — that I dwell in the House of* HASHEM *all the days of my life, to behold the sweetness of* HASHEM *and to contemplate in His Sanctuary.* Appreciate what is truly important, then you will find Hashem amidst all the opulence of the world.

For the same reason we read the book of *Koheles* on Succos, in which we learn that the pleasures and comforts of the material world are subordinate to the needs of the soul and its pleasures.

---

1. *Editor's Note:* Admittedly we sometimes fall short of this ideal and allow ourselves to be mired in shallow material pursuits. This is only temporary short-sightedness, however, caused by our sins. Each of us has the ability (and obligation) to overcome it through broadening our vistas by learning Torah and by seeking the advice of genuine Torah scholars.

In summary, the message of the *lulav* is this: Learn to cherish what is genuine; value the inner significance of this world rather than its outer facade. (5654)

War and Peace

☙ Succah: Peace as a First Resort Lulav: Battle as a Last Resort

The Jewish people always prefer peaceful solutions in conflicts with its enemies, based on the Torah's commandment to seek peace always, even in the face of belligerent enemies (cf. *Devarim* 20:10).

The *succah*, described as a "Canopy of Peace," symbolizes this dream vividly. Indeed, an underlying theme of Succos is the welcoming of all of humanity under Hashem's protective wings; thus, the prophet Zechariah foretells that in the time of *Moshiach* all nations will come to Jerusalem to celebrate Succos (14:16).

Sadly, much of the time our efforts to reach out to the nations meet with failure. When they spurn our offers of peace, we are left with no choice but to do battle against the forces of evil. The *Zohar* (*Tikkun* 13) suggests that the Four Species are our weapons against our enemies.

Thus the two *mitzvos* of Succos — dwelling in the *succah* and taking the Four Species, represent these two approaches to conflict. If the peace offensive of the *succah*, the "Canopy of Peace," fails, then we are prepared to do battle with our "weapons," the Four Species.

The Psalmist expresses these two sentiments very succintly (120:6): אֲנִי שָׁלוֹם וְכִי אֲדַבֵּר הֵמָּה לַמִּלְחָמָה, *I am peace — but when I speak, they are for war*. When our attempts to speak of peace with our foes fall on deaf ears, we have no choice but to prepare for battle.

Elsewhere the Psalmist presents the same concepts in a beautiful allegory (149:5-6): יַעְלְזוּ חֲסִידִים בְּכָבוֹד יְרַנְּנוּ עַל מִשְׁכְּבוֹתָם: רוֹמְמוֹת אֵל בִּגְרוֹנָם וְחֶרֶב פִּיפִיּוֹת בְּיָדָם, *The righteous rejoice in honor, let them sing joyously upon their beds. The lofty praises of God are in their throats, while a double-edged sword is in their hand.*

Let us paraphrase these verses as they relate to the *succah* and the Four Species: The righteous rejoice in the *succah*, which commemorates the Clouds of Honor. They will praise God while lying on their beds, because even in their sleep they observe the *mitzvah* of dwelling in the *succah*, the only *mitzvah* which can be performed while asleep. Praises of God are in their throats, as they joyously sing *Hallel* on Succos; and the double-edged sword of the *lulav* and the other species is in their hands to defend themselves, after all attempts at peace have failed. (5653)

◆§ Succah: Bringing Israel to Hashem Four Species: Bring Hashem to Israel

The *Zohar* (*Vayikra* 320a) describes Moshe as Hashem's "best man" (שׁוֹשְׁבִינָא, representative or spokesman) because of his role in transmitting the Torah to Israel. Aaron is called the "best man" of the Matron, Israel, because he brought them close to Hashem through his relentless pursuit of peace.[1]

These roles of Moshe and Aaron can also be seen as parallels of the meaning of *succah* and the Four Species. The Talmud calls the *succah* Hashem's home (*Succah* 9a), a theme discussed at length in the essay on *Succah*. Bringing Israel into Hashem's "abode," the *succah*, is analagous to Aaron's role as peacemaker. On the other hand waving the *lulav* and its companion species heavenwards, we bring Hashem's Presence into our earthly lives. The opening words of the Torah's description of the *lulav*, "take for yourselves," suggest that when we wave these species, we give Hashem a part in our lives, analagous to the role of Moshe.

The following Midrash sheds light on the message of the Four Species: פְּרִי עֵץ הָדָר זֶה הקב״ה כַּפּוֹת תְּמָרִים זֶה הקב״ה דָּבָר אַחֵר פְּרִי עֵץ הָדָר אֵלּוּ יִשְׂרָאֵל כַּפּוֹת תְּמָרִים אֵלּוּ יִשְׂרָאֵל, *"The fruit of the citrus tree" refers to the Holy One, Blessed is He; "the branch of a date-palm" refers to Hashem. Another interpretation: "The fruit of the citrus tree" refers to Israel; "the branch of a date-palm" refers to Israel* (*Yalkut Shimoni* 651). By identifying the Four Species with both Hashem and Israel, the

1. The special roles of Moshe and Aaron are described at greater length in the essay on the *Succah*.

Midrash depicts an inexorable bond that exists between Hashem and Israel.

Evidently, the unique characteristics of the Four Species can be found both in heaven and on earth. In heaven, they apply only to Hashem, since no angel can manifest these characteristics, just as no people on earth possesses them but Israel. The fact that only Hashem in heaven and the Jewish people on earth can fulfill the potential of the Four Species attests to the extraordinary bond between Hashem and Israel. As Moshe says (*Devarim* 32:9), כִּי חֵלֶק ה׳ עַמּוֹ, "Hashem's portion is His people."

(5653)

◆§ Remembering the Beis HaMikdash: Taking the Four Species for an Entire Week

In the *Beis HaMikdash* the Four Species were taken every day of Succos. Outside the *Beis HaMikdash* (or outside Jerusalem, according to one opinion), they were taken only on the first day of Succos. After the *Beis HaMikdash* was destroyed, Rabban Yochanan ben Zakkai instituted the custom of taking the Four Species during the entire week of Succos everywhere to commemorate the practice in the *Beis HaMikdash* (*Succah* 41a).

To better understand this decree, let us consider this *mitzvah* in the light of the three fundamental dimensions of Jewish life: space, time, and soul. In the hierarchy of locations, the *Beis HaMikdash* was clearly the most important place in the world. The Festivals were the most prominent times of the year, and the Jewish soul, especially in its inherent yearning for sanctity and closeness to Hashem, was the epitome of the human dimension.

Now, the Torah says (*Devarim* 19:15), "By the word of two witnesses the affair shall stand [be judged]." Any two of the three variables described above enables the Four Species to link Hashem to Israel. On the first day of Succos, the holiness of the day and the always precious Jewish soul combine to elicit the full effect of the Four Species. Similarly, all week long in the *Beis HaMikdash*, the location and the Jewish soul together drew out the full power of the Four Species.

By extending the *mitzvah* of the Four Species to a full week, Rabban Yochanan ben Zakkai was teaching a message to all Jews after the destruction of the *Beis HaMikdash*, including our generation: When we long to perform the *mitzvah* in the rebuilt *Beis HaMikdash*, it is as if we had actually done it there. The strength of our desire alone allows us to feel even today the effect this *mitzvah* had on the Jewish soul in the *Beis HaMikdash*. Indeed, Rabban Yochanan ben Zakkai's decree was not merely a *halachic* rule about the requirement to take the *lulav*, it was an edict for all later generations that the effect of the *lulav* — accomplished in one day out of Jerusalem at the time of the *Beis HaMikdash* — would still continue in the period of exile, even though now it would take a full week to be achieved.

The Talmud relates that Rabban Yochanan ben Zakkai concluded that there was a need to establish a remembrance of the *Beis HaMikdash* from a verse in Yirmiyahu (30:17), צִיּוֹן הִיא דֹּרֵשׁ אֵין לָהּ, *Zion has no one seeking her*. This implies that we must always seek to remember the *Beis HaMikdash*. Really this means that by "seeking" the *Beis HaMikdash*, we can achieve the same spiritual fulfillment that the *Beis HaMikdash* itself delivered.

In another verse Yirmiyahu bemoans (*Eichah* 5:15), נֶהְפַּךְ לְאֵבֶל מְחוֹלֵנוּ, *Our dancing has been transformed into mourning*. The prophet's plaintive cry can also be interpreted in a more positive sense: Our mourning over the destruction of the *Beis HaMikdash* has the same effect on our souls that our rejoicing did while it stood.

Although our mourning allows us to still feel the effect of the *Beis HaMikdash* today, another factor plays an even greater role in allowing its spirit to continue in the present era. Our forefathers in the *Beis HaMikdash* were blessed with ideal spiritual conditions: the ideal place, the best time of the year, Succos, and the sacred Jewish soul. With great foresight, they combined these three elements to leave a legacy so that future generations, bereft of Hashem's glorious abode could still derive maximum benefit from the *lulav* and the festival. They had the magnanimity to lay a sturdy spiritual foundation for their less fortunate descendants. Thus now, even though the ideal place, time and soul no longer exist, nonetheless the Jew can still feel some of the aura of the *Beis HaMikdash*. (5652)

◆§ Four Species: A Means of Helping the Jewish People Absorb the Succah's Message

The *succah* represents the supernatural Divine Clouds, whose true meaning is completely beyond the grasp of the ordinary Jew. While the Divine Clouds no longer exist, in the *succah* we experience an inkling of the glory and protection our forefathers enjoyed in the Wilderness. More than simply believing that the Divine Clouds once happened in a particular historical period, we can feel in our times the same sense of Divine protection that our forefathers once enjoyed. As the Torah itself states (*Vayikra* 23:43) לְמַעַן יֵדְעוּ דֹרֹתֵיכֶם כִּי בַסֻּכּוֹת הוֹשַׁבְתִּי אֶת־בְּנֵי יִשְׂרָאֵל, *in order that your generations know that I placed the Children of Israel in succos.*

How can we grasp the message of the *succah*, its supernatural ambiance? Only through the catalyst of the *lulav*, which, pointed towards heaven by ordinary mortals, acts as a conduit for the message of the *succah*. It represents an otherworldly lifestyle that can be appreciated by even the orphaned, exiled but nonetheless yearning souls of our generation. This is demonstrated by the Torah's first remarks regarding the Four Species — (*Vayikra* 23:40) וּלְקַחְתֶּם לָכֶם, *And you shall take for yourselves*. This refers not only to taking the *lulav* in one's hand but also to absorbing the message of the *succah*. The variety of species utilized in conjunction with the *lulav*, representing various personalities, (as described previously) underscores that diverse individuals absorb the message of the *succah* (and all of Torah) differently. Yet, regardless of their unequal capacities for assimilating the essence of *succah* and its theme of Divine protection it pertains to all Jews.

(5636, 5649)

Lulav

Succah: Hashem's Generosity Lulav: Israel's Own Merit

Israel has benefited from Hashem's largesse and bounty since the beginning of its history. Sometimes this has been the result of our good deeds; other times Hashem gives us undeserved gifts, showering us with blessings far beyond what we earn through our merits. In the following verse, the Psalmist makes this distinction between outright grants of Divine charity and deserved favors (85:8): הַרְאֵנוּ ה׳ חַסְדֶּךָ וְיֶשְׁעֲךָ תִּתֶּן־לָנוּ, *Show us Your kindness, HASHEM, and give us Your Salvation.*

The opening clause, *Show us your kindness,* alludes to the kindness shown to Abraham (who, for example, was saved from the burning furnace of Ur Kasdim) and also to the Divine Cloud, a kindness that we commemorate in the *succah.* The second clause, a request for Hashem's salvation, implies that Israel merits this exchange.[1]

While the *succah* symbolizes Hashem's kindness to Israel (i.e. the Divine Cloud), the *lulav* symbolizes Israel's efforts to be worthy of Hashem's kindness. The spectacle of a congregation of Jews waving the *lulav* is a victory parade, celebrating our survival and vindication in judgment on Rosh Hashanah and Yom Kippur. Thus, *Give us your salvation* is a plea that Hashem spare the Jewish people on the High Holy Days.

The theme of deserving Hashem's kindness can help us understand the relationship between the commandment to take the *lulav* and Hashem's command to take an *eizov* (hyssop) branch on the night before the Exodus from Egypt. (The Jews were commanded to dip the *eizov* in the blood of the *Korban Pesach* (Paschal Lamb) and with this to make a sign on their doorposts so that the Angel of Death would pass over Jewish homes when he came to kill the Egyptian first born.)[2]

One important distinction exists between the *eizov* and the *lulav.* Whereas we are told merely to *take* the *eizov,* concerning the *lulav* the Torah says וּלְקַחְתֶּם לָכֶם, *take* **for yourselves,** implying that our taking is in our merit.

This comparison shows the great progress made by the Jewish people. At the time of the Exodus, Israel was not deserving of Hashem's kindness, as we find in the description of the prophet Yechezkel (16:7),וְאַתְּ עֵרֹם וְעֶרְיָה, *and you were naked and barren* (we may understand *naked* to mean that the Jews lacked merit). Thus, on Pesach,

1. We see this from Isaac's blessing to Jacob, who was disguised as Esau (*Bereishis* 27:28), וְיִתֶּן־לְךָ הָאֱלֹהִים מִטַּל הַשָּׁמַיִם וּמִשְׁמַנֵּי הָאָרֶץ, *May HASHEM give you from the dew of heaven and from the bounty of the earth. Rashi* comments that Isaac intended for the blessing to be fulfilled only if Esau and his descendants were to merit it. This was the character of Isaac — strict justice. Divine salvation is given only to those who deserve it. (In reality, even the ability of Israel to deserve Divine favors is itself an act of Divine charity. Thus the Psalmist asks that *Hashem* grant us salvation even though on the surface it seems that we have to merit it.)

2. The Torah uses the same word וּלְקַחְתֶּם, *and you shall take*, in reference to both the *lulav* and the *eizov* (see *Shemos* 12:22 and *Vayikra* 23:40).

we commemorate Hashem's outpouring of love for us, despite our lack of merit.

The taking of the *lulav* on Succos, however, emphasizes Israel's merit. In the aftermath of the repentance of Rosh Hashanah and Yom Kippur, Jewry has earned Hashem's kindness. In fact, the transition from Pesach to Succos can be perceived as an advancement from taking the lowly *eizov* (symbolizing our lack of merit) to the exalted level of the Four Species, well deserved by the newly rededicated Israel. The liberation of Pesach, dependent on Divine kindness, is preparation for Succos, which is enjoyed by Israel because of its own merits. As the Psalmist sings (113:7-8), מְקִימִי מֵעָפָר דָּל מֵאַשְׁפֹּת יָרִים אֶבְיוֹן לְהוֹשִׁיבִי עִם־נְדִיבִים, *He raises the needy [i.e. the undeserving] from the dust, from the trash heaps He lifts the destitute. To seat them with nobles.* On Pesach we were spiritually impoverished, but on Succos we sit with princes.

(5654, 5650)

Aravah — Hoshana Rabbah's Symbol

Introduction

וּלְקַחְתֶּם לָכֶם בַּיּוֹם הָרִאשׁוֹן פְּרִי עֵץ הָדָר כַּפֹּת תְּמָרִים וַעֲנַף עֵץ־עָבֹת וְעַרְבֵי־נָחַל

On the first day you are to take for yourselves the fruit of a citron tree, the branches of date palms, twigs of a plaited tree, and brook willows (*Vayikra* 23:40).

In the previous essay, we discussed the general theme and the rich symbolism of the Four Species. Now we will focus specifically on the fourth of the Species, the *aravah* (willow).

While the *Beis HaMikdash* stood, the *aravah* played a dual role in the services of Succos. On the one hand, as one of the Four Species, it was taken together with them. But it also had a separate role, as we see from the *Mishnah* (*Succah* 4:15), *Every day [the Priests] would make one circuit around the Altar [while holding only the aravah] and on that day [the seventh day of Succos] they made seven circuits.* Since the destruction of the *Beis HaMikdash,* the *aravah* is taken by itself only on the seventh day. Currently, the Four Species are held while making circuits around the *bimah,* which substitutes for the Altar of the *Beis HaMikdash.* On the seventh day, the *aravah* is taken by itself, after completing the circuits with all the Species. This day, which occupies a unique role in Jewish thought, is called *Hoshana Rabbah* — the day of the Great Salvation.

The following essay will address a number of basic questions, including: What does the *aravah* signify — both alone and as a part of the Four Species? What is the significance of *Hoshana Rabbah* and why does the *aravah* play so prominent a role in that day's services? Most profoundly, what is the message of the *aravah* and *Hoshana Rabbah* for today's Jew?

◆§ Hope for the Contemporary Jew

Yalkut Shimoni (*Emor* 651), discusses the Four Species, though not specifically the *aravah.* From this discussion, we can gain a powerful insight into the message of the *aravah* and its pertinence to each individual.

The *Yalkut* begins by citing a passage in *Tehillim* (102:18-19): פָּנָה אֶל־תְּפִלַּת הָעַרְעָר וְלֹא־בָזָה אֶת־תְּפִלָּתָם — *He [HASHEM] turned to the prayer of the desolate and has not despised their prayer.*

The Midrash cites the interpretation of Rabbi Yitzchak that this verse refers to those generations [i.e our] that no longer have a Jewish king, a prophet, a High Priest, or the *Urim V'Tumim* — precious stones — containing the names of the Twelve Tribes, which would light up to reveal a Divine message of importance to the Jewish people. All we have is prayer.

The Midrash continues: תִּכָּתֵב זֹאת לְדוֹר אַחֲרוֹן וְעַם נִבְרָא יְהַלֶּל־יָהּ, *This should be written for the final generation* [referring to our times that are leaning towards spiritual death] *and the nation that is created will praise God,* because Hashem will create them anew.

This Midrash reveals Hashem's special compassion for today's Jew, who lacks the direct link to Hashem provided by a High Priest, the *Urim V'Tumim* or a Jewish King. For him, prayer assumes an extraordinary role that replaces all the institutions that previous generations enjoyed.

In previous essays, we have seen that the Sages taught that each of the Four Species symbolizes a different kind of Jew. We may then ask which species best represents the contemporary Jew referred to in our Midrash? Surely the *aravah*, described by the Midrash as tasteless and lacking fragrance, is an appropriate symbol for today's Jew, who also lacks the "taste" and "fragrance" — the religious sophistication and closeness to Hashem — of his counterpart during the time of the *Beis HaMikdash*. True, even when the *Beis HaMikdash* stood, the *aravah* was taken by itself, as well as part of the Four Species. But, when the Jews of those times did take it alone — offering hope even for the Jew bereft of taste or fragrance — they had no need to do so for themselves, since they enjoyed the benefits of having a Priest, a King and the other blessings of life in the time of the *Beis HaMikdash*. Rather, they performed the service of the *aravah*, circling the Altar with it, so that a small ray of the spiritual "light" of the *Beis HaMikdash*, would filter down to our own "*aravah*-like" generation.

From where did those idealists derive such foresight? How did they recognize the urgent necessity of providing for us? The source of their idealism was the Four Species themselves. The stately *lulav* and the fragrant *esrog*, which symbolize learned and devout Jews, are taken together with the *aravah*, a plant without taste and fragrance. This indicated to them that the "haves" — Jews of "fragrance" and "taste," those blessed with Torah knowledge and the opportunity to perform *mitzvos* — should attach themselves to the "have-nots," their deprived brethren who are not privileged to realize their full potential in Torah and *mitzvos*.

If the fortunate of one generation can reach out and extend their spiritual umbrella over their "poorer" compatriots, it is reasonable to assume that such linkage among Jews can be extended even from generation to generation. The *aravah* could be taken alone in the *Beis HaMikdash*, even though its message of hope for barren Jews had little meaning for the spiritually "wealthy" Jew of those days, since that message would be of enormous benefit to future generations.

Thus, our forefathers had us in mind when they took the solitary *aravah*. Surely, they prayed for us as well, just as we pray for the spiritual well-being of our descendants. The Psalmist alluded to the prayers of past generations for us in the verse (102:18): פָּנָה אֶל־תְּפִלַּת

הָעַרְעָר וְלֹא־בָזָה אֶת־תְּפִלָּתָם, *He turned to the prayer of the desolate and has not despised their prayer.*

It is worth noting that at the end of the verse the word תְּפִלָּתָם, *THEIR prayer*, is used, while at the beginning the Psalmist said תְּפִלַּת הָעַרְעָר, *THE prayer of the desolate.* The plural form *their* alludes to the prayers of past generations on our behalf. The Jew of today survives not only in the merit of his own prayer, but also because of the *aravah* taken during Temple times — and the prayers of previous generations for our spiritual well-being.[1]

We say in the daily prayer service, וּמְקַבְּלִין דֵּין מִן דֵּין, *They accept from each other.* Literally, this recounts how the angels on high grant each other permission to praise Hashem. Homiletically, however, we may understand this fragment as a reference to the relationship among generations: Every generation receives from the past: We are nurtured by the legacy of our forebears and derive strength from our parents, and in turn we leave a legacy for the future.[2] (5665)

◆§ In Search of the Aravah-Like Jew? The Superficial Jew

What is the nature of the "*aravah*-like Jew? Such an individual seems so bereft of ties to his traditions that, unlike the ordinary *aravah* which is taken on all the days of Succos together with the other Four Species (suggesting a bond with other Jews), he stands alone, having severed his links with his fellow-Jews.

Our generation has been likened to the singular, lonely *aravah.* Why is this? Has our generation drifted so far as to be totally barren of Torah and *mitzvos*, that it deserves to be called the solitary *aravah*?

Surely the Midrash did not mean to suggest that all Jews would cease to observe *mitzvos*, or that they would abandon the study of Torah. On the contrary, the Talmud relates (*Eruvin* 19b) that every Jew is laden with *mitzvos* like a pomegranate (which according to tradition has 613 seeds corresponding to the 613 *mitzvos*).

---

1. We may further suggest that the word "prayer" is written in the singular to indicate that the Jews of those generations were united in their prayers for future generations, as if it were only one *prayer*.

2. Torah tradition sees the relationship of later generations to earlier generations "as a midget perched on a giant." While the giant is undoubtedly taller, the midget perched on his shoulders stands at a higher point. Likewise, later generations stand on the merits and accomplishments of their ancestors.

Who, then, is meant by the comparison to the solitary, barren, *aravah*? It is the Jew who observes *mitzvos* — but does so mechanically. For him, performance of *mitzvos* has become an automatic, "robot-like" process, devoid of feeling or emotion, what the prophet calls (*Yeshayahu* 29:13) מִצְוַת אֲנָשִׁים מְלֻמָּדָה, *a commandment of men learned by rote*. Such a person observes Torah and *mitzvos* with only a superficial commitment, with little perception of their inner meaning, and their connection to Hashem's will.

The custom of taking the *aravah* alone in the Temple is based on oral tradition, first transmitted to Moshe at Sinai (*Succah* 44a). The custom of taking the *aravah* on *Hoshana Rabbah*, the seventh day of Succos,however, was adopted by the Jewish people at the behest of the prophets, Haggai, Zechariah, and Malachi, (מִנְהָג נְבִיאִים).

It is entirely appropriate that the service of the *aravah* in contemporary times has its origin in a "custom." The criticism has been offered that Torah and *mitzvos* has evolved in our generation into a rote-like exercise, observed only because it is traditional to do so rather than out of any appreciation of its real meaning. It is appropriate, therefore, that the beautiful service of the *aravah* should have originated as a "custom," a human innovation encouraged by the prophets, to counteract the formal, "rote-like" observance of *mitzvos*.

How can the *aravah*-like Jew shed the superficial and ritualistic quality of his performance of *mitzvos* and return to his heritage? Surely, the mere act of clutching the *aravah* on *Hoshana Rabbah* is not by itself sufficient.

For one thing, the sheer will and desire to attain the high standards of past generations provide a starting point. Also, by emulating in some manner the behavior and actions of our forefathers, we can hope to reach a higher level. If Jews in the time of the *Beis HaMikdash* took the *aravah* by itself for all seven days of the festival based on Sinaitic tradition, we can at least follow that custom once, on *Hoshana Rabbah*.

The process of desiring to emulate and then actually emulating the standards of past generations, of attaining in part what our forefathers did so well, might seem no more than an ostentatious surface gesture. In reality, though, it can reap rich dividends. Outward actions (חִיצוֹנִיוּת) to emulate the *mitzvah* observance of past generations — in spite of our knowledge that we cannot possibly measure up to their standards — eventually lead to inner changes (פְּנִימִיוּת) as well. One who attempts to emulate luminaries of past generations including the Patriarchs will succeed in his spiritual goals. Slowly but surely, he will realize his dreams and aspirations and he will raise himself closer to the spiritual heights of the past. By yearning for increased spirituality and taking measures to achieve that aim, we actually can succeed in improving ourselves.[1]

However a caveat is in order: we must know our own limitations and shortcomings. While yearning to attain the level of past generations, we must also be aware of our current situation. The *halachah* specifies that a willow-like plant known as *tzaftzafa* may not be substituted for the *aravah* because it grows on mountains (*Succah* 34a). The *aravah*, on the other hand, thrives near water, and is therefore called in the Torah עַרְבֵי נָחַל, *willow of the brook.* (Even though willows grown in any location are acceptable, only species typically found near a brook may be used for the *mitzvah* of *aravah.*)

Mountain-grown *tzaftzafa*, on the other hand, suggests an exaggerated sense of self-worth, an overblown ego soaring into the mountains, and is therefore unacceptable. Instead, the simple *aravah* from the lowly riverbank is used, since it knows its station and recognizes its need to draw itself close to the other species, representing righteous and learned Jews. This is the personality type that will eventually attain lofty goals of personal growth, of connection with the deeds of past generations.

(*5665*)

◆§ The Uncommitted Jew

Thus every Succos brings a message of hope for the Jew whose observance of *mitzvos* is mechanical and robot-like, the Jew who is committed but not connected. Still, is there really hope for our brothers whose links are completely cut, who no longer observe *mitzvos* at all? Does the *aravah* hold out any promise for them as well?

After Yom Kippur, hope exists even for the unrepentant sinner, as we can see from a careful examination of the Midrash's description of the *aravah*. The *aravah* is described as lacking taste and fragrance, representing the Jew who lacks Torah knowledge and does not observe *mitzvos*.. However, his errors are errors of omission, the result of *mitzvos* not performed and Torah not studied. It cannot be said that such and in-

---

1. Our Sages taught "One is obligated to say 'when will my actions *reach* those of my forefathers?' " This is of course an impossibility. One's actions can, at most, barely touch the level of his forefathers. Yet if he "shoots for the stars" he will at least begin to attain his personal potential.

dividual has committed sins, that he has taken active steps to sin. Even if he had, it is in the power of *Yom Kippur* that such sins be swept away.

The "*aravah*-Jew" starts with a clean slate every *Succos* — even though he has performed no *mitzvos* and has not studied Torah, his past sins were expunged on Yom Kippur. This new start permits him to pray for Divine help, for salvation (יְשׁוּעָה) every Succos. He clutches the Four Species all through Succos and on *Hoshana Rabbah*, after the regular services, he holds the *aravah* and recites the special prayers for Divine salvation called *Hoshanos*. Let us turn now to consider the nature of these special prayers. (5663)

◆§ Hoshanos: Prayers for Divine Salvation — Relentless Pursuit of Evil

Every day of Succos we recite *Hoshana* prayers (so called because they begin with the word *Hoshana*) while circling the *bimah*. While these prayers are not explicitly mentioned in the Talmud, there exist many allusions to them in the Torah itself.

The following passage from *Parashas Ki Seitzei* (*Devarim* 22:25-27) concerning the assault of a betrothed girl may also be the conceptual basis for the *Hoshana* services: וְאִם־בַּשָּׂדֶה יִמְצָא הָאִישׁ אֶת הַנַּעֲרָ הַמְאֹרָשָׂה. . .וּמֵת הָאִישׁ אֲשֶׁר־שָׁכַב עִמָּהּ לְבַדּוֹ: וְלַנַּעֲרָ לֹא־תַעֲשֶׂה דָבָר. . .כִּי בַשָּׂדֶה מְצָאָהּ צָעֲקָה הַנַּעֲרָ הַמְאֹרָשָׂה וְאֵין מוֹשִׁיעַ לָהּ — *If the man [the assailant] find the betrothed girl in the field . . . only the man who lay with her shall die but nothing [i.e., no punishment] shall be done to the girl. For he found her in the field — the betrothed girl screamed [for help] and there was no one to help her.*

The hapless girl was taken against her will. She received no assistance in resisting and consequently is blameless. The Talmud (*Sanhedrin* 73a) deduces from this passage that if it is possible to prevent the assault, everyone in a position to do so is required to assist her, even by killing the would-be assailant if necessary.

Allegorically, the girl lying helpless in the field represents, in a sense, Israel, which wanders aimlessly all year in the wide-open world devoid of Torah's moral standards. In "the field" — outside the realm of Judaism — there is much moral assault, much sinning and no saviors. No one can help Israel if it strays from the Torah. However, every year on Yom Kippur, Jewish hearts and souls are purified. They forsake the field and return to their Creator.

Then, in the days following Yom Kippur, the Jewish people are able to contend with the forces of evil that pursue them. The forces of evil (whether in the form of the *yetzer hara* tempting to sin, or in the garb of nations that oppress the Jewish people) are still in hot pursuit. Now, however, we have assistance — Hashem Himself pursues the pursuer, frontally attacking the forces of evil.

The purpose of the *Hoshana* prayer is quite simple. We invoke our Helper above and plead with Him to pursue and eliminate all those evil forces that threaten Israel, that wish to stifle the Jewish people's quest for growth.

Screaming for help and pleading for Divine assistance pays off, as was conclusively demonstrated during one of Israel's most trying periods. It is well known than the First Temple was destroyed largely because of the Jewish people's affinity for idol worship (*Yoma* 9b). After seventy years of captivity in Babylon, part of the exiled community returned to *Eretz Yisrael*. Their leaders sought some guarantee that the same dreaded sin of idolatry would not recur. How could they be assured that the Second Temple (whose construction had already started) would not fall prey to the same offense? Their pleas for Divine assistance were answered. The Talmud (*Yoma* 69b) relates that as a result of their prayers for Divine assistance, Hashem agreed to destroy forever the temptation to worship idols. Since then, Jews have not known the urge to worship molten images — an urge which had been uncontrollable in many cases — because our forefathers cried and pleaded on behalf of their descendants.

We too, every Succos,stand newly purified and morally cleansed after Yom Kippur. We plead in the *Hoshana* prayer for an end to all pursuers of the Jewish people. On Yom Kippur we forsook the "wide open field," the world of temptation, of removal from Torah. We came back to Hashem's home and hearth. Now on Succos we plead for His continued assistance in eliminating all evil forces. Thus we plead "*Hoshana* — Save us!" (5663)

◆§ The Human Mouth: Power of Prayer

As we have stated in previous segments, the *aravah*, lacking taste and fragrance, represents the Jew devoid of Torah knowledge or *mitzvah* observance. The analogy has been drawn between such an *aravah*-like existence and contemporary generations. It is reassuring that the *aravah* can be taken by itself on Succos, separated from its association with the other species, which represent more devout and learned Jews. We are given the message that hope exists even for our generations.

The question remains, however, why do Jews totally lacking in Torah and *mitzvos* deserve to be saved every Succos? Do they merit the hope symbolized by the *aravah*? (It was suggested above that the prayers of past generations or the desire of the *aravah*-like Jew to emulate his sainted ancestors may help him as well. In the following discussion we will pursue a somewhat different approach.)

It may be asked, why save the *aravah*-like Jew at all? Perhaps he is saved in the merit of his own prayers — not only those of past generations. The very shape of the *aravah*, which resembles human lips curved to a point on both sides, reminds us of the power of prayer. Taking the solitary *aravah*, with its mouth-like shape, suggests pointedly that even today's Jew, lacking the formal trappings of King and High Priest and lax in his observance, can still accomplish a great deal through the prayers he can offer with his mouth.

The theme of the power of prayer can be extended even further to suggest that, in many respects, the spirit, the true inner meaning of the *Beis HaMikdash* lives on — even though the edifice itself is in ruins. The offerings that were brought in the *Beis HaMikdash* have been defunct since its destruction. Yet their true intent — coming closer to Hashem — lives on through prayer. All of us, and especially the *aravah*-like Jew, are deprived of the outer trappings of Judaism, but we retain at least the power of the Jewish mouth to replicate through prayer what offerings once accomplished.

In addition to prayer, Torah study, also verbally expressed, can take the place of the offerings and service of the *Beis HaMikdash*.

The Talmud (*Shabbos* 31a) relates a parable that powerfully illustrates the relationship between the external trappings of Judaism (e.g. the *Beis HaMikdash*) — important as they are — and the inner intent of *mitzvos*. A King decided to "double-lock" his most valuable possessions, so that two sets of keys would be required to open the vault. Judaism's most treasured possession is its closeness to Hashem. To arrive at this treasure, two "keys" are required — an outer and an inner one. The outer "keys," fear of Hashem, were best attained when Hashem's Presence was perceived by everyone, when the *Beis HaMikdash* and the service of the offerings were in existence. No place on earth was so conducive to instilling fear of Hashem as Jerusalem during the time of the *Beis HaMikdash*. As the Psalmist sings (118:20), זֶה־הַשַּׁעַר לַה׳, *This [i.e. the Beis HaMikdash) is the gate to Hashem.* In fact, the very name Jerusalem is partially derived from the Hebrew word for fear (יִרְאָה) (*Yalkut Shimoni*, 102).

Even now, however, with Jerusalem's glory defiled and the *Beis HaMikdash* in ruins, without the outer keys, Jews can still function by emphasizing the inner keys — Torah study and prayer. As the prophet Hoshea proclaims(14:3), וּנְשַׁלְּמָה פָרִים שְׂפָתֵינוּ, *Our lips will compensate for the bulls [of offerings].*

The ability to come close to Hashem by utilizing the inner keys of Torah study and prayer is granted only to the Jewish people. The rest of mankind (i.e., the Gentile world) suffered a far more grievous loss with the destruction of the *Beis HaMikdash* than Israel did. While the *Beis HaMikdash* stood, Israel offered seventy bulls every Succos, corresponding to the seventy basic cultures of the Gentile world. With the destruction of the *Beis HaMikdash,* these offerings ceased and no substitutes are available to the Nations, such as Torah study or prayer, to compensate for their loss. As the Talmud notes (*Succah* 55b), the greatest victim of the destruction of the *Beis HaMikdash* was the rest of humankind. Lacking the option of substituting the deeper meaning of the *Beis HaMikdash* (i.e. Torah study and prayer) for outer trappings (offerings), the non-Jewish world has never recovered from the ruin of the *Beis HaMikdash.* The Talmud (ibid.) suggests that humankind has never even fully comprehended what the loss of the *Beis HaMikdash* entailed for them. Without offerings, lacking Torah or prayer, they have suffered an irreparable blow.[1]

Israel, however, subsists on the inner keys of Torah and prayer, but is still not content. As the Psalmist sings (118:19), פִּתְחוּ־לִי שַׁעֲרֵי־צֶדֶק אָבֹא־בָם אוֹדֶה יָהּ — *Open for me the gates of righteousness; I will enter them to praise God.*

The Jew is ready to burst forth in song. The inner keys — Torah and prayer — have been prepared. The outer gate, however, is still locked. Undoubtedly, the path of righteousness is ideally attained in the *Beis*

1. This sweeping statement merits a longer discussion than is possible in the scope of this work. On the basis of *Proverbs* (28:9) we may suggest that while the prayers of Gentiles are heard by Hashem, since they lack the merit of the study of Torah or the services of the *Beis HaMikdash* their impact is limited.

HaMikdash through the sacrificial rite. "Open for us," King David pleads, "the outer gate — as well as the inner ones — so that I may praise Hashem." (5662)

⊲§ Seeking Hashem / Yearning for Hashem

What merit is there to the lowly *aravah* and its human counterpart, the spiritually impoverished Jew, (apart from those things mentioned in previous essays)?

The *aravah*-like Jew has one saving grace: he eagerly anticipates Divine help. He anxiously awaits hearing anything, even a fragment of Hashem's Torah. He may not comprehend all the Torah's teachings and his observance may not be on a high level, but his excitement, his anticipation and enthusiasm for Torah, knows no bounds. The willow is rooted by the water, growing next to a brook, eager to draw every drop of moisture into its roots. Torah is frequently compared to water (see *Taanis* 7a). The willow-like human, though he lacks Torah knowledge, eagerly seeks out the Torah and thirsts for Torah knowledge. In fact, the Torah's name for the willow, עַרְבֵי נָחַל, *willows of the brook*, is itself a veiled reference to the Jew seeking out Hashem. The word נָחַל, *brook*, is an acronym for the phrase (*Tehillim* 33:20) נַפְשֵׁנוּ חִכְּתָה לַה׳, *Our soul awaits* HASHEM.

However, enthusiasm does not come overnight. It starts with a faint yearning for closeness to Hashem and His Torah, and grows until it becomes an overwhelming enthusiasm, an unquenchable craving for Hashem's Torah. Every Succos the Jew is showered with blessings (a theme that will be developed more extensively in the section on *Shemini Atzeres*). These blessings do not all come at once — one has to deserve Hashem's bounty — and as a Jew increases his desire and enthusiasm for Torah, Hashem, in turn, increases the flow of His blessings.

Many Biblical verses and Rabbinical sayings point out Israel's thirst for spirituality — regardless of an individual's level of knowledge or observance.

For example, the prophet Isaiah urges the thirsty (55:1), הוֹי כָּל־צָמֵא לְכוּ לַמַּיִם, *All you thirsty, go to the water.* The Midrash (*Yalkut Isaiah* 480) interprets this as a reference to Israel's incessant and insatiable desire for Torah. King Solomon (*Mishlei* 30:16) speaks of אֶרֶץ לֹא־שָׂבְעָה מַּיִם, *a land never satiated with water,* because the soil can never absorb enough moisture. This is a reference to the Jewish people (whom the prophet Malachi describes (3:12) as אֶרֶץ חֵפֶץ, *a desirable land*), who are never content with their share of Torah, just as the soil is never saturated with water.

Similarly, Jacob gave Joseph the blessing (*Bereishis* 48:16) that his children should live as fish in the midst of the earth. This blessing underscores the same theme: Despite their aquatic environment, fish retain an unquenchable thirst for every additional drop of water. So too, the Jewish people (even if they do not fully comprehend Torah's treasures) are never content with their present state of Torah knowledge but always seek more. The greater Israel's enthusiasm for Torah — first expressed as yearning and then an unquenchable thirst — the more Hashem showers His nation with His bounty.[1] (5660)

◈ Hoshana Rabbah: A Day of Divine Favor For Those Who Lack Everything Aravah: A Species Representative of This Special Day

In previous sections, we have discussed various answers to the question of what merit the *aravah* and its human equivalent have. Now we will suggest the possibility that no merit at all may exist. In some cases, the merit of prayer, or even a sense of yearning for Hashem is not present even after the purifying aura of Yom Kippur. And yet there is hope: especially on *Hoshana Rabbah* hope exists even for such people — hope of receiving a gift of Divine favor.

In several places Hashem promised Moshe to give the gift of Divine kindness to recipients unworthy of such kindness. This is called in Hebrew מַתְּנַת חִנָּם, a free gift.

For example, Hashem told Moshe (*Shemos* 33:19), וְחַנֹּתִי אֶת־אֲשֶׁר אָחֹן, *And I will favor those whom I favor*. The Talmud (*Berachos* 7a) interprets this to mean "even if he [the recipient] is undeserving of His favor." Similarly, in asking Hashem to annul His vow not to let him enter the Promised Land, Moshe begged for Divine favor (*Devarim* 3:23). He pleaded that even if he should be denied entry on the basis of strict justice, Hashem should grant him a special gift of Divine favor

1. This is in keeping with the plea of *David Hamelech* "May Your kindness, Hashem, be upon us, just as we awaited you" (*Tehillim* 33:22).

and allow him to enter the Land. The Midrash (*Yalkut Shimoni* 395) says that Hashem showed Moshe the reward of the righteous in the World to Come and then showed him an even greater "storehouse" of Divine reward. This storehouse is reserved for those who receive reward as an act of Divine kindness even though they do not deserve it. Their greatest merit is their recognizing how undeserving they are.

Thus *Hoshana Rabbah*, the Day of the Great Salvation, derives its name from the consideration that on this day Hashem opens His treasure house of rewards even to the undeserving and saves even them, without question an exceptional spiritual feat.[1]

Upon further reflection, every Jew, whether learned or spiritually poor, needs to "tap" Hashem's storehouse of favors. True, many righteous individuals merit Divine reward. However, our actions and our good deeds are never sufficient to justify all of Hashem's kindness to us. Our good deeds and Torah would permit us to reap some, but not all, of the kindness that He bestows upon us. Eventually, every Jew needs to benefit from Hashem's eternal storehouse of Divine favor.

The double usage of the *aravah*, at times alone and at times in conjunction with the Four Species, may represent different methods of benefiting from Hashem's treasure house of reward. Taking the *aravah* alone is for the Jew who is absolutely dependent upon Divine kindness, because he lacks the merit of his own Torah and *mitzvos*. Taking the *aravah* together with the Four Species is for those people who, despite their redeeming qualities (represented by the *esrog*, *lulav* and *haddasim*), still need an extra measure of Divine kindness. (5657)

◆§ Reflections Why Hashem Chose Israel / Love of Truth

The *aravah*, which lacks fragrance or taste and represents the Jew who lacks Torah and *mitzvos*, is important in a dual sense. Firstly, it offers hope for all Jews, even those lacking basic prerequisites such as Torah and *mitzvos*. Beyond this, the fact that so barren an object can exist at all is itself a powerful statement about Hashem's selection of Israel from among the nations. Why did Hashem choose us rather than

1. *Editor's Note:* This is a resounding indication of the unconditional love that Hashem has for His children the People of Israel.

any other people? Surely, not on the basis of merit alone. If that were so, why would Hashem exude love even to Jews who have sinned?

Speaking through the prophet Yirmiyahu, Hashem gives a reason for selecting Israel in the following verse (2:21): וְאָנֹכִי נְטַעְתִּיךְ שׂוֹרֵק כֻּלֹּה זֶרַע אֱמֶת, *I have planted you as a vine, [because you are] all children of truth.*

Hashem chose us to be His children because of our ability to recognize the truth. We were selected because, like the *aravah*, we do not pretend to be what we are not. The *aravah's* appearance accurately reflects its character: It looks like a shabby willow. It does not attempt to disguise its nature with artful packaging. We were selected because, like the *aravah*, we make no attempt to mask our failings. Indeed, the *gematria* (numerical equivalent) of עֲרָבָה, *aravah* (277) is equal to that of one of the words for children, זֶרַע.

We are Hashem's children because of our love of the truth. Even the Jew who is like the *aravah*, with very little knowledge of Torah, at least realizes how little he knows, which in itself is a tribute to the power of Torah. When Hashem gave Israel the Torah, He implanted in every Jew a love of the truth, regardless of the consequences.

The verse cited above contains an allusion to this connection between Hashem's granting the Torah and our ability to discern the truth: The first word, אָנֹכִי, is the same form of the word *I* that begins the Ten Commandments. Thus the phrase *I planted you as... children of truth* is an allusion to the commandment אָנֹכִי ה׳ אֱלֹהֶיךָ, *I am Hashem, your God* (*Shemos* 20:2). The Jew's inherent sense of truth stems from Hashem's revelation at Sinai, which was shared by all Jews, regardless of their intellectual stature. The Rebbe of Lublin (one of the earliest Chassidic leaders of Poland, often called the *Chozeh* (Seer) because of his near-prophetic vision) said that a Jew can attach himself to Hashem simply by realizing that he doesn't know everything.

A quest for truth is all that is required of the Jew. This proposition sheds new light on an otherwise difficult Rabbinic saying which seems to suggest that a Jew must adopt a premeditated, calculated approach to life, planning every step ahead: כָּל הַשָּׂם אוֹרְחוֹתָיו בָּעוֹלָם הַזֶּה זוֹכֶה וְרוֹאֶה בִּישׁוּעָתוֹ שֶׁל הקב"ה — *Anyone who sets his path in this world will merit to see Hashem's salvation [in the World to Come]* (*Moed Katan* 5b, see also *Maharsha*, ibid.).

Must a Jew plan every phase of life ahead of time? In light of the above discussion, we can better appreciate this Rabbinic saying. While it is not absolutely essential to pre-calculate every step in life, it is nevertheless critical always to seek out the truth, to admit one's shortcomings, and to be aware of what one does not know. There can be no better path in life than an incessant quest for truth and a candid appraisal of one's own limitations. This is what the Talmud meant to describe with the term "path of life": a love for the truth coupled with absolute candor.

The power of the *aravah* as a symbol of the quest for truth can be demonstrated from the exalted position the "lowly" *aravah* is accorded on *Hoshana Rabbah*. On the one hand, the *aravah* is the least important of the Four Species, lacking taste and fragrance. Yet, the entire ritual of *Hoshana Rabbah* is centered around the *aravah*. (In the *Beis HaMikdash*, seven circuits were made around the Altar on *Hoshana Rabbah* while the Priests held *aravos*. Still today, most of the liturgy of that day focuses on the *aravah*.) How does the inferior *aravah* rise to such a superior status? Solely because it symbolizes the quest for absolute truth.

But what of the Jew who lacks even that basic prerequisite and no longer cares to seek out the truth? Is there hope on *Hoshana Rabbah* for the inveterate sinner who has totally abandoned his Jewish moorings? If the *aravah* plays so prominent a role despite its total lack of status, might this not suggest that Hashem selected Israel despite our massive shortcomings, because of his love for us and because of our forefathers' acceptance of the Torah at Sinai. Consider what Godliness would mean without Israel. What impact would the Torah's ideals have on humankind without the Jewish people? Torah and Godliness would be mere abstractions. The very shape of the *aravah* suggests that Israel's acceptance of the Torah, despite any failings in its observance, allows for the formation of a special bond between the Jewish people and Hashem. Its mouth (i.e., outer edge) is required to be smooth in texture and not jagged (פִּיָה חָלָק, see *Succah* 34a). A smooth surface makes an excellent receptacle; any object can be mounted on it. By accepting the Torah, Israel agreed to be a receptacle for Hashem's Torah: to receive it wholeheartedly and to act as a vehicle to disseminate Godliness.

The *aravah* portrays Hashem's love for Israel. But, the other side of the equation, Israel's love of its Creator, should also be stressed. As noted previously, outside of the *Beis HaMikdash*, the *aravah* ceremony on *Hoshana Rabbah* is not a Torah requirement. It came about through the initiative of the Jewish people, encouraged by the prophets, in order to show their love for the Creator even after the destruction of the *Beis*

HaMikdash. Israel and Hashem enjoy the unique ability to "read each other's mind" and to anticipate each others' wishes. By choosing to preserve the *aravah* ceremony even in contemporary times, Israel gives its "beloved," Hashem, great satisfaction. By allowing the *aravah* so prominent a role, Hashem displays His great affection for His people.

(5655)

↜ To Talk or Not to Talk Open Lips, Closed Lips

The *aravah*, plays a very significant role on *Hoshana Rabbah*, disproportionate to its nondescript appearance and total lack of taste or fragrance. What is the significance of the *aravah* and, by extension, the significance of the *aravah*-like Jew?

Consider the prominent role played by the number *two* in the symbolism of Succos. *Aravos* are used on two different occasions: once in conjunction with the other species (when *two aravos* are taken), and once by themselves. The Midrash (*Yalkut Shimoni, Emor* 652) compares the shape of *aravos* to that of the human lip, of which there are two.

A further significance of the number two in the context of the *aravah* relates to the fact that human lips are commonly used in one of two positions, either open in speech or closed in silence, corresponding to the two uses of the *aravah*: Taking the *aravah* together with the other species signifies "open lips," the power of speaking Torah thoughts, of accomplishing a great deal with one's lips. The second, taking the *aravah* by itself on *Hoshana Rabbah*, suggests that at times sealed lips and silence are more effective.

To extend this analogy even further, two leaders of Israel used their lips effectively, one by speaking, the other by remaining silent. Moshe spoke, articulated and taught the Torah; while Aaron distinguished himself by remaining silent at the moment of great tragedy, the death of his two sons, Nadav and Avihu.

Finally, the *aravah* itself is used in two different contexts, alone and as part of the Four Species. As long as the *aravah*, the simple unlearned Jew, can converse about Torah subjects with his peers, albeit in an elementary fashion, he may be taken in conjunction with the *esrog lulav*, and *haddasim*, representing devout and learned Jews. However even the solitary, "*aravah*-like Jew," who is unable to articulate Torah thoughts at any level, still has a place in Jewish life. His task is to seal his lips, to desist from speaking *lashon hara* (slanderous speech). In fact, a direct linkage can be drawn between sealing ones lips to avoid speaking evil and the eventual ability of using his lips to discuss Torah. By refraining from talking evil, the unlearned "*aravah*-like Jew," will eventually attain the ability to express Torah thoughts as well. The unlettered Jew begins life as a solitary *aravah*, but subsequently, by virtue of abstaining from evil talk, becomes part of the Four Species, and is accepted into the Torah family. As King Solomon suggests (*Mishlei* 24:26), שְׂפָתַיִם יִשָּׁק מֵשִׁיב דְּבָרִים נְכֹחִים, *Sealed lips reply correct answers.*

Lips that stay closed and refrain from speaking evil will eventually give correct answers to questions regarding Torah. If, as the Talmud says (*Arachin* 15a), evil speech is among Judaism's gravest offenses, surely sealing one's lips must rank as one of the greatest *mitzvos*.

No blessing is recited upon taking the *aravah* by itself on *Hoshana Rabbah* (*Succah* 44b). From this we can learn that, at times, remaining silent can be as effective as speaking words of Torah. (5654)

◆§ Israel Attracted to its Father The Role of Customs in Israel's Survival

In its exacting list of requirements for an acceptable *aravah*, the Talmud insists that it have elongated leaves, long and drawn out (מָשׁוּךְ כַּנַּחַל) like the shape of a brook (*Succah* 33b). Why the elongated shape? What is the symbolism of the brook-like leaf? And why should the *aravah* be "drawn-out"?

The answer to these questions is simple. The *aravah* is drawn out like a brook to symbolize that the Jewish people are also drawn (i.e. attracted) — after their Creator. As King Solomon states (*Shir HaShirim* 1:3), מָשְׁכֵנִי אַחֲרֶיךָ נָּרוּצָה, *Draw [attract] me, so that we will run after You.* This verse speaks of an inner magnetic pull, the powerful drive innate in every Jew to follow Hashem, regardless of where such a journey's destination may lie. Consider further the implications of being "attracted" to Hashem." This intrinsic attraction to the Creator demonstrates that Israel's faith in Hashem is primarily intuitive and emotional, rather than intellectual. We are believers, and descendants of believers (מַאֲמִינִים בְּנֵי מַאֲמִינִים), attracted to Hashem in the same intuitive, emotional manner as our fathers were. We are governed by unswerving faith, regardless of the consequences, and ask no questions as we follow our Creator.

This trait was first manifested in the Wilderness immediately after the Exodus, as the Jewish people were willing to follow Hashem wherever He might take them, even though their capacity for comprehending His will was limited before being given the Torah at Sinai. Despite the increased sophistication that Israel developed afterwards, Hashem has always retained a special fondness for the blind loyalty His people showed him at their inception as a nation. As King Solomon sings (*Shir HaShirim* 4:3), וּמִדְבָּרֵךְ נָאוֶה, *[The loyalty you gave Hashem in] your Wilderness is pleasurable.*

That first generation asked no questions. Drawn to their Creator, they found His presence attractive though they did not comprehend His will. This willingness to follow Hashem without necessarily comprehending was a critical ingredient in the makeup of that first generation of Jews that should inspire our generations as well. We, too, cannot fully fathom His will. Without prophets to foresee the future, we, too, can only survive through our *emunah*. Our generations (after centuries of exile awaiting the arrival of *Moshiach*) are described by the prophet Tzefaniah (3:12) as עַם עָנִי וָדָל וְחָסוּ בְּשֵׁם ה׳, *a poor and [spiritually] impoverished nation, [yet] trusting in Hashem's Name.* As the drawn out shape of the *aravah* reflects, Israel gives Hashem its unwavering trust, in spite of any concerns and worries it may have to push aside to do so.

The concept of *emunah* is more extensive, though. Let us in particular examine why the Jewish people are described as "believers, and descendants of believers" (מַאֲמִינִים בְּנֵי מַאֲמִינִים). In what way does our fathers' *emunah* affect our belief?

The relationship between fathers and children assumes two forms. On the one hand, is the intellectual relationship: Parents share ideas with their children, who, in turn, inherit their parents' intellectual capacities and ways of looking at the world. Such a relationship is possible, however, only with mature, older children. An entirely different relationship exists between parents and younger children, described in the phrase בְּרָא כַּרְעֵיה דְאַבוּהָ, *a child is his father's knees.* This association between parents and younger children is primarily emotional, the visceral, "knee-jerk," reaction of children who instinctively follow in their parents' ways.

As "believers, and descendants of believers," we, too, follow our Heavenly Father instinctively. *Aravah*-like, we are drawn to believe in the God of our fathers, just as a small child naturally follows his father. As King Solomon wrote (*Shir HaShirim* 1:8), אִם־לֹא תֵדְעִי לָךְ . . . צְאִי־לָךְ

בְּעִקְבֵי הַצֹּאן, *If you [Israel] do not know yourself [which path to follow] . . . go in the footsteps of the sheep,* that is, follow the roads that have been traveled — go in the directions of your parents.

Our Sages (*Succah* 44b) emphasize that the custom of taking the *aravah* on *Hoshana Rabbah* was *inspired* by the prophets, not an *edict* instituted by the prophets. Perhaps they intended to point out that the *aravah,* and the attraction to Hashem it symbolizes, could not simply be decreed by the prophets. Dedication to Hashem must be felt instinctively: If our forefathers in the Temple took the *aravah*, then we know intuitively that we should emulate them — not because a prophet insisted that we should. *Emunah,* too, is not something that can be learned. It must be transmitted "genetically," so to speak, from generation to generation.

The special role of sacred Jewish customs, instituted on the initiative of the people rather than imposed by their spiritual mentors, is captured by the the saying, מִנְהָג יִשְׂרָאֵל תּוֹרָה, *Jewish customs bear the force of law.*

In certain instances, a particular custom is described as מִנְהַג אֲבוֹתֵיהֶם בִּיְדֵיהֶם, *the custom of their fathers in their hands.* An example of this is the institution of observing the second day of a Festival (e.g. Succos) in the Diaspora when, from a strictly technical viewpoint nowadays, one day would suffice (*Beitzah* 4b).

This seemingly abstruse expression, "their father's custom in their hands," is actually very meaningful. Many customs are peripheral and of relatively recent origin, often stemming from the populace rather than from Torah leadership. In the course of time, however, some of these customs have assumed critical roles in preserving Judaism.

The expression "their father's custom in their hands" implies that what started as only a custom for our fathers has become for us a main source of support. Our survival depends on Jewish customs. Customs that had relatively minor importance in past generations are the "hands" and spiritual lifeblood of later generations. Thus, the custom of taking the *aravah,* while it was observed during Temple times, has attained increased emphasis since the Temple's destruction. In particular the day of *Hoshana Rabbah* and the service of the *aravah* performed on it are especially important for the contemporary Jew.

An intriguing way of looking at our relationship to earlier generations emerges from the famous scene of Jacob grabbing at Esau's heel as they emerged from their mother's womb. We, too, try to grab onto the "heels" of past generations — the customs which sometimes had relatively minor importance are often our major supports. (5654)

◈ Self-Negation / Purifying Man's Animalistic Instincts

While the *Hoshana* liturgy is recited every day of Succos, the service of *Hoshana Rabbah* is far more elaborate. Also on this day the *aravah* is given added emphasis, being taken by itself. The following passage from the Talmud (*Chulin* 5b) sheds light on the relationship between these two aspects of *Hoshana Rabbah — the aravah* and the elaborate liturgy: "אָדָם וּבְהֵמָה תוֹשִׁיעַ ה'" אָמַר רַב יְהוּדָה אָמַר רַב אֵלוּ בְּנֵי אָדָם שֶׁהֵן עֲרוּמִין בְּדַעַת וּמְשִׂימִין עַצְמָן כִּבְהֵמָה — *"Man and animal are saved by Hashem"(Tehillim 36:7). Rav Yehudah said in the name of Rav: This refers to people who are very intelligent and yet consider themselves to be no more than animals.*

In this passage, the Talmud tells us that self-negation, holding oneself to be little better than an animal, is a prerequisite for Divine salvation. With this key, we can understand the connection between the *aravah* and the *Hoshana* prayers, which center on the theme of Divine salvation. (The word *hoshana* itself means "Save us!") There exists no better symbol of man's lack of pretentiousness than the lowly *aravah*, which, as we have said many times, lacks fragrance and taste. Only those as meek as the *aravah* deserve Divine salvation on this great day.

Self-negation is no easy task, yet Israel, more than any other nation, is capable of it. As Moshe noted (*Devarim* 7:7), כִּי־אַתֶּם הַמְעַט מִכָּל־הָעַמִּים, *For you are the least of the nations*. In this he was referring to the Jewish people's natural instinct to consider itself small and unworthy. The Psalmist sings (116:6), דַּלּוֹתִי וְלִי יְהוֹשִׁיעַ *I am poor — and He will save me*. Precisely because of my "poverty" (i.e. self-negation), I will be saved. The custom of beating the *aravah* on the ground at the conclusion of the special service on *Hoshana Rabbah* may also serve to underscore the *aravah's* theme of self-negation.

Self negation is advantageous in another respect as well. While it is comparatively simple to consecrate one's spiritual side, it is far more difficult to sanctify the body, sometimes called the animal soul (נֶפֶשׁ הַבַּהֲמִית). Only self-negation, minimizing bodily concerns and personal indulgences, for the sake of fulfilling Hashem's will can sanctify the body.

As a symbol of self-negation, the *aravah* has a greater power to promote Divine salvation than the other species. Indeed, the *aravah* is bound with the other species not only for its own benefit — in order to give the fragile and humble *aravah* the protection and impressiveness of the other, sturdier, species — but also for their benefit as well. It teaches the *esrog, lulav,* and *haddasim* the virtues of humility, as exemplified in the *aravah*.

Even the arrogant, wicked Bilaam grudgingly admitted the virtues of self-negation. As he said (*Bamidbar* 24:7), יִזַּל מַיִם מִדָּלְיָו, *water flows from its poor ones.* The Sages (*Nedarim* 81a) adduced from this verse a warning to be careful to honor the children of poor (or humble) people, for Torah shall emerge from them. Torah (which is frequently compared to water) flows from the poor, from the humble, from those who negate themselves to Hashem's presence. (5651)

◆§ Hope Even When Unity Seems Impossible

The Four Species symbolize the dream of Jewish unity (as is discussed at greater length in the section on the Four Species). This ideal, while unquestionably noble, at times proves elusive or even unattainable. Unfortunately, the various species (and the various personality types they represent) are unable to come together all year round. Tragically, the curse of *sinas chinam* (baseless hatred), which caused the destruction of the *Beis HaMikdash* (see *Yoma* 9b), still affects us. But perhaps on Succos the dream of Jewish unity is more attainable than at any other time.

The message of *Hoshana Rabbah,* the day of Great Salvation, is that even when Jews are unable to unite, even when the "*aravah*-like Jew" cannot coexist with his more righteous brethren, there is still hope. On this day, we take the *aravah* alone, suggesting that even when Jews find it impossible to coexist, there is still a glimmer of hope. A beam of Divine light from the bright flame of Succos' unity lingers on throughout the year, even when the solitary *aravah* stands alone.

(5649)

Shemini Atzeres

◆§ Introduction

בַּיּוֹם הַשְּׁמִינִי עֲצֶרֶת תִּהְיֶה לָכֶם

On the eighth day, an "Atzeres" [cessation] shall be for you (*Bamidbar* 29:35).

תָּחֹגּוּ אֶת־חַג־ה׳ שִׁבְעַת יָמִים בַּיּוֹם הָרִאשׁוֹן שַׁבָּתוֹן וּבַיּוֹם הַשְּׁמִינִי שַׁבָּתוֹן

And you shall celebrate H*ASHEM's festival seven days. On the first day there shall be a cessation [from work] and on the eighth day there shall be a cessation* (*Vayikra* 23:39).

In these few words, and virtually nowhere else, the Torah describes the festival of *Shemini Atzeres.* A vast amount of Midrashic and other homiletic literature has emerged to explain the essence of this festival. In this essay we will discuss numerous issues, including the relationship between *Shemini Atzeres* and the *Shalosh Regalim* (Three Pilgrimage Festivals), especially the close association between Succos and *Shemini Atzeres.* We will also explore the links between the High Holy Days and *Shemini Atzeres* and the relationship between *Shemini Atzeres* and the day which follows it, *Simchas Torah.*

Other issues discussed include possible interpretations of the word *atzeres* and the deeper significance of praying for rain on *Shemini Atzeres.* In this essay (as well as subsequent pieces on *Simchas Torah* and *Parashas Zos HaBeracha*) we hope to convey an appreciation of the profundity and massive scope of the extraordinary day, *Shemini Atzeres.*

◆§ Atzeres: A Day of Unity

On this day the Torah proclaims an *atzeres. Onkelos* renders the word *atzeres* as כְּנִישִׁין, *gathering.* According to this translation, the festival is a time of ingathering, a season of Jewish unity.

Indeed, the entire festival of Succos celebrates the theme of unity (as discussed at greater length in the essay on *succah*). For example, the Talmud (*Succah* 27b) discusses the possibility of all Jews residing in one *succah*, which we may understand allegorically as an allusion to the possibility that all Jews can learn to live together on Succos. The Torah calls Succos חַג הָאָסִיף, *the Festival of Gathering* (*Shemos* 34:22), a reference not only to the harvest but also to the unification of Jewish souls in pursuit of a common purpose — to perform the will of Hashem.

Similarly, the Mishnah (*Avos* 4:14) speaks of a כְּנֵסִיָּה שֶׁהִיא לְשֵׁם שָׁמַיִם, *a gathering that is for the sake of Heaven*, one whose purpose is to glorify Hashem's Name. Homiletically, however, we may understand this Mishnah as a reference to the *succah*, in which we hope all Jews will gather together. (Even if we will say that this is not a reference to a gathering in an actual *succah*, we can still take it as a statement that Succos promotes unity among Jews.) Because it provides a focus for Jews to unite together around a common goal, the *succah* is called Hashem's home. (See the Talmud's dictum, *Succah* 9a, that Hashem's Name is manifest upon the *succah*.)

This Mishnah states, כָּל כְּנֵסִיָּה שֶׁהִיא לְשֵׁם שָׁמַיִם סוֹפָהּ לְהִתְקַיֵּם, *any gathering that is for the sake of Heaven will be perpetuated*, that is, its effects will continue to be felt beyond the actual duration of the gathering itself. If Succos is a time of gathering for Hashem's Name, how may we be assured that the effect of this time of gathering, achieved on Succos, will actually remain beyond the festival itself. How can Hashem ensure that, when the Jewish people leave the *succah* after the festival, they will "take into their houses" with them the dream of Jewish unity that was awakened in the *succah*? *Shemini Atzeres*, the festival immediately following Succos, is the guarantor that the unity achieved during Succos will endure beyond the festival.

The Torah's very brief description of the Festival, *On the eighth day an atzeres shall be for you*, can be paraphrased as follows, "On the eighth day, the spirit of unity achieved on Succos will become yours." *Shemini Atzeres* helps a Jew integrate the unity first attained on Succos into his thought pattern and emotions. (In this interpretation, the word *atzeres* connotes a storehouse in which sundry materials are kept, or, in this context, a time in which Jewish souls are gathered together.)

(5665)

◆§ Shemini Atzeres: Taste of the Hereafter

The nature of *Shemini Atzeres* can be deduced from its position in relationship to Succos. Not only does it follow Succos, but it is also the *eighth* day. The number eight alludes to *Olam HaBa,* the World to Come, while seven represents the greatest degree of achievement attainable in this world (just as Shabbos is the culmination of Hashem's creation of this world). The seven days of Succos are a time of material abundance, a time when Jew and Gentile alike are showered with Hashem's bounty, and all the pleasures of this world are available. *Shemini Atzeres,* however, symbolizes the spiritual pleasures of *Olam HaBa,* which are granted exclusively to the Jewish people on the (day which is reserved for them), the eighth day.

Thus, one of the few references to *Shemini Atzeres* in the Torah suggests that this festival is of particular importance to the Jewish people. The Torah says (*Bamidbar* 29:35), בַּיּוֹם הַשְּׁמִינִי עֲצֶרֶת תִּהְיֶה לָכֶם, *On the eighth day, shall be an "Atzeres" [cessation] for you.* The words *for you* imply that, unlike Succos which contains a message for all humanity (as demonstrated by the seventy bulls offered corresponding to the seventy distinct human cultures), this festival and its "preview" of the hereafter is uniquely Jewish. The *Ari* (the sixteenth-century mystical scholar whose work left a lasting impact on Chassidic thought) adduces an allusion to *Shemini Atzeres* and its uniquely Jewish connotations in the following verse (*Koheles* 11:2): תֶּן־חֵלֶק לְשִׁבְעָה וְגַם לִשְׁמוֹנָה, *Leave a portion for the seventh and also for the eighth.* The *Ari* paraphrases this verse to say, "Leave a portion for the Gentile world during the first seven days of Succos, since all men share in Hashem's bounty on Succos. But on the eighth day, scrape away anything that is not indigenously Jewish.[1]

The Midrash (*Yalkut Shimoni, Emor* 782) depicts *Shemini Atzeres* as a day of added blessings, an additional festival aside from the Three Pilgrim Festivals. In light of the above discussion, we can see why *Shemini Atzeres* might be considered an "additional" festival. Numerous terms for the concept of soul are used in *Tanach,* however the most frequently found are *nefesh, ruach,* and *neshamah.* The Kabbalists

---

1. This interpretation relies on a rarely found usage of the word גַּם to mean *to scrape away,* as we find this term used in the Talmud, (*Chullin* 92b.)

maintain that these three terms correspond to three distinct components of the human soul, in ascending order. Thus, *nefesh* refers to man's most animalistic instincts while *ruach* and *neshamah* denote successively higher levels of the human intellect.

It is possible to suggest that the three elements of the human soul correspond to the three Festivals. If so, however, how does *Shemini Atzeres*, the additional festival, fit into this scheme?

This festival corresponds to the *neshamah yeseirah*, the additional *neshamah* with which a Jew is blessed every Shabbos (*Beitzah* 16a). The *neshamah yeseirah* not only adds a higher level of spirituality to the day, but also allows the Sabbath observer to partake of food and drink without becoming excessively materialistic (*Rashi* ibid.). The Talmud suggests further that while humankind was certainly made aware of the Sabbath day, this unique dimension of Shabbos can be appreciated only by Jews.

Likewise, *Shemini Atzeres*, which as we have said is a uniquely Jewish occasion, a taste of the hereafter, corresponds to the additional soul. The Three Pilgrimage Festivals, occasions on which all humanity is blessed, correspond to those aspects of the soul shared by all people.[1]

Shemini Atzeres, then, is a uniquely Jewish experience. It is the day of "the additional soul," the day that is a foretaste of the hereafter and the period in which *Simchas Torah* is celebrated. There could be no better time for the joyous completion of Torah than this very special day. Is not Torah the mechanism whereby Israel merits the hereafter? Is it not through Torah that the Jewish people are able to appreciate the "additional soul"? Is it not the Torah itself that makes Israel unique among nations? Thus *Simchas Torah*, is the logical sequel to *Shemini Atzeres* — rejoicing in the Law following a day of intense spirituality.

If *Shemini Atzeres* is a day of such intense spirituality, why do we not sit in the *succah*, which, as discussed in previous essays, symbolizes *Olam HaBa*? The answer to this question flows from the previous discussion. On Succos, the *succah*, a taste of the hereafter, shields the Jew from the imperfections of this world. On *Shemini Atzeres*,

---

1. According to some commentators, Gentiles possess only the first of the three components of the soul mentioned above, the *nefesh*. While this is not the place for a detailed discussion of this subject, in suggesting that Gentiles have all three parts of the soul, lacking only the *neshamah yeseirah*, the *Sfas Emes* seems to rely on an inference derived from the Talmud (*Beitzah* 16a) which states that Gentiles lack a *neshamah yeseirah*. That they lack only this part of the soul implies that they possess all the other parts.

however, the entire universe is saturated with the spirit of the *succah.* The Jew and his entire world are, in effect, transformed into one large *succah.*

The Talmud rules (*Succah* 47a) that a Jew in the Diaspora must dwell in the *succah* on *Shemini Atzeres.* In Chassidic circles, however, this ruling is generally given only token observance. Homiletically, we may understand the Chassidic practice in the following way: Even though on Succos we needed the protection of the *succah,* on *Shemini Atzeres* that protection is extended over the whole world and the hereafter merges into the material world we know. Hashem asks Israel to prepare a "small meal" for Him on *Shemini Atzeres* (*Succah* 55b), to bring Godliness into our small world. It is generally thought that this world and the hereafter are mutually exclusive entities that will never coincide. *Shemini Atzeres* demonstrates that a Torah-oriented Jew can live an other-wordly existence while still in this world.

This is seen also in the Mishnah commonly said before reading *Pirkei Avos* (*Sanhedrin* 10:1), כָּל יִשְׂרָאֵל יֵשׁ לָהֶם חֵלֶק לָעוֹלָם הַבָּא, *Every Jew has a portion in the World to Come.* The Mishnah's use of the present tense, "has," rather than the future "will have," also suggests that the two worlds can converge. To the extent that a Jew lives a Torah-centered life, he can enjoy the spiritual treasures of the World to Come even in this world. While this is so especially on *Shemini Atzeres* and other festivals, it holds true every day that he lets the Torah turn his life into a blessed and meaningful experience. (5632, 5660)

◆§ Atzeres: A Day of Respite

בַּיּוֹם הַשְּׁמִינִי עֲצֶרֶת תִּהְיֶה לָכֶם

On the eighth day, shall be an "Atzeres" [cessation] for you (*Bamidbar* 29:35).

To better appreciate the meaning of the word *atzeres,* let us consider another use of the same word in a similar context: שֵׁשֶׁת יָמִים תֹּאכַל מַצּוֹת וּבַיּוֹם הַשְּׁבִיעִי עֲצֶרֶת לַה׳ אֱלֹהֶיךָ, *Six days you shall eat matzos and the seventh day it shall be an "Atzeres" for HASHEM your God* (*Devarim* 16:8). Here the Torah also describes the seventh day of *Pesach* as an *atzeres.* By understanding the concept of *atzeres* as it relates to Pesach, we may hope to broaden our understanding of *Shemini Atzeres* as well.

In the context of Pesach, the word *atzeres* might connote the opportunity to rest. Newly liberated, the Jewish people were hardly out of danger until Pharaoh's armies were annihilated at the Sea of Reeds on the seventh day of Pesach. While Hashem generally took pains to minimize the Jews' exposure to war situations (e.g. by diverting them away from Philistine territories at the beginning of *Parashas Beshalach*), here He allowed them to be threatened but blanketed them with the protection of the Divine Cloud. Nonetheless, the people had left Egypt heavily armed, ostensibly ready for any conflict. The verse we cited earlier in connection with Pesach can be interpreted as follows: "Six days you lived under the threat of imminent warfare, and the seventh day was a day of rest from your fears of war."[1]

If *atzeres* in the context of Pesach means a day of rest from fear of physical strife, then *atzeres* as the eighth day of Succos may well imply a respite from fears of spiritual danger.

As we said in the essay on the *succah*, not only Pesach but also the High Holy Days commemorate an Exodus, an Exodus from evil. On Rosh Hashanah and Yom Kippur, the Jewish people are liberated from the deadly grip of the *yetzer hara* that constantly tempts man to sin. Like Pharaoh, evil does not give up — it continues in hot pursuit for the seven days of Succos. The elaborate ceremonies of Succos are intended to shield us from the evil tempter and, when necessary, to combat him. (As discussed in previous essays, the *succah* shields the Jew and the *lulav* symbolizes outright strife with evil, with the Four Species as weapons of battle). The Torah itself hints at a relationship between the Exodus and the *succah* by emphasizing that Hashem placed the Jewish people in *succos* when they left Egypt (see *Vayikra* 23:43).

Only on *Shemini Atzeres* does the Jew attain a feeling of respite. The term *atzeres* (literally "cessation") evidently refers to the cessation of evil's harassment — on *Shemini Atzeres*. All through Succos, various tactics are employed in the struggle against evil. The *succah* shields the Jew from the *yetzer hara*, and the Four Species symbolize the offensive struggle against evil.

On *Shemini Atzeres*, a unique bond is forged between Israel and its Creator and no diversionary tactics, neither the *succah* nor the *lulav* is necessary to deflect the *yetzer hara*. On this day the Jew is able to

1. This interpretation relies on an alternative meaning of the word *matzah* as "strife," as it is used in *Shemos* 21:22 and *Devarim* 25:11.

repulse evil just by being himself, as indicated by the verse: *On the eighth day, shall be an "Atzeres" [cessation] for you.* Merely by virtue of being Jewish, of being yourself (לָכֶם), the mood of *atzeres*, of the cessation of evil, will prevail. (5655)

Pleas for Water

The Mishnah describes an elaborate ceremony conducted each day of *Chol HaMoed* Succos while the *Beis HaMikdash* stood. Known as נִיסוּךְ הַמַּיִם, the Libation of Water. A golden pitcher containing three *lugin* of water was filled from Shiloah, a well near Jerusalem. First a *tekiah,* then a *teruah* and then another *tekiah* were sounded on bronze trumpets. The officiating *Kohen* mounted the ramp leading to the Altar and, when he reached the top, turned to his left where there were two silver basins into which the water was poured.

The Water Libation played such an important role in assuring a steady flow of rainfall that Hashem made a point of asking Israel to perform the ceremony every year (*Rosh Hashanah* 16a).

Ordinarily, *mitzvos* are explicitly commanded in the Torah. In this case, however, Hashem *requested* that we pour water in order to assure an adequate rainfall. This ceremony was an addition to the original commandment, based either on the Oral tradition transmitted to Moshe at Sinai or on a derivation from the Torah itself (see *Taanis* 2b). Why did Hashem make this additional request? Furthermore, what is the significance of the Libation of Water Ceremony?

To appreciate the significance of this ceremony, it would be useful to analyze the first time rainfall is mentioned in the Torah. At the beginning of time, at the conclusion of the six days of creation, the stage was set for vegetation to flourish. On the third day, Hashem had set into motion the process whereby grass would grow by commanding the trees to bear fruit (*Bereishis* 1:11). But initially nothing happened.

The Torah later explains why the earth was not dotted with greenery despite Hashem's command issued days before: וְכֹל שִׂיחַ הַשָּׂדֶה טֶרֶם יִהְיֶה בָאָרֶץ וְכָל־עֵשֶׂב הַשָּׂדֶה טֶרֶם יִצְמָח כִּי לֹא הִמְטִיר ה׳ אֱלֹהִים עַל־הָאָרֶץ וְאָדָם אַיִן לַעֲבוֹד אֶת־הָאֲדָמָה—*The growth of the field was not yet on the earth and the grass of the field had not yet sprouted, because Hashem, God, had not caused it to rain on the earth and there was no man to work the earth* (ibid. 2:5). Evidently, the crucial precondition lacking was man. *Rashi* on this verse suggests that the prayers of man were absolutely essential — without them there could be no rain.

Thus a direct association existed between man's prayers and precipitation. When his descendants later failed to live up to the title *man*, they thereby diminished the power of their prayers for rain and the burden of asking for rain fell entirely upon Israel. While the *Beis HaMikdash* stood, the righteous would beseech Hashem for rain and were often immediately answered. (The Talmud, especially in the tractate *Taanis*, is replete with instances in which the righteous succeeded in obtaining rainfall under the most adverse circumstances).

Hashem's request of Israel to perform the Libation of Water Ceremony is really a plea to act as the first man did, and as the righteous of all generations have done. Rather than wait for Divine action, we must take the initiative to ask for rain. Pouring the water libation and praying for rain indicate our compliance with Hashem's request to "seek out rain." On this theme, the Torah says (*Devarim* 28:12), יִפְתַּח ה׳ לְךָ אֶת־אוֹצָרוֹ הַטּוֹב אֶת־הַשָּׁמַיִם לָתֵת מְטַר־אַרְצְךָ בְּעִתּוֹ, *Hashem will open for you His good treasure the heavens, to give the rain of your land in its season.* While this verse seems to suggest that Hashem *opens up the heavens* regardless of Israel's effort, closer examination suggests otherwise. The word לְךָ, *for you,* is seemingly superfluous, since the verse later says, *to give the rain of YOUR land*. We may, however, interpret it to mean בִּזְכוּתְךָ, *in your merit*. Only if Israel prays for rain and (when the *Beis HaMikdash* stands) performs the Libation of Water, can its rainfall be assured. (5648)

⸎ Water: Harmony in the Heavens

In light of the above discussion which emphasizes the importance of beseeching rain, some very esoteric and abstruse comments in the Midrash can better be appreciated.

On the second day of Creation, Hashem commanded that there be a firmament separating the waters that had been present since creation commenced (*Bereishis* 1:6). As a result of this command a permanent separation, the firmament (רָקִיעַ, also called heaven) divided the lower waters from the upper waters.

This time, however, Hashem's plan to separate the upper and lower waters was challenged. The waters below the firmament "cried" (i.e. they protested that they too wanted to be in Hashem's presence). *Rashi* (*Vayikra* 2:13) notes that the lower waters were placated by Hashem's promise that they too would play a prominent role in the services of the *Beis HaMikdash.* In fact, Hashem established a covenant with the waters stating that they would appear in His Temple as salt (placed on all offerings) and as water in the libation ceremony of Succos.

Now, we can better understand the "complaint" of the lower waters. They reasoned that man, who lives in the universe below the Heavens and who is surrounded on all sides by these lower waters, should not receive rainfall as a Divine gift emanating from the upper waters, without any effort on his part. If his efforts (in the form of prayer and the Water Libation) were to be made a prerequisite for rainfall, then the lower waters surrounding his habitat would also be assuaged. When the *Kohen* poured water from a pitcher into the silver basins alongside the Altar, he performed an event of cosmic importance. Harmony was restored among Hashem's creations, and the waters above and below the firmament could continue to coexist.

But why were the lower waters so insistent that man beseech Hashem for rain? What was so vital about his input?

Perhaps by complaining about their exclusion from Hashem's "inner circle," the lower waters were really acting on behalf of humanity, and especially the Jewish people, who also dwell below the firmament. Their complaint was simply a plea to Hashem: "Remember, that there is potential for sanctity on earth as well as in Heaven." True, the universe (below the heavens) is a mixture, with evil existing alongside good. True, man is no angel and his conduct is frequently less than impeccable. Nonetheless, the potential for living a sacred life on this earth still exists. By finding a niche for the lower waters in a sacred setting in the Libation of Water ceremony, we affirm that the earth as well as the heaven is sacred, and that great things can happen below the heavens.

◆§ Water: Pure and Unrefined

One question remains, however. What is the significance of using *water* in this ceremony? On all other occasions, wine is poured into the basins above the Altar — why on Succos is water poured in addition to wine?

In answer, let us consider a significant difference between the two substances. Wine requires considerable processing to be made suitable for human use, and more so for use on the Altar. Grapes must first be harvested and trampled to release their juice, then waste materials must be separated from the edible components. Finally, the remaining liquid must be fermented under exacting conditions for a rigidly controlled period of time. Water, on the other hand, may be consumed by man and brought to the Altar in its natural state, totally without special processing.

The year-long use of wine testifies to the "processing" (i.e. spiritual preparation and growth) man requires to achieve his potential. The use of water on Succos, on the other hand, symbolizes the inherent spark of goodness in every person that gives him the potential for greatness that remains, whatever other failings he may have. The Water Libation Ceremony, emphasizing as it does the intrinsic purity of the human soul, was not meant to be an isolated event. On the contrary, while water was poured onto the Altar only once a year, its symbolism has meaning throughout the year. Purity endures on earth in the beautiful form of the "unprocessed" Jewish soul.

One of the thirteen rules of Torah interpretation has significance here: כָּל דָּבָר שֶׁהָיָה בִּכְלָל וְיָצָא מִן הַכְּלָל לְלַמֵּד, לֹא לְלַמֵּד עַל עַצְמוֹ יָצָא, אֶלָּא לְלַמֵּד עַל הַכְּלָל כֻּלּוֹ יָצָא, *Everything that was included in a general rule and was once exempted from the rule [i.e., an exception was made once] was exempted not to teach only about itself but also to teach about everything else covered by the rule.*

Although water was poured onto the Altar only once a year, the symbolic meaning of the act, the viability of the pure Jewish soul, remains valid all year long.

In our material world, a naturally pure substance is generally an exception. Usually, a wine-like process of crushing and filtering is required to achieve purity. The prophet Zechariah (14:8) predicts a day when pure, living, water will emanate from Jerusalem וְהָיָה בַּיּוֹם הַהוּא יֵצְאוּ מַיִם־חַיִּים מִירוּשָׁלַםִ, *And it shall come to pass in that day, that living waters shall go out from Jerusalem*. On that future day, the unadulterated goodness inherent in every Jewish soul will become openly revealed.

Israel (i.e. the lower waters) cries because the sanctity inherent in the Jewish soul is not yet apparent. We cry because it appears that Godliness and everything connected to it has abandoned this earth and retreated to the heavens. These cries are the ultimate praise of the Jewish people: What other nation would cry over the absence of spirituality? Libation of Water, seen in this light, is not merely a testament to the purity of the Jewish soul — it is a Divine means of comforting the Jewish people: "You have shed just tears. On Succos I comfort you." (5651)

◆§ Water: A Blessing to Appreciate

As discussed earlier, Israel's blessings are fundamentally different from those bestowed on the Gentile world at this time of year. The Gentile world is content to benefit from Hashem's bounty without being aware of its source and, equally tragic, without considering the *purpose* of Divine blessings. Humankind has no inkling of what to do with the manifold blessings of this season, other than to enjoy them in an ostentatiously physical fashion. Israel, however, is determined to keep its blessings distinct from those of the Gentile world and to remember that whatever we enjoy comes from Hashem. Moreover, we are committed to utilize our blessings of rainfall (like all of our material blessings) for a higher purpose. Specifically, we seek prosperity and freedom from economic concerns to give us time and energy to follow spiritual pursuits and grow in the study of Torah.

To distinguish ourselves from the Gentiles, it is not sufficient merely to think differently about the source and purposes of Hashem's bounty. We must also have a visible sign of the distinction between our blessings and those of the Gentiles. Such a sign is our delay in offering our prayer for rain, and our acceptance of Divine Blessings, until *Shemini Atzeres*, while the other nations begin to enjoy their bounty from the first day of Succos.

Another distinguishing feature is the means by which we obtain these blessings: we strive for our portion by praying for rain and performing the Water Libation Ceremony. Blessings that result in reward for effort are usually better appreciated than outright gifts. Our blessings, since they come as a result of prayer and service, have a greater impact on us, while the newfound affluence the rest of the world obtains without effort has the danger of causing them to forget the Creator.

> אֶת־קָרְבָּנִי לַחְמִי לְאִשַּׁי רֵיחַ נִיחֹחִי תִּשְׁמְרוּ לְהַקְרִיב לִי בְּמוֹעֲדוֹ
> *My offering, My food [i.e. My fuel], for [i.e. to be placed on] My fires [of the Altar for the purpose of] My sweet smell, you are to be scrupulous to offer Me in its appointed time* (*Bamidbar* 28:2).

This verse, which refers primarily to the daily offering, may also be interpreted as a Divine plea not to forget that our sustenance comes through the *sweet smell,* the intense spirituality of Hashem's Torah and *mitzvos,* more than as a result of our own material efforts.

An additional safeguard ensures that we remember the source of our unique blessings. In the prayer for rain of *Shemini Atzeres,* we ask to be granted rain in the merit of the Patriarchs: בַּעֲבוּרוֹ אַל תִּמְנַע מָיִם, *In his [Abraham's] merit, do not withhold water.*

The Patriarchs, blessed at times with great wealth, never forgot the source of their blessings and were always careful to utilize them for Hashem's purposes rather than their own. We therefore ask to appreciate and utilize our blessings as well as they did theirs.

Finally, the Water Libation, the prayer for rain, and all the blessings of the season including Succos and *Shemini Atzeres,* can be understood as referring to Torah, as well as to physical bounty. This understanding is in light of the renowned Rabbinic statement, אֵין מַיִם אֶלָּא תּוֹרָה, *Whenever water is referred to in the Scriptures, — it means Torah* (*Bava Kamma* 17a). Our various requests for rain at this time of the year are really pleas for Torah and spiritual growth. The complaint of the lower waters that they too deserved Divine access were, according to this interpretation, really requests that the Torah of mortals (i.e., the Oral Law deduced by the Sages of the Talmud in accordance with principles transmitted at Mount Sinai) be given equal weight in Hashem's presence along with the Written Law given to Moshe. (5646, 5654)

◆§ Shemini Atzeres: Climax of Succos

In earlier essays, we have shown the uniqueness of *Shemini Atzeres,* giving special emphasis to the differences between it and Succos. The following verse, however, seems to indicate a close association between the two festivals: תָּחֹגּוּ אֶת־חַג־ה׳ שִׁבְעַת יָמִים בַּיּוֹם הָרִאשׁוֹן שַׁבָּתוֹן וּבַיּוֹם הַשְּׁמִינִי שַׁבָּתוֹן, *You shall celebrate HASHEM's festival for seven days; on the first day there shall be a day of rest and on the eighth day there shall be a day of rest* (*Vayikra* 23:39).

An obvious question arises. This verse begins with the obligation to observe *seven* days of Succos and concludes with mention of the *eighth* day, *Shemini Atzeres*. Evidently, despite its uniqueness, the eighth day somehow remains associated with Succos.

The Talmud (*Rosh Hashanah* 4b) explicitly describes *Shemini Atzeres* as a "completion" (תַּשְׁלוּמִין) of the first days. In what sense is *Shemini Atzeres* the "completion" of Succos? Seemingly, the blessings of Succos are segmented into seven equal portions, with each day representing one such portion. These segments of the total blessings of Succos can be shared with all of humankind. *Shemini Atzeres*, however, is a day on which blessings are retained (the word עֲצֶרֶת being closely related to the word אוֹצָר *storehouse*), when the totality of the blessings of Succos is enjoyed by Israel. Individual blessings may be parceled out and shared with other cultures, but the blessings of this day, the apex of Succos, are not shared with other nations. (5654)

◆§ Shemini Atzeres: The "Locking Up" of Succos

אָמַר לָהֶם הקב״ה לְיִשְׂרָאֵל אַתֶּם נוֹעֲלִים לְפָנַי בַּפֶּסַח וְאֲנִי נוֹעֵל בִּפְנֵיכֶם בָּעֲצֶרֶת

HASHEM said to Israel, "You 'lock up' before Me on Pesach and I 'lock up' before you on Shemini Atzeres" (*Shir HaShirim Rabbah* 7:2)[1]

This Midrash suggests that *Shemini Atzeres* is important not only in its own right but also for its ramifications for the coming winter season, just as the final days of Pesach set the tone for the forthcoming spring and summer.

The expression "lock up" in this context means to preserve the achievements of the holiday season, just as we lock up valuables to keep them secure. The gains of Pesach are preserved through Israel's efforts,

1. The text of this Midrash as given by the *Sfas Emes* seems to be the opposite of that in the Midrash before us. In order to present the interpretation of the *Sfas Emes*, we have preserved the text as it appears in his writings.

while those of Succos are secured by Hashem. The contrast in the two descriptions is intriguing. Why do Hashem and Israel assume different roles at different times?

To grasp the thrust of this Midrash, let us draw a parallel between the cycle of the agricultural year and the seasonal activities of the Torah-oriented Jew. Both have active phases in the summer and quiet, passive times in the winter. The farmer harvests and gathers his grain all through the summer. Israel also has its most active phase, when most *mitzvos* are observed, in the Festival cycle that begins with Pesach and culminates at Succos, a period centered around the summer months. In saying that Israel "locks up," the Midrash refers to a process of permanently absorbing the blessings of the Pesach festival, not only by physical work but also by performing numerous *mitzvos*.

After Succos, however, the farmer enters into a more dormant phase, resting from physical exertion while awaiting the abundant rainfall implied in the blessings of Succos. Just as the Jewish farmer is physically inactive, we also seem to slacken off in a spiritual sense, since the Torah provides no festivals during the winter. The obvious solution is to immerse ourselves in Torah while we await Hashem's spiritual bounty, analogous to the farmer's rainfall. Thus, in this time of year we read in the Torah the story of the Exodus, a necessary prerequisite for Torah, and the giving of the Torah. Hashem "locks up" by producing rainfall (a symbol for Torah) while we study Torah in the winter.

Shemini Atzeres is a time of judgment for rainfall and, by extension, growth in Torah. The contrasting descriptions of the *atzeres* of both Pesach and Succos shed light on the distinct functions of the winter and summer seasons. The Torah calls the last day of Pesach an "*Atzeres* for Hashem" (*Devarim* 16:18), a time for the Jew to perform Hashem's *mitzvos*, while the *atzeres* following Succos is an *atzeres* for us to immerse ourselves in Torah. (5649)

◆§ Atzeres: Israel Accepts Hashem's Blessings

The Three Pilgrimage Festivals, Pesach, Shavuos, and Succos, are occasions during which Hashem showers the Jewish people with His blessings. (See for example *Devarim* 16:15: שִׁבְעַת יָמִים תָּחֹג לַה׳ אֱלֹהֶיךָ ... כִּי יְבָרֶכְךָ ה׳ אֱלֹהֶיךָ בְּכָל־תְּבוּאָתְךָ וּבְכֹל מַעֲשֵׂה יָדֶיךָ *Seven days you shall celebrate a festival to Hashem your God . . . for Hashem your God will bless all your grain and all your handiwork.*) On *Shemini Atzeres*, which comes immediately following Succos and marks the conclusion of the Festival cycle, an even greater Divine gift is granted — the *ability* to receive Divine blessings. It is no small matter that mortals can receive Hashem's blessings. This is the unique gift of *Shemini Atzeres* — Hashem enables Israel to absorb and assimilate His blessings.

The following verse, recited in the *Kiddush* for Festivals, וַיְדַבֵּר מֹשֶׁה אֶת־מֹעֲדֵי ה׳ אֶל־בְּנֵי יִשְׂרָאֵל, *And Moshe declared HASHEM's appointed festivals to the Children of Israel* (*Vayikra* 23:44), appears to be a general statement pertaining to all the Festivals. It is written, however, specifically in the context of *Shemini Atzeres*, suggesting that only on *Shemini Atzeres* can the Jewish soul truly integrate the blessings of all the previous Pilgrimage Festivals. Moshe acted as a conduit to channel blessings to the Jewish people. This is indicated in the phrasing of the verse itself, וַיְדַבֵּר מֹשֶׁה, *and Moshe declared*. The root דבר often has the meaning "to lead" (cf. *Tehillim* 47:4, יַדְבֵּר עַמִּים תַּחְתֵּינוּ, *He leads nations beneath us [i.e. to follow us].*) *Shemini Atzeres* is the "adhesive" that cements the bond between Israel and the Festivals.

How did Moshe accomplish the feat of binding Israel to the Festivals? Actually, it was not the day of *Shemini Atzeres* itself or the person Moshe that had this extraordinary effect — but rather what Moshe symbolized and what the day truly commemorates. Moshe, acting as the transmitter of the Torah, which is called (*Mishlei* 4:2) לֶקַח טוֹב, *a good acquisition*, (in that it gives Israel the ability to appreciate what is truly good) was able to implant in Israel the capacity to absorb the blessing of the other holidays.

We can now better understand the relationship between *Shemini Atzeres* and the day following it, *Simchas Torah*, a day of joyous celebration upon completing the annual cycle of weekly Torah readings. *Simchas Torah* is celebrated after *Shemini Atzeres* since it is only in the merit of the Torah that Moshe transmitted that *Shemini Atzeres* can accomplish its true function — to help the Jew derive year-round inspiration from the Festivals.

This theme, and in particular Moshe's role, can be expanded upon. Why was Moshe the ideal teacher for the laws of the Festivals? The entire Torah was transmitted through Moshe, why was special emphasis given to his role in the context of the particular festival of *Shemini Atzeres?*

Upon closer examination, it becomes clear that Moshe's personality — his entire lifestyle — served as an example of how we can derive the most benefit from the Festivals. The consensus of Talmudic opinion maintains that every Festival is really a dual occasion. On the one hand, it is a "festival for Hashem" (see *Devarim* 16:8). At the same time it is an occasion to eat, drink, and enjoy physical pleasures (cf. *Bamidbar* 29:35). The Talmud captures the essence of every Festival in a concise phrase (*Beitzah* 15b): חַלְקֵהוּ חֶצְיוֹ לַה׳ וְחֶצְיוֹ לָכֶם, "Apportion the day into two equal parts — half devoted to Hashem, and the other half for yourselves."

This passage seems to assign Jewry the difficult task of "bisecting" a single day into equal components, despite the fact that the two are seemingly dichotomous in nature. How can we reconcile a spiritual orientation (prayer and Torah study) with physical pleasures (eating and sleeping)? However, it was precisely to teach that it is possible to combine intense spirituality with a major presence in the physical world that Moshe was chosen to transmit the laws of the Festivals to Israel. No one could better show how to combine a nearly Divine personality with very human characteristics than Moshe, who according to the Midrash, (*Yalkut Shimoni* 951) was both human and Godlike (i.e., he personified the characteristics of an angel and a human simultaneously). If ever there was a paradigm of fusing spirituality with physical necessity, of living the spirit of the Festival *every day*, without question it was Moshe. (5660, 5664)

◆§ Succos: International Implications Atzeres: Unique to Israel and Torah

Shemini Atzeres follows immediately after Succos. While a certain kinship exists between the two holidays (for example, if necessary, some of the offerings of Succos could be brought on *Shemini Atzeres*), there are also major differences between them. The Talmud (*Rosh Hashanah* 4b) lists six significant halachic differences and, of greater significance to our discussion, the natures and meanings of the two festivals are very different.

The transition from Succos to *Shemini Atzeres* can be viewed as a journey from the *succah*, with all its implications, to the Jewish home. (While many Jews in the Diaspora eat in the *succah* on *Shemini Atzeres*, this is by Rabbinical decree. The Torah requirement, never abandoned in *Eretz Yisrael*, is to leave the *succah* prior to *Shemini Atzeres*). This transition is not merely a change of home and hearth, but rather a complete change of ambiance. On Succos the Jew is possessed with the goal of influencing humankind to accept Hashem's sovereignty, as symbolized by the seventy bulls offered on Succos (as we have discussed in many places in the essays on *Succah* and *Lulav*). On *Shemini Atzeres,* however, the Jew comes home to Hashem and His Torah and only one bull is offered, corresponding to Israel.

The "journey" from festival to festival can be compared to another journey "traveled" daily by the devout Jew. The Talmud (*Berachos* 64a) praises the individual who goes every day from the synagogue to the *beis hamidrash* (house of study): הַיּוֹצֵא מִבֵּית הַכְּנֶסֶת וְנִכְנָס לְבֵית הַמִּדְרָשׁ וְעוֹסֵק בַּתּוֹרָה זוֹכֶה וּמְקַבֵּל פְּנֵי שְׁכִינָה שֶׁנֶּאֱמַר ,,יֵלְכוּ מֵחַיִל אֶל־חָיִל יֵרָאֶה אֶל אֱלֹהִים בְּצִיּוֹן", *"One who leaves the synagogue and then enters the beis hamidrash and studies Torah will merit to greet Hashem's countenance, as it says (Tehillim* 84:8), *"They will advance from strength to strength; each one will appear before* Hashem *in Zion."*

The analogy between the synagogue and *beis hamidrash* can be extended to the relationship between Succos and *Shemini Atzeres.* Succos, with its world-wide significance and international implications, can be compared to the principal activity of a synagogue — prayer — which is also universal in nature. Gentiles as well as Jews may pray and, in fact, the *Beis HaMikdash* and its contemporary equivalent the synagogue are called (*Yeshayahu* 56:7) בֵּיתִי בֵּית־תְּפִלָּה לְכָל־הָעַמִּים, *a house of prayer for all men. Shemini Atzeres,* on the other hand, is meaningful only to Jews. It is thus analogous to the *beis hamidrash* where the Torah, given only to Israel, is learned.

The progress from festival to festival, like that from sacred place to sacred place, promises those who embark on the journey with King David's blessing: *They will advance from strength to strength; each one will appear before* Hashem *in Zion.* (5663)

◆§ Shemini Atzeres and Shavuos: Comparison and Contrast

While comparisons are frequently made between Succos and *Shemini Atzeres,* it is also possible to note a connection between *Shemini Atzeres* and Shavuos. Similarities clearly exist — for example, both festivals are called *Atzeres* (*Shemini Atzeres* in the Torah itself, and Shavuos in Rabbinical parlance — e.g., *Pesachim* 68b). Both holidays revolve around the theme of Torah — Shavuos is the time of the giving of the Torah while *Simchas Torah* (which in *Eretz Yisrael* is observed on *Shemini Atzeres)* celebrates the completion of the reading of the Torah. Moreover, unlike Pesach and Succos, neither Shavuos nor *Shemini Atzeres* possesses a *mitzvah* particular to itself, such as *matzah* and *succah,* which dominate their respective festivals.

The similarities between *Shemini Atzeres* and Shavuos are by no means coincidental. The following verse elucidates the relationship (*Mishlei* 6:23): כִּי נֵר מִצְוָה וְתוֹרָה אוֹר, *Because a mitzvah is a lamp and the Torah is light. Mitzvos* are compared to a source of light, whereas Torah is the light itself emanating from the source. Most occasions require a unique *mitzvah* to distinguish the occasion. However on Shavuos and *Shemini Atzeres,* occasions that celebrate the Torah itself, the light of Torah is so powerful that the additional light of specific *mitzvos* is unnecessary. On these two very special days, Torah alone more than compensates for the lack of unique commandments, and any such commandment would be superfluous.

The connection between these festivals can be understood more deeply by considering them in relation to a major Torah personality who epitomizes and captures the essence of each festival. Jacob observed the Torah before it was formally given at Mount Sinai, and thus reflected the theme of Divine Revelation at Sinai — the theme of Shavuos. Before Sinai the Torah was in a state of potential — it had long been waiting for Israel to observe it, but only time would tell whether the commitment Israel gave it there would be fulfilled.

The same was true of the Patriarch Jacob. Alone with his small contingent of family and followers, surrounded by a world of pagans — his Torah was also one of potential. Only time would tell whether his clan would grow into a nation of believers. Thus Jacob, looking in from the outside, prepared the way for a Torah-based world. Moshe, on the other hand, viewed Torah from within. He had the satisfaction of seeing generations of Jews accept the Torah both for themselves and for their posterity. He lived to see the entire Written Torah, as well the Oral Law, become an integral part of Jewry's heritage. Thus he viewed the completion and the fulfillment of the Torah, as we do every *Simchas Torah* when we celebrate the conclusion of the annual reading of the Torah.

Jacob, on the other hand, perceived the Torah's potential, much as we celebrate Shavuos, the festival that marks the commencement of Israel's relationship with Torah. From Jacob's perspective, a world of Torah was still in the future. Thus the prophet Michah said (7:20), תִּתֵּן אֱמֶת לְיַעֲקֹב,

You shall give truth to Jacob. The word תִּתֵּן, *give,* is in the future tense, implying that the Torah's truth was still to come. In contrast, Moshe had already transmitted truth — the ultimate Truth — to a world that had been beset by falsehood. Therefore the Torah says of Moshe (*Devarim* 33:4), תּוֹרָה צִוָּה־לָנוּ מֹשֶׁה, *Moshe commanded the Torah to us,* in the past tense.

Even the physical symbols of these holidays differ markedly. They too reflect the contrast between the "external view" of Shavuos and the "internal view" of *Shemini Atzeres.* The Talmud describes Shavuos as a New Year (i.e., a period of judgment) for fruit trees (*Megillah* 31b). It is a time for fertility on the outside: one can easily see nature's growth at Shavuos. At *Shemini Atzeres,* which comes at the onset of winter, however, there are no visible manifestations of growth. This day's prayers revolve around rain, which moistens the soil so that eventually vegetation may flourish next spring.

Shavuos and *Shemini Atzeres* — superficially so similar, yet fundamentally so different. One is a celebration of potential; the other, the joy of fulfillment. (5663)

◆§ The Three Pilgrimage Festivals: The Three Patriarchs Shemini Atzeres: Moshe

The relationship between the Three Pilgrimage Festivals and *Shemini Atzeres* is similar to the relationship between Moshe and the three Patriarchs, Abraham, Isaac, and Jacob. Each in his own special way taught the world that mortals can attain Godliness if they seek out Hashem. Abraham, through his relentless love of the Creator and of ordinary people, showed that love can engender true reverence for Hashem. Isaac's fear of Heaven and Jacob's unceasing pursuit of truth demonstrated that man can approach Hashem and become close to Him, but only by seeking Him out. To commemorate the pioneering spirit of the three Patriarchs in seeking out Hashem, three times a year we also abandon our material pursuits to seek out Hashem by visiting His Temple in Jerusalem. This is the basis for the Three Pilgrimage Festivals.[1]

1. Of course today it is not possible to observe the festivals in the *Beis HaMikdash,* may it soon be rebuilt. The character of our observance of the festivals in the present period of exile is discussed at length in the general essay on the festivals.

Shemini Atzeres celebrates an entirely different and loftier concept. Reverence for Hashem, fear of His Exalted Nature (יִרְאַת הָרוֹמְמוּת), can be attained everywhere — even at home, away from the *Beis HaMikdash,* without overt efforts to seek out Hashem. That was Moshe's mission — unlike the Patriarchs, who taught the world that Hashem can be sought out — Moshe emphasized that His Presence can be felt anywhere through immersion in His Torah. *Shemini Atzeres* commemorates the Torah's annual completion (on *Simchas Torah*), the day on which we read Moshe's final blessings to the Children of Israel. No special pilgrimage, no extra effort to seek out Hashem is required — it can be achieved simply by learning Torah! On this occasion Hashem's Presence can be perceived anywhere Jews are devoted to Torah, not only in Jerusalem.

King Solomon extolled the Torah as precious beyond pearls — יְקָרָה הִיא מִפְּנִינִים (*Mishlei* 3:15). The Talmud interprets this statement as follows (*Horyos* 13a): יְקָרָה הִיא מִכֹּהֵן גָּדוֹל שֶׁנִּכְנָס לִפְנֵי וְלִפְנִים, *The Torah is more precious than the Kohen Gadol, who entered the Holy of Holies [on Yom Kippur].*

Torah, and the closeness to Hashem its engenders, is more precious than even the most sacred locale on earth. The Mishnah voices this theme (*Avos* 3:7), וּמִנַּיִן אֲפִילוּ אֶחָד שֶׁנֶּאֱמַר בְּכָל הַמָּקוֹם אֲשֶׁר אַזְכִּיר אֶת שְׁמִי אָבוֹא אֵלֶיךָ וּבֵרַכְתִּיךָ, *How do we know this even of one? For it is said: 'In every place where I cause My Name to be mentioned, I will come to you and bless you'.*

Any Jew — even one who lives a solitary existence — can perceive Hashem's Presence, no matter how dismal the surroundings, as long as he occupies himself in Torah. This was perhaps Moshe's greatest accomplishment — giving the Jewish people the potential to perceive Godliness anywhere. Thus the Pesach *Haggadah* interprets the Torah's final verse *(Devarim* 34:12), וּלְכֹל הַמּוֹרָא הַגָּדוֹל אֲשֶׁר עָשָׂה מֹשֶׁה לְעֵינֵי כָּל־יִשְׂרָאֵל, *The great fear which Moshe caused [i.e. accomplished] in the eyes of all of Israel,* as a reference to Divine Revelation — מוֹרָא גָּדוֹל זוּ גִילּוּי שְׁכִינָה.

How appropriate, then, that on the festival that celebrates the blessings Moshe gave Israel, a Jew does not need to seek out Hashem, or even travel to Jerusalem. On that day, Hashem's Presence can be found everywhere. (5662)

☙ Shemini Atzeres — Prayer for Rain, Celebration of Torah

The Talmud (*Taanis* 2a) rules that one begins to pray for rain starting on *Shemini Atzeres*. It is also a time-honored custom, cited in the *Zohar* (*Parashas Pinchas*), to observe a festival of rejoicing in celebration of the completion of the Torah on *Simchas Torah*. Are these two practices entirely separate from each other or does an inherent connection exist between them?

To appreciate the relationship, we need to contemplate the consequences of praying for rain. As the prophet Yeshayahu said (55:10), כִּי כַּאֲשֶׁר יֵרֵד הַגֶּשֶׁם וְהַשֶּׁלֶג מִן־הַשָּׁמַיִם וְשָׁמָּה לֹא יָשׁוּב כִּי אִם־הִרְוָה אֶת־הָאָרֶץ וְהוֹלִידָהּ וְהִצְמִיחָהּ וְנָתַן זֶרַע לַזֹּרֵעַ וְלֶחֶם לָאֹכֵל, *For when rain and snow come down from heaven, and they do not return there without having refreshed the earth and make it bring forth and bud and give seed to the one who sows and bread for the one who eats.*

This verse speaks for itself. What begins as a few raindrops ultimately results in bountiful fruit. Torah, too, produces the fruit of *mitzvos* and good deeds. Just as the rain that fuels growth originates in Heaven, the Torah could not produce bountiful fruit without Divine assistance and inspiration. Only with the help of Hashem, Who is described as "residing in Heaven," can Torah fulfill its mission, and help its adherents flourish spiritually.

It is noteworthy that both the prayer for rain of *Shemini Atzeres* and the celebration of *Simchas Torah*, together constituting a festival in their own right, are delayed until immediately after Succos. Why do we not pray for rain and rejoice on the first days of Succos?[1] Evidently, the delay in asking for Hashem's bounty until after Succos somehow helps clarify the nature of the blessings that Israel is seeking.

We do not merely ask for Divine blessings as a gift. Moreover, Divine blessings are by no means confined to the Jewish people. All year long, but especially at Succos time, Hashem showers the universe with His blessings. The world benefits from Hashem's bounty — and grossly abuses it. Man enjoys Hashem's beneficence every Succos, and attributes everything it receives to its own effort and zeal, without even thinking that it is Hashem who provides sustenance.

1. While the Talmud (*Taanis* 2a) says this is because we do not want the rain to drive us out of our *succos*, the *Sfas Emes* here adds a homiletic reason.

Israel, on the other hand, deliberately bides its time. Never forgetting that its blessings emanate from the Giver of the Torah, it wants no part of the blessings bestowed on the rest of the world throughout Succos and delays its prayer for rain and other forms of sustenance until *Simchas Torah*, the Festival of the Torah.

Israel is sensitive to what blessings entail. The true significance of Hashem's gifts is the very fact of receiving Divine assistance and the obligation to recognize from what source it comes. The *Zohar* (*Parashas Pinchas* 218b) captures the essence of Israel's yearning for blessings in a Torah context with a pithy metaphor: The Jewish nation is like a human heart, which receives only the purest filtered components of food materials from the blood. Other organs filter out waste products, which are then excreted without having served a productive, life-sustaining role. The blood that enters the heart, however, contains only the most refined remnants of all the nutrients that entered the digestive system. The heart is sustained by the "innermost food" (פְּנִימִית הַמַּאֲכָל). Israel, too, is not content with the generalized, under-appreciated blessings granted at the beginning of Succos and insists that its blessings be filtered through Torah until they are as pure as the blood that enters the heart. Therefore we delay our prayer for rain until the conclusion of the holiday.

The renowned Rabbinic saying (*Yalkut Shimoni* 258), "The Torah was given only to those who ate manna," takes on new meaning in light of the above remarks. A unique quality of the manna was that it was totally absorbed in the body, without waste or excretion. Someone who appreciates blessings in their finest and purest form, in the spirit of the Torah, rejects the unacknowledged and unappreciated blessing bestowed upon the rest of the world over the first days of Succos and instead insists on blessings that can be totally absorbed, as the manna was. This is the rain of *Shemini Atzeres*, set in the context of the Torah.

Those blessings start on *Shemini Atzeres* but they do not end on that day. The Jew immersed in Torah knows how to appreciate Divine blessings and will ultimately merit the same reward as those who partook of the manna. He discards the waste and ingests only the purest elements of Hashem's abundance, without wasting any of His blessings. He fully appreciates whatever he receives from the Almighty, be it much or little, and puts it to effective use.

Shemini Atzeres and *Simchas Torah* are not merely days of blessings, but a time of the most refined form of Divine blessing, available only to those who devote themselves to Torah. (5662)

◆§ Shemini Atzeres: Deserved Blessings

The Mishnah (*Tannis* 2a) describes the prayer for rain recited on *Shemini Atzeres* (as well as the daily prayer recited in the second blessing of the *Amidah*) as גְּבוּרַת הַגֶּשֶׁם, "the strength of rain." This unusual expression can be understood by noting that rain ordinarily comes down in great strength (מִפְּנֵי שֶׁיּוֹרְדִין בִּגְבוּרָה).

Let us try to comprehend the true intent of the Talmud here. Why is this physical phenomenon of rain — its tendency to come down torrentially — of such spiritual importance that it gives its name to the prayer of *Shemini Atzeres?* Why emphasize the rain's strength?

The term "strength of rain" may refer not only to the manner in which rain comes down from the heavens, but also to the extraordinary human strength required to extract rain from certain "hostile" sources. On several occasions the Torah depicts Moshe as having extracted water from rocks (*Shemos* 17:6, *Bamidbar* 20:11). King David praises Hashem as the One הַהֹפְכִי הַצּוּר אֲגַם־מָיִם, *Who turns the rock into a pond of water* (*Tehillim* 114:8).

Apart from the miracle of drawing water from a stone, the fact that the source of the water was a rock is of great significance. Hashem bestows His bounty on all mankind and causes rain, regardless of man's merit — an undeserved act of Divine kindness. For the nations of the world, rainfall is associated with Succos, when Hashem's kindness and magnanimity manifests itself. The prophet Zechariah (14:16-19) suggests that those nations that will not make the pilgrimage to Jerusalem when the *Beis HaMikdash* is rebuilt will not enjoy Hashem's rains.

Israel, however, seeks no favors — our rainfall is deserved. Whereas water that comes as a Divine favor can come only from natural sources (e.g. the heavens, a flowing spring), deserved rain can be extracted from even the most hostile environment. Israel, and only Israel, possesses the ability to extract water from a rock and to find moisture in inhospitable places. While humankind obtains its yearly blessing of rainfall on Succos, a time of heightened Divine kindness, Israel waits a little longer. It derives its yearly allotment of rain (and other material blessings) on *Shemini Atzeres*, described by the Talmud as a Day of Judgment. On that day, Israel is judged by its Creator and, having been found deserving, is granted the ability to extract rain — with all its necessary strength

(גְבוּרַת הַגֶּשֶׁם) even under the most improbable conditions, during a period of judgment.

The renowned Rabbinic dictum (*Tannis* 2a) "The key of rain is granted only to Hashem" (i.e. angels cannot affect the flow of rainfall) conveys the same message. Hashem, and only Hashem, can reverse the natural order. Only He can provide rain from a rock, or on *Shemini Atzeres.*

The Psalmist alludes to the unique source of Israel's rainfall by associating strength with a multiple of the number eight (90:10), וְאִם בִּגְבוּרֹת שְׁמוֹנִים שָׁנָה, *And if with Strength — eighty years.* While the surface meaning of this verse refers to man's lifespan, the Psalmist may also be hinting at rain, which comes with strength. In other words, rain that is deserved and that can be extracted with strength from a rock if necessary, is decreed on the eighth day of Succos. (5655)

Simchas Torah

◆§ The Torah Itself Rejoices

To better appreciate this most joyous of festivals, let us first clarify who rejoices on *Simchas Torah.* Is it the Jewish people or possibly Hashem? Strictly speaking, however, the festival's name suggests that it is the Torah itself that rejoices. Let us first consider this possibility.

The Midrash (*Yalkut Shimoni, Bereishis* 2) says, "וָאֶהְיֶה אֶצְלוֹ אָמוֹן", הָיָה הקב"ה מַבִּיט בַּתּוֹרָה וּבָרָא אֶת הָעוֹלָם, "*And I was His artisan*" (*Mishlei* 8:30)*: Hashem looked at the Torah [for guidance] and created the world.* In considering whether or not to create a universe centered around man, with all his frailties, Hashem heeded the Torah's advice to proceed. (The renowned Rabbinic comment that "Hashem created the world in the merit of the Torah" (ibid.) can be interpreted as meaning that the universe was created because of the Torah's advice). The Torah not only wanted the universe to exist, it was also concerned that it should be a productive environment for Israel, the nation that would accept the Torah at Mount Sinai. A conscientious advisor thinks not only about the initial acceptance of his advice, but also that his counsel should lead to positive and enduring results. From the Torah's perspective, it was not enough merely for the world to be created; it also had to remain a viable entity. Every Rosh Hashanah and Yom Kippur, the continued viability of the universe is at stake, since the High Holy Days are a time of judgment not only for individuals but also for all of mankind. Indeed, human transgressions — if they were to reach sufficient proportions, Heaven forbid — could lead to the eradication of the universe.

Every year during the High Holy Days, the Torah fears that the universe, and especially Israel, will not survive. Since the Torah "worries" with us about the survival of the Jewish people, it has good reason to rejoice with us on *Simchas Torah*, knowing that whatever the fate of specific individuals may be, the community and its allegiance to Torah will continue. On *Simchas Torah*, the Torah rejoices that its advice to create the universe was once again vindicated, as the people of the Torah renew their collective lease on life. (5662)

◆§ Israel Rejoices as It Discovers Its "Light"

Returning to the question of who rejoices on *Simchas Torah*, let us examine an answer found in the liturgy of that day: נָגִיל וְנָשִׂישׂ בְּזֹאת הַתּוֹרָה כִּי הִיא לָנוּ עוֹז וְאוֹרָה, *Let us rejoice with the Torah, for it is our light and our strength.* The short stanza, chanted after completing the reading of the Torah on *Simchas Torah*, reveals not only who rejoices on *Simchas Torah*, but also the underlying reason for their joy. Israel rejoices ("let *us* rejoice"), for it has rediscovered its light. The Jewish people, having drifted away from the Torah into total darkness, now comes back to Torah's light and strength.

But how is this possible? How can a nation that lost its spiritual moorings find its way back to the light of Torah? The answer is through *mitzvos*. King Solomon (*Mishlei* 6:23) describes precisely the relationship between Torah and *mitzvos*: כִּי נֵר מִצְוָה וְתוֹרָה אוֹר, *Because a mitzvah is a lamp and the Torah is light*. It is impossible to obtain light without a source. As we celebrate our rediscovery of Torah's light on *Simchas Torah*, we must remember the source from which this light emanates.

To rephrase the question, how can mere mortals approach Hashem's

Torah? The conduit to Torah, the source of Torah's light, is *mitzvos*. As Moshe indicates in his farewell address, the Torah is a "fiery law" (אֵשׁ דָּת). Without the law, we could not survive the intensity of the Torah's fire — Hashem's word in its most abstract form without any physical symbols such as *mitzvos*. The well-known verse (*Devarim* 33:4), תּוֹרָה צִוָּה־לָנוּ מֹשֶׁה מוֹרָשָׁה קְהִלַּת יַעֲקֹב, *Moshe commanded the Torah to us the heritage of the congregation of Jacob*, alludes to the relationship between Torah and *mitzvos*. Moshe "disguised" the Torah's intense light (אוֹרָה) in the form of Divine commandments (which are relatively simple to observe) so that the Torah could remain Jacob's (and his descendants') possession (מוֹרָשָׁה) in perpetuity. The Jewish people could not survive on the basis of abstract Torah study, no matter how significant it is, without actual *mitzvah* performance.

This association between the source of light (*mitzvos*) and the light itself (Torah) explains the verse we commonly recite during the lifting of the Torah scroll after communal reading: וְזֹאת הַתּוֹרָה אֲשֶׁר־שָׂם מֹשֶׁה לִפְנֵי בְּנֵי יִשְׂרָאֵל, *This is the Torah that Moshe placed before the Jewish people* (*Devarim* 4:44). The term "placed" indicates that Moshe enabled Israel (i.e. placed a road before them) to benefit from Torah's light through the observance of *mitzvos*. An indication that he urged *mitzvah* observance as a means of coming closer to Torah can be seen from the *gematria* (numerical value) of the epithet by which he is commonly known, מֹשֶׁה רַבֵּינוּ, *Moshe Rabbeinu*, "Moshe our teacher" (of Torah), which equal 613 corresponding to the 613 commandments.

Recognizing the association between *mitzvos* and Torah, the Jewish people said (*Shemos* 24:7), נַעֲשֶׂה וְנִשְׁמַע, *We shall do [mitzvos] and we shall listen [to Torah]*. Through the empirical performance of *mitzvos*, we will merit to understand Torah.

The relationship between the source, *mitzvos*, and the light, Torah, also helps to explain *Simchas Torah's* position in the Jewish calendar, following the High Holy Days and Succos. One can bask in Torah's light only after a month of immersion in *mitzvos*. *Tishrei* (the month of the High Holy Days and Succos) also called in *Tanach* (*I Melachim* 8:2) the יֶרַח הָאֵתָנִים, *the month of the strong*, because of the powerful impact of its many *mitzvos* (e.g. *shofar, lulav, succah, aravah*, Libation of Water). Only after such a "saturation" in *mitzvos* can Israel benefit from Torah's light on *Simchas Torah*.

In closing, the liturgical piece cited above refers to the Torah's light with a feminine noun, אוֹרָה (*ohrah*), instead of the more common masculine word, אוֹר (*ohr*), a subtle but important distinction. Whereas *ohr* refers to Torah's light in the abstract, the term *ohrah* (elsewhere used in reference to the Jews' reaction to the defeat of Haman, see *Esther* 8:16) describes the extraordinary joy felt by Israel because it can grasp the profundities of Torah. (5662)

◆§ Israel Celebrates Torah's "Completion"

The custom of celebrating *Simchas Torah* is not explicitly mentioned in the Talmud. One of the most frequently cited sources for the Festival is the following Midrash (*Yalkut Shimoni Melachim I* 75): שֶׁעוֹשִׂין סְעוּדָה לְגָמְרָהּ שֶׁל תּוֹרָה, *One makes [i.e. celebrates by arranging] a meal upon the completion of the Torah.* This expression, "the completion of Torah," particularly as it is related to the celebrations of *Simchas Torah*, bears further clarification.

Simchas Torah is not an isolated festival that happens to follow the High Holy Days and Succos. On the contrary, the goal and final destination of the spiritual journey that started on Rosh Hashanah is *Simchas Torah*. Just as the commemoration of the physical Exodus every spring is only a prelude to reliving the acceptance of Torah at Sinai, so, too, the spiritual Exodus celebrated during the High Holy Days (i.e. freedom from the *yetzer hara* that stifles man, a theme developed in previous essays) is only a preparation for *Simchas Torah*. (According to this approach, *Simchas Torah* is the completion of the entire festival cycle, the goal toward which all other holidays pave the way.) The expression, "the completion of Torah," signifies that Torah and this holiday represent the climax of all other festivities. Indeed, in one sense, the purpose of the whole process of spiritual purification of Rosh Hashanah and Yom Kippur is to prepare us to accept the Torah on *Simchas Torah*. (5658)

The expression "Torah's completion" in the above Midrash is usually understood to refer to the annual completion of the cycle of weekly Torah readings. Why is that important? Hashem transmitted to Israel the Torah and its commandments in segments rather than all at once. For example, positive commandments were given as two hundred forty-eight separate entities. Similarly the three hundred sixty-five distinct negative commandments enable the Jewish people to absorb them in manageable doses.

Today also, the Torah is not transmitted all at once. A gradual process occurs whereby Israel absorbs the message of Torah spread out over fifty or fifty-four weeks. Each annual Torah cycle has its own message, its own lessons that it seeks to impart to Israel as each generation finds new meaning in the weekly reading. Thus, on *Simchas Torah* we celebrate not only the completion of Torah but also the cumulative effect of all the weekly Torah readings. All the lessons of each individual Torah reading coalesce to give meaning to the entire Torah. The Torah and all its teachings are completed every *Simchas Torah.*

Alternatively, one can think in terms of a pyramid consisting of different levels of Torah comprehension. On the one hand, the angels enjoy a far more sophisticated understanding of Torah than Israel does. However, Israel is unique in one respect: No angel and no other people can practice Torah in the same way the Jewish people do. Torah without observance of *mitzvos* (as discussed above) is incomplete. On *Simchas Torah,* in celebrating the completion of Torah, we really celebrate the renewed existence of Israel, who completes the Torah through adherence to a Torah life style and through observance of *mitzvos.*

(5658)

◆§ A Day of Perfect Unity

Israel rejoices on *Simchas Torah* because on this day Hashem (the Transmitter of the Torah), Israel (the receiver of the Torah), and the Torah itself become inseparable. This relationship is articulated in the renowned Rabbinic saying, יִשְׂרָאֵל וְאוֹרַיְתָא וְקוּדְשָׁא בְּרִיךְ הוּא חַד הוּא, *The Jewish people, the Torah and Hashem are one.* (*Zohar, Acharei Mos* 73)

The essence of *Simchas Torah* can be best captured in one word: דְבֵיקוּת, *clinging.* Israel clings to the Torah, and to Hashem, the Giver of the Torah, regardless of the consequences. It is this adversity against all odds that leads to that intimate relationship between Hashem, Israel and the Torah, that we celebrate on *Simchas Torah.*

Of equal importance, is that on *Simchas Torah* we celebrate *achdus,* unity among Jews. As we complete the Torah, we remember that the true goal of Torah study is to create a united Jewish community. The well-known dialogue between Hillel and a prospective convert, related by the Talmud (*Shabbos* 31a), serves to underscore this point. A non-Jew came to Hillel and pleaded, "Teach me the entire Torah while I stand on one foot." To this Hillel responded, "Don't do to others what you don't want them to do to you. This is the essence of Torah, and the remainder is merely commentary. Go and study it!"

Hillel's response suggests that Torah and *mitzvos* are powerful vehicles that can lead to a united world Jewry. As cited above, the Midrash advocates feasting on the occasion of the Torah's completion, traditionally observed on *Simchas Torah.* In light of the above remarks, it may be possible to reinterpret the expression "completion of the Torah" as a reference to the final effect of Torah study on the Jewish people, the emergence of one nation united through Torah. (5654)

☙ Simchas Torah and Shavuos
Shavuos: Celebrating the Supernatural Torah
Simchas Torah: Torah's Relevance to the Natural World

The association between Shavuos and *Simchas Torah,* both of which celebrate Israel's relationship to Torah, is best expressed in an observation by King Solomon (*Koheles* 7:11): טוֹבָה חָכְמָה עִם־נַחֲלָה וְיֹתֵר לְרֹאֵי הַשָּׁמֶשׁ, *Wisdom is good together with an inheritance, and even better for [because of] those who see the sun.*

This verse contrasts two different roles Torah might play in the world. The first (though it is stated second, in the words *see the sun*) is as a solitary and ruling force in a world. This would have been possible had Israel not been ensnared in the worship of the Golden Calf. Shavuos celebrates precisely such a Torah-dominated world. The annual celebration of the Giving of the Torah on Shavuos reminds us of that first Shavuos, when Israel forsook any remaining association with the material world, in favor of a new supernatural order, and opted to live as angels. Israel chose to be among those "who see the sun," who perceive Hashem with the clarity that only angels enjoy.

This approach, however attractive it may seem, was found not to be viable on a permanent basis as shown by the sin of the Golden Calf. Men cannot live as angels do. In the aftermath of this gravest of sins, a very different role for Torah was envisioned, expressed by King Solomon as *wisdom together with inheritance.* In this new world, Torah (wisdom) would prove that it could not only exist alongside Hashem's inheritance (the natural world) but that it could be the dominant force.

Certain changes were required for Torah to survive and prevail in the natural world. No longer would just Ten Commandments suffice. A far more detailed exposition of Torah (including the Oral Law) was necessary to enable the Jew to meet the challenges of the secular world. Many more *mitzvos* dealing with the material world were transmitted to Israel to help them grapple with daily life. The Midrash (*Koheles Rabbah* 7:22) describes the world after Israel's sin by citing the Mishnah (*Avos* 2:2) יָפֶה תַלְמוּד תּוֹרָה עִם דֶּרֶךְ אֶרֶץ, *It is pleasant to study Torah along with the ways of the world [i.e. daily life].*

In light of the above discussion, we can now appreciate the role of *Simchas Torah* vis-a-vis that of Shavuos. On Shavuos we celebrate the ideal Torah as it was first transmitted to Israel. On *Simchas Torah,* though, we celebrate Israel's ability to survive in the real world because of the Torah.

One question remains. If through Torah one can cope with the challenges of the world, why was it necessary to give the Torah originally in a supernatural fashion? Or, to rephrase the question, if we celebrate *Simchas Torah* and its message that Torah pertains to daily life, why do we also observe Shavuos?

The answer is that *Simchas Torah* would not have been possible without Shavuos. The Torah's domination over the natural world was possible only because it was given supernaturally at first. The fire and drama of that first Shavuos instilled such piety and fear into the Jewish heart that later it was possible to remove the outer trappings of Sinai — and still have the Jews observe Torah. A careful examination of the beginning of the verse cited above reveals that King Solomon understood that the supernatural beginning we celebrate on Shavuos was a prerequisite for day-to-day observance of the Torah. *Wisdom is good together with an inheritance, and even better for those who see the sun.* The expression *even more* (וְיוֹתֵר) may refer to the extraordinary accomplishment of maintaining a Torah lifestyle in a secular world. If this feat was possible, it was only because of those who *see the sun,* the pioneering efforts of the first generations that received the Torah at Sinai. (5649)

We can give another explanation of the apparent redundancy of *Simchas Torah* and Shavuos. Shavuos commemorates the first giving of the Ten Commandments, transmitted to a generation of righteous Jews. The festivities of *Simchas Torah,* however, remind us that the Torah was given a second time on Yom Kippur, this time to repentant Jews. The Jewish people, having returned to Hashem in the aftermath of the sin of the Golden Calf, now deserved a festival of their own, in addition to Shavuos, to celebrate Torah's renewed significance for them.

The early nineteenth century scholar *Chiddushei HaRim* (grandfather of the *Sfas Emes*) noted that Moshe tarried on Mount Sinai just as long for the second Tablets as for the first. If the second giving of the Torah on Yom Kippur had been merely a repetition of the ceremony at Sinai, this additional learning period would not have been necessary. We can say, however, that Moshe had to relearn the Torah in order to teach Hashem's word to an entire new generation, a generation composed of the same people but still radically different in spirit: the generation of returnees.

The Talmud (*Berachos* 34b) states that the returnee enjoys a "place" not available to those who have always remained righteous: מָקוֹם שֶׁבַּעֲלֵי תְשׁוּבָה עוֹמְדִין צַדִּיקִים גְּמוּרִים אֵינָם עוֹמְדִין, *In the place where the returnee stands, [even] the totally righteous do not stand.*

Perhaps we can say, then, that the place enjoyed by the returnee is the holiday of *Simchas Torah*, given to Israel after it repented from the sin of the Golden Calf.

Already during the six days of creation, Hashem showed special "affection" towards Adam after he confessed his sin. Whereas the creation of each day is described as "good," the creation of Adam (who partook of the forbidden fruit and then repented, all on the day of his creation) is described as "very good" (*Yalkut Shimoni* 15).

This portrayal of *Simchas Torah* as a celebration of *teshuvah* (repentance) may also explain the placement of this festival (and that of the preceding day, *Shemini Atzeres)* in the Jewish calendar. While a seven week period is required between *Pesach* and Shavuos, which celebrates the Torah of the already committed Jew, *Simchas Torah*, celebrating the Torah of the returnees is observed *immediately* after Succos. Perhaps this is because the *baal teshuvah* is able to accomplish in a moment what for others may require weeks. Every year, after the High Holy Days, Israel is able to proceed immediately to *Simchas Torah.*

The relationship between *Simchas Torah* and Shavuos can be understood in yet another manner. Shavuos celebrates Israel's acceptance of the Torah. Yet, what is the value of Torah unless it leaves a lasting impact on its students? On *Simchas Torah*, which comes a number of months after Shavuos, during which period the Torah is gradually absorbed, it is finally appropriate to celebrate Torah's effect on the Jewish people.

A parallel can be drawn between the yearly cycle of the farmer and that of the Torah Jew. The grain harvest commences on Pesach, continues through Shavuos, and reaches its climax on Succos, which the Torah calls חַג הָאָסִיף, *the Festival of Gathering.* So too, the first fruit of Torah is celebrated on Shavuos, and its complete fruit on *Simchas Torah.* King Solomon's dictum (*Koheles* 7:8), טוֹב אַחֲרִית דָּבָר מֵרֵאשִׁיתוֹ, *Better something's end [Torah's maturity] than its beginning [Torah's initial stages],* suggests the relationship between Torah's "infancy" on Shevuos and its "maturity" on *Simchas Torah.*

The association between Shavuos and *Simchas Torah* can also be compared to the blessings recited before and after eating. The purpose of the blessings before eating is to thank Hashem for the food one is about to eat, while the blessing after eating is to thank Hashem for the sustenance and strength obtained from the food — its "impact." Similarly, the blessing before a public reading of the Torah thanks Hashem for giving Israel the Torah, while the blessing recited after the reading, *Who has given us a Torah of truth and implanted permanent life within us,* gives thanks for the Torah's impact on an individual.

It may be possible to extend the analysis further by suggesting that the distinction between Shavuos and *Simchas Torah* lies in the nature of the Torah being commemorated. On Shavuos, it was the Written Law that was given to Moshe, whereas on *Simchas Torah* we celebrate the Oral Law, which teaches us how to interpret and apply the Written Law.

In conclusion let us note that, despite significant differences that exist between these two occasions, they also share notable points of similarity. On both *Simchas Torah* and Shavuos, the Torah is revealed among men (i.e. people can feel the sanctity of Torah in this world) unlike other times, when Torah's sanctity is hardly apparent to the uninitiated. King Solomon hints at the unique nature of these two days in the following verse (*Mishlei* 8:30): וָאֶהְיֶה אֶצְלוֹ אָמוֹן ... מְשַׂחֶקֶת לְפָנָיו, *I [Torah] was hidden [by Hashem from man] ... I will be a plaything before him [available to delight humankind].* On most occasions, the Torah is hidden to all but the most discerning; on Shavuos and *Simchas Torah,* though, ordinary mortals can sense Torah's revelation in this world.

(5634, 5636, 5639, 5640, 5647, 5649)

◆§ The Universe Returns to Torah Standards

Why should we rejoice on *Simchas Torah?* To answer this question, we must keep in mind that the High Holy Days are not only a time of judgment, but also a period of renewal for the world. On Rosh Hashanah the world returns full cycle to its historical beginnings, to its first day when Hashem said, "Let there be Light." The short period between Rosh Hashanah and *Shemini Atzeres* — when there is a great opportunity for Jews and Gentiles to participate in the renewal process — is comparable to the period spanning more than two millennia from the Creation of the world until the Torah was given at Sinai, during which time the world existed on the basis of unmerited Divine kindness. On Rosh Hashanah, Yom Kippur and Succos, Hashem opens the floodgates of repentance, allowing everyone, Jew and Gentile alike, to return to Him.[1]

On Succos all of humanity is graced with numerous undeserved blessings. On *Shemini Atzeres* and *Simchas Torah* this "grace period" expires. Every year at that time, the relationship between merit and reward is re-established and Hashem's management of the universe returns to the standard set at Mount Sinai by which merit leads to reward. On *Simchas Torah* Israel celebrates the return of its special relationship with the Creator that was temporarily suspended during humankind's judgment season.

Judaism's love of truth — expressed through rewards gained or as a result of Israel's effort, rather than unmerited kindness — is alluded to in the blessing recited after a communal reading of the Torah, אֲשֶׁר נָתַן לָנוּ תּוֹרַת אֱמֶת, *Who gave us a Torah of truth.* This expression is usually understood incorrectly to mean that Hashem gave us a truthful Torah. If that were so, however, the blessing should read תּוֹרָה אֲמִיתִּית, *a truthful Torah,* rather than the way it actually reads, תּוֹרַת אֱמֶת, *a Torah of truth.* This way suggests that studying Torah is a means to an even higher end, attaining and understanding Truth. In a universe too often beset with falsehood, it is only through Torah that Israel can grasp what is true.

---

1. The shape a *succah* must have in order to meet the minimum requirements — two complete walls and a partially open third wall — resembles the letter *heh*, ה, which also consists of two complete sides and a partially open third side, symbolizing the wide opening through which the penitent may return. See *Menachos* 29b.

Let us contemplate the ramifications of the above statement. Through Torah, and only through Torah, can the true meaning of a situation be evaluated. It is only through Torah that a person's nature, his true potential, can be revealed. An allusion to Torah's ability to bring man's true nature to the forefront can be found in the word צֶלֶם, man's image (cf. *Bereishis* 1:27), which is also an acronym for צִוָּה לָנוּ מֹשֶׁה (תּוֹרָה), *Moshe commanded us [Torah].* It is only through the Torah transmitted by Moshe that a man's "image," his profile and full potential, can be realized. (5646, 5648)

◈ Response to the Angels' Complaint

To gain a better appreciation of the special role played by *Simchas Torah* in the annual "renewal" of the world (as discussed in the previous essay), let us consider several passages in *Tehillim* (8:3-7) that deal with man's creation: לְהַשְׁבִּית אוֹיֵב וּמִתְנַקֵּם — *To silence foe and avenger [who pleads],* מָה אֱנוֹשׁ כִּי תִזְכְּרֶנּוּ וּבֶן אָדָם כִּי תִפְקְדֶנּוּ — *What is frail man that You should remember him, and the son of mortal man that You should be mindful of him?* וַתְּחַסְּרֵהוּ מְּעַט מֵאֱלֹהִים וְכָבוֹד וְהָדָר תְּעַטְּרֵהוּ — *Yet, You have made him but slightly less than the angels, and crowned him with honor and splendor.* תַּמְשִׁילֵהוּ בְּמַעֲשֵׂי יָדֶךָ — *You gave him dominion over Your handiwork.*

The Midrash (*Yalkut Shimoni Tehillim* 651) suggests that the complaint, "Who is man?" was voiced by the angels at the time of man's creation. When Hashem was about to create man He "consulted" with the angels. Hashem suggested, "Let us create man." They (the angels) said, "What is man that You remember him?"

As we have said, the process of creation is renewed every year, beginning on Rosh Hashanah and culminating on *Shemini Atzeres* and *Simchas Torah.* It is reasonable to assume that not only the creation of the universe is renewed annually, but also that the angels' complaint is repeated every year at this time. Thus, on Rosh Hashanah, the Day of Remembrance, they would say, "Who is man that You remember him," and on Yom Kippur, the day that man approaches the level of angels, they would say "You caused him to lack nothing but being like Hashem." "And crowned him with honor and splendor" is an apt description of Succos, when the Jewish people are graced with the "Cloud of Honor" and the Four Species, including the "fruit of a splendid tree" (פְּרִי עֵץ הָדָר). Finally, the angels complain, "You gave him dominion over Your handiwork," referring to *Shemini Atzeres*, ("Atzeres", in this approach, is associated with the attribute of Sovereignty). On *Shemini Atzeres*, Israel is vindicated and its prominence restored, while the rest of humanity is rejected. (Thus the Torah says, (*Bamidbar* 29:35) *It shall be an Atzeres for* ***you***).

The ultimate response to the angels' complaint is that man was created in the merit of Torah. Only Israel proved worthy of the challenge of being called man — only Israel accepted and upheld the Torah.

The reason for the joy of *Simchas Torah* should now be apparent. Every year at this time, despite the angels' objections, the universe and with it man's lease on life is renewed — all in the merit of Torah. Consequently on *Simchas Torah* we delight in the Torah to which Israel owes its survival and rejuvenation. (5646)

◆§ Israel's Initiative

As we have said, the festival of *Simchas Torah* is neither a Biblical nor a Rabbinic obligation. Rather, according to the *Zohar* (*Parashas Pinchas*), *Simchas Torah* is a custom started by the Jewish people themselves, because of the special bond they sensed between Israel and the Torah on this day. Many *mitzvos* help to cement the connection between Hashem and His people during *Tishrei*, including *shofar, succah, lulav*, and the Libation of Water. Now, however, in the final days of the festival season, none of these *mitzvos* remain — yet Israel feels closer than ever to its Creator. Moreover, Israel rejoices during Succos by participating in the festival's many *mitzvos*: *succah, lulav*, and the *aravah* ceremony of *Hoshana Rabbah* all lend a joyous ambiance to the festival.

On *Shemini Atzeres* and *Simchas Torah*, however, these external trappings of joy no longer exist — yet Israel radiates joy. Surely, the joy that permeates *Simchas Torah* must be an internal thing, generated by Torah. Bursting with that internal joy, the nation of Torah had no choice but to designate that day as a festival, *Simchas Torah*.

An allusion to the internal joy of these days can be found in the Torah's proclamation of *Shemini Atzeres* (*Bamidbar* 29:35): עֲצֶרֶת תִּהְיֶה לָכֶם, *It shall be an Atzeres [an ingathering of the emotion] for you [alone]. Shemini Atzeres* and *Simchas Torah* are a private time of rejoicing, originating in Israel's initiative, but encouraged enthusiastically by Hashem.

Not only does Hashem embrace Israel's initiative but even more, on *Simchas Torah,* He rewards them with a hint of the special ecstasy their forefathers felt in the *Beis HaMikdash.* Such intense joy independent of the physical stimuli of *succah* or *lulav* is today possible only on *Simchas Torah.* This is the same joy that was felt in the *Beis HaMikdash* three times a year — on Pesach, Shevuos, Succos. On *Simchas Torah,* as a reward for Israel's initiative, the Jew basks in the inner serenity and joy that once existed in the Temple. (5636, 5637, 5643, 5648)

◂§ A Day of Renewed Commitment for an Entire Year

Really, though, *Simchas Torah* is not an isolated moment of joy in the Jewish year. Rather, coming at the culmination of a joyous Succos, the happiness with which this day is saturated gives the Jewish people strength and enthusiasm to study Torah joyously throughout the coming year.

The Mishah (*Avos* 3:6) emphasizes the vital importance of commitment to Torah. *If someone takes upon himself the yoke of Torah — the yoke of government [e.g., oppressive taxation] and the yoke of worldly responsibilities are removed from him [i.e. he will prosper materially].*

A commitment to any worthwhile undertaking should be made in advance. There is no better day to commit oneself to Torah — and to do so joyously — than *Simchas Torah.* The Talmud (*Shabbos* 130a) suggests that any *mitzvah* started with joy will always be performed joyously. If Israel accepts the Torah with joy on this happiest of festivals, it will assuredly continue studying Torah joyously in the year ahead. (5637)

In fact, *Simchas Torah,* with its heartfelt joy, serves to ensure that the Torah one learns will not be forgotten in the year ahead. Even the businessman with his many worries will retain his Torah knowledge if he makes a commitment to Torah on *Simchas Torah* with joy and sincerity. (5634)

◂§ Completion of Teshuvah

The happiness of *Simchas Torah* is the culmination of a process begun on Rosh Hashanah, the process of *teshuvah.* The *Zohar* (*Parashas Naso*) identifies two types of *baalei teshuvah* (penitents). One rights the wrongs he has done but does not attempt to develop a new relationship with Hashem. The more committed *baal teshuvah* is not satisfied with merely correcting his sins, but tries to reinstate himself in Hashem's good graces and, above all, to renew his dedication to Torah study with the same devotion he had before his sin. Israel, as well as the rest of humankind, achieves the first phase of return during the High Holy Days. However, the return to Torah study is achieved only on *Simchas Torah*, when the annual cycle of Torah readings is completed. Thus, part of the joy of *Simchas Torah* comes from the perception that the lengthy process of return, begun before Rosh Hashanah, has at last reached a successful conclusion. (5636)

◆§ Culmination of the High Holy Days

Links generally are drawn between *Simchas Torah* and the festival immediately preceding it, Succos. However, it may also be possible to view *Simchas Torah* as the fulfillment of the entire season beginning with the High Holy Days and continuing through Succos. The purpose of these occasions is to bring the Jew closer to Torah, the goal that is realized on *Simchas Torah*.

The association between *Simchas Torah* and the High Holy Days is hinted at in the *Shema*. וְאָהַבְתָּ אֵת ה׳ אֱלֹהֶיךָ בְּכָל־לְבָבְךָ וּבְכָל־נַפְשְׁךָ וּבְכָל־מְאֹדֶךָ, *You shall love* H*ASHEM*, *your God, with all your heart, with all your soul and with all your resources* (*Devarim* 6:5). The first part of this commandment, to love Hashem *with all your heart*, is most relevant to Rosh Hashanah, on which we attempt to channel all of our thoughts, even our evil passions, to higher and more spiritual ends. *With all your soul* refers to Yom Kippur, when we afflict our souls (cf. *Vayikra* 16:31) *With all your resources* alludes to Succos, when the Jew, despite his successful harvest, abandons the material comforts of his home in favor of the simple *succah*.

This verse talks about the Jew's obligation to give up his wealth and even his life for his beloved God. The next verse speaks of the ensuing reward: וְהָיוּ הַדְּבָרִים הָאֵלֶּה . . . עַל־לְבָבֶךָ, *Let these matters . . . be upon your heart*. The reward for observing the previous holidays is that Torah will be implanted in every Jewish heart, and that reward is given on *Simchas Torah*. (5635)

⇜§ Compensation for the Loss of the Beis HaMikdash

Perhaps the simplest reason that the custom of observing *Simchas Torah* originated in the Diaspora is that, as long as the *Beis HaMikdash* stood, there was no need for special celebrations to engender joy. The *mitzvos* of Succos as observed in the Temple, such as the Libation of Water and the offerings, gave the people of those times several opportunities to experience happiness. In our generations, however, as the liturgy of Yom Kippur says so poignantly, אֵין לָנוּ שִׁיוּר רַק הַתּוֹרָה הַזֹּאת, *we have only this Torah as a remnant.*

Only through Torah study can we compensate for the absence of the rituals of the *Beis HaMikdash*. For example, if one studies the laws of the offerings, it is considered as if he had actually brought them. Thus, by studying the *mitzvos* performed joyously in the *Beis HaMikdash* on Succos, we can experience some of the joy felt by previous generations. On *Simchas Torah* then, Torah compensates for Judaism's greatest loss — the destruction of the *Beis HaMikdash.* (5635)

⇜§ Shemini Atzeres and Simchas Torah: The Jew Enters Hashem's Home

The role of these final days of Succos in the overall setting of the holiday season can be appreciated by remembering that the *succah* is frequently compared to Hashem's home. On Succos, Hashem's Presence is made manifest in this world, but on *Shemini Atzeres* and *Simchas Torah,* an even greater spiritual feat occurs: Instead of bringing Hashem's Presence into our homes, we accompany him to His domicile.

Rashi (*Bamidbar* 29:35) says that on *Shemini Atzeres* the Jewish people bid farewell to Hashem after an elaborate and successful holiday season by making a "farewell feast" for Hashem. But Israel refuses to leave! Instead, armed with the Torah, it enters Hashem's home and obstinately makes a dwelling place for itself there. This is the message imparted by these final, sacred days of Succos — that the student of Torah dwells permanently in Hashem's abode. (5637)

Moshe's Blessings

⊲§ Moshe's Farewell Blessings — Introduction

The Talmud (*Megillah* 31a) rules that Moshe's farewell blessings to the people be read on the second day of *Shemini Atzeres.* In post-Talmudic times, the custom arose of completing the annual cycle of Torah readings on this day, accompanied by a celebration in honor of the event. These festivities eventually caused the day to be known as *Simchas Torah.* It is evident however, from the above cited ruling of the Talmud that Moshe's blessings had already been read on the second day of *Shemini Atzeres* (i.e. *Simchas Torah)* even before the custom evolved to complete the Torah at this time. Possibly Moshe's farewell was chosen as the most appropriate reading for the "farewell" holiday — the last of the festivals of *Tishrei*.

The following essay explores in detail several elements of Moshe's farewell blessings, which are as pertinent today to the Jew about to go into the workplace at the holiday's conclusion, as they were to the people who stood on the Plains of Moab, on the threshold of their entry into the new land.

⊲§ The Uniqueness of Moshe's Blessings

וְזֹאת הַבְּרָכָה אֲשֶׁר בֵּרַךְ מֹשֶׁה אִישׁ הָאֱלֹהִים אֶת־בְּנֵי יִשְׂרָאֵל לִפְנֵי מוֹתוֹ

And this is the blessing which Moshe, the man of God, bestowed upon the Children of Israel before his death (*Devarim* 33:1).

In preface, let us consider why we read Moshe's blessings on *Simchas Torah* and in what way these blessings are unique. The Torah is filled with blessings (such as those of Jacob and Bilaam, to name but a few) — why do we read only these on this day?

One answer is that this is the festival that Israel enjoys in the merit of Moshe. As noted in a previous essay, *Shemini Atzeres* (and *Simchas Torah)* was given to Israel as a "bonus" supplement to the Pilgrimage Festivals in the merit of Moshe. It is only fitting that his blessings are read on the holiday which is attributable to him.

More profoundly, not only Moshe's personal greatness but also his role as the transmitter of the Torah to Israel makes these blessings relevant to *Simchas Torah*. These were not the only blessings related in the Torah: The Midrash (*Yalkut Shimoni, V'zos HaBerachah* 949) notes that Moshe was one link in the chain of those who gave the Jewish people their blessings, starting with the Patriarchs. Moreover, the concept of blessings is not unique to Israel. Hashem blesses all of mankind, and indeed showers them with blessings.

Moshe's blessings however have one unique aspect: His blessings were earned with the merit of Torah, rather than received as undeserved gifts. Whereas the Patriarchs' blessed their heirs long before the Torah was given at Mount Sinai, Moshe blessed a nation that had spent the previous forty years immersed in Torah study. It is therefore appropriate that we read blessings earned through Torah study on the day that marks the completion of the annual Torah reading cycle. Naturally, these blessings are granted only to Israel, the nation that most cherishes and appreciates blessings.

This concept, that Moshe's blessings were earned through Torah study, sheds light on the suggestion of the Midrash (*Devarim Rabbah* 11:4) that the Torah itself blesses the Jewish people. The Torah joined with Hashem to transmit its blessings to Israel, through Moshe.

If these blessings came to Israel through the Torah, *Simchas Torah's* position in the festival cycle becomes more understandable. Through the whole month of *Tishrei*, Israel beseeches the Creator for the blessings of life, peace and joy. Hashem in turn responds by showering mankind with blessings (e.g. the fall harvest), especially during Succos. By continuing the festival season beyond Succos, celebrating *Shemini Atzeres* and *Simchas Torah* (holidays which have no significance to mankind at large), Israel demonstrates that it is not content with mere blessings: It desires blessings earned by means of a Torah-true lifestyle.

How do Torah-generated blessings differ from ordinary blessings? What would it matter if Israel simply shared in the general blessings humanity receives every Succos? The answer is that the blessings of Torah are infinitely more powerful than any others. While ordinary blessings can only benefit those who have not previously been cursed, those derived from Torah are able to convert curses into blessings.

This unique ability of the Torah to overturn curses is vividly illustrated by the comparison of the opening letter of the Ten Commandments with that of the Creation story. *Bereishis* begins with a letter *beis*, for בְּרָכָה, *blessing* alluding to the physical world's desperate need for blessings merely to survive. The Ten Commandments, however, which mark Israel's initiation to Torah, begin with the letter *aleph*, connoting the word אָרוּר, *cursed* because Torah has the power to transform curses into blessings. Thus the wicked Gentile prophet Bilaam failed in his attempt to curse the Torah nation. His curses became blessings even before he had the opportunity to express them (see *Devarim* 23:6).

Numerous other examples show that the Torah, the Torah nation of Israel, and Torah-oriented individuals have the power to convert curses into blessings. In a poignant scene, the Midrash (*Yalkut Shimoni V'zos HaBeracha* 951) depicts Moshe holding off the Angel of Death while he gave Israel his final blessings. Death can at least be forestalled through the power of Torah.

On *Shemini Atzeres*, the day before the annual reading of these blessings, Israel prays for the "strength of rain" (גְבוּרַת גְשָׁמִים). The Torah nation is not content with just the usual rain, but asks for rain acquired through strength — rain acquired from the least propitious source. Again, the Jewish people convert "curse" — a source incapable of producing rain — into blessings (see our earlier essay on *Shemini Atzeres*).

The Torah itself was given at Mount Sinai through the medium of fire. In this instance fire, ordinarily a destructive force, became a source of perpetual life, again because the Torah possesses the power to convert curses into blessings. Even if this were not so, however, the position of Moshe's blessings in the Torah would be conducive to transforming curses into blessings. Generally, good endings override bad beginnings. Because they come at the end of the Torah, the power of Moshe's blessings supersede any negative effect of the curses mentioned earlier in the Torah.

The lives of the righteous are compared to a path strewn with thorns at the beginning but clear at the end. After years of frustration and suffering their accumulated blessings finally prevail. This is another example of the power of Torah to turn curses to blessings.

The Festival *Shemoneh Esrei* prayer contains an allusion to this added potency of blessings that come in the merit of Torah: וְהַשִּׂיאֵנוּ ה׳ אֱלֹהֵינוּ אֶת בִּרְכַּת מוֹעֲדֶיךָ לְחַיִּים וּלְשָׁלוֹם לְשִׂמְחָה וּלְשָׂשׂוֹן כַּאֲשֶׁר רָצִיתָ וְאָמַרְתָּ לְבָרְכֵנוּ, *Bestow upon us, O* HASHEM, *our God, the blessing of Your appointed festivals for life and for peace, for gladness and for joy, as You desired and promised to bless us.* The phrase, *As You desired*, is a subtle plea to be blessed in the manner in which Hashem wishes man to be blessed — blessings earned through Torah.

What made Moshe's blessings so unique is that they were given in the full light of day, (*Devarim* 32:48) that is, with an extra infusion of spirituality. *Rashi* (*Shemos* 2:2) notes that at Moshe's birth his house was suffused with light. Similarly, Moshe ascended Mount Nebo to meet his death during the בְּעֶצֶם הַיּוֹם הַזֶּה, "brilliance of the day" (*Devarim* 32:48), which we can understand to mean that he departed in a burst of light. Thus, he fulfilled one of the Torah's most moving blessings (*Devarim* 28:6): בָּרוּךְ אַתָּה בְּבֹאֶךָ וּבָרוּךְ אַתָּה בְּצֵאתֶךָ, *Blessed are you when you enter and blessed are you when you leave.* As *Rashi* renders this — may you leave the world without sin — the same as when you entered the world. Just as Moshe's birth was accompanied by a great light, his passing too was graced with light.

(5647, 5652, 5660, 5665)

◆ Moshe's Blessings: Continuation of a Tradition

Moshe's farewell blessings begin abruptly, as if in the middle of a sentence. The phrase *AND this is the blessing* suggests that these blessings, unique as they were, were also a continuation of the farewell blessings of the righteous of earlier generations, especially of Jacob's. Indeed, the exact same word that opens these blessings, וְזֹאת, *and this*, is found in the closing of Jacob's blessings (see *Bereishis* 49:28).

The structure of Moshe's blessings also parallels that of Jacob's in that both bestow individual blessings on each of the twelve tribes.[1] Furthermore, Jacob and Moshe shared the same primary function in life — both were pillars of Torah. As revealed in the verse (*Michah* 7:20), תִּתֵּן אֱמֶת לְיַעֲקֹב, *Give truth to Jacob* Jacob incessantly sought out the truth of Torah, even before it was given. (5663)

1. Thus it is appropriate that we read Moshe's blessings on *Simchas Torah,* as we seek blessings for the forthcoming twelve months. (See *Tur Orach Chaim Hilchos Rosh Chodesh*).

The conjunction *and* that opens this verse suggests another critical transition that occurred with Moshe's passing. He was the sole transmitter of the Written Law. (While all of Scriptures, including the Prophets and the Writings are considered part of Written Law, the *mitzvos* are derived only from the Torah itself.) Since his death and Joshua's rise to leadership, the text of the Torah was in place to be interpreted according to a set of rules that are the basis of the Oral Law, the thirteen hermeneutic principles.

Thus, the death of Moshe marked the completion of the Written Law and the beginning of the period in which the Law would be transmitted on an oral basis. By beginning his farewell blessings with the linking word "and," Moshe was suggesting that his blessings' which though they were included in the body of Torah were not an integral part of the law. They served as a bridge between the Written Law he had transmitted and the process of Oral Law that would characterize the period of his successors. (5665)

Alternatively, we can say that the conjunction *and* is a link back to the beginning of the Torah. As discussed earlier, the Torah begins with a letter *beis*, symbolizing בְּרָכָה, *blessing*. However, the blessings in the early part of the Torah were long in coming to fruition. The Jews underwent frustrations and hardship in Egypt and through the forty-year trek in the Wilderness. In addition to the physical privations, they also experienced the even more difficult *spiritual* struggle to understand and practice the Torah. Now, as he was about to close his eyes for the last time, Moshe could look upon a mature nation ready to enter the Promised Land and proclaim, "And *this* is the blessing alluded to at the beginning of time with the opening *beis* — finally Israel has truly become a nation of Torah, as it was promised from the beginning of creation." (5647)

◆§ The Second Verse of Moshe's Blessings

וַיֹּאמַר ה׳ מִסִּינַי בָּא וְזָרַח מִשֵּׂעִיר לָמוֹ הוֹפִיעַ מֵהַר פָּארָן וְאָתָה מֵרִבְבֹת קֹדֶשׁ מִימִינוֹ אֵשְׁדָּת לָמוֹ

And he said: HASHEM approached from Sinai — having shone forth to them from Seir, having appeared from Mount Paran, and then approached with some of the holy myriads [of angels] — from His right hand He presented the fiery Torah to them [Israel] (33:2).

This verse is interpreted as an allusion to Hashem's first offering the Torah to other nations before giving it to Israel. Specifically mentioned are the nations of Seir (Esau, ancestor of the Romans) and Paran (Ishmael and the Arab nations), as well as the angels, all of whom rejected viable contenders for the prized possession of Torah.

We must wonder what purpose would have been served had the angels received the Torah. As Moshe himself argued when he went to Heaven to receive the Torah, (*Shabbos* 89a) "Do you work six days a week [that you need rest on the Sabbath]? Do you have parents to honor?" Similarly, it is difficult to conceive of the non-Jewish world appreciating Torah in the same form as we do. What would many of the more esoteric concepts of Torah mean to the world at large?

It appears that each nation would have benefited from Torah presented in a way based on its level of sophistication. Perhaps Edom and Paran would have been offered a simpler version of Torah, containing language similar to that of our Torah but lacking access to its more esoteric concepts. Conversely, the angels would have focused on only the most sublime aspects of Torah.[1]

In this interpretation, Hashem's original intention was to offer Israel an "intermediate" Torah — a version deeper than that offered to the Gentile world, yet less profound than that of the angels. The *Zohar* (*Balak* 192b), however, suggests that the clause *having shone forth to them from Seir* refers to the shining of Hashem's countenance on Israel because Seir and other nations had rejected Torah. The above discussion helps us understand this passage from the *Zohar*. Israel would have been offered a version of the Torah in any case, regardless of what the rest of mankind chose. However, because Seir rejected the Torah completely, Israel was able to benefit from even the simple meaning of the Torah, originally intended for the non-Jewish world alone. Similarly, the deeper elements of Torah, originally intended for the angels, were now also given to Israel.

(This insight suggests another meaning of the word *and* in the phrase *And this is the blessing*. In addition to the portions of the Torah originally designated for Israel, Hashem also gave them portions intended for the non-Jewish world.)

The assumption that Israel was not the intended recipient of the simplest level of Torah can help us more fully understand the first *Rashi*

---

1. See *Ramban on Bereishis* 1:1 for further discussion of this theme.

in the Torah. *Rashi* states that the reason the Torah starts with *Bereishis*, rather than with the first *mitzvah* given the Jewish nation, was to justify giving the Jews "the inheritance of nations," *Eretz Yisrael*, which they were to inherit from the seven Canaanite nations. This suggests that the story told in *Sefer Bereishis* was originally intended for the Gentile world. When they declined to accept the Torah, Israel became heir to the "inheritance of nations" and was given the story of *Bereishis* as part of its Torah as well. Had Edom or Ishmael accepted the Torah, the *Bereishis* story, including the entire Torah until the Exodus, would have been mankind's portion rather than Israel's.

(5632)

The knowledge that the other nations rejected the Torah, and that Israel accepted it, may help us better understand why the final day of Succos is called *Simchas Torah* — the day of the Torah's rejoicing. As discussed earlier, in the period of the High Holy Days and Succos Hashem offers all mankind an opportunity to come closer to Him. Presumably, then, Seir and Paran, are given another opportunity to accept the Torah and each time reject Hashem's "outstretched hand — they simply do not want to find their way back. At the festival's conclusion the Torah can also rejoice that Israel, and only Israel, retains possession of it.[1] (5639)

This verse can also be interpreted allegorically. The four places mentioned, Sinai, Seir, Paran, and the dwelling place of the angels, allude to four distinct approaches to Torah: the simple meaning (פְּשַׁט), homiletic interpretation (דְרַשׁ), allusion (רֶמֶז), and *kaballah* (סוֹד). It is well known that the other nations can penetrate the first three aspects of Torah to some extent, but not the Torah's deeper secrets. The first three places mentioned in this verse, Sinai (at which the Torah was originally offered to all men), Seir and Paran, are all accessible to the non-Jewish world. The last place mentioned, however, the dwelling place of the angels (who are most relevant to the secret meaning of the Torah) is not accessible to mankind at large. No matter how much effort the nations of the world expend on interpreting (or misinterpreting) the Torah, their endeavor will have been an exercise in futility, its secrets will always be Israel's. (5639)

1. Editor's Note: In this sense the Torah's rejoicing is similar to that of the Matriarch Leah, that she did not fall to the lot of the wicked Esau in marriage (see *Rashi* on *Bereishis* 29:17).

Alternatively, we can interpret this verse as suggesting that Hashem originally intended to give Israel only the simple meaning of the Torah, which in turn would be shared with the rest of humanity. This plan came to naught, however, because the world, far from appreciating Israel's magnanimity came to despise the Torah nation. As the Psalmist says (109:4), תַּחַת אַהֲבָתִי יִשְׂטְנוּנִי, *In return for my love they hate me.* Because of its unswerving loyalty to Torah, Israel suffered many trials before it came eventually to appreciate the secrets of the Torah, alluded to at the end of the verse: אֵשׁ דָּת לָמוֹ, *a fiery Torah to them.* (5655)

❦ ❦ ❦

Homiletically, this verse might refer to the festival cycle of *Tishrei. HASHEM approached from Sinai,* alludes to Rosh Hashanah, characterized by the *shofar* blast, first heard by the Jewish people at Sinai (see *Shemos* 19:16). *Having shone forth to them from Seir* is a reference to Yom Kippur, during which a goat (Hebrew: *seir*) is pushed over a cliff to expiate the sins of the people (see *Vayikra* 16:21) and also to the defeat of Esau (whom *Bereishis* 27:16 associates with the hair of a goat), at the hands of Jacob.

Having appeared from Mount Paran refers to Succos, a time of Divine kindness to all mankind, including Ishmael, who came from Mount Paran. *And then approached with some of the holy myriads [of angels]* refers to *Shemini Atzeres* and *Simchas Torah,* days on which we celebrate our special sacred bond with the Creator. (5646)

❦ ❦ ❦

Alternatively, the first three phrases may allude to the three Pilgrimage Festivals. The fourth phrase, however, refers to *Shemini Atzeres,* when the *holy myriads of angels* appear, a day of total intimacy between Hashem and His people, as discussed at length in the essay on *Shemini Atzeres.* (5639)

❦ ❦ ❦

Similarly, Sinai, Seir, and Paran might allude to the three Patriarchs, and the holy myriads of angels to Moshe, who attained a closer relationship with Hashem than any other mortal. (5665)

Finally, the four phases of Divine revelation — Sinai, Seir, Paran, and the holy myriads of angels, may allude to four types of *mitzvos*: *chukim* (statutes whose reasons are not known), *mishpatim* (laws governing peer-to-peer relationships), *toros* (laws related to the study of Torah), and all other *mitzvos*. (5647)

Our verse concludes, *from His right hand He presented the fiery Torah to them [Israel]. Rashi* comments on this phrase that the Torah is written before Hashem as "a black fire on top of a white fire."

What does this description of Torah imply? Perhaps this metaphor was intended to teach a lesson about the importance of a good heart. Even though the outside of a person may appear black and besmirched with sin, his inside must be pure if his Torah is to survive. No matter how far a Jew strays from his faith, the teachings of Torah remain permanently implanted within him — provided his original learning was done with sincerity.

Simchas Torah is celebrated shortly after Yom Kippur, rather than at Shevuos when the Torah was given. On Yom Kippur, Jewish hearts and souls are purified and Israel attains the purity of heart described as a "white fire," that makes the joy of *Simchas Torah* possible.[1] (5639)

◆§ The Third Verse

אַף חֹבֵב עַמִּים כָּל־קְדֹשָׁיו בְּיָדֶךָ וְהֵם תֻּכּוּ לְרַגְלֶךָ יִשָּׂא מִדַּבְּרֹתֶיךָ׃

Indeed, You greatly loved the peoples, all His sacred ones were in Your hands; for they placed themselves at Your feet, accepting the burden of Your utterances (33:3).

This somewhat obscure verse lends itself to numerous interpretations. Firstly, this verse may seem to be the conclusion of the previous verse. The Torah has been described as a "fiery law" which, in both its content and its impact on the Jewish people, defies human understanding. Like fire, it cannot be grasped — it is inscrutable. Thus Moshe's thorn bush, which "burned but was not consumed," (see *Shemos* 3:2), is a metaphor for the Jewish people's relationship to Torah: Though we cannot grasp all of the intricacies of Torah, we are inextricably bound to it as the thorn bush was to the fire. Not only are we warmed by the Torah's light, our connection with Torah makes it "burn brighter" and rise to a higher level of sanctifying Hashem's Name. Such is the power that even simple, unsophisticated Jews have when they study the Torah and attach themselves to it.

---

1. See also the discussion of the relationship between *Simchas Torah* and Shavuos in the essay on *Simchas Torah*.

This verse also considers the relationship of Torah Jews who lack fire and enthusiasm. Even they can relate to Torah, by subordinating themselves to the Rabbinical authority of their generation. Following this approach, the verse can be understood as follows:

Hashem loves the "dimming embers" in Israel, those in whom the fire of Torah is weak,[1] if they subordinate themselves (תֻּכּוּ) to Hashem (לְרַגְלֶךָ) and allow themselves to be guided by Israel's righteous Sages (קְדֹשָׁיו בְּיָדֶךָ).

The verse concludes with a description of the reward granted to those "dimming embers" who flock to Hashem. The words of the Torah will burn (יִשָּׂא).[2] (5634)

In a similar vein, this verse may be interpreted as a reference to Israel's humility and deference to Hashem. This approach is based on the contrast between *Your hands* (an exalted place) and *Your feet* (the lowest point).

Israel has achieved a high level of spirituality, as indicated in the expression *His sacred ones [i.e. Israel] were in Your hands*. Nonetheless, Israel subordinates itself to Hashem — *they placed themselves at Your feet.*

This concept of Israel's self-abasement before Hashem explains an otherwise difficult statement by the prophet Yeshayahu (43:10) — אַתֶּם עֵדַי נְאֻם־ה׳, *"You are My witnesses," says HASHEM*. Israel testifies that Hashem exists. Yet elsewhere the Jewish people are depicted as Hashem's "close ones" (relatives).[3] The well-established principle of Jewish law holds that one's blood relatives may not testify for or against a person. It should therefore be impossible for Israel to testify about Hashem's existence!

We can answer that the law prohibits only spoken testimony. Israel's testimony, however, is not in words; its very actions bear silent witness to Hashem's Omnipresence. What other nation could rise to such heights and still negate itself before its Creator?

But Israel has a dream that has not yet been realized, a dream that one day the entire universe will testify to Hashem's existence and all nations

1. This interpretation rests on a Talmudical use of the word עֲמֵים to mean *dimming embers* — see *Pesachim* 27a, עוממות.

2. The Mishnah (*Rosh Hashanah* 2:2) uses the word יִשָּׂא to mean burning.

3.. (Cf. *Devarim* 14:1) בָּנִים אַתֶּם לַה׳ אֱלֹהֵיכֶם, *You are children to HASHEM your God.*

will recognize Him. The end of our verse promises that this dream will eventually come true.

Thus the phrase יִשָּׂא מִדַּבְּרֹתֶיךָ also means *They will lift His stewardship,* as we sometimes find the root דבר used to mean "leadership" (cf. *Tehillim* 47:4). Every time a Jew proclaims his belief in Hashem, he raises the banner of His sovereignty and sets in motion a series of events that brings more of the Gentile world to accept His rulership.

A classic example of this interaction lies in the words of the Psalm (114:1-4): בְּצֵאת יִשְׂרָאֵל מִמִּצְרָיִם . . . יִשְׂרָאֵל מַמְשְׁלוֹתָיו. הַיָּם רָאָה וַיָּנֹס הַיַּרְדֵּן יִסֹּב לְאָחוֹר. הֶהָרִים רָקְדוּ כְאֵילִים גְּבָעוֹת כִּבְנֵי צֹאן, *When Israel went out of Egypt . . . Israel [became] His dominions. The sea saw and fled: the Jordan turned backward. The mountains skipped like rams, the hills like young lambs.* These verses portray a clear cause and effect relationship: Israel accepts Hashem's sovereignty and Nature follows its lead. (5641)

Alternatively, we can interpret this verse in the context of the High Holy Days and Succos. As mentioned previously, Rosh Hashanah, Yom Kippur, and Succos have momentous significance not just for Israel but for all of humankind. Moshe here points out that despite the fact that Hashem "embraces" all peoples, His relationship with Israel remains the closest.

Let us see how this emerges from our verse, אַף חֹבֵב עַמִּים; Though Hashem favored all the nations, it is especially so at this time of year, since Rosh Hashanah is a time of judgment for *all* the world. On Succos this was evident when Israel offered seventy bulls corresponding to the seventy nations. כָּל־קְדֹשָׁיו בְּיָדֶךָ וְהֵם תֻּכּוּ לְרַגְלֶךָ, and even though all of Israel's sacred ones were in Your hands and she was as beloved as ever, including during the High Holy Days and Succos, they permitted themselves to be crushed at Your feet. They "lowered" themselves by offering sacrifices on behalf of the other nations on Succos in obedience to Hashem's will.

Succos demands extraordinary sacrifice on Israel's part. Imagine the consequences if, instead of spending Succos bringing offerings for the other nations, the Jews used the opportunity to nurture their unique relationship with Hashem. Instead, however, they behave as loyal servants and forego their own spiritual growth and advancement in order to fulfill His will that they act on behalf of the whole world.

At the end of our verse and the beginning of the next one, the Torah promises to reward this altruism: יִשָּׂא מִדַּבְּרֹתֶיךָ. תּוֹרָה צִוָּה־לָנוּ מֹשֶׁה, *Accepting the burden of Your utterances — Moshe commanded the Torah to us.* As a result of Israel's self-sacrifice throughout Succos, it renews its bond with Hashem and the Torah on *Simchas Torah.*

The association between bringing offerings on behalf of the nations and celebrating the Torah on *Simchas Torah* can be developed further. These offerings are more than just a way to merit the joy of *Simchas Torah* — they are a vital preparation to understanding the Torah.

Jewish metaphysics perceives the universe as a four-level pyramid. At the base are inanimate objects (*domeim,* silent), followed by vegetation (*tzomeach,* growing). On the next level is the animal world (*chai,* living) Finally, man (*medabeir,* speaking) is at the pyramid's apex. Beyond this hierarchy, Israel occupies an exalted place at the very summit, above the four ordinary levels. This can be seen from the distinguished title given to the Jewish people in this verse. Israel is called *midabrosecha,* the nation that not only speaks (or alternatively, leads, see above), but speaks in Hashem's language and conducts itself according to His will.

But how does one ascend to the very peak of the pyramid? How does a *medabeir* evolve into a *midabrosecha*? Only by devoting himself to others, to elevate the lower level. Thus, the offerings Israel brings on behalf of the Gentile world (*medabeir*) on Succos earn for her the title of *midabrosecha* — on *Simchas Torah.*

This principle of ennobling oneself by elevating those on a lower level explains the Talmudic requirement that one must feed his animals before he himself may eat (*Gittin* 63a). The act of eating has a much higher purpose than mere sensual gratification — it is itself a form of Divine Service. Thus the Talmud (*Berachos* 55a) compares a man's table, used for serving mundane food and drink, to the Altar in the *Beis HaMikdash.* Although eating provides necessary nourishment for the *medabeir,* one who wishes to achieve the spiritual benefits of eating must first give his attention to the needs of those below him on the pyramid. (5637)

❧ ❧ ❧

A slightly different approach explains the connection between Succos and *Simchas Torah* in the context of our verse by emphasizing the *succah* itself rather than the festival's offerings. *Onkeles* renders this passage into Aramaic as follows: וְאִנּוּן מִדַּבְּרִין תְּחוֹת עֲנָנָךְ נָטְלִין עַל מֵימְרָךְ, *Those who followed You under Your cloud [i.e. the Divine Cloud discussed in the essay on succah] let themselves be borne by Your word [i.e. they followed You throughout the Wilderness].* They will merit the Torah mentioned in the following verse, *Moshe commanded the Torah to us.*

The Torah itself is totally beyond human comprehension. No mortal can possibly grasp the word of Hashem described in the previous verse as a "fiery law," on the strength of his own abilities and merit. Only by following wherever Hashem leads regardless of the consequences is it possible to achieve any understanding of the Torah. By following Hashem steadfastly into the Wilderness, Israel eventually merited to grasp some of the Torah's insights. וְהֵם תֻּכּוּ לְרַגְלֶךָ, by allowing themselves to be crushed by hardships while following at Your feet into the Wilderness, יִשָּׂא מִדַּבְּרֹתֶיךָ, they were lifted to understand Your word. Israel's self-negation eventually enables it to comprehend Hashem's word.

Every year on Succos we follow in our forefathers' footsteps. We too forsake comfortable homes and live in flimsy *succos* to show our desire to follow Hashem wherever He takes us. Then on *Simchas Torah* we too are rewarded for our self sacrifice with the ability to comprehend the Torah.

King Solomon (*Shir HaShirim* 1:4) alludes to this connection between dwelling in the *succah* and *Simchas Torah:* הֱבִיאַנִי הַמֶּלֶךְ חֲדָרָיו נָגִילָה וְנִשְׂמְחָה בָּךְ, *The King has brought me into His chambers [i.e. the Succah, the house where His Name is manifested, as described in the essay on Succah] and therefore I rejoice in You [Your Torah] on Simchas Torah.*

(5638)

❀ ❀ ❀

Alternatively, this verse alludes to the relationship between different generations in Jewish history. This is especially apparent in the phrases כָּל־קְדֹשָׁיו בְּיָדֶךָ, *all His sacred ones in Your hands,* and תֻּכּוּ לְרַגְלֶךָ, *placed to Your "feet."*

The Patriarchs were critical links in Israel's development, as were the twelve tribes. Moshe, in his farewell address, says the Torah is transmitted from the Patriarchs to their children, the tribes. They, in turn, taught Torah to their own progeny, so that eventually a great Torah congregation evolved, as described in the following verse: תּוֹרָה

צִוָּה־לָנוּ מֹשֶׁה מוֹרָשָׁה קְהִלַּת יַעֲקֹב *Moshe commanded us the Torah, it is an inheritance of the congregation of [i.e. emanating from] Jacob.* Both the hands [the Patriarchs] and the feet [their children, the Tribes] were vital links in the formation of the Torah congregation.

◆§ The Fourth Verse

תּוֹרָה צִוָּה־לָנוּ מֹשֶׁה מוֹרָשָׁה קְהִלַּת יַעֲקֹב

Moshe commanded us the Torah, it is an inheritance of the Congregation of Jacob (33:4).

Before considering homiletical interpretations of this verse, let us first examine its simple meaning. To what event does this verse refer? When did Moshe "command" the Torah to Israel?

Possibly it is speaking of the time at Sinai when the Jewish people asked Moshe to accept the Torah on their behalf. After the first two commandments were given directly to the nation by Hashem they were afraid that if they received any more, they would perish from the sheer intensity of Hashem's Presence (see *Devarim* 5:22).

It was a miracle that Israel survived hearing the first two commandments directly from Hashem. The Talmud (*Shabbos* 88b) relates that after each of the first two commandments, the Jewish people's souls expired and had to be revived by angels. Since the Torah was intended as Israel's permanent legacy, an heirloom to be transmitted from one generation to the next, they felt that something so enduring should not exist on the basis of miracles alone. It would be better if Moshe, who was of sufficient stature to survive the impact of Divine Revelation, was to receive the Torah for them.

Furthermore, they sensed that Moshe, was capable of grasping much more of Hashem's word than they were.

Thus, our verse may be read, "It is because *Moshe* transmitted the Torah to us that it is a heritage to the Congregation of Jacob." Had Israel accepted the Torah directly from Hashem in this miraculous manner, it would have been virtually impossible to transmit the Torah from generation to generation in a natural manner. (5635)

Alternatively, this verse may be understood as a continuation of the second verse, which described the Torah as a "fiery law". Mere mortals can come close to such a Torah only through *mitzvos.* As discussed extensively in the essay on *Simchas Torah,* the ordinary Jew relates to Torah primarily through observing *mitzvos*. Had the Torah been given in a more abstract form rather than as concrete *mitzvos*, it could not have been passed on from one generation to the next. In this light our verse may be read, "By being commanded in the form of *mitzvos,* the Torah became a heritage to the Congregation of Jacob."

As we said in the essay on *Simchas Torah,* there is an allusion to Moshe's role as a transmitter of Torah and *mitzvos* in that the *gematria* (numerical value) of the epithet *Moshe Rabbeinu* (מֹשֶׁה רַבֵּינוּ) exactly equals the number of *mitzvos* in the Torah, 613. Is this merely a play on numbers, or does a more profound connection underlie this apparent coincidence?

As is well known, our Sages understood that the 613 mitzvos of the Torah correspond to the components of the human body. Specifically, the 248 "positive commandments" are relevant to the 248 limbs, and the 365 "negative commandments" are relevant to the 365 sinews of the body.

Each limb is nourished by observing one of the positive commandments. Similarly, every sinew is kept alive by refraining from violating a particular negative commandment. In most instances, however, the relationship between a component of the body and its corresponding *mitzvah* is subtle and unseen.

The life of Moshe, however, was so intensely spiritual that it was apparent to all that the commandments sustained every limb and sinew of his body. For him, the 613 *mitzvos* were not merely the numerical equivalent of his name, but his very lifeblood. Moshe's very existence was tied to the 613 mitzvos he observed. The Torah alludes to this unique lifestyle by calling him "A Man of God" suggesting that the spiritual forces driving his body were fundamental to his existence.

(5662)

Alternatively, this verse may refer to Moshe's ability to strengthen the already existing bond between Hashem and Israel. This allusion is based on the similarity of the word צִוָּה, *commanded,* and the Aramaic word צַוְתָּא, *close relationship*. Thus the verse reads as follows: "Moshe *bound* us (Israel) to the Torah."

Torah is called a great light. However, light cannot exist in a vacuum, it must be contained by some type of receptacle. The Jewish soul is the best receiving agent for Torah's light. By binding Israel's souls and Torah together — the receptacle and the light — Moshe became the ultimate *shadchan* (matchmaker). In fact, the closer the relationship between Israel and the Torah, the more the light of Torah is revealed in the world. If Israel strays from Torah (Heaven forbid), then the Jewish soul grows dark and the "light" available for the rest of humanity also diminishes. (5655)

While the above discussion may help clarify Moshe's role in transmitting the Torah, the verse itself contains an apparent contradiction. The beginning of the verse suggests that the Torah was transmitted by Moshe while the end implies that it was inherited from Jacob.

Both implications are true in different senses. Torah is latent in the Jewish psyche and every Jew possesses an inner, "intuitive," feeling for it. It was this inner sense that enabled the Patriarchs to observe the Torah and to pass it on to their children even before it was given. Unlike their forefathers, however, the Jews [in Egypt] lacked the ability to recognize this inner sense. Only when Moshe commanded the Torah at Sinai did this long-dormant, "instinctive," Torah re-emerge into the open to guide Israel to live a Torah-true lifestyle.

Moshe's role in helping Israel actualize its latent feelings for Torah can be deduced from several sources. For example, the Torah is called a light (*Proverbs* 6:23) — תּוֹרָה אוֹר because it breaks through the darkness that obscures a Jew's inner potential for greatness. When the Torah was given, Israel proclaimed (*Shemos* 19:8), כֹּל אֲשֶׁר־דִּבֶּר ה׳ נַעֲשֶׂה, *Whatever Hashem has said we will do.* Grammatically, the word נַעֲשֶׂה can also mean, "it has already been done," suggesting that the Torah had already been implanted into the Jewish soul by the Patriarchs. Moshe's role at Sinai is described as וַיָּקֶם עֵדוּת בְּיַעֲקֹב, "*Making the testimony [the Torah] stand*" (*Tehillim* 78:5). The Torah already existed; Moshe merely brought it to the forefront. (5655)

The term "Congregation of Jacob" may also refer to the *reward* bestowed on Israel when it accepted the Torah. Our Sages derived from this verse the saying "One who studies Torah merits [to enjoy] Jacob's portion" (*Yalkut Shimoni V'zos HaBerachah* 952). Unlike Abraham and

Isaac, who were promised finite portions in *Eretz Yisrael*, Jacob was offered a portion without limits.

The Midrash derives the lesson that every Jew can obtain Jacob's portion of boundless blessings through Torah study. This concept, however, requires further discussion. Possibly the Midrash means that someone who studies Torah will receive not only his own portion but also that of his enemies, in the same way that Jacob, the consummate Torah student, received the blessings his father intended for Esau. So too, if Israel immerses itself in Torah it will merit to receive blessings intended for its enemies. This may provide a rationale for the custom, of many congregations to read the blessings Isaac bestowed on Jacob (but intended originally for Esau) on *Simchas Torah*. We may infer from this custom that in the merit of Torah, Israel's detractors will cede their share of the world to the Jewish people.

From one perspective, the struggle between Jacob and Esau for Divine blessings is replayed every *Tishrei*. In this month, Hashem reviews the fate of the world in general and Israel's role in particular. It is possible, then, that other major historical confrontations are also (at least symbolically) re-enacted at the same time.

On Rosh Hashanah, as humanity stands in judgment before the Creator, Esau (representing the Gentile nations) seeks to wrest Hashem's blessings away from Jacob. Hashem, however, far from acceding to this presumptuousness, protects Israel's heritage on Rosh Hashanah and ensures that Esau does not succeed in his insidious attempts to misappropriate it. The shofar blast is a veiled but urgent reminder to the Jewish people to follow in the footsteps of the father Jacob and eschew the use of force that was Esau's trademark (*the hands are Esau's hands*) in favor of prayer and Torah study, the source of Jacob's power (*the voice is Jacob's voice*). If Jacob obtained his blessings through Torah, then we too, the Congregation of Jacob, can "defend" ourselves from Esau's onslaught by returning to our source, the Torah.

Aided by the shofar of Rosh Hashanah, Jacob triumphs and maintains his blessings. However, the Jewish people's victory is kept secret until *Simchas Torah*, a day of intimacy between Israel and Hashem. Then, as we read from Jacob's inheritance (as the Torah describes itself), we can publicly rejoice. Now it can be revealed to the world that Hashem's blessings will remain in Jacob's hands for another year.

This may be the intent of the verse recited on Rosh Hashanah night:

תִּקְעוּ בַחֹדֶשׁ שׁוֹפָר בַּכֶּסֶה לְיוֹם חַגֵּנוּ *Blow the shofar at the moon's renewal, at the time appointed for our festive day.* (*Tehillim* 81:4). Israel's triumph over Esau is hidden on Rosh Hashanah; only on *Simchas Torah* (*our festive day*) does the Jewish people's vindication become apparent. (5662)

The Mishnah (*Avos* 2:17), however, seems to contradict our verse's implication that the Torah is מוֹרָשָׁה קְהִלַּת יַעֲקֹב, *the inheritance of the Congregation of Jacob.* The Mishnah says, הַתְקֵן עַצְמְךָ לִלְמוֹד תּוֹרָה שֶׁאֵינָהּ יְרֻשָּׁה לָךְ, *Prepare yourself to learn Torah for it is not an inheritance for you.* How can we reconcile this Mishnah with our verse?

There is no question that the Torah is Israel's birthright, inherited from past generations. In order to receive an estate, however, one must be worthy of it. Only after the intensive preparations recommended by the Mishnah is Israel able to realize its birthright. As the Talmud (*Megillah* 6b) emphasizes, יָגַעְתָּ וּמָצָאתָ understanding Torah comes only with effort and exertion.

The Talmud (*Berachos* 57a) voices the same theme by suggesting that the word מוֹרָשָׁה, *inheritance*, can also be understood as מְאוֹרָשָׁה, *betrothed.* The Torah is not wed, inherited, or even given as a gift to Israel, but only betrothed to it. A couple that is betrothed knows that great effort is required to develop their relationship. So, too, Israel must study Torah intensely so that its relationship as the "betrothed" of the Torah can develop into a full-fledged marriage. (5635, 5647)

The metaphor of betrothal to Torah can be carried further. A betrothed couple, through diligent and persistent effort, can develop a relationship that will endure for many years. So too, by delving into Torah we can develop new solutions for the unique challenges that emerge in every generation. By working with its betrothed partner — the Torah — Israel can find all the answers it ever needs. (5648)

Another way to resolve the apparent contradiction cited above between the Mishnah and our verse is to make a distinction between the Jewish community as a whole and its individual members. Torah is certainly the "inheritance of the Congregation of Jacob," but not necessarily that of any individual Jew. The likening of Israel's relationship with Torah to a betrothal thus becomes a plea to each and every Jew to make himself into a participating member of the community. A betrothed couple knows that an intimate relationship can be developed only after they are married — and even then, great effort is required for two personalities to mesh. So, too, an individual who wishes to inherit his portion in the Torah, must subordinate himself to the greater community. When the Mishnah calls upon the Jew to prepare himself for Torah, it is, in effect, urging him to prepare himself to be a part of the community. (5632, 5635)

It is entirely fitting that we read this verse, which calls for communal involvement, at the close of the festival of Succos. As discussed in the essay on *Succah*, this is a particularly conducive time for Jewish unity. Both the *Succah* and the Four Species symbolize Jewish unity. Moreover, one of the holiday's names — חַג הָאָסִיף, *the Festival of Gathering* — suggests this is a time for different factions to unite. Now on *Simchas Torah*, immediately following such an appropriate occasion for unity, Israel can read and appreciate the words, תּוֹרָה צִוָּה לָנוּ מֹשֶׁה מוֹרָשָׁה קְהִלַּת יַעֲקֹב, *Moshe commanded us the Torah, it is an inheritance of the Congregation of Jacob.* (5636)

◈ The Fifth Verse

וַיְהִי בִישֻׁרוּן מֶלֶךְ בְּהִתְאַסֵּף רָאשֵׁי עָם יַחַד שִׁבְטֵי יִשְׂרָאֵל
He became King in Jeshurun when the leaders of the nation gathered — the tribes of Israel in unity (*Devarim* 33:5).

Who was the King in Jeshurun? The Sages disagreed (cf. *Ibn Ezra* and *Rambam Devarim* 33:5) whether this verse refers to Moshe or to the Torah itself. In reality, however, both opinions are correct. Moshe, even though he is no longer with us physically lives on through the Torah; and the nation of Torah continues to thrive because his ideals still are alive. This is especially true at communal gatherings, where the leaders of the community come together.

If such conclaves are successful, it is because a spark of Moshe remains in today's leaders. In this light the previous verse can be understood differently by repunctuating it: תּוֹרָה צִוָּה־לָנוּ – מֹשֶׁה מוֹרָשָׁה (שֶׁל) קְהִלַּת יַעֲקֹב *The Torah commanded us: Moshe shall be a heritage of the Congregation of Jacob.* Moshe had a permanent impact on all future generations.

The most obvious interpretation of our verse, however, is that Hashem is the "King" in Jeshurun. In this approach, our verse suggests that only when Jews unite (*when the leaders of the nation gathered*) will Hashem's sovereignty be acknowledged by all men (*He became*

King in Jeshurun). Such unity requires not only that the leaders unite but also that ordinary Jews coalesce (*the tribes of Israel in unity*).

Finally, the term יְשֻׁרוּן, *Jeshurun*, needs clarification. If it is meant to praise Israel's יַשְׁרוּת, *uprightness*, the name יְשָׁרִים, *upright people*, would be more appropriate. However the name *Jeshurun* reflects the Jewish goal of influencing all mankind to be righteous. By leading an upright life in a world of injustice, even as a minority of one, Israel will one day merit to see all men adopt their ways. (5641, 5658, 5665)

The above remarks focus on Jewish unity and its impact on the rest of the world. But how is Israel to accomplish this often elusive goal of unity? The answer may lie in the previous verse — there is no greater unifying force among Jews than Torah. Despite all other differences, as Jews we all share a common heritage — in Torah. Every Jew, even the most unlearned, has a portion in Torah. The name "Congregation of Jacob" may even be taken as a reference to the Torah itself, rather than to Israel. Inasmuch as everyone has his "niche" in Torah — some aspect of Torah that he excels in — the Torah itself is the "Congregation of Jacob," capable of unifying all Jews. The more that Torah is studied, the more unity prevails. (5651)

☙ Zevulun's Blessing

וְלִזְבוּלֻן אָמַר שְׂמַח זְבוּלֻן בְּצֵאתֶךָ וְיִשָּׂשכָר בְּאֹהָלֶיךָ

Of Zevulun he said: Rejoice, Zevulun, in your going out, and Issachar, in your tents (33:18).

Zevulun, the merchant, rejoices when he goes out on commercial ventures and Issachar rejoices when he studies Torah in his tent. *Rashi*, comments that this verse alludes to the partnership forged between these brothers by which Zevulun provided financial support for Issachar's Torah study.

Why should Zevulun rejoice on embarking upon a venture? Such joy would seem more appropriate at the successful completion of a project rather than at its outset. Perhaps, however, this verse is not only a blessing but also a piece of timely advice from Moshe: the best guarantee of success in any undertaking, be it in business or in Torah, is to begin it with joy. By rejoicing at the start of a venture, one shows that he trusts that Hashem will provide for all his needs; in reward for that trust, Hashem will surely crown his efforts with success. (5634)

Moshe's parting advice thus explains why everyone — the merchant as well as the student of Torah — rejoices on *Simchas Torah.* The full-time student rejoices at his future growth in Torah, while the businessman knows that by rejoicing on *Simchas Torah* he ensures his prosperity, as well as his portion in Torah, for the year ahead.

To give a homiletical interpretation of this verse, just as Zevulun goes out and interacts with the world, Israel, too, leaves its home every Succos and enters the succah. On *Shemini Atzeres* and *Simchas Torah,* however, the Jew returns to his home, no longer concerned about interacting with others, but rather focusing on cementing his relationship with Hashem. On *Shemini Atzeres,* like Issachar, the Jew rejoices in his tent — the Torah oriented home. (5634, 5646)

◆§ Blessing of Perpetual Youth

בַּרְזֶל וּנְחֹשֶׁת מִנְעָלֶךָ וּכְיָמֶיךָ דָּבְאֶךָ

Iron and copper shall be your lock, and as your days so shall be your (flow) strength (33:25).

In the closing segment of his farewell address, Moshe gives Israel the above blessing. *Rashi* suggests that the latter part of this verse is a blessing that one's waning years דָּבְאֶךָ, when time *flows away* from a person should be as joyous as one's youth (יָמֶיךָ, one's prime years). How can one ensure that his old age will be as fruitful as his youth? The beginning of our verse may contain the answer — *Iron and copper should be your lock.* Anything valuable is kept under lock and key. Moshe advises Israel to "lock up" its youth, to treat it as a valuable not to be wasted. A well-spent youth ensures that the later years will also be productive.

King Solomon voices the same theme (*Koheles* 12:1): וּזְכֹר אֶת־בּוֹרְאֶךָ בִּימֵי בְּחוּרֹתֶיךָ עַד אֲשֶׁר לֹא־יָבֹאוּ יְמֵי הָרָעָה, *Remember your Creator in the days of your youth [and utilize them well], so that the evil days [of tormented old age] will not come.*

The Psalmist also emphasizes the importance of a well-spent youth (92:14-15): שְׁתוּלִים בְּבֵית ה׳ בְּחַצְרוֹת אֱלֹהֵינוּ יַפְרִיחוּ עוֹד יְנוּבוּן בְּשֵׂיבָה דְּשֵׁנִים וְרַעֲנַנִּים יִהְיוּ, *Planted in the house of* HASHEM, *in the courtyards of our God [those who spend their youth in spiritual pursuits] they will flourish. They will still be fruitful in old age, vigorous and fresh they will be.* The word עוֹד is usually translated as *still* — *they will still be fruitful in old age.* If we substitute another commonly found meaning, *more,* the verse then tells us that those who capitalize well on their youth will accomplish even *more* in their senior years.

A similar connection can be made between the "youth" of the Jewish people, the generation that followed Hashem into the Wilderness, and its later generations long removed from the Exodus. The achievements of that first generation in the Wilderness "locked" in the Torah so that today's Jew living in the waning generations far removed from Sinai, can still preserve his connection with Torah. Similarly we must strive in turn, to accomplish as much as we can in Torah, according to our abilities and circumstances, in order to leave as great an impact as we can on future generations. (*Parashas Berachah* 5653)

◆§ The Relationship Between the Torah's Ending and Its Beginning

The Torah concludes (*Devarim* 34:10-12): וְלֹא־קָם נָבִיא עוֹד בְּיִשְׂרָאֵל כְּמֹשֶׁה . . . וּלְכֹל הַיָּד הַחֲזָקָה וּלְכֹל הַמּוֹרָא הַגָּדוֹל אֲשֶׁר עָשָׂה מֹשֶׁה לְעֵינֵי כָּל־יִשְׂרָאֵל — *Never again has there arisen in Israel a prophet like Moshe . . . And by all the [miracles he performed with a] strong hand and all the great fear [of HASHEM] that Moshe instilled in the eyes of all Israel.*

The Torah begins (*Bereishis* 1:1): בְּרֵאשִׁית בָּרָא אֱלֹהִים אֵת הַשָּׁמַיִם וְאֵת הָאָרֶץ, *In the beginning, God created the heaven and the earth.* In this section we will explore the connection between the Torah's ending and its beginning, both of which we read on *Simchas Torah.*

King Solomon wrote (*Koheles* 3:14): וְהָאֱלֹהִים עָשָׂה שֶׁיִּרְאוּ מִלְּפָנָיו, *God made [the universe] so that man should stand in awe of Him.* There are several means to achieve fear of Hashem. Some individuals fear His power to punish them in this world, or in the hereafter. This, however, is considered an inferior form of fear, because it is fear of something which is only a creation, rather than of Hashem Himself. Hashem created the universe in order that man should fear not His ability to exact retribution, but rather His very Majesty. This fear, known in Torah literature as יִרְאַת הָרוֹמְמוּת, develops when man recognizes how insignificant he is relative to Hashem.

Thus, Moshe's greatest accomplishment was to bring Israel to this highest form of fear of Hashem through the Torah he transmitted to us. In particular, studying and contemplating the intricate perfection of the universe infallibly leads us to appreciate how insignificant we are in comparison to Hashem. Can there be a better place to begin this study than the story of Hashem's creation of the universe, as told in *Parashas Bereishis?* Thus the Torah's end, urging us to fear Hashem's Majesty, impels us to start learning the Torah again from the beginning.

The very word alludes to this connection בְּרֵאשִׁית. By rearranging its letters, we get the words יָרֵא, *one who fears,* and בֹּשֶׁת, *ashamed,* suggesting that someone who is *afraid* of Hashem will be *ashamed* to sin. Rearranging the letters in yet another pattern, we get the words יָרֵא, *fear* and שָׁבַת, *cease* — all other thoughts and activities *cease* when one ponders the *fear* of Hashem's infinite grandeur.

From this perspective, lesser kinds of fear, such as that of powerful people, etc., can also bring us to fear Hashem and His Majesty, through the realization that all of these fear-inducing agents were themselves created by Hashem. How much more so, then, must we fear Hashem Himself, and be filled with awe at His greatness.

The Midrash (*Sifrei, V'zos HaBerachah*) interprets these words, *all of the great fear that Moshe instilled,* as a reference to the Giving of the Torah at Mount Sinai. Those who cannot reach the level of fearing Hashem's Majesty through marveling at His wonders can still do so by studying Torah. In fact, Hashem explains the necessity of His personal revelation at Sinai by stating, וּבַעֲבוּר תִּהְיֶה יִרְאָתוֹ עַל־פְּנֵיכֶם, *So that His fear can be on your face.* (*Shemos* 20:20) Not only the marvels of creation described at the beginning of the Torah, but also the entire Torah whose reading we conclude on *Simchas Torah,* instills fear of Hashem.

Alternatively, the Torah's conclusion, *And by all the [miracles he performed with a] strong hand,* can be seen as a natural continuation of the process of creation. Hashem created the universe and gave righteous people the ability to perform miracles, also a form of creation. Thus, the story of the creation, with which the Torah begins, is inextricably linked to the continuation of creation wrought by Moshe.

Moreover, the Torah served as the catalyst for both Hashem's creation and Moshe's miracle. Hashem consulted with the Torah to create the universe, likewise all of Moshe's miracles occurred in the merit of Torah. King Solomon alludes to Torah's role in the ongoing process of creation in the following verse (*Mishlei* 8:30): וָאֶהְיֶה אֶצְלוֹ אָמוֹן וָאֶהְיֶה שַׁעֲשׁוּעִים יוֹם יוֹם, *And I (the Torah) was His artisan — I was His plaything every day*. The Torah was the master craftsman whose imprint was stamped on the universe at Creation. It is also Hashem's "plaything", a source of new creations that comes into play whenever the righteous continue to perform miracles. Thus on *Simchas Torah* we also celebrate Torah's power, which the righteous harness to preserve the world. (*Parashas V'zos HaBerachah* 5653)

Let us develop even further the relationship between the last words of the Torah, לְעֵינֵי כָּל יִשְׂרָאֵל, *before the eyes* (in the sight) *of all Israel*, and its beginning. The story of the Creation is among the most mysterious puzzles of the Torah. No human can ever hope to duplicate creation or even begin to explain how Hashem formed this universe. Only through the prism of Torah can the Creation be fathomed at all. The mysteries of creation can be unraveled, to a partial extent at least, only through in-depth study of the Torah.

The Torah's last words may also be seen as an allusion to the well-known Rabbinic dictum (*Yalkut Shimoni Bereishis* 2): בִּשְׁבִיל יִשְׂרָאֵל שֶׁנִּקְרְאוּ רֵאשִׁית בִּשְׁבִיל תּוֹרָה שֶׁנִּקְרָא רֵאשִׁית, *[The world was created] because of Israel, who is called the beginning [cf. Yirmiyahu* 2:3] *and because of the Torah which is called the beginning* [cf. *Mishlei* 8:22]. This saying can also be interpreted to mean that only through Israel's study of the Torah can the creation of the universe be appreciated. The first letters of the Torah's concluding words לְעֵינֵי כָּל יִשְׂרָאֵל can be rearranged to spell the word כְּלִי, *vessel*, suggesting that Israel is a vehicle through which creation could be understood.

Similarly, the *gematria* (numerical value) of the final letters of these words (י,ל,ל) is seventy: Since the seventy nations of the world are unable to perceive the magnitude of Creation, Israel acts as their "eyes" to do so for them. This implies that not only does Israel possess a unique ability to comprehend Creation, but that also every individual Jew is capable of understanding some aspect of Creation better than any non-Jew. (5662)

The relationship between the Torah's conclusion and its beginning holds within it a message for every Jew. The Midrash (*Yalkut Shimoni* 2), focusing on the role of Moshe, suggests that the universe was created in the merit of Moshe, who was called "beginning" (*cf. Devarim* 33:21). This does not contradict the previous statement that the universe was created in the merit of Torah. On the contrary, it was the teachings of Moshe that brought humanity to realize that it owes its existence to Torah. How fitting, then, that the Torah concludes with a synopsis of

Moshe's accomplishments (*the great fear and that strong hand that Moshe instilled . . .*) and begins with an allusion that the universe was created in his merit. (5660)

In a similar vein, the connection between the Torah's conclusion and its beginning may be understood in terms of the role played by Israel in the creation process. In the beginning, Hashem created the universe. But who would testify to this basic truth? Surely, not early mankind who, for the most part, defied or denied Hashem 's existence. It was not until Israel accepted the Torah that an entire nation was committed to informing humankind of its true origin. Thus, the Torah's last phrase, *In the eyes of all of Israel,* and its first verse, *In the beginning Hashem created the heavens and the earth,* are closely related. Only because of Israel's dedication does the world know anything of its beginning. The Rabbinic comment (cf. *Bereishis Rabbah* 1:5), בְּנִשְׁמָתָן שֶׁל יִשְׂרָאֵל נִמְלַךְ, *Hashem consulted with the souls of Israel* before creating the universe, underscores this theme. Hashem consulted the souls of Israel before creating the universe because it is Israel's mission to teach the world about its Divine origin — about the story of *Bereishis.*

(5655)

"Hashem consulted with the souls of Israel before creating the universe!" To what does this obscure expression "the souls of Israel" refer? Also how does this Rabbinic dictum correlate with the assertion that Hashem consulted the Torah before creating the universe?

Evidently, the universe was created for the sake of Israel's involvement and immersion in Torah. As Israel goes deeper into the study of Torah, Hashem's presence in the world becomes more apparent and it becomes more obvious that His conduct of the world is completely above the processes of nature. Hashem's "consultation" with Jewish souls actually means that He evaluated the overall spiritual level of the Jewish people to determine to what extent the universe would have to be regulated on the basis of Torah.

Even though the Torah was an essential partner in the initial creation, it was not clear to what extent the Torah and its moral values would continue to shape the future of the world. That would depend on the souls of Israel, their aspirations and degree of immersion in Torah. Thus the term "the eyes of Israel" alludes to the association between Israel's spiritual level and the extent of the Torah's influence on the universe. Every generation perceives the Torah in a different light. For some, Torah is the essence of existence; for others, unfortunately, the Torah is only one of many considerations in their lives. By consulting with the souls of Israel at the time of Creation, Hashem determined that the degree of His apparent involvement in the universe's affairs, the extent to which the world and Israel's lives would be governed "supernaturally," be dependent upon Israel's spiritual level. This analysis makes the relationship between the Torah's concluding words (לְעֵינֵי כָּל יִשְׂרָאֵל) and its beginning (בְּרֵאשִׁית בָּרָא אֱלֹהִים) strikingly clear. Creation, and the concomitant extent to which the world is aware of its Creator, is dependent on "Israel's eyes" — its immersion in Torah. (5651)

Finally, the association between the Torah's beginning and end can be viewed in terms of the linkage between generations. The description of the universe as a "void" in the Torah's second verse is an apt metaphor not only for its physical condition but also for the spiritual wasteland that would engulf much of the world in its early epoch.

Eventually, however, the Patriarchs began to exert a positive influence on humanity but even then only a few courageous individuals upheld a belief in Hashem and His Creation. Not until the generation of Moshe, the last one mentioned in the Torah, did a significant portion of the world acknowledge the Creator. To have a *Bereishis*, a genesis for a universe that would be populated by highly imperfect beings, could have been only in the merit of "Israel's eyes", the generation of Moshe that witnessed so many of Hashem's miracles.

Thus the Rabbinic dictum cited earlier, *[The world was created] because of Israel, who is called the beginning*, is exactly equivalent to the other dictum, *because of Torah, which is called the beginning.* Contemporary generations, though far removed from Moshe's time, still have a vital role to play in upholding the world by acknowledging our indebtedness to our predecessors. The prophet calls Israel שְׁאֵרִית נַחֲלָתוֹ, "the remnants of [Hashem's] estate" (*Michah* 7:18). By subjecting ourselves to the teachings of our ancestors, to the Torah, we fulfill the purpose of, and indeed justify, the Creation. (5650)

Z'man Simchaseinu — The Time of Our Rejoicing

וַתִּתֶּן לָנוּ ה׳ אֱלֹהֵינוּ . . . אֶת יוֹם חַג הַסֻּכּוֹת הַזֶּה זְמַן שִׂמְחָתֵנוּ
And You gave us, HASHEM, our God . . . this day of the Festival of Succos, the time of our rejoicing. . . (Festival Prayers).

Why is Succos called the time of Israel's rejoicing? Halachically, the commandment to rejoice on the festivals applies equally to Pesach and Shavuos as well as Succos (cf. *Pesachim* 68b). Yet the Torah alludes to the special status of Succos by repeating the *mitzvah* of rejoicing three times in connection with it: וְשָׂמַחְתָּ בְּחַגֶּךָ . . . וְהָיִיתָ אַךְ שָׂמֵחַ, *You shall rejoice in your Festival . . . and you shall experience pure joy* (*Devarim* 16:14-15); and וּשְׂמַחְתֶּם לִפְנֵי ה׳ אֱלֹהֵיכֶם שִׁבְעַת יָמִים, *You shall rejoice before HASHEM, your God, seven days* (*Vayikra* 23:40). The concept of joy is also associated with the Libation of Water ceremony performed in the *Beis HaMikdash,* as well as the extra dimension of joy of *Shemini Atzeres* hinted at by the phrase "*And you shall experience pure joy.*"

◆§ Following Hashem into the Wilderness

Israel's traditional rejoicing at Succos time is based on historical precedent. As we said in the essay on Succah, the following verse (*Shir HaShirim* 2:3) describes Israel's loyalty to Hashem in following Him trustingly into the Wilderness: בְּצִלּוֹ חִמַּדְתִּי וְיָשַׁבְתִּי, *To be in His shade I coveted and there I sat.* Israel's wish to be sheltered by Hashem was granted not only immediately, in the form of the Divine Cloud, but also perpetually, by Jews around the world who build *succos* every year.

From this verse, however, it seems that Israel did not merely long for the Divine Presence, it *coveted* it. Someone in love feels neither hunger, nor thirst, only a passionate longing to be with his beloved. Israel too, in its passion for Divine shelter and closeness to Hashem, ignored all its other needs. Thus, they went out into the Wilderness with no provisions at all except for the *matzah* they had baked (see *Shemos* 12:39).

Their wish was granted, but how would their enthusiasm to be with Hashem be repaid? The Talmud (*Shabbos* 130a) relates that any Divine commandment that one performs initially in a joyous manner will always be performed joyously. Israel's reward for its initial enthusiasm for the Divine Presence is to rejoice in the *succah* every year.

Closer examination of this verse reveals that Israel not only yearned for Hashem's Presence before it was granted the protection of the Divine Cloud, but also continued to yearn for Him even while He was protecting them. As King Solomon notes, *In His shade I coveted.* Although already shielded by the Divine Cloud, Israel yearned for an even closer relationship with Hashem, to remain forever in the Divine Presence. This wish is granted every Succos — as Jews leave their physical homes and dwell in Hashem's house, the *succah*. (5641)

◆§ The Appeal to Build the Mishkan

When the Jews followed Hashem enthusiastically into the Wilderness, their "romance" with their Creator was in full bloom. But, as frequently happens, a rift soon developed. Israel strayed after the Golden Calf and Moshe shattered the Tablets. The special relationship with Hashem seemed to be finished, but not for long. The process of reconciliation reached its climax on the first Yom Kippur, when Moshe descended from Mount Sinai with the Second Tablets. As *Rashi* notes (*Devarim* 9:18), נִתְרַצָּה הקב״ה לְיִשְׂרָאֵל בְּשִׂמְחָה, *HASHEM was reconciled with Israel joyously.*

The *Mishkan* was physical testimony to Israel's renewed relationship with Hashem. Immediately after Yom Kippur, Moshe called for donations to erect the *Mishkan* and the people responded swiftly, generously, and above all, joyously. This resoundingly successful appeal, which began the day after Yom Kippur, was completed by Succos and the necessary materials were available by then. It is therefore fitting that Succos, the anniversary of Israel's first and most enthusiastically received appeal, is called "The Time of Our Rejoicing." (5644)

◆ Romance Restored

The connection between Succos and the joyous outpouring of donations for the *Mishkan* can be developed even further. Israel's magnanimity was not simply an isolated event that happened to occur immediately after the atonement granted on Yom Kippur for the sin of the Golden Calf. On the contrary, those generous donations formed an essential part of the process of reconciliation that began on Yom Kippur. Even though Hashem had forgiven them for their involvement in the Golden Calf, how could Israel compensate for the misguided joy connected with that sad incident? The only way to repair the strain in their relationship with Hashem was through proper joy. The joyous outpouring of donations to the *Mishkan* which occurred during the period between Yom Kippur and Succos, helped erase any lingering effects of Israel's wrongdoing.

On that first Yom Kippur Israel's sins were forgiven. It was only on Succos, however, through Israel's generosity that the romance between Hashem and Israel resumed its full force. This pattern continues in our times also. Every Yom Kippur Israel returns to its Creator and its sins are expiated. However, the joy that should characterize our relationship with Hashem is still not present since our misdeeds have left an almost indelible stain on it. Once again, we draw close to the Creator through joy. This time, the anticipation of dwelling in the *succah* (which is called "Hashem's home," as discussed in previous essays) restores the joy to our "romance" with Hashem. (5644)

◆ A Time of Unity

One of the "byproducts" of the joy of Succos is that the various factions within the Jewish people are able to put aside their differences and unite. The sin of the Golden Calf occurred in an atmosphere of disunity. Many of the people were opposed to this reckless venture and even among those who sinned, there existed many factions (see *Sanhedrin* 63a). Only in the aftermath of Yom Kippur's atonement was Moshe able to unify Israel in the joyous undertaking of building the *Mishkan* (cf. *Shemos* 35:1). Even today, a welcome byproduct of the atonement of Yom Kippur is the emergence of a newly unified Jewish nation preparing for the upcoming festival. Succos is called חַג הָאָסִיף, *The Festival of Gathering,* referring not only to the gathering of the harvest, but also to the gathering together of all segments of Jewry. In a similar vein, as we discussed previously, the Four Species are a powerful symbol of Israel's desire for unity every Succos. (5644)

◆§ The Joyous "Water Drawing" Ceremony

During Israel's formative period the joy of Succos was connected with the *Mishkan* in the Wilderness. After the nation settled in the Promised Land, the *Beis HaMikdash* also had a special connection with Succos. Not only did the dedication of the national center take place on Succos (see *I Melachim* 8:65), but every year the most joyous ceremonies celebrated there took place on Succos.

The following description of the *Simchas Beis HaSho'eivah* (Water Drawing Ceremony), adapted from the Mishnah in Tractate *Succah*, gives an indication of the joyous nature of Succos in the *Beis HaMikdash*:

> *The Kohen performing the ceremony filled a golden flagon holding three lugin of water from the Shiloach, a well near Jerusalem. When they reached the Water Gate, one of the Southern Gates of the Temple Courtyard they sounded a tekiah, teruah, and tekiah. He went up the ramp and turned to his left. There were two silver bowls there: The western one was for water; the eastern one was for wine (4:9).*
>
> *Whoever did not see the rejoicing of Beis HaSho'eivah never saw rejoicing in his lifetime (5:1).*
>
> *There was not a courtyard in Jerusalem that was not illuminated by the light of the Beis HaSho'eivah (5:3).*
>
> *Devout men and men of good deeds would dance before them with the flaming torches in their hands and would utter before them words of songs and praises of Hashem. The Levites with harps, lyres, cymbals, trumpets, and countless other musical instruments would stand on the fifteen steps that descend from the Courtyard of the Israelites to the Women's Courtyard. Two Kohanim stood at the Upper Gate that descends from the Courtyard of*

the Israelites to the Women's Courtyard with two trumpets in their hands. When the crier called out at dawn, the two Kohanim sounded a tekiah, teruah and tekiah. When those who brought the water that had been drawn from the well of Shiloach reached the tenth step between the Women's Courtyard and the Israelites' Courtyard, the Kohanim sounded a tekiah, a teruah, and a tekiah. They would continue sounding tekiah until they reached the gate leading out to the east (5:4).

Why did such intense joy surround the simple ceremony of drawing water for the Water Libation? In the special essay on the Libation of Water, we describe this ceremony as an opportunity to demonstrate that sanctity exists on earth as well as in Heaven. The sublime praises of Hashem sung during the ceremony, usually the exclusive prerogative of angels, voice a powerful statement that mortals, despite their failings and temptations, can aspire to spiritual levels unattainable even by angels.

Many of the Psalms sung by the Levites in the *Beis HaMikdash* begin with the word לַמְנַצֵּחַ, *to the victor.* The Water Libation Ceremony gives new meaning to this obscure expression. Israel has long desired to be as close to its Creator as the Heavenly angels, as expressed in *Shir HaShirim* (8:6): עַזָּה כַמָּוֶת אַהֲבָה קָשָׁה כִשְׁאוֹל קִנְאָה, *Strong till the death is my love [i.e. Israel is willing to die if necessary for its love of Hashem], hard as the grave is jealousy [i.e. Israel's jealousy of the angels, who enjoy unlimited Divine access].*

Throughout the year Israel is jealous of the angels' closeness to Hashem that it can never attain. At the Water Libation Ceremony, however, we no longer need to feel jealous. We have become the "victor" in our struggle with the angels for Divine access. Hashem accepts our service with at least as much if not more enthusiasm as that with which He favors the angels. The phrase we say in the *Yishtabach* prayers הַבּוֹחֵר בְּשִׁירֵי זִמְרָה, usually translated *Who chooses musical songs of praise,* may also allude to Hashem's preference for Israel's song over that of the angels. The word שִׁירֵי has two meanings: *songs* or *remnants*. While the song of mortals is but a mere remnant of the angels sublime praises, nonetheless Hashem *chooses [man's] remnants of songs* over those of the angels'.

Now we can appreciate the joyous pageantry associated with the

Water Drawing. When Israel asserts its legitimate claim to Divine proximity, and demonstrates that there is sanctity on earth as well as in Heaven, when the songs of the *Levi'im* are preferred over those of the angels, this is appropriately a *Time of Our Rejoicing.*

The sage Hillel captured the essence of the Water Drawing Ceremony in a few succinct words: אִם אֲנִי כָּאן הַכֹּל כָּאן, *If I am here, everything is here.* (*Succah* 53a) The sage was not referring to himself with the word "I," but rather to Israel. As long as Israel participated in the Service of the *Beis HaMikdash* Hashem's Presence was apparent. If (Heaven forbid) the Jews strayed from Torah, the *Beis HaMikdash* itself would become defunct, as it eventually did. The predominant theme of the Water Drawing ceremony, and the reason for its pervasive joy, is the centrality of man, and especially Israel, in Hashem's universe. There is no greater joy than to be chosen as an instrument through which Hashem's Presence can be felt on earth. (5646)

◆§ Source of Ruach HaKodesh

But what aftereffects did the Water Drawing Ceremony leave behind? Did anything of the exuberance of Succos in the *Beis HaMikdash* somehow linger on for the rest of the year? To answer these questions, the Sages suggested an additional meaning of the name *Simchas Beis HaSho'eivah,* usually translated "The Joy of the Water Drawing": שֶׁמִּשָּׁם שׁוֹאֲבִין רוּחַ הַקֹּדֶשׁ, *from there [participating in this ceremony] one could draw upon Ruach HaKodesh, the Sacred Spirit* (*Yerushalmi Succah* 19b). Not only water, but also *Ruach HaKodesh*, a form of Divine inspiration, was drawn and was available to those who participated joyously in the Water Libation Ceremony.

This was the legacy of Succos in the time of the *Beis HaMikdash.* Any ordinary Jew who participated in the Water Libation Ceremony could receive a permanent inspiration for a lesser form of prophecy, all in the merit of joyous involvement in the Divine Service.

The second verse of the story of Creation also alludes to the relationship between the Water Drawing Ceremony and *Ruach HaKodesh:* וְרוּחַ אֱלֹהִים מְרַחֶפֶת עַל־פְּנֵי הַמָּיִם, *and the Divine Presence hovered upon the surface of the waters* (*Bereishis* 1:2). One way of attaining *Ruach HaKodesh* is to participate joyously in the Drawing of the Water. (5642)

◈ The Jew Again Learns How to Speak

We may obtain further insights into the Water Drawing Ceremony by considering the nature of *Ruach HaKodesh*. Although no one in our times can truly fathom the meaning of prophecy, there may still be some benefit in exploring it as best as we can. One of the first mentions of this concept in the Torah is in the account of the creation of man (*Bereishis* 2:7): וַיִּיצֶר ה׳ אֱלֹהִים אֶת־הָאָדָם עָפָר מִן־הָאֲדָמָה וַיִּפַּח בְּאַפָּיו נִשְׁמַת חַיִּים וַיְהִי הָאָדָם לְנֶפֶשׁ חַיָּה, *And* HASHEM *God formed the man of dust from the earth and He blew in his nostrils the soul of life and the man became a living being* (*Bereishis* 2:7).

Perhaps *Ruach HaKodesh* means the return of man to his original state. During creation, man was infused with (i.e. had blown into his nostrils) the Divine Spirit. With this infusion, a mass of dust formed from the earth came alive. Throughout the year, we are party to the struggle between good and evil, between the "dust from the earth" and the "Divine soul of life." On Succos, after the purification of Yom Kippur and the exhilaration of the Water Drawing Ceremony, we are able to push aside the material side of our personality (the dust of the earth) and let the spiritual in us prevail. On Succos, we receive Divine Inspiration, and once again find the Divine soul of life implanted in us as when we were created.

Extending further our analysis of Divine Inspiration, we will see why this concept is often associated with a lesser form of prophecy. *Onkeles* renders the final segment of this verse, *man became a living being*, as וַהֲוַת בְּאָדָם לְרוּחַ מְמַלְלָא, *it [the soul of life] became in man a talking spirit*. Every Succos, as our pristine soul is restored under the impetus of the joyous Water Drawing Ceremony, we regain the gift of speech. (While even the wicked can talk, their speech is far removed from the talking spirit of the First Man.) The essence of prophecy is the ability to use Hashem's gift of speech to articulate words of Torah.[1] In some circumstances, an individual becomes so imbued with this gift of articulating Torah that he attains the status of a "prophet" and is able to communicate directly with Hashem. In other cases, especially today when prophecy has ceased, we can still utilize the gift of Divine Inspiration to realize our potential to derive new insights into Torah.

---

1. Thus the term נָבִיא, prophet, is related to נִיב שְׂפָתַיִם, *the speech of the lips*. See *Yeshayahu* 57:19.

Truly, Succos may be called the "Time of our Rejoicing" because of the Jew's enhanced ability, as a result of the Water Drawing Ceremony, to articulate Torah thoughts. As King Solomon wrote (*Mishlei* 15:23): שִׂמְחָה לָאִישׁ בְּמַעֲנֵה־פִיו, *Man's joy is the response [talk] of his mouth.* There can be no greater source of joy than the ability to articulate Torah thoughts properly, the culmination of which is the gift of prophecy. (5639)

Tragically, the Water Drawing Ceremony no longer exists and a major theme of the Festival prayers is heartfelt pleading that Hashem's Presence be revealed again. One who truly believes never ceases to be aware of Hashem Presence. However, he prays for the time when that Presence will be manifested to all men, when the Glory of Hashem's Kingdom will be revealed again.

These sentiments are voiced in the Daily Evening Services: יִרְאוּ עֵינֵינוּ וְיִשְׂמַח לִבֵּנוּ וְתָגֵל נַפְשֵׁנוּ בִּישׁוּעָתְךָ בֶּאֱמֶת בֶּאֱמֹר לְצִיּוֹן מָלַךְ אֱלֹהָיִךְ, *May our eyes see, our heart rejoice and our soul exult in Your salvation in truth, when Zion is told, 'Your God has reigned!'* (cf. *Yeshayahu* 52:7). We people long for the day when all men will perceive that which we already know — that Hashem reigns in Zion. (5632, 5634, 5639, 5662)

❧ The Water Drawing Ceremony: Significance to Today's Jew

We pray that the *Beis HaMikdash* will soon be rebuilt and the Water Drawing Ceremony restored. Then we will truly *feel* Succos as the Time of our Rejoicing. Yet, even in the darkness of our times, we can still feel a ray of the great light that shone in the *Beis HaMikdash,* a reminder of the overwhelming joy that pervaded it every Succos. The *succah* itself, described as "Hashem's house," (cf. *Succah* 9a) is a miniaturized version of the *Beis HaMikdash.* Even now, we can still rejoice over our glorious past and promising future. Although for the present we cannot enjoy the unique joy of Succos in the *Beis HaMikdash,* we still rejoice in the knowledge that we did once participate in the indescribably joyous Water Drawing Ceremony, and also that, hopefully soon, we will merit to see the rebuilt *Beis HaMikdash* in its full glory. (5660)

The above observations clarify an apparently inexplicable statement of R' Yehoshua ben Chananya (*Succah* 53a) that he never slept during the entire period of the Water Drawing Ceremony, which is the entire

Chol HaMoed. Why should he have remained awake during the day, since the ceremony itself took place only in the evening and the early hours of the morning? We can say, however, that this Sage realized that, even though the ceremony was confined to a particular time frame, the Divine Inspiration and the joy that accompanied it could be experienced during every moment of the festival. Just as Moshe did not sleep on Mount Sinai even after he received the Torah, knowing that every moment was an invaluable opportunity to absorb Divine Torah knowledge, so too the Sages remained awake throughout Succos in order to derive joy and inspiration for the year ahead. (5634)

Yet, even without the *Beis HaMikdash*, we can replicate a bit of its joy by performing a *mitzvah* instituted to memorialize it. By taking the *lulav* seven days, as was done in the *Beis HaMikdash*. we replicate a bit of that joy. Indeed, every joyous occasion celebrated by the Jewish people draws from the joy of Succos, as we see from the term the "Time of Our Rejoicing" which suggests that all of our joy is derived from this season. (5644)

◆§ Source of Joy for the Entire Year

The Torah hints at the festival's ability to arouse joy in the phrase (*Vayikra* 23:41) שִׁבְעַת יָמִים בַּשָּׁנָה, *Seven days of the year*. This unique construction, not used for any other festival reveals that these seven days provided inspiration for the entire year. Likewise, the month of *Tishrei*, in which Succos occurs, is called יֶרַח הָאֵתָנִים, *the month of the strong*, (*I Melachim* 8:2), a hint that this month provides the strength necessary for the year ahead. Even now, without the *Beis HaMikdash*, we still have an obligation to utilize the potential of this sacred period to the fullest to cull from these days a reserve of joy for the entire year. (5643)

Indeed, the Torah considers lack of joy to be a primary reason that Jews drift away from Torah and undergo suffering as a result: תַּחַת אֲשֶׁר לֹא־עָבַדְתָּ אֶת ה׳ אֱלֹהֶיךָ בְּשִׂמְחָה, *Because you did not serve* H*ASHEM*, *your God, with joy* (*Devarim* 28:47). This verse reveals that joy is a crucial factor in proper Divine Service — those who exude joy will eventually merit Divine inspiration. (5643)

◆§ Time of Joy — Aftermath of High Holidays

The joy of Succos stems in part from its position in the calendar, immediately following Rosh Hashanah and Yom Kippur. The Psalmist suggests that only those "straight of heart" can experience true joy (97:11) אוֹר זָרֻעַ לַצַּדִּיק וּלְיִשְׁרֵי לֵב שִׂמְחָה, *Light is sown for the righteous; and for the upright of heart, joy.* Only those who lead sincere lives, devoid of all deviousness, can be truly happy. Rosh Hashanah and Yom Kippur are not merely days of judgment and forgiving but also a time when Israel's innate purity is restored (see *Vayikra* 16:30). After this spiritual cleansing, Israel can rejoice on Succos. (5638)

◆§ Return to Purity

In the larger perspective, the process of purification undergone on Rosh Hashanah and Yom Kippur may be viewed as a return to mankind's original pristine state at the time of Creation. As King Solomon observes (*Koheles* 7:29), לְבַד רְאֵה־זֶה מָצָאתִי אֲשֶׁר עָשָׂה הָאֱלֹהִים אֶת־הָאָדָם יָשָׁר וְהֵמָּה בִקְשׁוּ חִשְּׁבֹנוֹת רַבִּים, *But, see, this I did find: God has made man straightforward, but they sought many intrigues.* All year long we veer from the "straight" road to flirt with sin. On Rosh Hashanah and Yom Kippur, however, we return to our original incorruptibility — we become "straight" again and now can rejoice over it. Similarly, King David's dearest wish was to remain always on the "straight path" attained in this season: אַחַת שָׁאַלְתִּי מֵאֵת ה׳ אוֹתָהּ אֲבַקֵּשׁ שִׁבְתִּי בְּבֵית ה׳ כָּל יְמֵי חַיַּי לַחֲזוֹת בְּנֹעַם ה׳ וּלְבַקֵּר בְּהֵיכָלוֹ, *One thing I asked of* H*ASHEM*, *that shall I seek: That I dwell in the House of* H*ASHEM all the days of my life; to behold the sweetness of* H*ASHEM and to contemplate in His Sanctuary* (*Tehillim* 27:4). Hashem's "House" symbolizes the straight, undeviating path of life we renew on Rosh Hashanah and Yom Kippur.

The *Hallel* prayer made up of six Psalms recited on Succos and other festivals, is the joyous song of the newly purified Jewish soul. As the Psalmist proclaims (102:19): וְעַם נִבְרָא יְהַלֶּל יָהּ. This phrase is, usually translated *The newly created nation will praise God.* The word נִבְרָא, *created*, can also have the meaning of *purity* as we learn in the verse מִצְוַת ה׳ בָּרָה מְאִירַת עֵינָיִם, *the command of Hashem is pure (clear), enlightening the eyes.* Only Israel, after being purified on the High Holy Days and finding its way back to the "straight path," may praise Hashem by reciting *Hallel.*

In a similar vein, the joy of Succos is also derived from the restoration of the Jewish soul that occurs at this time of year. All year long, we are mired in materialism. On the High Holy Days, however, we are able to utilize our spiritual potential again, to return to the true values of Judaism and to rejoice over them on Succos. Moreover, the *mitzvos* of Succos, in particular waving the four species towards Heaven, generate spiritual joy. (Cf. *Vayikra* 21:40).

The connection between spirituality and joy can also be seen from other instances when the Scriptures speak of joy. For example, the Psalmist talks of joy in the future: יִשְׂמַח ה׳ בְּמַעֲשָׂיו, *HASHEM will rejoice in His works* (104:31); and also יִשְׂמַח יִשְׂרָאֵל בְּעֹשָׂיו, *Israel will rejoice in its Maker* (149:2). Joy is deferred until that time in the future when spirituality will prevail. In the present world, with its rampant materialism, it is difficult to rejoice.

Similiarly, the Sabbath is identified as a day of joy. In the Psalm dedicated to the Sabbath, King David writes, (92:5) כִּי שִׂמַּחְתַּנִי ה׳ בְּפָעֳלֶךָ בְּמַעֲשֵׂי יָדֶיךָ אֲרַנֵּן, *For You have made me rejoice, HASHEM, with Your deeds; at the works of Your hands I sing glad song*. Likewise, the Midrash identifies "the day of your joy" (וּבְיוֹם שִׂמְחַתְכֶם) (*Bamidbar* 10:10; *Yalkut Bamidbar* 725) as the Sabbath. Only with that weekly foretaste of the World to Come, suffused with the intense spirituality of the *neshamah yeseirah* (additional soul), (cf. *Beitzah* 16b), can the Jew truly rejoice.

The association between spirituality and joy (as evidenced by singing Hashem's praises) is also a major theme of *Hallel*. Thus it says (115:17,18) לֹא הַמֵּתִים יְהַלְלוּ יָהּ . . . וַאֲנַחְנוּ נְבָרֵךְ יָהּ מֵעַתָּה וְעַד עוֹלָם, *Neither the dead can praise God . . . but we will bless God from this time and forever*. The word "dead" here refers to the wicked, whose lives are a spiritual void and who are thus functionally dead. It may also refer to the body, which eventually disintegrates into dust. Those whose lives are spiritually empty cannot praise Hashem with joy. Only Israel, whose life is imbued with spirituality, whose souls dominate their existence, can praise Him joyously. (5660, 5664)

◆§ Awe Leads to Joy

The joy of Succos comes not only because of the effects of the High Holy Days, the return to a straight path and dominance of the soul, but also because of the mood associated on Rosh Hashanah and Yom

Kippur. These solemn days are generally characterized by a heightened awe of Hashem. Succos, in marked contrast to the High Holy Days is a time of unmitigated joy. However, fear and joy are not necessarily conflicting emotions. On the contrary, as *Sefer HaIkarim,* a medieval work of Jewish philosophy, recognized, true fear of Hashem promotes joy. Thus, the joy of Succos stems directly from the fear and awe experienced on the High Holy Days.

The relationship between these seemingly conflicting emotions requires further explanation. In what sense does fear of Hashem lead to joy? To answer this, let us redefine the concept of joy. From the Torah's perspective, joy comes only from a spiritual state called *shleimus* (completeness). Only someone who utilizes *all* of his God-given talents for spiritual purposes can truly rejoice. This idealistic, virtually perfect, state of being can be attained only by those who first fear Hashem. The God-fearing individual, by utilizing his capabilities to the utmost, can attain the level of *shleimus*, at which he experiences a sense of spiritual ecstasy. His life becomes suffused with joy. Thus the fearful perfection of the High Holy Day period is the precursor of the joy of Succos.

The connection between fear and joy may be expressed in similar but somewhat simpler terms: We rejoice on Succos to celebrate the lofty level of fear of Hashem that we were able to attain on the High Holy Days. No greater joy exists for the devout Jew than this ultimate accomplishment — true fear of Hashem.

The integral relationship between fear of Hashem and joy can be shown from other sources as well. Judaism's most joyous occasion, the Water Drawing Ceremony (discussed previously) took place in Jerusalem. The Hebrew name יְרוּשָׁלַיִם is a composite word consisting of יְרוּ, *fear,* and שָׁלוֹם, *peace* (see *Yalkut Bereishis* 102). We are told that a Jew entering the *Beis HaMikdash* would experience both emotions simultaneously — an overwhelming sense of fear coupled with exuberant peacefulness and serenity. Only in our mundane world, in which the true meaning of joy is usually obscured, are these sentiments dichotomous. (5643)

◆§ The Fear of Isaac

The life of the Patriarch Isaac is a prime example of how fear and joy can be integrated. Isaac's outstanding trait was his fear of Hashem, as exemplified by his near-sacrifice on the altar. His son, Jacob, swore by the "fear of Isaac" פַּחַד יִצְחָק (*Bereishis* 31:42). Yet, this model of fear was given the name *Yitzchak*, which means "he will laugh," because of his ability to remain joyous — to smile and laugh — despite all the trials he faced in his life.[1] Even the ritual of blowing shofar, whose awesome sound inspires fear of Hashem even in the slumbering soul, is actually only a means of sensitizing the Jew to his Divine origins. Once that has been accomplished, the Jew, renewed in his devotion to Hashem, can rejoice on Succos. Thus, the awe induced by the shofar is merely a catalyst to prepare for the joy of Succos.

The verse that recounts Sarah's reaction to Isaac's birth also alludes to this relationship (*Bereishis* 21:6): כָּל־הַשֹּׁמֵעַ יִצְחַק־לִי *All who hear will laugh with me*. In view of the previous comments, this verse may also be given a homiletic interpretation: Anyone who hears the sound of the shofar (a reminder of the ram sacrificed in place of Isaac at the *Akeidah*) will eventually laugh, at the conclusion of the High Holy Day season, on Succos.

The Psalmist's call, תִּקְעוּ בַחֹדֶשׁ שׁוֹפָר בַּכֶּסֶה לְיוֹם חַגֵּנוּ, *Blow the shofar on the New Moon on the hidden [occasion leading] to our Festival day*, (81:4) may also be understood in this light. This verse is usually understood to refer solely to Rosh Hashanah, which always occurs on the New Moon. However, the term "festival" may also refer to Succos, which is frequently described simply as "the festival." Thus these words also convey the following message: Sound the shofar! Though its ultimate goal is hidden on Rosh Hashanah and veiled in the form of fear of Hashem, on the "festival" (Succos), the shofar's true reason the creation of joy, will ultimately surface. (5643, 5651)

◆§ Restoring Roots

The joy of Succos stems from an important ramification of the High Holy Days — the restoration of authentic Jewish roots. The soul of a Jew has its roots in Heaven. Emanating from Hashem, it never ceases to yearn to return to its original closeness to Him. However, sin causes it

1. Presumably he was given this name because Hashem foresaw that he would always remain joyous. While the story of his birth indicates a different reason for the name, because Sarah laughed at the news that she and Abraham would have a child at their advanced ages, this was only an immediate rationale for the name. Underlying the name was the knowledge that Abraham's son, even though he would be a paragon of fear, would nevertheless always rejoice in his lot.

to drift away from its Heavenly roots, and creates a barrier between Hashem and man (see *Yeshayahu* 59:2). The Rabbinic dictum (*Yoma* 86a), גְּדוֹלָה תְשׁוּבָה שֶׁמַּגַּעַת עַד כִּסֵּא הַכָּבוֹד, *Great is repentance for it reaches the Throne of Glory* (i.e. Hashem's Presence), alludes to one of the most potent results of Yom Kippur — the restoration of a Jew's soul to its Heavenly roots and its return to closeness with its Creator. What greater joy can there be than to return to one's heavenly roots!

King Solomon's advice to the penitent (*Koheles* 9:7) may be better understood in light of the above remarks: לֵךְ אֱכֹל בְּשִׂמְחָה לַחְמֶךָ וּשְׁתֵה בְלֶב־טוֹב יֵינֶךָ כִּי כְבָר רָצָה הָאֱלֹהִים אֶת־מַעֲשֶׂיךָ, *Go, eat your bread with joy and drink your wine with a glad heart, for God has already accepted your deeds.* The classic commentaries understand this verse as a reference to the Jewish people, who having fasted on Yom Kippur, are assured that they may now eat in joy for Hashem has accepted their efforts to repent. However, the word *already* seems to suggest that Hashem *already* accepted their deeds even before Yom Kippur. In what sense did He *accept* Israel's deeds before Yom Kippur?

In light of the preceding discussion however, the word *already* assumes a new meaning. Yom Kippur does not bring about a *new* status but rather a *return* to previously existing Heavenly roots. Hashem already accepted you — even before the universe was created, He had planned a unique role for Israel. On Yom Kippur, as Israel's sins are purged, they return to their previous place of honor.

The verse recited as a *sefer Torah* is being placed into the Ark suggests the same theme (*Eichah* 5:21): הֲשִׁיבֵנוּ ה׳ אֵלֶיךָ וְנָשׁוּבָה חַדֵּשׁ יָמֵינוּ כְּקֶדֶם, *Bring us back to You,* Hashem, *and we shall return; renew our days as of old.* Israel beseeches Hashem for a return to its previous state, when its heavenly roots were more openly perceived. (5640)

◈ Time of Rejoicing: The Festival of Succos Generates Joy; Trust Effects Joy

Whereas in previous sections we have attributed the joy associated with Succos to historical events or to the preceding High Holy Days, the origin of this joy must lie in the festival itself. On one level, this joy stems from the message of the *succah*. The act of leaving a comfortable home to dwell in a flimsy *succah* demonstrates clearly that one trusts in Hashem (as we discuss extensively in the section on *Succah*). There are few happier moments than that, when a Jew determines not to rely on his possessions but rather to trust Hashem.

The *Hoshana* prayers said on Succos, with their pleas for Divine salvation, also remind the Jew to trust Hashem rather than the rich harvest he has just completed reaping. Even the Water Libation Ceremony (discussed in the section on *Shemini Atzeres)* conveys the same message. As the prophet Yirmiyahu says (*Eichah* 2:19), שִׁפְכִי כַמַּיִם לִבֵּךְ, *Pour out your heart like water* — arouse all your emotions in your prayer to Hashem and show that you trust Him fully. The pouring of water during this ceremony symbolizes this pouring out of emotions like water. (5645)

◆§ Succos: Eden Revisited

Another reason Israel rejoices on Succos is the yearly opportunity to dwell in Hashem's home, the *succah*.[1]

By entering the *succah*, Israel re-enacts the story in which Hashem "housed" the first man, Adam. Just as the Garden of Eden was the best place in the universe to be close to the Creator, so also is the *succah*. On Succos, a Jew may perceive a ray of Eden's "light," a glimmer of that lost sanctity, as he enters his *succah*. If so, the source of Succos' joy becomes more clear to us. There was never a more joyous place than Eden, as we say in the blessing given every newlywed couple, שַׂמֵּחַ תְּשַׂמַּח רֵעִים הָאֲהוּבִים כְּשַׂמֵּחֲךָ יְצִירְךָ בְּגַן עֵדֶן מִקֶּדֶם, *Gladden the beloved companions as You gladdened Your creature [Adam] in the Garden of Eden from aforetime*. Eden, the first source of joy, is experienced again every Succos, the annual festival of joy.

Actually, every dwelling in which Hashem's presence is manifest — including the contemporary Jewish home — is a place of joy. As we recite in the prelude to the Grace After Meals during the wedding week, נְבָרֵךְ אֱלֹהֵינוּ שֶׁהַשִּׂמְחָה בִּמְעוֹנוֹ, *Let us bless God, in Whose abode is joy*. Every home that is conducted in accordance with Hashem's wishes is a "mini-Eden," and a true source of joy. (5643)

◆§ Succah: A Shield from Materialism

By extension, the *succah* is not just a replica of Eden but also a shield, insulating its residents from the materialism of the world. A comparison can be made between the *succah* and Shabbos. Shabbos is a

1. The essays on Succos discuss the Divine Presence in the *succah* at length.

place in time protected from the vanities of this world — a foretaste of the World to Come. So too, the *succah* is a uniquely spiritual place on earth — also a foretaste of the World to Come.

The nature of the *succah* as a shield from the passions and vices of the world sheds new light on the term "Time of Rejoicing" At any other time it could be difficult for a Jew to rejoice. The spiritual joy attained through performance of *mitzvos* is often overshadowed by the physical aspects of joy.[1] As observed, only on Succos, in the cocoon of the *succah*, protected from the frivolities of the outside world, can a Jew safely rejoice. Only on Succos can the spiritual aspects of joy prevail. Israel alone among the nations knows how to appreciate the joy of Succos. Whereas everyone else rejoices in the harvest, Israel celebrates the source of its bounty — Hashem's kindness. (5643)

We have previously noted that the concept of joy is frequently expressed in the future tense, as in the verse (*Tehillim* 149:2) יִשְׂמַח יִשְׂרָאֵל בְּעֹשָׂיו, *Israel will rejoice in its Maker*. This is because it is impossible to experience true joy in this world. The weekly Sabbath and the *succah* are the ideal time and place to experience what joy we are given in this world and to feel a semblance of the true joy of the World to Come. (5662)

☙ Israel Renewed

Finally, the joy of Succos may be related to Israel's unique role in the human race. As we said in the essay on *Shemini Atzeres*, the High Holy Days are universal in scope. The fate of all men and all nations is judged on these days. Theoretically, all of mankind could come close to the Creator every year at this time, obviating Israel's unique role. But this never happens and only Israel presents itself at the Judgment Hour. Only Israel returns to its Creator during the Ten Days of Penitence. Consequently, while Israel's unique bond to Hashem is renewed every year at this time, the first opportunity that presents itself to rejoice and express gratitude for our annual "re-selection" is Succos. Then we rejoice not only in our selection, but also retroactively in the entire process of judgment that led to this result.

Succos is a time of joy not only for Israel, but also for Hashem, Who

1. For example, the physical pleasure of eating the Shabbos meal may be so predominant that one can lose sight of the *mitzvah* being performed.

delights in His "lot," that He has selected Israel again for its unique and leading role. (5644, 5660)

☙ A Joyous Light for the Nations

However, Israel does not react to its renewed lease on life, to being chosen from among the nations with false pride. Instead, we want to perfect not just ourselves but all of humanity. The very name *Yeshurun* — nation that engenders righteousness — suggests that our ultimate joy is reserved for that future day on which our ideals will be shared by all men. For now, our mission is to serve as an example for mankind. Eventually the climax of our joy will come when our sterling conduct will be recognized and emulated by all the world.

Finally, Succos might be called "The Time of Our Rejoicing" because it is the last of the Pilgrimage Festivals. On Pesach, Hashem liberated us from Egyptian servitude and prepared us to receive the Torah. On Shavuos, we actually did receive the Torah, thereby fulfilling the purpose of the Exodus. From Rosh Hashanah through Yom Kippur, we internalize the Torah and truly integrate it into our way of life. This is the greatest joy, and Succos is its celebration. (*Succos* 5657)

☙ The Unique Joy of Shemini Atzeres: Israel's Private Joy

The joy of Succos is specified explicitly in the Torah: וְשָׂמַחְתָּ בְּחַגֶּךָ, *You shall rejoice in your Festival.* (*Devarim* 16:14) The obligation to rejoice on *Shemini Atzeres*, however, is deduced from the following verse: וְהָיִיתָ אַךְ שָׂמֵחַ, *and you shall experience pure joy* (*Devarim* 16:15).

Why is the joy of *Shemini Atzeres* so unique, and how is it derived from the phrase אַךְ שָׂמֵחַ? On the one hand, the Talmud understands this phrase to refer to the extraordinary, almost supernatural, joy of that day which, as we discussed in the essay on *Shemini Atzeres*, is a foretaste of the World to Come. Its joy does not come from the observance of *mitzvos* (e.g. *succah, lulav*), but rather is a purely spiritual, unparalleled, joy.

In a similar vein, אַךְ שָׂמֵחַ could mean "only joyous." Generally, the word אַךְ is a limiting term, excluding something from our consideration. It suggests that only Israel can partake of the extraordinary joy of *Shemini Atzeres*. (We see this also in the word וְהָיִיתָ, *and you [singular] shall be*, indicating that only Israel rejoices on this day.) While the joy of Succos is experienced by all peoples, *Shemini Atzeres* is a day of private joy, experienced only by Hashem and Israel. (See our essay on *Shemini Atzeres* for further discussion of its theme.) (5637)

◆§ Shemini Atzeres: Climax of the High Holy Days

Homiletically, the meaning of this phrase can be derived from the *gematria* of the word אַךְ, which is twenty-one. The first twenty one days of the month of *Tishrei* — from Rosh Hashanah until *Hoshanah Rabbah* — are colored by the awe and fear of the judgment period as well as by the joy of Succos. This period reaches its climax on the last day — *Shemini Atzeres.* (5639)

The word אַךְ also connotates a purity, as we see from a verse describing the purging of foreign vessels (*Bamidbar* 31:22). While the previous days of Succos were also joyous, they cannot compare to the rarified, pure joy of *Shemini Atzeres.* (5639)

◆§ Joy Amidst Suffering

The word אַךְ however also has negative connotations, indicating a sense of aching, worry, and sickness. (Thus this word is used to describe Noah's pain after being attacked by a lion under his care — see *Rashi* on *Bereishis* 7:23.)

There is a message of joy in the phrase אַךְ שָׂמֵחַ for the contemporary Jew, even though he has no hope currently of equaling the joy of his forefathers in the *Beis HaMikdash.* In our times, daily life has become a constant struggle for survival, and the word אַךְ suggests suffering and anguish much like Noah experienced in the Ark. Thus, we find a related word נִהְיֵיתִי used to describe the suffering of Daniel (8:27).

The message to us in this word is one of powerful encouragement: Even though you are broken, rejoice! Indeed, precisely because you are broken and you sorely miss the *Beis HaMikdash*, you will merit to feel a ray of its light on the Festivals. Every time we recite the *Mussaf* Service, commemorating the additional offerings of the festivals, we experience mixed emotions. While we are sad that we do not have a *Beis HaMikdash* in our times, we also feel joy that we once had it, and in the merit of lamenting its loss, we are privileged to feel a small part of the joy that pervaded it. May it soon be rebuilt, and we will then feel its full, unmitigated joy.

The Talmud expresses this theme when it derives the ruling that we must rejoice on the last day of the festival from this phrase (*Succah* 48a). Even if our lives in exile are dark as the night, on the Festivals we will still be given the ability to rejoice. (5637)

The phrase אַךְ שָׂמֵחַ also warns us not to abuse the gift of joy. Joy often is associated with frivolity, and even idolatry (as we find in the incident of the Golden Calf, see *Rashi* on *Shemos* 32:6). Even though the Torah admonishes us constantly to be happy, we must always be careful to do so only in a propitious manner. (5637)

◆§ A Promise: Joy for an Entire Year

The phrase אַךְ שָׂמֵחַ may also convey a promise as well as an obligation. In this sense, the verse tells us, "If you rejoice on Succos, you are guaranteed to rejoice on *Shemini Atzeres* also. Moreover, if you rejoice on your Festival, you will merit to rejoice all year long."

◆§ Conclusion

In closing, we will suggest an approach somewhat different form the ones presented until now. Our rejoicing on Succos and *Shemini Atzeres* is based not on past experiences or even present or future events but simply on the hope that if we begin the year with joy, it will remain a joyous year throughout. Every year has its own challenges that call for renewed diligence in Torah study. As Moshe says (*Devarim* 32:7): בִּינוּ שְׁנוֹת דֹּר־וָדֹר, *Understand the years of every generation.* Each generation's era has its own problems and challenges that require original solutions, which must obviously be based on the Torah. In order to succeed in this quest, we must begin the year on a joyous note, and there is no better time to do this than Succos and *Shemini Atzeres.* (5641)

Index

☙ Index

תורה

BEREISHIS / בראשית

SHEMOS / שמות

VAYIKRA / ויקרא

נביאים

YEHOSHUA / יהושע

SHMUEL / שמואל

MELACHIM I / מלכים א

YESHAYAH / ישעיה

YIRMIYAH / ירמיה

YECHEZKEL / יחזקאל

HOSHEA / הושע

כתובים

SHIR HASHIRIM / שיר השירים

RUTH / רות

EICHAH / איכה

KOHELES / קוהלת

ESTHER / אסתר

MISHLEI / משלי

DANIEL / דניאל

DIVREI HAYAMIM I / דברי הימים א

משנה

תלמוד

מדרש רבה

VAYIKRA / ויקרא

EICHAH / איכה

SHIR HASHIRIM / שיר השירים

SHEMOS / שמות

ילקוט שמעוני

TANACH / תנ״ך

זוהר

תפילה

SHABBOS AND FESTIVAL

MISCELLANEOUS